THE HISTORY OF THE
SOUTH WALES BORDERERS
1914–1918

THE HISTORY OF THE SOUTH WALES BORDERERS
1914–1918

BY
C. T. ATKINSON
LATE CAPTAIN, O.U.O.T.C.

The Naval & Military Press Ltd

Published by

The Naval & Military Press Ltd
Unit 10 Ridgewood Industrial Park,
Uckfield, East Sussex,
TN22 5QE England

Tel: +44 (0) 1825 749494
Fax: +44 (0) 1825 765701

www.naval-military-press.com
www.military-genealogy.com

Cover illustration taken from *Deeds That Thrill the Empire*.
Private J. H. Fynn going out to bandage wounded men under heavy fire.
For his most conspicuous gallantry Fynn was awarded the V.C.

In reprinting in facsimile from the original, any imperfections are inevitably reproduced and the quality may fall short of modern type and cartographic standards.

COMPILER'S PREFACE

THE long interval which has elapsed between the end of the war of 1914–1918 and the publication of this account of the achievements of the TWENTY-FOURTH in the course of it is to be explained mainly by two reasons. The writing of the story was originally undertaken by Mr. F. Loraine Petre, the author of several well-known works on Napoleon's campaigns. Unfortunately he died before he had made any progress with the work. Major Ferguson, who then took it over, was unable to continue it, and, after writing the story of the 1st Battalion and doing a great deal in the way of collecting material, had to abandon it. Then when I was honoured with the invitation to attempt the task I found myself more than usually pressed for time owing to other engagements I could not avoid, and in the years 1927, 1928 and 1929 the time I had available was very small. This is my apology to the Regiment for the very long time I have taken over compiling the story.

One disadvantage of this delay has been that it has been unusually difficult to trace or get touch with many survivors of the different campaigns who could have supplied valuable information and helped to fill in the gaps in the story. Several who might have helped have died before my account could be submitted to them for correction and amplification, others have found that after so long an interval memories have become blurred and inexact and that details have escaped them. I owe much to all those who have been so kind as to help with criticisms and additional matter: the imperfections of the story would have been even more conspicuous but for their assistance. To certain people in particular I am specially indebted; to the three who have in succession acted as Secretaries of the Regimental History Committee, Colonel Tudor, Colonel Gross, Major Edwards, and to Major Ferguson, who not only had made a collection of materials which has proved invaluable but has read most of the chapters in proofs and pointed out errors and omissions. Among others I would like to make special mention of Major Croft of the 5th Battalion, who placed at my disposal an excellent account of that battalion's doings which he had written, with much statistical material; most unfortunately he died before my account could have the advantage of being revised by him. For the story of the 4th Battalion's doings I have to thank Colonel Kitchin, who, in addition to leading the battalion in its campaigns, has done much to record its doings. This Preface would, however, be swollen to undue dimensions were I to mention by name all those who have helped me and I hope that the many others will be content with this general acknowledgment.

The basis of my account has, of course, been the War Diaries

COMPILER'S PREFACE

kept by the different battalions, supplemented by the "Part II's" of the Daily Orders, which have been very useful in tracing the early adventures of the Service battalions, and in compiling the appendices of Honours and Awards. Diaries vary in value and fullness, and if, as I fear, some may feel that not enough is made of the doings of their own battalion at a particular time, my excuse is that where very little has been recorded it is very hard to make much of a story. I have also had recourse to reading the diaries of the Divisions and Brigades in which the different battalions served, and these have often filled up gaps. But where gaps still exist it is not for lack of effort to fill them, and I have preferred to make full use of information where it has been plentiful rather than to cut all units down to a common level.

I have tried to make the appendix on Honours and Awards as accurate as possible, but I fear that some names may have escaped me; searching through the *London Gazette* for individual names rather resembles the proverbial hunt for a needle in a bundle of hay. The omissions are probably most numerous among officers and ex-officers serving on the Staff and not therefore recorded in any battalion's Diary.

The sketch-plans and diagrams are for the most part copied from plans in the Diaries; in some cases they represent an amalgamation of more than one plan. It was considered better to include a larger number of mere black and white plans than to go in for coloured plates and more elaborate maps of which a few only could be given. Reasons of expense have also been decisive against the inclusion of photographs of individuals or places.

C. T. A.

OXFORD,
February 1931.

CONTENTS

CHAPTER		PAGE
I.	Mobilization and the Retreat from Mons	1
II.	The Marne and the Aisne	16
III.	First Ypres	35
IV.	Expansion	54
V.	Tsingtao	73
VI.	Festubert and Givenchy	85
VII.	Gallipoli: the Landing	100
VIII.	Gallipoli and Aden	113
IX.	From May 9th to Loos	137
X.	Gallipoli: Suvla	154
XI.	After Loos	168
XII.	Gallipoli: after Suvla	182
XIII.	Mesopotamia: 1916	199
XIV.	Preparing for the Somme	212
XV.	The Somme: the opening phases	235
XVI.	The Somme: the middle stage	248
XVII.	The Somme: closing phases	260
XVIII.	Salonica 1915–1916	270
XIX.	The Third Winter	280
XX.	Arras and Messines	295
XXI.	Mesopotamia: Kut and Baghdad	312
XXII.	Third Ypres	328
XXIII.	Third Ypres: continued	342
XXIV.	Cambrai	351
XXV.	Salonica in 1917	371
XXVI.	The Last Winter	379
XXVII.	The Great German "Push"	393
XXVIII.	The Lys	403
XXIX.	The Aisne, 1918	423
XXX.	The Summer of 1918	433
XXXI.	The Turn of the Tide	441
XXXII.	Through the Hindenburg Line and Further	456
XXXIII.	The Last Great Battle in the West	474
XXXIV.	The Last Year in the Balkans	479
XXXV.	Mesopotamia: 1917–1918	495
XXXVI.	After the Armistice	505
	Honours and Awards	517
	The Roll of Honour	534
	Index	591

LIST OF MAPS AND PLANS

MAPS

THE WESTERN FRONT	*At end of Book*
MESOPOTAMIA	,, ,,

PLANS

	PAGE
MONS	7
THE MARNE	20
THE AISNE, 1914	32
LANGEMARCK	37
THE GHELUVELT AREA	42
GHELUVELT CHÂTEAU	44
KIAOCHAU AND TSINGTAO	75
THE ATTACK ON TSINGTAO	80
FESTUBERT	89
GIVENCHY, JANUARY 1915	95
THE ADVANCE ON KRITHIA	117
THE BOOMERANG AND THE TURKEY TRENCH	120
GULLY RAVINE	125
ADEN	133
RUE DE BOIS, MAY 9TH, 1915	139
LOOS	146
DAMAKJELIK BAIR	158
KAIAJIK AGHALA	165
SUVLA	183
HELLES, JANUARY 1916	195
OPERATIONS FOR RELIEF OF KUT	207
HART'S CRATER	213
BEAUMONT HAMEL	236
MAMETZ WOOD	243
THE SOMME BATTLEFIELD—S.W. PORTION	259
THIEPVAL AND GRANDCOURT	264
MONCHY LE PREUX	297
OPERATIONS OF 12TH S.W.B., SUMMER 1917	301
MESSINES	306
RECAPTURE OF KUT	315
OPERATIONS NORTH OF BAGHDAD	320
THE BOOT, APRIL 30TH, 1917	323
PILCKEM AND LANGEMARCK, 1917	337
GOUDBERG SPUR	348
CAMBRAI, NOVEMBER–DECEMBER 1917	364

LIST OF MAPS AND PLANS

	PAGE
Cambrai, the German Counter-Attack	368
The Doiran-Vardar Front	373
The March Retreat	400
The Lys, April 1918 (Southern half)	404
The Lys, April 1918 (Northern half)	411
Loisne Château	418
The Aisne and the Ardre	431
Advance of Thirty-Eighth Division, August–September 1918	446
Maissemy and Gricourt	451
The Attack on the Hindenburg Line	457
Villers Outreaux	463
Ypres, 1918	471
Wassigny and Catillon	476
Grand Couronné	485
The Pursuit from Doiran	491
Upper Mesopotamia and Kurdistan	502

BATTLE HONOURS
OF THE
SOUTH WALES BORDERERS[1]

The Great War—18 *Battalions.*—" MONS," " Retreat from Mons," " MARNE, 1914," "Aisne, 1914, '18," " YPRES, 1914, '17, '18," " Langemarck, 1914, '17," " GHELUVELT," " Nonne Bosschen," " Givenchy, 1914," " Aubers," " Loos," " SOMME, 1916, '18," " Albert, 1916, '18," " Bazentin," " Pozières," " Flers-Courcelette," " Morval," " Ancre Heights," " Ancre, 1916," " Arras, 1917, '18," " Scarpe, 1917," " Messines, 1917, '18," " Pilckem," " Menin Road," " Polygon Wood," " Broodseinde," " Poelcappelle," " Passchendaele," " CAMBRAI, 1917, '18," " St. Quentin," " Bapaume, 1918," " Lys," " Estaires," " Hazebrouck," " Bailleul," " Kemmel," " Béthune," " Scherpenberg," " Drocourt-Quéant," " Hindenburg Line," " Havrincourt," " Épéhy," " St. Quentin Canal," " Beaurevoir," " Courtrai," " Selle," " Valenciennes," " Sambre," " France and Flanders, 1914-18," " DOIRAN, 1917, '18," " Macedonia, 1915-18," " Helles," " LANDING AT HELLES," " Krithia," " Suvla," " Sari Bair," " Scimitar Hill," " Gallipoli, 1915-16," " Egypt, 1916," " Tigris, 1916," " Kut al Amara, 1917," " BAGHDAD," " Mesopotamia, 1916-18," " TSINGTAO."

---

[1] The Honours in capitals are those borne on the King's Colour.

THE HISTORY OF THE SOUTH WALES BORDERERS
1914—1918

CHAPTER I

MOBILIZATION AND THE RETREAT FROM MONS

WHEN, at the end of June 1914, England heard with horror of the murder at Serajevo in Bosnia of the Archduke Francis Ferdinand of Austria and his wife, only the most far-sighted of men can have had the faintest inkling of what was to follow from this crime. With their attention absorbed by the stormy situation in Ireland, the majority even of thinking people were slow to realize that the little cloud in the Balkans was an even greater menace. After the delivery on July 25th of the Austrian ultimatum to Servia, however, few soldiers can have failed to see the grave nature of the situation and the immediate importance to the Empire, and in particular to the Army, of the turn affairs had taken: even so, it was the issue of orders on July 29th to put in force the arrangements for the "precautionary period" which was the first overt indication of the country's need to be prepared for critical developments. These arrangements, which included the recall from leave of officers and men, the manning of coast defences and the posting of armed guards on cable stations, magazines and similar points of importance, fell far short of mobilization; but it was recognized that they were probably only a prelude to that measure, and in most units of the Army steps were unobtrusively taken to get ready for it. Many things could be done to turn to good purpose these tense days of waiting; equipment could be overhauled and serving officers and men medically examined so that the numbers required to complete war establishments could be ascertained. Thus, when the afternoon of August 4th brought what to many impatient officers and men seemed the belated order to mobilize, the Army was well on the alert and the process of mobilization virtually took a flying start.

Of the component portions of the TWENTY-FOURTH, the two Regular battalions were naturally separated by half the circumference of the globe, the 1st under Lieutenant Colonel H. E. B. Leach being stationed at Bordon in Hampshire, and forming part of the 3rd Brigade of the First Division[1] in the

---

[1] Major General Lomax commanded the Division, and Brigadier General H. J. S Landon the brigade, the other units of which were the 1st Queen's, the 1st Gloucestershire and the 2nd Welch.

Aldershot Command, while the 2nd (Lieutenant Colonel H. G. Casson) was at Tientsin in China; the 3rd (Special Reserve) Battalion under Lieutenant Colonel S. W. Morgan had finished its training and had dispersed again, and the Regiment's only Territorial battalion, which had the rare distinction of being unnumbered and known by its county name of Brecknockshire,[1] had been in camp with its brigade[2] at Portmadoc in Carnarvonshire since July 25th. Its Commanding Officer was Lieutenant Colonel Lord Glanusk, C.B., D.S.O.

The issue of the mobilization orders was almost immediately productive of scenes of the greatest activity and no little excitement at the regimental Depot at Brecon. Here Major F. M. Gillespie was in command, with Captain B. W. Collier as Adjutant and Captain G. C. Thomas as Quartermaster, and it was on the small Depot staff that the main burden of the mobilization fell. It was not merely that within a few hours of the issue of the summonses Reservists came pouring in,[3] there was a rush of eager recruits anxious to take their part in the coming struggle—it was one advantage of the delay in the decision to mobilize that it gave people more time to accommodate themselves to the sudden change in the country's situation, so that the actual outbreak of war found the vast majority of men convinced of the necessity of the action the Government had taken. Moreover, the Depot was the natural centre to which inquiries of all sorts were addressed, to which men came who wished to offer their services in various capacities. A thousand and one problems had to be dealt with, everyone was snowed under with work, and what was accomplished in a short time was really most remarkable.

The Reservists' response to the call was magnificent. Except for a few men away at sea practically every man on the Reserve reported, to a total of 1038. These had to be medically examined—only six of the whole number proved to be unfit—to be equipped and fitted with uniforms, and the majority[4] had then to be entrained for Bordon to bring the 1st Battalion up to war establishment. Simultaneously the 3rd Battalion had to

[1] On the organization in 1908 of the Territorial Force the other Volunteer Battalions of the Regiment had been taken away from it to form the Monmouthshire Regiment, one of the five purely Territorial Infantry regiments.

[2] This was the South Wales Infantry Brigade, an extra unit attached to the Welsh Division: the other battalions of the brigade being the 4th, 5th and 6th Battalions of the Welch Regiment.

[3] No less than 381 Reservists reported on August 5th and 470 more turned up next day.

[4] 631 were sent to Bordon, out of whom the 10% "first reinforcements" were provided.

MOBILIZATION

be mobilized and dispatched on August 8th to its war station at Pembroke Dock. The 3rd's strength on mobilization was just about 600, to which were added such Reservists who remained over after the 1st Battalion's needs had been met, while later on the "details" left behind by that battalion were also attached to it.

To allow the officers on the Regular establishment of the 3rd Battalion to proceed with it to Pembroke Dock officers on retired pay were given charge of the Depot, Colonel F. C. K. Hunter being appointed to command it, with Major C. E. Fitz G. Walker as Adjutant and Captain T. Murray as Quartermaster. They found their hands only too full, for even the departure for Bordon of the bulk of the Reservists did not bring any great or long-continued relief to the over-crowded Depot. To the crowd of Reservists, who after all were disciplined soldiers accustomed to doing things in orderly fashion, there succeeded a mob of recruits, full of keenness but utterly inexperienced, devoid of any kind of discipline except willingness, unknown to each other and to the Depot Staff, with their attestation papers, when they had not already lost them, often imperfectly or wrongly filled in. The accommodation at the Depot, adequate enough for 300 men, was hopelessly overtaxed by the influx of five times that number, every available inch of space was soon occupied and twice as much more was needed. Men had to sleep anywhere, and as they had nowhere to keep their blankets, it proved necessary to issue and withdraw the whole stock daily so as to ensure the full number being available. The cooking facilities were quite inadequate for such a crowd, and the cook-house staff found themselves cooking in relays all day, while additional crockery, knives and forks and other requisites had to be obtained in large quantities. The issue of rations was a great difficulty, and the local constabulary had to be called in to maintain some degree of order in the clamouring crowd of healthy and hungry recruits. But with general goodwill and anxiety to help it was not long before things began to get into working order. As men could be sorted out, given regimental numbers and otherwise identified correctly, it proved possible to obtain additional sleeping accommodation outside barracks and eventually to pitch a camp which further reduced the pressure on the Depot's space. Several old N.C.O.'s who had rejoined the colours proved most useful in shepherding the flocks of raw recruits, and on the decision, announced on August 7th, to form a new battalion in each regiment of the Line, to be known as a "Service battalion," things were simplified by the departure for Park House Camp on Salisbury Plain of about 1000 recruits, now distinguished as the 4th[1] (Service) Battalion, The South Wales Borderers.

Meanwhile at Bordon mobilization had proceeded smoothly. The Reservists turned up on August 6th and 7th in the charge of two Special Reserve officers who were to accompany the battalion overseas, Lieutenant James and Second Lieutenant Vernon; four officers of the 2nd Battalion who happened to be at home on leave, Captain Prichard, Lieutenants M. T. Johnson, Coker and Travers, reported for duty along with Captain Bill, who was on leave from Sierra Leone. Indeed so smoothly did things move that the battalion was able to report itself completely mobilized by midnight on August 8th, the fourth day of mobilization; only two other units in its Division were already in a similar state. The achievement reflected great credit on the excellent organization and hard work of the staff of the Depot which had made this possible.

Three days of standing-by in readiness to move followed, largely devoted to giving the Reservists practice in route-marching and to refreshing their musketry. To provide a nucleus for the new "Service" battalion, whose formation had just been authorized, fifteen N.C.O.'s were detailed on August 7th to proceed to Brecon. At the same time the war establishment of officers was reduced by two, and Captain R. H. Evans and Lieutenant R. G. Lochner were sent off to the new 4th S.W.B., together with Second Lieutenant C. J. P. Copner as surplus to war establishment. Then at 4.30 a.m. on August 12th the battalion began entraining for Southampton, and at 2 p.m. sailed for France on the *Gloucester Castle* along with the 1st Gloucestershire. In all there went overseas with the battalion 26 officers, 1 warrant officer, 49 sergeants and 911 men, besides an officer and 5 men attached from the R.A.M.C. and 6 N.C.O.'s attached from the Ordnance Corps.[2] In addition to this were the 10 per cent "first rein-

[1] Owing to the Regiment having no numbered T.F. battalion its senior Service battalion had the distinction of being the lowest numbered of all the Service battalions.

[2] The officers were Lieutenant Colonel H. E. B. Leach, C. O.; Major A. J. Reddie, second in command; Lieutenant C. J. Paterson, Adjutant; Second Lieutenant J. R. Homfray, Transport Officer; Lieutenant R. B. Hadley, Machine Gun Officer; Lieutenant W. R. Wilson, Quartermaster. A Company, Captains G. B. C. Ward and W. C. Curgenven; Lieutenants M. T. Johnson, C. J. Coker and C. K. Steward. B Company, Captains F. G. Lawrence, D.S.O. and M. B. Yeatman; Lieutenants V. B. Ramsden and H. H. Travers; Second Lieutenant H. D. Dawes. C Company, Major W. L. Lawrence, Captain R. S. Gwynn, Lieutenant C. W. Anstey, Second Lieutenants C. A. Baker and N. G. Silk. D Company, Major G. E. E. Welby, Lieutenant A. E. L. James, Second Lieutenants M. G. Richards, C. C. Sills and J. M. L. Vernon, with Captain Elliot, R.A.M.C., attached.

MOBILIZATION

forcements" under Captain W. O. Prichard, who followed the battalion to France a week later, while such "details" as remained over, the few unfits, boys under nineteen and recruits who had not completed their training, numbering in all 194 men, proceeded under Captain Bill to join the 3rd Battalion.

The passage to Havre was soon over, and by 1 a.m., August 13th, the battalion had disembarked and was helping to unload the transport. The unloading arrangements were indifferent, possibly because they had not yet been tested, in particular there were not as many cranes as were needed, but by hard work the ship was cleared before midday. Most of the battalion had before this proceeded up a very steep hill to a rest-camp three miles out of the town, where the next two days were spent. The troops received the warmest of welcomes from the inhabitants, and were soon on the friendliest terms with them, despite the minor difficulty of the language. A mixture of Welsh and Hindustani seemed to be easily understood, and the Quartermaster's fluent Arabic, a relic of Egypt in the 'Nineties, was equally successful in producing the desired results. A little route-marching was attempted for the Reservists' benefit, but on the evening of August 14th came orders to entrain next morning, and by 1.30 p.m. on the 15th the battalion was steaming out of Havre for an unknown destination. Its reception all along the line was most cordial: at every halt fruit, coffee and cigarettes were offered and crowds thronged down to the stations to cheer the troops. After a long halt at Rouen the train went on through the night, ultimately arriving about 7 a.m. at Etreux on the Oise, seven miles north of Guise. Here the battalion detrained and marched off in pelting rain to Leschelle, a village seven miles S.E. of Etreux, where it was billeted in considerable comfort, the rest of the brigade being close at hand.

The battalion was now in the concentration area assigned to the "B.E.F.," as the so-called "striking force" was now named.[1] Of the strategical situation regimental officers and men knew no more than that the Germans were advancing through Belgium and had encountered stubborn resistance at Liége. It was generally expected that as soon as the B.E.F. had completed its concentration it would advance to meet the Germans, and there was a hazy idea that all along the common frontier the French and Germans were already in contact. Of General Joffre's plans for an offensive, in which the B.E.F. was

[1] Of the six Divisions of the "striking force" only four had as yet proceeded to France, the First and Second from the Aldershot Command forming the First Army Corps, commanded by Sir Douglas Haig, the Third and Fifth Divisions making up a Second Corps.

to assist the French Fifth Army under General Lanrezac to hold up the advance of the German right while other French Armies delivered counter-attacks against the German centre, only the highly placed were aware: of the overwhelming strength in which the German right was advancing not even they knew anything, for the rapidity with which the Germans could mobilize their Reserve Corps and the numerical superiority that this would allow them to develop at the very outset seem to have escaped the French Intelligence Section. Actually when the B.E.F. started to move N.E. from its concentration area the French " plan 17 " had already miscarried completely. Liege had fallen on the 16th, four days later Von Kluck's great Ist Army came pouring through Brussels, moving forward in a generally S.W. direction, as ignorant of the strength and position of the B.E.F. as that force was of its numbers, while on Von Kluck's left Von Bülow's IInd Army was advancing against the French Fifth Army, whose right flank was soon to be threatened by the advance of Von Hausen's Saxons from further Eastward.

It was in happy ignorance of the odds against it that the B.E.F. began its advance. The first day's move (August 20th), a short but hot march of eight miles, which over the pavé roads felt much longer, brought the S.W.B. to Malgarni, ten miles S.E. of Le Cateau. Thence another hot and trying march took it next day to St. Aubin, 3½ miles North of Avesnes. Here for the first time the sound of distant guns was heard, the beginning of Bülow's attack on Lanrezac near Charleroi.[1] Next morning an early start was made, the men only just getting their breakfasts before they had to march off. The line of advance lay through Maubeuge to Bettignies, twelve miles away, where dinners were served. It was very hot, and what with the heat, the cobble-stones and the unwonted weight of rifle, pack and ammunition, nearly 60 lbs in all, which they had to carry, many of the Reservists had had quite enough already. However, more was to be asked of them. Contact had been established between the British and the German cavalry N.E. of Mons, to which town the Second Corps had advanced, its line stretching away Westward along the Mons Canal nearly to Condé, and it proved necessary to push the First Division forward to a position S.E. of Mons, so as to support the right of the Second Corps. For the S.W.B. this meant moving on Eastward about 4 p.m. to Villers sire Nicole and thence North to Givry, where touch was obtained with the Royal Irish of the Third Division and an outpost line was put out. This position was not reached till after 7 p.m.,

[1] On this day the Second Corps reached a line running West from Maubeuge, the First Corps being echeloned to its right rear.

and the extra seven miles march left the men pretty tired, though cheered up by the stories which came in from the cavalry of their encounters with the German Uhlans.

The night of August 22nd/23rd passed quietly enough, but about 8 a.m. the battalion was ordered forward with two platoons of cyclists to occupy a hill near Vellereille le Sec. This it held till relieved soon after midday by the arrival of the Second Division, now coming into line nearer to Mons and on the immediate right of the Third Division. This allowed the S.W.B. to move back through Givry to the extreme right of the British line at Peissant, about four miles S.W. of Binche,[1] and relieve

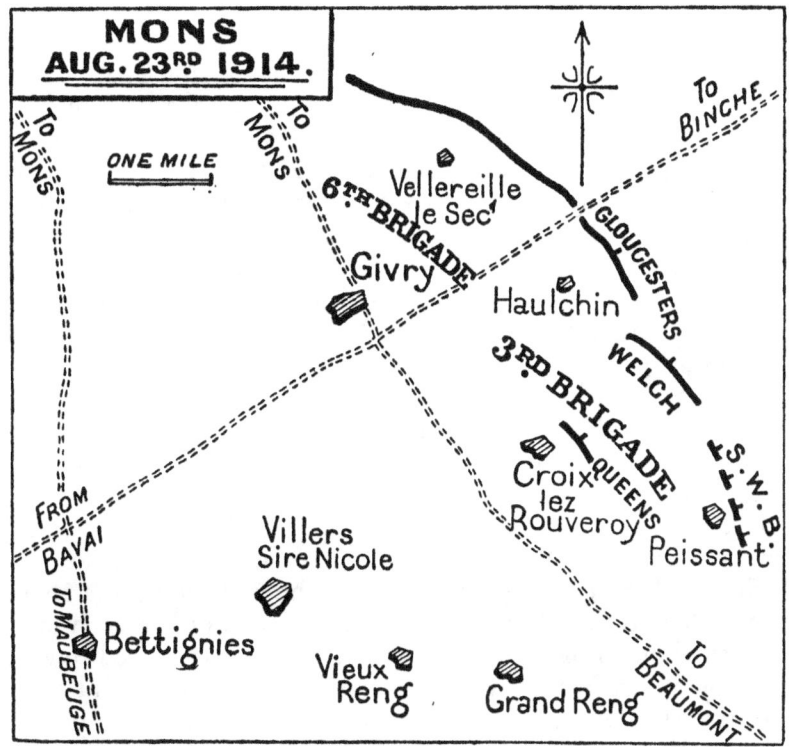

the 2nd Welch. Here a line was taken up which one of the officers declared to be exactly all the books said it ought not to be. The field of fire was bad, a large wood only 400 yards away provided cover in which an attack might mass, a sunken road ran from the wood into the position, giving an approach screened from the defenders' fire, and though the French were supposed to be covering the right nothing could be seen or heard of them, though every effort was made to obtain contact. Still these

[1] The 3rd Brigade was holding the front assigned to the First Division from Peissant to Haulchin.

defects were of little account, for, as it happened, the German attack on the B.E.F. came exclusively against the Second Corps, which successfully withstood the assaults of no less than three of Von Kluck's corps. The First Corps meanwhile had nothing in its front but German cavalry, for Von Bülow's right corps was far back in rear; though subjected to some long-range shellfire, it was practically not engaged, and the battalion's endeavours to put Peissant into a state of defence proved labours lost. Despite the Second Corps' successful resistance to Von Kluck's onslaught the general situation of the Allied forces rendered the B.E.F.'s position so precarious that a speedy retreat was imperative. The French counter-strokes in Lorraine and in the Ardennes had failed completely; Lanrezac, pressed in front by Von Bülow and threatened in flank by Von Hausen, had actually begun giving ground while the B.E.F. was moving up to Mons: indeed, Sir John French had only agreed to take up the Mons position and to remain there for twenty-four hours at Lanrezac's urgent request. Moreover, it became known early on the 24th that German columns were advancing in force well to the Westward of the B.E.F.'s line, and to have continued to hold the position would inevitably have led to disaster. Accordingly orders were issued for a retreat to an East and West line running from Le Longueville, five miles West of Maubeuge, to Bavai, and about 4 a.m. the First Division began its move rearward.

The S.W.B. had passed a quiet night, and though early on the morning of August 24th there was a sudden outburst of rifle fire on the right, it proved to be, not the precursor of an attack, but only an Uhlan patrol on the edge of the wood in front, on which D Company had opened fire. The incident, however, was notable, as it proved to be almost the only occasion during the whole retreat when any of the battalion got a chance to use their rifles. Shortly after this episode orders arrived for the battalion to move off, and at about 8 a.m. it started to withdraw by Vieux Reng towards Bettignies. By 9.20 it had passed through the Queen's, who were holding a rear-guard position near Croix les Rouveroy and beat off the rather feeble efforts of the German cavalry to follow up the retreat. By 1 p.m. the brigade was concentrated near Bettignies where it proceeded to entrench. No attack came, however, and about 3 p.m. the march was resumed to Neuf Mesnil, $1\frac{1}{2}$ miles West of Maubeuge, where the battalion billeted for the night. The men were extremely tired, for the day had been hot and they had had to dig hard in the midday heat.

They were on the move again early next day, for the projected stand West of Maubeuge had had to be abandoned, and crossing the Sambre above Maubeuge the S.W.B. found themselves moving through thick enclosed country to Marbaix, West of Avesnes.[1] The whole Division moved by a dusty and narrow road with a bad surface and many sharp turns: " the worst march to date " one account calls it. From Marbaix after a brief halt the battalion trudged on to Le Grand Fayt, five miles East of Landreçies. The village was almost deserted, Lanrezac's retreat and the prospect of the approach of the Germans had sent the civil population flying Southward, greatly increasing the congestion of the roads and complicating the problems of moving the troops. A fair supply of eggs, coffee and milk proved obtainable, but to get shelter there was nothing for it but to break into the houses. About midnight, however, the brigade was disturbed by a sudden order to proceed to the help of the 4th (Guards) Brigade who were said to have been heavily attacked at Landreçies. To lighten the burden on the men lorries were sent up to take their packs and greatcoats, and shortly before daylight the brigade was on the move. On reaching Favril, S.E. of Landreçies, however, it was halted and warned to prepare to fight a rear-guard action, as the Guards were falling back from Landreçies. The position was bad, for the country was flat, much wooded and enclosed and afforded no field of fire whatever, while to make matters worse the battalion's line was overlooked from some high ground 1000 yards away. German guns had come into action and were doing a certain amount of shelling, but the battalion was so fortunate as to escape without any casualties. This was largely thanks to Regimental Sergeant Major Shirley, who seeing D Company standing in fours on a road in full view of the enemy,[2] promptly ordered the men to fall out along the side of the road. Hardly had this been done when a couple of shells landed just where the company had been standing. Eventually about 2 p.m. the brigade was ordered to withdraw and the battalion moved on down the main Landreçies–Etreux road.

This road was terribly congested, transport was moving in two lines with infantry on either side, to say nothing of refugees, and only the good discipline and steadiness of the men enabled company commanders to keep their units together. At one point on the line of march tins of bully-beef and other rations were arranged along the roadside, and the men were instructed to help themselves to their rations as they passed, by which means

---

[1] Owing to the impossibility of passing through the great Forest of Mormal from North to South the First and Second Corps had to diverge on this day, the former going East of the forest by the valley of the Sambre, the latter over the more open country West of it.

[2] Major Welby had taken his company officers to see the line on which D was to entrench.

time was saved and the men provided with food. That evening the battalion bivouacked on the Wassigny–Oisy road and spent a wet and uncomfortable night. Heavy firing had been heard throughout the day from the Le Cateau direction, but of what was passing there nothing definite was known. Actually Von Kluck had fallen in force on the Second Corps, now reinforced by the newly arrived Fourth Division; and though in the end Sir H. Smith-Dorrien's men had had to retire they had put up so good a fight that Von Kluck believed he had had the whole British force against him and made no effort to feel to his left for the First Corps. The advance of Von Bülow's right had been retarded by the resistance of Maubeuge, so the First Corps was but little pressed during the day, though its retreat was considerably retarded by the blind and enclosed country in the Sambre valley and by the congestion of the roads by the refugees.

Despite the check to Von Kluck[1] the B.E.F. had still no option but to continue retreating as fast as it could till Joffre could carry out the necessary redistribution of his forces. He had now adopted a defensive attitude on his right and right centre, and was shifting troops as fast as he could to the Westward to form a new army and hold up the German wheeling movement before it could swing round Paris, but many days must elapse before this transfer could be completed, and till then the B.E.F. must trudge on Southward.

August 27th was a particularly toilsome day, marked for the First Corps by the gallant rear-guard action at Etreux, where the 2nd Royal Munster Fusiliers held up nearly a whole German division, and, though virtually wiped out, diverted it from pressing the rest of the First Corps, now retreating on one terribly congested road through Etreux and Guise. When about midway between Etreux and Guise the S.W.B., who had moved off very early, were ordered to halt and take up a position on some high ground S.W. of Iron. They were told that the rear-guard was in trouble and that they would have to cover its retirement and act as escort to four batteries who were in position close by. Trenches were dug and gaps cut in wire fences that might otherwise have impeded movement and the battalion waited. The artillery got some distant targets but no attack developed, and at last the rear-guard appeared, coming along in column of route and quite able to dispense with help. Accordingly the battalion formed up and, passing through Guise ahead of the rear-guard, moved on down the St. Quentin road to billets at Bernot, into which it eventually crawled about

[1] Though the Second Corps began its retreat about 2 p.m. it was not till next morning that Von Kluck's Army was ordered to advance beyond the line held by Sir H. Smith-Dorrien's men.

11.30 p.m., everyone dead beat It was to get but little rest, however; another early start was necessary next day (Aug. 28th) and the already tired men had to toil on down the Oise valley past La Fère to Crepy which they reached at midnight, after covering twenty-five miles. Everybody was quite done, the heat, the want of sleep and the difficulties of issuing and cooking rations added to the fatigue of the long marches; moreover the men were not a little depressed at the continuous retirement and the uncertainty of the situation. There was something mysterious and monotonous about this marching away from an enemy most of the First Corps had never seen, but whom the Second Corps had apparently trounced most successfully. The physical efforts demanded had been considerable, on many of the Reservists the strain was all the greater because they had been but recently recalled from civilian jobs in which they had had little chance of keeping in good condition for marching. That there was straggling is not to be denied, but it was not wilful straggling, it was with the vast majority sheer physical inability to keep up. In reality it was extraordinary that more men did not break down under the strain, and it is to the influence of the regimental spirit and traditions that one may largely attribute the way in which exhausted men, stumbling along on sore feet under a burning sun and heavily burdened with rifle and ammunition, managed somehow to keep going with the battalion.

August 29th brought the weary " foot-sloggers " of the First Corps a welcome day of rest, for the Corps remained halted in the bivouacs reached overnight. This was possible partly because Von Kluck's misconceptions as to the British bases and line of communications had caused his pursuit to be directed to the S.W., away from the generally Southward line by which the B.E.F. was retreating, partly because Lanrezac was standing at bay at Guise and was sharply engaged in serving Von Bülow much as Smith-Dorrien had served Von Kluck at Le Cateau. The battle at Guise was not to mark the beginning of that resumption of the offensive at which General Joffre was aiming; the retreat had to be continued for another week before all the necessary readjustments could be completed; but it exercised a critical influence on the campaign. By standing at Guise[1] Lanrezac had fallen a little behind the line of the general retirement, and had apparently presented Von Kluck with a chance of intercepting the Fifth Army should he promptly wheel round to his left and strike S.E. To do this meant to abandon the original German scheme of a great enveloping movement outside and West of Paris, in which Von Kluck would have crossed the

[1] The Fifth Army remained there till midday on August 30th and then withdrew without being in any way pressed.

Seine below the French capital, but even apart from the chance of cutting off Lanrezac that movement was already beginning to look a little beyond the compass of Von Kluck's Army, weakened as it was by march-wastage, by its heavy losses at Mons and Le Cateau and by the large detachments left behind to secure Belgium. Thus while the S.W.B. were resting at Crepy, welcoming the chance to get a wash and perhaps a change of shirts and socks, more was happening elsewhere than they could know. At the time the halt seemed only a temporary interlude in the retreat, for by 4 a.m. on August 30th the battalion was on the march again through the forest of St. Gobain, the 3rd Brigade acting as rear-guard to the Division. It was hotter than ever; in the forest there was little movement of the air and the day was stifling. Indeed the troops were so exhausted that they failed to reach the assigned line, Soissons–Rethondes, the First Division halting some eight miles short of it, with the S.W.B. billeting at Brancourt.

August 31st saw the retreat continued through Soissons and across the Aisne. It was hot again, but no special incidents varied the monotony and toil of the continued marching, and that evening the S.W.B. reached Missy aux Bois, five miles South of the river, and bivouacked by the roadside prior to another 4 a.m. start. This next day (September 1st) saw Von Kluck's move S.E. bring his advanced guards into touch again with the British rear-guards, whence arose the actions at Verberie, Nery, Crepy en Valois and Villers-Cotterets. The First Division, having moved off early East of Villers-Cotterets by the Soissons–La Ferté Milon road, was well on its way before the Germans became engaged with the Second Division's rear-guard on the next road to the Westward. Thus though rumours that Uhlans were close at hand led to special precautions against surprise both on the march and when halted, the S.W.B. only heard the sounds of the fighting and saw nothing of it. It was a long march and again very hot; the battalion covered over sixteen miles and only reached its bivouac at Fulames quite late in the afternoon, though it had been on the march from 5.40 a.m. It was off again, without breakfasts too, before sunrise on the 2nd. This was because Von Kluck, having to his surprise bumped into the B.E.F. again, was making great efforts to catch it up, so Sir John French, wishing to avoid being brought to action, had called on his Corps commanders to push on and get clear of the enemy by a night march or an early morning start. Thus September 2nd saw the B.E.F. tramping in intense and suffocating heat down the Ourcq valley and reaching that evening a line from Meaux to Dammartin. Its exertions had once again carried it out of Von Kluck's reach, and that commander, after wasting half a day in a vain effort to overtake the British, was now swinging S.E. again in the hopes of intercepting Lanrezac. In this also he failed, the brief diversion of his troops to the pursuit of the B.E.F. had helped to ensure for Lanrezac's troops an unhindered passage of the Marne, and the chance that they might be intercepted was over.

The S.W.B. had been employed on this day's march in protecting the Eastern flank of the column, a company with a section of 18 pounders being dropped at three successive points for that purpose, with orders to come along with the rear-guard. The battalion finished up a tiring day at Cregy near Meaux, after some quite unnecessary counter-marching owing to confused orders as to its billets. The inhabitants were clearing out as fast as they could go, and the owners of two well-stocked chicken runs handed them over to A Company, saying they would rather the British had the fowls than the Bosch. Quantities of fruit were also given to the men, and one villager before departing placed her cellar at an officer's disposal with any amount of good cider in it. The men thus enjoyed an uncommonly good meal that evening, the change from the normal rations[1] being most welcome. They were on the move early again next day (Sept. 3rd), marching back through Meaux to Varredes, crossing the Marne there and proceeding now in an Easterly direction up the left bank of the Petit Morin to the little village of Sammeron, where sheds provided fair cover for the night, after a particularly trying march of over twenty miles. The reason for this Eastward move was partly the necessity of closing the big gap between the B.E.F. and the Fifth Army, now more than ten miles wide, partly because a further move S.W. would have brought the B.E.F. inside the Paris defences. As Von Kluck's Army was also moving S.E. another collision with it seemed probable, so special precautions had to be taken to protect the left flank. However, no serious encounter occurred, and next day (Sept. 4th) the B.E.F. moved South again, the First Corps reaching the Grand Morin at and West of Coulommiers. For the S.W.B. the chief incident of the day was a long halt at Mouroux, where a stream gave everyone the chance of a welcome wash. Moving on again in the evening, the battalion fired some ineffectual shots at a German areoplane which passed overhead and eventually bivouacked just South of Coulommiers, across the Grand Morin. Here Captain Prichard and the "first reinforcements" turned up, bringing the battalion well above its establishment.

After a fine but cold night (Sept. 4th–5th) the battalion had another early start, marching South by Ormeaux to a bivouac

[1] The bread ration issued at this time was French; it was as hard as stone and usually covered with a blue mould, so the change was the more appreciated.

S.E. of Rozoy, where it settled down for the night (September 5th/6th), expecting to continue the retirement at 2 a.m. Before that hour, however, the unexpected news had come round that the retreat was at last over, that the enemy had apparently abandoned his march against Paris, that the French were about to take the offensive and that the B.E.F. would advance N.E. to co-operate, the First Corps moving to the line La Chapelle Iger–Lumigny, with the Second and Third Corps[1] swinging round in echelon on the left so that the whole force would face East. Von Kluck's move S.E. had brought him in between the Paris defences and the French Fifth Army, and instead of enveloping the French left he was now himself in danger of being outflanked and enveloped, for the newly formed French Sixth Army under General Maunoury had already begun to advance from Paris against the rather inadequate flank-guard which he had left North of the Marne to cover his movement. Ignoring the possibility of a counter-attack from behind the shelter of the Paris defences, and apparently regarding the B.E.F as a negligible quantity, Von Kluck in his haste to fall on the flank of the Fifth Army had put himself in peril, and the B.E.F. might look forward to repaying him in kind for its exertions and hardships.

Little over a fortnight had passed since the 1st S.W.B. had left its concentration station; since then, including the 40 miles covered in the advance to Mons, it had marched nearly 250 miles with but two[2] days' halt. During that time the men had rarely had a proper night's rest, they had been lucky if they got more than two or three hours' sleep, they had frequently had to prepare positions for defence and then march away directly their work was finished; they had often moved off without breakfasts, meals had been irregular, and if rations had usually been available there had seldom been time to cook them. The weather had been intensely hot and, as already mentioned, more than half the battalion started the march in inadequate training for all they had to endure. The weight to be carried had been considerable, even after packs and greatcoats had been discarded at Favril. That some men fell by the wayside and were never seen again was only natural, that others who fell out managed to rejoin says much for their determination, their temper and their *esprit de corps*. That the continued retreat told at times

---

[1] This had been formed on September 1st out of the Fourth Division and 19th Infantry Brigade.
[2] The day of the actual battle of Mons, August 23rd, and August 29th: this figure does not take into account such movements as the S.W.B. carried out from Givry to Peissant on August 23rd and any extra distance covered by occasional counter-marches, etc.

on the spirits of the men is not remarkable; what might have been surprising, had it not been so characteristic of the good-humour, cheeriness and buoyancy of the British Regular soldier of 1914, was the way the men kept going, despite all their privations and exertions. If there was any despondency or any serious " grousing " it vanished with the news that the retreat was over and that the Army was to advance and fight the enemy before whom it had so long been retreating.

Not many of the S.W.B. saw any Germans during the advance to Mons and the subsequent retreat, fewer still had a chance of firing a single round and not a man fell by the enemy. Yet no one can cavil if " Retreat from Mons " has an honoured place among the " honours " of the TWENTY-FOURTH. The mere fact that the battalion was denied contact with the enemy, that it had no chance of testing its musketry, its tactical efficiency and its endurance under fire, made its trials all the harder. On Moore's retreat from Corunna it was noticed that those units whose discipline and efficiency stood the test best were those who had been most in contact with the enemy and had had most fighting. To emerge, as the 1st S.W.B. did, from the Mons retreat with discipline and spirit unimpaired, though denied the bracing tonic of a successful encounter with the enemy, could only have been possible to a thoroughly well-ordered battalion, inspired by great traditions and determined to live up to a great past.

CHAPTER II

THE MARNE AND THE AISNE

THE orders to stop retreating and resume the offensive found the B.E.F. a full day's march to the rear of the position from Changis to Coulommiers in which General Joffre had expected it to be. This was due to a striking example of that "friction" which, as Clausewitz says, "distinguishes real war from war on paper." Writing to Sir John French early on September 4th, General Joffre had requested the B.E.F. to continue the retirement so as to make room for the mobile troops of the Paris garrison between it and the left bank of the Marne. Accordingly the British Commander-in-Chief had issued orders for the move to the line Rozoy–Brie Comte Robert which the B.E.F. had proceeded to carry out at once, the Second Corps starting at ten that evening and the First and Third Corps early next morning: partly to profit by darkness to conceal the move from the Germans, partly because a night march would be cooler and less exhausting than one in the full heat of the day. Thus by the time (3 a.m. September 5th) that General Joffre's "Instructions" for the next day's attack reached the British G.H.Q. one Corps was just completing its march and there was not time enough to get orders out to stop the other two. Thus instead of moving N.E. across the Grand Morin, which would have brought it into immediate conflict with the German IInd Corps, advancing South from between Meaux and Changis to the Grand Morin, the B.E.F. was a whole day's march to the S.W., out of touch even with Von Kluck's outposts, and to retrace its steps that day was out of the question. The importance of this becomes the more obvious when the German movements on September 5th and 6th are considered. On the 5th four of Von Kluck's five corps advanced to and across the Grand Morin, reaching a line S.W. of Mouroux—South of Coulommiers and La Ferté Gaucher-Esternay: meanwhile his IVth Reserve Corps, left North of the Marne to protect his right flank and rear, had already become engaged with Maunoury's Sixth Army advancing N.E. from Paris towards the Ourcq. News of this reaching Von Kluck that evening revealed to him to some extent the dangers of his situation and caused him to order his IInd, IVth and IIIrd Corps[1] to retrace their steps, re-cross the Marne and hasten to the assistance of the IVth Reserve Corps. To cover this shift the IInd and IVth Corps were to leave rear-guards on the Grand Morin to co-operate with two cavalry divisions, and during September 6th this movement was in progress across the British front, but with the B.E.F. too far

---

[1] In that order from West to East

away to be able to interfere. Clearly, if the " Instruction " of September 4th had arrived in time to prevent Sir John French's orders for the 5th being carried out so promptly, the B.E.F., even if not already at grips with the IInd Corps on September 5th, must have closed with it and probably with the IVth Corps also on the 6th. In that case the IVth Reserve Corps must have been left unsupported to sustain the full weight of Maunoury's attack and could hardly have avoided defeat. As to the results that would have followed, or as to the probable course of an encounter South of the Marne between the B.E.F. and the greater part of Von Kluck's Army, it would be idle to speculate, though it may be pointed out that the Germans would not have enjoyed those advantages of position they were to utilize so well when the B.E.F. did come to grips with them a week later on the Aisne.

For the 1st S.W.B. the chief event of September 5th had been the already mentioned arrival of the " first reinforcements." This party had embarked at Southampton on August 20th, reached Boulogne next day and moved thence to Rouen, to be hurriedly pushed up to Amiens on the news of Le Cateau and then as hurriedly taken off by train to the new advanced base at Le Mans. On the way the train passed through the outskirts of Paris, and the party gathered the impression that most of the capital's inhabitants were on their way South by road or rail to escape the Germans. From Le Mans several days of hard marching brought the party to Rozoy and the 1st Battalion, which its arrival brought well over establishment again, more than filling the gaps made by sickness[1] and by the few who had fallen behind.

Otherwise the day passed quietly enough. The troops having reached their billets fairly early, had time for a good meal and a real rest, and when the advance started at 7 a.m. next day (Sept. 6th) all were in good spirits, rejoicing that the retreat was a thing of the past. The First Division was moving by two roads, the 3rd Brigade on that to the right making for La Chapelle Iger by way of Compalay. The Queen's provided its advanced guard, the battalion heading the main body. The country was mostly wooded and progress was slow, especially as the troops neared La Chapelle Iger. Firing could be heard in front, and before long A Company, leading the battalion, bumped into the rear of the Queen's and had to halt. It appeared that the First Corps, being nearest to the Germans to start with, had run into them in some force near Vaudoy. With the head of the Second Corps five

[1] No exact figures of the sick and missing are obtainable, but the 3rd Brigade Diary for September 10th states that up to that date the sick averaged between 70 and 80 per battalion. Moreover, some of those unable to walk had been conducted to the Base by rail or motor-lorry.

miles to the left rear of the First Corps, and with the big forests of Crecy and Malvoisine on his left flank in which large forces might be concealed, Sir Douglas Haig had to proceed cautiously lest his Corps should be committed to an unsupported attack on superior numbers. There was a long halt therefore till the Second and Third Corps could wheel up into line and thereby secure the First Corps' left flank, and an outpost line was taken up and positions put into a state of defence so as to be ready for a German counter-attack. However, no attack came, and eventually, rather after 3 p.m., the advance was resumed. On this A Company, pushing ahead by General Landon's special orders, passed through the Queen's and, throwing out its own advanced-guard, pressed on through the Bois Blandereau towards Vaudoy. Indications that fighting had taken place were not wanting, a wounded British cavalry trooper to whom the Germans had given first aid, with some broken-down motor-lorries, but no opposition was encountered, and about dark the battalion passed through Vaudoy and bivouacked just North of it, the Queen's finding the outposts of the brigade.

The first day of the advance had not resulted in any heavy fighting, but the Third and Second Corps had reached the line of the Grand Morin and hopes ran high of catching the Germans at a disadvantage next day. Unfortunately information as to the French progress was slow in reaching the British G.H.Q., and with the situation uncertain it was 8 a.m. before orders could be issued. Thus the S.W.B., who had had breakfasts about 5 a.m., did not actually get going till nearly midday. The 3rd Brigade then moved off N.E. as right flank-guard to the Division, the battalion leading with B Company in front. Progress was not rapid, though once again no enemy were encountered, but it was encouraging to pass through German bivouacs, showing signs of hasty departure. The route lay through Dagny and Lendon to Choisy,[1] where the battalion bivouacked after dark. The march had been long and trying and, to make matters worse, a satisfactory supply of water proved hard to find. Once again the B.E.F. had had little fighting, though it had had the best of such encounters as had taken place, mostly small affairs of cavalry, and had ended the day over or just about to cross the Grand Morin.

September 8th found the S.W.B. on the move by 6 a.m., but the 3rd Brigade was at the tail of the column and the 1st forced the passage of the Petit Morin at Sablonnières without having to call for assistance. All along the Petit Morin there was sharp fighting: the position was strong and the Jäger and dismounted cavalry, on whom Von Kluck was counting to hold up the

---

[1] W. of La Ferté Gaucher and five miles short of the Grand Morin.

British advance, offered a stubborn and skilful resistance. But by evening this had been overcome, the passage had been forced at several places, and over 500 prisoners with a dozen machine guns taken. The way to the Marne was clear, for the day's fighting had broken down the screen behind whose shelter Von Kluck was preparing to crush Maunoury.

The S.W.B., who had crossed the Grand Morin at Jouy and then moved forward to Sablonnières, had got as near to going into action as to adopt "artillery formation" after crossing the Petit Morin and had passed by British guns in action, but they reached their bivouac at Hondevillers without having fired a shot, and spent a cheerless night in pouring rain, matters not being improved for A Company by the late arrival of its "cooker." During the day a "second reinforcement" of 90 men under Lieutenant H. M. B. Salmon had swelled the battalion's ranks, while such signs of the haste and disorder of the German retreat as abandoned equipment and accoutrements helped to encourage the men.

On the 9th it was again the 3rd Brigade's turn to lead the First Division. To the general surprise the bridges over the Marne were not only intact but undefended, and the Queen's, pushing across the river, quickly secured the heights beyond. The battalion, following hard behind them, crossed Nogent bridge about 7.30 a.m. No opposition being encountered, the 3rd Brigade pressed on and by 10.15 a.m. had reached Beaurepaire, $2\frac{1}{4}$ miles further North. Here it halted till about midday and then pushed forward to Bontemps to be brought to a stop by orders. Large hostile forces were reported to be advancing against the right flank from Château-Thierry and this caused a long halt while the Second Division was coming up on the left and the true situation was being ascertained. Actually no counterstroke ever developed from Château-Thierry, and about 3 p.m. the brigade moved forward again, as far as Le Thiolet on the Château Thierry–Paris road, where it found shelter for the night. If it had not been engaged its advance had yet been of the greatest importance. Almost without firing a shot the First Corps had decided the battle of the Marne.

Absorbed in his struggle against Maunoury, Von Kluck had been unprepared for the collapse of the German defence along the Petit Morin, and unable to retrieve the situation thus created. Though the strong detachments he now hastily threw across its path did hold up the Second Corps, he could do nothing to prevent the First Corps crossing the Marne, and the position which it had secured was so full of menace both to him and to his neighbour, Von Bülow, that he had reluctantly to order a retreat. He was apparently more than holding his own against Maunoury,

THE HISTORY OF THE SOUTH WALES BORDERERS

but he had no reserves available to throw in against the First Corps which had an undefended gap open before it and might well have rolled Von Kluck's line up from the left had he tried to hold on. He dared not risk it, broke off the battle against Maunoury with no little skill, and before evening the whole Ist Army was retreating towards the Aisne. On Von Bülow, too, the B.E.F.'s advance had had a decisive influence. As he himself

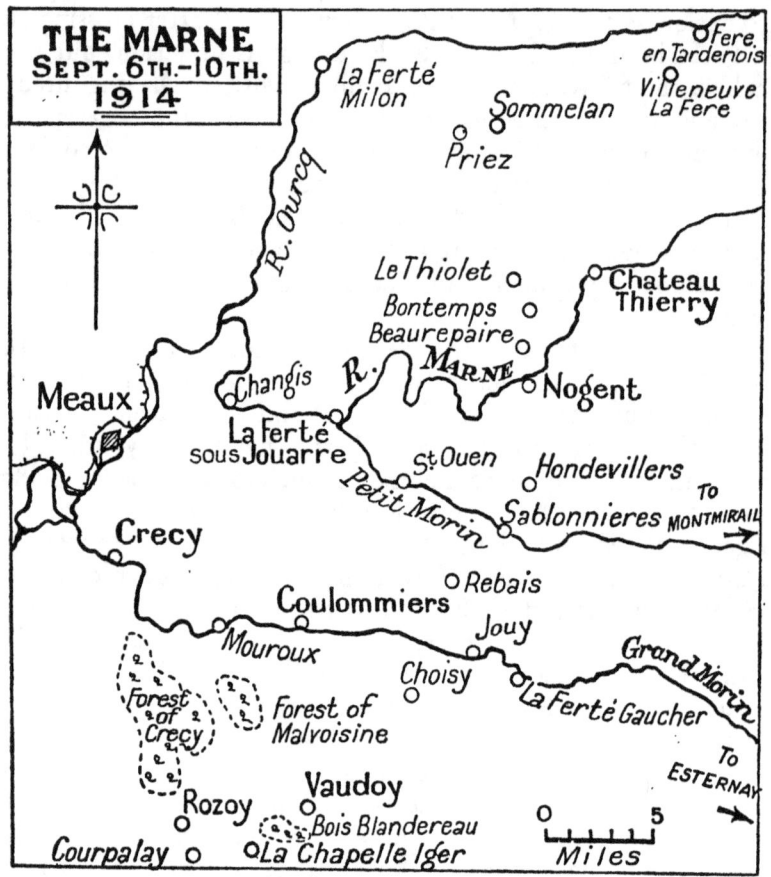

has written: "When numerous enemy columns crossed the Marne between La Ferté sous Jouarre and Château-Thierry there remained no doubt that the retreat of the Ist Army was unavoidable and that the IInd Army must also go back."[1] In a sense it was less what the B.E.F. had done than what it might do unless the Germans decamped at once that forced its opponents to retire. By promptly breaking off the battle before the B.E.F. could profit by its advantageous position the German generals avoided tactical defeat, were able to get their armies

[1] Von Bülow's *Report on the Battle of the Marne*, pp. 59-60.

back behind the Aisne ready to stand and fight there, and thereby prevented the Marne from being much more decisive. If between September 5th and 9th their original plan of campaign went utterly to grief, the Germans owed much to Von Kluck's timely extrication of his Army from the dangerous predicament in which his misreading of the situation, his obstinacy and his precipitation had plunged it.

To the S.W.B. September 9th had brought no more stirring experiences than its predecessors : once again the battalion had not come into action, nor did it do so next day, when the 2nd Brigade took its turn to lead the Division's advance and was sharply engaged with the German rear-guard near Priez. Here, however, the enemy gave way on the 1st Brigade beginning to advance on the 2nd's right, the 3rd not getting within 1000 yards of the area in which the German shells were falling. That evening the battalion bivouacked at Sommelan, a few miles South of the Upper Ourcq. The Germans were in full retreat now, covered by strong rear-guards which managed to delay the pursuers, but their main bodies were getting well away, and on the 11th, when the B.E.F. continued the pursuit N.E. across the Ourcq, there was no fighting. Many stragglers and wounded were picked up, but our advanced-guards failed to regain touch with the German rear-guards. This was partly because its N.E. move was taking the B.E.F. East of the line to which most of the Ist Army was retiring and yet well West of the IInd Army. The S.W.B. had an early start that day, got to Villeneuve la Fère about 11 a.m. and bivouacked in a field. Shortly after the men had had a meal it began to rain and everyone got well soaked before, about 4 p.m., the battalion was ordered to move into some tumbled-down sheds for shelter. However, it proved possible to light fires and get more or less dry, and the arrival of the baggage-wagons allowed the officers a welcome change of clothes.

September 12th saw the advance continued, with some fighting along the River Vesle, which the First Division crossed near Bazoches. The Welch were advanced-guard, and the battalion could see them extending on the high ground North of Bazoches and driving the Germans back before them. However, though progress was slow the S.W.B. did not have to get out of column of route and eventually reached Vauxceré, three miles South of the Aisne, about dusk, wet through and tired. Quite fair shelter was obtainable, two platoons of A Company occupying a large cave. On the B.E.F.'s extreme left the Fourth Division had actually succeeded in crossing the Aisne near Venizel before midnight, but the centre and right had yet to effect a passage and the S.W.B. spent most of September 13th in waiting to advance, while the cavalry supported by the 2nd Brigade were securing a crossing at Bourg. This was eventually effected, and about 3 p.m. the S.W.B., who had been under arms since 6 a.m., got orders to advance.

Moving through Longueval, over a slippery road congested with transport and guns, the battalion crossed the Aisne by the aqueduct which carries the Aisne–Oise Canal over the river. This had been damaged, but could be used, and by 6 p.m. the battalion was across and moving towards the high ground beyond the river. Just North of Bourg it formed up under cover of a steep hill. Firing was going on, a few shells innocuously fell in the water as the S.W.B. were crossing the river, and eventually the battalion settled down to a night in bivouac near Bourg, covered by A Company which climbed up the spur about dusk and threw out an outpost line. Further to the North the 2nd Brigade had reached Moulins, so the day had seen the First Division well established across the Aisne. On its left the Second Division was also across, though hardly as far forward, but the Second and Third Corps had only been able to gain rather precarious footholds. The opposition offered had not been very strong and the main reason why no more ground had been gained had been the delays in passing the troops over the half-ruined and improvised bridges. The Germans seemed to have no more than rear-guards on the ridge North of the river along which the Chemin des Dames runs from East to West, and the orders for September 14th talked most optimistically of reaching Laon, many miles to the North.

Had the situation of the Germans remained unchanged during September 13th these optimistic hopes might well have been fulfilled. In retreating from the Marne the German Ist and IInd Armies had done nothing to diminish the gap between them which Von Kluck had created by retracing his steps N.W. to ward off Maunoury's outflanking movement. Indeed they had rather diverged, and the fifteen miles which separated them were watched rather than held by three cavalry divisions, two of which had been roughly handled on the Petit Morin. Such a force could never have withstood a vigorous thrust by the First Corps, practically at full strength in men and guns, and had it firmly secured the Chemin des Dames ridge Von Kluck could hardly have maintained his position. But, luckily for the Germans, Maubeuge had fallen on September 7th and set its besiegers, the VIIth Reserve Corps, free for use elsewhere. Hurried forward by forced marches, they just reached the Chemin des Dames in the afternoon of September 13th, and were therefore in position to oppose Sir Douglas Haig's advance next day.

The First Division's orders were that the 2nd Brigade should advance before daybreak and secure the ridge for a mile Westward from Cerny. On this the 1st Brigade, acting as advanced-guard, was to move forward by Moulins and Cerny on Chamouille and the 3rd would follow behind it. The S.W.B. were timed to start about 7.30 a.m. which allowed a chance of giving the men a meal and issuing rations. But when the battalion began to advance it soon became evident that things were hardly proceeding " according to plan " : the road was blocked with troops, and at the cross-roads half a mile South of Vendresse the battalion came to a standstill and remained halted for some time. Heavy firing could be heard in front and German shrapnel was bursting overhead, though luckily their range was just too long by fifty yards, and the battalion escaped almost without casualties. What had happened was that the 2nd Brigade had encountered strong opposition and had been unable to cross the ridge, though it had captured several hundred prisoners and put two batteries out of action. General Lomax had then put in the 1st Brigade on its left, West of the sugar factory near Cerny, and it had pushed across the head of the Chivy valley, carried the German trenches on the plateau N.W. of the valley and had, like the 2nd Brigade, established itself on the ridge. But losses had been heavy, German guns and machine guns developed a great volume of fire, and German reinforcements soon began a series of counter-attacks. Accordingly the 3rd Brigade had to be put in, and about 10.30 a.m. the S.W.B. got orders to advance.[1] Immediately in their front rose a wooded ridge running S.W. from Troyon and separating the Vendresse from the Chivy valley. This ridge the battalion proceeded to climb, skirting round to the West of Vendresse to get to it, and on reaching the crest formed up under cover of the woods in readiness to advance. It was shelled as it moved, but the bursts were again too high to be effective and there were no casualties.

From the top of the ridge[2] a fine view could be obtained of the Chivy valley and across to the Chemin des Dames Ridge from which the Beaulne spur ran S.W. and S. It was now nearly 11 a.m., and the 1st and 2nd Brigades were heavily engaged to the right front, while the British guns could be seen to be making good practice. There were no signs of the Second Division, which should have been making progress up the Beaulne spur, indeed the enemy seemed to be counter-attacking down that ridge. The German guns also were active, and before long casualties began to mount up, the Adjutant's charger being the

[1] The Queen's had been sent off to the N.E. as right flank-guard, so the S.W.B. were now leading the brigade.
[2] The ridge was sometimes called the Vendresse spur, but was also known as Mont Faucon, though this name belonged more properly to its S.W. end.

first. About twelve o'clock orders to advance were received, the direction being N.W. across the Chivy valley. C Company led off, followed by B and D, A being left on the ridge to assist the machine guns to support the attack, which was also covered by the 39th Brigade R.F.A. The country was very difficult owing to the dense woods, and progress was slow, though the Welch on the left, having easier ground to cover, got on faster, and by 1 p.m. had established themselves on the S.E. slopes of the Beaulne spur with the battalion to their right rear along the Chivy–Beaulne road, facing about N.N.W. If they could get no further the two battalions had effectually checked the German counter-attack down the Beaulne spur by catching it in flank; indeed their intervention was largely responsible for its complete defeat.[1] For some time the two battalions maintained their ground, though by this time the enemy's fire had become very heavy, and casualties were numerous, the first officer to fall being Lieutenant M. T. Johnson of A Company, who was mortally wounded shortly after the advance began. But while the battalion and the Welch were holding their own, further to the right the German counter-attacks were more successful, driving back the 2nd Brigade from the sugar factory, some 500 yards beyond the edge of the ridge, just far enough to enable them to outflank the Camerons and other units of the 1st Brigade S.W. of Cerny. These troops, many of whom had run out of ammunition, were forced back after a stubborn resistance. This rendered the battalion's position precarious and caused a retirement to the Vendresse ridge, where the 3rd Brigade prolonged the new line taken up by the 1st. Here, as one officer writes, "we stayed firing and being fired at for some hours and then another effort."

This took the shape of an advance by the battalion and the Welch down into the Chivy valley, across it and up the slopes beyond, but well to the right of the previous advance, so that the battalion passed N.E. not S.W. of Chivy. This effort was made because by the middle of the afternoon the counter-attacks on the First Division had worn themselves out, upon which Sir Douglas Haig had determined to try one more attempt to break through. If only the Sixth Division, now on its way up from the new base at St. Nazaire, could have been up and in hand, instead of being still three days' march to the rear, much might have been done. As it was, unluckily, the S.W.B. and Welch, with two companies of the Gloucestershire, were the only reserves the First Division had available.

[1] *The Official History.* 1914. Vol. I., p. 363, cites German evidence for this: the three battalions of the 25th Reserve Brigade who delivered the counter-attack had to retire in complete disorder after suffering heavy losses.

It was nearly sunset by this time, but light enough for the Brigadier to point out a barn on the far ridge as directing point to Captain Ward, whose company, A, was leading with C, D and B following. As the troops pushed down the slope they were greeted with a sharp burst of shrapnel and some H.E. shells, one of which, bursting in the middle of Lieutenant Vernon's platoon of D, knocked out nearly the whole platoon, the officer being very severely wounded. However, the battalion pushed ahead, leaving Chivy on the left, and was soon pressing on uphill through a thick wood with dense undergrowth. The light was failing too and direction and touch was hard to keep. There was not much opposition, though several Germans were rounded up, some of them unarmed,[1] and eventually A reached a bank within a short distance of the objective, and, as it gave a good position, halted there for the other companies to close up. C soon arrived, but not B and D, with which touch had been lost. However, a little later the Welch came up on the left, and Colonel Morland of that regiment decided to hold the bank at which Captain Ward had halted. Accordingly A and C started to improve the position, though it was raining hard and everyone was cold and tired. B and D meanwhile, after losing touch with C, had diverged to the right and established themselves to the right rear of A and C, across the track leading from Chivy to Cerny, and, like them, just below the crest of the ridge. Shortly after they occupied this position a German attack developed, only to be quickly beaten off, after which they settled down to entrench, having two companies of the Gloucestershire in support nearer to Chivy.[2] Further to the left and beyond the Welch two battalions of the 5th Brigade had also reached the Chemin des Dames opposite Courtecon, but though their arrival became known to the portion of the 3rd Brigade on the ridge a wide gap separated them from it, and their commander found the enemy in such force round him that he decided to withdraw from what seemed a quite untenable position.

Actually B and D Companies were to maintain their ground for nearly a week,[3] and though a German attack in the early morning of September 15th drove A and C and the Welch back from their overnight position to a new line nearer to Chivy, this

---

[1] Between 150 and 200 prisoners were taken in this advance, the majority by the Welch.

[2] It gives some idea of the uncertainty of the situation that the Brigadier and his Staff Captain seem to have ridden up the track towards Cerny just before this counter-attack developed, and passed through our front line without realizing it. They were lucky to escape with their lives, for they ran into the Germans and had their horses shot under them.

[3] This position came to be known as "The Haystacks."

was well up the slopes of the ridge. These positions were not of any great strength, and it was a great testimony to the tenacity and spirit of the two battalions that they held on to them so long. The ground was open arable land, bare stubbles being interspersed with ungathered crops of beet and lucerne which afforded cover from view. The left trenches held by B and D faced North, those on the right of the track facing N.N.E., but, though covered to some extent from frontal fire, the position was liable to be enfiladed from the right and afforded a poor field of fire. By this time, however, it was beginning to be realized that with the B.E.F.'s 1914 standard of musketry only a very short field of fire was needed.

The night of September 14th/15th was a trying experience for the troops clinging on to the slopes of the Chemin des Dames Ridge. Apart from the precarious nature of their position they were surrounded with the dead and wounded of both sides, most of the British being Highlanders, and though some of these unfortunates were successfully rescued[1] many others could not be reached, and to make matters worse the night was bitterly cold, with not a little rain. Shortly after sunrise (5.30 a.m.) a weak German attack developed, mainly on the Welch, followed about 7 a.m. by a more serious advance, that battalion and A and C being so badly enfiladed from the right that it was clear that the position was untenable, especially as it was known that the 5th Brigade had already withdrawn; accordingly the detachment fell back, taking with it the prisoners gathered overnight. The retirement was not pressed and a new line was soon taken up by the Welch on the edge of the wood North of Chivy, while A and C went back into reserve near Battalion Headquarters which Colonel Leach had established three-quarters of a mile up the road N.E. of Chivy.

B and D had also been attacked in the early morning, the Germans coming forward in force and some of them making signs as though they wished to surrender; one officer actually called out that he wished to speak to a British officer. B and D, however, were not to be taken in by such tricks and opened fire at 200 yards range with deadly effect, wiping out nearly the whole party. Throughout the day the German artillery were active, but B and D were not to be shifted and succeeded in substantially improving their position. Snipers in the woods proved very troublesome and Captain Yeatman went out with his servant to see if he could deal with them. This he did most

[1] Admirable work was done by the Battalion M.O., Captain Elliot, and the regimental stretcher-bearers who were untiring in their care of the wounded and in their efforts to bring in the men lying out in No Man's Land. This work was continued for the next two nights, a large number of wounded being got in.

successfully; he crawled forward and stalked them systematically, shooting four with his revolver. He had barely got back to his company, however, before he was shot and killed. A Company meanwhile had been sent up to the Blanc Mont spur to keep touch with the Welch. This left C in reserve, and as by this time the whole battalion was in touch with Headquarters again it was possible to take stock of the situation and estimate casualties. The first estimate showed two officers, Captain Yeatman and Lieutenant Johnson, and 18 men killed, Lieutenants Richards and Vernon and 76 men wounded, and 122 missing: of these last, however, no less than 68 turned up safe and sound, having become detached in the dark and joined up with the 5th Brigade, and the net loss proved to be just under 150.

The next five days brought no important changes in the battalion's situation. The Germans shelled its trenches intermittently, but the men soon became fully alive to the necessity of "burrowing deeper into the hill," as one account puts it, in order to obtain protection from the shell fire, and casualties were low, though on September 19th Brigade Headquarters were forced to clear out of Chivy and go back behind the Vendresse spur. By day snipers were troublesome, and at night rifle fire was often almost continuous, both sides being apparently apprehensive that their enemy might advance under cover of darkness. The Germans did try this several times, but without any success; in the small hours of September 19th, for example, between 250 and 500 infantry advanced against A and D Companies, the latter of which had on the 17th been shifted to A's right. The firing was very heavy and C had to push up two platoons to reinforce the firing line, but the Germans failed to make any impression, and another attack on A Company on the following evening, in which about 150 enemy were engaged, was beaten off without any necessity to call upon the supports. Really an infantry attack was a welcome interlude in the shelling, which caused most of the casualties. One shell for example wounded 11 men in one platoon of A which was withdrawing from an exposed trench in the open to the shelter of the woods. A regular deadlock had now set in all along the British front, and with both sides gradually consolidating into regular connected lines the positions in which the hard fighting of September 14th had left them, it was doubtful whether anything was to be gained by retaining positions as exposed and as difficult to support as those on the Northern edge of the Chivy valley. Accordingly General Lomax decided to evacuate them, and to let the front line on the left of the Division follow the Vendresse spur to Mont Faucon. Early on September 21st the advanced positions were evacuated without attracting the enemy's attention, and by 7 a.m. the battalion had taken up its new positions. D Company was now on the Mont Faucon ridge,[1] with B in support and A and C back in Brigade reserve near Vendresse. Here, as Captain Paterson put it in his diary, " we sit under a cliff with shells coming thick and fast over us, but they can't touch us as the slope is too steep."

In retaining for so long its precarious position at the head of the Chivy valley the battalion had owed, as the Division put it, " more to audacity than to any natural advantages of ground ... the moral effect of maintaining these positions so long must have impressed the enemy with the tenacity and hardihood of our troops. Heavily shelled every day, suffering losses continuously in spite of their entrenchments, the S.W.B. and Welch maintained their positions with the utmost confidence, and were always ready for a night enterprise as a welcome change from the monotony of the day's inactivity." They had had not a few hardships and inconveniences to suffer during these days. " Trench warfare " was in its absolute infancy, not yet accepted as a chronic condition of existence, and no one had as yet thought of the systematic mitigation of its hardships. There was no chance of getting a wash or a shave or a change of clothes : one officer who arrived on September 20th with a draft was deeply impressed by the flourishing beards with which the C.O. and Adjutant were adorned, while his company commander " looked like a tramp " and the men were " as white as millers from the chalk mud."

This draft, which had left Pembroke Dock on September 11th, reaching St. Nazaire two days later, consisted of Lieutenants Blackall-Simonds (R. of O.), and Gilbert (S.R.) with 190 men, mainly Reservists, but including many Special Reservists. Its arrival about filled the gaps in the companies, the battle casualties to date having amounted to 35 killed and 131 wounded, while colds and rheumatism due to continued exposure in wet trenches had sent several more to hospital, though with two companies in reserve it now became possible to get the rest and the chances of cleaning up that were out of the question on the slopes by the Haystacks.

Some quiet days followed the withdrawal from the advanced position. Its evacuation allowed the Germans free access to the Chivy valley, where woods offered cover in which they might mass for attacks. But the British batteries had the valley under observation, and, as the *Official History* says,[2] " if this ground was henceforward a source of anxiety for the First Corps, it became a trap for the Germans." From the Vendresse ridge a good

---

[1] Approximately on the line from which the battalion had started to attack on September 14th.   [2] *1914*. I. p. 394.

view could be obtained. There was a German trench on the skyline opposite, well out of rifle range, and the Germans could sometimes be seen walking about in the open, though if the section of 18 pounders in close support of the S.W.B. opened fire " they popped under like rabbits and seemed to be jolly deep," as one diary puts it. There were many German dead lying on the face of the hill opposite and at the head of the valley, while between the Haystacks and the factory they were particularly thick, with many British mixed up with them. In front was the wooded valley, easily observed in daytime, but by night the brigade had to maintain a post at its lower end and to send patrols to search the woods with the object, among others, of preventing snipers from establishing themselves close to our lines. The two companies now in front line were established in some quarries on the front edge of the woods. The right company used the two quarries it was holding as its main position, a fire-step being cut round their front edge: on the left the quarry was used for the supports, the main firing position being in front and more in the open. On the right there was a gap before the Gloucestershire were reached, but this was open ground and easy to observe. The real weak spot lay in the cover afforded by the woods in front, and look-out posts were therefore established some little way down the slopes to give warning of any attack. On September 24th one of these was rushed and three men were killed, but B Company rushed up reinforcements, cleared the wood in front and re-established the post. Two days of heavy shelling but no important incidents followed, and then came a stern trial for the S.W.B.

Quite early in the morning of September 26th, just as B Company was beginning to relieve A in the right pair of quarries, heavy firing began further to the right. At first, however, there was no sign of the attack extending Westward; half A had withdrawn to reserve and the company commander was superintending the relief of a detached post on the left of his company when very heavy fire broke out from that direction also, and almost at once Germans came swarming forward to attack. Captain Ward and Lieutenant Steward, however, formed their men up behind a bank which gave a good fire position, and at this point the enemy were checked. On the left the Germans were more successful. D had its sentry groups in front of its trench-line, and it was the practice to withdraw them as soon as ever it was light enough for the sentries in the trenches to see the ground in front. The Germans, who had evidently massed in the woods close at hand, seem to have followed the outposts so closely that they were up to the trenches and had got their machine guns into action before it could be seen that more than the group sentries were advancing. The defenders of the front trench seem to have been mostly overpowered by sheer weight of numbers, and both Major Welby and Second Lieutenant Sills were killed, but the survivors put up a gallant fight, snatching up any weapon that came to hand.[1] Reinforcements were not long in coming,[2] and Lieutenant Simonds with the leading platoon of C arrived to find a stout fight going on for the quarry. Lieutenant Simonds was killed, but Major Lawrence brought up the other platoons and they, working round the the edge of the quarry, cleared the Germans out of our trenches, Captains Gwynn and Prichard being well to the fore. The Germans now fell back into the woods under fire from a machine gun which Major Lawrence got into position, but rallied there and maintained a fire-fight for some time longer. Before this the attack had spread to the right quarries where B Company and part of A were kept busy, Lieutenant Coker, who did splendid work, bringing up another platoon of A to support one already there. Here, despite all their efforts, the Germans failed to reach the quarries. For some time the struggle continued: by 7.15 a.m. it had almost died down, only to be resumed again an hour later. Indeed the German pressure was still heavy when, about 9 a.m., a new phase in the situation developed.

The early morning had been foggy, and the mists did not clear away from the Chivy valley till after 9 a.m. Then the position became clearly visible to the troops on their left, where the Camerons from the Beaulne spur could look up the valley and see the Germans collected in numbers in dead ground about fifty yards below the battalion's line; further back too reserves were massed, including at least one battalion in quarter column. In front firing was still going on, though not as heavily as it had been. But the artillery could now be ranged on the admirable targets which had disclosed themselves, and the gunners did not miss their opportunity. Assisted by machine guns and long range rifle fire they hammered the Germans most effectually, inflicting enormous casualties and forcing them to quit. Soon after midday all pressure on the battalion had ceased, and the Germans, except for their dead and wounded, had cleared out of the valley. It was now possible to take stock of the situation and reorganize the companies, which had got not a little mixed.

Another urgent task was that of burying the dead. Nearly 30 from D Company alone were buried along with Major Welby and Lieutenant Sills in the communication trench leading from

[1] Some men are said to have fought with their fists and one actually defended himself with a table fork.
[2] The Welch Regiment from reserve sent up two platoons which worked round the foot of the hill on the left and prevented the Germans outflanking the line.

the quarry to the front trench, as it had been decided to make the quarry the firing line and fill in everything in front. But numerous as were the British dead the Germans lay even more thickly. An officer of the Camerons, who relieved the battalion on the evening of September 27th, has written of a line of dead Germans lying almost shoulder to shoulder about forty yards from the quarries, and has described how the German dead were piled most thickly in front of the centre of the line. In all the Camerons buried nearly 300 Germans lying quite close to the British line and further out were many more: their patrols also brought in many rifles and other equipment taken from the German dead and affording ample evidence of the destruction wrought by the battalion and the supporting artillery. But the S.W.B. had suffered grievously: besides the three officers already mentioned, Captains Gwynn and Prichard and Lieutenants James and Coker were wounded, the last named mortally, while Captain Prichard lost a leg, and in all nearly 200 men were casualties.[1] Still it was no small feather in the battalion's cap to have successfully repulsed about the most serious effort that the Germans made during the later stages of the fighting along the Aisne. A whole brigade, the 50th of the 25th Division, seems to have been brought up specially for the attack, and it was estimated that 4000 Germans were engaged in it. The Mont Faucon spur had great tactical importance: its loss would have gravely impaired the whole position of the First Division, which could hardly have retained a foothold North of the Aisne without recapturing it. Small wonder, therefore, that the battalion received many congratulations on its gallant resistance to the odds against it. The Divisional commander, General Lomax, paid a special visit to the battalion to congratulate it, and in addressing it compared its action to Rorke's Drift. Sir Douglas Haig wrote, "The conduct of the South Wales Borderers in driving back the strong attack on them made by troops massed in the Chivy valley is particularly deserving of praise. Please tell the Brigadier how proud I feel at having such splendid troops under my command."[2]

On being relieved by the 1st Brigade[3] the 3rd was at last given

---

[1] Originally nearly 100 were returned as missing, most of whom were subsequently found dead, while others were brought in wounded. On September 29th, for example, nine were brought in by inhabitants of Chivy. The final figures were 87 killed, 12 missing and 95 wounded.

[2] Major Lawrence was awarded the D.S.O. for the great part he had played in the repulse of this attack. Sergeant Duffy, who had already distinguished himself in an encounter with some German snipers, received the D.C.M.

[3] General Landon issued a most appreciative Brigade Order congratulating the battalions on the splendid way in which they had endured the trials and hardships of the past fortnight.

a real if brief rest. The battalion was taken right back across the Aisne and given quite comfortable billets at Coilly, where Sir Douglas Haig visited the battalion to thank it in person for having saved the whole position on the Aisne. The men were able to get washed, and to clean their clothes and accoutrements, deficiencies in equipment could be made good, promotions and transfers made to fill the all too numerous vacancies; Captain Curgenven for example succeeded Major Welby in command

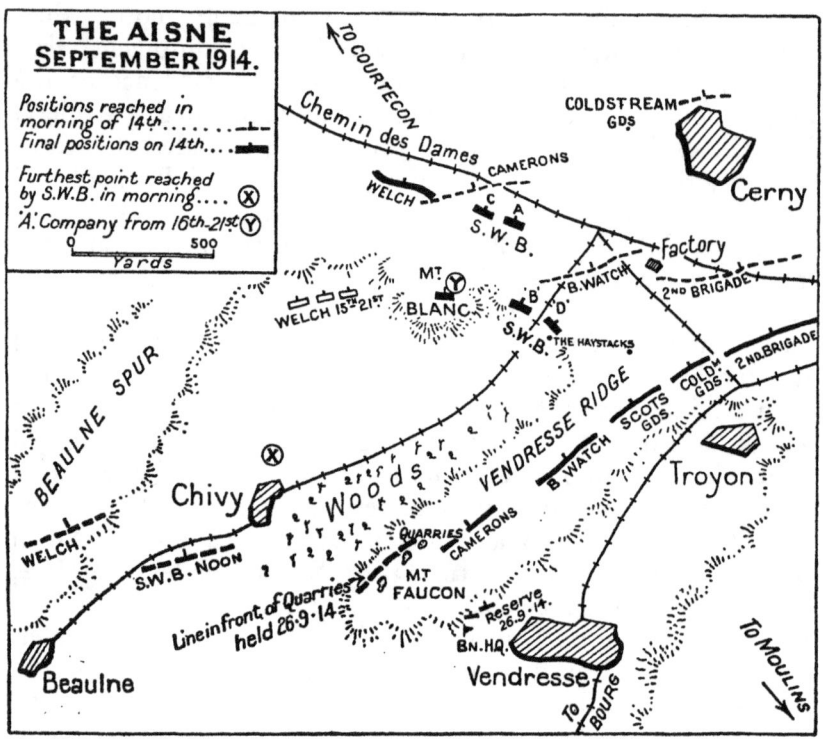

of D. A corrected casualty return was made out which showed the total to date as 6 officers and 110 men killed, 5 officers and 267 men wounded, and 35 men missing. With the wastage from sickness added in the battalion, despite the large drafts which it had received, was much below establishment. On October 6th its strength is given as 781 of all ranks, while only ten officers were doing duty with companies, as Lieutenants Baker, Anstey and Dawes had gone sick.

By October 6th the battalion had been back in the trenches for some days, having been placed in support to the 1st Brigade at Vendresse on the evening of October 1st. The First Division's line had been much improved by now, as well as being extended to the left. This was part of the redistribution needed to allow the Second Corps to be taken out of the line and sent off to Flanders, to which the centre of interest was now shifting. By this time it was clear that it was not on the Aisne that the deadlock established by the fighting of September 14th was going to be resolved. Each side had endeavoured in turn to outflank its enemy by pushing its available troops to the still open Western flank of the line, out of which had developed that " Race to the Sea" whose closing stages were to be fought out East of Ypres. But though it had been decided to transfer the B.E.F. to Flanders, bringing it again to its original position on the Allied left, the First Corps had to remain on the Aisne until the middle of October, lest German suspicions should be aroused by the disappearance of the British from their front. Thus the S.W.B. spent the first fortnight of October in comparative quiet and inaction. No offensive operations were attempted by the British, who were now extended over a very wide frontage for the numbers available; and though their guns were intermittently active and their snipers troublesome, the Germans were much less inclined to try even small infantry attacks, and the rifle fire at night from their trenches decreased considerably. Casualties during this fortnight were not numerous, despite the shell fire. The situation indeed was well summed up by Captain Paterson, who wrote of this period in his diary, "Just the same. Every day and all day, long bombardments. The Germans must have gone back a bit as their shells and rifle fire come very close to the slope of this hill, which they could not do if they were near. We have a few casualties now and then, but nothing much. It is really wonderful how many narrow escapes one can have and yet not be hit."

It was getting a good deal colder now, though the weather remained pretty fine, and officers and men set about providing themselves with "dug-outs" which afforded rather more protection against the weather and against bullets and lighter shells. But the battalion was not to see much more of the Aisne. By October 12th the Second Corps had begun its advance towards Lille, and once the Germans were aware of the presence of British troops in Flanders there was no longer much point about keeping the First Corps on the Aisne. The Second Division's relief by French troops began on the evening of October 12th, that of the First Division followed three nights later. It fell to the battalion and the Gloucestershire to take up a position near Bourg to cover the retirement. This was occupied about 6 p.m. on the 15th, and two hours later the relieving French units began to pass through on their way up to the trenches. There was some delay because one French battalion got heavily shelled: it had heavy casualties and dispersed for a time to take shelter, but eventually the shelling ceased and the relief was completed in time to let the British rear-guard file away through Bourg and over the river before daylight. The S.W.B.'s destination was Lime, in which village Battalion Headquarters were established in a most palatial château. But these comforts were not to be enjoyed long. That evening came orders to be at Fère en Tardenois by 5 a.m. on the 17th ready to entrain, and, thanks to Captain Paterson's skilful piloting of it in pitch darkness over an intricate and difficult road, the battalion arrived there to time, though after the long period in trenches the men found the unaccustomed marching very trying, and many had much difficulty in completing the march. By 8 a.m. the battalion was steaming out of the station for a destination only revealed to the Adjutant at the moment of departure as being Etaples.

The battalion entrained just over 950 strong, including 23 officers. A large draft over 150 strong had joined on October 10th, and at the same time six officers had arrived, including one Regular, Captain Barry, with Captain Crewe Read and Lieutenants Kelly and Graham, " pre-war " Special Reservists, and two officers, Lieutenant Hayes and Second Lieutenant Watkins, who had been Gazetted to the Regiment since the outbreak of war. The men were mostly Special Reservists, but included a fair sprinkling of re-enlisted old soldiers.

CHAPTER III

FIRST YPRES

ONCE the Germans had succeeded in checking the Allied pursuit North of the Aisne the centre of strategical interest had shifted away Westward. As already explained, both sides had then developed that series of efforts to outflank their enemies so well described as the " Race to the Sea." The B.E.F.'s transfer to Flanders was part of this process, and before the S.W.B. left the Aisne the Second and Third Corps had already encountered the Germans in the Lys Valley and were disputing with them that Aubers ridge whose strategical and tactical importance was so utterly disproportionate to its geographical significance. To their left General Allenby's Cavalry Corps was also in contact with the Germans and had established touch with the troops under General Rawlinson, the newly formed Seventh Division and Third Cavalry Division. This force, though too late to do more for Antwerp than cover the Belgian Army's retreat to the Yser, had taken up a line to the Eastward of Ypres in readiness to move forward when the British forces on its right came up level with it. On its left it had French cavalry, with the Belgians beyond them; in its front, though as yet their presence was unsuspected at the British Headquarters, large German forces were gathering for the capture of the Channel ports, with which the German leaders hoped to compensate themselves for their check on the Marne. British Headquarters indeed in sending the First Corps to Flanders were still hoping for a decisive stroke. It was no defensive battle that was contemplated, but the outflanking of the German right. Actually the Germans had organized, partly out of surplus Reservists, partly out of volunteers,[1] several complete new Corps which were now available. It was a remarkable achievement, and gave them a preponderance in numbers at the critical point, but for which the First Corps' move to Flanders might have achieved much of what Sir John French hoped for from it.

The S.W.B. reached the new area only to be on the move again at once. A round-about train journey had landed the battalion at Cassel early on October 18th, whence a five-mile march took it to good quarters round Hondeghem. By the following evening the concentration of the Corps was reported complete, and on October 20th the advance began, the 2nd Brigade, which led the First Division's column, reaching Elverdinghe, four miles N.W. of Ypres, with the 3rd close behind it.

---

[1] These were chiefly youths not yet liable for service or men exempted in previous years for different reasons.

THE HISTORY OF THE SOUTH WALES BORDERERS

The march had been tiring, not so much from the mileage as from the number of hours under arms, but the S.W.B. were lucky in their billets not far out of Poperinghe.[1] During the day German attacks had developed in some force against Rawlinson's command, while the French cavalry had been forced back behind the forest of Houthulst. Byng's cavalry, their left thus exposed, had had to retire to the line Langemarck–Zonnebeke, where they connected up with the Seventh Division, which though forced to bring back its left to conform with Byng's retirement, had successfully maintained its position, repulsing some vigorous attacks. The day's fighting had, however, left the British G.H.Q. still under the impression that the First Corps need not expect any really serious opposition, and the orders issued to the First Division for October 21st directed its advanced-guard, the 3rd Brigade (less one battalion) and three batteries of artillery, to clear Elverdinghe by 5 a.m. and advance on Poelcappelle, passing through Langemarck at 7 a.m. The Second Division on its right would be advancing on Passchendaele and was to cross the Langemarck–Zonnebeke road at 7 a.m.

This meant an early start for the S.W.B., who had to pass the brigade's starting-point at 3.40 a.m. They were the second battalion in the column, the Queen's being ahead. The roads were congested with refugees and French Territorials, and it was 6.30 a.m. before the vanguard crossed the Ypres–Yser Canal at Boesinghe and 8 a.m. before Langemarck was reached. The cavalry had already encountered German patrols not far ahead, and stronger forces seemed to be advancing behind them. Orders therefore were issued for the battalion to come up on the right of the Queen's and push forward against Poelcappelle village, the Queen's making for the railway station. On its right the battalion had the 2nd Oxfordshire Light Infantry, the Second Division's left battalion.

The advance started just after 9 a.m., D Company (Captain Curgenven) being on the left astride the Langemarck–Schreiboom–Poelcappelle road, with B (Captain F. G. Lawrence) in support; A (Captain Ward) was on the right, with C (Major Lawrence) in support, moving out by the side road running East from Langemarck so as to obtain touch with the Second Division. The moment the troops debouched from Langemarck they came under heavy shell fire, but it was neither accurate nor effective and at first the advance made good progress. Much of the country was enclosed and this gave fair cover from view, but before long the leading lines emerged into the open and came under heavy rifle fire also. Casualties began to mount up, the

[1] On this day two officers, Lieutenant Travers and Second Lieutenant Gilbert, were evacuated sick.

second line suffering rather more heavily than the leading line.

The advance was carried on in the approved fashion, "fire and movement," and was well supported by the artillery, including some French batteries near Langemarck; indeed the advanced-guard had forced the Germans back to an entrenched position between Poelcappele village and station when its further progress[1] was arrested by the development of a counter-attack on the left from

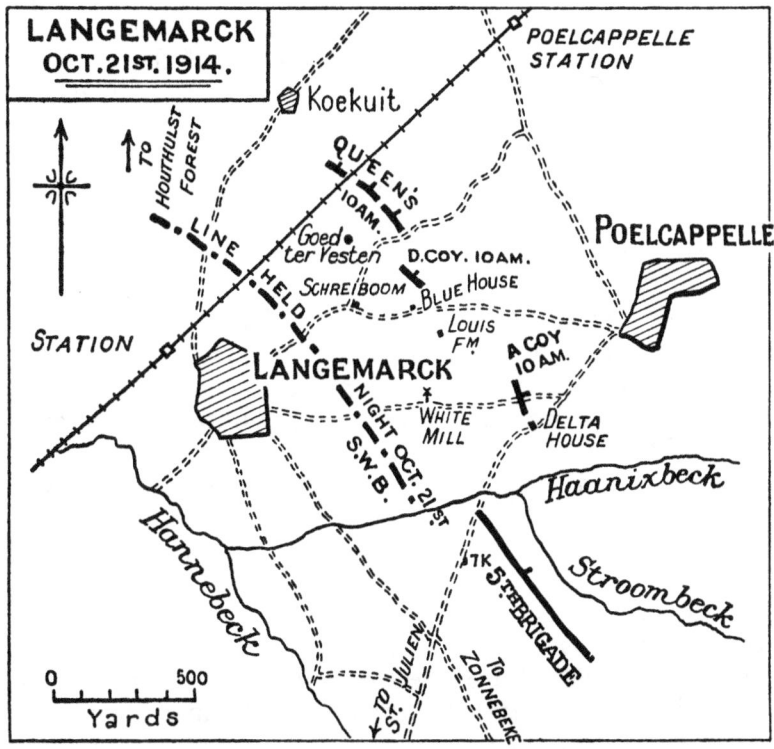

the Houthulst direction. General Landon had to use the Gloucestershire to cover the threatened flank near Koekuit Farm and to fetch the Welch up from the main body to support the advanced-guard. But the Germans were coming on in strength: a new Reserve Division, the 46th, was advancing through the forest of Houthulst and pressing the French cavalry back. In the end, instead of the 1st Brigade reinforcing the 3rd and pushing home the advantage the advanced-guard had secured, General Lomax had to put it in on his exposed left, and, as the 2nd Brigade were held back in Corps reserve, only the Welch were left to support

[1] The advance had covered about 1000 yards.

the S.W.B. and Queen's. The latter battalion had by 10 a.m. got nearly half-way to Poelcappelle Station[1] and D Company were keeping pace with them, while A, though not in touch with D, had also got on well despite losses. Indeed, when the German counter-stroke developed there seemed every indication that the attack was on the verge of success. Colonel Leach had just reported that the enemy were retiring North under heavy fire and that a party who had massed in a gap which had opened between his leading companies had been caught by the machine guns and effectively dealt with. However, the threat to their flank seems to have drawn the Queen's off to their left, for shortly afterwards Colonel Leach, in reporting[2] that the enemy were retiring opposite his left, added that he was out of touch with the Queen's.

The German attacks soon developed into a really formidable effort. At 1.15 p.m. a message reached Brigade Headquarters from Colonel Leach that German infantry were advancing and that their shell fire was heavy, but that he was holding his ground. The pressure increased steadily, and B Company had to be pushed up to support D which detached a platoon to cover its left. Losses were heavy, Captain Curgenven was killed, Captain Barry badly wounded, and eventually, somewhere between 2 and 3 p.m. after having maintained their ground stubbornly for some hours, B and D were forced back. About the same time the Gloucestershire evacuated Koekuit, whereupon the Queen's also had to retire. However, some platoons of the Welch were thrown in, and their support enabled B and D to push forward again nearly to a windmill about 500 yards N.E. of Langemarck. Reinforcements from the 1st Brigade enabled the Gloucestershire to reoccupy Koekuit, while about 3.40 p.m. the Queen's were reported to be advancing again also. Thus with the situation on their left less unsatisfactory, and with the gap on their right effectually covered by the effective fire of Lieutenant Hadley's machine guns, which frustrated the enemy's efforts to penetrate further, B and D could maintain their new position until nightfall.

Meanwhile on the right A Company also had been brought to a standstill. Its second line was held up for a time along a bank bordering a cabbage field, the ground in

---

[1] This is stated by the 3rd Brigade Diary and a map in the 1st Division Diary shows the Queen's as having been North of Goed ter Vesten Farm. In that case D Company must have been about as far as the points later on known as Blue House and Louis Farm. A message received by the First Division at 10.25 a.m. puts D as about "the bend in the main Langemarck–Poelcappelle road," i.e. somewhere beyond Schreiboom.

[2] Message received by 3rd Brigade 12.10 p.m.

front being very open and flat and swept by fire from a farm on which Captain Ward tried without success to range the British guns, his messengers being shot down on their way back. The leading platoons had diverged to the right and from their bank the second line could do some shooting, but eventually Private Hullah made his way back from the front, and, guided by him, Captain Ward was able to get his men up to the leaders. They had first to crawl forward through the cabbages and then a rush took them into a friendly fold in a ploughed field. They then crept forward till they could get a good field of fire and there scraped up what cover they could with their entrenching tools. Casualties had been fairly heavy, including Second Lieutenant Watkins, a very promising young officer who had only been with the battalion ten days, but, though during the afternoon the Germans attempted several advances, A's accurate fire made them think better of it. A message got through to Captain Ward from Battalion Headquarters and Drummer Foster and Private Hullah did good work in bringing up ammunition, but no reinforcements reached A, and the guns never got properly on to the farm with a windmill on its left which here marked the main German position.[1]

During the afternoon the Germans—they were, as afterwards discovered, the 51st Reserve Division—made various efforts to drive the battalion back, but without success. They showed great bravery, coming on in masses and singing as they came, but the battalion's rapid fire was too much for them. However, the situation on the left was none too satisfactory, as the 1st Brigade was spread out over a long front, and it was decided to bring back the more advanced troops of the 3rd Brigade nearer to Langemarck, with the battalion on the right, the Welch next, and the Gloucestershire thrown back at an angle opposite Koekuit to connect up with the 1st Brigade. This allowed the Queen's to be withdrawn into reserve.

Orders to this effect were issued by the 3rd Brigade about 5 p.m., but it was some time before they could be carried out and A Company brought back to the new line.[2] A was not pleased at having to retire. Though it had lost heavily, 25 men killed and missing and twice that number wounded, it saw no reason why it should give up the ground it had gained, nor did it like its new position any better when morning light disclosed a belt of enclosed land about 400 yards in front which

[1] If B and D's final position was somewhere short of Schreiboom, A, which in the evening proved to be well ahead of B and D, must have been somewhere about Delta House, but it is very difficult to establish the exact positions.
[2] This ran from the Haanixbeck on the right to the Langemarck–White Mill road, in front of and roughly parallel to the Langemarck–Zonnebeke road.

would give the enemy good cover.[1] It was some compensation to find plenty of food in the deserted farms, and as the Germans left the battalion in peace that night it was able to entrench itself quite well. Losses had been heavy, Captain Curgenven, Second Lieutenant Watkins and 19 men were known to be killed, 65 men were missing, Captain Barry and 62 men wounded. Captain Barry, who was at first reported "missing," owed his life to the devotion of some of his men who refused to give up searching for him, and eventually found him seventy-two hours after he had been wounded, disabled by a badly damaged knee.[2]

For the next three days the battalion remained in its position, being intermittently shelled and under considerable rifle fire, while occasionally it had to beat off an attack. "They came on in masses of 200 and got simply cut to pieces," writes one account, but though both to its left and right the fighting was very heavy, the battalion lay just between the main attacks, its left[3] being just on the fringe of the XXIIIrd Reserve Corps' attacks on the Koekuit–Kortekeer Cabaret line. Here on October 22nd, the Germans broke through the 1st Brigade's terribly extended line near the Kortekeer Cabaret but were expelled next day by a counter-attack, in which the Queen's, the 3rd Brigade's only reserve, played a leading part. To the immediate right the 5th Brigade was attacked in force on the evening of October 23rd but repulsed the attack most successfully, doing tremendous execution. Langemarck, however, was heavily bombarded and was quickly reduced to ruins, Battalion Headquarters having to quit the house in which it had established itself and to take refuge in the open where the signallers and orderlies soon provided it with some protection. "When coal-boxes are about the open country is the place," writes one survivor. Good work was done in searching for the wounded and in patrolling, notably by Private Smith, who took a small party out to the White Mill and surprised and captured a German observing officer and three men. By this time French reinforcements had become available in sufficient numbers for the relief of the First Corps from the line Zonnebeke–Langemarck–Bixschoote and for its concentration in readiness for a new thrust Eastward, behind the Seventh Division, whose front ran from Zonnebeke by

[1] On the night of October 23–24. A and C advanced to and occupied this belt, getting a much better field of fire.

[2] Captain Ward, Lieutenant Salmon, Lance-Corporal Coxhead, Private Hullah and Drummer Foster were recommended for rewards by the Brigade on account of this day's fighting. Captain Ward received a brevet, the three men the D.C.M.

[3] The battalion had to extend to the left to allow the Welch to do the same and so relieve the Gloucestershire opposite Koekuit, that battalion withdrawing into reserve.

Kruseik to Zandvoorde. The Second Division was relieved first, on the night of October 23rd/24th, and next night French troops appeared to replace the First. There were some misunderstandings before the relief could be accomplished, but by 3 a.m.[1] the S.W.B. were clear of Langemarck and on their way to a bivouac in a wood near Hooge. Since the 21st the battalion had only had another half-dozen casualties, but all ranks were exhausted and after the strain of the last four days the day's rest was much appreciated; moreover, a mail had just come in, with many welcome parcels.

The First Division's rest was not to last long. The German attacks were now being concentrated against the Seventh Division's scantily held front, and even before the S.W.B. came out of the line part of the Second Division had had to be put in to drive back the Germans who had broken through the 21st Brigade and penetrated into Polygon Wood. Between October 24th and 26th some progress was made by the Second Division East of Zonnebeke and by the French IXth Corps on their left, but the Seventh Division was hard put to it to hold on, especially near Kruiseck where its line formed a sharp salient; so, instead of supporting the Second's attack towards Becelaere, the First Division was gradually absorbed in the Seventh's defensive fight astride the Ypres–Menin road. On the 26th the 1st Brigade had to take over the frontage between that road and Reutel and late that evening A and B Companies of the S.W.B. were sent forward to reinforce it. After some counter-marching, due to uncertainty as to where they were wanted, the two companies eventually relieved the remnants of the 2nd Scots Fusiliers (21st Brigade) in the grounds of Poezelhoek Château, having on their right the 1st Scots Guards (1st Brigade) and on their left the 2nd Grenadiers (4th Brigade). By 3 a.m. (October 27th) they were in position, A on the right, B on the left, each having two platoons in front. The field of fire was good, though rather spoilt by houses, and the supports had good dug-outs in which to shelter. This was as well, for German snipers were busy and made walking about in the Château grounds decidedly "unhealthy." Their guns too were active and one shell, hitting an outhouse in which the officers not in the front line were snatching a little sleep, put Captain Lawrence out of action with a nasty wound, though Captain Ward and Lieutenant Salmon miraculously escaped unhurt. On the whole the day passed off quietly. The Germans did not develop any attack in force and gave the men in the front trenches little to shoot at, and about 9 p.m. the Camerons arrived to relieve the two companies, which started back for the bivouac near Hooge.

[1] The relief should have been completed by 8 p.m.

Headquarters and C and D Companies had meanwhile been sent forward along with the Welch to relieve part of the Seventh Division between Zandvoorde and the Western slopes of the Kruiseck knoll. These orders were issued too late for the relief to be carried out under cover of darkness, and the shelling and rifle fire prevented it being completed in daylight. Some of the battalion got into the front line, relieving the 1st R.W.F., but part of the 2nd Queen's remained in line between them and the Welch and the situation was rather confused. However,

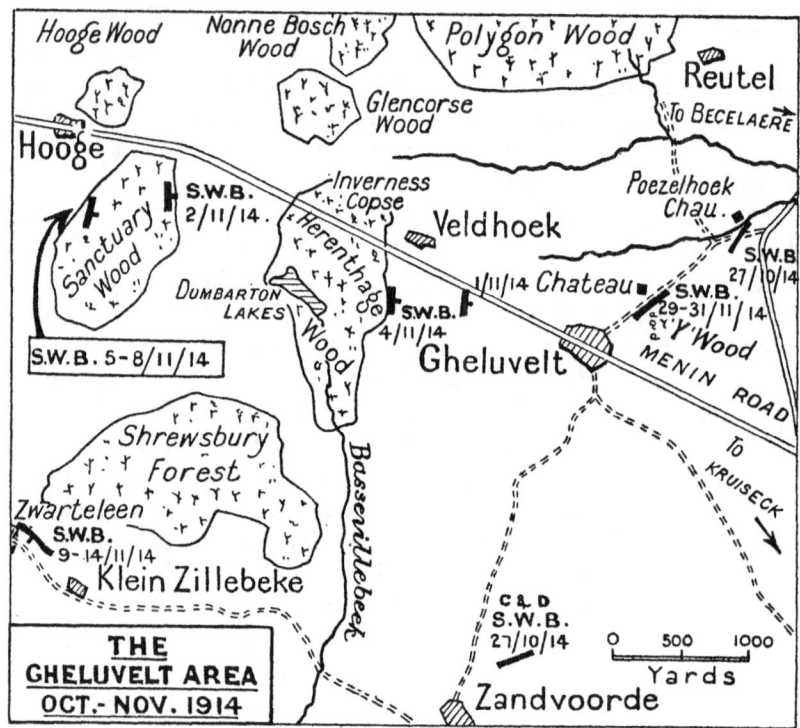

the day passed off quietly, and that night (October 27th/28th) the units of the 3rd Brigade were extricated and withdrawn to the old bivouac near Hooge. Here the half-battalion arrived about 3.30 a.m. (28th) to find A and B already there, and settled down to enjoy a quiet day, undisturbed and undamaged by the occasional German shells which fell near, apparently searching for British guns. Another big mail was in and a draft of 34 men arrived with Captains Lake and Maxwell of the 3rd Battalion and Second Lieutenant Fowkes, recently Gazetted from the R.M.C. That evening an urgent demand for the battalion's machine-gun section was received from General FitzClarence of the 1st Brigade. Lieutenant Hadley and his men pushed off at once. Of the whole detachment only

4 men were ever seen again, the rest were wiped out next day in resisting the big German attack along the Menin road, Lieutenant Hadley being last seen fighting desperately with a bayonet.

This attack, launched about 5.30 a.m. by the newly arrived 6th Bavarian Reserve Division, backed up by the XXVIIth Reserve Corps and three Cavalry Divisions, besides some Jäger and Landwehr units, was among the most formidable of all the German onslaughts. The attackers succeeded after hard fighting in breaking through near the junction of the First and Seventh Divisions at the cross-roads S.E. of Gheluvelt and gradually rolled up the lines of the 1st and 20th Brigades respectively North and South of the Menin road. The Gloucestershire were promptly thrown in to counter-attack towards the cross-roads and about 10 a.m. the battalion was ordered to fall in ready to move. At 11.15 it started down the road, halting for a time in Inverness Copse. About noon orders were issued for the 3rd Brigade to counter-attack through Gheluvelt and recover the lost trenches; accordingly the Queen's and Welch advanced on the right South of the road, with the battalion North of it. C Company led, followed by A, D, now under Captain Crewe-Read, and B, now commanded by Captain Gwynn. Streams of wounded were met coming back, and before long the battalion had passed through Gheluvelt, which was being heavily shelled and had already been badly knocked about. Here about 2 p.m. it diverged to the left past a derelict windmill and, filing out in the open, advanced to and occupied a small wood[1] about North of the 8th kilometre stone. Despite shell fire, casualties were few and the wood gave fair shelter. However, the Germans were in force from the cross-roads to Poezelhoek and without more accurate knowledge of the ground and more artillery support, shortage of shells was already a serious problem, further progress North of the road was impossible[2] and Colonel Leach, after consulting with Colonel Morland of the Welch, decided to take up a position East of and covering Gheluvelt. This was being done when, about 3.45 p.m., General Landon came up and gave orders for an advance against the German trenches along the Becelaere–Kruiseck road. C Company and two of the Welch started to carry this out but were soon held up,[3] Captain Lake being wounded. Eventually therefore, after a conference of battalion commanders near Gheluvelt Château, it was decided to abandon

---

[1] Y on plan.
[2] South of the road more progress seems to have been made in conjunction with a counter-attack by the Seventh Division.
[3] The First Division Diary states that the firing-line was 700 yards East of Gheluvelt when the attack stopped.

the counter-attack and consolidate the position which had been reached. The battalion accordingly set to work soon after dark to entrench a line which on the left ran along the Gheluvelt–Poezelhoek road in front of Gheluvelt Château, facing S.E. This was held by a platoon of A Company, on whose right D, B and C continued the line Southward, C's right resting on a copse about 200 yards North of the Menin road, beyond which the Welch continued the line to and across the road. On the left were the 1st Scots Guards (1st Brigade), whose headquarters were established along with those of the battalion in the stables

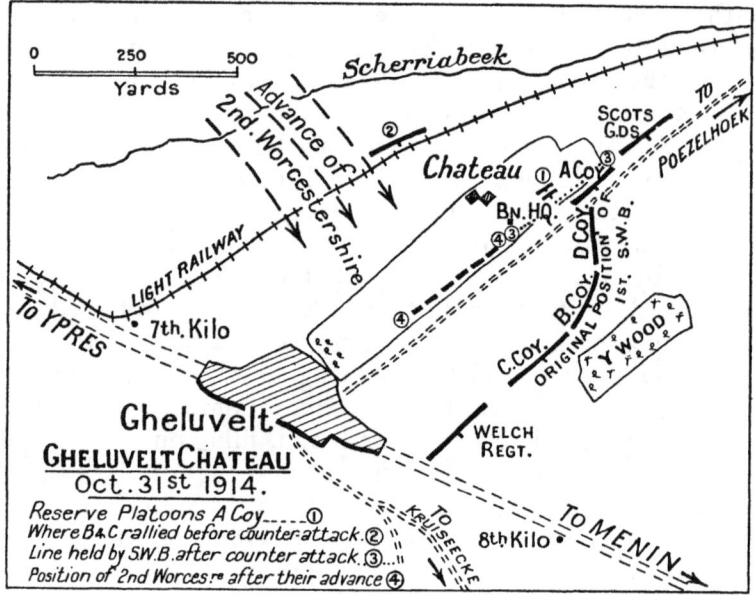

of Gheluvelt Château, the remainder of A Company being retained in reserve.

There was a great shortage of tools for entrenching, but as C's trenches, being on the upper part of a gentle slope and not covered by a wood[1], were the most exposed, they were given all the available picks and shovels, the others doing their best with their " grubbers." Unluckily, in superintending the issue of tools, the Adjutant was shot through the body; he survived to be taken back to hospital in Ypres but died a few days later after showing the same courage and self-control in his sufferings that he had displayed in the face of danger. He was a great loss to the battalion: his calm fearlessness had made a wonderful

[1] Y on plan.

impression on the men and proved a great encouragement and a steadying influence. Captain Gwynn now took over the Adjutancy, Lieutenant Ramsden succeeding to the command of B.

The battalion's new position was none too satisfactory. Its right was well in the open, and if the long copse in front of the centre and left afforded them some shelter, this equally gave cover behind which an attack might mass. Actually to be concealed from view meant less exposure to artillery fire and compared with this the cover the copse gave to German riflemen was unimportant. The soil was stiff clay and digging was made no easier by pouring rain all through the night of October 29th/30th. Next day, however, it was fine, with a warm sun and drying wind, so things improved slightly. The battalion was heavily shelled but by this time it was " pretty clever at digging," as one officer puts it, and escaped with very few casualties. There was heavy fighting, especially away to the right where Zandvoorde was lost and the Seventh Division forced to throw back its whole line,[1] but the battalion was not seriously pressed, though about 8 a.m. the German 54th Reserve Division appears by German accounts to have attacked the Gheluvelt front and been beaten off.[2]

October 31st, however, was to be very much the reverse of quiet. The Germans renewed the attack in greater force and with a greater weight of artillery behind it than ever. They had brought up fresh troops to replace and reinforce the units which had borne the brunt of the earlier struggles, while on the British side the same units, or rather their remnants, which had been in action when the fighting began, had to face the attacks of October 31st and succeeding days. The S.W.B., as battalions now went in the B.E.F., were strong; though sadly short of officers, having only 14[3] all told, it still mustered over 750 men, despite its losses at Langemarck, but few other battalions in the First Division were over half their proper strength, and the Germans who attacked on October 31st enjoyed an overwhelming advantage in numbers as well as in artillery.

---

[1] One consequence of this was that the position held by the Queen's, the right battalion of the 3rd Brigade, South of the Menin road became a pronounced salient.

[2] Cf. *France and Belgium.* 1914. Vol. II. p. 285. As the *Official History* (*ibid*. II., p. 175) remarks "many successful repulses by fire of German attacks receive no mention whatever in the diaries—they were regarded as a matter of course."

[3] The officers present on the morning of October 31st were Colonel Leach, Majors Reddie and Lawrence, Captains Ward, Gwynn, Crewe-Read and Maxwell, Lieutenants Ramsden, Salmon, Steward and Homfray, Second Lieutenants Silk, Graham and Fowkes, Lieutenant and Quartermaster Wilson.

It had been a troubled night with constant sniping and frequent shelling which developed shortly before daybreak into a bombardment of tremendous severity, followed by repeated infantry attacks. C Company in its exposed position suffered very heavily, but the battalion stuck stubbornly to its line and beat back all the infantry attacks. One of these left a party of Germans established in a trench facing B Company, but so sited that Lieutenant Salmon's platoon of A in the front line could enfilade it. Lieutenant Salmon hurried over to the Scots Guards, who still possessed a machine gun, and having got them to place it in position to enfilade the trench, opened fire with destructive results, whereupon the surviving Germans, nearly 60 in all, came rushing forward with their hands up in haste to surrender. This success was a great encouragement and in Colonel Leach's words, "instilled new life into everyone."[1] Second Lieutenant Graham[2] and a platoon of C actually counter-attacked and cleared the enemy out of a small copse on the right front.

Before long, however, the situation took a change for the worse. Though under heavy rifle fire, D Company and B's left were shielded from the shelling by the copse in front, but the rest of B and C beyond them could be accurately ranged on by the German guns, and casualties were so heavy that A from support had to be thrown in by driblets to replace them. The Welch were in as bad or worse plight. About 10 a.m. Colonel Morland visited Colonel Leach and informed him that his battalion had been nearly wiped out by the shell fire and that its position was becoming desperate. Some time after this the right of the Welch seems to have been overwhelmed, apparently by Germans who had penetrated into Gheluvelt from the South and cut off the Queen's, in the salient S.E. of the village. Thus in addition to the shelling and the infantry attacks on its front, C found itself under enfilade rifle and machine-gun fire from the Menin road. Major Lawrence, however, stuck stoutly to his almost untenable position, setting a magnificent example of steadfast courage which was largely responsible for the continued maintenance of the defence. Even when Germans got into a copse in rear of C he told off some men to turn round and fire over the parados and, hopeless as the position had now become,

---

[1] The prisoners, who belonged to the 6th Bavarian Reserve Division, were promptly handed over to an escort of half a dozen S.W.B. under Corporal Price, one of the regiment's best boxers, who not only escorted his charges across the shell-swept ground in rear, several of them and half the escort being hit in the process, but having discharged his duty returned to the firing-line.

[2] Second Lieutenant Graham, who with Sergeant Dwain as his spotter did some most effective sniping, was hit in the head about midday and mortally wounded.

his influence and example kept the men at their posts. But before long the remaining company of the Welch was overwhelmed and then from front, flank and rear the enemy swarmed upon the battered trenches to which the remnants of C were clinging. Major Lawrence went down fighting to the last, and only a handful of C managed to force their way back through the Germans already behind them, and the enemy, pushing on, drove them and B back into and across the Château grounds.[1]

On the left, however, Lieutenant Steward and the remainder of A Company's reserve had prepared a fire position along the bank of the Gheluvelt–Poezelhoek road, which they now manned. Some of the men who were retiring were stopped by Company Sergeant Major Hicks and took their places in A's line, while Captains Crewe-Read and Maxwell with most of D also joined A, a party under Captain Maxwell being posted by Major Reddie on a mound 70 yards S.E. of the Château so as to cover the avenue leading to the village and fire upon any Germans who attempted to cross the Château grounds towards the light railway which runs along their North-Western edge. Here Colonel Leach, Major Reddie and Captain Gwynn, assisted by Lieutenants Ramsden and Steward and Second Lieutenant Fowkes, were doing great work, rallying the survivors of B and C. Merely to have held on to the railway line and to have stopped the Germans there would have been an achievement, but Colonel Leach was not going to be content with this. A little earlier he had been visited by General FitzClarence's Staff Captain, Captain Thorne, and had sent back a report by him, pointing out the urgent need of support for the right, but without waiting for any possible reinforcements and thereby giving the Germans time to reorganize and to improve their advantage, he now counter-attacked at the head of the rallied remnant of B and C, aided by the handful that Battalion Headquarters could produce and a few Scots Guardsmen. The effect of the charge was immediate. It seemed to catch the Germans by surprise : many were shot or bayoneted, others bolted, throwing away rifles and equipment as they fled. In their flight they came under the fire of Captain Maxwell's party, while when they crossed the Poezelhoek road they afforded targets to A and D further to the left and to the Scots Guards beyond them. These stood up on the bank and did great execution on the retiring enemy, while Colonel Leach's men now came up and lined the edge of the Château grounds to the right. Casualties had been so heavy and the trenches in front were so badly battered that Colonel Leach did not think

---

[1] This seems to have been between 1 p.m. and 2 p.m.

it advisable to advance any further, especially as the enemy were still in possession of Gheluvelt and might at any moment renew the attack. The exact situation there was difficult to ascertain: patrols were dispatched thither but were cut off or returned without much news, until Lieutenant Ramsden volunteered to investigate and returned to report that the enemy, though in some strength in Gheluvelt, seemed disorganized and more concerned with obtaining water than with preparing to push on. Even so with the flank open the battalion's position was very insecure and an order to withdraw to Polderhoek was actually received over the telephone. However, at the same time the Scots Guards got an order from General FitzClarence to maintain their position, whereupon Colonel Leach decided to hold on.

His decision was justified when a little later the Germans began bombarding the ground to the battalion's right rear, and lines of British infantry were seen advancing from the woods West of Polderhoek. These were the 2nd Worcestershire under Major Hankey, practically the last reserves of the Second Division, whom General FitzClarence had sent up to counter-attack. Their advance completed the work which the stout resistance of A and D and Colonel Leach's counter-attack had begun. The Germans to the right of the battalion fled in confusion, affording splendid target, and the Worcestershire, prolonging the battalion's line towards Gheluvelt, made that flank secure,[1] so that the First Division's line was virtually re-established. Indeed, had things gone as well South of the Menin road as, thanks very largely to the TWENTY-FOURTH, they had North of it, the results of October 31st would have left the Germans little to boast about. South of the road, however, the Seventh Division had suffered terribly, and though a counter-attack had somewhat restored the situation, at least to the extent of arresting the German advance and thrusting them back, not enough ground had been regained to allow of Gheluvelt being retained. After dark therefore the 1st Brigade with the S.W.B. and Worcestershire was drawn back to a new line in front of Veldhoek, running from the Menin road about 600 yards West of Gheluvelt to Polygon Wood.

Orders for the evacuation of Gheluvelt Château had reached Colonel Leach about 5 p.m.; the Worcestershire moved first, then the Scots Guards, lastly the S.W.B., A Company covering the retirement. Many of the wounded were safely got away, others too badly hurt to be moved were left behind under the care of Captain Meaden, R.A.M.C., who gallantly volunteered

[1] Of the Germans in Gheluvelt, the majority seem to have bolted when the Worcestershire reached the Poezelhoek road, leaving the village clear.

to remain with them even with the certainty of falling into German hands.[1]

Near Polderhoek Château the battalion passed through some of the Black Watch and halted behind them to have the roll called,[2] while Major Reddie went off to get instructions. He eventually found the acting Brigadier, Colonel Lovett of the Gloucestershire,[3] a little way back along the Menin road and was told that the S.W.B. were to continue the line held by the Black Watch and to dig in South of the road. Returning with these orders he found himself in command as there had been some heavy shelling, by which Battalion Headquarters had been much knocked about and Colonel Leach severely wounded.[4]

Of all the fighting that the 1st Battalion had been through since its landing in France its defence of Gheluvelt Château stands out as the greatest achievement. It had been hard pressed on September 26th and its repulse of the attack on Mont Faucon had been a memorable feat, but the situation on that day was nothing like as critical and perilous as it was at Gheluvelt five weeks later. The B.E.F. was not then standing with its back to a wall. How critical that situation was has been universally acknowledged: Sir John French in his dispatch and again in his book " 1914," has described it with authority and emphasis. But when he wrote his dispatch, and again when he wrote " 1914," he had had no opportunity of going carefully into the details of the fighting or of ascertaining with accuracy the parts played by the different units. Hence while giving great credit to the Worcestershire for their gallant and successful counter-attack, he ignored the TWENTY-FOURTH. Subsequently, in the second edition of " 1914," he corrected the omission and acknowledged " the indomitable courage and dogged tenacity " which the battalion had displayed. Since then, too, the Official History has made quite clear the parts played by the two battalions, even if, naturally enough, it has not space to do more than summarize the story. " Gheluvelt " is a name to be

---

[1] He was awarded the D.S.O. for his devotion: it was from him also that information was ultimately received that even after the Château and its grounds had been evacuated the Germans had left it respectfully alone till five o'clock next morning.

[2] Two hundred and twenty-four men answered to their names: those definitely known to have been killed numbered 40, while 127 wounded were accounted for; the remainder being " missing " and for the most part dead.

[3] General Landon had succeeded General Lomax (wounded) in command of the Division.

[4] Colonel Leach's wounds were too severe for him to return to the battalion but his services were rewarded by a C.M.G. His period in command had been memorable and the battalion owed him not a little for what he had taught and helped it to do in the stern test of active service.

remembered with special pride by both regiments. There is credit enough and to spare for both the TWENTY-FOURTH and for the old Thirty-sixth. Each battalion's work supplemented the other's. Without the TWENTY-FOURTH's stand and counter-attack the situation might have been beyond the Worcestershire's power to save, that battalion's counter-attack in causing the Germans to evacuate Gheluvelt did something the remnant of the S.W.B. could not have accomplished.

Gheluvelt was far from ending what the 1st S.W.B. had to endure in First Ypres. Weak as it was—8 officers and 320 men—[1] it was stronger than many battalions in the B.E.F. and it could not be spared from the line. After digging in vigorously all night—as one officer puts it, " after a day of incessant fighting we spent a night of incessant digging "—it had next day (November 1st) to endure a heavy bombardment which tested the new trenches severely. When daylight came it had found level ground in front for about 200 yards with woods away to the right and a cottage in the foreground. On the left near the road A Company got occasional targets in Germans who appeared near the cottage, further to the right there was more to fire at, though the sandy soil made it difficult to keep the rifles in working order. The bombardment notwithstanding, casualties were few, though Captain Ward was buried by shells striking the parapet near him. It took twenty minutes to dig him out.

That evening the brigade was relieved and placed in reserve on the Eastern edge of Sanctuary Wood. After spending the morning (November 2nd) in improving the dug-outs in the wood it was called out about 1 p.m. for a counter-attack. This was necessary because the Germans had broken through the line S.W. of Veldhoek, had outflanked and overpowered the battalion of the K.R.R.C. who had relieved the S.W.B. the previous evening, and were advancing into the Herenthage Woods. Well supported by the guns and assisted on the flanks by French units who had recently reinforced the First Corps, the 3rd Brigade and some attached details successfully expelled the Germans from the Herenthage Woods, whereupon the indefatigable General FitzClarence tried to push on and recover the lost trenches.

---

[1] The discrepancy between this figure and the 224 given above (cf. p. 49) is to be accounted for by the transport detachment and others not in the line on October 31st. Of the officers, besides those mentioned Captain Maxwell had been killed and Captain Gwynn and Second Lieutenants Silk and Fowkes wounded. The eight still present were Major Reddie, now commanding, Lieutenant Steward, now Adjutant, Lieutenant Wilson, the Quartermaster, Captains Ward and Crewe-Read, Lieutenants Ramsden and Salmon, and Second Lieutenant Homfray, who now joined A Company, the Quartermaster taking over his transport work.

However, the men, a mixture of units with very few officers to lead them, were much too weary for a big effort and, despite all the General's efforts, enfilade fire from the South soon brought the advance to a standstill. Lieutenant Salmon, who with half A Company had taken part in the attack, the remainder of the battalion being held back in reserve, was wounded in the arm and several of his men were hit. Accordingly another new line had to be taken up on the Eastern edge of the Herenthage Woods with the battalion in support in the woods. Next evening it relieved the Welch and some French in the front line and spent a busy night connecting up the little detached trenches of which this consisted, besides making communication trenches to the rear and starting a second line to be occupied by day. The situation was now slightly less critical. Substantial French reinforcements had appeared, and though their efforts to advance on Gheluvelt met with very scanty success, the Germans seemed for the time to have shot their bolt on this part of the front. Early on the 4th they took advantage of a thick fog to attempt to advance, but without success, A Company aided by a machine gun on its left effectually keeping them in check, though the shelling this day was heavy and the battalion had several casualties. About midday the Germans were reported to be advancing again, and the Welch from reserve hastily reinforced the 3rd Brigade's right, but the line held and by 2 p.m. the pressure was relaxing. That evening the Gloucestershire relieved the battalion which went back into Divisional reserve near Hooge. Here it spent four days (November 5th–8th), mainly occupied in digging a reserve line on the Eastern edge of Hooge Wood. It had more than once to turn out on a false alarm that the Germans had broken through, but on the whole these were peaceful days,[1] though bivouacking in November was proving very unpleasant.

On the British front the Klein–Zillebeke quarter had of late been the most active. Here Lord Cavan with a mixed detachment from both First and Second Divisions had been covering the Seventh's right flank and connecting up with the French. On November 6th the other battalions of the 3rd Brigade were sent to join him and were put into line on his right, running from the Ypres–Comines railway near the afterwards famous "Hill Sixty," past Zwarteleen. On November 9th the battalion also was placed under his orders[2] and that evening it relieved the

[1] Casualties since October 31st had been low, barely thirty, but besides Lieutenant Salmon, Captain Crewe-Read and Lieutenant Ramsden had been wounded (on November 3rd).

[2] Three provisional brigades from the Second Corps had now relieved both the Seventh Division and the 3rd Brigade and were holding the centre of the First Corps' line South of the Menin road.

Munster Fusiliers[1] and Irish Guards near Zillebeke.[2] The position here was curious. The front line ran along the front edge of a narrow strip of wood, with a second line on the rear edge. Separated from the battalion's wood by a turnip field barely fifty yards across was another wood in which the Germans were posted. But, with a single strand of wire in front—it was "considered a luxury in those days" to have as much, one officer writes—the battalion regarded itself as almost impregnable against infantry attacks and was little worried by the shortness of the space between the lines. On the right more in the open were dismounted cavalry, British and French, the latter Cuirassiers who were believed by the British to have no rifles. The S.W.B. had barely settled down in their new surroundings before, about 10.30 a.m. on November 10th, the Germans began a furious bombardment, " the worst shelling I ever remember," Major Reddie describes it. Such efforts to advance as their infantry ventured upon met with no success and, except that Captain Ward was wounded in the head, the S.W.B. suffered little. They were equally fortunate again next day (November 11th) when the German XVth Corps attacked Cavan's detachment and those on its flanks in great force. This was part of the big attack in which the Prussian Guard, after breaking through the 1st Brigade near Veldhoek and reaching the Nonne Bosschen Wood, were counter-attacked and driven out by the Oxfordshire L.I. The main stress of the attack on " Cavan's Force" came rather to the battalion's left, but it was quite sharply engaged. Though very heavily bombarded, it stuck to its trenches and when the German infantry came pouring out of the woods to attack, received them with a rifle fire that soon sent them to the right-about. It was lucky to have but few casualties, though one of its few remaining officers, Lieutenant Homfray, was killed by a shell.[3] A feebler attack next day was

---

[1] This battalion had been reconstructed and had now joined the 3rd Brigade in place of the 1st Queen's, who had been practically wiped out at Gheluvelt on October 31st.

[2] Its right flank rested on the hamlet of Zwarteleen.

[3] The only officers now left were Major Reddie, Lieutenant Steward, the Quartermaster, and Second Lieutenant Shipley who had joined a few days earlier: three of the companies were therefore commanded by N.C.O.'s, of whom Company Sergeant Major Hicks was the only survivor of the original Company Sergeant Majors: Regimental Sergeant Major Shirley also survived but had the misfortune to be wounded on November 14th, the day the battalion was relieved. Company Sergeant Major Hicks became Acting Regimental Sergeant Major in his place. The Regimental Quartermaster Sergeant, Orderly Room Sergeant and all the Company Quartermaster Sergeants were also among the casualties, and on November 16th, Major Reddie, on parading the remaining N.C.O.'s to pick out men to fill the vacancies, found himself selecting a Corporal to become a Company Sergeant Major.

also repulsed, a few prisoners being taken. Thus the weary survivors of the battalion were still able to give a good account of themselves, nor did they leave the initiative entirely to the enemy, for when a machine gun posted in a house was making itself troublesome, Corporal Pugh and Private Black went out from our trenches, crawled up to the house and, rushing it, killed the entire team and put the machine gun out of action.[1]

On November 14th, to everyone's relief, the battalion was withdrawn from the trenches and went back to Hooge, moving next day into billets at Ypres. By this time the relief of the First Corps by French troops was in full swing and that evening the S.W.B. moved out of Ypres to Locre, proceeding two days later to a new billeting area S.W. of Bailleul where the Division was to be given a chance to recuperate and refit. A draft of 136 men had joined on November 12th and the battalion came out of the line just over 400 strong. The defence of the Channel Ports had cost it nearly twice that number; indeed, hard as it had been hit on the Aisne, Ypres had been a far harder trial, and but few who had landed at Havre in August were now left to march with the battalion to its well-deserved rest billets. They could, however, feel that in the three memorable months since what seemed now a very far-off day, they had helped to sustain to the full the Regiment's traditions and to add notably to its laurels.

---

[1] They were awarded the D.C.M., as was also Private Gunter who had twice shown great gallantry in going back under heavy fire to fetch ammunition and guide up reinforcements.

CHAPTER IV

EXPANSION

ON the 1st Battalion's departure for France its "details," the young soldiers who were under age or had not completed their training, with the few medically "unfits," had, as already mentioned, been sent to the 3rd Battalion at Pembroke Dock, arriving on August 23rd. The 3rd's ranks had already been swelled by the Regular Reservists not required to complete the 1st Battalion to war establishment[1] and the arrival of the 1st's "details" brought it up well over 1000 strong, while recruits came in as fast as the Depot could attest and dispatch them. Drafts fairly poured in, and in October the establishment was raised to 2500, new companies being formed as required.[2] This naturally put a big strain on the battalion staff, whose energies were severely taxed. The Regular officers on the battalion's establishment were nearly all transferred to the new "Service" battalion, whose formation had been authorized on August 7th, or, like Lieutenant Salmon, had departed with the drafts of which the 1st Battalion seemed always in need. In their place came the newly Gazetted Regular subalterns from the R.M.C., like Second Lieutenants Fowkes and G. D. O. Lloyd, N.C.O.'s promoted to commissioned rank, and a flood of newly appointed Special Reserve officers, a dozen being Gazetted to the Regiment on August 15th and half a dozen more in the first week of September.[3] With them came several of senior standing and experience who came in as Lieutenants or Captains and gave valuable help in the instruction of the new hands. By the end of September no less than twenty-two new subalterns had been appointed to the 3rd Battalion, and before the year ended the number had risen to fifty.[4]

By the end of the year not only had the remaining Regular Reservists and nearly all the "young soldiers" departed for the

---

[1] These numbered over 200, the "details" mustered 194, and about 50 Regulars from the Depot, including Sergeant Major Marr and Quartermaster Sergeant Mellsopp, had also proceeded to Pembroke Dock.

[2] The "double company" organization was adopted on September 21st.

[3] Most of these had already learnt the rudiments of their work in the Officers' Training Corps, and one of them, Second Lieutenant Watkins from the Oxford University O.T.C., went to the front within a month of being Gazetted and was killed at Langemarck on October 22nd.

[4] Regimental Sergeant Major Marr, Company Sergeant Major Thomas and Sergeant Hooper all departed on October 2nd to join the 4th Battalion, having been promoted to Second Lieutenant. Regimental Quartermaster Sergeant Mellsopp had preceded them by some weeks, having been appointed Quartermaster of the new unit on August 23rd. Company Sergeant Major W. Bruntnell became Regimental Sergeant Major of the 3rd Battalion and Sergeant J. Martin succeeded to the vacancy as Regimental Quartermaster Sergeant.

front, but most of the Special Reservists also had been utilized for drafts, so the battalion staff had to concentrate its energies on licking into shape the post-August-4th recruits who alone remained available. It was arduous work. The men, though willing, were very raw: there was a great dearth of rifles and of equipment for training purposes: the calls on the battalion for the duties which had to be performed by the garrison were many and varied, and there was all too little time for training. The burden which fell on the permanent staff of the Special Reserve battalions was heavy, particularly perhaps in that first winter of unpreparedness and deficiencies in every kind of equipment, though there were few periods in all the four and a half years when the strain was appreciably relaxed. Later on more equipment was available, convalescent officers and men from "the front" were available to help with the training, administrative arrangements had been systematized and worked more smoothly, so that if the demands of the battalions overseas for drafts were insatiable and unending, meeting them had almost become a matter of routine. But in the winter of 1914–1915 conditions were about at their worst and the officers and N.C.O.'s on whom the work fell, many of them men over military age or for medical reasons unfit for active service, deserve to be gratefully remembered as having "done their bit" full well and helped appreciably in the great task of enabling the battalions overseas to maintain unimpaired the Regimental reputation and traditions, and even enhance them by new examples of devotion, gallantry and self-sacrifice. That all the drafts dispatched were fully up to the August, 1914, level of efficiency, particularly in musketry, is not to be maintained: that their average was, all things considered, so high is enormously to the credit of those responsible for their training.[1]

Training drafts was not the 3rd Battalion's sole occupation. Pembroke Dock, though not on the coast most exposed to German raids or attacks, was an important naval station, and the duties of its garrison were arduous enough. In November, when alarms of intended German raids, if not of actual invasion, were specially rife, orders were received to send four "Service companies" of trained soldiers to Edinburgh where they were to join a mobile Reserve Brigade. These companies went off on November 19th under Colonel Morgan, the rest of the battalion being left behind under Major Gibson-Watt. Drafts for overseas were normally furnished by these "Service companies," which were kept up to strength by transfer from the companies at

[1] Some idea of the increased work which fell upon the battalion is afforded by the fact that the Orderly Room staff, of which Quartermaster Sergeant Chatfield was in charge, had to be increased to twenty.

Pembroke. Before this the 3rd Battalion had already furnished a substantial nucleus nearly 600 strong for a new Service battalion, the 9th, formed on October 31st,[1] but recruits continued to pour in, and a new element began to appear in the shape of the convalescents from the 1st Battalion.[2] These were very useful as instructors, their first-hand knowledge of " trench warfare " being far more useful than all the pamphlets and "Notes from the Front " which the War Office could produce. On the 2nd Battalion's return in January, 1915, a new demand on the 3rd developed, as it required a draft of 234 men to bring it up to war establishment before proceeding overseas again. The flow of recruits had somewhat slackened off by now, but the 3rd's strength rarely fell below 2000; and with the constant Gazetting of new officers there were generally from 50 to 60 present with the battalion, which had at one time as many as 200 officers on its strength. On March 11th, 1915, the " Service companies " from Edinburgh returned to Pembroke Dock, the acute anxiety about invasion having long ago evaporated.[3] In June, however, came a fresh move, this time for the whole battalion, which was transferred from the " Severn Defences " to the " Mersey Defences." On June 9th the battalion took up its quarters at Hightown near Liverpool, where it was to remain for " duration," as it did not move away till some months after the Armistice.

While the Special Reserve battalion was thus engaged in its dual task of manning coast defences and preparing drafts the Regiment's only Territorial battalion had already proceeded overseas. Before the declaration of war the Brecknockshire Battalion had returned to Brecon to be ready to mobilize, and on completing mobilization had moved to its war station at Fort Scoveston, Pembroke Dock, on August 5th. Here the battalion remained till September 28th, when it shifted to Dale near the entry to Milford Haven, having a detachment under Major D. W. E. Thomas at East Blockhouse on the opposite side of the Haven. The Brecknocks had been well up to establishment on mobilization and were very well off indeed for officers, but recruits poured in so that even after a few medically unfits had

---

[1] On the formation of the 9th Battalion the two junior companies of the 3rd Battalion, G and H, were reduced, but in February the influx of recruits and recovered wounded allowed a new G Company to be formed, and H reappeared before the end of March.

[2] The first recorded joined on September 14th, but it was not till much later that any large number appeared.

[3] About this time Captain Thomas departed overseas to join the 1st Battalion, relieving Lieutenant Wilson who, though invalided home, was able to take over duty with the 3rd Battalion.

been discharged the battalion was soon well over strength. Like other Territorial units the Brecknocks were invited to volunteer for foreign service, and responded so readily to the call that the battalion was placed high on the list of T.F. units available for duty abroad. Expectations of an early departure for France ran high, but the particular duty for which the battalion was required proved not to be to reinforce the B.E.F. in France, but to proceed to Aden, and by undertaking garrison duty at that important coaling station release a Regular unit for service at the front. On October 19th, therefore, the battalion moved back to Fort Scoveston to prepare for foreign service. All those under age or otherwise unfit for service abroad and the few who had not taken on the foreign service obligation were now transferred to a Home Service unit to which the mass of untrained recruits were posted. Major G. Turner, an officer on retired pay, was posted on October 3rd to command this " Reserve Battalion," and Major Pugh Morgan[1] took over the Adjutant's duties. As Major Isaac was unfit for foreign service he also joined the new unit as Quartermaster. In his place the foreign service unit was so fortunate as to secure the services of an old member of the Regiment, Lieutenant Elvidge, who joined on October 5th and whose experience of the ways and customs of the East was to prove of the greatest use to the battalion. His help was the more valuable because, after the battalion had reached Southampton on October 29th to embark on the transport *Dilwara*, a telegram was received from the War Office ordering Captain Lloyd and all but one of the Sergeant Instructors to return to Brecon and await further orders. Lieutenant M. F. Thomas was therefore appointed Adjutant in Captain Lloyd's place and Company Sergeant Major Green took over the Regimental Sergeant Major's duties. That evening the *Dilwara* sailed for the East in company with several other transports carrying the Wessex Territorial Division, bound for India on the same errand as the Brecknocks were to discharge at Aden.

In the meantime several other battalions had been added to the four " pre-war " battalions of the TWENTY-FOURTH. As previously described the formation of a 4th S.W.B. had been authorized on August 7th when the party already mentioned had been detailed from the 1st Battalion to serve as its nucleus. On August 19th Major Gillespie was promoted " temporary Lieutenant Colonel " to command the new unit, and before August was out it was already in effective existence at Parkhouse Camp on Salisbury Plain. Of Regular officers Colonel Gillespie had to assist him Captains H. P. Yates, who became Adjutant, and

---

[1] Promoted to that rank on October 20th.

R. H. Evans, who was subsequently attached to the 1st Dorsets, Lieutenants Godwin-Austen, Lochner and Mundy, and Second Lieutenant Copner, while several old officers of the Regiment were appointed to the new battalion from the Reserve of Officers. Major Cooke was the first Gazetted, to date August 29th, Major Beresford followed next day and Captain Kitchin ten days later.[1] The 4th was therefore fortunate in having so many trained officers to start its new hands on the right path, more particularly in having as its C.O. an officer of the zeal, energy, professional knowledge and personality of Colonel Gillespie, who from the start set up the very highest standards as the ideal for the new battalion. But the task before Colonel Gillespie and his helpers was greatly lightened by the zeal and keenness with which the raw recruits threw themselves into the uphill task of becoming efficient soldiers in the shortest possible time. When " K. 1," as the " First New Army " was generally known, was originally formed it was announced that it was to be ready for the front in six months. There were some who did not believe a serviceable battalion could be produced in so short a space, others argued that even if this were possible the war would be over long before that. Undeterred by these doubts " K. 1 " set about learning its trade as fast as the shortage of every kind of appliance for instruction would allow it. It was largely a matter of making bricks without straw. Drill could be learnt in plain clothes, though when men could be put into any kind of uniform discipline and *esprit de corps* certainly benefited, but musketry instruction without rifles was a different affair, and some time elapsed before even " K. 1 " battalions could get enough rifles for musketry to be taught to the platoons in turn. Equipment for specialists like machine gunners and signallers was even longer in putting in an appearance, and at first all sorts of makeshifts had to be devised for quite ordinary articles of which the official stock had become exhausted.

Parkhouse Camp was quite a pleasant spot in fine weather and September, 1914, was on the whole warm and dry. With general keenness and readiness to learn on the part of those to be instructed progress was rapid, especially when the obstacles and handicaps to training are taken into account. Recruiting was proceeding rapidly meanwhile, so rapidly that early in September a second "Service" battalion was formed and was encamped alongside the 4th during the first weeks of its career. The 5th South Wales Borderers belonged to the " Second New Army," whose formation had been authorized early in September. "K.1" had already been organized into six Divisions, the 4th

---

[1] The first Quartermaster was Lieutenant Mellsopp, who was appointed to that post on August 23rd.

EXPANSION

S.W.B. being posted along with other Welsh and Western units to the Thirteenth (Western) Division, commanded by Major General R. G. Kekewich, the defender of Kimberley in the South African War. It was brigaded along with the 8th Cheshires, 8th R.W.F. and 8th Welch in the 40th Brigade, the staff of which was entirely drawn from the TWENTY-FOURTH, who provided a Brigadier in Brigadier General J. H. du B. Travers, a Brigade Major in Captain Morgan-Owen, and a Staff Captain in Lieutenant Godwin-Austin. In organization " K.2 " was an almost exact replica of " K.1," and the 5th S.W.B. were allotted to the 58th Brigade of a Nineteenth (Western) Division,[1] composed of the corresponding battalions of the regiments represented in the 40th Brigade.

The 4th S.W.B. were very fortunate in their first C.O. ; the 5th had equal cause to congratulate themselves in that Colonel Trower was available to make the battalion. Colonel Trower, who had joined the Regiment in 1877 and had only just missed reaching Rorke's Drift in time to share in that memorable defence, had retired in 1905 from the command of the 1st Battalion. When he arrived on September 4th, 1914, at Parkhouse Camp the 5th Battalion was indeed starting under good auspices. No one could have been better fitted to handle that motley crowd, two-thirds of them colliers to whom military discipline was wholly unfamiliar and not a little irksome, to whom for example the notion that absence without leave was a really serious offence was almost an absurdity. He was quick to see how this magnificent raw material was best to be treated, to reduce punishments to a necessary minimum, while at the same time setting up a very high ideal of conduct and discipline, of which he was himself the embodiment. He taught by precept and by example : he was patient, forbearing and considerate, and before long he had obtained a remarkable hold over his men.

Colonel Trower was not without help from other Regular officers. Major C. V. R. Wright was one of the first officers Gazetted to the 5th, and, as the 4th was unusually well supplied with Regulars for a Service battalion, Lieutenants Lochner and Copner were transferred to the 5th as from September 12th, the former becoming Adjutant. Major F. P. Smyly also joined in September, and in October Major Cooke was also transferred from the 4th, becoming second in command of the 5th. By this time the 4th had been joined by two more senior officers of experience, Brevet Colonel F. W. Birch, a retired officer of the

[1] Major General G. C. M. Fasken was the original G.O.C. of the Nineteenth Division, Brigadier General C. T. Becker commanded the 58th Brigade.

Indian Army, and Sir W. L. Napier, a retired Colonel of Territorials, who both joined as Majors and took command of companies. October also saw the arrival of most of the subalterns required to complete the 4th and 5th Battalions. The subalterns for "K.1" and "K.2," who came for the most part from the Universities and Public Schools, were a splendid set of young men. One of the original Regular officers of the 4th Battalion has written of them, " Without exception they showed themselves to be leaders of the right type, keen and quick to learn, ready to take responsibility, soon earning the respect and confidence of their men." Most of them had learnt something of their work in the O.T.C., and the reason for the delay in their appearance was that on being commissioned they had all been sent for a month to a camp of instruction. This was very valuable and the young officers on joining were already fairly proficient in platoon and company drill, had learnt the elements of musketry and tactics, and were ready to take a share in instructing their men from the moment they arrived. Later-formed Service battalions, whose original subalterns were not given any such course of instruction, were therefore at a disadvantage in comparison with " K. 1 " and " K. 2."

But of later-formed Service battalions the TWENTY-FOURTH was to produce a substantial number. Under the 1881 organization Wales and Monmouthshire had, unlike Scotland, fewer regiments to support than their population in 1914 might have warranted, and as few districts had done as well in recruiting as Wales the number of Service battalions in the three Welsh regiments was unusually high. In September a call was sent out to form a third " New Army," and to this, " K. 3," the TWENTY-FOURTH's recruiting area actually contributed enough men for the formation of three battalions. The 6th, 7th, and 8th S.W.B. may be reckoned as having come into existence by the middle of September, the earliest dates on which any officers were Gazetted to them being respectively September 12th (6th Battalion), September 14th (7th) and September 19th (8th), and October 1st found them all provided with C.O.'s and with nearly a dozen subalterns apiece. The 6th were originally commanded by Lieutenant Colonel J. D. A. T. Lloyd, an old officer of the Regiment, the 7th by Brevet Colonel H. E. Hancock, an Indian Army officer, and the 8th by Brevet Colonel D. F. Lewis, who had retired from the Indian Army.

Training the 4th and 5th Battalions was difficult enough in the prevailing shortage of weapons and all kinds of equipment. The " K. 3 " battalions naturally fared worse in these respects than the earlier-formed units, and were even worse off as regards trained instructors. There were not enough to go round and "first formed, first supplied." However, there were not wanting veterans, of all ranks, who came forward at this crisis to do most valuable work in training the new units. Many of these veterans were unable to stand the strain of those strenuous winter months, accentuated as it so often had to be by real hardships in the way of camps and quarters: others, who had stood this strain, were unequal to the medical tests required of those who were to go overseas, and, after having done yeoman service in training, had the chagrin of being left behind by the battalions they had helped to form. To enumerate all who did good work for the TWENTY-FOURTH in this great emergency would fill too many pages, to attempt a selection from among them would be invidious, but the Regiment owes these veterans a great debt. It was from them that the new battalions in large measure acquired their zeal for the Regiment and its traditions, their determination not to let those traditions suffer in their keeping, their pride in being members of a great company.

That winter's task was up-hill work indeed. What has been said of the 3rd Battalion's difficulties in regard to training and equipping the drafts it had to supply in ever increasing quantities applies very forcibly to the Service battalions. It was long before they were properly clothed, longer before they were properly equipped, and longest before they were properly armed. The camps in which they had come into existence were not exactly suited for occupation at the end of autumn, and troops who found themselves still under canvas towards the end of November were experiencing a quite realistic foretaste of some features of active service. Thus the 4th S.W.B., who moved in October from Parkhouse Camp to Chiseldon near Swindon, found their new camp badly sited on low-lying ground which heavy rain soon turned into a marsh. They had no difficulty in believing the inhabitants, who assured them that snipe were often shot on the site of their encampment. Indeed the fields in which the battalion was encamped were actually the source of a stream of sufficient dimensions to be named, and when the weather broke and heavy winter rains set in this rivulet, the Og, rapidly filled and overflowed the low-lying fields through which it wandered. At this time the troops were still in tents, though a hutted camp was in process of erection. With the camp flooded life in tents proved extraordinarily unpleasant, culminating in a violent gale which flattened out most of the tents and turned the swampy fields into a lake. A move was made to such of the huts as were habitable, but many of them could not be used, as the flooded stream was pouring over their floors. What made things worse was that the men had only one suit of service dress with other clothing on the same scale, and except for the fortunate few who possessed extra underclothing or boots of their own there was no chance of changing into dry clothes when wet. Whatever the weather training went on continuously and at high pressure, a half-holiday on Sundays being all that could at first be allowed, while to devote the maximum time to training barrack-room duties, such as kit inspections, were mostly relegated to the evenings, and the C.O. and Adjutant usually carried out their Orderly Room work after dinner, so as to enable them to supervise effectually the training of the companies. What with the bad weather and the strenuousness of the training the strain on the men was severe and their health suffered in consequence. Septic throats in particular were prevalent, with rheumatism and chills. Indeed the marvel was that the sick-rate was no higher. The battalion therefore welcomed the news that they and the 5th Wiltshires[1] were to move into billets at Cirencester, whither they proceeded early in December.

The 5th meanwhile had remained at Parkhouse and were finding it bleak and exposed. The winds blew vigorously from every quarter, sometimes it seemed from all together. November brought rain in copious quantities. Many tents had no tent boards, and although various drainage schemes were devised the lines became ever more deeply submerged in mud. Training was hampered by the constant calls for working parties to try and improve the camp, but despite all they had to endure the men remained patient and on the whole cheerful. The climax came with an awful evening of wind and storm when in quick succession the Y.M.C.A. marquee, the library tent and the band tent were carried away, together with a number of bell tents, while only by tremendous efforts was the officers' mess just prevented from following suit. After this orders to move into billets at Basingstoke were very welcome, and on December 7th the battalion entrained in the pouring rain, in which it was to be its usual fate to move, for that town. It left 100 men behind under Major Smyly, who were detailed to carry out a scheme of hut construction and did their work so well that the battalion's selection to be the Divisional Pioneers was partly attributed to the authorities' satisfaction with their efforts. But the battalion contained a higher proportion of officers and men trained in mining and engineering than any other in the Division, and its selection, which was announced in January, was only natural.

[1] This battalion, originally Army Troops of "K.1," had replaced in the 40th Brigade the 8th Welch, who had been selected to become Pioneers.

The experiences of the " K. 3 " battalions were not dissimilar. Of these three the 6th had been allotted to the Twenty-Fifth Division, originally commanded by Major General F. Ventris, which was being formed at Codford on Salisbury Plain.[1] This camp, to which the battalion moved from Brecon towards the end of September, was hardly happily chosen. The site was damp, and, to make matters worse, no floor boards were available for the tents. Indeed the enormous demand for all the various articles of equipment needed for camp life had completely outrun the supply, so that officers and men had to put up with all kinds of makeshifts, some of them not too satisfactory. The 6th were quite without office stationery and found the lack of an adequate supply of " Army Forms " a serious impediment to progress, making the daily routine hard to conduct. Uniforms of a kind were issued towards the end of October, when the battalion was put into what were described as " Kitchener's blue suits," made out of a supply of blue cloth believed to have been made for the Police. Effective rifles were not available, and it was hard to do much training with nothing better than " D.P." weapons. Recruits and young officers flowed in and by the beginning of November the 6th was fairly well up to establishment, while as far as the deficiencies in its equipment would allow it was making good progress with its training.

The 7th and 8th found themselves in the Twenty-Second Division under Major General R. A. Montgomery, and were brigaded together in the 67th Brigade with the 11th R.W.F. and 11th Welch, Brigadier General R. B. Williams being their first Brigade commander. This Division was originally assembled at Lewes in Sussex, where it was brought together towards the end of September, moving to Seaford on the last day of the month. Seaford, though attractive enough as a camping place in spring or summer, had its drawbacks in autumn, when storms off the sea became frequent and nearness to the sea meant that everything tended to get and remain damp. However, the Sussex Downs provided ample elbow-room and there was no lack of good ground to train on, and both battalions set seriously to work to make themselves soldiers. They were greatly handicapped, as all the later-formed Service battalions were, by the lack of trained instructors as well as of appliances and equipment, and their steady progress towards efficiency was greatly to the credit of all concerned.

The 7th were particularly fortunate in having a large number of experienced senior officers to conduct their training, and both

---

[1] It was in the 76th Brigade under Brigadier General E. M. Archdale, along with the 10th R.W.F., 10th Welch and 7th K.S.L.I.

battalions had attracted a very good stamp of recruits. Owing partly to the big demands on the 3rd Battalion for drafts the bulk of the re-enlisted ex-soldiers were transferred to it—the 7th for example alone sent back about 60 on October 19th—their places being taken by fresh recruits, of whom the Depot could produce almost unlimited numbers.

Officering " K. 3 " was not a very easy matter at first. By the time it came into existence not only were very few senior officers of recent experience available, but the supply of young men with any measure even of O.T.C. training had been pretty well exhausted and the valuable O.T.C. training camps had unfortunately been broken up, so that in " K. 3 " battalions most of the young officers started on the same level of military knowledge—or rather ignorance—as the men they had to command. But there were now coming forward many men of a rather different type from the " K. 1 " and " K. 2 " subalterns. They had represented the pick of the undergraduates and older Public Schoolboys : " K. 3 " got fewer of these, but rather more older men with some experience of professional life and work. Many of them had come back from the Colonies or China or the Argentine, while others had not at first been able to find substitutes to take over their work : certainly all three " K. 3 " battalions of the TWENTY-FOURTH were very fortunate in their subalterns. That there were some " misfits " was hardly wonderful, seeing the hurry and rush with which the new battalions had to be got together and the scanty opportunities for testing the numerous applicants for commissions ; it was more remarkable they were so few. At first it was rather a matter of chance what officers were appointed to the different battalions, but once the units began to take shape the C.O.'s and other senior officers were often able to get hold of young men of their acquaintance, one officer might bring in one or two friends of the right type, and gradually the officer cadres filled up and began to acquire cohesion and character. By the end of 1914 the 6th S.W.B. had two Majors, a Captain and twenty-five subalterns, the 7th three Majors, seven Captains and seventeen subalterns, the 8th two Majors, five Captains and twenty-three subalterns.[1] Among the senior officers were several old members

---

[1] The original Adjutants of the three battalions were: 6th Battalion, Lieutenant F. Carter, whose appointment dated from November 15th; 7th Battalion, Captain Boys, who held his post from September 19th till the end of November; 8th Battalion, Captain L. T. Thorp, appointed on September 29th. The Quartermasters were Lieutenant V. W. Bloxham (6th, appointed September 20th), G. Martin (7th, appointed September 22nd) and J. Wilson (8th, appointed October 5th). The first Regimental Sergeant Majors of these battalions were Casey (6th), Sherwood (7th) and Cushman (8th), but in November Company Sergeant Major Talmage became Regimental Sergeant Major of the 7th.

of the TWENTY-FOURTH, notably Majors A. M. Addison and A. H. M. Hamilton Jones of the 8th, and Captain J. Grimwood of the 7th; while several others had previous military experience, such as Major Kaye and Captain H. H. Boys of the 7th, the latter a retired Indian Army officer, who did excellent work as Adjutant in its very early days, and Lieutenant Colonel C. Davidson, who became second in command of the 6th.

Like the " K. 1 " and " K. 2 " battalions those of " K. 3 " remained in camp for some time after the legitimate camping season was over and found life under canvas as autumn was passing into winter peculiarly uncomfortable and unattractive. At length the authorities seemed to realize that, however patient and long-suffering the keen recruits of the New Armies might be, it was essential to give them roofs over their heads and something dry to sleep on, and a move into billets followed. The 6th's fate took them to the Bournemouth neighbourhood, whither their whole Division moved early in November, a fortnight's practically consecutive rain having made Codford quite impossible as a camping ground and thereby precipitated a move if the Division was not to be washed away altogether. At Bournemouth the Division found comfortable quarters, if the difficulties of training were somewhat increased when the men were scattered in billets. It was to remain in this area till well into the spring, for though it moved out of Bournemouth itself to Parkstone in February, and went on to Larkhill early in March, it returned to Parkstone at the end of that month. Actually it did not move away till the end of April, when it marched through the New Forest to Hursley Park and encamped there for three weeks. Long before this time the 6th S.W.B. had altered their status and quitted the 76th Brigade to become " Divisional troops," the battalion having been selected in January for training as Pioneers, a part for which the high percentage of miners in its ranks naturally marked it out.

The 7th and 8th had also been forced to quit the too open-air life at Seaford and seek shelter in billets. St. Leonards provided the 7th with most comfortable quarters and much hospitality, the 8th being next door to them in Hastings. The move into billets was made on December 1st, and the two battalions remained in these quarters, to their great content, until March, though the 8th transferred to Battle in February for a week's special training. On March 1st, the 8th moved to Hawkhurst, in Sussex, shifted to Maidstone after a fortnight, were there for ten days and then marched back to Seaford, where they arrived on April 11th. They had been employed during this time on digging part of the London defences, the 7th being sent to Bromley and Knockholt on a similar errand from March

19th till April 7th, when they also returned to Seaford, by this time a much more congenial spot than it had been when the two battalions left it. Here, brigade and Divisional training were the order of the day, while "specialists," who had been already selected for their different tasks,[1] were able to acquire much more proficiency as they were now being adequately supplied with equipment. The 8th now blossomed out into the possession of a band, formed in April. Promotions to non-commissioned rank, most of which had at first been only provisional, had now been confirmed and made definite. Some of the original selections found themselves reverting somewhat abruptly to a lower level, others whose ascent had been less meteoric were more firmly established. Several younger officers who had joined as Second Lieutenants developed into possessors of a second or even a third "star," and altogether the battalions were settling down into shape. The 8th got a specially good report from an inspecting General in March, being complimented on its handling of arms and its drill.

During the winter months several changes took place among the officers of the Service battalions. Thus Colonel Lewis was forced by ill-health to relinquish command of the 8th: Major W. D. Sword, of the North Staffords, replaced him, being Gazetted temporary Lieutenant Colonel to command the battalion on December 25th; a couple of months later (February 20th) Colonel Lloyd vacated command of the 6th, also for ill-health, and was succeeded by Lieutenant Colonel E. V. O. Hewett of the Queen's Own (Royal West Kent). Captain Boys had had to leave the 7th in November, Captain Grimwood replacing him as Adjutant, and other senior officers who had to retire eventually after doing good service in the infancy of their battalions included Colonel Davidson of the 6th, Majors Kaye, Carruthers and Benson of the 7th, and Captains Scott-Napier (7th) and Ralston (6th). Meanwhile, despite all the difficulties against which the new battalions had to contend, steady progress was made towards efficiency. Naturally the earlier formed units, being first for service overseas, got preferential treatment in regard to uniforms, effective rifles and other articles of equipment. "K. 3" had to put up with all sorts of weapons and in the all-essential matter of musketry they were greatly handicapped until, quite late in the summer, Service rifles could be provided.

The 4th and 5th Battalions meanwhile had spent the winter months in far greater comfort than had been possible in the

---

[1] The 7th's machine-gun section was formed in January, Lieutenants G. D. Taylor and Treglown being posted to it, and about the same time Lieutenant Giles was appointed Transport Officer.

camps in which they had come into being. When the 4th had marched into Cirencester the inhabitants had remarked on the worn appearance of the men, which had testified clearly as to the hardships they had been enduring. The change to comfortable and dry quarters combined with the good food provided by the hospitable people on whom the men were billeted, soon worked wonders both with the health and the appearance of the men. It was now clear that not even " K. 1 " could be ready for active service as soon as had been hoped, as it was out of the question to provide it with all the equipment it needed, the delay in providing field guns would alone keep it back some time. It was possible, therefore, to mitigate somewhat the strenuous character of the training, to let Sunday become a day of complete rest, to give a Saturday half holiday and to allow of week-end leave, so that the strain was substantially relaxed. In the end the 4th spent over three months in their pleasant quarters at Cirencester before moving to Woking in March for brigade and Divisional training. Here they were lodged along with the 5th Wiltshire in Woking Barracks, which was rather a close fit for two strong battalions.

The 5th, who had been as hospitably received at Basingstoke as the 4th at Cirencester, were, somewhat to their annoyance, sent back to the Plain in January for a musketry course at Perham Down. Here they were quartered in half-finished huts, devoid of fire-places or heating facilities and situated in a sea of mud. There were so few rifles that only one company could shoot at a time and the precious weapons had then to be handed over to the next. Heavy rain and bitter cold did not improve matters, but as one account says, " if the conditions could not have been worse, we occasionally hit the target in spite of everything."

This musketry course was followed by a move on January 20th to fresh billets at Burnham, in Somerset, where again the 5th were most hospitably received. Burnham was an admirable training ground, with its hard asphalt sea front to do duty as a barrack square and its sand dunes to afford ample space for open order work and tactical schemes. Across the Severn Sea the lights of Newport were visible, and if leave was not often to be had, the mere sight of them was better than nothing. A noticeable incident of the stay at Burnham was the arrival of a handful of mules who " turned out to be more than a handful," but whose appearance was greeted as a step forward. In March came orders for a return to " the Plain " and on March 4th the 5th bade farewell to their kind Somerset hosts and moved to Sling Camp, near Bulford. Shortly before this it had lost Major Smyly, who had received command of the 7th Dorsets: his knowledge and experience and genial personality had been of the greatest value to the young battalion and his departure was much regretted. Captain G. S. Crawford succeeded to the command of A Company.

As already mentioned, a 9th Battalion had come into existence on October 31st, its nucleus being formed by drafting 600 men from the over-flowing 3rd Battalion. Command of this was given to an old officer of the 1st Battalion, Major E. S. Gillman,[1] who had as his second in command Major A. T. Walling of the Indian Army, while Second Lieutenant F. E. V. Blowen was appointed Adjutant and Lieutenant J. Scott Quartermaster.[2] The 9th as originally constituted had two companies only, a third being added in the summer of 1915 as new officers and men flowed in, although its training was severely handicapped by the usual difficulties of " New Army " battalions as regards clothing and even more equipment. Having come into existence at Pembroke Dock it remained in that area for the first eight months of its existence, being allotted along with the 3rd S.W.B. to the land defences of Pembroke Dock. On January 1st, 1915, however, it officially became part of the 104th Brigade of the Thirty-Fifth Division, part of the Fourth New Army or " K. 4," which had been organized out of the battalions formed from the Special Reserve units. It soon became clear, however, that when the New Armies went abroad the strain of keeping them supplied with drafts would be more than the Special Reserve could stand, and in April orders were issued for the reconstitution of " K. 4 " as draft-finding formations, to be known as " 2nd Reserve." The 9th thus found itself transferred along with the rest of the former 104th Brigade, now the 11th Training Reserve Brigade, to a camp at Kinmel Park, in Denbighshire. It had at the time, in addition to half a dozen Captains and ten Lieutenants, over 70 Second Lieutenants, whose instruction was an even greater difficulty than that of teaching the rank and file. The facilities at the disposal of a battalion for teaching young officers were necessarily limited and not till the early part of 1916 was the problem satisfactorily solved, Officer Cadet Battalions being then established to which all aspirants for commissions could be sent and given a proper grounding before being Gazetted.

Though the raising of the 9th provided the Regiment with six Service battalions, more than most regiments raised, there were

[1] His appointment was dated November 11th.
[2] Company Sergeant Major Hipkiss became Regimental Sergeant Major of the battalion and Sergeant Howatson its Regimental Quartermaster Sergeant.

EXPANSION

more to come. In addition to the "New Army" battalions raised by the ordinary machinery and organized and administered from the start by the War Office, various local committees and similar bodies had been constituted in different places for the purpose of raising additional battalions with special qualifications or characteristics. Thus the London and North Eastern Railway raised a special Pioneer battalion, Manchester and Liverpool between them produced the infantry for a complete Division, and the Church Lads' Brigade and the British Empire League recruited battalions of the K.R.R.C. In this work Wales was not going to be left behind, and a movement was on foot for the organization of a complete Welsh Division, if not a whole Army Corps. The War Office regarded the proposal favourably, and on October 10th the G.O.C. Western Command was informed that sanction had been given and that the raising of the troops might be begun. Steps were taken to raise three new battalions for the TWENTY-FOURTH, the 10th, 11th and 12th, the latter being a "Bantam" battalion formed of men below the normal standard of height but otherwise of sound physique.

Of these three battalions the 10th was the first to be raised. Recruiting for it was started at Ebbw Vale and Cwm, the places on which it mainly drew including Abercarn, Abertillery, Crumlin, Newport, Pontnewydd and Tredegar.[1] By the end of the month nearly 300 men had been collected, the greater number of them being from the Monmouthshire collieries and ironworks, men of a fine and sturdy stamp. The first officers gazetted to it were Lieutenant E. W. Broacker and Lieutenant and Quartermaster J. R. Ingledew, whose appointments dated from November 27th and 26th respectively; but a big step forward was taken when Sir Hamar Greenwood, M.P., who had formerly held a commission in the old 4th Battalion, the old Montgomeryshire Militia, was given command of it on December 10th. Several other officers were also gazetted to it, among them Major W. H. Pitten and Captain T. H. Morgan, who undertook the Adjutant's duties. By the end of the year, it was able to take 600 of all ranks with it to Colwyn Bay where its brigade, then numbered 130th, was being organized.[2] Here recruits continued to pour in steadily, batches of 50 or more arriving at frequent intervals, so that before long the battalion was not only up to establishment, but was able at the end of

---

[1] Its title of "1st Gwent" was an indication of its recruiting area.
[2] The Welsh Division was originally numbered as the Forty-Third, but on the "K. 4" battalions being allotted to draft-finding duties the Division was renumbered, becoming the Thirty-Eighth, whereupon the 130th Brigade became the 115th.

March to form a fifth company, E,[1] intended for draft-finding purposes. By this time the battalion was well supplied with subalterns, no less than 30 having been Gazetted to it, though many of them did not join till some time after their appointment, as courses of instruction were now being arranged for newly Gazetted subalterns. Among these officers were several like Second Lieutenants Charlton and Cottam, who were commissioned from the battalion's own ranks, while many others came from the Artists or Inns of Courts or from other Service battalions, a very good stamp of officer being obtained.

The formation of the 11th S.W.B. or "2nd Gwent," did not proceed quite as rapidly as that of the 10th. Breconshire and the Pengam district were assigned to it as recruiting areas and the nucleus of the battalion was originally constituted at the Depot at Brecon on December 5th, Major J. R. Porter, a retired officer of the Indian Army, being Gazetted Lieutenant Colonel to command it as from that date, though no other officers were appointed to it till after the New Year. The 11th indeed had only collected about 160 men before it moved to Colwyn Bay, where it took up its quarters at Old Colwyn in the first week of January. Subsequently recruiting improved considerably, the arrival of 180 men on January 19th, allowing of the formation of a second company, B. January also saw the arrival of Lieutenant J. E. W. Palmer from the 4th R.W.F., to take over duty as Quartermaster, and the appointment as Regimental Sergeant Major of Sergeant A. T. Dawes, while half a dozen subalterns appeared, among them Second Lieutenants T. H. C. Griffiths, T. H. I. Monteith and R. T. Evans. The third company came into existence in the middle of March and in April the battalion was completed by the formation of D Company. By this time the 11th had some 20 subalterns, and in April four of them, Second Lieutenants W. G. Williams, L. Roberts, Monteith and Cullimore, were given their "second star" and placed in charge of companies; while Regimental Sergeant Major Dawes was given a commission and took over the Adjutant's duties on May 6th. Company Sergeant Major Barry, of A Company, one of several rejoined veterans whose services the 11th had secured,[2] succeeded him as Regimental Sergeant Major. The beginning of June saw the battalion staff completed by the appointment of pioneers, stretcher-

---

[1] Companies had been given letters on January 23rd.

[2] Most of the original Company Sergeant Majors and Company Quartermaster Sergeants were men with considerable previous service, and several others who did good work as W.O.'s or N.C.O.'s, such as Sergeants (later Company Sergeant Majors) Dorchester and Feast, were veterans with twelve years to their credit.

bearers and signallers, and subalterns were now so numerous that most platoons had a second officer. The battalion was still at Colwyn Bay, but its time there was approaching an end.

The 12th was not completed till some time after the 10th and 11th. Its first " Daily Orders " were issued at Newport on March 15th, by which time a nucleus of recruits had been collected together by its first officer, Lieutenant C. D. Phillips, who had been Gazetted to it on January 30th, 1915. Quartermaster Sergeant Albutt had joined from the Depot on March 9th as Quartermaster, followed soon after by Sergeant Westhorpe, who became R.Q.M.S., with Sergeants Parker as C.S.M. and Bethell as C.Q.M.S. of the first company to be formed. On April 21st, Major E. A. Pope, of the 3rd Welch, arrived to take command, and on May 1st a second company came into existence. In the battalion's early days good work was done by drill instructors attached from the local Police, but it was very difficult for the battalion to make much progress. The latest formed Service battalions fared rather better than their " K. 3 " predecessors had in matters such as equipment with necessaries and clothing, if not as regards arms and accoutrements. The Ordnance services were now more nearly abreast of what was required of them, contractors had been found to produce various essentials and there was not quite the same need to fall back on makeshifts, but the men had to be in billets from the first, which did not offer quite the same chance of developing a corporate feeling and discipline as being together under canvas did. May, however, saw the 12th Battalion advancing steadily. Officers were now being Gazetted in considerable numbers, two of them, Lieutenants H. C. Rees and C. E. Hoffmeister, who were transferred respectively from the 10th Bedfords and the 7th Dorsets, taking command of companies and being soon afterwards promoted to Captain. C Company was formed on May 18th and the influx of recruits was such that D Company could be formed three weeks later. Regimental Sergeant Major Vatcher,[1] who joined on May 1st, proved a tower of strength to the young battalion, for which he did splendid work, while Lieutenant C. D. Phillips, who had become acting Adjutant when Colonel Pope joined, was now definitely appointed Adjutant as from February 2nd, 1915. Early in July came orders for the battalion to quit Newport for Prees Heath Camp, near Whitchurch, in Shropshire. An advanced party under Second Lieutenant Symes and the Quartermaster, left for this spot on July 8th and the main body followed five days later. On moving thither the battalion was definitely

---

[1] He had served in South Africa with the K.D.G.

struck off the strength of the 115th Brigade, to which it had till now been attached, being transferred to a Welsh Bantam Brigade formed of other surplus battalions of the Thirty-Eighth Division.

Meanwhile the " Brecknockshire Reserve Battalion," originally constituted from the " Home service details," 300 in all, left behind by the Brecknock Battalion, had rapidly attained its full establishment. This unit was intended to take over the home defence duties originally allotted to the battalion which had gone overseas but also to provide drafts for that unit, which was now distinguished as the " First Line." Practically the whole Territorial Force had undertaken the overseas obligation, and before long the Reserve battalions were organized as " Second Line " Brigades and Divisions. On the departure for France of various selected Territorial battalions to be attached as fifth battalions to brigades of the Regular Divisions,[1] various " Second Line " units replaced them in the " First Line " Divisions, but this did not happen to the Brecknockshire Reserve Battalion, which, after being billeted at Brecon till November 13th, was then transferred to Haverfordwest.[2] It spent a fortnight in billets here and then moved to Ft. Hubbertstone at Pembroke Dock and took charge of such part of the duties of that garrison as its lack of proper weapons and equipment allowed it to discharge. Though it contained a fair proportion of trained men—besides the " pre-war " Territorials who had been unable to pass for foreign service or to undertake the overseas obligation, its first 600 men included over 100 re-enlisted Territorials and about 40 veterans from the National Reserve— it was very badly off for rifles, equipment and uniform, and with all the Service battalions bound for overseas claiming priority Home Service units had to wait some time to have their deficiencies supplied. However, all worked hard, while the battalion was not lacking in competent and experienced instructors,[3] and its progress towards efficiency was highly creditable to all concerned.

[1] All three battalions of the Monmouthshire Regiment, formerly Volunteer battalions of the S.W.B., were among these picked battalions.
[2] Lieutenant Colonel T. G. Powell, a retired Territorial officer, joined as second in command.
[3] Regimental Sergeant Major Griffiths and Regimental Quartermaster Sergeant Maund had been among those transferred from the " First Line."

CHAPTER V

TSINGTAO

THE chance which had placed the 2nd Battalion at Tientsin[1] on the declaration of war brought it an experience peculiar to it and one battalion of the Indian Army, that of co-operating with our Japanese allies in the capture of Tsingtao.[2] The German acquisition of Kiaochau in 1898 had caused the bitterest resentment in Japan, and to oust the Germans from a position so full of menace to Japan was an urgent object to the Mikado's ministers. Kiaochau indeed explains Japan's entry into the war, and it was not remarkable that preparations were almost immediately started for an expedition against that place. Only ten days after the time-limit of the Japanese ultimatum to Germany expired (August 23rd), Japanese troops landed at Lung Kow, on the Northern side of the Shantung Peninsula, and began advancing on Kiaochau (September 2nd). Simultaneously a Japanese squadron relieved the British warships which had already established a watch upon Kiaochau Bay.

British co-operation with the Japanese was not to be confined to naval assistance, although as the British troops in the North China command only amounted to eight battalions, three British and five Indian,[3] the British Army's contribution to the attacking force could not be large.

Though no actual orders to mobilize were received, the 2nd Battalion had been holding itself in readiness for active service ever since August 4th, the detachments from Peking and Fengtai having been recalled to Tientsin, and directly Japan declared war it was warned to be prepared to move at short notice, though definite orders were not received till September 17th. Two days later the battalion embarked on three small transports and proceeded down the Peiho to Taku Bar, where H.M.S *Triumph* and the destroyer *Usk* were waiting to act as escort. The embarkation return showed 22 officers[4] and 910

[1] B Company was on detachment at Fengtai and half D was at Peking as Legation Guard.
[2] By a curious coincidence the battalion's barracks in Tientsin were next to the German barracks, and when Tsingtao fell several of the German prisoners who came into the battalion's hands were personally known to our men. The German troops from Tientsin had moved to Tsingtao just before the declaration of war.
[3] The 2nd D.C.L.I. and four Indian battalions were at Hong Kong, and the 2nd S.W.B., the 2nd Gloucestershire and 36th Sikhs at Tientsin.
[4] The officers were Lieutenant Colonel H. G. Casson; Majors J. Going, E. W. Jones, E. C. Margesson; Captains R. J. Palmer, T. C. Greenway, A. H. Ellis, J. Bradstock, G. H. Birkett (Adjutant), D. G. Johnson, C. M. Tippetts, C. B. Habershon; Lieutenants A. E. Williams, R. K. B. Walker, R. L. Petre, A. N. Cahusac, D. H. S. Somerville, W. Rawle; Second Lieutenants R. P. Behrens,

men, 66 of all ranks, including the band boys and a few men who were unfit for active service, having been left at Tientsin.

After crossing Taku Bar the convoy and escort stood across the Gulf of Chihli to Wei-hai-wei, picked up some mules there (September 20th) and proceeded to Laoshan Bay, on the East coast of the Shantung Peninsula about forty miles N.E. of Tsingtao, the well-fortified main German settlement on Kiaochau Bay which was the objective of the expeditionary force. Here the Japanese main body had begun disembarkation on September 18th, by which time the original landing force had already seized Kiaochau town and established itself at the head of Kiaochau Bay, thereby isolating the German territory completely. Laoshan Bay, which was crowded with Japanese transports guarded by a strong squadron, was reached on September 22nd. At 8 a.m. next day disembarkation began, the men being soon ashore. Landing the mules, however, proved difficult. They had to be slung over the ship's side by a crane and lowered into lighters which were then towed as near to the beach as the shallowness of the water would permit. Then the real fun began, that of inducing the suspicious and unaccommodating animals to jump out of the lighters and wade ashore. They did not yield easily to persuasion; and what with overcoming their reluctance and landing ammunition, carts and stores of all kinds, the battalion had a strenuous time. The bodies of the carts had to be taken ashore separately and then have the wheels fitted to them; fourteen days' supplies had to be landed as well as forage for 300 mules and ponies. The men had no coolies to help them, the Chinese who were working the donkey-engine kept on refusing to work and had to be forcibly encouraged to keep going, but by unflagging exertions the ships had been cleared by 8 a.m., September 23rd. The battalion's labours were not over then, for the stores had to be transferred to the Base Supply Depot and there was a shortage of appliances for moving them. However, as General Barnardiston's dispatch of October 9th testifies, the battalion " worked hard and cheerfully," and on September 25th it could move forward to Puh-li, six miles from the landing-places.

This march was a foretaste of difficulties to come; the road, or rather track, was bad, narrow and congested with traffic; while to add to the confusion hardly anyone in the battalion knew a word of Japanese and only a very few Japanese officers knew much more English. Moreover, the Japanese commander,

C. R. Macgregor and M. C. Morgan; Lieutenant and Quartermaster E. H. Laman. Four officers of the 2nd Battalion who were at home on leave had been retained for service with the 1st (cf. p. 4).

General Kamio, proposed to employ the British force in the centre of the line, and not, as General Barnardiston wished, on the left where it would have been in touch with the ships. This not only entailed a longer march than would have been needed, but greatly increased the difficulties of supply,[1] and consequently the privations the British contingent was to endure. Indeed the very first day of the advance found the battalion already on half-rations for want of transport, and for the same reason

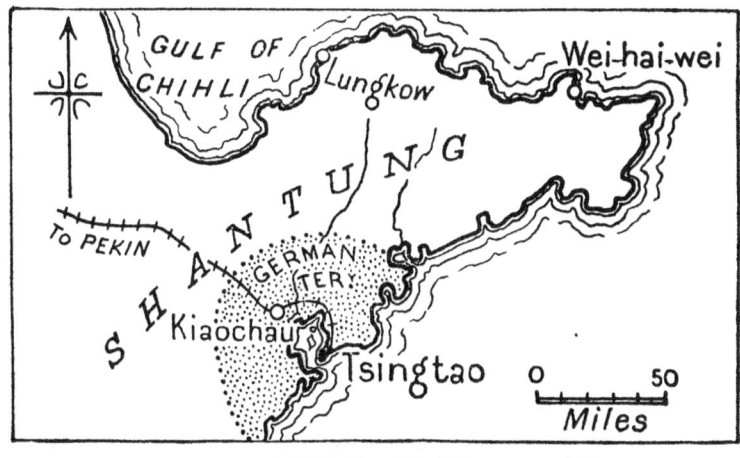

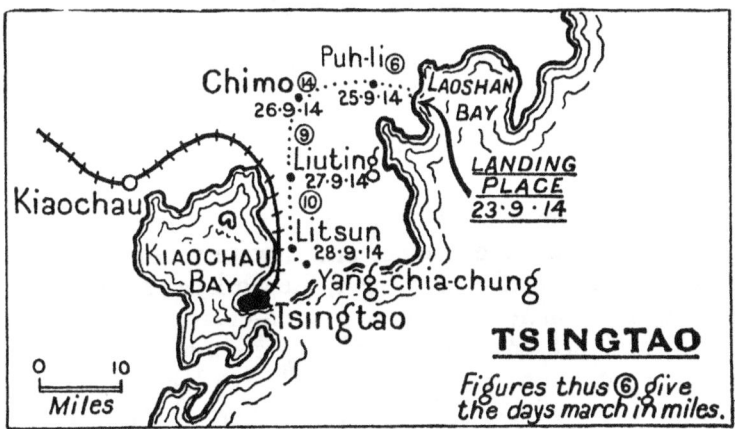

all crowbars and felling-axes and most of the picks and shovels had to be left behind. The second day's march to Chimo, fourteen miles further on, was peculiarly trying. Chinese roads at the best are apt to consist of a succession of boulders in a river of mud; these, moreover, were blocked with Japanese transport and guns, making halts and checks frequent. Japanese ideas of march-discipline too were not ours, and the driving of their guns was distinctly poor; they frequently broke right into

[1] The British supplies had thus to come up over a line of communications 40 miles long and a bad road at that.

our marching column and drove the men off the road into the potato fields where the long tendrils of sweet potatoes wound themselves round the men's legs and seriously hampered progress. At Chimo the battalion encamped beside a good stream and managed to supplement its rations by purchasing on its own account bullocks, fowls, eggs and grapes. On the third day (September 27th) the battalion had only nine miles to cover to Liuting, where it could hear guns firing and see the masts of German vessels in Kiaochao Bay which were replying to the Japanese fire. The intention was that the German advanced position N.E. of Tsingtao should be attacked at dawn next morning, the battalion being assigned a front of 1600 yards and having a redoubt to carry. However, as the Germans decamped during the night, the battalion was not engaged and bivouacked after a ten-mile march at Yang-Chia-Chung, a village about three miles from the German lines. On the way it had passed General Kamio, who expressed warm admiration of the appearance of the men and commented particularly on their " shorts," though he wanted to know how the men kept their knees warm in the winter. However, the bivouac was well within range of the enemy's guns, which bombarded the village freely; so on September 30th General Barnardiston shifted the battalion a mile further East where it could dig in on a reverse slope and get some cover. Here the 2nd S.W.B. spent ten days while heavy artillery was being brought forward, ammunition and siege equipment accumulated, and the initial stages of the investment begun. The weather was bad, heavy rains reduced the so-called roads to rivers of mud and greatly impeded the forwarding of the guns and other materials, besides making the troops very uncomfortable. The S.W.B., being in thin summer clothing with only one blanket and a waterproof sheet apiece, came off specially badly. However, the work was steadily pushed on, though German aeroplanes and observation balloons were much in evidence and their activities were a nuisance, reducing greatly the amount of work that could be done by day. The Japanese, who had plenty of coolies to help them, before long constructed a light railway to connect the base with the advanced positions and were able to bring forward their heavy guns. An interesting episode was the visit, on October 2nd, of an A.D.C. of the Emperor of Japan who brought a present of saki for the officers, with cigarettes for them and the N.C.O.'s, and expressed the Emperor's great satisfaction at the co-operation of British and Japanese troops. Eventually, on October 10th, General Barnardiston received orders from General Kamio for the 2nd S.W.B. to take its place in the front line, about 600 yards frontage being assigned to it. It had already had a few casualties from the German shell fire, but considering the bad weather and the conditions in which it was living the sick-rate had been extremely low.

This outpost line had by now been advanced in the centre to the Shibosan or Shuang Shan Ridge about a mile from the German redoubts. This was a clay ridge intersected by ravines which would have given good cover in dry weather, but in heavy rain the loose soil was easily washed away, dug-outs in the sides of the ravines collapsed, streams carried down quantities of mud to fill up trenches and reduce roads to quagmires, and a piece of work was no sooner completed than it was washed away and had to be begun afresh. To struggle against such difficulties and in unfavourable conditions was a severe trial. The troops were thinly clad and usually soaked through, much digging was needed, and, as no wheeled transport was available, rations, ammunition and stores, including heavy beams for use in the trenches, had to be carried up to the front by hand over a mile and a half of tracks often knee-deep in liquid mud. Two companies only were actually in line, A and B going in first, while D and half C took up their position in a nullah about 300 yards from the village of Huang Chia Yiang, the rest of C remaining at the old bivouac to dismantle the splinter-proofs it had erected, bring the precious wood up to the new line and provide the necessary carrying parties. All were within range of the German guns, but the battalion suffered far more from the bad weather and the discomforts and hardships it entailed than from the enemy. Moreover, largely owing to transport difficulties the troops had to carry on their heavy task on barely adequate rations, certainly on much less food than they were accustomed to in peace. Bully beef and biscuits they did receive, but no bacon or cheese; bread was occasionally issued and was usually not more than soddened dough; while the men dug up the Chinese sweet potatoes and ate them raw. They sometimes got some rice from the Japanese, but it was difficult to find anything dry to make fires, so when a tea ration was available, which was not often the case, it could not always be used. "Tea when made was a peculiar affair," writes one survivor of Tsingtao, " the only water available was from a stream that was in flood, and this was of a rich muddy colour which looked like good milky tea." Luxuries like sugar and jam were very occasionally issued, but for the most part the men were on the barest minimum of rations, and in the six weeks there were only two issues of tobacco.[1]

---

[1] One of these was a gift of 5000 cigarettes from the Mikado, each cigarette being stamped with the Imperial chrysanthemum. The Mikado also twice presented the battalion with 2000 sugar cakes shaped like chrysanthemums, an attention which was very much appreciated by all ranks.

The Shibosan Ridge on which the battalion's front companies were established was partly covered with fir trees, and some degree of protection from the enemy's observation and artillery was obtainable behind it, but to the South it sloped gently down towards the bed of a river without affording a vestige of cover. The German front line was very strong; it consisted of a line of low-command redoubts constructed of ferro-concrete and armed with field guns and machine guns, the heavier guns being in the larger forts in rear. Trenches defended chiefly by machine guns linked up the redoubts; 200 yards in front the ground was sharply cut away, the face of the cut being revetted, and at the foot of it was a really good wire entanglement, with a mine-field and a live wire in front. It was therefore necessary to proceed by regular siege operations, digging a succession of trench lines at intervals, known respectively as the "Artillery Covering Position" and the "First," "Second" and "Third Attack Positions," connected up by communication trenches. The Southern slope being in full view of the enemy, night work only was possible; by day picquets held the most advanced completed position, the remainder of the outpost companies being in support and reserve further back and generally engaged on carrying fatigues or in improving and maintaining the communication trenches, tasks which kept them fully employed.

The frontage allotted to the battalion was in the centre of the ridge, being roughly delimited by two low knolls, known respectively as "54" and "45.5." The first task was to dig communication trenches up to the crest, prior to the construction of the "Artillery Covering Position" on its further side. The battalion was handicapped, especially at first, by a great shortage of tools, other than the ordinary small entrenching tools carried by the men. These, though admirable for the purpose for which they were intended, were hardly fitted to deal with rock, for to add to the difficulties the ground proved to be very rocky. Moreover, while only twenty picks and shovels per company were available, even sandbags were extremely scarce. Thus the British troops were at a great disadvantage as compared with the better equipped Japanese, who had ample supplies of every kind of material, plenty of coolies to bring forward stores and supplies, and larger and better maps than were available for our troops. A section of Japanese engineers was attached to the battalion and did excellent work, despite the language difficulty, the N.C.O.'s often managing to explain by dumb show what they wanted done. The Germans indulged in fairly liberal shelling—on the night of October 11th/12th, for example, they regularly bombarded the neighbourhood of Huang Chia Yiang, though the support companies, being well sheltered in the nullahs around, escaped with only two casualties—but the weather was the more serious trouble. From October 15th to 17th it rained almost incessantly. Not only did it delay the work, but it meant that the men, being without tents or dug-outs or a chance of drying their clothes, " just got wet and remained wet," as one account writes. Apparently the hard work kept the men fit, for the sick-rate remained remarkably low. On October 21st the companies changed positions, C and D relieving A and B, which went back to Huang Chia Yiang. By this time the communication trenches had been taken right up to and over the crest and work had to be begun on a trench on the down slope.

The working parties were always covered by standing patrols pushed well out to the front, while smaller parties reconnoitred the ground between our lines and the German position. To avoid any mishaps through chance encounters with patrols from the Japanese units on the battalion's flanks a Japanese N.C.O. and some men were usually sent out with the S.W.B. patrols; this precaution was fully justified, as our patrols were nevertheless fired upon more than once by Japanese patrols and sentries, though fortunately without much serious harm being done. As a further safeguard our patrols were fitted out with Japanese overcoats, " thin khaki drill affairs with a hood " they are described, and this served the purpose of preventing the Germans from distinguishing between British and Japanese.[1] The Germans proved very unenterprising and made little effort to interfere with our working or covering parties either by fire or by patrols, so the work proceeded without more delay than the state of the ground imposed. On October 28th a half-battalion of the 36th Sikhs, which had landed a week earlier, reached the front, and one of its companies took over the right of the S.W.B.'s frontage; two days later (October 30th) the " Artillery Covering Position " just over the crest of the ridge was occupied, whereupon the artillery were brought up into position and next day the bombardment began. It was exceedingly effective, the forts and redoubts suffered severely and some oil-tanks near the dockyard were set on fire, causing a tremendous conflagration.

As soon as the " Artillery Covering Position " had been occupied work was begun on the " First Attack Position "; some nullahs leading to it provided ready-made communication trenches, and on the evening of November 1st the companies from the covering position occupied it, while those in reserve worked in the communication trenches and Battalion Headquarters were brought right forward. Almost immediately

[1] It was afterwards reported that the Germans had failed to discover where the British were till November 6th, and that their specially furious bombardment of the British trenches on that day was the result of the belated discovery.

preparations were begun for the occupation of a " Second Attack Position" 400 yards further down the slope. The approach to this lay over the bare open, no convenient nullahs provided covered ways, and the new position was in places only 300 yards from the German lines. The soil was crumbly, and as the line was on the edge of the river bed water welled up in the trenches, making the parapets subside and seriously impeding progress. The only thing to be done was to spread potato

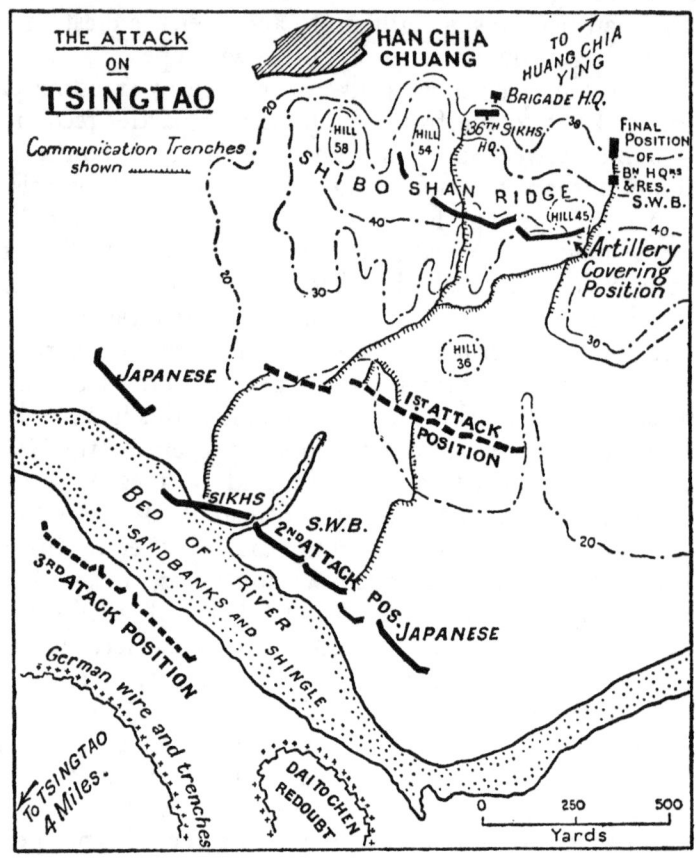

vines along the bottom of the trench and tread them in; this afforded a tolerable foothold, but quite failed to prevent water oozing in, and on the next night it was decided to substitute a sand-bag parapet for the trench. That evening A and C Companies were employed on the front line, B and D working at the communication trench connecting it with the "First Attack Position." The men worked well, and though so many sand-bags were required that the supply ran short good progress was made, useful help being given by the Japanese engineers who managed to drain part of the trench. The Germans, who were well supplied with searchlights, were constantly turning them on and opening machine-gun fire on the targets disclosed, with the result that the working parties had to lie down in the mud and wait till the searchlights were turned off and the machine guns stopped fire. This delayed the work greatly, but the battalion tried to make a point of being ahead of the Japanese regiments working on its flanks, although they had so many more men available for the work. On the night of November 4th/5th, the "Second Attack Position" was practically completed and the communication trench brought through, though lack of sandbags again hindered progress and delayed the starting of communication trenches leading to the "Third Attack Position," which was to be on the far side of the river bed. Useful work in reconnoitring was done by Lieutenants Cahusac and Rawle who forded the river, which proved to be very shallow, and located the wire entanglement.

Till now the battalion had been lucky as regards casualties, though after the "Artillery Covering Position" had been occupied the Germans had been very active both with artillery and machine guns, and used large searchlights freely, and on November 4th/5th the 36th Sikhs had had two officers wounded and several men killed. The night of November 5th/6th, however, brought the battalion heavier casualties than it had yet suffered. Digging the "Third Attack Position" involved an advance over the open across the river bed, and the position chosen was exposed to enfilade fire from both flanks. The work was to be carried out by C Company on the right, next the Sikhs, and by B on the left, nearer the Dai To Chen redoubt, A meanwhile working on the "Second Attack Position" and D at the communication trenches. Before taking out the two platoons of B detailed for the digging, Captain Bradstock went out reconnoitring with a few men, and discovered that the Germans had constructed a little fortified loopholed shelter in No Man's Land from which snipers could interfere seriously with the digging. Accordingly he and his men, after crawling to within a few yards of the post, sprang up and charged it. The Germans did not wait for them but bolted; and the obstacle having thus been disposed of, Captain Bradstock went back to our trench and fetched out his two platoons. As the men were crawling up the glacis of the German position to the line selected, heavy fire was suddenly opened from the left. Captain Bradstock promptly swung one platoon round to the left to reply, but the German fire increased and from another position more to his front two machine guns and more rifles opened, he therefore brought his second platoon up on the right and in front of the other. Just then a Japanese patrol was noticed close to the left front, and Captain

Bradstock seeing that the Germans on his left were apparently a stronger patrol driving in the Japanese, successfully directed his fire so as to force the Germans to relinquish pursuit and retire. The two platoons, Nos. 5 and 6, were admirably handled by their commanders, Lieutenants Petre and Morgan, the fire orders being carried out with accuracy and excellent fire-control and discipline maintained. However, with the enemy on the alert and their machine guns sweeping the ground, to have persevered in the attempt to reach the assigned position would have been futile, and after remaining in position long enough to find and remove the wounded, of whom there were several, Captain Bradstock took his men back to the "Second Attack Position." In assisting the wounded some very fine work was done, notably by Captain Johnson, who had already won general admiration by dashing and fearless work on patrol, while Lance Corporal Foley and Privates Green, Snow and West, all showed great gallantry in searching for wounded comrades and bringing them in under heavy fire at close range. Private Evans was perhaps the most conspicuous of all : after going out three times successfully he had just reached a fourth man when a machine gun caught him and riddled him with bullets.[1]

C Company and the Sikhs meanwhile, profiting by a fold in the ground and by the Germans' concentration of their attentions on B, had got on very well and had dug quite a satisfactory trench, at the cost of only half a dozen casualties compared with B's 30. However, as B had been unable to dig their trench, General Barnardiston reported to the Japanese Commander-in-Chief that he did not yet consider the "Third Attack Position" fit for permanent occupation. He received the reply that the general scheme of assault required it to be held, so that evening it was occupied by picquets. D Company was put in to complete C's work, and about midnight Lieutenant Somerville took out a patrol to ascertain the truth of the rumours, which were now current, that the Germans were evacuating their trenches. The position in front of the battalion proved to be still held, and the working parties were accordingly withdrawn after completing their night's task. However, both to right and left there was unusual activity, searchlights playing freely and heavy firing going on all night. Actually the Japanese were forcing a decision, and during the night they assaulted and took a fort at the Western end of the line, with the result that just as their main assault was about to be delivered at 7 a.m. next day (Nov. 7th) the white flag went up and the siege was over.

[1] Captain Johnson received the D.S.O., the five men, of whom West died of wounds, were awarded D.C.M.'s. Captain Bradstock was subsequently awarded the new decoration of the M.C.

The sudden termination of the operations robbed the little British contingent of any chance of distinguishing itself in the final stage. The Japanese intention to force a finish on the night of November 6th/7th, whether deliberate or the result of a sudden decision, was never communicated to General Barnardiston, and it certainly came as a complete surprise to the 2nd S.W.B., who, through no unwillingness or fault of their own, missed a share in the culmination they had worked so hard to bring about. The battalion was waiting to join in that assault, and found it hard to believe that the Japanese did not know it was ready or had inadvertently omitted to warn the British of their intentions. Not having shared in the assault, however, the battalion had come off fairly lightly as regards casualties, its total being 14 killed or died of wounds or disease and 2 officers, Lieutenants Williams and Petre, and 34 men wounded. Nevertheless the siege of Tsingtao had been an exhausting and trying experience. The battalion had had to work hard in the face of serious difficulties and handicaps. Many of these have been mentioned, want of tools and maps, shortage of rations, the absence of adequate shelter and fuel, summer clothing which was ill suited to the severe weather; perhaps the most serious was the difficulty of co-operating with Allies whose ways were not our ways and whose language was unfamiliar. The Japanese, it must be admitted, were interesting rather than easy people with whom to co-operate. Though they welcomed the presence of a British contingent at the siege and liked to serve alongside a British regiment, they seemed anxious to impress on us their extreme efficiency. It looked almost as if they wished the British to be there mainly as spectators, to see how well the Japanese could do the work. That they did it very well the S.W.B. would cordially admit, but in little things they were not easy to work with. They were inquisitive and apt to take offence, and it was a great misfortune that the battalion did not happen to include any officer qualified as an interpreter in Japanese who could have acted as a liaison officer and smoothed over minor troubles and the misunderstandings from which they arose.

However, despite all these very trying conditions the men remained cheerful and willing, their conduct General Barnardiston himself described as " exemplary," the small amount of sickness despite the great strain on the men was itself a testimony to their discipline and to the battalion's excellent interior economy. The " mentioning " in dispatches of six officers[1] and twelve N.C.O.'s and men was an additional testimony to General Barnardiston's satisfaction; and he subsequently expressed him-

[1] Colonel Casson, Major Margesson, Captains Bradstock, Birkett and Johnson, and Lieutenant Petre.

self warmly both to the G.O.C. of the Division to which the battalion was allotted on reaching England and to its new Brigadier, declaring that he had nothing but the highest praise for the 2nd S.W.B. and that their new commanders were lucky to have them under them. If, therefore, "Tsingtao" does not recall any very spectacular or dramatic achievement, it is a record of steady and arduous work under trying conditions, and the fact that the battalion is the only unit in the British Army entitled to the honour fully explains its presence among the chosen ten on the King's Colour.

That the battalion so soon came under new commanders was the natural sequel to the fall of Tsingtao. Every unit that India and the Colonies could spare was urgently needed at home. Territorials and Indian battalions were relieving those Regulars whom the outbreak of war had found on foreign stations, and within ten days of the surrender[1] the battalion, which in the meantime had been quartered in some well-built German artillery barracks, left for Shatzonkon Bay, there to embark for England. The route to the coast was lined by Japanese troops who gave the battalion a warm send-off, while flattering messages were received from the Mikado and from high authorities in Japan, both civil and military, expressing their appreciation of its work. From Shatzonkon Bay the hired transport *Delta* carried the battalion to Hong Kong, where it spent ten days ashore, while the *Delta* was fitted up for the voyage home. During this period the details left behind at Tienstin rejoined, bringing with them the families of the married men and the heavy baggage, and then on December 4th the battalion re-embarked. The voyage home was uneventful. The *Emden's* career was already over, submarines had not yet begun to infest the Mediterranean, and except that from Aden to Suez the *Delta* had the company of the old battleship *Ocean* and the Russian cruiser *Askold*,[2] the voyage was performed without escort. On January 12th, 1915, the *Delta* dropped anchor in Plymouth Sound and the battalion promptly disembarked and was railed off to Coventry. Thence a march took it to Rugby, the neighbourhood in which was quartered the 87th Brigade of the Twenty-Ninth Division, to which formation it had been assigned.

[1] On November 16th, a composite company of a platoon from each company with a company of the 36th Sikhs represented the British Army at the formal entry into Tsingtao.

[2] This vessel, known to the men as the "packet of Woodbines" from its five funnels, formed part of the naval forces which supported the 2nd S.W.B. at its landing on the Gallipoli peninsula.

CHAPTER VI

FESTUBERT AND GIVENCHY

THE First Corps had reached its rest billets after the close of the fighting at Ypres exhausted and terribly reduced in numbers—few of its infantry units could parade 500 men and even so were largely composed of recently arrived drafts. All ranks were in urgent need of rest, of sleep, of refitting. Many deficiencies in equipment needed to be made good, hardly a battalion in the First Division possessed a single machine gun, most men's clothing was in a deplorable condition from wet and mud. Battalions required not only large drafts to bring them up to establishment, but time to absorb and assimilate them. Some weeks must elapse before the Corps could be brought up again to full efficiency. Fortunately the French had been able to take over the whole Ypres Salient and the British line was now reduced to the 21 miles between Cuinchy and Wytschaete. The four Corps to whom its defence was now entrusted, the Second, Third, Fourth and Indian, were in little better state than the First Corps and almost in as much need of rest and recuperation, but after their unsuccessful efforts to force a way past Ypres to the Channel ports the Germans also were too exhausted to be capable of further efforts, and both sides were settling down to a winter marked by strategic if not tactical inactivity. Locally there was to be much "liveliness." The supremacy of the defence over the attack was hardly yet as fully established, or perhaps not as fully realized, as it was later on. Both sides sought every possible means of harassing their enemy. Though neither British nor Germans were too well supplied with ammunition what little they had was vigorously used, as far as it would go, and there was very little of the "live and let live" spirit which developed in later years in some parts of the line. Neither side had quite accepted the *status quo* as something only to be altered by means of a big offensive, and only worth altering if a big change could be produced. There was more "war" about the "trench warfare" of the winter of 1914–1915 than there was to be again, and the 1st S.W.B.'s rest after First Ypres was abruptly cut short.

Coming out of the line about 400 of all ranks the battalion had been joined on November 19th by a draft of 196 men under Captain A. M. Lloyd, recently released from his duties as a Territorial Adjutant, with Second Lieutenants G. D. O. Lloyd, recently commissioned from the R.M.C., and J. McNaught Davis, from the Cambridge O.T.C. On November 21st

5 officers[1] and 97 men turned up; followed a week later by another 3 officers[2] and 53 men. These drafts brought the battalion up to a respectable strength, but it was still short of officers.

Before the end of November the battalion's rest had been interrupted by a short return to the trenches. The Second Corps was due to relieve the Cavalry opposite Wytschaete, but, as nearly half its infantry had been employed at Ypres under the First Corps and had only just been relieved, it was not quite ready to carry this out and had to call on the First Corps for help. The 3rd Brigade, though little over 2500 all told, was the strongest in its Division and was accordingly detailed for a tour of trench duty, so on November 23rd the S.W.B. found themselves relieving the 9th Lancers and 18th Hussars in some very indifferent trenches near Kemmel. Here they spent 48 hours, mainly devoted to efforts to improve the line, the Germans opposite being employed in much the same way, though they were also trying to sap out in front of their line. This the battalion did its best to discourage, but the German snipers were not less busy, and on the 24th Second Lieutenant Grylls, who had arrived only three days earlier, was wounded. The chief episode of these days was the repulse on the 25th of an attack on C Company. Before dawn three parties of Germans were detected advancing, and were so hotly received that they promptly abandoned the attempt and did not renew it. That evening the 5th Brigade relieved the 3rd which returned to Outersteene, the battalion having had some 15 casualties and being very glad to be greeted by much appreciated hot baths and an issue of new clothing.

The first half of December was quiet, the chief incident being that the battalion turned out on December 3rd to line the roads for the King who was visiting the Army. His Majesty spent some time with the battalion, inspecting the men carefully. More drafts arrived, one of 138 men on December 4th and two smaller.[3] With them came several officers, some, like Second Lieutenant Drury, from Sandhurst, some, like Second Lieutenants Farrier and Johns, commissioned from other regiments,

[1] Captain Lord de Freyne (3rd Battalion), Second Lieutenants Grylls (newly commissioned from the R.M.C.), Taylor (King's Own), Garnett-Botfield (R.B.) and Owen (Lincolnshire).

[2] Lieutenant A. S. B. James (3rd Battalion), Second Lieutenants Loch (ex R.M.C.) and Jenkins.

[3] It is quite impossible to reconcile exactly the figures in the Divisional, the Brigade and the Battalion diaries: unfortunately the latter, which should be the most authoritative, seems not to be quite contemporary and had to be made up later on: it does not record the arrival of several officers who were certainly present with the battalion on December 21st–24th, Captain Fowler among them.

others, like Lieutenants Byrne and Garnett, typical of the pick of athletic England who had rushed to join up when war broke out and were now taking their places in the field. Captain Fowler again represented the " pre-war Regulars " now getting terribly scarce in most battalions of the Line. Practically all the " pre-war " enlisted men, whether serving soldiers, Regular Reservists or Special Reserve, had been exhausted by this time, and the drafts were largely composed of men enlisted since the beginning of the war, whose training, more particularly their musketry, was naturally not up to the level of the " pre-war " men ; a substantial proportion, however, were re-enlisted old soldiers, men who had finished their Reserve engagement but had hastened to rejoin the colours. Many had the South African medals and there was very good stuff among these veterans, but they also included others whose military knowledge was decidedly rusty and whose physique was not equal to the strain of trench-warfare in the swamps of Flanders. For men of 45 and upwards to have to stand for hours in water-logged trenches was much too severe, and if the sick-rate during that winter was high it was partly because these willing veterans were undertaking hardships beyond their powers of endurance.

Building up out of these agglomerations of reinforcements[1] a battalion in any way comparable to that which had landed at Havre in August was naturally a very heavy task for the few surviving trained officers and N.C.O.'s. The new officers themselves were mostly but partially trained and quite inexperienced, and it was hard on the First Corps to be called out on December 20th, when in the midst of reorganizing, to restore a nasty situation which had just developed at and North of Givenchy.

For some time past General Joffre, with an optimism which the tactical situation hardly seemed to warrant, had been planning an immediate resumption of the offensive both in Flanders and in Artois. He had requested Sir John French to co-operate in this, and accordingly the Second and Third Corps had been told to prepare to join in directly the French began to make progress on their left, while the Fourth and Indian Corps demonstrated vigorously and detained the enemy's attention by local attacks. The Indian Corps' contribution was an attack on the trenches between Festubert and Rue d'Ouvert, and the Germans had retaliated vigorously by counter-attacking both at Givenchy and in front of Festubert. They had captured the front and support lines of the Sirhind Brigade (Lahore Division) from Givenchy to La Quinque Rue, Givenchy itself was in great danger, and, as

---

[1] On November 30th the battalion had mustered 13 officers and 815 men, by December 20th it had risen to 21 officers and 967 men (First Corps A and Q Diary).

the reserves of the Indian Corps had all been exhausted, the First Division was ordered to its assistance.

The First Division had been "standing to" from December 14th–19th, in readiness to move at short notice in case the French offensive developed so satisfactorily as to make an opening for the whole B.E.F. "Standing to" had just been called off when orders to get ready to move at once reached the S.W.B. It was then 5 p.m. (December 20th) and at 7.30 p.m. the battalion was tramping off in the darkness for Merville. It was a trying march, the roads were in bad condition and crowded with traffic, but at midnight the 3rd Brigade had reached Merville. It was off again at 4.30 a.m. in pouring rain, however, and before 8 a.m. was at Bethune. Here it halted for a time by the roadside and had breakfast, while the Brigadier[1] went forward to investigate. The position proved to be very serious: the 1st Manchesters were still clinging tenaciously to Givenchy, but were very hard pressed, while North of Givenchy the Germans were close to Festubert and were only opposed by the exhausted remnants of the Sirhind Brigade and some Indian cavalry who had been rushed to their help. Thus although the 3rd Brigade had covered 16 miles since 7 p.m. over bad roads and very heavily laden, they had to push on hard to Gorre, five miles away, and with the prospect of an immediate attack.

Orders for this were issued by the First Division at 11.40 a.m.: the 1st Brigade on the right was to recover the lost trenches North of the knoll on which Givenchy stands, with the old German front line from East of Givenchy to the Northern end of Rue d'Ouvert as second objective. On its left the 3rd Brigade, passing through Festubert, was to recover the lost British trenches N.E. of that village as far as the Rue des Cailloux,[2] beyond which the Meerut Division was still holding out. It was then to press on against the German lines from Rue d'Ouvert Northward.

Starting off again about 12.30 p.m., and pushing on as fast as the congested roads would allow, the head of the 3rd Brigade's column reached Gorre at 1.45 p.m. The pace had been too much for many of the heavily burdened[3] and tired men and not a few had fallen out. Meanwhile things had gone wrong at Givenchy. The Germans had attacked the village from the North and the

---

[1] Brigadier General R. H. K. Butler had replaced General Landon on the latter's promotion.

[2] The frontage originally assigned to the 3rd Brigade was not much over 500 yards.

[3] The battalion had been told it would be billeted in Bethune and the orders to attack were issued while it was on the march, so the men had no chance of getting rid of their packs, which were full of recently received presents, or of the goat skins which they were wearing.

FESTUBERT

Manchesters were only just managing to cling to the Western edge: the 1st Brigade had therefore to be diverted to Givenchy and in consequence a wide gap soon developed between the two brigades. The 3rd Brigade pushed on to Festubert, starting at 2.15 p.m. with the Gloucestershire leading and the S.W.B. following. Half an hour later the head of the column was at the cross roads West of Festubert. Here the Gloucestershire turned off to the right, and the S.W.B. halted under cover while Major Reddie and the commanders of the two leading companies made a hurried reconnaissance. The orders were to attack at

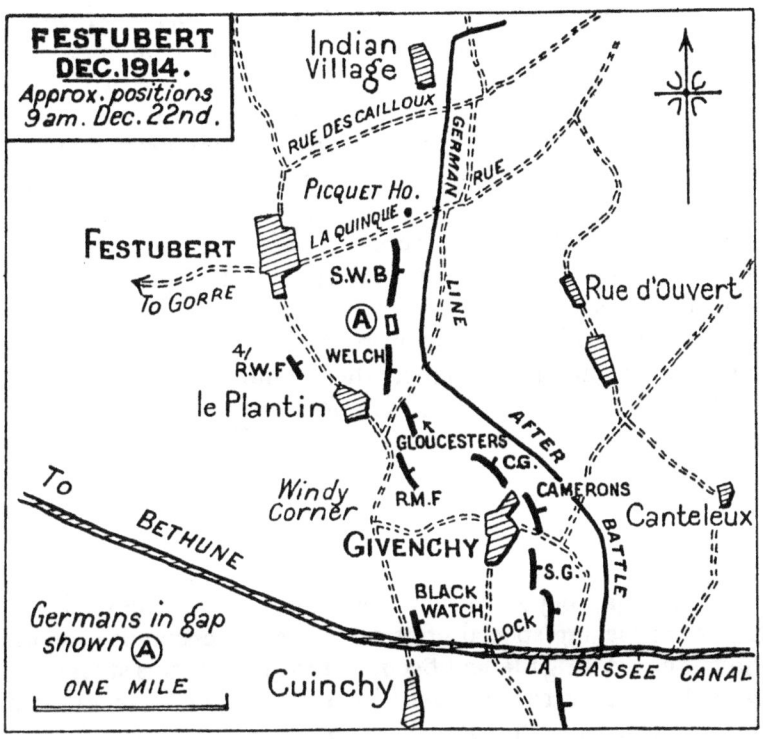

3 p.m. and at that hour the battalion, which had deployed and extended, debouched from Festubert with C and D Companies in the firing line and A and B in support. The Gloucestershire were supposed to be attacking on the right, but touch with them had already been lost and on that flank the battalion was quite unsupported.

Directly the leading lines came out of such cover as Festubert afforded they were pelted with shrapnel, while a considerable volume of rifle and machine-gun fire developed, especially from the right front. Tired as the men were the advance was gallantly pressed, though over that water-logged country, intersected by deep ditches and mainly mud where it was not water, progress was very slow. It was nearly dark, direction was hard to keep, the artillery support negligible.[1] The S.W.B. pushed on, nevertheless, though if a man tripped or fell the mud clogged his rifle and thus made it hard to develop proper covering fire. Casualties were numerous: Captain Fowler was hit early in the advance but continued to lead his company, Captain Lloyd was severely wounded and there was not much chance for a wounded man who fell into one of the frequent ditches. Still the S.W.B. pressed on, until they reached and occupied the original support trenches held by the Sirhind Brigade about 800 yards East of Festubert, the Germans retiring to the old British front line another 150 yards further on. On the extreme left of the recovered trenches a handful of the 1st H.L.I. was still holding on, but otherwise the battalion was quite "in the air." Moreover, the hurry with which the attack had been pressed, and the obstacles which the boggy ground had presented, had caused considerable disorganization and the battalion had also lost heavily. Major Reddie, therefore, finding he had hardly a full company up in the front line, realized that to try to recover the old front line also would be folly, unless he were sure of support on his flanks. The Germans were apparently in some force and there was no one on the right, where a more than usually boggy bit of ground had caused the Gloucestershire to diverge to the right towards the high ground N.E. of Givenchy from which they were being fired at, and that battalion was held up 250 yards from the German lines. General Butler had therefore to put in the Welch on its left, of whom about half a company ultimately came up on the S.W.B.'s right, but even then there was still a wide gap beyond them. Far away to the right the Germans were making special efforts for the possession of Givenchy. The whole 1st Brigade had become absorbed in this struggle and several hundred yards separated its left from the Gloucestershire. This gap had to be filled and so, instead of using the Munsters to secure his original objective, or even to link up the S.W.B. with the Welch, General Butler had to employ them to gain connection with the 1st Brigade.

Thus the S.W.B. spent the night in reorganizing and in trying to improve the position in the recovered support line. More men worked their way forward and Major Reddie was able to extend to his right, narrowing the gap between the battalion and the bulk of the Welch, which patrols had by now discovered to be partly held by Germans. These Germans were

[1] The Division's own artillery had been left in reserve and the guns which supported the attack were those of the Indian Corps, whose establishment included neither field-howitzers nor 60-pounders.

cleared out of about 100 yards but beyond this they could not be pressed. Orders had been issued to renew the advance at 7 a.m., but with no one coming forward on the right[1] and the Germans holding the continuation of our line, Major Reddie realized the uselessness of trying to push on, and on reporting the situation to the brigade he received orders to hold on. Meanwhile on his left the 2nd Brigade, who were relieving the Meerut Division in front of the Orchard to the North of La Quinque Rue, were having heavy fighting and were in some difficulties, which put an advance by the S.W.B. quite out of the question. Their own position too was not over satisfactory: ammunition and food were both urgently needed but communication with the rear was precarious; 1100 yards of open had to be traversed as the only known communication trench was little better than a running river, and many men were shot in carrying messages back. The men had had no food since breakfast on December 21st, so the iron rations had to be consumed, and not till the 23rd could picks and shovels be brought up: till then the men had to do their best with their "grubbers." Some good work was done during these days; Corporal J. Edwards and Private W. Adams, for example, distinguished themselves by bringing up rations over the open after the ration party had been dispersed by heavy fire. They subsequently volunteered to go back to fetch ammunition. Sergeant O'Toole again, after carrying messages under heavy fire, went back to fetch up ammunition and water, while in another sphere Corporal R. Lewis was equally conspicuous, directing the stretcher-bearers, rescuing many wounded and binding up wounds under heavy fire.[2] Meanwhile the battalion was fully occupied in maintaining and improving its position. To the right the fighting round Givenchy was very fierce, while the Munsters actually penetrated to the Lahore Division's old front line North-East of Givenchy but had to be withdrawn at night because they were so far ahead of the units on their flanks. The Gloucestershire and Welch struggled manfully to secure the trenches running North from the Givenchy knoll, but could make little progress over that soft ground and in face of that heavy fire. Still the 1st and 3rd Brigades had achieved their main object of checking the German advance and securing the tactically very important Givenchy knoll: if all the lost trenches had not been recovered at least a line had been re-established which was

---

[1] The S.W.B. found some Germans to their right rear and actually fired at their backs.
[2] These four men all received the D.C.M. Captain Orr-Ewing, R.A.M.C., now M.O. to the Battalion, did magnificent work also, and was ultimately awarded the M.C.

satisfactory. Accordingly about noon on the 22nd orders were issued to secure the position gained.

For another two days the 1st S.W.B. continued in the line. B Company did strenuous work in constructing a communication trench, which improved matters considerably, while the battalion and the Welch both started sapping out across the gap in front of Willow Corner which the Germans were holding. Spasmodic bomb-throwing and sniping went on by day, Lance Corporal Francis doing some most effective sniping as well as making a useful daylight reconnaissance. The guns also got on to the Picquet House on the battalion's left front and shelled it effectually, depriving the German snipers of a useful post. Altogether the situation had been considerably improved before, about 6 p.m. on the 24th, the Munsters turned up to relieve the battalion. It came out of the trenches with 10 officers and 553 men, having had 1 officer (Second Lieutenant Owen) and 114 men killed and missing, six officers[1] and 99 men wounded.

A bare 48 hours out of the line was all the battalion could be allowed. On the evening of December 26th it was back again in the same trenches, putting C and D Companies and a platoon of B into the front line, with the rest in support. The main need was to cover the gap in the line. Saps were being dug with that object,[2] and the completion of the communication trench made it easier to reach the point where work was in progress. B Company meanwhile constructed two large " strong points " behind the line and altogether the battalion improved the position as much as the persistent rain and the rising water level allowed. On being relieved by the Munsters on the evening of the 28th[3] it left two platoons of B behind under Second Lieutenant Farrier to dig a trench across the gap still separating its sap-head from the Welch. The work was very risky, having to be conducted within 40 yards of a watchful enemy, and before long a star shell revealed the diggers to the Germans. They promptly opened fire, killing Second Lieutenant Farrier and a platoon sergeant and compelling the party to cease work.

Coming back to the line again after another 48 hours out the battalion found the front trench so full of water and mud that it had to be abandoned, except for some snipers' posts

[1] Besides those already mentioned Lieutenants Byrne and Garnett and Second Lieutenant Johns were wounded, the two former being put out of action within a week and ten days respectively of their arrival at the front. The discrepancy between these figures and the total decrease in the battalion's strength since December 20th is to be accounted for by the very large number of men reporting " sick," mostly with rheumatism or " trench-feet " after their long exposure in water-logged trenches.

[2] Seventy yards were dug by the battalion on the 26th.

[3] It only went back as far as the support line, known as Tuning Fork.

fitted up in the drier parts of it and of the sap. The recently constructed strong-points in the rear were now held as the main line of defence.[1] By this time the area North of Givenchy and East of Festubert was such an absolute bog that no offensive movement could have been carried out across it. Early on the 31st a small party of Germans did try to crawl up to the battalion's sap-head, but they were spotted and shot down, and both sides had now to turn rather to combating the water than to harassing each other. The Germans were very active with trench-mortars and various kinds of bombs, a new feature since the Ypres fighting, which was to be only too characteristic of that " trench-warfare " to which the S.W.B. were now being introduced. The First Corps was not slow in demanding large supplies of bombs with which to retaliate and efforts were made to improvise them locally, though the early specimens were not always too satisfactory.

The battalion's first spell of trench-warfare was not to last much longer, however, as on January 4th it was relieved by the Berkshire of the Second Division and went back with the 3rd Brigade to Bethune for a rest. Since December 28th it had lost another officer (Second Lieutenant Pryce-Jenkins) and 3 men killed and 8 wounded, making its total battle casualties for December 3 officers and 128 men killed and missing, 6 officers and 110 men wounded.[2] It had been a hard time; some indeed have described this mid-winter Festubert fighting as the worst thing the battalion had yet experienced. Conditions certainly had been much more difficult and unpleasant than before and the balance from the outset strongly weighted against success, but the battalion could leave the line with the knowledge that it had played its part well.

The much anticipated rest only lasted four days. On January 8th the battalion returned to Festubert where it remained for a week in " local reserve " in some miserable and almost unfurnished cottages. Then on January 14th it moved up into the front line at Givenchy which the 3rd Brigade had just taken over. Here on the rather higher ground the water problem, though troublesome, was not so urgent as in the marsh in front of Festubert, but the Germans were at closer quarters, at places actually within bombing-range, so " a certain liveliness " prevailed, though by January 21st the First Division's Diary could

---

[1] Later on even these had to be abandoned and a new line taken up nearer Festubert, as the line to which the S.W.B. had advanced on December 21st was almost completely under water.

[2] Ninety-eight men under Captain Bill and Lieutenant Nisbet with Second Lieutenants Neilson (Lincolnshire) and Jackson (Royal Warwickshire) had arrived on December 29th.

record that "the 3rd Brigade's snipers have now got the ascendancy over the enemy." In rear of the front trenches points were selected to be specially fortified as "keeps," to serve as rallying points in case a sudden attack should break through the front line, which for various reasons was none too defensible.

This precaution was soon to be fully justified. Early on January 25th warning was received from a deserter that the enemy were going to attack in force; at 7.30 a very heavy fire was opened against the British lines astride the Canal, and shortly afterwards attacks developed on both sides of it. South of the Canal the 1st Brigade's front line was broken through and the enemy's further progress only arrested with difficulty. In the Givenchy sector the four battalions in the line had two companies each in the trenches, one in local reserve, one in brigade reserve. The S.W.B., at the N.E. corner of Givenchy, had C Company (Captain Lord de Freyne) holding Scottish and Main Trenches and D (Captain Temple)[1] in New Cut and Road Reserve. B (Captain Salmon) was in local reserve at Windy Corner 1100 yards back, A (Captain Bill) in brigade reserve at Le Preol. Two platoons of the 4th R.W.F.[2] were in reserve to C and D respectively. The Welch were on the right with the Gloucestershire beyond them and then the Munsters reaching to the Canal.

Directly the bombardment started the supports were pushed up into the front trenches and Captain Salmon brought up two platoons of B to Wagon Hill to support C. The bombardment was very heavy, Scottish Trench getting about the worst of it. The parapet was blown in at several points, but Lord de Freyne manned it strongly on either side of the gaps and successfully prevented the enemy from breaking through. Sergeant Wilcox did splendid work in charge of a machine gun at the salient in this trench; though the gun was overturned and he himself buried by the parapet being knocked down, he remounted the gun and kept it in action until more shells completed the destruction of the parapet, by which time the whole section was out of action, every man being killed or wounded. Corporal Williams also was conspicuous for the ability and gallantry with which he handled his platoon, taking charge when the officer and sergeant had both been wounded, and keeping the enemy away from vulnerable parts of the line by his skilful direction of its fire. As the Germans maintained their pressure Captain Salmon went back to fetch up the rest of B Company and, though himself wounded, brought it up through a heavy fire.

[1] 5th Worcestershire (attached): he had recently joined the battalion.
[2] This Territorial battalion had joined the 3rd Brigade in December.

Its arrival was timely for, if the Germans had failed to effect an entrance anywhere on the battalion's front, they had succeeded in driving the Welch out of some completely demolished trenches and had penetrated into the village and were only checked by the fire of the garrison of the Keep. The situation called for a prompt counter-attack, which was now delivered by the local reserves, parts of B and C Companies, some of the Welch and a company of the Black Watch which was serving as a working-party. There was sharp fighting from house to house, for the

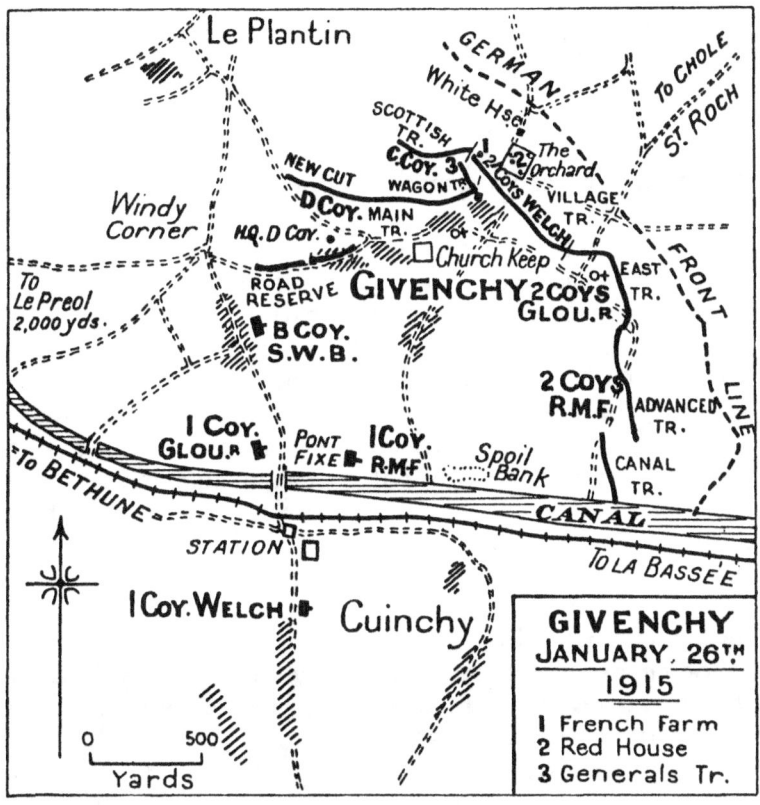

Germans were in force, but the counter-attackers were not to be denied. B and C, well led by Lieutenant Travers[1] and Second Lieutenant Loch, used their bayonets most effectively and, aided by some Black Watch who came round the church from the other side, cornered and captured a large party of Germans. Pushing on, the two subalterns and a few men occupied a building close to the trenches of the Welch from which they could fire down a communication trench by which the enemy were retiring. Their fire successfully pinned another

---

[1] He had rejoined on January 2nd after recovery from illness.

party to the ground, and when some of the Welch came up these also were captured. By about 11 a.m. the position at Givenchy had been completely restored, over 70 Germans had been taken, many more killed in the village alone, and all the lost trenches reoccupied, as far as in their damaged condition this was possible. Indeed so promptly and so effectively had the local reserves acted that the situation was restored almost before the Division knew that the line was broken, and the reinforcements which the Corps placed at General Butler's disposal to counter-attack arrived to discover they were not needed. South of the Canal things did not go so well: the Germans had had more time to secure their gains before they were counter-attacked, and not all the lost ground was recovered. The Givenchy counter-attack indeed was much quoted as an example of how such a situation should be handled[1] and the battalion's work was recognized by the award of the D.S.O. to Captain Salmon, who had remained in action although wounded and controlled his company most effectively, and of the D.C.M. to Sergeant Wilcox and Corporal Williams.[2] Considering the severity of the bombardment the battalion's losses were not heavy, 21 men killed, 2 officers (Captain Salmon and Second Lieutenant Nisbet) and 40 men wounded.

That evening A and B Companies took over the trenches and set to work to repair them, and for another ten days the battalion remained in the line with two companies in the trenches for 48 hours at a time. The chief incidents of this period were the battalion's first "raid" and the arrival on February 1st of a big draft of 240 men under Second Lieutenants Harwood-Banner, G. P. French and Piggott. Ninety-two men under Second Lieutenant Russell had joined on January 26th, so that after being 340 short of establishment on January 18th, the battalion was nearly up to it again. The raid was carried out on January 27th, Company Sergeant Major Whitehouse, Corporal Francis and two men acting as escort to Lieutenant Wingate, R.E., and two sappers who were to blow up a half-ruined building midway between the lines and connected with the German line by a short trench. It was a great resort of snipers and mining was also believed to be in progress there. At Major Reddie's proposal the Brigadier agreed to the raid being entrusted to a small party only, as this would lend itself better to

---

[1] Shortly before the attack the Brigadier had ordered the battalion to prepare a defence scheme, about the first ever called for, and as things turned out everything went exactly as foreshadowed.

[2] Rewards were not as lavishly distributed in 1914–1915 as in later years or Lieutenants Travers and Loch and not a few others might well have received some award.

surprise than would the employment, as originally suggested, of two companies and several batteries. The scheme worked very well. The party crawled out at dusk, occupied the house, fixed up the explosives and withdrew. The explosion was a complete success, the building was demolished and Company Sergeant Major Whitehouse, going out next morning to investigate, found the trench leading back to the enemy's lines full of German dead.[1]

For most of February the battalion was out of the line, reorganizing, refitting and resting at Lapugnoy, four miles S.W. of Bethune. Captain Salmon rejoined on the 14th, having made a quick recovery, Second Lieutenants Mumford and Master also reported and on the 25th Captain Gwynn reappeared and resumed duty as Adjutant. The establishment of machine guns was now completed up to four and some useful company training was put in, varied by recreation. A gift of footballs and boxing-gloves from the 3rd Battalion came in very handy and the rest did everyone good. On February 23rd the battalion was inspected by Sir Douglas Haig, now G.O.C. First Army, who spoke highly of its recent work, and just before the end of the month the 3rd Brigade returned to Festubert. This sector was in better case than in December; breastworks above ground having been substituted for trenches below the water level. These, however, afforded the enemy a good mark and to keep them in repair needed constant work, but their defence did not require the men to spend long hours up to the knees or even waists in water. Duck-boards had now been provided as well as water-proof waders, and the arrangements for drying and cleaning clothes and giving men baths when they came out of the line were being systematized. Sickness in consequence was much lower than when the S.W.B. had previously sampled the Festubert sector, and casualties were not numerous, although the German snipers were active and their guns were beginning to be better supplied with ammunition again; ten days in the trenches cost less than that number of casualties, while sufficient drafts appeared to make good the wastage.

During the Neuve Chapelle operations (March 10th/13th) the battalion was standing by in its billets at Essars, being in Divisional reserve. Had all gone well the First Division, which was holding the Festubert and Rue du Bois sectors, was to have pushed forward and linked up the Second Division on its right at Givenchy with the Indian Corps. But the Second Division failed to carry the trenches facing it and various delays and mishaps held up the Indian and the Fourth Corps far short of the objectives

[1] Company Sergeant Major Whitehouse and Corporal Francis both received the D.C.M.

which had at one moment seemed quite likely to be reached. After standing by till March 13th, the S.W.B. went back with the 3rd Brigade to spend ten days in Corps reserve; this over, it relieved the Jullundur Brigade (Lahore Division) in the Port Arthur sector, including the right of the line established by the recent attack. The First Division was shifting to its left, which meant that the battalion had a new piece of the line to learn and to improve; the trenches, being for the most part but newly dug, needed an unusual amount of work, so the men were kept busy, but on the whole things were quiet. The British had to economize ammunition most rigidly in preparation for the next "push," which was to eclipse Neuve Chapelle completely: the Germans, enlightened by Neuve Chapelle as to the deficiencies of their defences and warned to take the offensive capacities of the B.E.F. seriously, were working vigorously to remedy their weak spots, and were also not inclined to stir up trouble by local offensives. There thus set in on the First Army's front a period of relative quiet, which was to last nearly two months. Possibly but for the diversion of reserves and ammunition to Ypres, where the Germans delivered their first gas attack on April 22nd, the First Army's inactivity might have ended sooner: actually, the last half of March, April and the first week of May proved most uneventful for the S.W.B., tours in the trenches being varied by a fortnight out of the line early in April, at the end of which month the battalion was withdrawn to Hingette for special training for the First Division's projected assault on the German trenches near Richebourg L'Avoué. This was to be part of the greater Neuve Chapelle in which the First Army, attacking North of the La Bassée Canal, would co-operate with a French attack in force near Arras. Of this joint offensive high hopes were entertained: the lessons of Neuve Chapelle had, it was believed, been learnt and the obstacles which had there prevented the full exploitation of the initial success would this time be avoided.

Frequent drafts appeared during this time[1] and at one time the battalion was over establishment. Two of its original officers rejoined: Lieutenant Baker on March 20th, Captain F. G. Lawrence, who became second in command, on the 25th, while on April 15th Captain G. C. Thomas arrived from the 3rd Battalion to replace Lieutenant Wilson, who had been invalided, as Quartermaster. As against that it had the mis-

---

[1] Those recorded are: March 3rd, Second Lieutenant Playford and 15 men: March 10th, Second Lieutenants Pollock and Ford and 50; March 11th, Second Lieutenant Longlands and 63; March 22nd, Second Lieutenants Mayne and Williams and 7; April 7th, 55 under Regimental Sergeant Major Shirley; April 14th, 35; April 22nd, 30; April 27th, 138.

fortune to lose two other "pre-war" Regulars: Captain Bill being killed by a sniper on March 28th and Lieutenant Travers, who had done so well at Givenchy, being mortally wounded that same day. Apart from these losses casualties were not heavy, under 30 all told for March, 15, including Second Lieutenant Playford wounded, for April. An interesting and encouraging incident in April was the appearance of Colonel Trower of the 5th Battalion on a "Cook's tour," as the visits of the C.O.'s of "New Army" battalions to the trenches were usually termed. There were not a few old friends to welcome Colonel Trower and his visit marked the drawing nearer of the time when that "New Army," from which so much was expected, should take its place at the front and assist in that eagerly anticipated "great push" which was to drive the Germans Rhineward. Meanwhile, in another theatre of war the 2nd Battalion had been adding some memorable names to the Regiment's long list of battles.

CHAPTER VII

GALLIPOLI

The First Phase

BEING among the last to reach England of the Regulars recalled from peace stations overseas, the 2nd S.W.B. naturally found themselves joining the Twenty-Ninth Division, the junior of the five improvised "Old Army" Divisions.[1] It was not wholly Regular, its R.E., R.A.M.C., Signal Company and A.S.C. were all Territorials, as was also one infantry battalion, and of its three artillery brigades one, the 147th, was an improvised formation. Units and commanders were strange to each other, and as the Division was scattered over a wide area in which suitable manoeuvre ground was hard to find, opportunities for getting it together by brigade and divisional exercises were scanty. Much administrative work was necessary to fit the troops out for service in France, and they had also to learn something of the new conditions and methods of the "trench-warfare" to which the B.E.F. was now committed. The 2nd S.W.B. had had some foretaste of this warfare at Tsingtao, the only other unit in the Division which had already "smelt powder" in the war being L Battery, R.H.A., now re-formed after its heavy losses at Nery during the Retreat from Mons. Being decidedly under establishment owing to its casualties at Tsingtao, the battalion had to call on the 3rd Battalion for a substantial draft, 234 men joining on February 2nd, while Lieutenants, now Captains, Williams and Petre rejoined on recovery from their Tsingtao wounds. Short leave was given quite liberally, and some old members of the Regiment came to renew acquaintance with the battalion. Nothing could have exceeded the kindness and hospitality of the people of Coventry where the battalion was quartered till it joined the rest of the brigade at Rugby shortly before sailing. The men were most appreciative of the welcome they received and the survivors of the 2nd S.W.B. of 1915 are not likely to forget Coventry and its inhabitants.

Meanwhile, though regimental officers and men were mostly quite unaware of it, a violent controversy had developed over their Division's destination. Originally there had been no question but that it would proceed to France at the earliest possible date, as Sir John French was contemplating an offensive in Flanders with Zeebrugge as principal objective. Changes

---

[1] The battalion was posted to the 87th Brigade (Brigadier General W. R. Marshall), along with the 1st K.O.S.B., the 1st Royal Inniskilling Fusiliers and the 1st Border Regiment, so that the brigade included a unit from each of the four countries, England, Ireland, Scotland and Wales.

in General Joffre's plans caused this scheme to be dropped about the end of January, whereupon the advocates of a diversion in the Mediterranean, already a powerful factor in the British War Council, began to press for the Division's employment in that quarter. At one time it was proposed to send it to Salonica to assist in a Greek movement to the help of Servia, but this project was squashed by Greece refusing to take the plunge unless Roumania would come in also, whereupon it was decided (February 16th) to prepare the Division for immediate dispatch to Lemnos, where it would be available to support that naval attack on the Dardanelles upon which an earlier session of the War Council had decided. The arguments for and against a diversion in the Mediterranean in the spring of 1915 lie outside the province of a regimental history. Those for and against the particular form this diversion was to take, and as to the responsibility for that decision, are equally a matter of controversy, but the Regiment's doings in the Gallipoli campaign cannot be properly appreciated unless one realizes the effect of the decision of January 28th, 1915, that the Admiralty should "prepare a naval expedition . . . to bombard and *take* (sic) the Gallipoli Peninsula." Where a joint naval and military operation, enjoying the advantage of surprise, might have had fair prospects of success, the Navy's attempt to accomplish single-handed a task beyond the scope of any fleet unassisted by troops prejudiced the chances fatally. When troops were eventually sent out the enemy had had ample warning and a task never too easy had been made virtually impossible. When it was decided to send out the Twenty-Ninth Division there was still time to order the postponement of the naval attack till the troops could arrive, but the naval attack was allowed to go forward to its inevitable end, and the Turks, put only too completely on the alert, could devote two months to strengthening their defences. Not till the end of April was the Twenty-Ninth Division able to start the desperate venture in which the scales were from the first so heavily weighted against it.

Part of the delay must certainly be attributed to a sudden change of mind on Lord Kitchener's part. On February 19th he announced that the Twenty-Ninth Division could not be spared for the proposed operations: the news from Russia was bad and there were signs of an impending German attack in the West. Not till March 10th was it finally decided to employ the Division at Gallipoli, and the 2nd S.W.B. only left England on March 17th, the day before the disastrous repulse of the naval effort to force the Straits.

The chief event of the preceding weeks had been a review by the King. This took place on March 12th, the Division being drawn up near Dunchurch Station along the main London–Holyhead road. The King, after passing along the line from left to right, took position for the march-past at a spot locally reputed to be the exact centre of England,[1] where the Ermine Street crosses the Holyhead Road. It was a remarkable sight, battalions going past in double fours and presenting a magnificent appearance. The infantry were nearly all soldiers of several years' service, the S.W.B., for example, on landing in England averaged well over twenty-five years in age, and the long column of seasoned soldiers, eight abreast and with bayonets fixed, impressed the spectators enormously. It was in fact the last appearance in England of any substantial portion of the " Old Army," and as such well deserves to be remembered. Four days later the battalion left Rugby for Avonmouth, embarking there on the S.S. *Canada*.[2]

Sailing on March 17th, the *Canada* passed Gibraltar four days later and reached Malta on the 24th. Two days were spent here in coaling and the battalion disembarked about a dozen sick. Continuing the voyage on March 26th, Alexandria was reached early on the 29th. The " Mediterranean Expeditionary Force," as the troops allotted to the Gallipoli venture were now designated, had to be concentrated in Egypt, instead of at Mudros, close as that fine harbour was to the proposed scene of action. Alexandria offered all the facilities for the necessary preparations which Mudros lacked. The troops and stores had necessarily been embarked without reference to the tactical or administrative arrangements for a landing, which indeed could only be made after positions had been reconnoitred and plans drawn up. Accordingly the battalion disembarked at Alexandria and spent ten days at Mex Camp, devoting the time to brigade and battalion training, especially to practising embarkation and disembarkation. Then on April 8th the bulk of the battalion embarked on the Cunarder *Alaunia* for Mudros, which it reached

[1] A monument to the Division has since been erected here, and when the avenue of elm trees along which it marched past had to be cut down it was replanted in memory of the Twenty-Ninth.

[2] The embarkation strength was 27 officers, including the M.O., Lieutenant Blake, R.A.M.C., and 1008 men, of whom Lieutenant Rawle and 70 men forming the transport detachment embarked with their horses and wagons on the S.S. *City of Edinburgh*. The officers were the same as had left Tientsin for Tsingtao with the exception of Major Jones who was on sick leave, and Captain Petre, who had been appointed Staff Captain to the 87th Brigade, while Lieutenant Silk and Second Lieutenants Nevile, Bunce, Ross, Chamberlain, Stanbrough and Heal had joined from the 3rd Battalion, the last five having been promoted to commissions from the Regiment. Lieutenants Habershon, Williams, Petre and Walker had been promoted Captains, the original Second Lieutenants had all received their " second pip," and Captain Williams had succeeded Captain Birkett as Adjutant.

early on April 11th. The battalion's transport, following in the *Manitou*, narrowly escaped destruction, for an audacious Turkish torpedo boat, having slipped out of Smyrna, intercepted her off Skyros and gave her crew and passengers eight minutes in which to quit the ship before it was torpedoed. Hastily and amid some confusion the boats were launched. One at least upset and some other men seem to have jumped overboard. Then the Turks discharged their three torpedoes, but all without success, whereupon the torpedo boat found it expedient to quit the scene, towards which British destroyers were hastening. Most of the men in the water were picked up and the *Manitou* continued its voyage, but the incident had resulted in the drowning of over 50 men, among them one man of the 2nd S.W.B., Private Hogg.

The battalion remained at Mudros just a fortnight, being strenuously employed in practising disembarkation and rowing, with occasional route marches to keep the men fit. Rowing was an unwonted exercise to most of the battalion, but they took to it with zeal and quickly attained to a creditable proficiency. This was as well, for the battalion was to be called on to propel its own boats in the last stages of the approach to the shore.

The plan adopted by Sir Ian Hamilton, the Commander-in-Chief of the " M.E.F.," was that while the Australian and New Zealand Corps should attempt a landing near Gaba Tepe on the Western coast of the peninsula, some 15 miles from Cape Helles, the Twenty-Ninth Division should take the bull by the horns and get ashore at the end of the peninsula, utilizing for its main landing the beach at Sedd ul Bahr, just East of Cape Helles, and two smaller beaches on either side of Tekke Burnu, the promontory N.W. of Cape Helles. Two diversions were to be made, one by two battalions on the West coast at a little beach, afterwards familiar as " Y," about 3000 yards S.W. of Krithia, the other by one battalion at Eski Hissarlik, the Eastern end of the wide Morto Bay, which lies just inside the mouth of the Straits. Here on the cliffs which rise sharply from the shore was an old battery, known as de Tott's, and the beach just S.W. of it received the name of " S " Beach. It was here that the S.W.B. were to force their landing, the idea being that by disembarking in rear of the main defensive position the battalion would be well placed to threaten and harass the retreat of its defenders. But the " S " Beach troops might have to remain isolated and exposed for some time after landing, and it was no small compliment to be selected for this task. General Hunter-Weston, G.O.C. of the Division, indeed informed Captain Davidson of H.M.S. *Cornwallis*, on which the S.W.B. embarked, that the battalion was a specially picked one, chosen because of the difficulty of the operation.

The plan was that the *Cornwallis* should proceed two and a half miles inside the Straits, where the troops would be transferred to four trawlers, each of which had six boats made fast alongside. The men, 36 to a boat, lay behind the bulwarks opposite the boats to which they were detailed, ready for the signal to man them. Thanks to the constant practice in embarking and disembarking the men could man their boats in 45 seconds. The trawlers would steam in as near the shore as possible and then the men were themselves to row them ashore. Unfortunately the Navy's resources in boats proved to be limited, and only three companies of the battalion could be employed at " S " Beach. A Company (Captain Palmer) was, therefore, detached and added to the two battalions detailed for " Y " Beach, the K.O.S.B. and the Plymouth R.M.L.I. of the Royal Naval Division.

The first moves were made on the evening of April 23rd, the *Alaunia* steaming out of Mudros for Tenedos. As she passed the *Triumph*, the battalion's old friend on the China station and recently at Tsingtao, that battleship's band struck up " Men of Harlech." Her crew crowded the deck and cheered themselves hoarse, the S.W.B. responding with equal vigour. Arriving at Tenedos early on the 24th the battalion was transferred in the afternoon to the *Cornwallis*. Nothing could have exceeded the welcome given by her officers and crew. Each mess took charge of a proportion of men and entertained them at supper, after which all ranks settled down to get as much rest as possible. At 10 p.m. the ships weighed anchor and steamed slowly towards Sedd ul Bahr. By 3.30 a.m. they were reaching their assigned stations and the troops stood to arms and were given breakfast by their naval hosts. At 5 a.m. the warships started the bombardment under cover of which the landing was to be made. The trawlers, to which the S.W.B. had been now transferred, were hampered by the Dardanelles current, and further delayed by the mine-sweeping flotilla just inside the Straits. Indeed the flagship signalled to them to make for " V " Beach instead of for " S," but luckily the signal was not taken in and the trawlers held on their way towards " S," fortunately escaping at first the notice of the batteries on the Asiatic shore. It was misty early, which helped to conceal the tows, but as they neared the shore the mist lifted. About eight hundred yards from shore the order was given to get the men into the boats which, thanks to careful rehearsing and excellent organization, was done quickly and quietly. The Turks had spotted the flotilla now and shells were bursting all round, but fortunately without hitting the boats, though two trawlers were hit. Before long the water became too shallow for the trawlers, whereupon they let the tows go and the S.W.B., though hampered with packs and rifles, plied their oars with such vigour that in a few minutes the boats were grounding and the men, leaping out into waist-deep water, hastened ashore. Two companies, B and C, landed on the actual beach; D, under Major Margesson, was to get ashore further to the right on the rocks below De Tott's Battery, and scramble up the cliff which here rose fairly straight up for nearly two hundred feet. To make the ascent easier D were in shirt sleeves and without packs, and being thus lightly equipped they quickly scaled the cliff and rushed the ruins of the battery. From it the left platoon could take in flank the trench above the beach from which the defenders had opened a sharp fire on the other companies. " It was an unforgettable experience," a naval spectator has written,[1] " to watch this well-trained battalion working its way methodically and without confusion to the top of the battery from both sides." A party of Marines had landed almost immediately after D Company and followed them up the cliff, watching them " literally fly on ahead, line a wall at the top, place machine guns in position, run telephone communications down the hill and station snipers on a line running by a wall at right angles to the position."

Meanwhile B and C's leading platoons were also ashore. Closely packed in open boats they had afforded the easiest of targets and casualties had been numerous, including Lieutenant Behrens killed and Second Lieutenant Chamberlain wounded, both before landing. However, they promptly rushed the trenches ahead of them. Most of the Turks bolted, but B and C were too quick for others and shot and bayoneted several, while about a dozen surrendered.

Considering the task the battalion had been set its casualties were low,[2] though unluckily they included Major Margesson, who was shot in the chest when directing No. 15 Platoon's fire so as best to assist B and C. His was a great loss: a thoroughly competent officer, much was expected of him not only in the Regiment but by others outside it also.

By 8 a.m., then, the battalion was well established on its objective, and though guns on the Asiatic shore had by now opened fire on the captured position, the *Cornwallis* was quick to turn her guns on to them and soon afforded relief. It was

[1] *The Immortal Gamble*, p. 75.
[2] The total casualties at " S " Beach were 2 officers and 12 men killed, 6 men missing (probably drowned) and 2 officers and 40 men wounded. Captain Johnson was the other officer wounded, Captain Birkett, though wounded in the hand, continued at duty.

possible, therefore, to take stock of the situation, send the wounded off to the ship and start getting water and reserve ammunition out of the boats, which, however, had gone adrift, as the seamen detailed as beach party had been unable to resist the temptation to join in the advance, picking up the rifles of the first casualties.

The situation was none too satisfactory. From their cliff the S.W.B. could look back across Morto Bay to Sedd ul Bahr on their left rear. Heavy firing was still going on, the ships were still bombarding the fort and village, so these had clearly not been carried, and though the watchers from De Tott's could not grasp the details of the tragedy of "V" Beach they could not but realize that there was no immediate likelihood of their co-operating in a rapid advance from the Sedd ul Bahr–Cape Helles area. Indeed machine guns from Sedd ul Bahr kept on opening fire on B and C from the rear, though as they made poor shooting they were a nuisance rather than a danger. On the S.W.B.'s own immediate front there was some sniping from the direction of Hill 236, though whether the surviving defenders of the captured trenches had received any reinforcements it was impossible to ascertain. Such information as had been collected indicated that the beaches at the Southern end of the Gallipoli peninsula were held by at least three battalions, with the remainder of a division in close support, and the prisoners affirmed that 2000 men were in the near neighbourhood. Colonel Casson, therefore, decided to secure the position against the counter-attack which there seemed reason to expect, and disposed his men to this end. D Company and a platoon of C held De Tott's, three platoons of B and one of C formed the front line along a ridge facing North, the rest of B and C being in support nearer the beach, while a field hospital was established just below De Tott's in some trees, where an excellent supply of water was discovered. A sharp watch was kept on the Sedd ul Bahr–Cape Helles area, but though about midday Turks could be seen retiring from Hill 114, which success was followed later in the afternoon by the capture of the redoubts on Hill 138, the situation at "V" remained unchanged, and nightfall found the battalion still in the same isolated and exposed position, though well dug in. Actually, no counter-attack developed, for, as appears from Turkish disclosures since the war, their force in the Cape Helles area was smaller than G.H.Q. had been led to believe: there was only one company at Morto Bay[1] and but two battalions engaged in the defence of the Southern beaches. However, even in the light of this wisdom after the event it is difficult to

[1] Another from the local reserve at Krithia seems to have moved to Morto Bay when the bombardment began.

see what more the battalion could have achieved, with the rest of the Division held up over two miles away. Those in higher command made no attempt to utilize the lodgment which the S.W.B. had effected by diverting some of the " main body " to " S " Beach, and without reinforcements it would have been nothing short of foolhardy for three companies to advance into unknown country with no definite objective or instructions, for the contingency which had arisen does not appear to have been contemplated and no provision had been made for it. General Hunter-Weston's message received next day—" Well done, S.W.B. Can you maintain your position for another 48 hours ? " —is sufficient testimony to his satisfaction with the battalion's achievement.

During the night of April 25th/26th there were several heavy bursts of rifle fire from the Turkish positions which, as our patrols had ascertained, ran along a ridge 800 yards distant, but the battalion for the most part reserved its fire, and the Turks were usually quieted by a few rounds from the ships. One patrol from B Company had a sharp encounter and dispersed a Turkish patrol, bringing in two prisoners, but the chief event of the night was the arrival of a ship's pinnace towing boats loaded with rations and extra ammunition.

Morning found the situation unchanged. A report had been received that Sedd ul Bahr had been captured, but this was clearly untrue. The Turks were still holding on, so the battalion had to hang on and improve its defences, and not till the early afternoon did it have the satisfaction of watching the eventual success of the gallant survivors of the Hampshires, Dublins and Munsters. These, aided by the right of the troops who had landed further West, at " W " and " X " Beaches, succeeded about 3 p.m. in carrying the village and the fort on Hill 141, and as the Turks retired towards Achi Baba an artillery observing officer, attached to the battalion, directed the ships' fire effectively on to them. " They got a caning," writes an eye-witness, " we could see scores dropping as the shrapnel burst over them. The naval gunners got the range to an inch and followed them up splendidly." Even then, however, there was no advance up to the level of the battalion's position. Casualties among senior officers had been specially heavy, and the Major on whom the command at Sedd ul Bahr had devolved was unaware that the S.W.B. were established at De Tott's.

The night of April 26th/27th was for the battalion a repetition of its predecessor. Patrols were pushed out, there was a little firing, but the Turks did not attempt to attack and confined themselves to sniping. When morning came all remained quiet, and no orders reached Colonel Casson until

1 p.m. These were that French troops would relieve the battalion, whereupon it was to march across the Peninsula and rejoin its brigade, which was now taking over the left of the Division's line. Actually, owing to delays in the landing of the French, it was nearly seven o'clock before the first two French companies reached De Tott's. Their C.O. was very anxious for Colonel Casson to remain for the night to assist his battalion in securing the position, and it was well after midnight before, the taking over being completed, the S.W.B. moved off towards "X" Beach.

The distance to be covered was under four miles, but moving by night over rough and unreconnoitred country was necessarily slow and fatiguing. There was no interruption from the Turks, who seemed to have fallen right back, but the move disturbed the jackals and their howls were calculated to irritate nerves already on edge from lack of sleep. Hardly anybody had had any real rest since the night of April 23rd/24th, and though in better condition than the survivors of the "V" Beach landing, the battalion was far from fresh. But a new effort was about to be demanded from it. Though it only reached "X" Beach about 5.30 a.m. it was promptly ordered to be ready to advance against Achi Baba at eight o'clock.[1] After the checks experienced on the first day and the subsequent delays, largely increased by the shortage of small craft and other facilities for landing reinforcements and supplies, not a moment was to be lost if the Division's objectives were to be secured.

The 87th Brigade, even when the S.W.B. had rejoined, was considerably below strength, the detachment employed at "Y" Beach being still away; General Marshall was in temporary command of the Division, so Colonel Casson acted as Brigadier and Major Going commanded the battalion. The brigade was to advance North-East astride Gully Ravine, the deep depression which reached the sea some five hundred yards North of the point on which its left was resting, with Sari Tepe—Hill 472—as its objectives. The 88th Brigade on its right was attacking Krithia, and the whole line would pivot on the French right just North of Eski Hissarlik. Little artillery support was available other than the naval guns, there had been no time for reconnaissance, and the Turkish strength and dispositions were unknown. Yet such was the urgency of the situation that the attack had to go forward. At first it progressed well enough. Starting at 8 a.m. with the Border Regiment next the sea, the Inniskillings East of Gully Ravine, and the S.W.B. in reserve, the 87th Brigade gained ground steadily, though the men's exhaustion, the roughness of the ground and the steadily increasing

---

[1] There was just time to give the men breakfast and issue rations.

heat made its progress slow. At first there was little opposition, for though some distant Turkish guns opened fire their ranging was bad, and they did but little damage. For nearly two hours the advance crept slowly on, then strong opposition developed in front of the Borders and about the same time a gap opened in the centre owing to the Inniskillings swinging away to their right to conform with the 88th Brigade's movements. This gap Colonel Casson filled with C Company,[1] but soon B also had to be sent up, which left only D still in hand at the White House where he had established his headquarters. These reinforcements, however, could not carry the line further. The exhaustion of the men was beginning to tell, accentuated as it was by thirst and the increasing heat. "Everyone was done up," writes one survivor, "though we continued to advance it was very slow work. Sharp rushes were a thing of the past, a slow walk was all we could manage." The Turks had been reinforced by a whole division, and though they had not had time to do much entrenching, the broken ground with its gullies and undulations provided excellent ready-made fire positions, difficult to locate and impossible to indicate to the supporting ships.[2]

The S.W.B. before long found themselves ahead of the troops on their left and their immediate opponents were emboldened to try an advance, which the battalion's accurate rifle fire soon brought to a standstill. This repulse seems to have affected the troops facing the Border Regiment, for about 1 p.m. that battalion managed to get going again and was nearly at "Y" Beach when a vigorous counter-attack by a fresh battalion from Krithia drove it right back. A timely and accurately placed salvo from the *Queen Elizabeth* stopped the Turks dead and helped the Borders to rally, but there was no more gaining of ground on the left, so the centre could not advance without exposing its flank. Meanwhile the 88th Brigade had been held up also; the French after progressing well had been driven right back and an effort by the 86th Brigade to carry the firing line forward had lacked weight and driving power. It was more than the exhausted troops could manage. The centre was now reported to be wavering, B Company West of the ravine had been specially hard pressed when the Border Regiment was pushed back and was urgently demanding ammunition, so about 2.30 p.m. Colonel Casson had to put in his last reserve, D Company, part of it reinforcing B's right and arriving in time to assist in repulsing another Turkish advance, which "got within 200

---

[1] Captain Greenway was commanding C Company and Lieutenant Somerville D Company.

[2] There was no artillery forward observing officer with the battalion.

yards before we were able to turn them," as one eye-witness writes. In retiring the Turks came in for severe punishment from the battalion's rifles, but to follow them up to their main position 600 yards ahead was impossible. Could the men have made the effort it would still have been futile, for the Turks had succeeded in outflanking the 88th Brigade, whose right the French retreat had exposed, and that brigade and the 86th, which was by now mixed up with it, were gradually thrust back. By about 5.30 p.m. only the S.W.B. were still hanging on to the most advanced positions gained,[1] and after dusk they, too, were recalled to the new line which General Marshall had decided to entrench.[2] This ran more or less diagonally across the peninsula from just short of "Y" Beach to a little N.E. of De Tott's, the 87th Brigade as before being responsible for the left astride Gully Ravine.

Considering the heavy fighting the 2nd S.W.B.'s losses had not been severe, 16 men killed, 29 missing, 86 with Lieutenant Somerville and Second Lieutenant Neville wounded, which proportionately to the force engaged compared favourably with other battalions. The battalion could look back on the fight with some satisfaction: no unit had advanced as far, it had only evacuated its gains by command, coming off at a walk in good order and quite unmolested, it had punished the Turks heavily[3] and had repulsed their efforts to drive the invader back into the sea. On reaching the new line the three companies found no rest awaiting them, but orders to dig in at once. They had hardly started on their task before it began to rain in torrents, so that as one survivor writes, "after being parched and scorched all day we were drenched and nearly frozen. However, this was a blessing in disguise, for it compelled us to continue scratching at the earth to keep some warmth in our bodies, whereas had it been a warm night we should have been more inclined for sleep than for entrenching. Consequently we put up fairly good cover."

By this time the whole battalion was together again, Lieutenant Silk with two platoons of A Company having rejoined early in the afternoon, Captain Habershon with the remainder in the evening. It was a sadly depleted Company, however; Captain Palmer had been killed with 17 men, 9 were missing, 42

---

[1] Apparently somewhere between Fir Tree Wood and "Y" Beach: B Company finished up opposite Krithia.

[2] Privates Clent, Hendy and Spink distinguished themselves by good work in assisting the wounded, going out many times and rescuing men who must otherwise have perished.

[3] The Turkish official accounts testify to their infantry's heavy losses on this day: clearly with an additional brigade of fresh troops and more adequate artillery support the Division's object would probably have been achieved.

wounded, as was also Captain Tippetts, who had been very badly hit. The "Y" Beach force had had a hard time; though its landing had not been opposed, it had in the end been vigorously counter-attacked and had been heavily engaged nearly all the night of April 25th/26th. As at "S" the landing at "Y" had taken the Turks by surprise and by six o'clock the force had been well established on the cliffs above the beach. With nine companies as against the three who landed at "S" it might seem that much might have been done. Certainly had the force at "Y" been promptly reinforced by the diversion thither of the divisional reserve the opening might have been turned to decisive account. Unfortunately, however, here also the commanding officer lacked instructions for the precise circumstances in which he found himself, so after pushing reconnoitring parties almost to Krithia he finally decided early in the afternoon to entrench on the cliffs above the landing place and await further instructions, which were not forthcoming. A Company, less one platoon in support, took the right of the position, with the K.O.S.B. on their left and the R.M.L.I. beyond them again. It was a pity that this work had not been begun earlier: the soil was hard, and the tough roots of the scrub which covered it did not make entrenching with " grubbers " any easier, and before the troops had had time to construct satisfactory defences Turkish attacks began to develop. The first of these was delivered rather before 6 p.m. and though the Turks were kept at bay as long as the ships could give supporting fire, at 7.15 p.m. these ceased fire, whereupon the Turks pressed closer. All night long their attacks continued, well supported by cleverly handled machine guns. Their pressure was heaviest on the left, coming unfortunately against the raw and inexperienced Plymouth R.M.L.I., to whose assistance A Company's reserve platoon had soon to be dispatched. But the K.O.S.B. and the S.W.B.'s other platoons were hard pressed also. The Turks came on repeatedly with the utmost vigour and devotion, the fighting was often at very close quarters, losses on both sides were heavy, and though when morning dawned the Turks drew off, leaving the British lines still intact, the position was none too good. All ranks were feeling the strain of the hard and continuous fighting, ammunition was running very short, casualties had been especially heavy among the officers, and, not to mince matters, many of the R.M.L.I. recruits had had enough and were not to be relied upon. Seeing boats come in to evacuate the wounded, several unwounded men, some of whom had already made their way down to the beach, hastened to climb on board, apparently under the impression that evacuation had been ordered. Almost simultaneously a sudden Turkish attack, for which they had massed unseen in the ravine, broke through our centre, and disaster was only averted by Captain Habershon who formed up the S.W.B. and charged the enemy with the bayonet. His action was most effective, the Turks broke and fled and made no further attempt to attack. Unfortunately more of the exhausted troops seem now to have sought the beach and as no orders and reinforcements had reached him and the position seemed quite untenable, the senior officer accepted evacuation as inevitable and it proceeded uninterrupted. By midday all the troops had been re-embarked, and a foothold that would have been invaluable on April 28th had been abandoned.[1]

"Y" Beach is in its way the most tragic incident in all the landings at Gallipoli. A far more promising opening than that secured at "S," its adequate exploitation might have made an incalculable difference. Wisdom after the event comes easily, one realizes now that the whole scheme of the attack was on the ambitious side, that all possible contingencies had not been taken into account when the orders were passed, that the "covering force" was out of all proportion to the main body, that there were insufficient reserves to profit by the openings made at "S" or "Y." These two landings present a distinct analogy with Picton's escalade of the Castle and Leith's capture of the San Vincente bastion at Badajoz in 1812. Those "diversions" or "false attacks" were successful and, being properly exploited, more than balanced the bloody repulse of the Fourth and Light Divisions at the main breaches, perhaps our closest parallel to the slaughter at "V" Beach. Adequately exploited, the "S" and "Y" landings might have given us Achi Baba on April 26th, and the S.W.B. would have had the privilege of having shared in both: the "honour" of "Landing at Helles" would then record not merely a gallant achievement but a substantial and fruitful success.

[1] There is a full account of "Y" Beach in the History of the K.O.S.B.

CHAPTER VIII

GALLIPOLI AND ADEN

The Second Phase:

STALEMATE AT HELLES

FROM the strategical standpoint the failure to capture Achi Baba on April 28th definitely marks the end of the first phase in the Gallipoli operations: the original force had exhausted itself in establishing a precarious lodgment on the Peninsula. If, then, the main purpose of the attack was to be achieved, and the way through the Straits to Constantinople opened to the Navy, substantial reinforcements must be promptly forthcoming. From the end of April to the middle of July the story is that of the arrival in driblets of reinforcements, half of which might have secured success had they only arrived earlier, and of several efforts to get forward, none of which achieved more than very limited gains. July brought more substantial reinforcements, including another battalion of the Regiment, to start afresh at another point. With August the third, or Suvla, phase opens, ending like the others in the partial success which, in war, is often equivalent to failure, and followed by four months of stalemate, indecision and ultimate evacuation.

To the regimental officers and men there was nothing to show that any particular milestone in their Gallipoli experiences had been passed on April 28th. There was no change in their position, in the hardships they were enduring, in the labours required of them, no reduction of the dangers to which they were exposed. Another ten days were to pass before the 2nd S.W.B. enjoyed anything which the most optimistic could regard as rest: in the meantime they were to have more hard fighting and to lose yet more of their number with little to show for their labours and losses. Actually April 29th and 30th proved uneventful: the Turks hardly attempted to interfere with the improvement of the position, units were sorted out, detached parties returned to their own corps[1] and the line was readjusted. Early on the 30th the battalion shifted slightly to the right, D Company's right now resting on the Cape Helles-Krithia road, B and C being also in front line with A in reserve. The rain had ceased and the sun had dried and warmed the troops, though still no proper rest was attainable. That afternoon our stretcher bearers tried to get in some badly wounded men who were lying out between the lines, but they were stopped by the Turks, who

---

[1] The battalion is returned as mustering 17 officers and 636 men on May 1st: it was the second strongest in the brigade and third strongest in the Division.

advanced in force, whereupon the battalion opened fire and drove them back to cover. After dark the Turks started a sharp fire from guns and rifles and followed it up by advancing, but retired on rapid fire being opened. Everybody was thoroughly tired now, nerves were all on edge, all night long alarms were constantly given. Indeed a heavy fire was once opened on what proved to be an advance in open order by two large hedgehogs.

May 1st likewise passed quietly enough, but about 10 p.m. the Turks began a heavy artillery fire. The battalion had by this time got fairly good cover and could, therefore, sit tight, suffering very little from the shrapnel and waiting for an infantry attack to develop. Suddenly red flares went up in front and with shouts of " Allah, Allah " masses of Turks pushed forward. Fire was reserved till they were quite close, when the battalion let fly with deadly and decisive effect. A little later the Turks came on again but with even less success: the moon had now risen behind them and they could be clearly discerned at some distance. Against the S.W.B. they made no more advances, confining themselves to keeping up an almost continuous rifle fire. Further to the right, however, they pressed their attacks with greater vigour and success, at one time piercing the 88th Brigade's line, besides driving the French back at several points. In this quarter heavy fighting continued all night. " The noise was deafening," one of the S.W.B. writes, " they yelled and shouted like madmen, but above all the cry of ' Allah ' could be heard."[1] The battalion's right machine gun did considerable execution by firing to its flank across the Lancashire Fusiliers' front, and after desperate fighting the line was re-established and the Turks ejected.

Morning brought an end to the attacks and disclosed Turks in some force clustering in the low ground in front of the 87th Brigade. Heavy fire was promptly poured into them, bowling many over, while others bolted and others put up their hands in token of surrender. The situation seemed to invite local counter-attack, and the Border Regiment, together with A Company S.W.B. from battalion reserve, pushed forward. The Borders promptly came under heavy fire and, swinging to their right to face it, exposed their left flank and were soon hung up. A Company, rather luckier in their ground, gained good cover in a small nullah, whence they could fire effectively at Turks who were enfilading the Borders. More A could not do and, though about 7.30 a.m. orders were issued for a general advance, a long wait ensued before the troops on the right began to get forward. C and D Companies then pushed out two platoons to form a firing line and an advance began, many exhausted and

---

[1] They were also heard to shout " Rendez vos armes, Messieurs les Anglais ! "

demoralized Turks being captured. But there was little artillery support and the right was not only held up but driven back in some disorder, the French in particular suffering heavily. The 87th Brigade had therefore to come back and the battalion resumed its old positions. The remainder of the day passed quietly, but the night was again anything but restful. Soon after dark the Turks reopened their bombardment and from eight o'clock on their infantry joined in and appeared to be making efforts to advance. However, the bright moonlight showed them up clearly at a considerable distance and the battalion's rifle fire brought every effort to a standstill. In the morning Turkish parties came out under cover of the white flag to search for wounded, and the battalion took advantage of this to dispose of the Turkish dead, who were lying thickly all over the ground in front, some quite close to our parapets. That evening the Border Regiment relieved the battalion, which withdrew to Gully Beach, where for the first time since the landing it found itself out of the firing line and able to get a real rest and some sleep. It wanted the rest badly; indeed many men were so exhausted that next day (May 3rd), after rifle inspections and a bathing parade, they slept right on all day and could not even rouse themselves for a hot dinner. This spell of peace lasted another two days, during which the battalion had the satisfaction of seeing reinforcements, the 125th (Lancashire Fusiliers) Brigade of the Forty-Second (Territorial) Division and a Gurkha battalion, moving up the Gully to take post in readiness for a new advance on Krithia.

This started on May 6th, the 87th Brigade being held in reserve while the 125th attacked along the Gully Spur between the ravine and the sea, the 88th advancing from the 87th's trenches across Fir Tree Spur[1] and the French conforming on the right. The attack made little progress: the 125th Brigade was held up after advancing 200 yards, the 88th with its left thus exposed only gained about 400, the French accomplished even less. On May 7th, therefore, the attack was renewed with the same objectives, the 87th Brigade being ordered to support the 88th and 125th. Casualties among senior officers had been heavy and as Colonel Casson was commanding a brigade of the Royal Naval Division Major Going was acting as Brigadier. Captain Greenway therefore commanded the battalion, whose orders were to push up the Gully in readiness to pass through the 125th Brigade when it should have attained its objective and then wheel right-handed against Krithia. However, the attack fared little better than its predecessor, and the S.W.B. toiled slowly up Gully Ravine, unable to discover what was

[1] That between Gully Ravine and the Krithia nullah.

happening except that crowds of wounded Territorials were coming back down the ravine. Eventually about 7 p.m. the battalion was ordered to relieve the Territorials, but as their line was about 300 yards in rear of that of the Inniskillings East of the nullah it was decided, in the words of an eye-witness, "to try a little ground-snatching as taught by the Japs at Tsingtao." Accordingly, directly it was dark Lieutenant Ross went forward with Company Sergeant Major Millichamp and a few men to mark out the trench, a small covering party being pushed out ahead. C and D Companies, having equipped themselves with picks and shovels discarded by the Territorials, crept stealthily forward, leaving A and B to man the existing trench. All went well; the men worked splendidly, the Turks, except for an occasional shell, gave no sign of life and only two men were hit. By daybreak a good fire-trench had been completed from the sea to Gully Ravine with a communication trench, dug by B Company, back to the original line.

Early in the morning orders were received to co-operate in the renewed attack up Fir Tree Spur to be made by the New Zealand Brigade, which had been specially brought round from "Anzac," along with the 2nd Australian Brigade. The 87th Brigade was to cover the left of this attack, and meanwhile the battalion was to push scouts and small patrols up the nullah and along the cliffs to endeavour to locate the machine guns which were holding up the advance along the bare and coverless Gully Spur. Until these could be silenced an advance by day was out of the question, as was impressed on Brigade Headquarters over the telephone. The Brigadier seemed fully aware of this and it was a little surprising that soon after 5 p.m. orders were received for the battalion to endeavour to carry the Turkish trenches 1000 yards ahead.

An artillery bombardment of sorts opened at 5.30 p.m. and ten minutes later two platoons each of C and D under Second Lieutenant Heal and Lieutenant Ross went gallantly forward, closely followed by the other half-companies under Captain Walker and Second Lieutenant Stanborough respectively. The advancing lines went forward splendidly, despite a storm of shrapnel and an even deadlier fire from machine guns some 500 yards behind the Turkish front line. Numbers fell, especially in the second line, which was mown down wholesale as it crossed the parapet, Second Lieutenant Stanborough being dangerously wounded, and the advance was held up about one hundred yards from the Turkish trenches. Here Sergeant Bean did splendid work; seeing that both Lieutenant Ross and Second Lieutenant Heal were down and that he was the senior present, he took charge and ordered the men to scratch up what cover they could and hold on. His fine example of courage and steadiness was ably seconded by Lance Corporal Millward, who ran up and down the line with orders, seeming to bear a charmed life, though the Turks concentrated their fire on him. The C.O. meanwhile, realizing that to send more men forward in face of

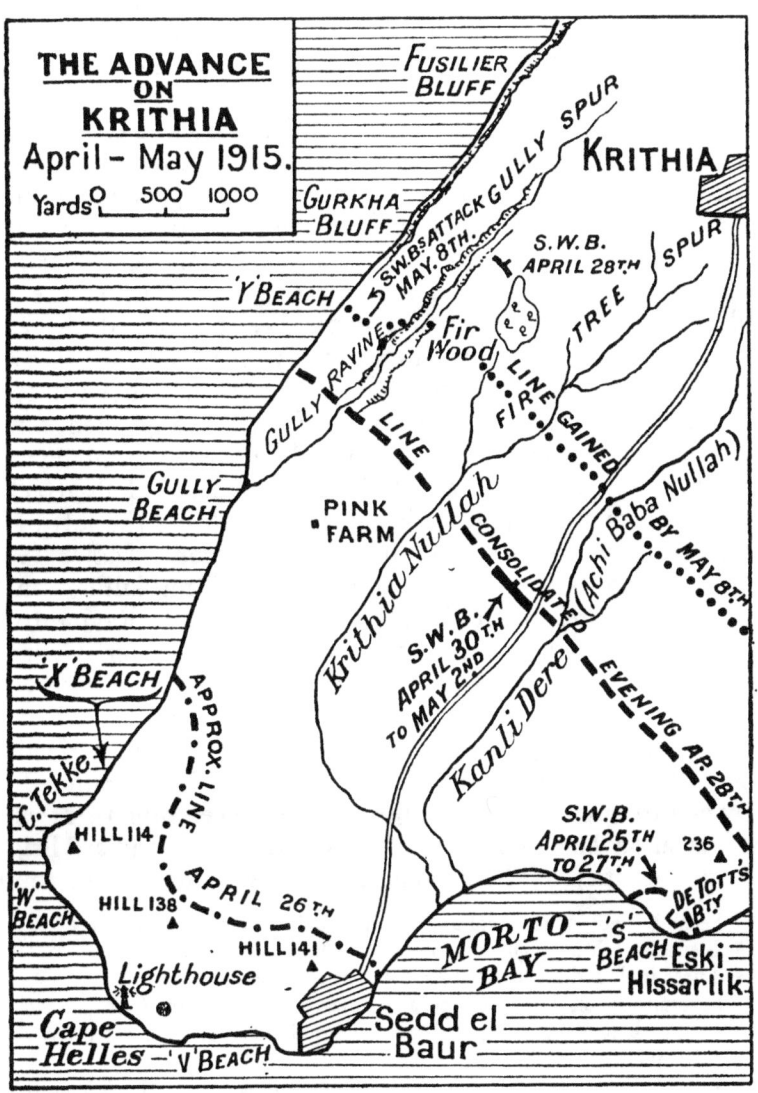

that fire would be mere waste of lives, stopped the advance of A and B. Further to the right the attack, though pressed with great gallantry, especially by the New Zealanders, had gained little ground. Like its predecessors, it had failed from sheer lack of enough guns and shells to allow the devotion and determination of the infantry a fair chance.

THE HISTORY OF THE SOUTH WALES BORDERERS

After dark Sergeant Bean brought back to the front trench the forty or fifty survivors of the advanced platoons, and shortly afterwards on relief by the K.O.S.B. the weary battalion moved back to support trenches near White House. It had lost heavily; besides the officers mentioned[1] Lieutenant Bunce had been killed with 14 men, 34 were "missing," all practically certainly dead, 83 were wounded, so that with the losses on May 2nd[2] and a few odd casualties since then,[3] the battalion was now well below 500 strong.

That evening the battalion was ordered back to Gully Beach, where it remained for ten days, having at first little more to do than improve the bivouacs and tidy up the ground around—which needed it badly—but later on having heavy fatigues, partly unloading stores on "W" Beach, partly road-making in Gully Ravine. Colonel Casson resumed command on the 11th and two days later General Hunter Weston visited the camp and congratulated the battalion warmly on its splendid conduct in the recent severe fighting.[4] On May 16th a first reinforcement arrived, consisting of Captain Fowler and 46 men, a mere trifle in comparison with the battalion's losses, but even so welcome enough. On May 22nd a sudden alarm of an attack on the 29th Indian Brigade, which was now holding the left of the line, brought the battalion back to the front, Major Going taking A and B Companies to support the Inniskillings on the left, Headquarters with C and D going up Gully Ravine to the 14th Sikhs. Actually the lost trenches were recovered without the battalion being put in,[5] but it was retained in reserve all night, returning to Gully Beach in the morning.

On May 26th a really substantial reinforcement arrived, 15 officers and 208 men,[6] while a few of the slightly wounded had returned to duty. On May 29th twenty picked miners, of whom the battalion had plenty, were attached to the Indian Brigade for special duty. These men, though without proper mining

---

[1] Second Lieutenants Heal and Stanborough died of their wounds.

[2] Lieutenant Macgregor and 9 men killed, 41 men wounded.

[3] These included Lieutenant Laman wounded on May 7th.

[4] Sergeant Bean, Lance Corporal Millward, and Privates Clent, Hendy and Spinks were all formally congratulated by the G.O.C. for their gallantry, and all were subsequently awarded the D.C.M.

[5] By this time, thanks largely to a dashing enterprise by the 6th Gurkhas, a considerable advance had been made along the coast to a bluff beyond "Y" Beach, afterwards known as Gurkha Bluff. East of Gully Ravine some progress had been made, mainly by sapping forwards or making small advances at night.

[6] The officers were Lieutenants K. Ffrench, R. C. Inglis, and J. F. Bradley, Second Lieutenants B. I. L. Jones, C. H. Nicholas, S. H. Geldard, S. H. Berger, H. J. Inglis, M. Spartali, H. L. Cass, J. C. Roberts, P. E. Burrell, H. C. Griffith and P. H. Turner, all Special Reservists save Second Lieutenants Roberts and Griffith, who were Regulars. Major Jones also rejoined at this time.

ANOTHER ATTACK ON KRITHIA

tools and appliances, did excellent work, though at the point where the galleries were being driven the stench from unburied corpses was overwhelming. The weather had got hotter now and flies were rapidly becoming a perfect plague. The end of the month found the battalion still at " the usual fatigues on Gully Beach," but with the beginning of June came a return to the trenches and more serious work.[1]

By this time Sir Ian Hamilton had been reinforced by the rest of the Forty-second (E. Lancashire) Division and more Australians, and the systematic working forward had not only straightened the line but advanced it considerably nearer Krithia, Fir Tree Wood being now inside British territory. But the Turks were working hard at their defences and it was decided to try another attack before they could make them impregnable. In this the Twenty-Ninth Division was again attacking astride Gully Ravine, the Indian Brigade West of it and the 88th East. These brigades had two main lines of trenches to capture, after which the 87th Brigade, which Colonel Casson was again commanding, was to pass through and attack Krithia. Until that time the brigade would remain in reserve, so the S.W.B. were not required to move, though they had plenty of occupation in making the necessary preparations.

The attack started at noon on June 4th, and on the right of the Twenty-Ninth Division and on the Forty-Second's frontage further East things at first went well. The 88th Brigade carried several lines of trenches, captured a substantial haul of prisoners and punished the enemy severely. West of Gully Ravine, however, affairs took a less satisfactory turn. Despite repeated efforts the Lancashire Fusiliers in the centre of the Indian Brigade failed to carry the Turkish trench known as J. 10. This neutralized the success of the 6th Gurkhas nearer the coast and of the 14th Sikhs in and just East of Gully Ravine, and reacted unfavourably on the situation further East, the 88th Brigade finding its left in the air and being enfiladed from across the ravine. Meanwhile the S.W.B. waited, listening to the sounds of fighting and watching batches of prisoners marching down to the beach. About 7.30 p.m. came orders to relieve the Dublin Fusiliers who, after an unsuccessful advance against J. 11, were hanging on astride the ravine, slightly in rear of the 14th Sikhs who were just South of the Eastern end of J. 10.

The relief took some time and the battalion had not been long in position before the Turks began to press hard upon the 14th Sikhs, to whose help first one and then another platoon of C Company were sent up under Captain Greenway and

[1] During this period on Gully Beach the battalion had 2 killed and 19 wounded, mainly caused by spent bullets.

Lieutenant Rawle. This allowed the Sikhs to be withdrawn—they had lost nearly 400—after which these two platoons with A Company on their right were busily engaged in improving their position and in replying to vigorous bombing and sniping. This advanced position, however, presented no particular advantages, so in the evening it was decided, with the concurrence of General Cox, B.G.C. 29th Indian Brigade, to withdraw to a better position in rear. In the readjusted line B took the right, East of the ravine, C and D were West of it, having relieved the Lancashire Fusiliers and having the 5th Gurkhas on their left: A Company was in support in the nullah, which was

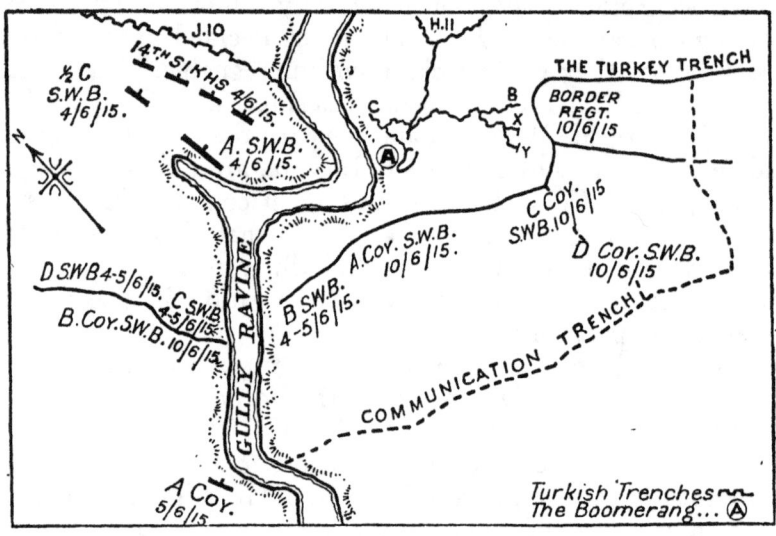

THE BOOMERANG AND THE TURKEY TRENCH, JUNE 1915.
X and Y = Sap-Heads.

blocked with wire and held by a machine gun. Heavy fighting was going on beyond the battalion's right and in the early morning of June 5th a sudden counter-attack ousted the 88th Brigade from H. 12, the most advanced of the trenches it had taken. Along the second line, however, the Turks were held up, being eventually driven back with heavy losses, but further readjustments proved necessary and that evening the S.W.B. shifted to their right, A and C relieving the Borders on a frontage of about five hundred yards with D in support, B holding about one hundred and twenty yards of front West of the ravine. This position the battalion held for nearly a week, improving it considerably, especially by digging a new trench in rear to avoid using the front line as a communication trench to the trenches on the right. There was much sniping, the Turks exposed themselves freely; on June 8th, indeed, the battalion claimed to have hit as many as eighteen, its own casualties meanwhile being trifling, though Lieutenant Silk was killed on June 9th.[1]

The chief incident of the time was an attempt on June 10th to dislodge the Turks from a sap opposite the angle of the firing line just East of the ravine. This was carried out in conjunction with the Borders on the right. One company of that regiment was to work down towards the ravine along the line B–C and connect up with a party of the battalion which, led by Lieutenant R. C. Inglis, was to seize the sap head at A and work along to C. Starting at 10 p.m., Lieutenant Inglis and his party crawled out to the sap head ninety yards away, jumped down into it and forced their way along it, but bombs and machine-gun fire soon checked them and eventually they were bombed out. A second attempt, in which Second Lieutenants Spartali and H. J. Inglis joined, again took the sap, but again it could not be held. The Inglis brothers, who had shown the greatest gallantry and determination, were both wounded[2] and Second Lieutenant Spartali and several men were killed. Meanwhile the Borders had reached C, cutting off and bayoneting the occupants of another sap, but after a stubborn bombing contest they too were compelled to evacuate most of their gains. After this it was decided to sap out to A, now styled " the Boomerang," in which task fair progress had been made before the battalion was relieved on June 12th. It then spent five days at Gully Beach " resting," which in practice meant finding large working-parties to strengthen the so-called " Old " or " Eski line," that held on the evening of April 28th, now forming a reserve position. General de Lisle, who had just taken over the Division on General Hunter Weston's promotion to command the Eighth Corps, was a remorseless digger, as the 2nd S.W.B. were to realize fully during the next two years and a half, and a line held for any time by his Division was likely to become more than ordinarily strong. But it meant unending work and some people were not sorry to get back on the 17th to the trenches, where life was not quite so strenuous.

The frontage now taken over by the S.W.B. was that held on June 12th, together with the so-called " Turkey Trench " on the right, formerly held by the Borders. This spell in the line proved short but exciting. On the evening of June 18th the Turks started a violent bombardment, doing great damage to parapets and trenches, temporarily severing all telephone wires, though communication between Battalion Headquarters and the firing line was re-established by orderlies and the devoted

---

[1] The operations of June 4th/5th had only cost the battalion a dozen casualties, but these included Captain Greenway and Lieutenant Rawle, both wounded.
[2] Lieutenant R. C. Inglis died of his wounds on June 29th.

linesmen soon had the wires in order again. About 8.30 p.m. an infantry attack developed but was beaten off, only to be soon renewed in greater strength. This time the attackers pressed hardest against the Turkey Trench and, having more bombs and better bombs than the defenders, succeeded in getting into its N.W. end and driving the garrison back, Lieutenant Jordan[1] being mortally wounded and most of his men killed or wounded. Pushing on, the Turks even penetrated to the main trench and cut the battalion off from the Inniskillings on its right. This was not to be endured, and soon a mixed party of S.W.B. and Inniskillings was driving the Turks back down the Turkey Trench. But they came on again, thrusting the Inniskillings back, and though about 11.15 p.m. Captain Walker and a bombing party forced their way along a new sap connecting the main line with the head of Turkey Trench, this could not relieve the pressure, and the Turkish bombers again cleared Turkey Trench to the junction with the main fire trench. Major Going had now come across from West of the nullah to take charge, and arranged, after consultation with the Inniskillings, that the Turkey Trench should be attacked in flank at 3 a.m. by a company of the S.W.B. Before that, however, the Turks had once again broken in between the two battalions, only to be ejected, while part of Turkey Trench had been recovered but lost again.

At 3 a.m. three platoons under Lieutenant Cass dashed out across the open. Shown up by a Turkish flare, they were met by a heavy fire; Lieutenant Cass and about 30 men went down and the few who reached the trench were all killed there. But the attack had relieved the pressure and, after one unsuccessful attempt to advance down Turkey Trench and a short bombardment, a fresh effort at 4.45 a.m. met with better success. This was made by Captain Fowler, Regimental Sergeant Major Westlake and some bombers, and supported by Captain Walker, Captain O'Sullivan of the Inniskillings and some men of both battalions. The party was headed by Private Woods, who cleared the way with the bayonet while Private Matthews kept down the enemy's enfilading fire. Both men did magnificently, exposing themselves fearlessly and pushing steadily on. By 5.15 a.m. thirty yards had been won back, by 6 a.m. seventy, half an hour later the whole trench was in British hands. Captain Fowler had been splendid and inspired his men by his gallantry; having exhausted his own bombs he picked up Turkish bombs and threw them back with great effect.[2] The Turks,

[1] He had arrived on June 10th along with Second Lieutenants Budd and Philpotts and a draft of 106 men.
[2] Captain Fowler who was recommended for the V.C., which his gallantry well merited, was awarded the D.S.O., while the two privates got D.C.M.'s.

THE TURKEY TRENCH

moreover, in retiring in daylight across the open had been heavily punished by our machine guns. Those who had got into the new sap fared likewise when they tried to escape. A last attempt on Turkey Trench from the Boomerang was easily repulsed and the S.W.B. and Inniskillings, exhausted but triumphant, could settle down to reconstruct their defences and deal with their casualties and prisoners. Of the latter there were about a dozen, but besides Lieutenants Cass and Jordan the battalion had Second Lieutenant B. I. L. Jones killed and Major Going and Captain Patterson wounded with nearly 80 men killed and wounded. The Inniskillings had lost nearly as heavily, but the 91 dead Turks who were actually counted in or within ten yards of Turkey Trench and the new sap, represented only the smaller fraction of their casualties, for many more were lying further out.

About 1.30 p.m. things became lively again, for Turkish reinforcements tried to cross Gully Ravine from West to East under cover of a fresh bombardment. Their efforts were frustrated by B Company's steady and effective fire from the left of the ravine, and an attempt to mass at the end of Turkey Trench was severely handled by machine guns and bombers and ended in nothing but heavy loss. Next morning (June 20th) came a welcome relief, followed by a short spell in the Eski Line. But the rest was only to be a prelude to a share in another big attack. More ammunition had arrived, with part of the Fifty-Second (Lowland Territorial) Division, and another attack was to be made. This time the 87th Brigade was to lead, the S.W.B. starting the attack West of Gully Ravine, with J. 9 and J. 10 as objectives. East of the ravine the Borders were attacking, and tackling the Boomerang. The K.O.S.B. and Inniskillings would then advance through the battalion to take J. 11, after which the 86th Brigade would go through in turn and capture the final objective, J. 12 and J. 13. Beyond the Borders the 156th Brigade (Fifty-Second Division) was attacking H. 12, the 88th being in reserve.

By 6 p.m. on June 27th the battalion had taken over the front trenches and was busy preparing for the assault. When the preliminary bombardment started at nine o'clock next day it was found necessary, as the lines were so near together, to withdraw from the front line to avoid our own shells falling short, but just before "zero" company commanders took their men back to the front line, preferring to risk a few "shorts" rather than have an extra 50 yards of very broken ground to cover. "Quite unlike any other in this campaign," as the battalion diary writes, "the bombardment appeared to be excellent," and when the time came for the assault the battalion found that this had been the case. A Company on the right suffered most for, although the Borders had attacked the Boomerang fifteen minutes before the main assault started, that redoubt and its satellites were still holding out at 11 a.m., and A therefore came in for flanking fire. But this did not check them and despite a hail of shrapnel the whole line, passing over J. 9 as ordered, was into J. 10 with incredible quickness, making short work of such few Turks as had survived the bombardment. Hard on the S.W.B.'s heels came the supporting battalions, which were soon in possession of J. 11 also. Then, while the 87th consolidated its gains, the 86th Brigade passed through, the Gurkhas co-operating on their left. This attack also was successful, the advance reaching a bluff at the N.W. end of J. 13, hereafter known as Fusilier Bluff. East of the ravine, however, things did not go as well. The 156th Brigade, with less artillery support, had only secured the left half of its objective and had lost very heavily, while subsequent attempts by the 88th Brigade to capture the right of H. 12 were unsuccessful. Still the "Battle of Gully Ravine," as the fight came to be called, was quite the most successful since the landing. "The Twenty-Ninth Division again proved what it could do in spite of its enormous losses," writes the battalion diary, and the S.W.B.'s share in the success had been considerable. The dash and promptitude of its assault had given a good send-off and though its losses were heavy—Lieutenants Budd and Bradley killed or died of wounds, Captains Habershon and Williams, Lieutenant Ffrench and Second Lieutenant Nicholas wounded, with 160 casualties among the men—this time there was something substantial to show for them.

Heavy fighting did not stop with June 28th. For several days the Turks made determined efforts to recover the highly important ground they had lost. Time after time they hurled themselves at J. 13 and J. 12, gained ground by bombing, were thrust back by bayonet charges, came on again, to achieve nothing in the end, while suffering tremendous losses. In this fighting the S.W.B. were scarcely engaged. On the 29th they had taken over some half-dug trenches[1] from the Dublins, Lancashire Fusiliers and Borders, and found plenty to do in completing them and clearing up the surrounding area. The ground was littered with dead who urgently required burial or burning, as with that hot sun the stench was almost unbearable. The trenches were mere apologies for defences, and were, moreover, enfiladed from both flanks. But the men worked splendidly and soon had greatly improved the line. On the night of June 30th the barrier in Gully Ravine was successfully advanced and

---

[1] This position was in front of J. 11 and extended across the ravine, the portion West of the ravine being known as J. 11b.

the bodies of many Dublin Fusiliers found and buried. None
of the counter-attacks actually came against the S.W.B., though
on several occasions, notably on July 2nd, when the Turks made
their biggest effort, their machine guns put in some effective work
by catching them in flank. But June 28th had left the battalion
very weak, and with little over 350 rifles for 600 yards of front
there was small chance of rest or relief. In officers it was still
fairly strong, as Captain Elgee from the Egyptian Army had
arrived on June 30th, along with Captain Somerville, now

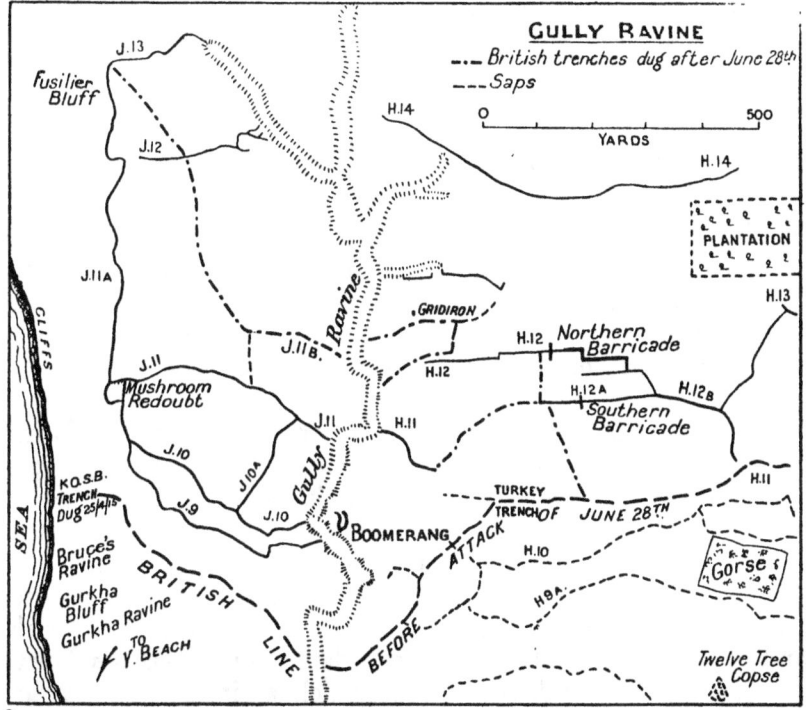

recovered from his wounds, while three officers of the 14th
Cheshires (Lieutenants Buckley, Kerr and Knowles) joined on
July 2nd.

But if the battalion missed meeting the main counter-
attacks it had one sharp fight before being relieved. Just
opposite its trenches the Turks were toiling away with the
object of securing a knoll, subsequently called the Gridiron,
which commanded the ravine. By July 5th they had pushed
within bombing distance, so it was decided that ten picked men
under Lieutenant Turner should attack their sap head and drive
them down their communication trench. This was then to be
wired, while a second party built a sandbagged wall on top of
the sap. Starting at 2.30 a.m. on July 6th, the attack was at first

successful, the sap being rushed and the garrison killed or taken, though Lieutenant Turner was unfortunately hit after having killed four Turks himself. Sergeant Lucas, however, took charge and carried on splendidly, wiring the communication trench as arranged. Directly this was done the other party under Sergeants Bell and Stratford started building the sandbag wall, but the Turks opened a heavy fire from three machine guns, inflicting many casualties. They also counter-attacked, and having a decided superiority in bombs ultimately forced our men back. Casualties were heavy, Lieutenants Turner and Kerr and 13 men killed, 30 men wounded, while shortly afterwards Captain Elgee was killed by a sniper. But our position had been improved by putting up wire and machine gun and rifle fire denied the knoll to the Turks.

Two days later (July 8th) the battalion was relieved by the 88th Brigade, and after two days at Gully Beach was shipped across to Lemnos, for its first real rest out of gunshot since landing. Lemnos to those who served in France would have seemed wholly devoid of facilities for rest and recreation; after the Peninsula it was a welcome haven of repose, and though the battalion's bivouac was a dusty camp and the water supply inadequate the change was thoroughly appreciated.

The relief of the much-tried infantry of the Twenty-Ninth Division was possible because the Thirteenth Division, the first to arrive of the three "New Army" Divisions recently detailed for service at Gallipoli, was now taking over the left of the Allied line. After many consultations and much telegraphing between Sir Ian Hamilton and Lord Kitchener it had been decided to reinforce the M.E.F. with three "K. 1" Divisions and two of Territorials, and to employ these forces in a new landing in Suvla Bay North of the "Anzac" position, from which a simultaneous attack would be made on the dominating Sari Bair ridge.

The Thirteenth Division, and with it the 4th S.W.B., had had a busy four months since arriving at Aldershot in February. With all that station's facilities for training, notably the excellent rifle-ranges, the instruction of its battalions had made rapid progress, especially after, early in June, they received Service rifles of the latest pattern. Gradually deficiencies in equipment were made good; machine guns, signalling equipment and various other requisites appeared and before long rumours of impending departure overseas began to be rife. The first definite intimation of the battalion's destination came with the sudden substitution of mule transport for the horses and carts already issued (June 7th): tropical Service helmets and khaki drill clothing were then served out, and, aided by these clues, the 4th had realized they were bound for Gallipoli some time before official information was received. Leaving Woking on June 28th, the battalion embarked that[1] same day at Avonmouth on the s.s. *Megantic*, a roomy and comfortable White Star liner, along with the 8th Royal Welch Fusiliers. There was a delay in starting as a submarine had just sunk a big transport with mules off Lundy, so the *Megantic* did not sail till 9 p.m. next day, and as far as Ushant she was escorted by destroyers. After that transports had to rely for protection on the guns at the stern with which they had been fitted. These were manned by infantrymen, who had to be trained in artillery duties *en voyage*, but while precautions against submarines were never relaxed the *Megantic* was fortunate in escaping an encounter with them; eventually she reached Mudros safely on July 12th, after calling at Alexandria, where base kits and most of the transport were landed with an officer and 31 men to look after the animals. The 4th was not to land at Mudros, however, for on the 15th, orders were received for it to proceed at once to the Peninsula, and by 4.30 p.m. C and D Companies under Major Beresford had started for the front on a trawler.

Landing at "V" Beach, these companies had a dusty and weary four-mile march to Gully Beach, where A and B soon joined them, and about 8 a.m. the 4th started off up Gully Ravine, heavily laden with blankets, waterproof sheets and other equipment.[2] The heat, the depth of the ravine and the loads carried made the move trying and tedious, but before long the 4th found itself threading its way through communication trenches, sometimes shallow and affording little protection against

---

[1] The officers who proceeded overseas were: Lieutenant Colonel F. M. Gillespie, commanding; Major M. J. de la P. Beresford, second in command; Captain H. P. Yates, Adjutant; Lieutenant and Quartermaster J. A. Mellsop; Lieutenant W. N. V. Bickford-Smith, Machine Gun Officer; Lieutenant S. Hemmingway, Transport Officer. A Company, Major Sir W. L. Napier, Bart., Captain A. W. Hooper, Lieutenant N. Y. Tessier, Second Lieutenants E. P. Bury and D. A. Addams-Williams. B Company, Major F. W. Birch, Captain J. Fairweather, Second Lieutenants L. H. Stockwood, D. S. Phillips, A. Buchanan and G M. Owen. C Company, Captain C. E. Kitchin, Lieutenants J. H. Miller and T. C. M. Austin, Second Lieutenants L. G. Cooper, E. G. Staples and C. M. Lucas. D Company, Captains P. R. M. Mundy and J. B. Blaxland, Lieutenant J. Farrow, Second Lieutenants A. F. Bell, T. M. Jenkins and J. W. L. Napier. 970 other ranks embarked, including Regimental Sergeant Major G. Halford, Regimental Quartermaster Sergeant G. Halford, Company Sergeant Majors C. Parish (A), J. Maher (B), A. A. Cornish (C) and T. Bush (D), Company Quartermaster Sergeants H. Wakefield (A), J. Callaghan (B), R. J. Goodchild (C), and D. J. James (D). The officers and men surplus to establishment were sent to the 9th Battalion, now allotted to draft-finding duties and known as "Second Reserve."

[2] Twenty-six officers and 875 men landed on Gallipoli, as, beside the transport detachment left at Alexandria, a party under Captain Hooper had been left at Mudros to act as "first reinforcements."

snipers. However, it gained the support trenches west of Twelve Tree Copse without casualties and settled down there to await its summons to the firing line as comfortably as the great heat, the smells, the scarcity of water and the flies would allow.

This was not long delayed, and by 8.30 a.m. (July 17th) the 4th found themselves in front-line trenches, having relieved the Dublin Fusiliers of the Twenty-Ninth Division in the trenches known as H. 12, H. 12a and H. 12b. These formed " a large square sandbagged salient," nowhere more than 120 yards from the Turks, while on the right at the Southern Barricade only 15 yards separated the two sides. Stout sandbag blocks had been erected and for the moment neither party was attempting more than harassing the other by bombing. The Dublins had recently made a gallant but ineffectual effort to rush the Turkish barricade, and their unburied dead lay thick between the blocks. Besides throwing occasional bombs the Turks kept up an almost incessant rifle fire, which as one account says, " chiefly damaged the upper row of sandbags, made an unholy noise, and apparently did little else " save waste ammunition. Snipers, either concealed in the scrub or firing from behind blinded loopholes, were far more effective and troublesome, and within a few minutes the 4th had had several periscopes hit. The battalion replied vigorously to the bombing, managed to pick off some of the obnoxious snipers, and, though it did not escape without some casualties, came quite successfully through its " baptism of fire," though the Turks seemed much better supplied with gun ammunition and with bombs and hand-grenades. The battalion was three days in the trenches on this first tour, followed by a rest on Gully Beach, where the men greatly appreciated the sea bathing, and soon became accustomed to the sensation of being shelled while in the water. Then, on July 21st, it reoccupied its former front-line trenches. It found the enemy again very active round the Southern Barricade and decidedly " nervy," apparently expecting an attack. The heat and the flies were very trying, making rest almost impossible by day, while by night working parties were needed to repair and improve the trenches, so that few of the 4th got more than the scantiest measure of sleep. Food was a difficulty: the heat converted " bully beef " into a liquid and glutinous mass few dared to tackle, and most people lived on dry biscuit with a little jam when the flies would let them eat it.

The chief incident of its second four-day tour was a vigorous attack on the 39th Brigade West of Gully Ravine, which gave its left company, B, something to fire at. This it did so effectually that the Turkish flanking party was checked and driven back. Later in the day (July 23rd) a field battery shelled the Turks near the Southern Barricade with good effect. The garrison of the front trench opposite had been withdrawn before the bombardment started, and had the sensation of hearing the shells skim just over their heads. Next day the Turks proved to be unusually quiet, their sniping was much reduced in volume and the battalion's snipers had things pretty well their own way. On July 25th the battalion moved into Brigade reserve, returning to Mudros on the night of July 30th/31st on the 86th Brigade relieving the 39th. Its fortnight on the Peninsula had given its raw hands valuable experience of the difference between practice and the real thing, they had got some idea of how to look after themselves in the presence of the enemy, and had worked well, despite the great heat and the want both of water and of good food. The time had only cost the 4th four killed, but these unfortunately included Regimental Sergeant Major Halford, mortally wounded by an accidental bomb explosion. He had done notable work in bringing the new battalion up to a high level of efficiency and was a serious loss.[1] The wounded came to nearly 30, including Major Birch, and about as many had been sent to hospital, for if the Turks had been fairly quiet the flies had not. Indeed between them and the all-pervading dust, which like the flies got over and into everything that was eaten or drunk, the health of the troops was seriously affected. Nearly every man suffered from an incipient dysentery, and the newly arrived " K. 1 " Divisions were even more affected by the Gallipoli climate than were the survivors of the original landing, who had had more chance to become acclimatized.

Some time before this the 2nd Battalion had returned to the Peninsula. Its rest had been cut short by an alarm that the Turks were likely to celebrate the festival of Ramazan by attacking in force, and accordingly on July 21st the 86th and 87th Brigades were brought back from the islands, being placed in Corps reserve near Gully Beach. The battalion had benefited considerably by its ten days at Lemnos; a draft of 199 men under Lieutenants Tragett and Mumford had arrived on July 17th, two new officers, Second Lieutenants H. P. Evans and R. A. Patterson, had joined from the Ceylon Planters' Rifle Corps,[2] and the rest and change of scene had made a great difference to all ranks, especially those who had been through everything since April 25th. These were not numerous, though several who had been away sick or wounded had now rejoined,

[1] Company Sergeant Major Cornish of C Company succeeded him as Regimental Sergeant Major.
[2] As against this Major Jones and Second Lieutenant Geldard had been invalided.

among them Second Lieutenant Nevile. While at Lemnos another of the battalion's original officers, Lieutenant Morgan, had been appointed Staff Captain, 87th Brigade, on Captain Petre's promotion to be Brigade Major, 88th Brigade. Colonel Casson too finally left the battalion on his definite appointment to command the 157th Brigade in the Fifty-Second Division. Careful and thorough, assiduous for his men's welfare, he had done well by the 2nd Battalion, which was sorry to lose him. Lieutenant Colonel Ward of the Denbigh Yeomanry now took command, but on July 26th Major Going returned and relieved him.

For nearly ten days after returning to the Peninsula the 2nd was in reserve, first on Gully Beach and then at "Y" Ravine, where water was inconveniently scarce. These were days of hard work, mainly road-making, or rather mule-track making. On July 30th, however, it moved up into the firing line, taking over the same position it had last held. The line East of the ravine had been straightened out in the meantime, but plenty of work was wanted; the firing platforms needed improvement and the parapets rebuilding. It was generally understood that some big movement was impending, probably a new landing, and the Division had orders to prepare an attack on the trenches immediately East of the ravine, but for the moment things were unusually quiet. The day after the battalion returned to the line the R.E. successfully exploded three mines under the Turkish trench opposite C Company's firing line, here only 30 yards away. This demolished about twenty yards of trench, including a sniper's post, but apart from this the next few days passed uneventfully, though the ascendency in sniping which the last occupants of the line had lost was soon recovered, while on August 3rd a draft arrived of 100 men under Captain H. A. Davies and Lieutenant McShane (N.F.), with Second Lieutenants Gibbs and Creany.

While the Regiment's senior Service battalion was getting introduced to active service conditions the 1/1st Brecknockshire were having a taste of fighting in a climate which surpassed even Gallipoli as a trial of physical fitness and endurance. That battalion, as already mentioned, had proceeded to Aden in October, 1914, arriving there on November 25th after being nearly seven weeks on the way. The British battalion from whom the Brecknocks took over was the 1st Lancashire Fusiliers, who were posted to the Twenty-Ninth Division on reaching England and shared with the 2nd S.W.B. in the landing at Cape Helles. Even before the Brecknocks landed there had been some encounters with the Turkish forces in the Yemen. This district borders on the Aden

Protectorate and was held in some strength by the Turks, whose presence there was full of menace to the British position at Aden and in the Protectorate, and necessitated the maintenance of a substantial garrison at Aden, consisting besides the Brecknocks of two battalions and a half of Indian infantry with other arms. With the British forces already committed to operations in East and West Africa and in Mesopotamia, in addition to the main struggle in France and the need for securing Egypt against Turkish attack, the idea of an offensive in the Yemen could not be entertained, though the enforced adoption by the garrison of a defensive attitude left the Protectorate open to the incursions of the Turks and was not calculated to inspire much confidence in or respect for the British among the " friendly " Arabs of the Protectorate. By the time the Brecknocks landed, however, a sharp blow had been already inflicted on the Turks at Sheikh Saad by the 29th Indian Brigade on its way to Egypt, and this had for the time discouraged their offensive propensities, so for the first few months of the battalion's stay at Aden the situation was quiet enough.

Aden, however, was no bed of roses for a Territorial battalion of whose officers and men hardly any had any previous experience of the Tropics: for the great majority of the rank and file indeed it was their first experience abroad or even away from the familiar surroundings of their own county, and perhaps had the battalion contained a larger proportion of men already acquainted with life in hot climates and able to advise their comrades what to do and what to avoid the Brecknocks might have fared better. As it was they owed much to the experience of their Quartermaster, Lieutenant Elvidge, one of the very few officers who had served abroad. Certainly they found the climate trying, and the sick-rate, not unnaturally, was high. Four men died in the first half of 1915 and several more had to be invalided home. The duties to be performed were quite heavy enough and the station offered no great facilities either for training or recreation. Some of the officers were sent off to India for various courses of instruction, others were taken for garrison jobs, like censoring, but for the battalion the chief event of the spring was the adoption on April 15th of the four company organization, Major Carless (No. 3) and Captains Woodliffe (No. 4), J. I. P. Thomas (No. 1) and Cockcroft (No. 2) being the company commanders under the new system.[1]

---

[1] The Warrant Officers were: No. 1, Company Sergeant Major Robinson and Company Quartermaster Sergeant Prosser. No. 2, Company Sergeant Major Magness and Company Quartermaster Sergeant Linnell. No. 3, Company Sergeant Major Evans and Company Quartermaster Sergeant Edwards. No. 4, Company Sergeant Major Best and Company Quartermaster Sergeant Ingram.

Meanwhile the inactivity of the British garrison was apparently encouraging the Turks to adopt a more aggressive attitude, and their pressure on the friendly Arabs of the Protectorate began to stiffen. They had reoccupied their fortifications opposite Sheikh Saad, and in June they not only shelled Perim at long range but actually attempted to land on the island. They were beaten off with loss by the 23rd Sikh Pioneers, who were holding the island, but the fact that they were taking the offensive without provoking counter-measures was having a discouraging effect in the Protectorate, and somewhat reluctantly the General commanding had to dispatch the Aden Troop, who formed the only cavalry of the garrison, to Lahej to assist the local Sultan and to order the Aden Movable Column to be in readiness to follow.

The Movable Column, which had been organized earlier in the year, consisted of only about 1000 rifles, to which the Brecknocks contributed the largest share, about 400 men, the rest of the battalion being retained at Aden, mainly on outpost and guard duties. For naval reasons several Red Sea islands had recently been occupied and half the 109th Infantry were detached to garrison them, the 23rd Pioneers were at Perim, and the half battalion of the 126th Baluchis, the other unit in garrison, had recently found a large draft for France. For artillery the force possessed two batteries, one of 15 pounders and one of 10 pounders, carried by camels and manned by the R.G.A., while the Aden Troop provided the column with its few mounted men. For transport it depended on a hastily organized camel convoy with undisciplined Arab drivers of uncertain loyalty. It was therefore not exactly well fitted for the task in hand, especially under the very unfavourable conditions prevailing, for at the moment (July 3rd) the Movable Column was ordered out to Lahej the weather happened to be peculiarly hot even for Aden in July.

The first stage of the move, which started on the afternoon of July 3rd, was an advance to Sheikh Othman, six miles away, on the border between the British territory and the Protectorate, the point from which the aqueduct with the Aden water supply starts. It was not a long march and was undertaken after the heat of the day was over, but even so it proved trying enough, and on arriving at Sheikh Othman about 7.30 p.m. quite a number of men collapsed[1] and were incapable of going on again when, about 3 a.m. next day, the column resumed its march. Wisdom after the event would suggest that in view of the terrific heat and the exhaustion of the men it would have been prudent to wait till evening before starting on the longer and more

---

[1] Two actually died, both, as it happens, particularly strong and athletic fellows.

difficult portion of the march. From Sheikh Othman to Lahej was nearly nineteen miles, over three times as much as the troops had already covered with some difficulty. However, it was considered essential to press on, and leaving the more exhausted men behind the column started off again. A start in the dark is never an easy thing and with hastily impressed transport and men already tired, while few had had any food, this move was no exception. As the day grew hotter the strain on the men became more acute. The going was very bad, the " road " would have been flattered by being described as a " track," the men had soon consumed the contents of their water-bottles and suffered agonies from thirst, while the camels

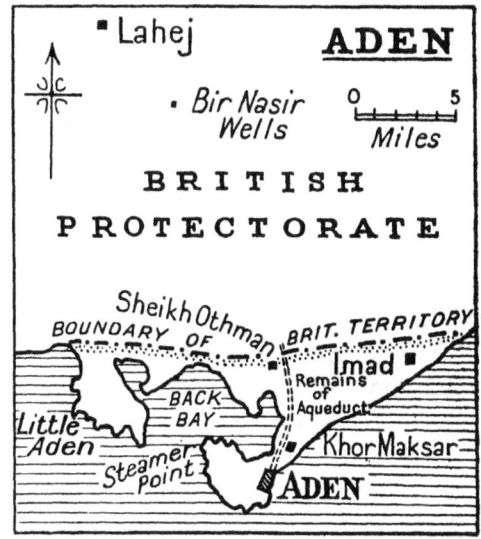

straggled, the wheeled vehicles stuck in the sand and formations were hard to keep. Before long heat stroke began to claim its victims. Man after man went down, and about midday the main body came to a halt some distance from Lahej, the bulk of the men being too done up to struggle any further. But firing suddenly broke out from the direction of Lahej, to which the advanced-guard, half the 109th Infantry and the four 10 pounder guns, had pushed on much earlier, getting in before daybreak. On this an effort was made by the main body to resume the march, and in the end it straggled into Lahej, the great majority of the men arriving completely exhausted and incapable of any effort whatever. It had been a terrible experience : seasoned and acclimatized troops would have found the unusual heat bad enough—there were many Indians among those who collapsed—but the Brecknocks had had little chance of preparing for an effort such as that which had been required of them; they had done hardly any route-marching at Aden and it was hardly wonderful that so many of them proved unequal to the exceptionally severe test to which they had been subjected. Luckily there was plenty of water at Lahej and Lord Glanusk managed to improvise satisfactory arrangements for issuing it, while Dr. Townley, R.A.M.C., did splendid work in attending to the exhausted men. Practically everyone was in need of his help, many men collapsed completely when they staggered into camp, and few could stir a finger till they had been rested and copiously watered.

Actually the firing which had been heard had been little more than a skirmish between the Aden Troop and some inquisitive Arabs who were hovering round the outposts. Just as it became dark, however, Arabs began advancing in considerable force, and before long developed quite a serious attack, being supported by Turkish Regulars and backed up by several guns. The British troops had established themselves in a large walled garden which was quite vigorously shelled, while the attacking infantry pressed in quite close to the walls. Counter-attacks were delivered with some success by the 109th and the Baluchis, while such of the Brecknocks as were capable of any effort, barely 100 all told, whom Lord Glanusk had collected, manned the walls on the left, and by steady rifle fire assisted to keep the Turks at bay. The fighting was quite sharp, the Turkish artillery plastered the position with shrapnel and in places their rushes came to very close quarters, several men being shot down within five or six yards of the gate of the Brecknocks' garden, but they were unable to make any impression on the defence, and towards morning they abandoned their efforts and drew off. As far as affairs at Lahej went the situation was fairly satisfactory: there was plenty of water available and the defence had definitely got the better of the attackers. Unluckily news came in which completely altered the complexion of affairs. The camel convoy had been approaching Lahej when the evening fighting started: on hearing the firing the Arab drivers[1] had taken to their heels, most of them cutting the cords which bound the loads on to the camels and letting the animals go loose. The camels carrying the 15 pounder battery had also bolted, and the net result was that all the food, the water, the medical stores, the reserve ammunition and the battalion's machine guns had been lost and that the 15 pounders were stuck in deep sand, four miles from Lahej. Their loss might have been survived, but not that of

[1] It came out afterwards that most of the camel-drivers were men from the interior of Arabia or from Somaliland who had been so heavily blackmailed by the Sultan of Lahej as they passed through on their way to Aden that they were anxious to take a chance of revenging themselves.

the reserve ammunition, for expenditure of ammunition during the night fighting had been considerable, and without a fresh supply the position at Lahej was quite untenable. Evacuation was the only alternative, and about 5 a.m. on July 5th the painful process of retirement began.

Fortunately the reception which the Turkish night attack had encountered had evidently been distinctly discouraging: they made no effort to molest the retiring troops, who were for the most part in no condition to have resisted a serious attack. The march was a repetition of the previous day's ordeal, almost an aggravation. It was as hot as ever, and the men started tired, short of food and sleep. As they struggled along through the deep sand they passed several dead bodies, victims of the march out. However, by this time the administrative staff at Aden had managed to collect some more camels and send them out with water, while a few motors capable of travelling over the desert were also sent out with more water and with ice. To these many men owed their lives, the motors after distributing their water serving as ambulances. On reaching the wells at Bir Nasir the retiring troops halted for a time. Here the bulk of the men who had fallen out during the previous day's march had been collected during the night and to some extent reorganized, water being issued to them and a camp marked out. In the evening the retreat was resumed, and by 9 a.m. on July 6th the column had regained Sheikh Othman. Though there had been no pursuit it was decided, in view of the loss of the transport camels and their loads and the exhausted state of the men, that Sheikh Othman also must be evacuated, even though this involved letting the Aden water supply pass into Turkish hands. Accordingly the troops came right back to the Khor Maksar lines at the isthmus connecting the promontory on which Aden stands with the mainland. Here under the protection of British warships, whose guns flanked the isthmus on either hand, a final halt was made and stock could be taken of the situation and of the condition of the troops.

Casualties had actually not been very high, under 100 in all, but they included nearly 30 deaths from heat-stroke, over half of them in the Brecknocks. Four of the battalion were missing, one of whom reappeared after the Armistice as a prisoner in Turkish hands, and three others had been wounded, but these figures hardly represented the state of the battalion. Hardly any of those who had taken part in the march were fit for more than the lightest duty, and two officers, Captains J. I. P. Thomas and Musgrove, and over 30 men had to be promptly invalided home, while steps were taken to relieve the battalion by a fresh unit from India. On the arrival of this unit, the 5th Buffs, the

Brecknocks embarked on the transport *Varsova* and sailed for India on August 5th. Some time before this the situation at Aden had been improved by the arrival of other reinforcements, including one brigade and two batteries from Egypt, and on July 21st these troops had pushed out and recovered Sheikh Othman, dislodging and defeating the Turks and finding the aqueduct and the water supply intact.

Reaching Bombay on August 11th the battalion was dispatched to Mhow, an important military centre in Central India, which it reached on August 14th, much refreshed by the sea voyage. It was destined to see a good deal of Mhow, as it was not till August, 1919, that it quitted that station for Calcutta. The Lahej episode was thus to prove its only experience of active service as a battalion, though many of its officers and men were to see plenty of fighting, for the battalion found several drafts for units in Mesopotamia, notably for the 4th S.W.B., besides which a large number of N.C.O.'s and men received commissions in the Indian Army Reserve of Officers. Its one action had been an unfortunate episode: with better management and rather more foresight on the part of those in charge the battalion might have been spared a test which would have taxed the capacities of any troops, and was certainly made far more strenuous than was necessary.

CHAPTER IX

FROM MAY 9TH TO LOOS

THE First Army might well have fared better against the German lines in front of the Aubers Ridge could it have attacked them some weeks sooner. Actually the artillery and ammunition available, though proportionately to the frontage attacked as strong as at Neuve Chapelle, failed to produce results approaching those achieved by the bombardment of March 10th. In the interval the Germans had completely reconstructed their defences. What they had accomplished in strengthening and thickening the sandbag breastworks of which their line here consisted was really prodigious. At the base of these breastworks they had constructed well-concealed dug-outs from which machine guns could sweep No Man's Land with a deadly grazing fire, while themselves practically immune against anything but a direct hit from a high explosive shell. Hard as the British patrols and observing officers had tried to obtain information about the German defences, the revolution effected in them had not been realized by anyone, and the troops had no idea that instead of the light field works of March 10th they were now faced by fortifications of a semi-permanent character, only to be demolished by really heavy guns amply provided with high explosive shell, that 18 pounders and shrapnel were useless against these works and that 200 yards behind the front trenches ran a scarcely weaker support line.

The British plan for the new effort which had been fixed for May 9th involved a main attack by the First and Meerut Divisions on a 2000 yards frontage from Chocolat Menier Corner (N.E. of Festubert) to the Port Arthur cross-roads (South of Neuve Chapelle), coupled with an attack by the Eighth Division astride the Sailly–Fromelles road three miles N.E. of Neuve Chapelle. The Second and Lahore Divisions would support the main attack which was to push East to the line Rue du Marais–Lorgies–La Cliqueterie Farm, where it was hoped to meet the Eighth Division advancing Southward, and that the joint advance would cut off the Germans holding the unattacked front line from Port Arthur to Rouge Bancs. The First Division was using the 2nd and 3rd Brigades, the latter being on the left and next the Meerut Division. In the 3rd Brigade the Munsters (right) and Welch (left) were the attacking battalions, the S.W.B. and the Gloucestershire thus being in support and occupying the third and fourth rows of breastworks that had been constructed behind the Rue du Bois as assembly positions. Their construction, though essential to provide shelter for the reserves within a short distance of the front, can hardly have escaped the notice of the

Germans and prevented their being caught unawares again, as they had been at Neuve Chapelle. At any rate when, at 5.40 a.m., the assaulting battalions went over the top, after an all too short and sadly ineffective 40 minutes' bombardment, the German rifles, machine guns and artillery were ready to receive them. So deadly was the fire which met the advancing infantry that only very few reached the German wire to find it most inadequately cut, while the bombardment had left the parapets but little damaged. About 100 Munsters and a handful of Northamptonshires (2nd Brigade) forced their way through the wire into the trenches, only to be overwhelmed. Most of the attackers were either shot down or forced to halt and seek what poor cover No Man's Land provided. A fresh bombardment from 6.15 a.m. to 7 a.m. was followed by an equally unsuccessful attempt by the support companies of the attacking battalions which merely swelled the casualty lists. Meanwhile the S.W.B. had moved forward into the vacated front breastworks, being heavily shelled in doing so and having many casualties, among them Second Lieutenants Pollock and French, both of whom were killed.

Arrived at the front breastworks the battalion found itself in for a long wait under a steady artillery fire, for the German guns, lifting off No Man's Land where the survivors of the assault were now lying out pinned to the ground by the machine guns, turned on to the British trenches and did their best to impede the preparations to renew the attack. On a fresh effort the authorities in rear had decided, despite the disastrous experience of the first attacks. The reports which had gone back had not adequately emphasized the completeness of the failure, and it was hoped that another bombardment might be more effective against the wire and machine guns. Accordingly orders were issued for the S.W.B. and the Gloucestershire here to relieve the remnants of the Munsters and Welch, while two battalions of the 1st Brigade from reserve replaced the 2nd Brigade. Similar reliefs were ordered in the Meerut Division, which had fared fully as badly as the First. Carried out in broad daylight these movements could not escape the watchful Germans and drew down heavy shelling on breastworks and communication trenches. This and the congestion in the trenches delayed the reliefs, and the fresh assault had more than once to be postponed, being finally fixed for 4 p.m. Well before this A and B Companies had taken up their position in front line, with C and D in second line and machine-gun detachments on the flanks of companies. Before the hour for the assault A Company worked out by a sap into an advanced trench so as to be nearer the enemy's line. They were heavily fired on, for the

British bombardment seemed to have no effect on the machine guns and even failed to prevent German riflemen manning their parapet, though at last the wire seemed to be fairly well cut and the parapet showed more signs of damage. A got their machine gun into position in this trench and did something to keep down the defenders' fire, but when the assaulting lines sprang to their feet and started to rush across No Man's Land they met a fire as fierce and deadly as had greeted their predecessors ten hours

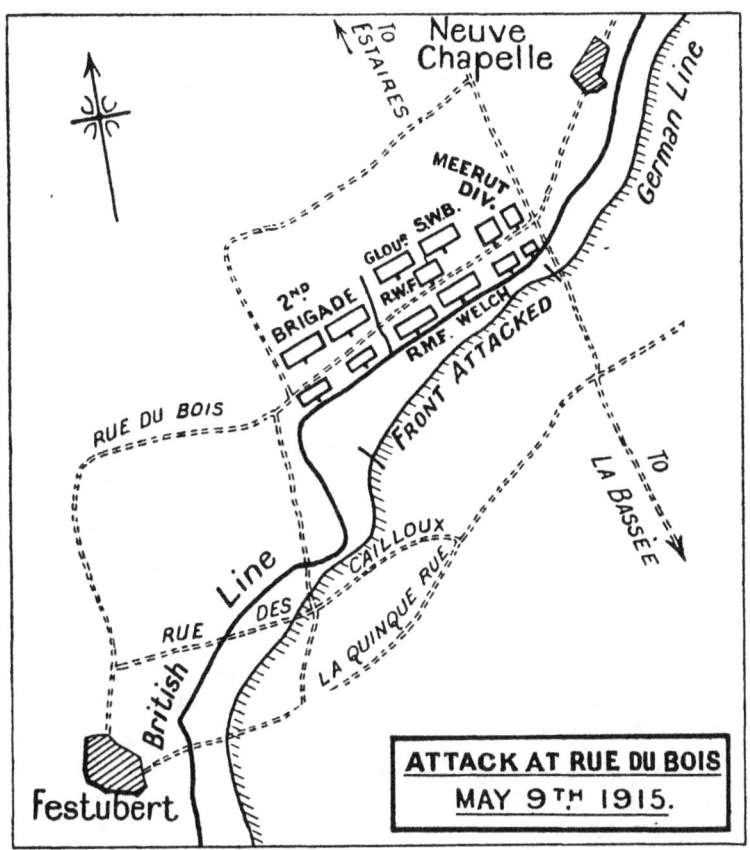

earlier. Well led by their officers, A and B pushed on, men falling at every step. Lord de Freyne was killed, Captain Conway Lloyd was badly wounded, and before half the distance between the lines had been covered nearly all the officers and over half the men who had crossed the parapet had been hit, while the remainder only escaped by taking what cover they could find.[1]

[1] About 50 Black Watch actually entered the German trenches in the 4 p.m. assault, but they were too few to effect anything and were soon overwhelmed or ejected.

Even now the Divisional commander wanted to try yet another ten minutes' bombardment and then to put in the rest of the battalions who had replaced the original attackers. However, the two brigadiers, Generals Thesiger and Davies, realizing how little this last bombardment had done, reported that it would be useless to renew the attack, and accordingly the guns opened fire again to allow the survivors of the assaulting battalions to withdraw to the British lines. Many got back, others had to remain out till darkness afforded cover for their return. Some gallant work was now done in rescuing wounded; Private Doyle, for example, had stood for an hour in a flooded ditch holding up a wounded man, who must otherwise have been drowned, and now succeeded in bringing him safely in, while Second Lieutenant Masters was wounded while assisting a badly hit man. Eventually about midnight the battalion received orders to withdraw and marched back to Hingette, the weaker by 10 officers[1] and 224 men. Yet it had fared relatively well, only one of the ten battalions of the First Division actually engaged in the attack had fewer casualties. Nor were the day's disasters confined to that Division: the Meerut Division also had incurred crippling casualties without achieving anything, while further North the Eighth Division had been unable to follow up its initial success in effecting quite substantial lodgments in the German lines. In face of the machine guns no reinforcements could cross No Man's Land, and eventually the survivors of the successful detachments had had to regain the British lines. But the French had made some progress North of Arras, and to assist them Sir John French decided to renew the offensive, using the Second Division to attack from the Rue du Bois and bringing the Seventh Division down South to attack from Festubert. He also agreed to take over from the French the sector South of the Bethune–La Bassée road next to the British right.

To do this the First Division after a very brief rest moved South of the canal and on May 14th relieved the French 58me Division in the new sector. Here the battalion found itself holding 700 yards of front with its left on the La Bassée road. The ground rose slightly here, sloping up from the swampy ground near the canal, and mining was therefore possible. Indeed there was a large mine crater just in front of the line which was promptly occupied and prepared for defence. Things were fairly lively, the German trench-mortars proving very troublesome, but casualties were light. After a week the battalion shifted to the left into the Cuinchy sector and spent a week

---

[1] Captain Lord de Freyne, Lieutenants Turner and Woodward, Second Lieutenants Garnett-Botfield, French, Jackson, Langlands and Pollock killed, Captain J. C. Lloyd and Second Lieutenant Masters wounded.

there, much worried by bombing and frequently shelled, but being again fortunate as regards casualties. It had another spell here early in June, from the 4th to the 10th, being now astride the La Bassée road. The British guns were distressingly short of shells just now; it was mainly on account of the exhaustion of his ammunition reserves that Sir John French had had to break off his offensive, and the battalion had to make the best of being heavily shelled night after night without any adequate reply from our guns. This turn of trench duty cost it nearly 30 casualties, but was followed by three weeks' respite, the battalion shifting from Bethune (June 10th to 16th), to Beuvry (June 16th to 24th), Auchel (June 24th to 28th), and at Labourse near Beuvry (June 28th to July 2nd). While at Beuvry large working parties were needed in the front line to construct dug-outs and carry up ammunition, but these escaped without casualties. Still only two drafts had arrived since May 9th—118 men on May 12th and 50 on May 28th—and the battalion was much below establishment, though several new officers had appeared.[1]

On returning to the line on July 2nd the battalion found itself in a new sector, that East of Vermelles which the B.E.F. had just taken over from the French. A new front trench had to be dug 70 yards out into No Man's Land, here much wider than North of the canal. This was done by the two companies in reserve, those in front providing covering parties, and was so quietly carried out that the Germans never detected what was going on. From July 9th to 19th the battalion was "out," during which time it was inspected by Lord Kitchener, and then had a week in the Cambrin sector (July 19th to 25th). Things here were lively, culminating in, on July 24th, a heavy bombardment, which battered in 30 yards of D Company's trenches and seemed to prelude an attack, though none developed.

August, like July, proved fairly "quiet." "New Army" Divisions were coming out now in a steady stream, another Battalion of the TWENTY-FOURTH was in France, though the 1st did not have the interest of introducing it to trench warfare, and the B.E.F., which had already formed a Third Army to relieve the French on a twelve-mile front beyond Arras, was also extending its line Southward past Vermelles till its right ultimately reached Grenay, six miles South of the La Bassée Canal. The 1st S.W.B., who held the Cambrin sector when in the trenches in August, spent most of September at Philosophe and Le Rutoire behind the most recently acquired sector, not

[1] Major Southey and Lieutenant Cahusac (May 12th), Second Lieutenants Holden and Edwards (both R.W.F.) and Vick (Hampshire) in May; Ackerley, Hayes, Hewitt and Saunders in June.

actually in the trenches, but finding large working parties to help with the preparations for a new offensive.

August had brought one important change; Colonel Reddie's appointment on August 10th to command the 1st Brigade.[1] He was succeeded by Major Gwynn, second in command since Major Lawrence's departure in June for a Staff appointment, while Captain Ramsden, who had rejoined in July, became second in command. Casualties on the whole were few, which was the more fortunate because drafts were anything but plentiful, only one of 30 being recorded between the end of May and the end of September.[2] On August 22nd, however, both Captain Salmon and Lieutenant Hewitt were wounded, during some bombing of B and D Companies in the Cambrin sector, and on the 29th Captain Banner was killed, while in September Second Lieutenant L. Williams was also killed while supervising a working party.

Meanwhile the first Service battalion of the Regiment to reach France had already had its first experience of "the real thing." The "K. 2" Divisions had found their way to France during July, and the 5th S.W.B. had landed at Havre on July 16th and proceeded to an area N.W. of Bethune, Tilques providing it with its first French billets.

Since leaving Burnham for Bulford the 5th had got through a prodigious quantity of work, and had made better progress with some important branches of its training, such as musketry, than had been possible earlier on. Service rifles for everyone, so that each man could become familiar with the weapon he was to take overseas, produced a vast improvement in the battalion's shooting, and the arrival of full equipment for signallers and machine gunners gave those " specialists " a chance to get properly trained. Sling Camp, in which the battalion was at first quartered, was only partly finished, and the 5th were kept busy constructing roads and paths and generally making the camp habitable. Horses and wagons now appeared for the transport detachment, while riding classes for the subalterns, most of whom were complete novices, afforded no small amusement to themselves and others.

[1] On the formation of the Guards Division the two Guards battalions in the 1st Brigade were transferred to it with their brigadier, Brigadier General Heyworth, and replaced by two "New Army" battalions, the 10th Gloucestershire and 8th Royal Berkshire.

[2] Officers joining in this period were Second Lieutenants B. J. Davies and Simmonds, T. F. Rawle (July), Wales and Gotelee (August), Vanderpump, Daniels, Potts, A. E. Morgan and H. S. F. Morris (September). Major Southey and Second Lieutenant Masters were invalided home in May, Captain Cahusac went to hospital in August and Lieutenant Edwards left to join the R.W.F.

A move in April to Perham Down was followed by a respite from road-making which allowed the battalion to concentrate on training. The Nineteenth Division had now reached the stage of field-days, and as the weather was fine these were frequent. A musketry course was now fired with quite satisfactory results considering how hampered the battalion had been in its efforts to acquire proficiency with the rifle. Trench-mortar work and bombing also were assiduously practised, and in this line the 5th served both as workshop and as instructors. Early in July the Division was inspected by the King, when its splendid appearance reflected no small credit both on those responsible for its training and on the keenness and energy with which all ranks had thrown themselves into making themselves efficient soldiers. This inspection was naturally hailed as the immediate prelude to departure overseas,[1] and on July 13th the 5th entrained at Ludgershall for Southampton, though bad weather postponed its departure from that port till the evening of the 15th.

The 5th did not stay long at Tilques, moving first to St. Venant and then to Le Sart. Here it spent most of August, two companies at a time being sent up for ten days' instruction in the trenches to the Indian Corps, to which the Nineteenth Division had been allotted. Companies not in the line spent their time partly in continuing their training, partly in making hurdles in the Forest of Nieppe, while later on two parties of 25 bombers under Second Lieutenants I. T. Evans and E. C. H. Jones were attached to the Sirhind and Jullundur Brigades.

The Indian Corps was now holding the Neuve Chapelle and Festubert sectors, with which the 5th was to become very familiar. Though these lay outside the frontage of the main battle subsidiary attacks were to be made both at Festubert and at Fauquissart, N.E. of Neuve Chapelle, partly as diversions, partly in the hope of profiting by the openings which a big success might produce North of the Canal also. The 5th therefore found ample occupation in preparing for these local attacks, digging assembly and communication trenches, and sapping out from our trenches so as to furnish outlets under our wire into No Man's Land. At the end of August the Nineteenth Division took over the Festubert sector and the battalion established its Headquarters at Gorre Château, with three companies in billets

[1] The officers who proceeded overseas with the 5th Battalion were: Colonel C. V. Trower (C.O.), Majors S. F. Cooke (Second in Command) and C. V. R. Wright. Captains G. S. Crawford, O. H. M. Newmarche, H. F. Thomas, W. Parkes, C. J. P. Copner, C. M. D. Curtis, T. E. Lewis and R. G. Lochner (Adjutant). Lieutenants D. W. Croft, E. B Trower, E C. H. Jones, B. O. Jones, L. E. L. Hall, L. Rose. Lieutenant and Quartermaster T. W. Bryant. Second Lieutenants H. W. A. Littleton-Geach (Transport Officer), I. T. Evans, W. H. Day, R. F. W. Rebsch, T. Maughfling, C. B. Lochner, E. Simons, G. A. Livesay.

at Le Touret. Gorre Château had already come in for severe treatment from the German " heavies," its roof had been badly damaged, hardly a pane of glass remained, but it was quite habitable and before long Battalion Headquarters became quite attached to it.

Shortly before moving to Gorre the 5th had had the misfortune to lose Captain T. E. Lewis in a bombing accident, in which Private Dart also was killed and Lieutenant B. O. Jones wounded. Captain Lewis' death was much regretted. The first subaltern Gazetted to the battalion, he had shown himself a keen and efficient soldier and an admirable bombing instructor; it was hard to lose so promising an officer by an accident behind the lines. Apart from his death casualties were few. Though companies were up in the front line every night only one man was killed and five wounded in the first three weeks of September. Apart from the preparations for the attack the work consisted mainly of keeping the line in repair; revetting, sandbagging and generally making good the damages caused by the occasional German bombardments. The weather being mostly fine, water was not the serious problem it had been when the 1st Battalion had originally made the acquaintance of Festubert or that it was to be again later, but even without water troubles the 5th were busy enough.

The new offensive was to be on a much larger scale than any of the previous ventures of the year. No less than nine British Divisions, among them the First, were allotted to the main attack between the La Bassée Canal and the mining village of Loos, which the British right now faced. In the subsidiary operations portions of another six were to be employed. The Nineteenth Division, for example, was using the 58th Brigade, to which the 5th S.W.B. had originally belonged, though in case of a German retreat North of the Canal another brigade could easily have been made available.

Although by September the British munition factories had substantially increased their output and the B.E.F. had nearly twice as many heavy guns as had supported the attacks of May, even so both guns and ammunition fell far short of what had been already realized to be necessary. Indeed relatively to the frontage to be attacked less artillery was available than at either Neuve Chapelle or Festubert. It was hoped to more than compensate for this by using gas, but the effective employment of this " accessory " depended on a favourable wind and thus introduced yet another element of uncertainty into the already difficult situation. The rapid expansion of the British forces necessarily entailed the employment in important Staff appointments of officers with no previous Staff training or experience; while by this time it was not only the "New Army" Divisions who were lacking in experience of mobile warfare as opposed to trench warfare, and were mainly composed of recruits whose training had perforce been hasty and imperfect. The Aisne and First Ypres had left but few of the fully trained officers and men of the original B.E.F. to hand on their knowledge and example to the reinforcements who had replenished the depleted battalions. The trench warfare of the first winter had been costly, the abortive offensives of the spring and the long drawn out struggle of "Second Ypres" had further diminished the experienced and really trained, and though by September, 1915, many battalions had in their ranks men who had served for some months in the trenches and had little to learn about trench warfare, these had no experience of anything else and had had little opportunity of learning much about open warfare. The successive extensions of the British frontage[1] had prevented the new Divisions from being used to relieve the older ones, who might then have enjoyed a real rest and adequate opportunities for training. Many of the surviving Regular officers had had to be taken from their battalions for the Staff, and even the "Old Army" Divisions were in certain senses inexperienced and only partially trained. It is easy to be wise after the event and to see now that in the peculiar circumstances it was premature to ask the B.E.F. to participate in a big offensive in the autumn of 1915, and that in consequence good material was wastefully expended. Had Sir John French been free to consider merely the needs and situation of the B.E.F. he would certainly not have attacked, but the B.E.F.'s special interests had to be subordinated to those of the Allies as a whole, and it was by the French, still decidedly the dominant military partner, that the decision to attack in force was taken. All that the B.E.F. could do was to co-operate as best it could, and even on the minor but still most important matter of selecting the locality for the British effort Sir John French and Sir Douglas Haig had to waive their objections to attacking between the La Bassée Canal and the Artois plateau. Regimental officers and men could not be aware of all that was going on at G.H.Q., or grasp the reasons why certain things had to be done. Had they known more they might have had more misgivings about the prospects of success. As it was, they were distinctly encouraged by carrying up to their allotted places in the trenches the cylinders of gas which the War Diaries for September, 1915 describe by so many circumlocutory expressions. To pay the Germans back in their own coin was something all could understand and approve, and

[1] The new Third Army had drawn off six Divisions to the Somme.

the employment of gas seemed to promise "better luck this time."

The First Division had been since June in Sir Henry Rawlinson's Fourth Corps. This was to attack the Southern half of the British objective from the Grenay–Lens railway to the Vermelles–Hulluch road. It had three Divisions in line from right to left, the Forty-Seventh (London Territorials), the Fifteenth (Scottish), a "K. 2" Division, and the First, the latter having the Seventh Division of the First Corps on its left beyond the Vermelles–Hulluch road. The German line opposite the First Division followed the Eastern slope of

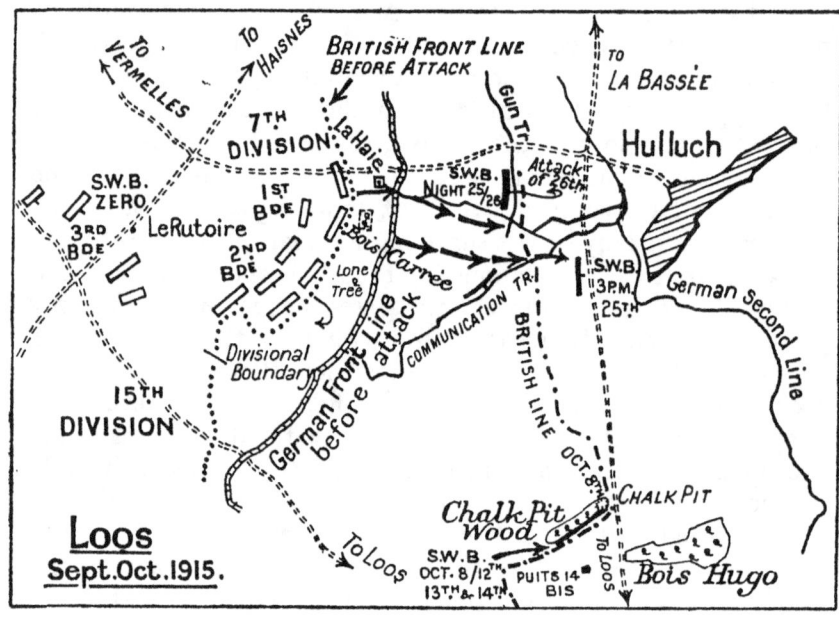

the ridge known as the Grenay spur, being concealed for the most part by the intervening crestline from the British front line along the Western slope. The 1st and 2nd Brigades were attacking on the left and right respectively, the 3rd being in reserve, between Le Rutoire and Vermelles. About 1500 yards behind the German front line the Lens–La Bassée road ran due North and South, with the second system of defence just beyond it and behind that the large village of Hulluch, South of which the German defences formed a large re-entrant reaching to the mining village of Cité St. Auguste, two miles away. It was hoped that the leading brigades of the First Division might secure Hulluch and the trenches South of it, in which case the 3rd Brigade was to push on through them towards the Haute Deule Canal.

Actually things went none too well with the first attack. With the German trenches just over the crest of the ridge, artillery observation had been particularly difficult in this quarter. The wire had been only indifferently cut, opposite the 2nd Brigade it was practically undamaged, and the front line trench with its defenders had escaped fairly lightly. However, the leading battalions of the 1st Brigade, the 10th Gloucestershire and 8th Royal Berkshire, carried the front line, though not without heavy losses, and pushed on towards Hulluch, supported by the Camerons, whom General Reddie promptly put in. Less than two hours after " zero " a line had been established on the Lens–La Bassée road just West of Hulluch. But the 1st Brigade could go no further, losses had been heavy, and the right was completely " in the air," for the 2nd Brigade had been brought to a standstill by the German wire near " Lone Tree."

The check to the 2nd Brigade was to have far-reaching, indeed almost decisive, results. Advantage was not taken of the fact that the 1st Brigade had cleared the German trenches for 600 yards to the North of the untaken portion to use the 2nd Brigade's supports to outflank their opponents: the unsuccessful frontal attack was renewed and, as on May 9th but with less excuse, merely expended itself in gallant efforts to achieve the impossible. The Black Watch, instead of reinforcing the troops already along the Lens–La Bassée road, had to be utilized to prevent the 2nd Brigade's opponents working Northward and reoccupying the trenches stormed by the 1st. Two reserve battalions of the attacking brigades, the London Scottish and the 9th King's, were actually used up in another unsuccessful frontal attack on the little damaged Lone Tree trenches, and not till the Munsters and Welch had also been thrown in against them did the defenders of the Lone Tree trenches eventually surrender about 3 p.m. They had not only inflicted very heavy casualties on their assailants but their resistance had completely disorganized the whole attack of the First Division.

The 1st S.W.B. meanwhile had moved forward from Philosophe towards Le Rutoire as early as 3 a.m. leaving A Company behind as a working party, but, being held up by the check to the 2nd Brigade, remained halted at Le Rutoire for several hours. When, about 11 a.m., the Welch moved forward to cross the German trenches North of La Haie copse the battalion received orders to follow. This was done, though movement over ground intersected with trenches, many of them congested with traffic, was necessarily slow. After crossing No Man's Land the battalion halted for some time in the support trench East of La Haie, but eventually advanced and got touch with the Welch who had prolonged the 1st Brigade's line Southward along the Lens–La Bassée road. By this time German reinforcements had reached Hulluch, had cleared out the handful of the 1st Brigade who had penetrated into the village and, though beaten back when they advanced against the troops along the road, were clearly in sufficient force to make it useless to renew the attack without adequate artillery preparation. There was still a wide gap on the right, for the remnants of the 2nd Brigade had pushed off right-handed to Chalk Pit Wood, a mile further South, and never established touch with the detachments opposite Hulluch. Eventually Generals Reddie and Davies decided to withdraw their men a little way to a communication trench which ran S.W. from the road and provided a ready-made defensive position, much better than the troops could have dug in the hard chalk along the road. Here the battalion was placed on the left in an intermediate line known as Gun Trench, having some of the Seventh Division on its left. Just behind it were three German guns captured by the Camerons and Berkshires in their morning advance but not yet removed owing to the heavy shell fire on the roads in rear.

The S.W.B. were not to pass a quiet night. Early on, about 9 p.m., Captain Playford took a patrol out to reconnoitre, but must almost certainly have run into the Germans in force and been killed or captured, as none of the patrol returned. A little later a counter-attack developed but was quickly repulsed by the battalion's machine-gunners, well handled by Captain W. T. Raikes. Notwithstanding this, a much stronger force approached the trenches, calling out "Don't shoot; we are the Welch." Colonel Gwynn and his men were not to be taken in and with admirable coolness reserved their fire until the enemy were quite close to the parapet. Then a sudden burst of rapid fire swept the approaching Germans down, hardly any escaping. However, German bombers continued to be troublesome, trying to work along a sap which ran out from the battalion's trench. Second Lieutenant Ackerley and the battalion bombers were equal to the emergency and, though the officer was wounded, the enemy's repeated efforts were successfully beaten off. Morning thus found the S.W.B. quite happy about their position and legitimately pleased with their night's work, to which the German dead who covered the ground in front were ample testimony; indeed practically every man in the front line acquired a German helmet as a souvenir, while some 15 wounded who were lying out close to the trench gave themselves up as prisoners. Elsewhere, unfortunately, things had not gone equally well during the night. At several

THE ATTACK ON HULLUCH

points counter-attacks had won back important ground, substantial German reinforcements had arrived and as the second line was now strongly held the chances of a British break-through had practically vanished. At First Army Headquarters, however, hopes of a big success were still entertained, largely because exact information had not been forthcoming, and it was decided to employ the two newly arrived divisions of the Eleventh Corps to attack the German second position between Hulluch and Bois Hugo. In this the troops on the flanks, the Fifteenth Division in front of Loos and the First facing Hulluch, were to co-operate.

By this time the units opposite Hulluch had been sorted out and reorganized. Except for the Black Watch the survivors of the 1st Brigade had been withdrawn and the Division was now represented in front line by the Welch, the Black Watch, and the 1st S.W.B., in that order from the right; none of them more than 400 strong. To achieve anything against Hulluch a really effective bombardment was absolutely essential. However, the Divisional artillery does not appear to have received any orders to bombard the position to be attacked; as far as the battalion could see Hulluch was never shelled, while a message postponing the attack from 11 a.m. till noon, which reached the Black Watch and the battalion, though hardly in time to give Colonel Gwynn a chance of explaining his intentions to his company commanders, was never received by the Welch. They therefore attacked along with the Twenty-Fourth Division[1] on the right and, being unsupported on the left, failed to reach Hulluch. However, the Twenty-Fourth Division's attack was gallantly pressed and at noon the S.W.B.[2] and Black Watch clambered out of their trenches as ordered. Between them and Hulluch lay 600 yards of open ground sloping down to the road, so that the German trenches at the bottom of the slope were hardly visible.[3] There was no artillery support and directly the four leading platoons started machine guns from the upper stories of houses in the little damaged Hulluch opened a deadly and accurate fire, inflicting many casualties. Captain Loch was wounded, Lieutenant Saunders killed, and before the leading lines had covered about 50 yards, much less got even half-way to the Lens–La Bassée road, the great majority of the men had fallen. Realizing that to push on further would merely sacrifice more lives quite uselessly, Colonel Gwynn on his own initiative stopped

---

[1] Of the Eleventh Corps.
[2] C. and D Companies were in the firing line, finding their own reserves, B, less one platoon which, like A, was detached to dig, formed the battalion reserve. The total strength of the battalion in action was hardly more than 400 rifles.
[3] The men lying down in the open could not see to fire back owing to the slope being convex.

the supporting platoons and reported his action to the Brigadier who, approving his action, gave the order to stand fast. On this any men who could manage it got back to the trenches and the remainder hung on in No Man's Land till darkness let them do likewise. Of the S.W.B. over 100[1] had fallen, the wounded including, besides those already mentioned, Second Lieutenants Drury, Simmonds, A. E. Morgan, H. S. F. Morris, who died of wounds later on, and Vick.

The First Division's failure against Hulluch was not the only reverse of September 26th. That day of disappointment saw nearly all Hill 70 lost, the line from there Northward to Bois Hugo driven in and the Eleventh Corps' attempt at a break-through completely foiled. Next day (September 27th) the Guards Division recovered a footing on Hill 70 and in Chalk Pit Wood, and in the next few days this last point was linked up with the advanced trenches facing Hulluch, but from September 27th onwards the battle consisted rather of British resistance to German counter-attacks than of any fresh British efforts to advance. On October 8th the Germans put in nearly five divisions in a vigorous effort to regain what they had lost on September 25th but were repulsed with heavy loss. Five days later (October 13th) the struggle virtually ended with another British attack which achieved only local successes quite incommensurate with the force engaged and the losses incurred.

These later stages of the offensive meant for the S.W.B. a long spell of duty in trenches, varied by short rests. During the Guards' attack on September 27th it opened heavy rifle and machine-gun fire to divert the German attention, thereby drawing down upon itself a heavy pounding which fortunately inflicted very few casualties, though Battalion Headquarters found their situation in a shallow communication trench in prolongation of the enemy's line of fire peculiarly unpleasant, several men being hit. "The worst three-quarters of an hour I had in France" one officer called it, and the battalion was really fortunate not to have its headquarters wiped out altogether. That evening the battalion was relieved in front line by the Munsters but only went back to support trenches, well within range of the German guns, and got a heavy dose of shelling on the 28th, though it again escaped with few casualties. Next night it was relieved by the Irish Guards and sent back to Noeux les Mines, just West of Vermelles, where it had six days in billets. On October 5th the Battalion returned to the trenches, as the First Division was relieving the Twelfth between Chalk

[1] The four platoons who went over the top had not amounted to more than about 150 all told, and as practically all the loss was incurred by them they were virtually wiped out.

Pit Wood and Hulluch. It was in support, however, when the Germans made their great counter-attack on October 8th, though it came in for some fairly ineffective shelling. That evening it relieved the Gloucestershire in front line, having its Battalion Headquarters in the Chalk Pit and all four companies in trenches. Colonel Gwynn had had to go to hospital on October 6th, and Major B. W. Collier,[1] who had just arrived with seven other officers,[2] was now in command.

The Chalk Pit Wood trenches wanted no little work to make them defensible or habitable, as the German bombardment had been very effective, the line being in places almost obliterated. Covering parties had also to protect working parties from the Gloucestershire, who were digging a new front line 80 yards further forward. Patrols were frequently sent out, towards Puits 14 Bis and Bois Hugo, and collected much valuable information including a German map showing the plans for the attack of October 8th. One of these patrols, consisting of Private Macaulay and two other men, encountered a much stronger German party and was forced to retire. Macaulay, however, remained behind to cover his comrades' retreat, killed two Germans at close quarters and eventually escaped, bringing off his opponents' helmets as a trophy.[3] On the 12th the battalion was relieved, but took post in North Loos Avenue in support, and next day it sent up 20 bombers and 10 carriers under Second Lieutenant Potts to assist the London Scottish in that day's attack upon Hulluch. This was part of the final effort already mentioned, in which the Forty-Sixth Division was trying to recover Fosse 8 and the Hohenzollern Redoubt, and the Twelfth to straighten out the line near the Quarries and to dislodge the Germans from Gun Trench. These last two efforts were only partially successful and the First Division was repulsed with considerable loss,[4] while the German retaliation was so heavy that the battalion had to go up that evening and relieve the Gloucestershire in the front line which had been much knocked about. It was only in the front line for twenty-four hours, however; next night the Forty-Seventh Division took over and the 1st was withdrawn for a rest, the battalion being at Allouagne till October 19th and then at Burbure till the end of the month. By this time

---

[1] Major Collier had just vacated the Adjutancy of the 3rd Battalion.

[2] Second Lieutenants Lynn Thomas, H. J. Inglis (who had already served with the 2nd Battalion at Gallipoli), Ward Jones, Buckley, Robertson, Davies and I. G. John.

[3] Private Macaulay received the D.C.M.

[4] Second Lieutenant Potts and Private Tamplin distinguished themselves by their gallantry in bringing bombs up to the firing line and in rescuing wounded men of the London Scottish under heavy fire. Second Lieutenant Potts received the M.C.

the Loos fighting was over and the B.E.F. was settling down to the prospect of another winter of trench warfare.

The 5th Battalion's share in the active fighting at Loos had ended long before the 1st's. The Nineteenth Division's orders were that the 58th Brigade should attack the German lines in front of Rue d'Ouvert in co-operation with the left brigade of the Second Division attacking from Givenchy. To assist in this Second Lieutenant Rose and 25 men of A Company took some trench-mortars up to the front line to bombard a strong point known as the Pope's Nose, while Second Lieutenant Lochner and the maching gun section were attached to the 56th Brigade who were holding the line to the left of the point of attack. A Company was detailed to work on the roads near Le Touret, B was placed in readiness just West of Festubert and D at Estaminet Corner, to which point Battalion Headquarters and C came up at 7 a.m. on September 25th, B and D having by then already advanced to the old British line.[1] The attacking battalions, the 9th Welch and 9th R.W.F., managed to advance about 200 yards but were then brought to a standstill by the heavy fire which they encountered, so there was no consolidating of captured trenches or digging communication trenches across No Man's Land for the battalion. Actually B had to reinforce the 6th Wiltshire, one of the supporting battalions, who had reached the front line and were suffering heavily from the German shell-fire, which had developed into a regular bombardment. B, considering the severity of the shelling, were lucky to escape with only one man hit, but there was nothing for them to do, and after the survivors of the R.W.F. and Welch had got back the two Pioneer companies were ordered back to the support positions, where the trench-mortar detachments, who had done excellent work, rejoined them, the machine gunners remaining rather longer in the trenches. C was sent up next day to assist in repairing the extensive damage done by the German retaliation, and until the end of September the battalion was busily employed on the communication trenches in the Festubert sector, but no further British attack was made on this frontage and the Germans were content to let things be. By the beginning of October a stalemate had set in here which was to last through the six months which the 5th spent in this and the adjacent sectors.[2]

That the results of Loos were very disappointing is not to be denied, though with just a little better luck, especially in the wind and the gas, much more might have been accomplished;

[1] That held from December 1914 to May 1915. Cf. Sketch 15.
[2] The 5th's total casualties for September were two men killed and six wounded.

even as it was a substantial success had more than once come within reach. The " New Army " Divisions had suffered severely from their inexperience, but the dash and courage and devotion of which they had given such ample proofs was an encouraging feature. These improvised formations had shown clearly that with more experience and more training they would be formidable and effective fighting machines : the Germans could no more disregard them because they were so raw than a year earlier they had been able to disregard the " Old Contemptibles " because they were so few. The B.E.F. could face its second winter of trench warfare hopefully because Loos had shown that great things might be expected when the full force of the British New Armies became available.

CHAPTER X

GALLIPOLI

The Third Phase—Suvla

ON returning to Mudros the 4th Battalion had found the harbour more crowded than ever with shipping, the camps bulging with men and every sign of the imminence of the great effort for which such ample reinforcements had been sent out. It was to take the form of a sortie *en masse* from the Northern end of " Anzac," for which General Birdwood's Corps was to be reinforced by the Thirteenth Division, a brigade of the Tenth and the 29th Indian Brigade, combined with a new landing in Suvla Bay by the rest of the Ninth Corps. The main objective was the rugged and intricate Sari Bair Ridge, from which the Turks overlooked the whole of " Anzac." Could this ridge be secured the right of the Turks facing " Anzac " would be turned and their position rendered most insecure; indeed, the new blow might even carry the British right across the Peninsula, isolating the Turks at Cape Helles, and August, it was hoped, would see the objectives of April secured and the Straits at last opened. The troops landing at Suvla, where comparatively little opposition was anticipated, would cover the left flank of the main attack on Sari Bair and by securing the high ground about the two Anafartas would threaten the Turkish communications with Bulair.

The sortie from " Anzac " was organized in four groups, " Right " and " Left Assaulting Columns," with the corresponding " Covering Columns," the last-named, as their names imply, having to protect the flanks of the main columns charged respectively with securing Chanak Bair and Koja Chemen Tepe, the chief points in the Sari Bair ridge. The 4th S.W.B. found themselves assigned to the " Left Covering Column," commanded by General Travers, along with their friends of the 5th Wiltshire and half the 72nd Field Company, R.E. This column had a task of no little difficulty. It was to march Northwards along the seashore for nearly two miles, skirting the intricate mass of spurs and ravines running down from Sari Bair, till it was across the Aghyl Dere, the largest of these ravines. It was then to wheel half-right and secure Damakjelik Bair, a ridge which formed the lower end of one of the main spurs. By occupying this it would at once cover the " Left Assaulting Column " against any attack from the Anafarta direction and be in position to gain touch with the Suvla advance. But unless and until that advance got going it might find itself isolated and much exposed; discipline and training would be severely tested by a flank march at night across that rugged and little-known country—there had been no opportunity for reconnaissance, beyond what could be done with field-glasses from Walker's Ridge at the Northern end of the "Anzac" lines or from destroyers patrolling the coast. The 4th S.W.B.'s selection to lead the column engaged in this difficult task was no little compliment to it and to its competent and resolute commander.

The first move was to smuggle the reinforcements into "Anzac" without the Turks detecting their presence. To do this the troops had to be transported there at night and to be hid in dug-outs all day. The 4th S.W.B.[1] left Mudros on August 3rd on a small steamer normally employed in plying between Ardrossan and Belfast, on which were also the 7th North Staffords. The boat was crowded to—possibly beyond—the limits of its capacity: indeed the troops were warned not to move about much for fear the vessel should capsize, a danger which was hardly serious as the men, wedged together like sardines, could barely stir. Arriving off Gaba Tepe about 10 p.m. the boat was greeted with a few shrapnel and an abundance of sniping, two men being hit while still on board, but the landing proceeded normally and before long the 4th were vigorously digging themselves in up one of the numerous gullies, trying to get concealment before dawn. Here they had to remain till the evening of August 6th, in very cramped quarters—only after dark was movement permissible—but though the Turks shelled the position freely, at times quite heavily, casualties were few. On the morning of August 6th a brigade conference was held at which General Travers explained what was expected of his column, and that afternoon Colonel Gillespie with Captains Kitchin and Mundy and some others were given a chance of reconnoitring through their glasses the unknown and intricate country to be traversed. They were taken along the coast in a destroyer and were able to spot several things which the maps did not reveal, notably that the Turkish trench which the leading company would have to attack was really at right angles to the position marked. Colonel Gillespie had been insistent that, as his battalion was to lead the way, he and his officers should have a chance to carry out this reconnaissance, and despite all objections, notably from the Navy who had plenty of other work for their destroyers, he—fortunately as it turned out—managed to get his way.

When the 4th started at 8 p.m., heavy firing was already to be heard on the right, where a furious fight was being waged for the Lone Pine trenches, and the battalion threaded its

[1] Battalions embarked with 25 officers and 750 other ranks, any surplus being left at Mudros as the "first reinforcements," which had not been provided on embarkation.

way down deep gullies to the shore to the accompaniment of the sounds of bursting shells and incessant rifle fire. As it plodded forward towards the deploying point, it caught some rifle and machine-gun fire from the foot-hills, where the New Zealand Mounted Rifles were clearing Bauchop's Hill, Table Top and other positions. Several men were hit, but the troops were as steady as veterans, though for a time the column had to halt and get what shelter it could in the prickly scrub along the shore, while the rear closed up. But it was soon moving on again, the 4th leading, though much delayed by the rugged ground which was littered with boulders and covered with holly oaks, a species of scrub standing about three feet high, with stiff and prickly leaves like a holly and bearing small acorns. The night was intensely dark, but the bursting shells and the naval searchlights playing on the hills which formed the Turkish position provided an intermittent illumination and made it possible to keep touch.

Soon after passing the mouth of the Chalak Dere the column found itself on more open ground, and the 4th then formed lines of companies moving to a flank in fours, 20 yards interval between platoons and 30 yards between lines, D Company under Captain Mundy acting as advanced guard. From the flank a desultory but apparently unaimed fire was still maintained, but the men's steadiness was admirable and the natural tendency to face to the right in the direction from which the fire was coming was well kept in hand and the proper direction maintained. Thus the battalion's movement escaped detection till, near the mouth of the Aghyl Dere, shots were suddenly fired into it from just ahead. Several men fell. There was a momentary check, but urged on by Colonel Gillespie,[1] and well handled by Captain Mundy, D Company dashed forward across the nullah and just as the next company reached the nullah a loud cheer proclaimed that D had carried the trench from which the fire had come. There was a sharp fight, but D made short work of the defenders, whose survivors bolted into the darkness.[2] Then, while D pushed straight ahead, the other companies bore off to the right towards Damakjelik Bair. This, as one officer writes, " was the most difficult part of the job. We had to cross the nullah, which was now about twelve feet deep with

---

[1] Thanks to Colonel Gillespie's prescience and the reconnaissance, the trench was attacked in flank and not frontally.

[2] It had been suggested to Colonel Gillespie that it might be risky to push on at once across the nullah, without clearing it up. The Commanding Officer, who had seen much service in W. Africa, said that from his experience of bush fighting he thought opposition in the nullah would die down directly D Company pushed across, which was exactly what happened.

very steep banks, and to reform on the other side on a bearing of 75 degrees." After some delay C Company started off in line in two ranks, but it was impossible to keep correct formations, for the scrub was 4 feet high and pretty thick. Still, so accurately was C led that it reached the ridge exactly at the point aimed at, a large tree. On the way several parties of Turks had been encountered and promptly dealt with, most of them being taken by surprise. By 1.30 a.m. Damajelik Bair had been seized and the 4th was consolidating the position. D Company, which had nearly all the fighting, had had 8 killed and 17 wounded, the other companies hardly losing anyone.

If the opposition encountered had not been formidable the battalion's achievement was none the less most creditable. For experienced veterans a night march over such rough and unreconnoitred ground would not have been easy, for a young battalion, new to war save for its fortnight in the Cape Helles trenches, it was a fine performance, as Sir Ian Hamilton warmly acknowledged. "The rapid success of this movement," he writes, "was largely due to Lieutenant Colonel Gillespie, a very fine man, who commanded the advanced guard, consisting of his own regiment ... a corps worthy of such a leader. ... Here was an encouraging sample of what the New Army under good auspices could accomplish. Nothing more trying to inexperienced troops can be imagined than a night march exposed to flanking fire, through a strange country, winding up at the end with a bayonet charge against a height, formless and still in the starlight, garrisoned by those spectres of the imagination, worst enemies of the soldier."

Having seized Damakjelik Bair the battalion had to dig in quickly before any counter-attack could develop. In the dusk it was hard to see what line to take up, and the ground varied greatly, in places quite easy to dig, elsewhere it was rocky and hard and several small gullies ran up into the position. D Company had occupied a hillock about 400 yards away, guarding the left flank and covering a small well, B and A had prolonged C's line to the right, where ultimately the 5th Wiltshire came up and continued the line up the spur, communication being eventually established with the 4th Australian Brigade on the ridge above the Asma Dere.

All night long the men worked steadily, though many, weak from the already prevailing dysentery, were hardly fit for the effort but had refused to be left behind. To their right rear heavy firing indicated that the assaulting columns were struggling forward up the slopes of Sari Bair : far away to their left intermittent firing could be heard and distant flashes seen, the landing at Suvla was in progress. Morning (Aug. 7th) found the battalion well dug in, though in places the trenches, sited in the darkness, were found to give such poor fields of fire that readjustments were imperative. Heavy fighting was going on both to the right and left, but the 4th found themselves in a backwater between the Sari Bair and the Suvla struggles, of both of which their position gave them a view. No counter-attack developed against them, either that day or the next, and though enough snipers were about in front to make movement in the open imprudent the chief casualties came from shrapnel: the Turkish

gunners had soon detected the presence of British troops on the Damakjelik Bair spur and shelled the position pretty steadily all day, giving the 4th reason to be glad of the hard digging they had put in. Second Lieutenants Buchanan and Lucas were wounded and the next two days saw the 30 odd casualties[1] of the night march more than doubled. Luckily good water was obtainable at two small farmhouses just behind the line, and a useful haul of entrenching tools, telephone wire and other articles was found in some abandoned Turkish bivouacs.

On the evening of August 8th the 5th Wiltshire moved away to take part in the main fight on Sari Bair and the battalion had

[1] These included Lieutenant Bickford-Smith and Second Lieutenant Jenkins.

DAMAKJELIK BAIR

to shift to its right to replace them. In the new position A Company was on the left, C in the centre astride a long spur running down into the valley to the Northward, with B on the right, while D was brought across from its hill to form a reserve. This left a gap of over a mile between the battalion and the sea, though the advance of the Suvla troops had by now provided some measure of protection. The Turks may have noticed the Wiltshire's withdrawal or may have been intending anyhow to try to recover Damakjelik Bair, but the 4th had hardly settled down into its new trenches when, just before dawn[1] (August 9th), a vigorous counter-attack developed. Turks came on in force and at one point on the left made their way up a gully and got within 150 yards. However, Captain Kitchin pushed forward No. 11 Platoon under Lieutenant Miller and part of No. 12 under Second Lieutenant Cooper some way down the spur so as to reinforce the picquets and get a better field of fire, and from this position they were able to stop further progress, though both officers were hit.[2] The attack was vigorously pushed and the action soon became very brisk, so about half an hour later Lieutenant Austin brought No. 9 forward to reinforce, taking post on the right. Fighting continued at close quarters, C being helped by the fire of A, who from rising ground on their left covered the Western slopes of the spur. About this time General Travers came up and ordered up a platoon of D to C's help. This platoon, No. 13 under Lieutenant Farrow, was at first held in reserve, but about 9.30 a.m. Captain Kitchin decided to use it and the rest of C in a counter-attack, as the Turks were too close to be healthy. This attack, pivoting on the right and swinging round its left, went splendidly. It swept through the bushes in front of C's line, clearing them of Turks and killing many. Company Sergeant Major Jones, a splendid N.C.O., of the best type of old soldier, was killed in the charge, but it had relieved the situation, and at the end of it No. 13 Platoon, shortly afterwards reinforced by No. 10, held a forward line across the spur, facing North, with the rest of C (facing East) roughly at right angles to them and lining a hollow road.

Elsewhere the battalion's steady fire had stopped the Turks before they could get near. But the 4th's success was marred by a sad loss. When the attack started Colonel Gillespie had hurried to the right flank and was directing the fire of a machine gun when, in looking over the parapet, he exposed himself to a

---

[1] Between 4.30 and 5 a.m.

[2] Second Lieutenant Cooper was killed outright, Lieutenant Miller, who lay out in the open for some time before he could be brought into safety, died that evening in the Field Ambulance. Both were officers of much ability and promise and were severely missed.

Turkish sniper and was hit in the head and killed. The 4th could ill afford to lose the man who had been its mainstay while forming and training. From the first he had devoted himself with all his energy and enthusiasm to the new battalion. A soldier of real ability, a born leader of men, with a splendid record in West and South Africa, he had inspired confidence in his new officers and men by his soldierly qualities, his just treatment of the men, and his constant care for their interests, and had won their affection as well as their respect.

After this repulse the Turks contented themselves with sniping and occasional shell fire, and made no attempt to renew the attack till after 6 p.m., when they came on again, attacking with great determination. Some Gurkhas, who were to have reinforced the left flank, had not arrived, and for two hours the battalion had, unsupported, to sustain the whole weight of the attack. D Company had to be brought up into line, and thanks to the steadiness of the men, who behaved like veterans, the Turks were kept at bay. The brunt of the fight again fell on C Company, next the gully, where the Turks, utilizing this approach, established themselves close to the line. Captain Kitchin, therefore, ordered Lieutenant Farrow to take his own platoon and No. 10 and make another counter-attack. This he did with great dash and success. Charging through the scrub the platoons dislodged about 80 Turks and sent them flying back off the spur with heavy loss. After covering 120 yards they came under heavy fire from the scrub at short range and were checked, Lieutenant Farrow being wounded in the leg, though he continued to lead his men with great gallantry. Seeing how things stood, Lieutenant Austin dashed forward with his platoon, and this timely help enabled Lieutenant Farrow's party to hold its own till after dark. Lieutenant Austin, who was also wounded, reported the situation at battalion headquarters on his way to the dressing-station, whereupon Major Beresford, now in command, sent the last reserve, two platoons of D Company, under Captain Mundy, to C's help. This reinforcement made the position secure and after dark the advanced party withdrew successfully to the position held after the first counter-attack. The night proved quiet, except for a small attack upon B Company about 2 a.m., which was easily repulsed. Reinforcements, some New Zealand Engineers and two companies of the 6th King's Own, had arrived, but were not used, and just before daybreak Major Beresford sent them back, the battalion having maintained its position unaided. Its stand received warm commendations from the brigade and Division and a special message of praise from Sir Ian Hamilton, but the cost had been heavy. The killed numbered 44, including

Colonel Gillespie, Lieutenant Miller and Second Lieutenant Cooper. Captain Hooper was wounded, along with Lieutenants Fairweather, Austin and Farrow, Second Lieutenant Staples, Lieutenant Fleming, R.A.M.C., the battalion's M.O., and 72 men,[1] which brought the total losses to date well over 200. Lieutenants Austin, Farrow and Bell, Company Sergeant Major Bush of D Company and Sergeant Myles all distinguished themselves in the fighting, the latter by most successful bombing, while Corporal Holliday did splendid work in reconnoitring, twice pushing fearlessly out at night right up to the enemy's lines.

For the next two days things were quieter. The gallantly pressed attempt to capture Sari Bair had definitely failed, and though the territory held by the Anzac Corps had been doubled, the essential vantage ground had not been secured and the British line ran below and not upon the crest. The Suvla advance also had been checked and the important high ground just West of the two Anafartas was still in Turkish hands. However, local operations for the improvement of the line were in progress in places, one of the most urgent being the capture of the Kabak Kuyu wells, at the foot of "Gillespie Spur," as the battalion's position was now officially named. The water supply was an urgent problem and accordingly General Cox, of the 29th Indian Brigade, under whose orders the 4th now found itself,[2] prepared to attack Kabak Kuyu on the afternoon of August 11th.

The plan required the battalion to swing its left forward about six hundred yards. This movement would cover a direct advance against the well by the Gurkhas. The advance was timed for 7 p.m., at which hour Lieutenant Bell and Second Lieutenants Addams-Williams and Owen, took out a covering party of 120 men. Moving in skirmishing order they at once came under rifle and machine-gun fire but reached the intended positions nevertheless, despite heavy casualties. The digging parties thereupon moved out and started work, though A Company on the right had some difficulty in reaching their line, owing to heavy fire at close range. Some of the covering party, however, had advanced too far and found it difficult to

[1] The heaviest loss fell on C Company, which had 2 officers and 21 men killed, 2 officers and 33 men wounded, D coming next with 11 men killed and 1 officer and 10 men wounded. The gap in C was temporarily filled by about 30 of the Herefordshire Regiment (Fifty-Third Division) who wandered into its lines on the evening of August 10th, having become separated from their battalion during the day's fighting on the Suvla front.

[2] General Cox had a most cosmopolitan command, including besides the 4th S.W.B. and his own Sikhs and Gurkhas, Australians and New Zealanders, to whom the 5th Connaught Rangers were added a little later.

maintain their position, while the Gurkhas attacking on the left were beaten back with heavy losses. Still the new line was taken up and entrenched as ordered, and that evening the 4th had the satisfaction of beating off an attack. But its losses had been severe, especially in the covering party, many of whom were missing, while both Lieutenant Bell and Second Lieutenant Addams-Williams were killed, Lieutenant Bury also was wounded. However, the details left at Mudros rejoined that evening and were distributed between companies.

Next day consolidation was continued and in the evening the battalion, by giving covering fire, supported a gallant but unsuccessful effort by the 9th Worcestershire to capture the wells. It was now apparent that to secure Kabak Kuyu would need a more substantial effort, so for the moment the 4th had to hold on, do what it could to improve its line, keep down the Turkish snipers and beat off occasional minor attacks: on the night of August 18th/19th, for example, C drove off two strong patrols which advanced against the line. On the 16th one diarist notes an issue of bully beef, bacon and marmalade to supplement the "not very sustaining continuous biscuit," hitherto the only issue, and the next day there were eggs, not very large ones and "not laid yesterday," but still eggs. An officer was sent off to Mudros to fetch the men's greatcoats, and on the 20th the packs arrived from Anzac, where they had been left. Meanwhile, the position was considerably improved by the 29th Indian Brigade coming up into line on the left and digging in; then on the 15th some New Zealand Mounted Rifles reinforced the battalion, which allowed first A Company and then C to be relieved and rested. The scrub in front was thick, and in places limited the field of fire badly, so a party sallied out one evening to deal with it with kukris borrowed from the Gurkhas. The kukri, however, proved an intractable weapon and the party's efforts combined the pathetic with the ludicrous. Better results were achieved when 100 Gurkhas went out to clear the scrub, the battalion supplying the necessary covering party; in accustomed hands, the kukris dealt faithfully with the scrub and greatly improved the field of fire. Casualties, however, continued to mount up: on the 13th the battalion lost another valued senior officer when Major Sir Lennox Napier was killed by a sniper, and altogether between August 10th and 25th 3 officers and 22 men were killed, 16 men missing and 69 wounded, which brought the battalion well down below 500 of all ranks, C Company for example, which had landed 184 strong, had lost 110 men and all its officers save Captain Kitchin, and even when reinforced by 38 men from Mudros was much below establishment. Meanwhile preparations for a new offensive were in progress and in this not only the 4th but the 2nd S.W.B. were to be involved.

Though the great new effort had failed, if by a narrow margin, Sir Ian Hamilton would not admit defeat and had promptly started to organize a fresh attempt. Its main object was the capture of Scimitar and " W." Hills, but a subsidiary operation was to be undertaken against the Kabak Kuyu position. A dismounted Yeomanry Division had arrived from Egypt, but the main hope for success lay in the employment of the veteran Twenty-Ninth Division, two brigades of which, the 86th and 87th, were accordingly withdrawn from the firing line at Helles and taken round to Suvla (August 16th–17th). The 88th Brigade, shattered in a gallant but unsuccessful holding attack on the " H." trenches on August 6th, undertaken to divert Turkish attention to the Helles area, was for the moment left behind.

Since the beginning of August the 2nd Battalion had had two spells in the trenches and a briefer one in reserve. It had not shared in the forlorn hope of August 6th, though a platoon and a machine gun had been sent up next day to help the Dublin Fusiliers repulse a counter-attack on H. 12. From August 12th to 16th it held the line near Border Barricade, and was busy sapping out in order to straighten the line. Turkish guns were active and gave the battalion ample occupation in repairing the line, but it was lucky to escape with only a dozen casualties, including Lieutenant Gibbs, wounded by the smashing of a periscope. On reaching Suvla early on August 17th, the battalion was attached to the Fifty-Third (Welsh Territorial) Division, to teach the newly arrived and inexperienced hands the tricks of the trade of trench warfare. This was an exacting task : the Territorials' position just East of Sulajik had been hastily taken up and entrenched, and the line was badly sited and dug, no communication trenches existed and there were Turkish snipers in the scrub behind the British front line. But in two days the S.W.B. accomplished much, cleared the area, suppressed the snipers, improved existing trenches and helped to dig a new line 600 yards long across a gap to connect up with the Fifty-Fourth Division on the left. On the evening of the 19th the battalion was relieved and taken back to the beach, moving up after dark next day to Chocolate Hill where it dug in ready for the attack.

The 87th Brigade's programme was that after half an hour's bombardment the Inniskillings would pass through the front line, held by the K.O.S.B. with the machine guns of the S.W.B. and of the Borders, and assault Scimitar Hill, the 86th Brigade simultaneously assaulting Hill " W." on the right. When these positions had been taken the S.W.B. were to capture the trenches between the two points attacked and consolidate a line from the Inniskillings' right to the ravine head East of Torgut Chesme. Punctually at 2.30 p.m. (August 21st) the bombardment started, the ships backing up the rather scanty artillery available. Judged by Western Front standards, even by those of 1915, it was inadequate, and to make matters worse the light was poor and the wrong way. The ships could hardly see the targets and their fire lacked accuracy and effect. Nevertheless the Inniskillings started forward at 3 p.m., but though their gallant assault reached the crest of Scimitar Hill, they came under a withering fire from both flanks and were thrust back half-way down the slope. In vain the Borders reinforced them and renewed the attack. Flanking fire from their left was largely instrumental in foiling their efforts, and meanwhile the 86th Brigade, forced off its proper line by burning scrub, had swerved to the right, becoming mixed up with the Eleventh Division, and was also held up. The Yeomanry, however, remained; and as they moved forward to attack Hill "W." the 2nd S.W.B. were put in against Scimitar Hill, C and D Companies leading with A and B in support. At first all seemed going well. It was getting dark, but from the front trench, in which Major Going had established his Battalion Headquarters, C and D could be seen charging over the crest of the hill. B Company, meanwhile, had been detailed to tackle the Turks on the high ground North of Scimitar Hill, which had given so much trouble to the earlier attacks. Before long, however, some Yeomanry, who had swerved to their left and got mixed up with the attack on Scimitar Hill, began coming back, declaring that they had been ordered to retire.

The situation being obscure, Major Going went forward with the Adjutant and found everything in confusion, 87th Brigade and Yeomanry being all mixed up on the slopes of the hill. He accordingly started to reorganize the line, placing Yeomen in the centre, Borders on the right and S.W.B. on the left and ordering the Inniskillings back to the support trenches,[1] Captain Williams meanwhile returning to Brigade Headquarters to report; on hearing his account the Brigadier after consulting with the Division ordered the advanced troops back. Without support on the flanks their hard-won lodgment on the slopes of Scimitar Hill would have been costly, if not impossible, to maintain and would have served no tactical purpose. Accordingly, under cover of darkness, the surviving

---

[1] Regimental Sergeant Major Westlake did splendid work at this time, helping to reorganize the troops and arranging to send forward parties with water and tools. For this and for his consistent good work throughout the campaign he was subsequently awarded the D.C.M. and the French Medaille Militaire.

attackers were withdrawn. Casualties had been heavy; the 2nd had lost nearly 300, nearly a third of its numbers. The killed and missing included Lieutenants Burrell, Nevile and McShane, while Captain Walker, Lieutenants Tragett, Mumford, Blake, Philpotts, Knowles, F. A. Hill and Evans, and all the four C.S.M.'s were wounded.

The 4th Battalion at Kabak Kuyu had also been warmly engaged. There the important tactical point was the hill on the far side of the Kaiajik Dere, N.E. of the wells, known as "Hill Sixty" or "Kaiajik Aghala." This was to be assaulted by two

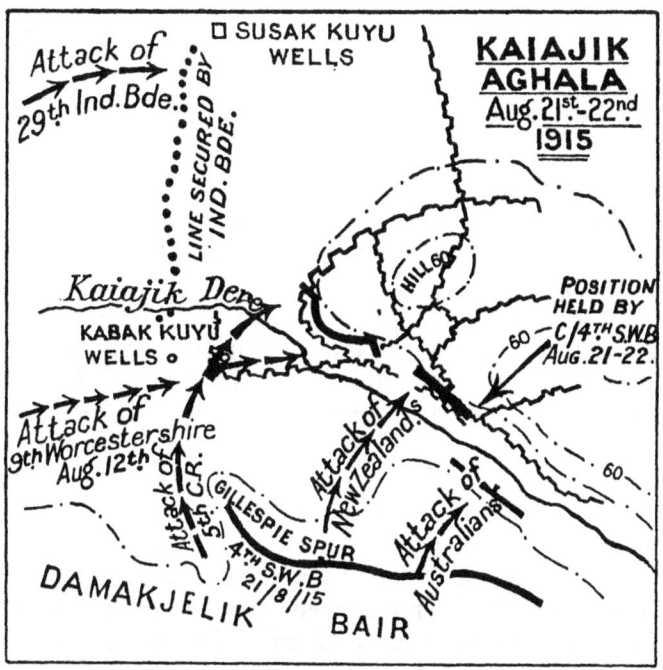

Australian battalions and the New Zealand Mounted Rifles, while the 29th Indian Brigade and attached units attacked further to the left, nearer Susak Kuyu. The 5th Connaught Rangers were to carry out the attack on the actual well of Kabak Kuyu; of the 4th S.W.B., A Company was to consolidate the ground round the well when captured, while B and D and the machine guns gave covering fire from the trenches, C, now barely 60 rifles strong, was retained in battalion reserve, being posted on the left flank.

Launched at 3.30 p.m., after a short preliminary bombardment, the attack was only partially successful. The Australians were held up and the New Zealanders, who attacked from the S.W.B. trenches, found themselves after a very gallant advance clinging to a trench just below the crest of the hill with both flanks in the air. The Connaught Rangers meanwhile had carried the well and the trenches guarding it, so A Company pushed up to consolidate the position round the well. The Indian Brigade also had gained its objective, but the New Zealanders were hard pressed and urgently needed support. An Australian Staff officer made his way to Major Beresford's headquarters to ask if he had any men in hand. On being told that the 4th had one weak company in reserve the Staff officer replied, " Then for God's sake send them forward to help the New Zealanders who are hanging on by their eyelids." Captain Kitchin was therefore sent for and asked if he knew how to reach the New Zealanders' position. He at once declared that he had suspected something of the sort might be needed and had reconnoitred the ground. Starting from just behind the Rangers' position, Captain Kitchin had first to file his company down a narrow lane between deep hedges into a field, turn there to the left and line up facing right ready for its dash over 300 yards of open. It was a difficult manœuvre, but it was accomplished and the company, dashing forward, reached its goal with only six casualties. For its success C had mainly to thank Captain Kitchin's previous reconnaissance and he had spotted every fold in the ground and knew exactly how to make the bounds. He was splendidly backed up by his N.C.O.'s—C had no subaltern left—and the men went forward in great style. Not a man faltered and their conduct testified to their confidence in their commander's leading. The company was promptly placed on the New Zealanders' right, holding about eighty yards of trench. On the right its flank rested on a communication trench which the Turks had barricaded and from which they were bombing. C had no trained bombers left, but the New Zealanders produced a sackful of " jam-pots," and Lance Corporals Beary and Gronow volunteered to throw them, though neither had handled a bomb before. So effectively did they throw their bombs that the Turks were kept at bay. Beary —a fine specimen of the Irishman turned Welsh miner—was conspicuously successful, and his ceaseless efforts gained him the D.C.M. All night long the struggle continued: the repeated counter-attacks could not shift C Company or the New Zealanders, and meanwhile A, though heavily shelled and losing Lieutenant Phillips killed, had erected a shell-proof shelter round the well. One specially vigorous effort about 3 a.m. was successfully beaten back, and after that things quietened down. Later in the day a newly arrived Australian battalion slightly improved matters by a partially successful attack on the right, but C Company, now down to 42 rifles, had a very trying time.

It was heavily shelled, the day was extremely hot and it had exhausted its water, so it was not sorry to be relieved that evening and to move back along with the rest of the battalion to rejoin the Thirteenth Division,[1] which was now holding Rhododendron Spur, the highest point on the Sari Bair Ridge which the attackers had succeeded in retaining. This move involved a march of nearly three miles before the battalion reached the reserve trenches for which it was destined. It was by now much reduced. Hill 60 had cost it another 16 men killed and missing and 71 wounded,[2] making its total casualties since the fighting began 7 officers and 102 men killed and missing, 11 officers and 286 men wounded.[3] But the 4th could feel that it had proved itself, had shown itself worthy of the Regiment and had emerged with great credit from its first real trial.

[1] Major General Maude had just taken command of the Division, General Shaw having been invalided.

[2] D Company came off worst, with 30 casualties, mostly from shell, C having 6 killed and missing and 18 wounded. Captain Kitchin, though slightly wounded, continued at duty.

[3] The battalion was now reduced to seven officers, the Commanding Officer, Adjutant, Quartermaster, and four company officers, as Major Birch had been evacuated to Alexandria for an operation.

CHAPTER XI

AFTER LOOS

THE last months of 1915 were perhaps the most uneventful period of the whole war on the Western Front. The B.E.F. had hardly enough guns or ammunition to support adequately the "raids" which were now becoming frequent, much less a minor offensive. The Germans, though better off for guns and shells, showed no marked disposition to stir up activities, and the dispatch to Salonica of nearly 150,000 Allied troops, including four British Divisions, had diverted to that quarter a substantial proportion of the recent augmentation of the B.E.F. which was not replaced for some time. The main interest, therefore, lay in the successive arrival of the remaining "New Army" Divisions and their initiation into "the real thing," and in the measures taken to make life in the trenches healthier, more endurable and less costly in lives than in the previous winter. The TWENTY-FOURTH have therefore few experiences and achievements to chronicle for the last quarter of 1915, though the battalions who represented it on the Western Front increased in number from two to five with the arrival of the 6th, 7th and 8th, and after relapsing to three in October, when the 7th and 8th left for Salonica, rose again to five in December, when the 10th and 11th Battalions came out with the Thirty-Eighth Division.

The 1st S.W.B., who had come out of the line on October 19th, did not return to the trenches till November 15th. The month's rest, the first of any length, had been most beneficial; especially as it had given a chance of some systematic instruction of the very partially trained recruits of whom the battalion was now so largely composed. The 1st now began a long spell of trench-warfare in the Loos Salient, marked by few incidents but full of hard work and much discomfort. It was a wet autumn and the rain added enormously to the normal labours of keeping the trenches in repair, besides making life in the line extremely unpleasant. Parapets and the sides of communication trenches were constantly collapsing and had to be repaired, revetted and strengthened. The struggle to keep the communication trenches reasonably clear of mud, enough that is to let them be used for the purpose for which they were designed, was never-ending. To make the line a little drier and more habitable trench-boards had to be laid down and dug-outs constructed. All the time the enemy had to be closely watched lest opportunities of harassing him effectively should be missed, patrols had to keep his defences under observation and to give warning if he seemed likely to become aggressive. However, apart from intermittent bombardments, which did much damage but fortunately did not cause many casualties, the Germans were neither active nor aggressive and the weather troubled the 1st more than did the enemy. Mud was their main opponent, but even against mud they kept up their end. The December diary records a careful visit of inspection by the Divisional Commander, General Holland, who, it states, " went away muddy but quite satisfied." Drafts were small and infrequent, though Second Lieutenants Lowe, Webb and Garnons-Williams joined in November and Second Lieutenants R. H. Cole, W. Cole, Walshe, W. R. Morgan, J. Smith and Wileman in the following month. Casualties, however, were few : Second Lieutenant Rawle was badly wounded in December and Second Lieutenants Ford and Lowe slightly wounded, while Captain Ramsden went off to a Staff billet.

The 5th Battalion, like the 1st, found the last quarter of 1915 strenuous rather than particularly exciting. The Nineteenth Division never got away from the Festubert–Neuve Chapelle area and the 5th's occasional shifts from Gorre to Le Touret or Cornet Malo brought no real change in its situation or work. " Companies employed under C.R.E." is the almost unvarying entry in the battalion diary. The work was varied enough, ranging from road repairs and constructing trench-tramways in back areas to improving trenches or mining in close proximity to the enemy. The work in the front trenches was almost exclusively done at night. Much of it was building up of breastwork defences in those places where the high water level made trenches quite untenable. This was often very dangerous because by day the Germans could note its progress and get their machine guns ready to play on the half-finished works when the men were busy on them, and despite such precautions as the prohibition of smoking it was hard to prevent the enemy discovering when work was in progress.

As regards casualties the 5th fared extraordinarily well; October brought a dozen, including Captain Curtis and Lieutenant Renwick wounded, but for November and December none are recorded. Various changes occurred among the officers. Major Cooke, who had been commanding while Colonel Trower was in temporary command of the 58th Brigade, left in December to become C.O. of the 9th Welch, whereupon Captain Deacon took command temporarily, as Major Wright was away ill. This gave Captain Newmarch command of B Company and Captain Croft command of D.

While the 1st and 5th had been in action at Loos three other battalions of the Regiment had been entered to active service, for, during September, all six " K. 3 " Divisions had found their way to France. Indeed before the Loos offensive opened the 7th and 8th S.W.B. had actually been under fire. They had not, however, had to undergo the searching ordeal endured by the Twenty-First and Twenty-Fourth Divisions, as the Twenty-Second had been allotted to the Third Army on the comparatively " quiet " Somme front.

That Division had shifted at the end of May from Seaford to Aldershot for the final stages in its preparation for service overseas. One of the great advantages of Aldershot was the splendid facilities for musketry, and the 7th now took the opportunity of selecting and training snipers. Final leave before embarkation was given, and in August came reviews by the King and Lord Kitchener, the usual indication of approaching departure. Surplus officers were sent off to the 9th Battalion, the 7th sending Captain d'Arcy and nearly a dozen subalterns, the 8th rather fewer. Shortly after the move to Aldershot Colonel Hancock's health had broken down and necessitated his relinquishing command: he had done admirable service and his departure was much regretted. He was succeeded as C.O. by Major Grimwood, whose place as Adjutant was taken by Lieutenant C. E. Williams, while in place of Major Benson, who had gone to the 3rd Battalion as a Draft Conducting Officer, Major Yatman of the Somerset Light Infantry joined as second in command on August 28th. Major Addison likewise was posted from the 8th to the " General List," and Major E. B. Ward of the D.C.L.I. joined in his place, taking over D Company, Lieutenant C. B. Morgan also becoming Quartermaster in place of Lieutenant Wilson.

The Twenty-Second Division's move from Aldershot began on September 3rd and the two S.W.B. battalions crossed from Folkestone to Boulogne on the night of the 5th/6th, their transport having started a day sooner. After a short stay in a rest camp both entrained for an area near Amiens, where the Division was concentrating, the 7th[1] marching to Vignacourt after detraining, the 8th[2] to Bertangles. By September

---

[1] The following officers proceeded overseas with the 7th Battalion : Lieutenant Colonel J. Grimwood (C.O.), Majors A. H. Yatman (second in command) and G. W. H. Wakefield (B Company); Captains J. B. Royle (C Company), F. A. Coe, (A Company), P Gottwaltz (D Company), J. B. Harris, P. Villar and G. D. Taylor, (M.G. Officer); Lieutenants C. E. Williams (Adjutant), W. A. Burn, P. S. J. Welsford, L. V. Williams, C. H. Morgan, E. E. Mills, W. T. Dick, D. S. Davies, C. J. H. Treglown, H. H. Hannay, H. S. Wingard, D. Noyes Lewis; Second Lieutenants B. J. Cadoux, P. D. Gillmore-Ellis, H. Giles, N. Griffiths, C. G. Robinson and C. H. Nicholas ; Lieutenant and Quartermaster G. Martin ; Regimental Sergeant Major Talmage, Regimental Quartermaster Sergeant J. J. Dunne.

[2] The officers of the 8th Battalion were : Lieutenant Colonel W. D. Sword (C.O.), Majors A. H. M. Hamilton-Jones (second in command) and E. B. Ward ;

10th the concentration had been completed and the infantry started upon the period of instruction in trench-warfare, now the customary novitiate of a new unit. For this the 7th were attached to the Fifty-First (Highland Territorial) Division, then in line N.E. of Albert, the 8th to the Fifth Division, then holding the Carnoy and Maricourt sectors nearer the Somme. Both battalions had some strenuous marching as their first experience of French roads, the 7th covering eighteen miles on September 10th and the 8th, who had done a route-march in the morning, no less than twenty-four in all. They stood it well, however, few men falling out, despite the great heat.

The instructional period followed the usual course, officers and men were first attached to the instructing units individually, next whole platoons went in together, finally companies took over a piece of line. Several officers were taken out on patrol and the routine of trench-life and duties was systematically followed. Neither battalion had specially notable experiences, though the new hands found the mere being in the actual presence of the enemy exciting enough. Both were shelled and sniped, but the 8th escaped casualties and the 7th had only two, Private Barnes opening its casualty list by being wounded on September 15th, while Private E. Davies, who was killed next day, was its first name on the Regiment's Roll of Honour.

This instruction over, both battalions proceeded South of the Somme, as the Division was relieving the 154me French Division from that river near Frise to the Luce. This line ran through undulating chalk country, mostly open, with occasional woods and large villages, though few isolated farms or houses. It was lightly held, being an unlikely sector for an advance, as, even if the Allies could carry the quite formidable German lines, the Somme running South to North behind them above Peronne, would present a troublesome obstacle. Indeed the opposing forces seemed to have adopted an attitude of mutual forbearance, though on the left some mining was in progress. Elsewhere, however, the 154me had evidently devoted the last four months with considerable success to making the line habitable and had dug most elaborate underground cook-houses and shelters.

The 8th were the first to go into the trenches, taking over

Captains L. T. Thorp (Adjutant), S. C. J. Hazard, J. R. England, C. H. C. Sharp, A. P. Percival, H. G. Down, C. L. Casey; Lieutenants F. H. V. Bevan, M. A. M. Dickie, G. M. Haydon, T. G. Wood, M. W. Brown, W. A. G. C. Kaye, T. N. B. James and L. V. Corfield; Second Lieutenants H. A. Llewellyn, W. W. Thomas, C. H. A. Lakin, C. C. Woolley, A. Bodenham, A. L. Amos, W. V. Franklin, C. A. L. Harvey, H. St. J. Kenny, G. E. Cardwell; Lieutenant and Quartermaster C. B. Morgan; Regimental Sergeant Major Cashman, Regimental Quartermaster Sergeant E. Lichfield.

the left or Chuignes sector on September 19th, the 7th Battalion being in brigade reserve near Chuignes. Advance parties had gone up on the previous evening and came in for a lively time. The Germans were apparently expecting to find the sector held by new troops, and attacked vigorously but quite unsuccessfully, though Sergeant Watkins and Corporal Davies of the 8th were both killed. Things were still quite animated when the 8th took over, while it was believed that the Germans had mines under B Company's sector. To anticipate them Colonel Sword, on the advice of the French mining officers, had two camouflets exploded about 9 p.m. September 21st. This provoked a great outburst of rifle fire, in which the German artillery joined, and before long their infantry began to leave their trenches, to be received with such a burst of rapid fire that their advance died away immediately: more experienced troops might have held their fire until more enemy had exposed themselves, but, as the Brigadier reported, there was no confusion and the men were quite steady, the machine gunners conspicuously so. Altogether the 8th came quite well out of their first brush with the enemy: they had inflicted several casualties, and their own, all from shrapnel fire, did not exceed a dozen.[1] The rest of the 7th, owing to Brigade Headquarters misunderstanding a message, believed that the enemy had entered the trenches and turned out in readiness to recover them: their services were not required, however, and when, on September 24th, their turn came to hold a section of the line just East of Herleville, they had an extraordinarily quiet time, having only one man killed in the course of two tours. The 8th, who came into line again on October 1st after a week in support, were also little troubled. There was much shouting of insulting remarks in English and snipers were active, but the German guns fired very little, probably they needed their ammunition more further North.

On October 11th, both battalions were attached to the Twenty-Seventh Division for further training under experienced units. The 7th, who were attached to the 4th K.R.R.C. in the 80th Brigade,[2] benefited greatly from the helpfulness of Colonel Widdrington and his officers. Two of its subalterns, Lieutenants Wingard and Davies, distinguished themselves when out on patrol. Reconnoitring a suspected sniper's post in No Man's Land, they came suddenly upon four Germans. Nothing daunted, they attacked with bombs and as the Germans bolted shot one of them. The 8th also received valuable instruction from the 1st Royal Scots in the 81st Brigade. But it was not in

---

[1] A working party of the 7th which was also in the front line had a few casualties.
[2] The Brigadier was an old S.W.B. officer, Brigadier General W. E. B. Smith.

France that the two battalions were destined to put their lessons to good use. The brigade had just gone into line again, the 7th being in trenches South of Cappy,[1] when rumours of a move became rife and were confirmed on October 20th by orders for the Division's relief. Next day the Twenty-Second handed over to a French Division, and units were hastily re-equipped for service in some Eastern theatre of war. October 26th saw both battalions entraining, and after three tedious and uncomfortable days they found themselves at Marseilles, where they embarked, the 7th on the *Lake Manitoba*, the 8th along with the Divisional Staff, the 11th R.W.F. and the 8th K.S.L.I. on the *Huntsend*, a captured German vessel. On October 30th both ships sailed for Alexandria.

Neither the 7th or 8th S.W.B. were to see France again, but their short experience on the Western Front had been most valuable. They had been under fire and had a chance of learning from experienced troops. Neither battalion had suffered heavily,[2] both had acquitted themselves well. The 7th, who were inspected on October 4th by General Gordon, got an extremely flattering report, as a " well commanded, well organized " battalion ; " it is a pleasure," the Divisional Commander wrote, " to see a battalion like this," a " particularly fine " body of men, " well turned out and keen."

The 6th S.W.B. were nearly three weeks later than the other two " K. 3 " battalions in going overseas.[3] After its three weeks in the New Forest the 6th had moved through Basingstoke and Bracknell to Aldershot, arriving on May 31st, being quartered in Tournay Barracks. It too had gone through the usual routine of a battalion about to proceed overseas : musketry, brigade and Divisional exercises, " set-piece " reviews and embarkation leave. Half a dozen officers went off to the 9th Battalion in July, among them Majors Wood and Thunder.[4] Captain Bloxham, who had

[1] While here, Second Lieutenant Robinson, a very promising subaltern, was killed by a stray bullet at night, the first officer to fall.

[2] The figures were : 7th Battalion, 1 officer and 8 men killed, 8 men wounded ; 8th Battalion, 9 men killed, 13 wounded.

[3] The officers who proceeded overseas with the 6th Battalion were : Lieutenant Colonel E. V. O. Hewett (C.O.), Major C. M. Samuda (second in command), Captains F. Carter (Adjutant), W. G. Evans, E. C. Choinier, E. L. Lloyd, S. C. Morgan, J. N. A. James, F. J. Easterbrook ; Lieutenants A. Case (Quartermaster), H. C. A. Davies, F. B. Thomas, T. J. Neale (T.O.), L. G. Blomfield, W. C. Charter, G. Rattenbury, R. Eskell, R. M. Cox ; Second Lieutenants N. D. Morris, H. S. Ede, T. Siddle, M. C. Ede, S. Evans, J. C. Owen, T. G. Evans, D. Jenkins, E. C. Amos, S. E. Rumsey, L. C. W. Deane, B. R. B. Jones, G. W. Jones, I. G. Randolph, D. A. Williams ; Regimental Sergeant Major Casey, Regimental Quartermaster Sergeant Segers.

[4] He had joined in February and had been commanding D Company.

handed over the Quartermaster's duties to Lieutenant Case as long ago as January, was now struck off as medically unfit for service overseas; while shortly before embarkation Major Samuda (Somerset Light Infantry) joined as second in command. Leaving Aldershot on September 24th, the 6th had just landed at Havre when the struggle at Loos began and spent the next day in the train, ultimately arriving at Chocques in the small hours of September 27th, and marching thence to the Le Sart area where its Division was concentrating.

Like the Twenty-Second, the Twenty-Fifth Division was not flung into the thick of the fighting straight away, but served its apprenticeship to war in the "quiet" Armentières sector, where little change had taken place since the Eastward advance of the Third Corps had been held up there in October, 1914. It was to have a long spell in this quarter, as not till the end of January was it relieved and given a month out of the line for rest and training. For the 6th S.W.B. this period was one of incessant work, sometimes in the actual trenches but more often just behind them, where the roads, the billets, the drainage and tasks like erecting such necessities as wash-houses and baths kept them fully employed. Keeping the communication-trenches in working order was in itself no small demand on the battalion's time and energies. It was a wet autumn, and in the low-lying Lys valley, whose natural drainage had been disordered by the digging of the opposing trench-lines, the main communication-trenches were often waist-deep in mud, or even deeper in water. Their sides tended to collapse and even without the intervention of the enemy they provided ample occupation. For the more skilled work required in the trenches companies were usually attached to the different brigades, and parties were continually up in the front line, supervising and assisting infantry working-parties or carrying out tasks which involved technical knowledge. Most of the battalion's casualties[1] occurred in this way, though as a rule the companies were withdrawn from the trenches during periods of special activity, as, for example, when a British bombardment was likely to provoke hostile retaliation. Some casualties occurred also in the back areas. On November 17th the Germans developed a heavy bombardment of Oosthove Farm, where Battalion Headquarters had been established early in October. Dozens of big high-explosive shells came crashing down on and round the farm, but the men behaved with great steadiness, the transport detachment distinguishing themselves by good work in removing their horses to a place of safety. Much damage was done but casualties were remarkably low,

[1] Private W. T. Ede, killed on October 3rd, was the 6th's first entry on the Regimental Roll of Honour.

only 2 killed and 5 wounded, and the damage did not necessitate a shift of quarters.

A Pioneer battalion's experiences in a "quiet" sector tended to lack variety; the never-ending work made the epithet "uneventful" most inappropriate, but week in and week out the same tasks confronted it. The machine gunners, who were occasionally attached to the battalions holding the line, alone came in for much real "fighting," but certain incidents stood out in the daily round of duty done and useful work performed. On December 2nd, after the Germans had blown a mine, killing a dozen of the 9th Loyal North Lancashires, Lieutenant Eskell's platoon of D Company promptly and skilfully entrenched the 60-yards-wide crater thrown up and rendered the line defensible. A month earlier (November 3rd) a man slipped during bombing-practice and dropped his bomb. It was timed to go off in five seconds, but Second Lieutenant S. Evans sprang forward, snatched up the bomb and hurled it at the bombing pit, though not soon enough to prevent it bursting in mid-air and wounding nine men; still, had it burst in the trench the casualties must have been trebled, and his presence of mind and gallantry were rewarded by a M.C., the first "honour" awarded to the battalion.

Casualties were not numerous. From the end of September to January 22nd, when the 6th at last left Oosthove Farm for other quarters, the battalion had in all 11 men killed and 1 officer, Second Lieutenant Amos, and 35 men wounded. Invalidings were more numerous and included Captain Carter, the Adjutant, who was sent back sick to England on December 12th, Second Lieutenant Deane taking over his duties.[1] However, considering the weather and the amount of hard work required of the battalion the sick-rate was not high, and the 6th had the satisfaction of knowing that its labours were fully appreciated by those in higher authority. On December 7th General Plumer, G.O.C. Second Army, inspected the battalion and complimented it on its splendid work and on the general condition of the area for which it was responsible, picking out the state of the horse lines and the recreation huts for special commendation.

To the TWENTY-FOURTH the chief event of December was the arrival in France of its 10th and 11th Battalions. The Thirty-Eighth Division had remained in North Wales until the end of July, when it received orders to move to Winchester for Divisional training, which had till then been impossible owing to its units being so much scattered. The Division

[1] Others invalided were Captain Blomfield and Lieutenants H. C. Davies and Siddle.

had also been greatly handicapped by being kept waiting for Service rifles, without which serious training in musketry was hardly possible. In other respects, however, both 10th and 11th S.W.B. had been making substantial progress. In May the 10th had had the benefit of the services of eight drill-instructors from the 4th Grenadier Guards, who proved extremely useful,[1] and the 11th reached the point of being able early in July to form a fifth company. On the receipt of orders to move to Winchester the two E companies, commanded respectively by Captain I. A. Morgan (10th Battalion) and Lieutenant W. G. Williams (11th Battalion), were sent off to Coed Coch Camp near St. Asaph, to form the nucleus of the new 13th "Local Reserve" Battalion, to the command of which Major Pitten was posted from the 10th. This battalion was to act as the draft-finding unit for the 10th and 11th Battalions, and all through the summer and autumn there was a constant interchange between it and the battalions destined for overseas, men who proved to be under age or fit temporarily for Home service only being sent off to the 13th and recruits drafted from it to fill their places. Some of the older N.C.O.'s who had done good service in training recruits proved medically unable to pass for service overseas and there were a good many promotions and changes among them and the Warrant Officers, the most noteworthy change in the 10th being Regimental Sergeant Major Orford's appointment to commissioned rank (June 1st, 1915), whereupon Company Sergeant Major Lockie of C Company succeeded him as Regimental Sergeant Major.

The 10th, who moved to Winchester on July 22nd, being quartered first in Hursley Park and then at Hazeley Down Camp, preceded the 11th by a month: it was not till August 30th that Second Lieutenant Browning and the Quartermaster took the latter's advance-party to Flowerdown Camp, whither the battalion followed shortly, moving to Hazeley Down a fortnight after its arrival at Winchester.

The country round Winchester was in every respect a great change from the Colwyn Bay area and the opportunities for practice in the more advanced work of Brigade and Divisional exercises were very welcome. Even now, however, the lack of Service rifles hampered the Division seriously, though in other respects its training was so well advanced that in September it was reported upon as being fitter to proceed overseas than several earlier-formed Divisions, and its date for embarkation was accordingly put forward. However, hardly any Service rifles were forthcoming before the end of October, so the 10th

[1] Three of them, subsequently transferred to the battalion, accompanied it to France.

and 11th spent their last few weeks in England mainly in an intensive but rather hurried training in musketry, parties being dispatched to the rifle-ranges on Salisbury Plain. During part of this time Captain D. G. Johnson of the 2nd Battalion, who was recovering from wounds received at Gallipoli, was attached to the 11th and acted as second in command. November also saw the final selection of officers and men for service, those surplus to War Establishment being sent off to the 13th Battalion, which had moved to Kinmel Park in September, while others were promoted to fill gaps in the establishment. Several important changes occurred in both battalions: the 10th were joined on the eve of departure by Captain C. D. Harvey of the Sherwood Foresters, who became Major and second in command in the vacancy caused by Major Pitten's departure. Captain T. H. Morgan had just previously been promoted Major and had handed over the Adjutancy to Lieutenant Orford, who was definitely appointed to that post on November 20th. The 11th lost the help of Colonel Porter, whose health was not equal to the strain of overseas service. He had done good work in raising and training the battalion, which owed him no small debt.[1] In his place Major J. R. Gaussen, an Indian cavalryman from the 3rd Skinner's Horse, I.A., joined on November 13th to take command, and just before sailing Captain E. F. Grant Dalton of the West Yorkshires was appointed Major and second in command. Lieutenant Palmer too proved unfit for service overseas, Regimental Sergeant Major Barry being promoted to be Quartermaster in his place, Company Sergeant Major Pearson getting the vacancy as Regimental Sergeant Major. A review by the Queen on November 29th indicated that the time for going abroad was near, and on December 3rd the two battalions[2] left Hazeley Down for Southampton, crossed to Havre that night, and proceeded by rail to Aire, the 10th on December 5th,

---

[1] Colonel Porter was transferred to command yet another new battalion of the Regiment. This was the 14th, and belonged to the same "Local Reserve" category as the 13th. Its nucleus consisted of a Depot Company formed by the 12th Battalion in September. Lieutenant Palmer was also transferred to this new unit as Quartermaster.

[2] The following officers proceeded overseas with the 10th Battalion: Lieutenant Colonel Sir H. Greenwood (C.O.), Majors C. D. Harvey (Sherwood Foresters), (second in command), T. H. Morgan; Captains G. F. H. Charlton, A. D. Givons, H. M. Long, E. T. Rees; Lieutenants A. Galsworthy, E. Gill, J. Godsal, W. O. Jones, R. Kenward, R. Simmonds, J. J. Williams; Second Lieutenants H. K. Budgen, A. Clayton, H. Cottam, H. H. Davenport, A. Hibbins, A. Hitchings, J. P. S. Hornsby, G. M. Garro Jones, I. J. Griffith Jones, W. H. Lillington, E. E. Orford (Adjutant), A. J. Ralph, C. N. Reed, W. H. Seager, L. Watts Morgan; Lieutenant and Quartermaster J. R. Ingledew, with Captain Howard, C.F., and Lieutenant T. B. Evans, R.A.M.C.; Regimental Sergeant Major Lockie, Regimental Quartermaster Sergeant Bardoe; Company Sergeant Majors Tilby (A), Lacey (B),

the 11th following next day. Detraining here, they marched Westward to their respective quarters and settled down to a fortnight's training, the 10th at Quernes and the 11th at Witternesse. On December 19th both battalions turned out to line the road in honour of Sir John French, who was passing through on his way home after relinquishing command of the British Armies in France. This fortnight over, the Division was ordered up to St. Venant and placed in reserve to the Eleventh Corps, to which it had been posted. The 10th were now billeted at Robecq, the 11th at Riez du Venant, and the end of the year found parties of both battalions up in the line for their period of instruction, the 10th under the Guards Division, the 11th being attached to the 57th Brigade of the Nineteenth Division and consequently seeing something of the work of another battalion of their own Regiment, Colonel Trower's Pioneers. The 10th had two men wounded, but the 11th did not have to record any casualties. A more important loss was the departure of the 10th's C.O., Sir Hamar Greenwood, who was recalled to England to take up a post at the War Office. He had done good work in raising and training the 10th and had the satisfaction of handing a very efficient battalion over to Major Harvey, who now took command.

The departure of the 10th and 11th S.W.B. for active service left remaining in England seven battalions of the Regiment, of which the 12th, now at Aldershot, was completing its preparation for going overseas. Of the others the 3rd was still near Liverpool, as busy as ever with its double functions of draft-preparing and guard-finding. It had formed two new companies, I and K, shortly before moving to Liverpool, but with the 2nd Battalion calling for drafts almost more insistently than the 1st it was hard pressed to get its recruits trained and ready. Recovered sick and wounded now formed a substantial proportion of the

Clissold (C), Cool (D); Company Quartermaster Sergeants Greenwood (A), Bowden (B), Keen (C), Rees (D).

With the 11th Battalion there went out: Lieutenant Colonel J. R. Gaussen (C.O.), Major E. F. Grant Dalton (second in command); Captains W. G. Williams, J. E. Mills, J. H. I. Monteith, A. J. Dawes (Adjutant), H. C. W. Williams, W. Cullimore, W. S. Edwards, C. F. B. Jenkins, L. R. Lewis; Lieutenants L. Roberts, J. H. C. Griffiths, C. E. Browning, R. V. Sayce, B. R. B. Jones, E. Goldsmith, J. Richards, W. T. Harris, T. P. Hamer; Second Lieutenants R. E. Thomas, G. W. B. Price, D. Powell, B. E. S. Davies, S. A. Miller-Hallett, W. H. A. Wilkins, L. R. Morris, G. Woodcock, Ll. Lloyd; Lieutenant and Quartermaster J. Barry, Regimental Sergeant Major Pearson, Regimental Quartermaster Sergeant Rees, Company Sergeant Majors Cooper (A), Dorchester (B) Primavesi (C), Davies (D); Company Quartermaster Sergeants Lett (A), Edwards (B), Jenkins (C), Golightly (D).

"intake" of men, and occasional drafts of transfers from "departmental corps" were received. Some of the recovered sick and wounded with other men hardly equal to active service were drafted in August to one of the Garrison battalions then being organized, the 1st Garrison Battalion, R.W.F. Colonel Morgan continued in command all through 1915, but in September the 3rd lost the help of Major Collier who had done great work as Adjutant under very difficult conditions and now proceeded overseas to join the 1st. Lieutenant S. B. Johns, who had been appointed Assistant Adjutant, took over his duties for the time, but in April, 1916, Captain Fowler, who had sufficiently recovered from his Gallipoli wounds to do duty at home, was Gazetted Adjutant. Regimental Sergeant Major Bruntnell remained with the 3rd Battalion all through 1915, as did also Regimental Quartermaster Sergeant Martin.

The 9th Battalion meanwhile at Kinmel Park was also occupied with the preparation of drafts and had begun to dispatch them overseas. Its first draft had had to be equipped by the 3rd Battalion, but from July on it was able to undertake this function also. Draft-finding, however, prevented its numbers from increasing rapidly, although a distinct stimulus was given to recruiting when the Newport Town Band joined *en bloc* and were employed on recruiting parties, while when the "K. 3" battalions completed their mobilization for active service and transferred their surplus officers and men to the 9th it proved possible to organize a third company. The battalion was at this time reconstituted with one "Service" company of trained men, one of recruits, and one of men temporarily fit for home service only, drafts being found by the first company, which was refilled from the other two as recruits completed their training or the convalescents recovered their strength. Colonel Gillman continued in command all the year, and in August Major Wood joined from the 6th Battalion and became second in command, while Lieutenant Blowen, the Adjutant, was promoted to Captain. The chief feature of the 9th's career, however, was the rate at which its list of subalterns continued to expand: they kept on coming in, until by the end of the year the battalion could have put a very respectable fourth company on parade out of the 150 subalterns on its books.

Of the two "Local Reserve" battalions the 13th was substantially augmented in December by the arrival from the 10th and 11th Battalions of their surplus officers and men, the latter numbering nearly 200. Major Pitten had been promoted to be Lieutenant Colonel, and he had as Adjutant Lieutenant J. R. O. Jones, with Regimental Sergeant Major Platt and Regimental Quartermaster Sergeant G. Thomas as those other corner-stones of the battalion. Recruiting had not been too brisk in the autumn and the process of completing the 10th and 11th for departure so depleted the battalion that a third company, which had been formed in October, had to be broken up again at the end of November. The 14th meanwhile was beginning to take shape under Colonel Porter's guidance. It was originally constituted at Prees Heath in September but, after about a month there, moved to Morfa Camp near Conway, where it arrived on October 22nd, 1915. Here the end of the year found it with Captain W. G. Evans as Adjutant and Company Sergeant Major Hitch acting as Regimental Sergeant Major, but shortly after the New Year it joined the 9th and 13th Battalions at Kinmel Park, where they constituted the greater part of a 14th Reserve Infantry Brigade, while about the same time Captain Evans handed over the Adjutancy to Lieutenant T. H. Woosey.

The 12th, which, as already mentioned, had shifted to Aldershot, where it arrived early in September, had made considerable progress during its two months at Prees Heath Camp. With far better facilities for training than could be enjoyed at Newport, especially as regards ample space for open-order work, and with the battalion concentrated under canvas instead of scattered about in billets, this was natural. It benefited considerably by having a couple of experienced instructors attached to it to help with its musketry and company training, Captains Haig-Brown and Bond, and it was fortunate in having Captain E. A. A. Whitworth transferred to it from the Rifle Brigade to command D Company. Shortly before the move to Aldershot the Depot Company had been formed under Captain Hoffmeister, and it was left behind on the battalion quitting Prees Heath. At Aldershot the battalion found itself part of the Fortieth Division, the last but one of the "New Army" formations, which was now being brought together and included, in addition to the three Welsh "Bantam" battalions,[1] units from Scotland and from all parts of England. The 12th S.W.B., who were posted to the 119th Brigade, were at first in Salamanca and Talavera Barracks but shifted in December to some new huts, glorified with the name of Marne Barracks, on the higher and bleaker ground of Blackdown. Two of its officers, Captains Foreman and Lieutenant C. M. Pritchard, went out to France on a "Cook's Tour" in November, and in December Major C. B. Hore of the Royal Warwickshires joined

[1] The others were the 18th and 19th Welch.

as second in command, but there were many delays over the completion of the Division for service abroad. Recruiting for some of its units had been somewhat overhasty; men had been enlisted after too perfunctory a medical examination and proved unequal to the work they had undertaken. Some units had to discharge quite a large proportion of their men as medically unfit, though this was not the case with the 12th, the majority of the Welsh " Bantams " being by no means lacking in stamina if they were below the normal in stature. In the end some units had to be amalgamated and others drafted in from elsewhere, and in consequence the Fortieth Division had to remain in England for some months after the Thirty-Eighth had gone overseas.

The 2nd Line of the Brecknockshire Battalion had undergone considerable changes in the course of 1915, beginning in February with a change in designation, being now styled " 2/1st Brecknockshire." In March it was reorganized in four companies on the double company and platoon basis and in April it had a change of quarters, though only to Dale, near the entrance to Milford Haven. About this time it was decided to reorganize the " Second Line " T.F. Divisions on an active-service basis. This involved two processes, firstly the formation of a " Third Line," sometimes described as " Third Line Depot " and later as the " 3/1st Brecknocks," which was to take over the draft-finding duties hitherto assigned to the " Second Line," secondly the transfer to a Home Service unit of the men unwilling or medically unfit to engage for foreign service. The Depot had been formed in February with Captain Graystone as Adjutant, the transfer of the Home Service men to their new unit did not take place till September when a few officers and over 300 men went off to the 50th Provisional Battalion at Sketty near Swansea. A shift from Dale to Fort Scoveston followed and in October nearly 250 men were transferred to the 2/7th R.W.F., with which battalion the 2/1st Brecknocks were for a time amalgamated under the title of the " 2nd Battalion, 203rd Brigade."[1] Shortly before the end of the year the battalion moved from Pembrokeshire to the East Midlands, its new station being Bedford, about as complete a change in scene from the country around Milford Haven as can be imagined. In December its temporary union with the 2/7th R.W.F. was terminated, but what with the transfers to that unit, to the Provisional Battalion and to the 3/1st, the battalion was not able to find enough men to form more than two companies, and not until after the passage of the Military Service Act were its numbers to be substantially augmented.

[1] On the Territorial Divisions being given numerical designations the Second Line Welsh Division had been numbered as the Sixty-Eighth Division.

CHAPTER XII

GALLIPOLI

After Suvla

THE attack of August 21st, despite the useful gains near Kabak Kuyu, had failed to affect the general situation. As definite a stalemate had resulted at Suvla as at Helles and once again the policy to be pursued was being debated between Whitehall and " M.E.F." Headquarters. Sir Ian Hamilton was strong for persisting, believing that with additional artillery and ammunition he could not only enlarge the foothold gained at Suvla but might achieve the decisive success so nearly reached already. Others were less sanguine, and before long the ominous word " evacuation " found its way into the discussion. Sir Ian Hamilton would not hear of it; naturally reluctant to abandon the enterprise in which he so firmly believed, he thought evacuation must involve enormous losses, even if it could be effected. Eventually he was replaced by Sir Charles Monro in October, shortly after whose arrival followed Lord Kitchener's visit to Gallipoli and then the decision to evacuate the foothold the M.E.F. had gained at so great a cost. No small factor in bringing the authorities to this decision was the new enterprise to which the Allies found themselves committed in Macedonia. Already in October the M.E.F. had had to find two Divisions, one French, one British, for that venture, and to prosecute the two campaigns simultaneously was beyond the resources of the Allies, especially in shipping.

Between the failure of the August attack, however, and its logical conclusion by evacuation, nearly five months intervened which to the troops at the Dardanelles were months of monotony, of disappointment, of hardship, of toil, of losses, not so much by the enemy's bullets and shells as from the climate and the general conditions. Regimental officers and men, if their outlook was necessarily more restricted than that of the Staff, could not fail to realize the ill-success of the " great push " and the thoroughly unsatisfactory character of the situation. Nowhere on the Peninsula had the British advanced enough to prevent the Turks shelling their rest camps (so-called) and landing places; and the conditions under which the troops had to exist, full of disadvantages both from the tactical and from the administrative standpoints, were bound to impress upon them the full meaning of the stalemate.

Regimental officers and men, however, were too busy combating practical disadvantages to have much thought to spare for the general situation. They were fully employed in

[SEPT. 1915]   AFTER SUVLA

improving the tactical situation at most points of the newly established line, in mitigating the worst features of the position as regards accommodation and water supply, and generally making life more endurable. Both 2nd and 4th S.W.B. were faced with much the same problems, though the older battalion's greater experience stood it in good stead, and heavy as its

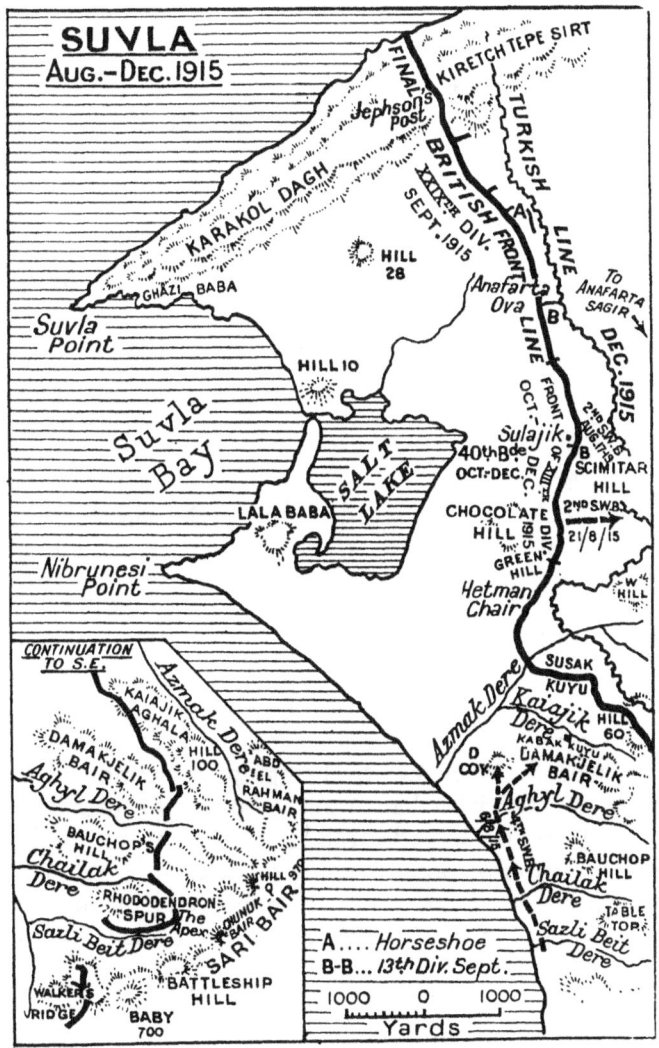

Scimitar Hill losses had been it was considerably the stronger, as the 4th, except for its "first reinforcements" from Mudros, had received no drafts and was down to 350 of all ranks, including 9 officers.[1]

[1] Second Lieutenant Keighley, promoted from the N.Z. Brigade, had joined on August 25th. He was a survivor of the original landing and had been all through the subsequent fighting.

Scimitar Hill was followed for the 2nd Battalion by a week in reserve trenches West of Hill 28. Conditions were uncomfortable, movement by day usually provoked shelling, water was scarce and had to be fetched by hand in cans from over a mile away. Some drafts turned up, amounting in all to 4 officers, (Lieutenant Byrne and Second Lieutenants J. E. K. Hall, Glazebrook, and B. R. S. Jones) with 132 men, one of them, 11 strong, being the sole survivors of 83 men torpedoed on the *Royal Edward* between Alexandria and Lemnos. After this week the battalion moved forward, relieving the 4th Worcestershire in some front line trenches to the left of the Fifty-Third Division's former line. It was a bad line, mainly consisting of small posts and detached trenches; here also water was hard to get, and to fetch it and rations, to say nothing of such trench stores as were available, meant taking away practically a whole company from work in the firing-line where every man was badly needed. But the Turkish trenches were 700 yards away, so there was no difficulty about working in the open at night. Moreover, the Turks were far from active. Content with their success in holding up the British, they made little effort to interfere with the consolidation of the position along the Eastern edge of the Suvla plain.

September indeed passed quietly for the 2nd S.W.B. Hard work was plentiful enough: the line needed both consolidating and improving and all ranks were kept busy. On the 2nd it received a compliment and a temporary accession of strength when the 4th Welch, now down to 9 officers and 350 men, were attached to it for instruction. This battalion had been badly knocked about, and as the Divisional diary says, "it was considered that its attachment to one of the best regiments in the Division would do much to bringing it round into a good state." The chief disturbance to the ordinary routine arose from Turkish efforts to impede the construction by night of an advanced position on some knolls 250 yards in front of the line. Six posts in all were constructed, being held by day by sentry groups. These posts were repeatedly attacked by bombing-parties and several times the garrisons were driven out but, reinforcements being sent up, recovered the posts and resumed work. In these encounters Second Lieutenant Ballantine and Sergeant Jackson were conspicuous for their gallantry in reconnoitring and on the night of September 15th/16th, Sergeant Jackson, after reconnoitring a lost post, led a party forward and successfully reoccupied it.[1] Quite the sharpest of these fights was on the night of September 17th/18th when about fifty Turks attacked the post known as Hill A. They were

---

[1] He subsequently was awarded the D.C.M.

checked by one platoon of B Company and driven off when a second reinforced it. By September 18th three of the posts had been linked up, two or three later attacks on the new line, now known as "The Horseshoe," were successfully beaten off, and before the battalion was relieved—on September 22nd—it had substantially improved the local position. This fighting had involved a couple of dozen casualties,[1] but sickness constituted the chief drain on the battalion's strength. This was growing serious : the want of rest, the monotony of the rations, the virtual impossibility of getting any luxuries, and the natural disappointment at the non-success of the Suvla offensive, all helped to lower the vitality of the men. Nearly everybody, whether he went sick or not, suffered more or less from diarrhœa, medical comforts were scarce, many men were too weak for hard work, especially for carrying laden sand-bags up to the advanced position, and it was a great relief to be shipped off to Imbros and spend the end of September in a real rest. A draft of 85 men joined here,[2] and Second Lieutenants Evans and Gibbs rejoined from hospital with 20 recovered sick and wounded. Colonel Going[3] went to hospital with dysentery on the 26th, being succeeded in command by Captain Williams,[4] who rejoined from the Divisional Staff, to which he had been appointed on September 6th, Captain Somerville replacing him as Adjutant.[5]

The 2nd Battalion were expecting to return to Suvla early in October. Actually they had seen the last of that region. Owing to the withdrawal of a French Division for Salonica and to the ravages of sickness in the three British Divisions stationed at Helles, the force there was falling dangerously low, and it was decided to reinforce it with the 87th Brigade, which proceeded thither on October 1st. The 2nd S.W.B., though the better for their rest, left 47 men in hospital at Imbros and had 91 men out of 557 attending sick parade. New clothing arrived early in October ; from the middle of the month a regular supply of

---

[1] These including Second Lieutenant J. E. K. Hall, died of wounds on September 22nd.

[2] Earlier in the month 4 officers (Lieutenant B. J. Davies, and Second Lieutenants F. Rice, A. Ballantine and I. E. M. Cochrane) and 13 men had joined, and on September 19th Captain Robertson and Second Lieutenant W. F. Page also arrived.

[3] He had been appointed "Lieutenant Colonel while in command of a battalion" on September 9th.

[4] Major Ellis had been invalided shortly before this.

[5] In his dispatch dated September 22nd, 1915, Sir Ian Hamilton "mentioned" Colonel Going, Captain Walker, Lieutenants Ffrench and Turner ; Lance Corporal Harris ; Privates Claffy, Poole and Turrell. Colonel Going subsequently received the D.S.O. and Captain M. C. Morgan the M.C.

eggs became available, and with the weather cooler, though still fairly warm, conditions were less unpleasant than when the battalion had left Cape Helles in August. It had a fortnight in reserve, went up into the firing-line just East of the Achi Baba nullah on October 19th, and from then on tours in the line, generally four days in duration, alternated with similar periods in support in the Eski line and with rather longer periods in reserve. Till about the middle of November things remained quiet: the British were too weak for an offensive—at one time the battalion was holding 500 yards of line with 320 rifles—and though there was some activity in mining and a little trench-mortaring or bombing the troops were chiefly employed putting out wire, building up parapets and generally improving the line. Occasionally the Turks offered targets to rifles and machine guns by coming out to do some wiring, but, until stirred up by the Fifty-Second Division undertaking a minor offensive near the junction of the East and West Krithia nullahs (November 15th), they were very inactive. When in reserve the battalion was kept busy preparing winter quarters, and the most was made of the rather restricted facilities for training. Instructional classes for machine gunners and bombers and in working trench-mortars and catapults were started: lectures were given to officers and N.C.O.'s on such subjects as "Trench construction," "Discipline" and "Courts Martial," instruction of which the inexperienced new hands stood in some need: rifle ranges were constructed and training in musketry given. Several drafts appeared, with some new officers, mostly from the 3rd and 9th Battalions,[1] but though casualties were low, only 1 wounded in October, 4 killed and 18 wounded in November, 9 killed and 1 officer and 48 men wounded in December, sickness kept down the battalion's strength.[2] Thus it mustered 21 officers and 604 men on October 31st, but only 20 officers and 550 men on December 2nd.

November, as already remarked, saw greater activity. After the 156th Brigade's successful attack (November 15th) both rifle fire and bombing increased, but the battalion's main attention was devoted to improving its trenches, in which it displayed no little ingenuity and skill, winning much praise from those in authority. Some bombers, who were lent to the 157th Brigade for several days to assist it in holding its bomb-heads, did excellent service and came back with high commendations and, what was equally satisfactory, no casualties. The weather turned colder,

[1] These included Lieutenant O. C. Bodley, Second Lieutenants Beardshaw, Cooke, Dutton, T. J. Edwards, Karran, Mason, Mayger, Main and Parry Davies.
[2] Captains B. J. Davies and Robertson, and Second Lieutenants Mumford, Roberts, Cochrane and B. R. S. Jones were all invalided during these months.

but Helles escaped the worst of the blizzard of November 26th to 28th which devastated Anzac and Suvla; the troops suffered severely enough from the frost and snow and the piercing wind, but extra rum was issued and comparatively few men had to be evacuated to hospital.

The increased activity of December was largely due to the evacuation of Suvla and Anzac. The 2nd S.W.B. had gone up into the firing line on the 18th, being on the left of the Krithia nullah. The next day the 157th Brigade attacked the trenches near the junction of the nullahs and gained some ground, but also roused the Turkish guns and bombers to retaliate vigorously. They did not, however, prevent the battalion from constructing a new fire trench 60 yards further in front or from plastering the Turkish trenches with bombs and trench mortars. The chief results of the increased activity were a bigger casualty list and about the longest spell in the front line the battalion had done on the Peninsula, fourteen days in all, for not till January 2nd was it at last relieved and sent back to the Eski line. During the last 48 hours it had had its 4th Battalion on its immediate left, the 40th Brigade having relieved the Inniskillings.

Since leaving Damakjelik Bair the 4th Battalion had had some varied experiences. It had had only a short spell in the Rhododendron Spur sector facing Sari Bair, the chief incident of which was the rescue of some wounded Wiltshires who had been lying out in No Man's Land since August 10th, while Major Yates was slightly wounded on August 26th. Then, early in September, the Thirteenth Division had left the Anzac Corps' area to join the Ninth Corps at Suvla. The 4th marched away thither on September 3rd, having been relieved by Australians in the trenches which it had just taken over on the remarkable feature known as Table Top. Arrived at Lala Baba the Battalion had to get what shelter it could on the seaward slope and then settled down to a variety of tasks. A defensive position round Lala Baba had to be constructed. The ground was littered with miscellaneous debris and needed much work before it could be rendered sanitary. Constant working parties were required for unloading ships, and as the Turks frequently shelled Lala Baba the battalion had to cut back into the cliffs to make shell-proof dug-outs, which could also serve as winter quarters. The soil, though sandy on the surface, was hard sandstone about two feet down and blasting was often necessary. The work was hampered by the shortage of timber, sandbags and other R.E. stores and consequently made slow progress, though the arrival from Lemnos of mess-boxes and officers' valises improved conditions for the officers, while all ranks enjoyed the bathing, which was excellent if decidedly dangerous during shell "strafes." What little time remained after all this work was devoted to training, but in that crowded area facilities were few and little could be done, especially as the constant labour was telling on the health of the men; many of them were already enfeebled by the prevalent dysentery, a complaint aggravated by the uncomfortable conditions and the monotony of the rations—on September 6th, for example, the first fresh meat for six weeks was issued, but unfortunately proved so tough that only the most determined could manage it. Indeed the battalion's exertions were only too well recorded in the increasing sick list and the dwindling number of effectives, the strength falling from 335 on September 1st to 277 three weeks later.

After a fortnight in Corps Reserve at Lala Baba the Thirteenth Division went up into the front line again on September 19th, relieving the Fifty-Third in trenches West of Anafarta Sagir.[1] These had by this time been made fairly strong, with good dug-outs, and were picturesquely situated among cornfields and trees; while in contrast to Anzac wells were abundant, but the Turks, whose lines were on slightly higher ground some distance away, enjoyed good observation over the ground behind our line. Attention had therefore to be concentrated at first on improving the communication trenches, while parapets were found to need strengthening, and badly sited loopholes had to be altered. Things were quiet enough: both sides indulged in occasional sniping, our patrols were out every evening, but rarely encountered any enemy, though they brought in many British rifles with much equipment and ammunition, relics of our unsuccessful advance against Anafarta Sagir. Occasionally the Turks indulged in a bombardment—one of particular violence on the evening of September 26th was accompanied by a tremendous fusilade—but they never left their trenches, being apparently deterred by the effective reply of the British gunners. Next day brought news of the capture of German trenches at Loos, which induced Lovat's Scouts on Chocolate Hill to indulge in playing their bagpipes. This naturally provoked the Turks to retaliate, and a tremendous fusilade started which was vigorously taken up all along the line. The Turkish guns joined in and shelled the reserve trenches heavily. Not knowing the cause of the outburst the 4th stood to arms and remained in readiness for an attack till, after about an hour, things gradually quieted down, the main result being that there were no digging fatigues that night. Anything like a British offensive, even on the smallest scale, was precluded by the weakness of most units,

[1] This was No. 3 Section, the right of which was at Sulajik: it was South of the line held by the Twenty-Ninth Division during September.

while even those who had received drafts of any size had not had time to incorporate and assimilate these reinforcements, mostly recruits with little training. It was as much as most battalions could do to hold and improve their lines, train their drafts and carry out the necessary fatigues. With so little transport available large carrying parties were needed, and all this work tended to keep the sick-rate up.

As regards drafts the 4th was about the least well-served battalion in the Division. A few officers arrived early in September, among them Lieutenant Usher, one of those left with the 9th Battalion, and some recovered sick and wounded returned to duty, while casualties in action were only 4 men killed and missing[1] and Captain Hooper and 5 men wounded; still it was down to 10 officers and 211 men by September 30th, 4 officers and 132 men having gone to hospital. October brought a slight improvement, though by the middle of the month the battalion had sunk to 178 men with 19 officers[2]: later on, however, drafts totalling 4 officers and 214 men arrived,[3] so that as casualties had continued low and admissions to hospital had been less frequent[4] the 4th could muster 22 officers and 378 men by the end of the month.

October had been spent in a new sector, the Thirteenth Division having relieved the Tenth at Chocolate Hill on September 30th to allow of the latter's departure for Salonica. This meant much work in stony soil with pick and shovel improving an unsatisfactory line, with the special disadvantage that the Turks had marked down the few available wells and systematically sniped men who tried to draw water. Otherwise their main activity consisted in occasional bombardments. Some batteries were posted just behind Chocolate Hill and the battalion got the benefit of what was meant for them. Two big Turkish guns somewhere away to the battalion's left front were constantly searching for our guns with 8-inch or 9-inch shells, which sometimes found the battalion's trenches instead. These pieces, though searched for by our naval guns, defied detection and were a standing nuisance.

The weather was getting colder now, which perhaps contributed to keep down sickness, as warm clothing had been issued and the supply of rations was improving, while firewood became

---

[1] These included Company Sergeant Major Bush of D Company, mortally wounded when the battalion was moving up to the front line on September 19th.

[2] Nine young officers had joined on October 6th.

[3] One of these included Lieutenants Austin and Farrow and 22 other recovered wounded. Captain Fairweather and Lieutenant Staples also rejoined on recovery from wounds.

[4] The figures were, killed 2 men, wounded 5, sick 5 officers and 58 men.

fairly plentiful. There was no lack of work, as once the line had been made good a new one was begun nearer to the Turks, saps being pushed out some distance to the front, and heads then dug and connected up. Patrols went out frequently and occasionally had brushes with the Turks; Captain Farrow on one occasion distinguished himself greatly by creeping up through the scrub to a Turkish sentry group and bombing it from behind.[1] In the subsequent confusion he got safely back to our lines. Among the officers who joined in October was Lieutenant Caldwell, a splendid rifle shot, who was put in charge of the battalion snipers and soon converted them into picked marksmen, more than equal to their Turkish "opposite numbers" in all the arts of concealment and disguise. Early in November the battalion lost its Adjutant, Major Yates, promoted to command the 6th King's Own (38th Brigade). One of its few remaining original officers, he had done consistently good service and was greatly missed.[2]

But what made November memorable was the blizzard. The month had begun with cold weather and enough rain to emphasize the inadequacy of such shelters as it had been possible to construct. Then came the days of real suffering, November 26th to 28th. Beginning on the 26th with "a cold dour Gallipoli day" and a bitter N.E. wind, things got worse as the day wore on. The wind increased steadily in force and with it came first sleet, then about 5.30 p.m. thunder and the deluge. So violent was the rain that in a few minutes every gully had become a mountain torrent in spate and ice-cold water was flooding trenches and dug-outs, drowning a few unfortunates and drenching everyone to the bone. The trenches, being situated on the slope of a hill, caught the water flowing down from the top of the ridge and filled up quickly, and the flow of water down the communication trenches was fast enough to carry men off their feet. The men could only scramble hastily out of their swamped trenches and, wet to the skin and bitterly cold, seek what cover the parados afforded, under heavy rifle fire; for the Turks, being higher up the slopes, were better off. With evening the sleet fell more thickly, the mud froze, and before long a regular procession of frost-bitten men was limping back to the ambulances. Some who fell by the way were found later on frozen to death, and many died in the poor shelter which the ambulances could offer. It was a night of horror, and morning brought no improvement. If anything it grew colder, the sleet

---

[1] He subsequently was awarded the M.C. for his generally excellent work.
[2] Major Kitchin, promoted to that rank on November 7th, when Major Beresford was posted as Lieutenant Colonel, succeeded him as Adjutant. Lieutenant Austin took over command of C Company.

had given place to driving snow, the wind, increasing in strength and coldness, seemed to pierce right through clothes and bodies. The water had gone down, leaving the trenches several feet deep in mud, in which men fished for weapons, food and equipment. The men rose to the occasion splendidly, the recovered rifles were promptly cleaned and rendered serviceable again, the gaps in the parapet were repaired; somehow or other the company cooks produced hot tea,[1] firewood in plenty was available, and enough was collected to light fires and get a little warmth, but the men's endurance was heavily taxed. Luckily the Turks were in scarcely better plight. Though their trenches had not been so badly flooded they were worse off for clothing and food than our men—several half-starved and scantily clad deserters had come over of late—and the cold took its toll among them. Almost by mutual consent both sides abstained from seeking to profit by the other's helplessness, yet things got no better that day or the next. The gale continued, the snow still fell, and many who had stuck it out till now were forced to go to hospital. There the R.A.M.C. toiled unceasingly, but over 200 men died, something like 10,000 had to be evacuated, and their awful experience left many others greatly weakened.

The 4th, who were relieved from the front line on the evening of November 28th, managed to obtain some shelter in the reserve trenches, roofing their line over with corrugated iron, while an issue of rum worked wonders. Still, though they had fared better than most battalions, their trenches having been fairly high up the slope, nearly 150 men had to be struck off the strength, bringing the battalion down to 15 officers and 231 men on December 1st. A draft from home of 3 officers and 110 men under Captain Cahusac, and the arrival of Lieutenant Buchanan with 72 recovered sick and wounded from Mudros, all before December 7th, were therefore exceedingly welcome as the evacuation of Anzac and Suvla had been decided upon and the battalion was to be the last to leave the trenches of the 40th Brigade. This selection was an undoubted compliment, as General Lewin[2] explained to the battalion, but the 4th might well find itself fighting a rear-guard action almost single-handed should the Turks discover what was happening and attack.

That the evacuation would escape their notice was too much to hope for, careful as were the measures for concealing from them its steady progress. Gradually supplies, carts, kits, surplus stores of all kinds, reserve ammunition and everything else that

---

[1] The H.Q. cookhouse was flooded but the cook nevertheless contrived to produce a hot dinner.

[2] He had recently succeeded General Travers, who had been invalided, as Brigadier.

could be salved were conveyed to the beach and re-embarked in night. A programme was carefully worked out by the Staff, in accordance with which the battalion relieved the Wiltshire at the firing-line on December 15th. The morning of the 19th found it and the Cheshire alone in the brigade's trenches,[1] the other two battalions having already embarked. Everything possible was done to make things appear quite normal, fires were lit in the usual places, men were posted up and down the lines as though the usual sentries were on duty and fired occasional shots. Our sniping had been purposely much diminished of late so that the Turks might get accustomed to our comparative silence.

Slowly the day wore on, being spent in such things as slitting the sandbags, so as to make them useless to the Turks, who were known to need them. Soon after dusk the Cheshire withdrew, leaving the S.W.B. alone in the front trenches. Still the Turks remained quiescent: after indulging in a brief but violent bombardment of Lala Baba earlier in the day, they had relapsed into inactivity. Apparently they had interpreted the extra activity in the harbour, the coming and going of more ships, as implying the landing of more troops for a fresh offensive: certainly the 4th's patrols had found them very active in digging new trenches and putting up more wire, as though expecting an attack. The first portion of the battalion to move was the machine-gun section, which started for the beach at 7 p.m., followed an hour later by Colonel Beresford and 250 men. Three hours later 150 more under Major Kitchin stole away, leaving Captain Cahusac with 6 officers and 70 picked men to patrol the otherwise empty trenches for another two hours and a half before they in turn might retire.

These last hours seemed interminable. The Turkish snipers were fairly active and our men made just enough reply not to make things seem unusual. Even after the rear party had gone rifles, skilfully fitted with a mechanical device to fire without a man to pull the trigger, replied occasionally, and to the last the Turks remained unobservant.

At last the time came for Captain Cahusac's party to start their three-mile tramp to the beach. The road to be followed had been carefully marked out with white flour and there was little chance of missing it. The leading party had manned the Lala Baba defences covering the place of embarkation, and when the rear-guard arrived the whole battalion was taken off on lighters and transferred to transports for conveyance to Imbros. It was 3 a.m. (December 20th) when the last of the 4th S.W.B.

[1] The 40th Brigade was holding the middle of the Division's line, directly opposite Scimitar Hill and just South of Sulajik Farm.

steamed out of Suvla Bay. The evacuation, which competent authorities had declared could only be accomplished at the cost of at least 40 per cent of those engaged, had been achieved virtually without a casualty. Its success was a great tribute to the skill with which the Staff had foreseen and worked out every detail, it was also largely due to the steadiness and good discipline of the troops, but it was greatly facilitated by the underground character of modern warfare. Modern weapons have driven the combatants underground in the effort to avoid casualties by concealment. Opponents who are normally invisible to each other can easily part company without its being perceived.

Arriving at Imbros about 8 a.m. the 4th landed and made their way to a camp where units could be sorted out, as the process of embarkation had involved much mixing up. Here they had hoped to get a good meal, but the Staff, apparently expecting heavy casualties in the rear-guards, had only provided rations for 400 men, whereas 1500 were clamouring for them. It was 10 a.m. before even Captain Mellsopp's energy and command of language could provide breakfasts, and barely were they finished before the 4th was ordered back to the landing stage and embarked along with three other battalions on an ex-North German Lloyd liner for conveyance to Mudros.

Their transport sailed at 7 a.m. next day (December 21st) along with another transport and escorted by two battleships and three destroyers. They had hardly started before so bad a storm sprang up that the destroyers were forced back to harbour, the battleships steamed on ahead, the other troopship altered course, and the battalion's transport pursued its way alone and unescorted. It was an unpleasant voyage, but luckily the very vileness of the weather lessened the chances of encountering a submarine, and by 1 p.m. the transport was safe in Mudros harbour, and next day the 4th disembarked and rejoined their brigade in a camp at Porteanos, three miles from the shore.

When the 2nd Battalion had gone back to the Eski line on January 2nd, evacuation was obviously imminent: it had received orders to send all officers' kits down to the beach, along with all gum-boots, mackintosh capes and packs, and nearly 100 sick and weakly men had been shipped off to Mudros. The succeeding days saw it busy in improving the tracks and communication trenches leading to the beaches and getting off such surplus ammunition and stores as could be shipped. Among other things the Orderly Room Clerk was sent down to the beach to collect all valuable documents out of the boxes so as to take them off the Peninsula on his person, while a seven days' reserve of rations which had been accumulated was built into a parados on the fire-step of the Eski line, which was to be held in case a rearguard action proved necessary to cover the re-embarkation.

The final stage for the 2nd S.W.B. came at 5 p.m. on January 8th. The battalion had already been divided into five parties of 100 each, the commanders being provided with slips which were to be handed in at the rendezvous, forming-up places and piers, so as to check the numbers leaving and ensure no one being left behind. Reaching the brigade rendezvous at 6 p.m., the battalion moved on to the forming-up place, and after a longish delay there marched down to the piers in single file. "Four shells came over from Asia," writes the battalion diary, "and struck very near the column but hurt nobody. We embarked on motor lighters, about 200 on each, and after inquiring at every ship in the harbour eventually got on board the *Prince Abbas*. The wind was rising as we embarked."

Thus ended for the 2nd Battalion the long drawn out Gallipoli campaign. Twenty-seven officers and 1008 rank and file had sailed for Gallipoli: 16 officers and 485 men embarked on the *Prince Abbas*, and in the meantime its drafts had amounted to 52 officers and 1028 men.[1] Its losses in battle and from disease had therefore been more than 150 per cent of its original strength, and over 200 per cent in officers, even allowing for those taken away for Staff appointments. Most of the sick and many of the wounded were eventually to return to duty, but 20 of its officers, including 8 present at the landing, had been killed.

The 4th Battalion also had been engaged in the evacuation of Cape Helles, as if one such experience had not been quite enough for anybody. On December 29th the 39th and 40th Brigades were ordered from Lemnos to the Peninsula, to relieve the Forty-Second Division. This brought the 4th S.W.B. back to the trenches[2] East of Gully Ravine in which it had undergone its "baptism of fire" five months earlier. It was very different now from the 4th S.W.B. of July, but Major Kitchin, who was in command[3] as Colonel Beresford had been invalided on the 28th, had a fair sprinkling of the "originals" under him, several officers and many men having rejoined on recovery from wounds or illness, including three former subalterns now Captains and in command of companies, Austin (C), Buchanan (B) and Farrow (D). In these trenches the 4th were, as already

[1] This excludes officers, but not men, returning from hospital: it seems likely also that the battalion diary has not noted all new arrivals of officers, two, at least, are mentioned as casualties whose reporting for duty is not recorded.
[2] It landed at "V" Beach about 8 p.m. and took over trenches next morning (December 30th).
[3] Captain Cahusac took over the Adjutant's duties.

mentioned, next door to their 2nd Battalion, who provided them with lunch, the more welcome because there had been no food on the steamer which had brought the 4th from Mudros, so it was their first meal since breakfast the previous day. This

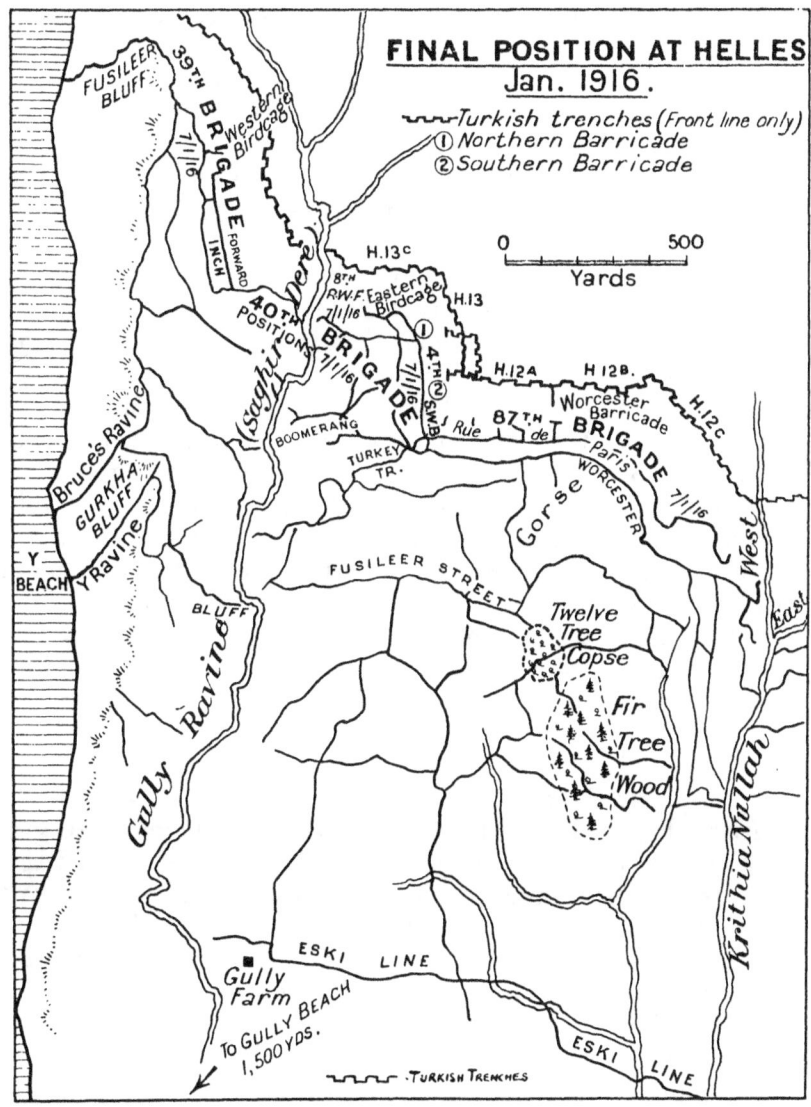

meeting was remembered afterwards as the only occasion during the war on which the 4th met another battalion of the TWENTY-FOURTH.

The 4th were much closer to the Turks here than at Suvla. Nowhere was the enemy's line more than 120 yards away, and at the well-known Northern and Southern Barricades, which B

Company was holding, the bombing posts were only 20 yards apart. This close proximity naturally increased the difficulty of concealing the evacuation, especially as after Suvla the Turks were bound to be on the alert. This was evident from the persistence with which they shelled the communication trenches every night, while on that of January 3rd the battalion by ceasing fire after 11 p.m. decoyed a strong Turkish patrol into leaving its trench to ascertain whether the British had gone. They, or rather the few who managed to regain their line, were soon enlightened. Meanwhile preparations for the evacuation were in progress, the battalion's particular task being the strengthening of an intermediate line of resistance between the front trenches and the Eski line.

Early on the 7th orders came round to be ready for evacuation on the following day, and about midday the Brigadier was discussing details with his battalion commanders and their adjutants when suddenly a violent bombardment opened. Heavy shells came pelting down on the Thirteenth Division's front line and communication trenches; one enormous 17-inch howitzer shell burst in the battalion's reserve trench, normally held by A Company, which fortunately was at the moment filing down Gully Ravine, taking its packs to the beach. A second landed in a sap in front of C's line, and then, to the battalion's great satisfaction, a third found its " spiritual home " in the Turkish front line, after which the howitzer left the 4th S.W.B. alone. For nearly four hours the bombardment raged, the incessant bursting of H.E. shell filling the air with dust, debris and smoke. Great damage was done, some communication trenches being rendered almost impassable, but the men behaved splendidly. Sergeant Myles and his picked bombers plied the Turks effectively from the Southern Barricade, and the machine gunners, though their guns were more than once dislodged, replaced them at once and kept them trained in readiness.[1] At last about 5 p.m. the bombardment stopped, shouts were heard in the Turkish trenches, bayonets showed and it looked as if they were coming. But only a few men appeared over the parapet, to be promptly shot down, and before long the shouting died away. The Turks were clearly " not for it "; only on the 39th Brigade's front at Fusilier Bluff could they be induced to attack, and there they were decisively repulsed. Apparently the Staff had intended to drive the invaders into the sea, but their failure seems to have greatly discouraged them and contributed to the ease with which the evacuation was eventually accomplished.

Considering the vehemence of the bombardment the 4th

[1] The C.O. had brought A Company up in close support of the front line in readiness for the expected attack.

had escaped lightly with only 30 casualties. Lieutenant Williams, a plucky young officer who, though wounded early on, had insisted, despite the M.O.'s orders, on returning to the firing-line, was killed with 9 men, Lieutenant McMullen and 20 men being wounded. However, the bombardment had provided enough work in repairing defences and clearing communication trenches to keep the battalion warm on a bitterly cold night, and the hour for the evacuation to start found the road to the beach cleared. The first move was the departure of the Quartermaster and an advanced party of 20 men. At 4.55 p.m. Captain Cahusac took 175 officers and men off to W Beach, followed three hours later by Battalion Headquarters and 77 men from the intermediate line. Before this a sharp half-hour's bombardment, the Turks' only interference with the proceedings, had cost the battalion its last casualties at Gallipoli, 1 killed and 3 wounded, the latter including the M.O., Lieutenant Hammond, who had done splendid work all through his five months with the battalion and especially in the previous day's bombardment. A forlorn hope of 80 men under Lieutenants B. I. Jones, Durand, Rogers and E. G. Jones was now left in the firing-line; this party, with another from the 8th R.W.F. on its left, was to remain in position till 11.45 p.m. The rest of the battalion meanwhile had scrambled down Gully Ravine to Gully Beach, whence it proceeded round the foot of the cliffs, past X Beach to W, passing *en route* many abandoned limbers and transport carts. During the whole march, perhaps six miles in all, there had been no shelling from the Turks and only occasional bursts of rifle or machine-gun fire. At W Beach the 4th embarked on a motor lighter, which carried it to the old battleship *Mars*, one empty lighter being rammed *en route* and collision with another narrowly escaped. It was pitch dark, the sea was getting up, and everybody was glad to be off the lighters, always clumsy vessels and particularly so in a rough sea when crowded with troops.

The little rear-guard of the 40th Brigade, after remaining at its post till the appointed hour, had crept silently away down Gully Ravine, but on reaching Gully Beach, where it should have embarked, found the sea too rough, so had to push on to "W." It was nearly 4 a.m. before it arrived, and hardly anyone was left on the beach save the parties detailed to set fire to the vast dumps of stores and ammunition. However, the rear-guard was quickly embarked, and as its lighter stood out to sea flames rose up at different points as dump after dump took fire, followed by tremendous explosions and the sound as of a universal fusilade as the fire reached the great small-arms ammunition dump. Then at last the Turk realized that he had been tricked again and the

THE HISTORY OF THE SOUTH WALES BORDERERS

Gallipoli tragedy ended with a touch of farce, a vigorous Turkish bombardment which merely made more complete the destruction of the stores abandoned to them. As at Suvla, the evacuation had been accomplished practically without a casualty, and, as at Suvla, the 4th S.W.B. had been in at the very end. From first to last in the Gallipoli venture there were few phases in which the TWENTY-FOURTH had not shared.[1]

[1] Those mentioned for their services at Gallipoli in the Dispatches published after the evacuation included, of the 2nd Battalion, Major Williams, Captains Greenway, Walker, Somerville and Ffrench, Second Lieutenant Ballantine, Regimental Sergeant Major Westlake, Company Quartermaster Sergeant Nothill, Sergeants Cook, Jackson and White, Privates Cable, Crisp, McCarthy, W. C. Millward, W. J. Morgan, Porter and Rice. Of the 4th, those mentioned were Colonel Beresford, Majors Yates and Kitchin, Captains Mundy, Buchanan and Farrow, Lieutenant Caldwell, Second Lieutenants J. Williams and Durand, Company Sergeant Major Murray, Sergeant Myles, Corporals Barratt and O'Grady, Lance Corporals Wardle and Simmons, Privates W. Morgan and Beary.

CHAPTER XIII

MESOPOTAMIA: 1916

THE natural sequel to the successful evacuation of Cape Helles was the speedy transfer of the troops from Imbros and Lemnos to Egypt, both in order to protect that country against the expected Turkish invasion and to enable the weary M.E.F. to rest and be reorganized before it could be seen in what theatre of war its services would next be required. For this, Egypt offered good facilities, besides being full of convalescent sick and wounded of the M.E.F., together with much of the transport belonging to its units. Neither 2nd or 4th S.W.B. therefore tarried long at Mudros: the 2nd indeed never landed but were promptly transferred (January 9th) to the transport *Scotian*, which sailed for Alexandria two days later. On landing the battalion entrained immediately for Suez, where the Twenty-Ninth Division was to encamp. The 4th saw more of Mudros, spending a fortnight in camp at Portiano before embarking. On January 26th, however, it also left for Egypt, and four days later disembarked at Port Said, the Thirteenth Division's concentration area.

Both battalions were terribly weak, though the 4th, only 320 strong on quitting the Peninsula, had received a draft of 45 men under Lieutenant Baker on January 17th; both, however, were rejoined by several convalescents and details, such as some 40 of the 2nd Battalion who had been permanently employed on beach duties at "W" since November. Major Williams had left the 2nd at Mudros for a Staff appointment in the Fifty-Second Division and Captain G. T. Raikes, who had till then been detained with the Egyptian Army, had assumed command. Several new officers turned up for both battalions, which settled down to the urgently needed refit. Training, too, could be seriously taken in hand; it had been impossible to impart systematic instruction to drafts on the Peninsula or even in the rare periods of rest on the islands, so both battalions had leeway to make up. The Thirteenth Division also was allotted to the Northern sector of the Canal Defences, now becoming an extensive and elaborate series of works. The 4th S.W.B., however, had no opportunity of displaying their skill in trench construction in the land of the Pharaohs, for their brigade was in reserve at first and a more distant area soon required the Division's services. Within a week of its arrival in Egypt the Thirteenth was under orders for Mespotamia. At such short notice were the new orders issued that many officers had actually sailed for England on leave on February 1st, among them from the 4th S.W.B. the C.O. and Quartermaster—the only officers who had landed with the battalion in July and remained with it throughout the campaign

—as well as Captains Austin and Farrow. Captain Cahusac was left in command, but before the 4th sailed Captain Grey arrived and took over.

The emergency which necessitated this hurried transfer was indeed serious. Operations in Mesopotamia had been begun with restricted objects: the all-important oil pipe-line had to be secured and the Turks prevented from making the region the base from which trouble might be fomented on the North-West frontier of India. Gradually these objects had been extended, the expedition had by degrees proceeded further inland, till September, 1915, had seen the whole of the Basra vilayet secured by the capture of Kut al Amara, 250 miles from the sea. To that point the advance can be substantially justified on military grounds; but only political motives alone can account for the further advance of that autumn upon Baghdad. Undertaken in inadequate force it had resulted in Townshend's "Pyrrhic victory" of Ctesiphon, his enforced retreat to and investment in Kut. His urgent need of relief had in turn necessitated the piecemeal dispatch upstream of the Indian Army Corps as its units arrived from France, regardless of their proper organization. The efforts of what was essentially a "scratch" force, without adequate artillery or ammunition, had, after partial and costly successes at Shaikh Saad (January 6th to 8th) and the Wadi (January 13th to 14th), been checked at El Hanna (January 21st); and, the relieving column being completely held up, it had proved necessary to find substantial reinforcements. By this time the fears for Egypt were beginning to subside. There were no signs of that advance in force from Syria so widely anticipated as the inevitable sequel to the British acknowledgment of failure at the Dardanelles. If as yet no one could appreciate the extent to which the defence of the Dardanelles had drained Turkish resources and incapacitated Turkey for any serious offensive, Egypt was clearly amply ensured and could well spare one Division for the greater emergency in Mesopotamia.

The Thirteenth Division's selection for dispatch to the relief of Kut was, like its employment in the evacuation of Cape Helles, no small proof of the reputation it had already established, as well as a tribute to its commander, General Maude. It was, however, hard on it to be hurried off to new exertions while still so much below establishment and without time to assimilate its drafts. The 4th S.W.B. were particularly unlucky as regards drafts; though quite well off for officers, the battalion started for Mesopotamia barely 400 strong. The other battalions in the Division averaged well over 800.

Definite orders for the Division's move were issued on February 7th and lively times followed: there was much to do to equip the troops for Mesopotamia and it was expedient that they should start without delay. The 4th S.W.B. embarked at Suez on February 15th, and after a warm but uneventful voyage, found themselves steaming up the Shatt-el-Arab on March 4th. Reaching Basra that day they went into camp beside the Tigris at Magil, three miles above Basra. On March 9th, Colonel Kitchin, whose homeward journey had been abruptly interrupted at Marseilles, rejoined, and next day came orders to proceed upstream to Sheikh Saad, where the Division was concentrating. The battalion had a bad time over its embarkation; after carrying all its stores down to the river bank it was suddenly ordered to embark half a mile lower down, and in torrential rain had to man-handle thither its stores and luggage, some hundreds of S.A.A. boxes and a quantity of firewood, only to find that its embarkation had been postponed. Eventually at 9 a.m. on March 12th a river steamer, P 19, arrived with two barges lashed on either side, and the battalion was soon aboard. The voyage was not enjoyable; the stream ran strong, making navigation difficult and progress slow, while the barges provided no shelter from sun or rain and the men got drenched through by a violent squall soon after starting. They were, moreover, extremely cramped for space, and facilities for cooking were very limited, indeed meals had to be prepared in instalments and the unfortunate cooks were on duty nearly all day. A short halt at Amara on the 14th was welcomed as a chance of stretching legs, and at 9 p.m. next day Sheikh Saad was reached. Here the battalion spent the next fortnight, partly in practising attacks on a trench system, but more often finding working parties to strengthen the "bunds" along the river bank, work which the steady rise of the Tigris rendered imperative.

Conditions at Sheikh Saad might have been worse, the men were in bell-tents, the officers in the "40-pound E.P." pattern, but the shortage of river transport, the millstone round the neck of the relieving force, meant that nothing beyond bare necessities of life was available, no "comforts" or extra rations being obtainable. On March 24th, Captains Austin and Farrow rejoined, and two days later came a sign of an approaching move, battalion commanders being sent up to Orah to reconnoitre the trenches to be assaulted. These lay across the narrow stretch of land between the Tigris and the broad Suwaikiya Marsh, which latter effectually precluded any turning or outflanking movement, even if the "Tigris Corps," as the relieving force was known, had not been tied down to the neighbourhood of the river by its deficiency in transport. Well protected on both flanks and only approachable over ground virtually devoid of cover, these trenches, five successive lines covering a depth of

2500 yards, presented a formidable obstacle, while the artillery and ammunition at the disposal of the Tigris Corps were none too abundant. On the right bank, however, the British had already pushed forward to Thorny Nullah some distance upstream of the Hanna trenches, and could therefore bring enfilade and reverse fire to bear on the position; but the Turks were well dug in and with their proverbial tenacity in defence were holding on regardless of this disadvantage.

The new attempt to relieve Kut was to begin with an assault on the Hanna lines by the Thirteenth Division, which therefore began moving up on the evening of March 31st in relief of the Seventh Indian (Meerut) Division, sadly reduced in the earlier fighting. Hardly had the S.W.B. quitted their camp before a terrific thunderstorm started, with drenching rain. The transport mules bolted in all directions, disposing of their loads, and when, after an hour, the rain eased off the ground was covered with water which in the darkness completely concealed the many deep ditches to be crossed. Men and mules went floundering headlong into them, and even when the transport officer and his men had been left behind to bring the mules in by daylight, conditions were so bad that the battalion took over four hours to cover the last three miles. In all the nine miles' march took from 10.30 p.m. to 6 a.m. and the men, who arrived exhausted, hungry and soaked to the skin, greatly appreciated the hot meal which the 38th Brigade, who were already encamped, had kindly prepared. Another violent storm that evening postponed the relief till the night of April 2nd/3rd, when after another dark and difficult march it was at last accomplished, Colonel Kitchin having successfully guided the battalion into the proper communication trench, after steadfastly resisting the advice of a guide who clearly had lost his way.

The 4th spent two very uncomfortable days in these trenches, waiting for the ground to dry. The men had no blankets, only their waterproof sheets: no firewood was available for cooking, drinking water could only be drawn at one point on which all the Turkish guns seemed trained, and the recent downpours had left the trenches terribly muddy. However, by April 4th the ground was fairly dry, and after dark the battalion crept out into the last of three rows of assembly trenches which the Meerut Division had dug in front of their main line. The attack was being delivered by all three brigades abreast, each with one battalion in front, the others following in succession. The 40th Brigade was on the left, next the river, and the S.W.B.[1] formed its third wave.

[1] Owing to the battalion's weakness, D Company of the 5th Wiltshire, who were over 1000 strong, was attached to it to equalize matters.

THE HANNA LINES TAKEN

"Zero" was at 4.55 a.m., nearly an hour before sunrise, and the long wait in trenches, so crowded that men could hardly lie down, was tedious and uncomfortable. It was a relief to climb out and lie down on the parapet five minutes before the attack started. Punctually at 4.55 a.m. the Wiltshire dashed forward and, though greeted with a brisk rifle and machine-gun fire, quickly mastered the front line. There they halted, and the R.W.F., passing through, carried the second line almost unopposed. As previously arranged our guns had now concentrated their fire on the third line, the objective of the S.W.B., some of whom could not be restrained but, pushing forward too soon, were caught by our own shells. At 5.15 a.m. the guns lifted and the 4th dashed forward to find their objective unoccupied. It was obvious now that the Turks had retired, leaving only a rear-guard to hold their front line, so, after patrols had ascertained that the remaining two lines of trenches had also been vacated, the 40th Brigade was ordered to push forward towards the next Turkish position. This was at Fallahiya some distance upstream and about level with Thorny Nullah. Accordingly, with the 4th S.W.B. and the Cheshire leading, the brigade started off about 7.30 a.m. The ground was devoid of cover, and before long the advance came under fire. The battalions extended and pushed on, but as they neared the position the fire grew heavier, especially from machine guns, and ground could only be gained by short rushes. The men behaved splendidly, persevering in face of a heavy and effective fire, though they were quite without artillery support, for the guns had been delayed in crossing the Hanna trenches. The battalion's machine guns took advantage of a communication trench to work forward to a position from which they could reply effectively, but about 800 yards from the Turkish lines the advance was definitely held up and the men dug in as best they could. During one of these rushes Captain Hemingway fell, dangerously wounded, and one of his men, going to his help, was hit and disabled. Captain Buchanan thereupon dashed out from behind cover and not only carried Hemingway in despite a heavy fire but, going out again, brought the private in also, for which gallantry he was subsequently awarded the Victoria Cross.

It had been intended that the Thirteenth Division should assault the Falahiya position at 12.30 p.m., but by General Gorringe's[1] orders the attack was postponed till the evening, when adequate artillery support would be available. Till then the 40th Brigade had to hang on, taking advantage of any targets it might get and pushing forward occasional patrols to keep touch with the

---

[1] He was now G.O.C. Tigris Corps.

enemy. At 7.15 p.m. the bombardment opened and 30 minutes later the 38th and 39th Brigades, passing through the 40th, stormed the position in fine style. As soon as possible after this the Meerut Division came forward and relieved the Thirteenth, preparatory to assaulting the next position, that at Sannaiyat, before dawn. Unluckily its advance was delayed by various difficulties and it was practically daylight before the assault could be delivered. It encountered a tremendous volume of fire and, though gallantly pressed, was brought to a standstill 500 yards from the trenches. Here under cover of a brisk artillery fire the troops dug in, preparing for another effort that night in which the 40th Brigade was to co-operate.

The 4th S.W.B. had barely got back to a bivouac,[1] where they found their indefatigable Quartermaster awaiting them with hot tea and rations, before they were ordered forward again. Actually a strong N.W. wind drove the waters of the Suwaikiya Marsh into the right trenches of the Meerut Division and caused the orders for the attack to be cancelled, and the 4th therefore remained in readiness in the Fallahiya trenches.

General Townshend's situation was now so desperate that there was no time to lose, so on April 7th the Meerut Division again advanced and, after heavy casualties, established a line decidedly nearer to the enemy's position while a further advance under cover of night (April 7th/8th) brought the British within possible assaulting distance. The assault was to be delivered by the Thirteenth Division, which accordingly took over the front trenches after dark on April 8th, with the 38th and 40th Brigades in front line and the 39th in support. Each assaulting brigade put all four battalions into line, drawn up in four waves 50 yards apart, each company having a platoon in each line. "Platoons" in the 4th meant barely ten rifles, only just over 170 men, much less than a company at war-establishment, taking part in the assault. The 4th were the second battalion from the left of their brigade, having the R.W.F. on their right and the Wiltshire on their left.

The troops moved off about 7 p.m. to get into position and after a march of two and a half miles lined up about 600 yards from the Turkish trenches. It was bitterly cold, the men were in khaki-drill and had no greatcoats, while the meat ration had not been issued in time to be eaten before the 4th moved off. Most men slept during the long wait that preceded the attack—the 4th put it as six hours—but when roused for the assault

---

[1] Three officers (Captain Hemingway and Lieutenants Bourne and Field) had been killed and seven (Captain Buchanan and Second Lieutenants Barry, Durand, Everett, Gilbee, Ford and T. G. Jones) wounded, with 158 casualties among the men, nearly 50 per cent of those in action.

THE ASSAULT ON SANNAIYAT

everyone was stiff with cold, many indeed being quite benumbed and confused. Losses in officers and N.C.O.'s in the previous attack had been heavy, and the recently joined drafts mostly lacked experience and training. But the men started off well and had covered nearly 400 yards before flares went up in the Turkish lines, followed quickly by a burst of rifle and machine-gun fire. Exactly what happened is uncertain except that the first line went straight on, its survivors actually entering the trenches. The second line, however, seems to have faltered and become mixed up with the third and fourth waves, which had pressed on. At the same time something started a right incline.[1] Direction was lost and in the din and darkness it was hard to make orders heard or to recover the line of advance. The net result was inextricable confusion and disorder: some men fell back on top of the 39th Brigade advancing in support, and despite all the officers' efforts the whole attack broke down completely. Then, as the light improved, the Turkish fire, at first too high, became more deadly and the attackers recoiled slowly to about 400 yards from the Turkish line, where they halted and endeavoured to reorganize. Meanwhile the first line, supported in places by detachments from the other waves, had actually driven the Turks back from their front line. Only prompt support was lacking to the attainment of success—the Turkish commander, Halil Pasha, admitted as much to General Townshend; but without support the handful which had gained the Turkish front line was forced out after a gallant resistance, its survivors retiring to where the rallied rear waves were digging in.

The night attack on Sannaiyat was a distressing experience for the Thirteenth Division: the reasons of its failure are clear enough, and the men were soon to show that the confusion was due mainly to their fatigue and benumbed condition. To the 4th S.W.B. the repulse had meant reduction to a mere handful. More than half those in action were casualties, and among the killed were Captains Austin and Farrow, subalterns of 1914, who had shown themselves splendid leaders and were badly missed. Lieutenants Morgan-Owen and Macaulay were also killed, Captain Cahusac, the Adjutant, was badly wounded, as were also Lieutenant Caldwell and Second Lieutenants Usher and T. L. R. Jones.[2] Lieutenant Caldwell, whose platoon was in the first wave, was hit in the head on the Turkish parapet.

---

[1] According to one account the Wiltshire struck a deep bog and were driven off their line, which caused them to crowd in among the 4th S.W.B., but it seems also that the Turks at first only disclosed their position on their extreme left and that the whole of the attack tended to converge towards this flank.

[2] Forty-two men were killed and missing and 43 wounded.

Recovering consciousness later on he crawled back to a ditch, but fainted again, to come to and find Turks and Arabs stripping the dead and killing the wounded. To escape murder he feigned death and soon afterwards British machine guns opened fire and sent the plunderers scuttling back to their trenches. Profiting by this Lieutenant Caldwell set out to crawl back to our lines, 300 yards away, and managed after five hours' toil to reach safety, thanks to the cover of the long grass and to our machine guns which kept the plundering Arabs at bay. The stretcher-bearers did splendid work, bringing in many wounded; but the outstanding incident was the gallantry of Private Fynn of C Company, who crept out in broad daylight to two men who were lying within 300 yards of the Turkish line, bandaged their wounds and brought one of them in.[1]

After dark (April 9th) the 38th and 39th Brigades were withdrawn to reserve, the 40th being left with some of the Meerut Division and the Thirteenth's Pioneers and R.E., to consolidate the line on which the attackers had rallied. A heavy rain-storm did not make matters better and many men were without food, but they hung on, toiled away at the trenches and rescued more wounded. Next evening the remnant of the 4th S.W.B. were at last relieved, to stagger back in pelting rain to "a lake which was to be our camping ground for the night," as one account puts it. Luckily the Quartermaster and his cooks had risen to the occasion again and had a hot meal ready, cooked before the storm broke.

After its crippling losses the 4th might well have expected to be out of action for some time, till drafts could arrive. Actually it got a few days' repose, during which Major Birch, Lieutenant Everett and Second Lieutenant Keighley rejoined. It was so weak, however, that when on the 17th the urgency of the situation necessitated its return to the firing line, it was combined with the 5th Wiltshire, who had also suffered severely, as a composite battalion commanded by Colonel Kitchin. A fresh effort on the right bank had now been decided upon, and on April 17th the Third Indian (Lahore) Division attacked and took the Bait Aiesa trenches, five miles upstream of the Falahiya lines. The 40th Brigade had meanwhile crossed the river by a pontoon bridge below Abu Rumman and had spent the day working on the bunds, as the river was rising still and the spreading inundations were reducing the area over which it was possible to manœuvre, besides making the supplying of the troops extremely difficult. The success of the attack led to orders being issued for the Thirteenth Division to take over the captured positions after dark to allow of the Lahore Division

[1] For this he received the V.C., the second awarded to the battalion.

concentrating for a fresh advance; and the 40th Brigade, detailed as Divisional Reserve, was to assemble a mile East of two sandhills known as the Twin Pimples. However, the relief had hardly been begun when the Turks started counter-attacking in considerable force.[1] Their attack, delivered with great vigour against the right centre of the new British line, N.W. of Twin Pimples, broke through the 9th Brigade's front line and was with difficulty stopped by the supports. The Turks also attacked the 7th and 8th Brigades, to right and left respectively of the breach, and pressed them both hard. Heavy fighting went on most of the night, and the 4th were soon involved. As they neared the brigade rendezvous it was obvious that a serious struggle was in progress, and

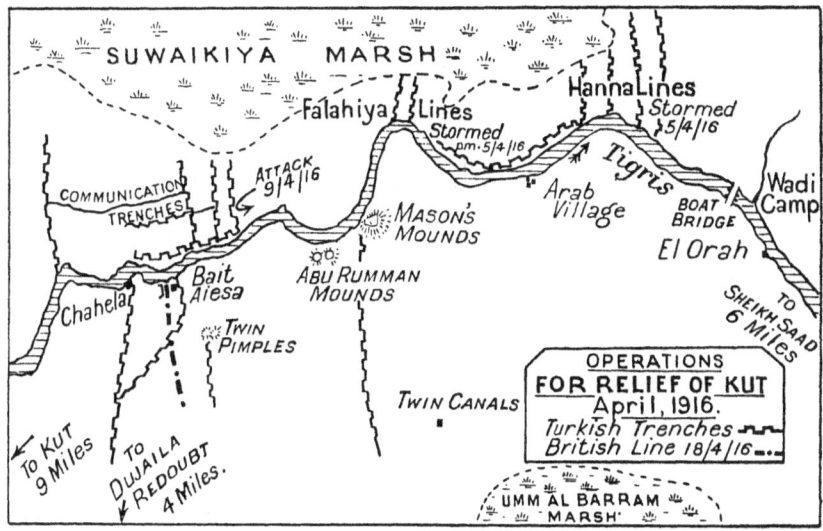

before long the battalion came under long-range fire, probably "overs" from the enemy's firing line. However, most of the men found shelter in an old trench and the remainder dug in behind, not without some casualties, among them Major Birch, who was mortally wounded about midnight. Shortly afterwards an urgent message arrived for the battalion to assist the 8th Brigade, holding from Twin Pimples Southward and reported to be very hard pressed. The battalion accordingly started off with only an approximate compass bearing to guide it and little definite information. It was pitch dark, but for flashes of light from rifles and machine guns, and the first incident of the advance was that the men had to wade through waist-deep water for over 400 yards: then the going improved and the pace quickened. The battalion had been told that the firing line

[1] They were said to have put in a picked Division which had not been in action since the Dardanelles.

was about 1500 yards ahead, but it had covered 2000 without finding it and was expecting to run on top of the Turks when it suddenly came upon a trench held by a mixture of Highland Light Infantry and 47th Sikhs, a little South of Twin Pimples. As this trench was well manned and the situation seemed satisfactory, Colonel Kitchin went off to find the nearest Brigade Headquarters and get definite orders, two companies of the battalion ultimately replacing the H.L.I. and assisting the 8th Brigade to withstand the vigorous pressure which the Turks maintained till after 5 a.m. The 8th more than held its own, and daylight saw the Turks in full retreat, suffering heavily from British rifles, machine guns and artillery. The battalion was among those specially commanded in General Gorringe's Order of the Day for its steadiness, and it had the satisfaction of assisting to secure over 130 prisoners who failed to retire with the rest of the Turks.

However, heavily as the Turkish counter-attack had been punished, it had for the moment stopped the British advance on the right bank and made it necessary to relieve the Lahore Division. The Thirteenth therefore now took over from the river bank to about 1000 yards South of Twin Pimples, the 40th Brigade holding the Southern half with the joint S.W.B. and Wilts battalion on its right. Desultory fighting on this front continued for several days, little ground being gained, as the Turks by flooding the country prevented any attack in force on the Chahela lines, their next position upstream. In one attempted advance by the 39th Brigade the battalion's machine guns, well handled by Lieutenant Stockwood, fired most effectively upon Turkish reinforcements advancing on their right. Lieutenant Keighley too did good work patrolling, and on the night of April 21st/22nd the battalion advanced about 500 yards and dug a line of picquet redoubts. During the proceedings a Turkish patrol ran into the covering party and evidently discovered what was afoot, for a heavy fire was at once opened from rifles and machine guns. Fortunately it was aimed very high, and the battalion, sticking to its work, had the satisfaction of completing it before morning with only 8 casualties.

By this time the situation was desperate. General Townshend's garrison was at its last gasp and a final assault on Sannaiyat by the Meerut Division (April 23rd),[1] though gallantly pressed, ended in failure ; the river steamer *Julnar* tried to run through to Kut with provisions, but without success, and April 28th brought the end. Kut surrendered and the relieving force

---

[1] The machine guns of the 40th Brigade, collected under Captain Marr of the S.W.B., caused terrible havoc among the Turkish reserves and reinforcements by their fire from across the river.

had to stand by impotently while the relics of the garrison were marched off into a cruel captivity which for the majority of the exhausted and enfeebled defenders meant death.

The end of the struggle found the Tigris Corps in a sorry plight. Apart from its disappointment, its exertions and its losses, it had had great hardships to endure, constant fatigues, shortage of rations and such a scarcity of safe drinking water that the men suffered acutely from thirst and some who drank from the ditches or flooded areas developed cholera. The flies rivalled those at Gallipoli, and the hopelessly overtaxed river transport could neither cope with keeping those still effective supplied nor with evacuating the sick and wounded. Few units were within 50 per cent of their establishment and most consisted mainly of inexperienced drafts with few trained officers. But the Turk was apparently no better off and certainly quite incapable of following up his defensive success by an offensive. The fall of Kut therefore began a cessation of active operations which was to last till December. Just at first, however, great exertions were required of the men in consolidating a defensive position, until it was realized that a Turkish offensive was most improbable, and that there was no need to wear the men out with constant digging, which was telling on their health and swelling the sick rate.

Shortly before Kut fell two drafts had arrived for the 4th, one of 250 men under Lieutenants Purves and Napier[1] and Second Lieutenant C. Evans joined on April 22nd, the other, 109 strong, under Second Lieutenants C. Griffiths and Wynne, appeared next day; whereupon, as the battalion now mustered 12 officers and 515 men, it and the Wiltshire were separated. On May 2nd, 28 men arrived from Egypt and next day Captain Bickford-Smith rejoined and took over the Adjutancy from Captain Grey, who retired to hospital suffering from severe dysentery,[2] being subsequently invalided home. Lieutenant Everett and Second Lieutenants Evans and Griffiths also went down with the same complaint, and the sick-rate soon assumed alarming proportions. Dysentery was the prevalent malady, but there were several cases of cholera, most of them fatal. The lack of comforts and amenities—even tobacco was often unobtainable—and the monotony of the rations which were, moreover, quite unsuited to a hot climate, combined with the heat to reduce all ranks to a pitiable condition. On May 21st, for example, the C.O., the Adjutant and the Quartermaster were the only officers not on the sick list. There was general satisfaction

---

[1] Lieutenant Napier was wounded on the 24th when arranging for the relief of the 8th Cheshire, about the battalion's last casualty in the Kut relief operations.

[2] He had been carrying on though far from fit.

therefore at hearing that the Division was to move down river for the hot season.

The end of May accordingly found the 4th at Sheikh Saad, where it spent the next three months. It was a bad period. The hot weather in Mesopotamia was bound to be trying to Europeans, however good the conditions under which they might be living and however ample the medical facilities. But in the summer of 1916 the medical arrangements in Mesopotamia were still anything but satisfactory. Ice-making machines and similar devices for alleviating the conditions were unheard of. The R.A.M.C. were terribly overworked, and the hospital accommodation was utterly inadequate. The heat was awful, the dust all-pervading. "We breathed dust, we ate dust, we exuded dust, when we slept we were covered with dust, the water and food were full of it, and the problem of keeping the rifles clean was almost hopeless," says one account. Fatigues too were frequent and multifarious duties claimed any who managed to be off the sick list. Arab marauders were always worrying convoys taking rations to outlying posts, and stealing anything they could, particularly rifles, so large escorts were required for ration parties and sentry duty was heavy. Naturally therefore the sick-rate was appallingly high and the mortality heavy. In June the battalion lost Regimental Sergeant Major Cornish,[1] who had done excellent work in that capacity; and of 55 men who arrived on June 19th, having come up river on barges without any protection from the sun, 4 had died by June 28th and 23 were in hospital. At one time the battalion's highly efficient M.O., Captain Shulstra, ran a battalion hospital so successfully that G.H.Q.'s curiosity was unfortunately aroused, for when the battalion's being so much healthier than other units was attributed to its having its own hospital an order was issued that in future no sick men were to be kept with a battalion for more than 24 hours, a piece of red tape which soon reduced the S.W.B. to the general level of ill-health.

August brought a slight improvement; days were still hot but nights pleasantly cool, and in September the maximum shade temperature dropped to 98 degrees. That month saw the Division move to Amara, 100 miles downstream, the S.W.B. and Cheshire going by land and covering the distance in eight night marches. The men stood the march well, and on reaching Amara found themselves much better off for comforts than at Sheikh Saad; and with the weather steadily getting cooler a definite programme of training could be undertaken, working up from battalion training to Divisional field-days, while recreation was not neglected. A Brigade Machine-Gun Company was now formed,

---

[1] Company Sergeant Major Murray succeeded him.

to which the battalion machine gunners were transferred, and at the same time Lewis guns were issued to battalions. The sick-rate had fallen now and the successive drafts more than balanced the invalidings. One of these drafts was of special note, 30 N.C.O.'s from the 1st Duke of Wellington's, one of the eight Regular battalions left in India, well-trained " serving soldiers," who were of great use in instructing recruits. In all 518 men are recorded as having joined between May 31st and November 30th. The battalion had mustered about 500 when active operations ended and 700 when it moved upstream again, making the loss by deaths and invalidings over 300. In the same period about 25 officers had joined or rejoined, among them Captains Blaxland, Buchanan, Fairweather and Philpott, and Lieutenants Napier, Tessier, Everett, Cracroft, Wilson and Staples. As against that some had joined the R.F.C. or received Staff billets, and several had been invalided.

At the end of November orders were received for the Division's return upstream. General Maude, who had taken over the command in Mesopotamia in August,[1] had completed his plans for reorganizing the forces and reforming their administrative arrangements,[2] and was now ready to start his campaign for the recapture of Kut and a fresh advance on Baghdad.[3] On November 27th the 40th Brigade struck camp and marched off for Sheikh Saad. The long stalemate was over, " Force D " was about to get some of its own back from the Turk, and the 4th S.W.B. could look forward to showing what they were worth under less adverse conditions than in the ill-fated attempt to relieve Kut.

---

[1] Major General A. S. Cobbe, an old officer of the TWENTY-FOURTH, who had been commanding the Meerut Division since the fall of Kut, succeeded General Maude as G.O.C. Tigris Corps, which in November became the First Indian Army Corps: the Thirteenth Division, however, was posted to the newly formed Third Indian Army Corps under General Marshall, the 2nd Battalion's original Brigadier at Gallipoli, and so missed coming under General Cobbe.

[2] A regimental history has no room to devote to these matters, but all ranks of the 4th S.W.B. engaged in Mesopotamia in 1917 and 1918 had reason to be grateful for the vast improvements effected.

[3] One reason for undertaking this offensive was the necessity of counteracting Turco-German activities in Persia and Afghanistan.

CHAPTER XIV

PREPARING FOR THE SOMME

THE New Year brought little change to the strategical situation in France. Though the stream of New Army Divisions was still flowing steadily across the Channel, months must elapse before these new units could be fit to share in a great offensive, and the improvement in the supply of munitions, though marked, was still insufficient to provide Sir Douglas Haig[1] with the overwhelming weight of artillery and ammunition essential to success in an attack on lines as formidable as those of the Germans, fortified by every device that the skill of the military engineer could invent. Indeed the German fortifications on the Somme front were as much stronger than those attacked on May 9th, 1915, or even at Loos, as those had been an advance on the lines carried at Neuve Chapelle. After his bitter experiences in 1915 Sir Douglas Haig was determined to avoid another premature attack, and had not the German pressure on Verdun compelled the British to deliver their attack in July as a counter-stroke, it is doubtful if the British offensive would have begun before September, if indeed even then.

"Mark time" was therefore the order of the day on the British front throughout the first half of 1916; such activities as took place were of merely local importance and as often as not were initiated by the Germans. These several times developed into quite considerable operations, as at the Bluff, S.E. of Ypres, or on the Vimy Ridge, but their strategical importance was limited. Still they gave many opportunities for fine performances by individual units, and in the TWENTY-FOURTH's war records these months are not without memorable incidents.

The New Year had found the 1st S.W.B. in trenches in the Loos Salient, but soon afterwards the battalion came out of the line and was back at Ferfay, S.W. of Lillers, for four weeks.[2] It then returned to the Loos Salient, at first occupying support trenches at Les Brebis, seven miles N.W. of Lens. The First Division was relieving the Forty-Seventh just South of Loos, where the Double Crassier, the largest slag heap in the Lens mining area, was a conspicuous feature. It had not been completely captured in the Loos offensive, and the French, who held the Loos sector from October to January,[3] had lost part of it. Its

---

[1] He had just (December 15th) succeeded Sir John French as Commander-in-Chief.

[2] Captain Steward left on January 5th to become G.S.O. III First Army, and was replaced as Adjutant by Lieutenant G. D. O. Lloyd, who gave place to Lieutenant S. B. Johns in March.

[3] The Forty-Seventh Division had relieved the French here on January 5th.

possession was very much in dispute. Frequent mining had produced a large crop of craters, prominent among them two known as Harrison's and Hart's, at the moment in German hands. From these craters the Germans overlooked the British front lines and their snipers could therefore make the British position quite unendurable. Accordingly, directly the 3rd Brigade took over (February 19th), the Brigadier ordered the battalion to attack them. Originally it was told to be ready in an hour and a half, and though Colonel Collier succeeded in getting half an hour's

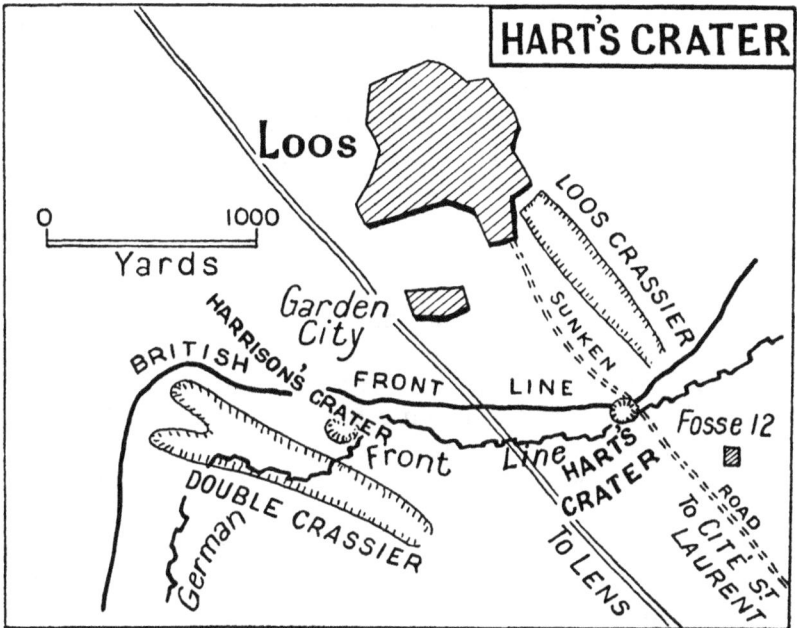

extension of time, even then the preparations were necessarily extremely hurried.

Hart's crater, the smaller and more Easterly of the two, was just South of a sunken road which crossed both the British and the German lines; Harrison's was nearer the point where the British front bent sharply back West round the Double Crassier. They were formidable positions: the German machine guns were skilfully placed and well handled, and their effective cross-fire repulsed the gallantly pressed attack on Hart's Crater. Against Harrison's the attack fared better. Captain Inglis, of D Company, who was in charge, attacked both from the North and from the West, where he used a platoon of the K.R.R.C.[1] He had expected this to be the least exposed flank; actually it was swept by machine guns from the Double Crassier and most

[1] The battalion being at this time very weak, a platoon from each battalion in the 2nd Brigade was attached to it.

of the stormers were shot down, Lieutenant Mayne being killed near the top of the crater at the head of his men. However, the party attacking from the North managed after a fierce struggle to establish themselves on the near edge of the crater. In this Private W. Phillips, a veteran warrior of 54, distinguished himself greatly. He had never previously thrown a bomb, but, having followed Captain Inglis up the slope of the crater, he threw bomb after bomb with great effect, and his gallant efforts went far towards beating off the Germans and securing the position. Company Sergeant Major Franklin did invaluable work in keeping up the supply of bombs and showed great coolness and steadiness in consolidating the position under heavy fire, while Second Lieutenant W. R. Morgan displayed great gallantry and devotion in rescuing wounded men. All night the contest continued, machine guns from Hart's Crater doing their best to impede the consolidation: they inflicted several casualties, but could not make the battalion relax its grip or prevent the crater being connected with the British lines.

Sufficient ground had been gained to prevent the enemy sniping down the British front line, but, with Hart's Crater still untaken, the position was too unsatisfactory to be endured. Accordingly on February 25th, after two mines had been exploded by the R.E., the Gloucestershire bombers, who had been lent for the purpose, attacked and occupied the crater. At dawn next morning they had just handed the post over to the battalion when a sudden German attack regained it. However, Captain Loch proved equal to the occasion and, counter-attacking before the Germans[1] had time to consolidate, thrust them out again. Colonel Collier, who hurried to the crater on hearing of its loss, found Captain Loch building up head-cover with sandbags which the enemy were shooting away as fast as he placed them in position. Though wounded in several places he stuck to his task and had the satisfaction of completing it, despite the enemy's efforts, thereby definitely securing the crater for the British. He was recommended for the V.C., but, though not awarded this, received an " immediate award " of the D.S.O.,[2] Private Phillips being given the D.C.M., while Second Lieutenant W. R. Morgan, the battalion bombing officer, and Company Sergeant Major Franklin received the M.C. The battalion's conduct in this crater fighting was thus well recognized, but the struggle had cost it nearly 70 casualties, the wounded including Second

---

[1] About 30 men had got in.

[2] Captain Loch, " one of the most gallant officers I ever met," as his C.O. has stated, was killed on July 2nd, on the Somme, when attached to the 2nd Brigade Staff. He had gone forward to lay out a taped line from which an attack was to be made, at a point close to the German lines and in a deep re-entrant.

IN THE LOOS SALIENT

Lieutenants Buckley, Dorrington (attached from K.R.R.C.) and Wileman.

Trench warfare in the Loos Salient at this period tended to be lively, hardly a day passed without some losses from either aerial torpedoes, trench mortars, rifle grenades, machine guns or snipers. In mining too there was great activity, while, as both sides were much better off for ammunition than they had been a year earlier, the shelling at times was very severe. Towards the end of a month the enemy's artillery usually tended to become specially active: one theory was that he was then getting rid of the balance of his monthly allowance of shells, but his trench-mortar and rifle-grenade activities were effectively curtailed and discouraged by adopting the principle of giving twice as much as we got, while before long his miners also had apparently had enough, as they confined themselves entirely to defensive measures, blowing camouflets to impede our miners' enterprises. In the aggregate this fighting involved substantial casualties, against which some small drafts arrived, and on March 26th the appearance of 118 men under Captain Mundy[1] was a really substantial contribution to the battalion's strength. Several new officers also joined, while Lieutenant C. A. Baker, who had gone out with the battalion in August, 1914, rejoined on March 4th, and Captain Lake, who had been wounded at Gheluvelt, reappeared a little later.

One particular tour in the trenches at the end of March and beginning of April stood out in the memory of those who endured it. Twice within a few days the battalion's front and support trenches were subjected to an intense and systematic bombardment by heavy howitzers firing H.E. shell and fitted with delayed action fuses, so that they had a burrowing effect. These rained down mercilessly, up and down the line, apparently searching for mine-heads, but incidentally demolishing whole stretches of the trenches and inflicting many casualties.[2] One big shell caught D Company's Headquarters in a dug-out at the side of the quarry near Hart's Crater and killed all the occupants[3] save two, who were at the very back of the dug-out. A second landed at the entrance to another dug-out, killed several men and completely blocked the entrance. Private Lomas and two others, finding themselves virtually buried, started groping about, and Lomas in doing so pushed aside a waterproof sheet and found himself in a narrow passage. Calling his companions to follow

---

[1] Captain Mundy became second in command and (temporary) Major as from April 10th.
[2] Seven men were killed and 5 missing (i.e. buried) on March 31st.
[3] Among them was Second Lieutenant W. R. Morgan; the company officers were luckily all up in the front line owing to the heavy shelling and so escaped.

him he crawled along it until he finally emerged in No Man's Land, though on the far side of our wire.[1] The second man had also reached the open when a fall of earth caught the third near the end of the sap. Being unable to release him Lomas had to leave him for dead, but made his way back to our lines to report, whereupon Private Ravenhill, Colonel Collier's runner, went out and eventually extricated the poor fellow after he had been half-buried for 12 hours.[2] The regimental transport at Les Brebis also came in for a share of the shelling, 3 men and 14 horses being hit.

When not in the front line the battalion was usually at Noeux, or Braquemont or Les Brebis. By this time the discomforts of trench warfare had been considerably mitigated in some sectors; it was often possible to keep the "cookers" in the support line along with the cooks, and hot meals were taken up to the front line on specially constructed carriers.[3] Once indeed when in support at Calonne, one of the suburbs of Lens, the battalion found itself in real luxury. The French who had been occupying this line had fitted up some cellars with every conceivable comfort; there were rose gardens and strawberry beds into the bargain. Being out of the line usually meant being on fatigue; as many as 250 men were often required for one single working party, and for three nights in May the whole battalion was on fatigue together.

Things were specially active about this time. Very sharp fighting was in progress on the Vimy Ridge, not far South of the 1st's sector, and the disturbed area tended to spread to both flanks. The battalion's patrols were very energetic and had several brushes with the enemy, notably on one occasion when Privates Quinn and Macaulay were out near the German wire and the enemy suddenly opened fire on a patrol from another regiment which was quite near. One man was hit and the Germans came out to capture him, whereupon Quinn and Macaulay turned the tables by promptly opening fire with good effect, and not only drove the Germans off, but were able to help the wounded man in. Lieutenant Ward Jones, Company Sergeant Major Miller, and Sergeants Freeman and Pratten were all among those brought to notice for good work at this period and received honours in the June list, while Private Quinn got an immediate D.C.M. and Macaulay, who had previously won a D.C.M. at Loos, received a bar. Another recipient of the D.C.M. was

---

[1] It was a disused and completely forgotten French sap.
[2] Private Lomas received the D.C.M.
[3] The Master Cook, Sergeant Banks, was indefatigable in his efforts for the men's benefit; while in this sector he commandeered a baker's oven and managed to provide every man with a daily ration of a pound of fresh bread.

Private Knott. He was caught in a barrage when driving an ammunition cart; he himself was wounded and one of his horses was killed, but he cut the dead horse loose and drove on, completed his errand and returned to the transport lines, where he collapsed.

The battalion had one nasty experience when relieving another unit in front-line trenches in the Maroc sector. The relief was incomplete; the S.W.B. were still encumbered with packs and greatcoats and had not yet taken over when a tremendous bombardment began. The other battalion cleared out, the guns lifted off the front line, and a strong party of raiders came dashing into the trench. Though caught at a disadvantage the S.W.B. rose to the occasion, and their stubborn resistance soon compelled the Germans to withdraw. As the raiders went back a machine gun on the right opened fire on them and knocked over nearly a dozen, though the S.W.B.'s casualties considerably exceeded that figure, including Lieutenant Davidson missing and a prisoner and Sergeant James killed. There was another bad day in the middle of June, when a heavy trench-mortar bombardment knocked out a whole Lewis gun team which had been posted to protect a mine-head in the centre of our line. Captain Lake also was killed and a dug-out in C Company's support line blown in, 10 men being killed or wounded. But on the whole the 1st reckoned that they gave as much as they got in the way of hard knocks. In June the battalion had the interest of acting as instructors to its newly arrived 12th Battalion, but when the preliminary bombardment of the Somme offensive began on June 24th the 1st was still in the Loos sector and did not quit it till some days after the battle proper had opened on July 1st.

Long before this the Regiment's other Regular battalion had reached the Western Front. The 2nd S.W.B. had outstayed the 4th in Egypt, but, after spending nearly two months either at Suez or in the El Kubri defences beyond the Canal, it also had moved to an area of greater activity. On March 9th it left Alexandria on two transports, the *Karoa* and *Kingstonian*, for Marseilles. It had not seen much of the reputed flesh-pots of the land of the Pharaohs. The time had been mainly devoted to training of all kinds, route-marches, ceremonial and close-order drill, some musketry, occasional field-days and much attention to bombing. Moreover Suez had not afforded many facilities for recreation, and when in the El Kubri lines the battalion was extremely busy improving the defences, besides being responsible for patrolling some four miles of the Canal. Water and fuel, too, were both so scarce that it proved necessary to give up drawing rations of fresh meat and revert to "bully." Still, there were some chances of football and boxing, a regimental grocery bar was started by a native contractor, new clothing was issued, and to be out of the cramped quarters of Gallipoli was no small relief. Those officers who had served six months with the M.E.F. were granted a month's leave to England. Lieutenant B. J. Davies and the transport party rejoined from Alexandria, ten new subalterns appeared, and before embarkation some small drafts and the return of recovered sick and wounded had brought the battalion's strength in "other ranks" up to nearly 650, though Second Lieutenants Mein and Breene and 36 men had been detached to the newly formed Brigade Machine-Gun Company.

The *Karoa* with the Headquarters wing reached Marseilles on March 15th, and the troops were promptly disembarked and entrained, arriving at Pont Remy on the 18th and marching to Domart en Ponthieu, where the Twenty-Ninth Division was concentrating. The 2nd S.W.B.—the other wing arrived next day—was the first unit in the Division to reach the concentration area, and the opportunity was thus given for several more officers, the Regimental Sergeant Major and a dozen men to get eight days' leave to England. More ample drafts were now forthcoming, and the fortnight which elapsed before the Division's concentration could be completed gave time to assimilate and incorporate them and to learn something of Western Front methods and conditions, so very different from those of Gallipoli. There, if the British had suffered from lack of trench-warfare appliances, the Turk had been equally hampered, while inadequately as the M.E.F. had been supplied with artillery and shells this weakness had been mainly felt when efforts were being made to advance: its enemies had usually been no better off, and their occasional violent bombardments had been but intermittent and brief. The Germans were not only better equipped, better organized, better led and better trained than the Turks, but their extraordinarily formidable defences quite outweighed the B.E.F.'s superiority over the M.E.F. in offensive weapons. In conditions the main change was that to be "out of the line" on the Western Front did mean real rest and comfort. If very different conditions were to prevail in later years, in 1916 the villages close behind the fighting line provided good billets with facilities for bathing and cleaning up, there was not the utter monotony of the Gallipoli rations, mails were frequent and regular, leave could be systematically given, and units in reserve were not, as in Gallipoli, just as liable to be bombarded as those in the firing line.

But, if conditions out of the line were more endurable, fortune had brought the Twenty-Ninth Division up against a particularly nasty portion of the German front. It had been assigned to the Eighth Corps, commanded as it happened by its old Divisional General, Sir A. Hunter-Weston, and on going into the line at the beginning of April found itself in the Auchonvillers sector, a little North of the Ancre and facing what had once been the village of Beaumont Hamel. The Divisional front was roughly concave, culminating on its right in a sharp salient known as Mary Redan, from which listening galleries ran out under No Man's Land. Opposite its left the so-called Hawthorn Redoubt projected from the German lines, in the centre another sharp salient marked the head of Y Ravine, a deep cleft which provided the Germans with good cover close up to their front line. Tremendous exertions had been lavished on these defences and a naturally strong position had been skilfully developed into a veritable fortress.

On the evening of April 3rd the 2nd S.W.B. moved up by platoons from its billets at Englebelmer into the right sub-sector, which included Mary Redan. Company commanders had gone on ahead 36 hours earlier and had acquainted themselves with the lines. The trenches were in a bad condition, having been much damaged by trench-mortar fire, especially at Mary Redan. The battalion therefore found plenty to do, and had also to push out saps in preparation for digging a new fire-trench. The unit it had relieved had reported the sector as quiet and the Germans opposite as unlikely to be aggressive, except by way of retaliation. However, the 2nd found the hostile trench mortars active enough, and on its second day was heavily shelled for over two hours. On its part it was active in patrolling, but on the early morning of April 5th Lieutenant Phillimore (H.L.I., attached) and an orderly had the bad luck to run into the enemy and be taken prisoners.[1]

The battalion's first tour in Western Front trenches was, however, to be memorable, for about 9 p.m. on April 6th the enemy suddenly opened a tremendous bombardment, barraging the communication and support trenches and systematically demolishing the fire-trenches and wire with minenwerfer. Great damage was inflicted, especially on the right of the line held by C Company, dug-outs were smashed in and some of their occupants buried, telephone-lines were severed, communication with

---

[1] Lieutenant Phillimore wrote a letter to a relative in which he said : "Tell my tenants . . . (giving the C.O.'s name with the letters transposed) that I think they should have the foundations of their house inspected, as I am not satisfied as to its safety." This message was conveyed to the battalion and was promptly realized to be a warning that the Germans were undertaking mining operations against Mary Redan.

the guns was interrupted.[1] Many of those in the front trenches managed to withdraw to the support line, but when the German guns lifted on to the support trenches, it was impossible to stop the enemy from entering the front line and capturing a dozen men who were trapped in a dug-out. A few Germans pushed on down Bond Street, a communication trench leading to the support line, but were met and driven back by a bombing party headed by two officers. At 10.30 p.m. the bombardment suddenly ceased, and the battalion could reoccupy the front trench and set about investigating and repairing the damage. This had been considerable. It was " a terrible shambles," one officer writes, " bay after bay being blown in and killed and wounded being buried under the blown-in trenches." Not only the front line but the communication trenches were badly knocked about, the wire had been practically completely demolished, and the Borders and the Inniskillings had to send up working parties to help reconstruct the parapet and clear away the debris. Casualties too had been heavy: 29 men killed and died of wounds, 18 missing, 31 and 5 officers, Captain Blake, Lieutenants Bodley and Llewellyn, Second Lieutenants Dickinson and Powell, wounded. Altogether it was a dismal opening to the battalion's career on the Western Front. It was pure bad luck to have been holding a sector which had evidently been marked down as the victim of a carefully prepared and organized raid; the weight of the bombardment—about 8000 shells, mainly high-explosive, were calculated to have fallen on the area bombarded—would have tried any defences.

Two days after this trying experience the battalion was relieved, and soon afterward went back to Louvencourt for a three weeks' spell in Divisional reserve. This was devoted mainly to training specialists, but was also marked by a parade before General Hunter-Weston on April 25th of all who had been present at the landing at Gallipoli. Captains Somerville and Laman, Lieutenant Ross,[2] the M.O., Captain A. J. Blake, Regimental Sergeant Major Westlake, and 167 other ranks were present, of whom the M.O., the Regimental Sergeant Major and 70 men had never left the Peninsula, so that the 2nd still contained quite a high percentage of old hands.

The battalion moved up to Mailly Maillet on April 28th in order that a picked party under Captain Byrne should raid the Hawthorn Redoubt on the following evening.[3] The raid had been carefully prepared, but, by some mischance, the party

[1] Our guns, however, opened a heavy fire in reply and apparently inflicted some damage on the raiders as they retired with their prisoners.
[2] He had just rejoined.
[3] The Border Regiment was holding the line.

started five minutes too soon, suffered heavily from our own shell fire and failed to effect its purpose. Captain Byrne was killed, Second Lieutenant Parry-Davies mortally wounded, and 24 men were casualties, 8 of them killed or missing. Three days later the battalion went into line again and held the left portion of the right sector for ten days. A new forward line was being constructed, but at first work was only possible at night, as the trench was too shallow to give cover by day. Such good progress was made, however, that before the battalion was relieved parts were fit for occupation by day. The G.O.C., who visited the sector on May 9th, expressed the greatest satisfaction with the battalion's work, not only on the new trench, but in improving the communication trenches and the old line, which had been taken over in very poor condition. Much wire was put up and patrols and snipers were active, the latter claiming several successes. The enemy's guns meanwhile were frequently in evidence, though luckily the casualties for the ten days only came to eight wounded and one missing, the recently issued shrapnel helmets helping to keep down the losses. From May 13th to 28th the battalion was " out," being mostly in Corps Reserve, which afforded better opportunities for training specialists, notably Lewis gunners, to work the new weapons, now being issued on the scale of four per company. Some reinforcements amounting to nearly 120 arrived, half of them recovered sick from Egypt, with three officers, including Captain Garnett who had been wounded when with the 1st Battalion at Festubert in December, 1914. Colds and rheumatism, partly due to a lack of straw which led to men sleeping on damp ground, were responsible for a rather high sick-rate which kept the battalion down below establishment.

At the end of May the 2nd returned to its former trenches and had an active ten days, improving the defences, making more communication trenches between the old and the new front lines, putting up more wire and draining the trenches, which persistent bad weather made particularly wet and muddy. The enemy seemed quieter, and this with various changes in their methods, such as using machine guns rather than snipers, was interpreted as indicating a relief. Patrols, however, failed to secure any prisoners or identifications, but the total casualties were only 5 wounded, and as 50 men joined from the Base Depot and 87 were transferred from the Corps Cyclist Battalion, several of them original members of the Divisional Cyclist Company formed in January, 1915, and Regular soldiers, the battalion's strength increased. From June 7th to 25th the battalion was " out," doing daily rehearsals of the attack. During this period Colonel Going and Captain Habershon rejoined, the former taking over command, while Captain Hughes and three subalterns joined from the 3rd Battalion.

June 23rd found the 2nd back in the firing line and next day the preliminary bombardment started, the artillery systematically pounding away at the trenches and cutting gaps in the wire. Gas was also discharged, somewhat to the relief of the occupants of the front line who were apprehensive of the possibilities of the cylinders being hit in a counter-bombardment. Infantry co-operation mainly took the form of keeping the gaps under close observation and blazing away with rifles and machine guns on any parties who might endeavour to carry out repairs, while frequent patrols sought to investigate the damage already done and discover what points still required special attention. This led to some sharp encounters, especially on June 27th, when the battalion's patrols penetrated into the enemy's trenches and engaged in bombing fights from which they were lucky enough to escape without losses. On one of these patrols Second Lieutenant Karran and Sergeant Howcroft penetrated into the German trenches and, finding themselves in an empty bay, waited in hopes of obtaining an identification. Before long an officer came along, whom Second Lieutenant Karran promptly shot, but before he could obtain any identifying marks several Germans came rushing up out of a dug-out and he and his companion only just escaped capture. Second Lieutenant Kelly also was conspicuous in this work: he was out with a party removing wire, which encountered the enemy at close range; he managed, however, to get his men under cover and when the enemy had ceased fire took them out again and continued the work.[1] The Germans retaliated vigorously, bombarding our lines and occasionally dosing places close behind, like Englebelmer, where B Company, then in reserve, had nine casualties on June 28th. For the troops in the line it was a trying time. The weather was wet, the mud was up to their knees, an unlimited amount of work left them only very few hours' rest, three or four a day, and the continuous rain made cooking almost impossible. The bombardment continued with varying intensity, gradually working up to its culminating point, though the original intention to attack on the 29th had to be given up and "Z day" postponed by 48 hours. June 30th, therefore, found the 2nd S.W.B. still awaiting the order to assault, not a little weary after a strenuous week but much encouraged by the volume of metal which they had seen pelting down upon the lines that confronted them.[2]

[1] He was awarded the M.C.

[2] Judged by Gallipoli standards the bombardment had been heavy, but in comparison with later attacks on the Somme the barrage was weak, only one field gun being available to every 40 yards of front as against one to every 3 in the attack on Beaumont Hamel on November 13th, 1916.

THE DUCK'S BILL

During the early months of 1916 the 5th S.W.B. had remained in the area with which 1915 had made them so familiar. From January 1st to 22nd headquarters were at La Couture; then followed nearly a month's rest and training in a reserve area round Cornet Malo, though C Company was left in the line till February 7th. The battalion then returned to Vieille Chapelle and remained there or thereabouts till it moved to Molinghen in the middle of April. "Night work under C.R.E." is the most frequent entry in the battalion diary for this time, but stirring incidents were not wanting and several individuals distinguished themselves by acts of coolness and courage. On March 8th, for example, a shell came through the roof of a pump-house and killed Private John, one of the crew of the pump which supplied air to the men in the mine-galleries. Private Rees continued to work the pump as if nothing had happened and thereby saved the lives of all those down in the mine. A similar incident occurred a week later: a shell burst inside No. 15 mine shaft, doing considerable damage: on this occasion it was Private Williams who remained at his post for nearly an hour, keeping the pump going. That same day (March 14th) the Germans exploded a mine under the salient North of Neuve Chapelle known as the Duck's Bill. Half the salient was destroyed, most of the garrison, including a working party of the 5th, were killed or wounded and the communication trench to our main position was much damaged and blocked. Captain Croft, however, promptly rushed across to the Duck's Bill and having done all he could to reorganize the survivors and maintain the defence, went back to fetch help. Several of the 5th at once volunteered and, led by Captain Croft and Second Lieutenant Lochner, a small party dashed across the open under heavy fire to reinforce the Duck's Bill. Two, Sergeant Howe and Private Skelton, were killed, but the rest got across and assisted the remnant of the garrison to put up a good fight and prevent the enemy exploiting the success of their mine.[1] A week later, the Germans having blown up part of the line held by the 8th North Staffords, Sergeant Bridgewater, who was in charge of a party of the 5th in the mine-galleries near, at once hastened to the spot with his men, manned the parapet and assisted the garrison to hold on.

On the whole, considering how constantly parties were up in the front trenches and that even back areas were by no means immune from bombardments, the 5th fared well. If casualties for March were pretty high, three weeks of April, though spent "in the line," barely cost the 5th half a dozen wounded. In

[1] Captain Croft was awarded the M.C. and Lance Corporal Hibbert the D.C.M.

April Major Wright, who had returned in February along with Captain Curtis, left to take a newly formed Pioneer battalion to Salonica. On this Major Deacon succeeded him as second in command, Captain Croft taking over D Company, while in May, Captain R. G. Lochner was promoted Temporary Major and succeeded as Adjutant by Lieutenant C. B. Lochner. Lieutenant Renwick rejoined from sick leave in May and several new subalterns appeared.

By the middle of May, however, the 5th were out of the Lys valley and on their way to the Somme after nearly three weeks' training and rest at Enquin les Mines. On arrival the battalion was placed under the Eighth Division,[1] in line opposite La Boisselle, to assist it in preparing for the now imminent offensive. Headquarters were usually in Albert and companies worked more or less independently on the varied tasks which the "mounting" of the great offensive entailed. Thus on June 1st the battalion diary records that half A was roadmaking and preparing fascines at Henencourt, the other half was making trench tramways. B was at St. Gratien, also cutting fascines and improving roads, C was deepening trenches at Ovillers Post, D constructing dug-outs. On June 6th again the whole battalion was employed to dig a new trench 750 yards long and 150 yards out into the wide No Man's Land in front of Border Trench.[2] This was a triumph of speed, efficiency and noiselessness, so quietly done that the Germans never spotted it and there was not a single casualty, though including the R.E., who were putting up the wire, and an infantry carrying-party, 1200 men were out in the open at the same time. The battalion did not, however, entirely escape casualties: on June 10th it lost Lieutenant Nisbet who had been wounded at Givenchy in January, 1915.

The 5th owed their comparative immunity from casualties largely to having learnt to work very silently and to be careful not to leave things about to attract the Germans' attention. Some deep dug-outs, which afterwards saved many lives during German bombardments, were constructed at one place: not a piece of tell-tale white chalk was allowed to show, every bit was put into sandbags and carried away to be used where parapets needed thickening or a too wide trench had to be narrowed. On another occasion it was discovered that the Germans meant to raid "the Nab," a salient 80 yards wide and 150 deep. Some 180 of the 5th were sent up one night to fill in the existing trenches with wire and dig shallow bombing trenches just behind them, but separated from them by a wire

[1] The Eighth had no Pioneer battalion at this time.
[2] Opposite Ovillers.

fence. If the Germans attacked, the wired trenches would prove a nasty obstacle, and while entangled in them they could be effectively handled from the bombing trenches. The work was the more difficult because it had to be done in a narrow space and in moonlight, but done it was, with less than half a dozen casualties; and the Germans, possibly discovering the reception prepared for them, did not try a raid on " the Nab."

In the last week of June, the 5th went back West of Albert to the Long Valley, hoping that once the bombardment had begun they might be given a little rest. They were to be disappointed. Others might rest, but not Pioneers: roads had to be kept in repair, and with the prodigious traffic which the bombardment and all the preparations for the offensive entailed they needed more repairs than ever; trench tramways also had to be pushed forward and routes prepared for the artillery to advance by if the break-through came off. Up to the last moment before the assault the Pioneers were kept busy. Still the 5th were gluttons for work and had established a great reputation for what they could get through. The G.O.C. Eighth Division wrote to General Bridges praising their work in the most handsome terms, and in Sir Douglas Haig's Dispatches of April 30th, dealing with the winter and early spring, five officers of the 5th were mentioned: Colonel Trower, Major Cooke, Captain H. F. Thomas, Lieutenant Harrison and Second Lieutenant Lochner. The June "Honours" List brought the M.C. to Lieutenant C. E. L. Hall and Second Lieutenant I. T. Evans, and the D.C.M. to Sergeant Silcox, all very well-merited rewards.

The 6th S.W.B. arrived on the Somme some time after the 5th had made the acquaintance of that region. The New Year had found them still in the Armentières sector, but with the end of January the battalion had been withdrawn for a rest, moving to Rouge Croix. The 6th were legitimately pleased that after their four months in the line, the 13 miles march from Oosthove Farm was accomplished with only 13 men falling out. They did much route marching in the five weeks they were " out," with plenty of musketry, in which most of the men had had no practice while in trenches, but training was often interrupted by urgent calls for working parties. Some reinforcements arrived, about 60 in all, and 7 officers including Lieutenant Beeston, while Captain S. C. Morgan had been promoted Major in December. Towards the end of February the Division went back to Armentières in snowy weather, and the 6th settled down to work on wiring the rear defences, only to be suddenly transferred early in March to Ypres and put into the line astride the Ypres–Comines canal.

Their new sector included "the Bluff," recently the scene of bitter fighting.[1] The line was in a terrible state. Unburied dead were lying everywhere, the bombardments had reduced trenches and parapets to chaos, there was much to rebuild and more to clear up. Moreover, the 6th, being billeted at Dickebusch, had six miles to go to reach their work and an even longer six, so it seemed, to cover to get back to quarters, so orders to move to an entirely new quarter were not unwelcome.[2]

The German pressure on Verdun had by this time become so serious that it was essential for the B.E.F. to do something to reduce it, directly or indirectly. If as yet a serious British offensive was for every reason inadvisable, Gallipoli had been evacuated and Egypt teemed with troops who were once more ready to go anywhere and do anything. With these additional forces as his disposal Sir Douglas Haig could take over a substantial extra frontage and so free several French Divisions for the fighting zone. The line taken over was that intervening between the First and Third British Armies, from Loos past Lens and Arras towards the Ancre, and the centre of this front on the lower slopes of the famous Vimy Ridge was now the Twenty-Fifth Division's destination.

Arriving at Hauteavesnes on March 13th the 6th found themselves in a crowded area, in which nearly all billets were full and water was scarce and bad. Battalion Headquarters were established at Tilloy lez Hernaville on March 17th and remained there, with road-making and constructing light railways as the main occupations, till April 22nd, when the battalion moved forward to Neuville St. Vaast.[3] This village was supposed to be a "strong point" in the line of defence, but consisted of a mass of debris under continuous fire from the German trenches, which overlooked it from 600 yards higher up the slope. Movement, let alone work, by day was impossible and officers and men had to spend their days in cellars and deep dug-outs, constructed by the Germans, only emerging after dark to toil at the defences. By night things were lively enough, what with constant sniping, much fire from machine guns and quite heavy shelling. Indeed the wonder was that casualties were not far higher. Up to the middle of May they had barely amounted to 20, including Lieutenant R. W. Thomas, wounded on May 5th,

---

[1] It had been taken by the Germans from the Seventeenth Division and then recaptured by the Third.
[2] Casualties had not been heavy but included Second Lieutenant S. Evans, wounded on February 22nd.
[3] During this time Lieutenant H. C. A. Davies and Second Lieutenant S. Evans rejoined, and several new officers appeared, among them some, like Second Lieutenant W. B. C. Morgan, who had been sent to the 9th Battalion in July, 1915.

but then additional liveliness brought increased losses. The first notable episode was the explosion of five mines under the German front line in the Berthonval sector on the evening of May 15th. Much damage was done and several big craters formed,[1] which the Germans kept under heavy artillery fire. C and D Companies went forward promptly, nevertheless, and started consolidating the craters. Second Lieutenant W. G. Edwards directed the work magnificently, standing up on the lip of a crater, setting a splendid example of devotion and gallantry. He was admirably supported by Second Lieutenants Marshall and Renwick, the former carrying on though wounded and encouraging the men by his courage and endurance. Sergeants Llewellyn and W. Thomas backed their officers up magnificently, and Privates Lewis, Griffiths, Yates and Evans all distinguished themselves. Despite the violence of the shelling the two companies stuck to their work and completed their task, their casualties, a bare dozen, being surprisingly low, though the three officers mentioned were all wounded, Second Lieutenant Edwards very severely.[2] Three days later C and D were again to the fore. They were at work on these craters which had been persistently shelled, and had to break off work to repulse a determined counter-attack. Casualties this time were heavier: Second Lieutenant G. W. Jones was killed and with him fell six men, including the two sergeants who had distinguished themselves three nights earlier, Captain E. L. Lloyd, Second Lieutenants S. Evans and Amos,[3] and 26 men were wounded. However, C and D were not deterred from completing their consolidation and leaving to the infantry who relieved them a quite defensible line. After this the Neuville St. Vaast corner was "livelier" than ever, the village being constantly shelled, and the 6th were not sorry to be relieved on May 31st and sent back to Villers Chatel for a fortnight's rest and training, in which its main occupation was the construction of rifle-ranges and some much needed musketry practice.

Before this the battalion had seen several changes. Major Samuda had gone sick,[4] Second Lieutenant Manners had transferred to the Intelligence Corps, and Lieutenants Randolph

---

[1] These were the group known as the Crosbie Craters which were lost in the German attack on the Forty-Seventh Division on May 21st, the Twenty-Fifth having then side-slipped to the right.

[2] Second Lieutenants Edwards and Marshall received the M.C., while the M.M. was awarded to Sergeants Dawson, Ellaway, J. T. Jones, Thomas and Private Yates.

[3] These last two had already been wounded once, Second Lieutenant Amos in December, Lieutenant Evans in February, but had rejoined (March 11th and April 27th) on recovery.

[4] He was ultimately struck off the strength on May 31st.

and Easterbrook[1] to the R.E. At Villers Chatel four more subalterns, Lieutenants Mumford and Carpendale and Second Lieutenants M. Griffiths and Belcher, joined, and the battalion heard with satisfaction of the award of the C.M.G. to Colonel Hewett. On June 12th it moved by rail to Longeau to be attached to the Thirty-Second Division, then in line in front of Aveluy Wood. On arrival, Longeau proved to be the wrong station and the battalion found itself faced with a twenty-mile march in pouring rain. After a night's railway journey in closely packed trucks this proved a severe ordeal and the 6th did not do too badly in accomplishing the march with only 48 men falling out. A fortnight's hard work followed, getting everything ready for the coming attack, after which the battalion moved back to Senlis, rejoining its own Division, now in reserve to the Tenth Corps.

The two S.W.B. battalions in the Thirty-Eighth Division arrived on the Somme even after the 6th Battalion. Their periods of instruction had not been completed before the end of 1915 and their first tours in the line on their own account did not begin till January, 1916, was nearly half over, the intervening time having been spent at Robecq in completing their training. But from January 14th, when the 10th took over the Moated Grange sector at Neuve Chapelle, till the middle of June the two battalions had a long round of tours in the trenches, in first one and then another of the sectors between the La Bassée Canal and Fauquissart, varied by short periods in brigade or Divisional reserve. Their furthest South was Givenchy, which both battalions found distinctly livelier than the other sectors they sampled, while Festubert bore off the palm for unpleasantness. The ground here was so water-logged that the front line consisted of "islands," detached posts which could only be approached by night, as the enemy profited by being on a low ridge, a few feet higher than the surrounding swamps, to overlook our line. At the end of February and the beginning of March, when the two battalions were in this quarter, the area badly needed draining, while the "islands" had to be connected up and the old British front line in use before May, 1915, repaired as a reserve line. On one occasion a party was returning from one of these islands just before daybreak and was spotted by the Germans, who opened fire, hitting two men, one of whom lay out helpless and disabled in the snow. Seeing this Lieutenant Gill, the battalion machine-gun officer, dashed out to his help, and

---

[1] He was awarded the M.C. for good work in maintaining a light railway in working order under heavy fire.

brought him safely in, despite heavy machine-gun fire.[1] Luckily the enemy were very unenterprising and casualties were lower than during the tours in the Givenchy trenches,[2] where the drier ground made mining possible. The 10th had the more active time here, having nearly 30 casualties, including 7 men killed on April 3rd, when the Germans blew a mine. Great damage was done; a sap head was completely destroyed and its garrison killed or buried, a large crater 30 feet deep and 30 yards across was formed and the front line trench was also damaged. The battalion rose to the occasion splendidly. Captain E. T. Rees promptly garrisoned the near lip of the crater with 20 men and a Lewis gun, just in time to repulse a strong party of enemy who advanced to seize the crater. Parties were then organized to consolidate the position and dig out the entombed men, while others, by using rifle-grenades effectively, kept in check the enemy's efforts to interfere. Privates G. A. Thomas, Beach and H. S. Evans distinguished themselves greatly; though partially buried in debris they not only extricated themselves but assisted to extricate others in worse case, scraping away the earth with their hands when tools could not be used.[3] Ultimately a new and quite satisfactory fire-trench was constructed 80 yards in front of the original line.

April was also noticeable for the 10th Battalion because on the 25th Lieutenant Colonel S. J. Wilkinson of the West Yorkshires, who had been commanding the 19th Welch, the Divisional Pioneers, was transferred to the battalion to take command, Major Harvey reverting to second in command. This transfer led to Major Grant-Dalton leaving the 11th S.W.B. for the 19th Welch as C.O., and as Colonel Gaussen was then officiating as Brigadier, Captain Dawes had temporary command of the 11th. May brought a move to the Moated Grange, just North of Neuve Chapelle, where the 10th were active in patrolling the craters which punctuated No Man's Land. On the 24th a strong fighting patrol attacked and drove in a German working party, but without securing identifications, while the German retaliation descended mainly on the 11th, causing some 16 casualties. Neither battalion, however, really suffered severely during this long period of trench warfare, the 10th's total casualties amounting to 2 officers[4] and 37 men

---

[1] He was awarded the M.C.

[2] Though casualties were not heavy a fair number of both battalions had to go to hospital, those invalided from the 10th including Captain Givons, while the 11th lost Captain Mills and Lieutenant Goldsmith. The 10th was also so unlucky as to lose three of its Warrant Officers, Company Sergeant Major Keen being wounded and Company Sergeant Majors Greenwood and Rees invalided.

[3] All three were subsequently awarded the M.M.

[4] Second Lieutenants Seager and Huggett.

killed, and 2 officers[1] and 106 men wounded, the 11th's to Captain Cullimore and 9 men killed, 6 officers[2] and 87 men wounded. Drafts had arrived in fair numbers and the vacancies among the officers had been quickly filled.

June saw the Welsh Division relieved from the trenches and concentrated in a training area round Tincques and Villers Brulin. Here ten days were spent in fairly assiduous training, varied by refitting and a little recreation, though to be really " out " after so long a dose of the line, was in itself recreation enough. Towards the end of the month[3] the Division began to move Southward, marching by Toutencourt and Acheux to Buire sur Ancre, where it arrived on July 3rd, to find itself in reserve to the Seventeenth Corps and on a verge of a far sterner struggle than it had yet experienced.

The 11th was now no longer the junior battalion of the TWENTY-FOURTH in France. The 12th S.W.B. had at last crossed the Channel. That battalion had spent the first five months of 1916 at Blackdown, completing its training and waiting rather impatiently for the more backward units of the Division to be brought up to the necessary level. There were various changes among the officers and N.C.O.'s, some men were discharged as unfit and quite a number of skilled munition workers were taken away to jobs where they were urgently needed and their places filled from the Local Reserve battalions. Eventually on June 1st the battalion[4] had left Frimley for Southampton, crossing to Havre that night and entraining for Lillers on the 4th. From Lillers it marched to Bourecq (on the main road to Aire), finding the *pavé* exceedingly trying,

---

[1] Second Lieutenants H. E. Davies and Ralph.

[2] Captains R. I. Evans and H. C. W. Williams, Second Lieutenants J. H. C. Griffiths, Miller-Hallett and Watts and Lieutenant and Quartermaster Barry.

[3] About this time Major T. H. Morgan was transferred from the 10th to the 11th as second in command and Lieutenant Barry rejoined on recovery from wounds.

[4] The officers who went overseas with the 12th were Lieutenant Colonel E. A. Pope (commanding), Major C. B. Hore (second in command), Captain and Adjutant W. E. Brown, Lieutenant and Quartermaster J. Albutt; Captains E. A. A. Whitworth (O.C. " A "), R. F. Murphy (O.C. " B "), H. C. Rees (O.C. " C "), C. E. Hoffmeister (O.C. " D "), J. W. Freeman, R. A. Godwin-Austen, C. M. Pritchard; Lieutenants T. O. Jones, J. S. Lewis, H. C. Lloyd, O. D. Morris, A. Newman, J. R. Symes, H. R. Taylor and D. R. Williams; Second Lieutenants H. J. Brown, P. J. Duckham (Transport Officer), H. S. Edmonds, H. P. Enright, E. H. Francis, W. E. G. Howell, H. R. Jones, A. G. Osborn, W. J. Proctor, J. E. Reeves, J. M. Renwick, J. R. W. Taylor, O. P. Taylor, J. B. V. Wood; and Lieutenant D. Viliesid, R.A.M.C. (M.O.), Regimental Sergeant Major Vatcher, Regimental Quartermaster Sergeant Westhorpe, Company Sergeant Majors Parker (A), Codling (B), Davenport (C) and Tomlinson (D); Company Quartermaster Sergeants Avery (A), Squibb (B), Job (C) and Smith (D).

and there spent a week, training, route-marching, practising putting on gas-helmets and generally preparing for the trenches. What impressed it most was the deluge of literature which descended upon the headquarters staff, who were bewildered by the quantity and variety of the returns demanded, far exceeding the capacity of the battalion stationery-box to cope with them, and were soon suffering from a severe surfeit of orders and instructions. The most important of these was that received on June 12th for the battalion to proceed to the front next day and be attached by companies to the 3rd Brigade for the usual instructional period. The following evening saw the 12th in a wet and uncomfortable camp at Houchin, listening to the rifle and machine-gun fire, and next day, after donning steel helmets at Petit Sains, A and B Companies found themselves attached for instruction to their own 1st Battalion, C and D going to the 2nd Welch, both in the Calonne sector. The four days' tour was full of interest and value for the new hands, but it cost the 12th two men killed, Private Edmonds being the first in the battalion to fall, and half a dozen wounded. Four days' rest was followed by a second instructional tour and then by ten days' training behind the lines. This was marked by a sad accident at bombing-practice on July 1st, Lieutenant Newman, the Bombing Officer, a keen and popular officer of great promise, being unfortunately killed. Then on the 3rd came orders for the Division to take over the Calonne sector from the First Division, under orders for the Somme, and on July 4th the 12th relieved the 10th Gloucestershire in the left sub-sector of the Division's line and with that may be said to have started its fighting career.

Shortly after the departure of the 12th Battalion for France the 9th, 13th and 14th officially ceased to be connected with the Regiment. This was in consequence of the decision to pool the resources of the different regiments by amalgamating all " Second Reserve " and " Local Reserve " units into a " Training Reserve." Drafts from any Training Reserve battalion, English, Scottish or Welsh, might go to any regiment. That there was great advantages about this is obvious enough, but the disadvantages must not be overlooked. Officers and men of a draft-finding unit were deprived of the stimulus of inculcating into the recruits they were training the traditions and standards of special regiments. Recruits from South Wales might find themselves in a regiment mainly composed of Londoners or Lancashiremen. Esprit de corps, to which the authorities professed to attach great importance, was hardly encouraged and the value of the territorial connections of the infantry of the Line as a factor in promoting homogeneity and corporate feeling was much reduced. Of the three battalions, the 9th became the 57th Training Reserve Battalion, the 13th was numbered the 59th and the 14th the 65th.

The 9th to the end of its time as a battalion of the Regiment had Colonel Gillman as C.O. and Captain Blowen as Adjutant. Its brigade had been renumbered as the 13th Training Reserve Brigade and together with the 14th constituted a Rhyl Training Centre under Major General Donald. Recruiting improved early in 1916, partly due to the energy and persuasiveness of the already mentioned former Newport Town Band who did great things in the mining valleys, and with the influx of men attested under the Derby scheme and those brought in by the Military Service Act the numbers of the battalion rose considerably. A good many men were transferred from units like the A.S.C., Army Pay Corps and R.A.M.C., who had everything to learn about musketry and open order work, and as the battalion staff was expected to turn these men into infantrymen in about ten weeks the strain on it was considerable. Luckily most of the " young officers " had been taken off its hands by the opening of a school of instruction at Bodelwydden Park, so the staff could concentrate its energies on its recruits.

The 13th meanwhile had sent its first draft overseas in January and the needs of keeping the 10th and 11th Battalions supplied had prevented it from completing its four companies till June. Then with the passage of the Military Service Bill through Parliament and the calling up of the men attested under the Derby scheme recruits had come rolling in with great rapidity. Till then many of the recruits posted to the battalion had been mainly of the " Labour " category, and there had been a good deal of transferring and cross-posting of these men between the various organizations formed for dealing with them, such as a " Works Battalion " of the King's, and a " Labour Battalion " of the Cheshire, while in June the 13th formed a Works Company of its own. Some of these Labour recruits were sent off to munition works, others " released " for short periods to help on farms, but the main work of the battalion consisted in the preparation of drafts for foreign service. In May, the 13th lost Colonel Pitten, who was succeeded by Lieutenant Colonel J. A. F. Field from the Cheshire, and on Lieutenant J. R. O. Jones going abroad, Lieutenant E. B. Rees became Adjutant but was succeeded in August by Captain Jordan.

The fortunes of the 14th had differed little from those of the 9th and 13th, though it had been somewhat more successful than the 13th in filling up its ranks. A substantial transfer from the 21st R.W.F., another Local Reserve unit, followed by another from the 19th R.W.F. at Blackdown, swelled its numbers in January, and allowed of the formation of B Company at the end of the month. Recruits flowed in steadily during the spring, mostly from South Wales, but with substantial infusions from London, Lancashire and Cheshire, and C Company came into existence on April 1st, followed by D later in that month. A big draft was supplied to complete the 12th to war establishment, and in return the details of the 12th together with those of the 19th R.W.F. were posted to the battalion in June. Some of the men recruited were classified as Labour recruits and sent off to munition works at Coventry, while others, who were colliers, were posted to "Class W, Army Reserve," and released for employment in collieries. However, the battalion was pretty well up to strength when at the end of August orders arrived for its transformation into the "65th T.R." On this taking place it despatched over 600 men to the 3rd Battalion, which, on top of having supplied a draft of 250 to France, left comparatively few men to follow Colonel Beresford-Ash, who had replaced Colonel Porter in command on July 8th, to the new unit.[1]

This left the 3rd Battalion and the 2/1st and 3/1st Brecknock as the only units at home officially belonging to the Regiment. To the 3rd Battalion 1916 brought little change in one sense, though its personnel changed constantly as drafts departed and recruits and convalescents reported. Captain Fowler, who, as already mentioned, was Gazetted Adjutant on April 21st, held that post to the end of the year, only relinquishing it in September, 1917, when he returned to the 1st Battalion in Flanders. Shortly before that Colonel Morgan's period in command had run out, and he had been succeeded by Major Maxwell-Heron, while Captain F. Carter, formerly Adjutant of the 6th Battalion, who had often deputised for Captain Fowler, carried on till Major Hamilton-Jones was appointed Adjutant in June, 1918. But apart from these changes there is little to chronicle in the story of a Special Reserve battalion in the last years of the war.

[1] The 9th, after being changed from the 57th T.R. into the 282nd Infantry Battalion in August, 1917, had the satisfaction of reviving its connection with the Regiment in the following month, when it was reconstituted as the "52nd (Graduated) Battalion The South Wales Borderers." This was under the scheme by which recruits were posted in batches of a company at a time to a battalion and passed through a definite training programme before going overseas together. Shortly after this Colonel Gillman relinquished the command he had held for over three years, being succeeded by Colonel H. T. Fisher: for his good work in command he received the thanks of the Army Council, and of Lord French, the Field Marshal commanding the Home Forces.

This does not mean that these units were not busy enough: their record is one long tale of monotonous duty: they had all they could do to keep the battalions in the field up to strength: too often their best trained drafts went off to some other regiment who reaped the fruits of the hard work of officers and N.C.O's, who were trying to inspire into the recruits who passed so rapidly through their hands the traditions and spirit of "the Regiment." It was not given to them to know, otherwise than by hearsay, how the drafts they had trained had borne themselves, but in the record of the war of 1914-1918 the share of the Special Reserve, if inconspicuous and often overlooked, was of fundamental importance.

The 2/1st Brecknocks had entertained hopes that their battalion would in due course proceed overseas, but the Sixty-Eighth Division was not among the half-dozen Second Line T.F. Divisions ultimately selected for active service. In July, 1916, the battalion was called upon to produce a draft of nearly 200 men for service in France, and another 60 were taken in August. This left it very weak, and as other battalions were in the same plight it soon became obvious that the Sixty-Eighth was not for France but would be sacrificed to provide drafts. The battalion had an influx of men from other units in October, 1916, and it was not till nearly a year later that it was finally broken up, when its Division was reformed, being reconstituted with Training Battalions. It had had several moves in the meantime, being for a time at Thetford, moving to Wrentham in November, 1916, and remaining there till May, when it shifted to Hesham Park, near Wangford, in Suffolk, its last quarters, where in August, 1917, it was finally broken up. The 3rd Line, however, continued to exist and to serve as a draft-finding unit, primarily for the 1st Line unit in India, to which it supplied substantial drafts to make up the wastage caused by invaliding and by men being transferred to units on active service in Mesopotamia or to the numerous "employments" in India whose demands seemed almost insatiable.

CHAPTER XV

THE SOMME

I: *The Opening Stages*

OF the seven battalions of the TWENTY-FOURTH on the Western Front only one actually "went over the top" on July 1st, 1916, when the great struggle of the Somme opened. Before July was out all but one were to have fighting enough and to spare in "the Somme," but on that day of desperate fighting, terrible losses and mixed success and failure, it fell to the 2nd Battalion only to sustain the Regiment's reputation for self-sacrifice, steadiness, determination and devotion to duty. Of the others, as already explained, the 1st was still in the Loos Salient, the 5th, 6th, 10th and 11th, though in the battle area, were in reserve, the 12th was only serving its apprenticeship to war. The 2nd Battalion had already seen enough of the Beaumont Hamel defences to know that an assault on them would be no child's play; both by nature and by art they were among the toughest nuts the British had to crack, while heavy as our bombardment had been it had not succeeded in sweeping away all the wire, in rendering the front trenches untenable, or in putting their garrison out of action.

The Twenty-Ninth Division was attacking with the 87th Brigade on the right and the 86th on the left. The 2nd S.W.B., on the left of their brigade, faced the Southern side of the salient round the head of Y Ravine. It had A, C and D Companies in line from left to right with B in support: on its right the Inniskillings were attacking, the Borders were to follow it, to go through it when the attack reached Station Road in the bottom of the valley 700 yards away, and to tackle the second objective. It was noticeable that the plans were far more definite than those for Loos and the tasks allotted to different units more precise. Could an entrance into the hostile positions only be achieved, no company need hesitate as to what to do next or how far to push forward. A, on reaching the Ravine, was to swing half-right and advance astride the second trench, C, also swinging half-right, to clear the ground between the Ravine and the front trench, D to push straight through to the third trench and consolidate there. Careful arrangements were made for "mopping up," and the points to be consolidated had been determined and allotted.

During the night companies moved up to their assigned positions, to the accompaniment of considerable artillery activity. The men were very heavily laden; indeed, they could hardly be seen for the things they had to carry, and they spent a cold and cheerless night in the closely packed trenches. At 5 a.m. on July 1st hot tea was served out, at 6 our guns began a steady bombardment, which developed into an intense one an hour later. At 7.20 our big mine near the Hawthorn Redoubt on the 86th Brigade's frontage was exploded. It was the biggest yet fired, and sent a huge cloud of earth and stones 100 feet high, and the explosion shook the earth for a long way round. It

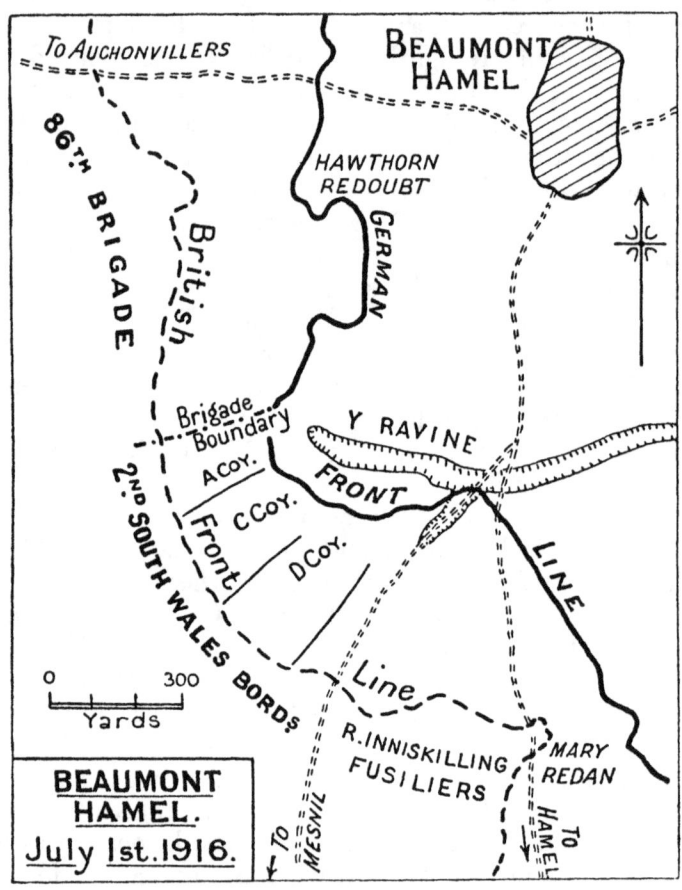

seemed impossible that any Germans could have survived it, and hopes ran high as the companies began getting out of our trenches and filed through the gaps in our wire in readiness to assault. It was ominous that directly they reached the outer edge of our wire, not 100 yards from our trenches, machine guns opened a fire which increased rapidly in intensity. Indeed, before "Zero" (7.30 a.m.) casualties had already been serious. Nevertheless the battalion went forward with admirable steadiness and determination, though deluged with shrapnel as well as mown down wholesale by the devastating machine guns.

There were 600 yards to be covered on the right,[1] and No Man's Land was pitted with shell-holes which, with the heavy loads the men were carrying, made the advance slow. The Germans manned their parapets in force before our men were half-way across, and though they gave targets to the rifles of the leading line it was only too clear that neither mine nor bombardment had done all that was hoped. A Company persevered till within 20 yards of the nose of the salient, where a shower of bombs brought the survivors to a standstill, a very few reaching the wire, only to be shot down in trying to get through it. A sunken road gave C some help to cross the hollow in its front, but C too was stopped, when about 60 yards from the wire, by machine guns from the right. D also pressed on, men dropping at every yard, till nearly 300 yards from our line, when scarcely any were left to go farther.

Meanwhile B had clambered out of the support trench at 7.30 and, undeterred by the fate of the leading companies, started to advance. Before its men were through our wire the machine guns were bowling them over. They pushed on, gallantly led by Captain Hughes, who was last seen 50 yards from the enemy's wire, heading a handful of men, all of whom were shot down a minute later. Within twenty minutes of Zero the 2nd S.W.B. had been virtually wiped out. The vast majority had been hit, the survivors could only hang on where they were, taking advantage of such cover as shell-holes or other inequalities of ground presented. Second Lieutenants Dutton and Mayger[2] did good work in getting the remnants of their companies into this sort of shelter and from there endeavouring to reply to the enemy's fire with bombs and rifles. Here and there a man managed to do some effective shooting at the enemy, but that was all. Very few regained our trenches during the day. Wounded and unhurt alike had to lie where they were among the killed, under intermittent machine-gun fire and shelling which swelled the already terrible casualty list. One of the few officers who survived narrates how after firing away all his ammunition and scoring several successes—he was sheltering in a hole made by a large trench-mortar bomb—he fell asleep from sheer exhaustion, and woke up later to watch our heavy artillery bombarding the hostile trenches with considerable accuracy. Rather after midnight, when there was a lull in the machine-gun fire, he managed to regain our lines.

In the meantime two attempts had been made to carry the line forward, the Borders advancing as arranged at 8.15 a.m., the Newfoundland Regiment being put in an hour later. The

---

[1] The left company had only half that distance to go.
[2] Both subsequently received the M.C.

Borders suffered terribly from the machine guns before they cleared the British trenches, and none reached the forward line of survivors of the S.W.B. Of the Newfoundlanders, whose heroic but hopeless attempt was made because erroneous information had reached D.H.Q. that a lodgment had been made in the German lines, a few worked forward by the sunken road and joined the survivors of C, the great majority went down before they were half-way across No Man's Land, and thereafter no further advance was attempted. The long day dragged on slowly, each hour adding to the casualties and to the sufferings of the wounded, till at last darkness enabled survivors to creep back to safety and allowed stretcher-bearers to go out on their errand of mercy, though the Germans started a heavy but intermittent machine-gun fire directly it became dark and kept on sending up flares, as though expecting a fresh attack. This greatly hampered the work of rescue, and many of the wounded, especially those lying in or near the German wire, could not be reached.

North of the Ancre indeed the British attack had ended in unmistakable failure and terrible losses. The Twenty-Ninth Division had, as General Hunter-Weston wrote: " shown itself capable of maintaining its high traditions." It had given " a magnificent display of disciplined courage," it had gone forward in the face of a devastating machine-gun fire and heavy shelling, without faltering or wavering, in perfect order and undismayed by the odds against it.[1] But it had been shattered to pieces and was incapable of further effort. The 2nd S.W.B. had not been the heaviest hit battalion in the Division, yet its casualty list included 15 of the 21 officers and 384 of the 578 men engaged in the attack, 235 of them killed and missing. There was little chance that any " missing " might later be reported as prisoners; scarce one had reached the enemy's lines, and " missing " merely meant that a man had fallen too far out for his body to be recovered. Of the officers, Captains Blake, Hughes and McLaren, Lieutenant H. P. Evans, Second Lieutenants Bowyer, Don, Karran, Murray, Rice, Robinson and Wells had been killed. Captain Somerville and Lieutenants Fowkes, Kelly and Mason could be reckoned fortunate in being merely wounded. Of the fallen officers several had served with the battalion for some time, and their loss was severely felt. Even when the reserve officers and the 10 per cent of N.C.O's and men left out as " battle nucleus " had rejoined the battalion was sadly changed from that which had been through the evacuation of

---

[1] Besides the M.C.'s already mentioned, the D.S.O. was awarded to Major Raikes for gallantry in leading up the reserve and for his conspicuous services in organizing the succour of the wounded.

Cape Helles and had landed in France full of hopes of achieving great things. Its gallantry and devotion had been conspicuous, but the task set it had been beyond even its capacity.

The British failure on the left and left-centre had been to some extent balanced by substantial successes on the right, while beyond that again the French had attained all their objectives, their unexpected attack having apparently altogether surprised the Germans. On the British right-centre also some hard-won footholds had been gained, and in exploiting and extending these the Regiment's two Pioneer battalions were both involved.

One of these lodgments had been made by the Thirty-Second Division on the spur South of Thiepval, at a sharp angle in the German lines, known as the Leipzig Salient; farther to the right the Thirty-Fourth Division had effected another at La Boisselle, South of the Albert–Bapaume road. Both Divisions had lost very heavily and had to be relieved, the Thirty-Second Division by the Twenty-Fifth, the Thirty-Fourth by the Nineteenth. Thus both 5th and 6th S.W.B. came into the fighting area almost together, though neither was to have the satisfaction of much that could be reckoned " fighting " in the sense of using rifles and bayonets and inflicting casualties on the enemy. An occasional bombing-fight, when the enemy counter-attacked at a point where Pioneers were assisting to consolidate, gave some men chances of " putting it across " the enemy, but usually the Pioneers had to endure, not to inflict losses, to be shelled and machine-gunned without a chance to reply. Trenches had to be cleared up, captured positions connected with our lines and rendered defensible, damages to be repaired and communication trenches kept open, all under heavy fire, indispensable work which offered few chances of " getting into the limelight."

The 5th Battalion, as already mentioned, had been attached to the Eighth Division for July 1st and had moved into position opposite Ovillers on the previous evening. Three companies were allotted to the different brigades and were in readiness to go forward and consolidate their gains, the fourth, A, was specially detailed for bridging trenches and pushing forward tramlines. The Eighth Division, attacking with great dash and gallantry, came up against specially strong defences and only at one point was a foothold gained in the German trenches. Counter-attacks were promptly begun against the handful who had established themselves here; machine guns on either flank swept No Man's Land and prevented reinforcements or fresh supplies of ammunition from following them across, and " consolidation " was never even begun. After the 5th S.W.B. had waited interminable hours D Company was ordered up in the evening, though not to consolidate captured trenches. It had to man part of our frontage which was defended by hardly any save the dead and the dying. It had also to go out into No Man's Land and bring in those of the casualties who survived and could be reached. D did splendid work. All night long they toiled, some men going out time after time, often right up to the German wire, and many owed their lives and escape from captivity to D's devoted courage, enterprise and resource. Lieutenant Rebsch was conspicuous in this work, and besides him Sergeants Jones and Williamson, Lance Corporals Drewett and Thoms, and Privates Boggett, T. J. Bowen, Clarke and Casey distinguished themselves particularly. Before daybreak the Twelfth Division arrived to relieve the Eighth, and the 5th S.W.B. were allowed to rejoin their own Division, by that time in line near La Boisselle.

This village, one of the strongest points between the Ancre and Fricourt, had defied direct attack on July 1st, though just East of it the Thirty-Fourth Division had taken and held portions of the front line and in places had penetrated even deeper. The 58th Brigade had been placed at its disposal, and the following day (July 2nd) saw it establish itself solidly in the second line East of La Boisselle and gain a footing in the village itself despite stubborn resistance. Next day (July 3rd) the 57th Brigade attacked in conjunction with the Twelfth Division on the left, and after a bitter struggle captured most of the village and 150 prisoners. The 5th were turned on to dig a communication trench across No Man's Land into La Boisselle and to assist in evacuating wounded, while bombing parties under Second Lieutenants Coulter and A. L. Richards joined in the clearing up of the village. This went on for another three days. The Germans clung stoutly to the ruins, which were wrested from them step by step, the 5th's bombers, now under Lieutenant Hall and Second Lieutenant I. T. Evans, doing fine work. Lieutenant Hall, " essentially a fighter rather than a Pioneer " one account calls him, one of the 5th's keenest and most efficient officers, who had already received a well-deserved M.C., was conspicuous for his skill and gallantry. He took his men through our own barrage to close with the enemy before they could recover from our shelling, drove the Germans back some way down the trench, handling rifle and bomb most effectively himself, and was killed just as he had attained his objective.

July 7th saw a fresh attack by the Nineteenth Division, the Twelfth co-operating on the left nearer Ovillers, the Twenty-Third on the right nearer Contalmaison. This proved definitely successful on the left and centre, and then on the night of July

9th/10th the Nineteenth Division was relieved and the 5th, who had been digging and carrying almost without intermission, were at last given a rest. The battalion had been lucky as regards casualties, barely 40 all told, including Second Lieutenant Day wounded, but the men had been terribly hard worked and welcomed the chance of real repose in the pleasant surroundings of Baisieux Wood.

The 6th Battalion's experiences somewhat resembled those of the 5th. Headquarters had remained at Senlis till July 4th, when they moved to Bouzincourt, though meantime A and C Companies had been up to Aveluy Wood, assisting the Thirty-Second and Forty-Ninth Divisions, and had been kept busy, escaping with half a dozen casualties, though these included Major Morgan and Second Lieutenant T. G. Evans, both wounded. By July 4th the Twenty-Fifth Division had relieved the Thirty-Second, the frontage held including part of the Leipzig Salient. B and D, who went up to the line that evening, found plenty to do in clearing the ground taken, connecting it up with the old British trenches and preparing for counter-attacks. On July 5th the 1st Wiltshire mastered yet more of the Salient, and then for two days that battalion and the 3rd Worcestershire held on despite repeated counter-attacks, punishing the enemy severely. This meant more consolidating and connecting up for the Pioneers under very trying conditions. The gains made had been important so the enemy did not spare their shells, but the 6th came off extremely lightly with two men killed and two officers, Captain F. B. Thomas and Second Lieutenant J. L. Evans, and 32 men wounded. On the night of July 6th/7th the battalion was relieved and proceeded by Aveluy to Albert, where it occupied billets just vacated by the 5th Battalion.

The Twenty-Fifth Division was now shifting to the right, relieving the Twelfth S.W. of Ovillers, astride the Pozières road. The toils were closing in now on Ovillers and the next advance would, it was hoped, complete the isolation of that village. In preparation for this the 6th had to consolidate captured ground, dig assembly trenches and improve the position generally. It was often vigorously shelled and casualties were more severe. Second Lieutenant N. Griffiths and 11 men were killed, Lieutenant Eskell, Second Lieutenant Renwick and 24 men wounded, among them Company Sergeant Major O'Neill who did splendid work on July 10th in bandaging others worse wounded than himself. On the same occasion Lieutenant Ede showed great courage and coolness, getting up on the parapet under severe shell fire and walking slowly up and down to encourage his men, who were having a bad time. So effective was his example that most of the men stuck steadily to their work despite the shelling. On July 12th the 7th and 75th Brigades attacked most successfully just North of Ovillers and by distracting German attention enabled the Forty-Eighth Division to work round behind Ovillers and compel the surrender of its defenders. After this the Twenty-Fifth, which had by now lost heavily, was withdrawn, though the 6th S.W.B. were left behind for several days, to help the relieving Division to consolidate. This meant more hard work, but the 6th were fortunate as to casualties, having only two more killed and three wounded before being taken back to Bus les Artois on July 20th.[1] On the 24th it moved to Beaussart, relieving the 5th Northamptonshire just North of the Ancre, which frontage the Twenty-Fifth Division had just taken over.

While the Pioneer battalions had been leaving their mark on the trenches, and suffering quite substantial casualties, two junior " Service " battalions of the TWENTY-FOURTH had had a much briefer but far more costly share in the great battle. The Thirty-Eighth Division, in reserve to the Seventeenth Corps when the battle began, had been transferred almost directly to the Fifteenth under Lieutenant General Sir H. S. Horne. That Corps, attacking on either side of the sharp bend in the German line at Fricourt, had been conspicuously successful, capturing Mametz on the right and breaking into the German positions North of Fricourt, which village it had proceeded to " pinch " out. By the evening of July 5th the British line was already close to the Southern projection of Mametz Wood, the largest of the many woods on the battlefield, which offered a serious obstacle to an advance against the main ridge. Lying in the dip between the Montauban-Mametz spur and the main ridge along which the German second line ran, it was within 300 yards of that line from which it could easily be reinforced. It was mainly composed of oak trees, nine feet and more in girth, interspersed with birches, a few beeches and some willows with thick undergrowth, and having as yet escaped heavy shell fire was still very dense. Previous efforts had shown that the wood was held in force, and the Thirty-Eighth Division, which relieved the Seventh in front of Mametz Wood on July 5th, spent its first days in reconnaissance. Then on July 7th the 115th Brigade attacked the wood from the frontage Cliff Trench (left)—Marlborough Wood, using the 11th S.W.B. on the right and the 16th Welch on the left.

The attack had as its first objective a line just inside the Eastern edge of the wood. This secured, the attackers were to

---

[1] The total casualties for the month were nearly 20 men killed and 80 wounded.

MAMETZ WOOD

push on North and West and endeavour to reach a ride running North and South about midway across the wood.[1] Starting at 8.30 a.m. the attack at once encountered a heavy fire from rifles and machine guns, while the German guns which had already replied vigorously to our bombardment redoubled their fire. The 11th pushed forward well nevertheless, but before long machine guns from Bazentin-le-Grand Wood and from Sabot and Flatiron Copses caught them in flank, inflicting many

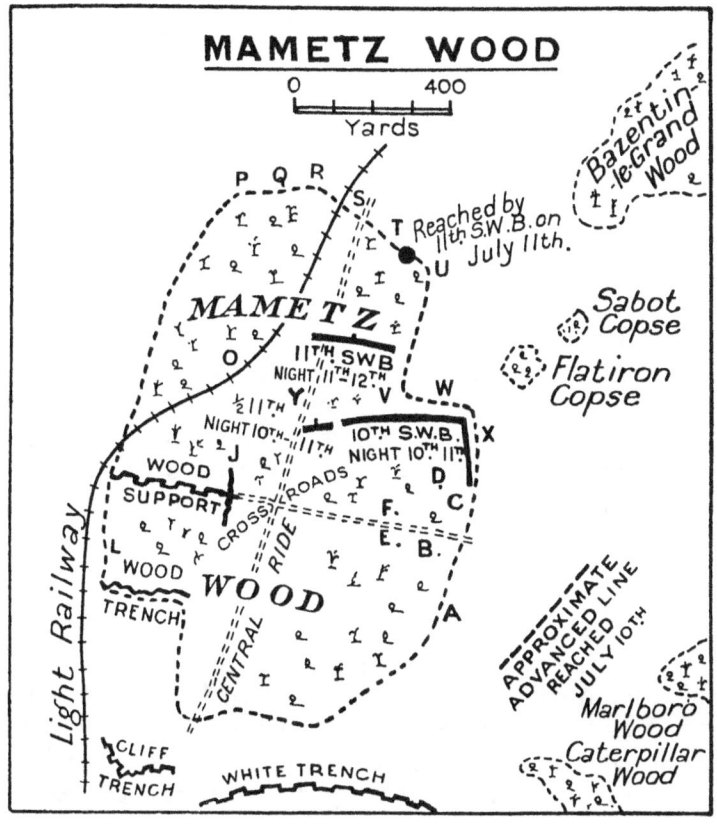

casualties, and brought the attack to a standstill. On the right the leading men were within 200 yards of their objective, on the left they were nearly double that distance off. Satisfactory observation and registration had been impossible and in consequence the British bombardment had been neither sufficiently accurate nor effective. A second attack was ordered for 11.15 a.m., but the half an hour's fresh bombardment again proved inadequate. The machine guns were not subdued, and this advance also was soon held up.

By this time the 10th S.W.B. had received orders to support

[1] Cross-roads Y—T—U on map.

the attack and Colonel Wilkinson had come forward to reconnoitre. When the second advance failed, A and D Companies under Captain Galsworthy were ordered up to reinforce the firing line, followed an hour later by the remaining two under the C.O. Setting out from their bivouac near Mametz the 10th advanced across a maze of battered trenches, progress being much impeded by heavy rain and the consequent mud, and eventually arrived at the point of deployment just before 3 p.m. At 3.15 p.m. A, B and D also attacked,[1] but with no better success than before. The machine guns were still in action and their fire made progress virtually impossible. Colonel Wilkinson was killed in bringing forward the second wave and the advance soon faded away.

Divisional Headquarters, however, issued orders for yet another thirty minutes' bombardment to begin at 4.30 p.m. This was to be followed by an assault, for which the infantry were to be reorganized. When this message found General Evans (B.G.C. 115th Brigade), it was already past 4 p.m., and before he could reach Caterpillar Wood it was 4.45 p.m. With the troops lying out within 250 yards of Mametz Wood, rather disorganized, very weary and wet to the skin, for it had poured with rain and the ground was saturated, the orders could not be carried out: the Brigadier therefore decided to cancel the attack and after dark the attacking units were successfully withdrawn, the whole brigade being placed in bivouac near Mametz. The 10th S.W.B. had come off lightly, except for losing their C.O., having only 2 men killed and about 30 wounded, but the 11th were harder hit with 13 officers[2] and 177 men casualties.

The 10th and 11th S.W.B. spent two days in their Mametz bivouacs, during which time the 113th Brigade systematically patrolled No Man's Land and reconnoitred Mametz Wood, only to find it still strongly held. On the evening of July 9th two companies of the 11th S.W.B. took over Marlborough and Caterpillar Woods from the 114th Brigade which was concentrating for a fresh effort at 4.15 a.m. next day. In this it was attacking the Eastern portion of the wood, the 113th Brigade simultaneously assaulting the Western side, while the 115th remained in reserve.

General Watts, G.O.C. Seventh Division, had temporarily taken charge of the Thirty-Eighth, and by concentrating a heavy

---

[1] C remained in reserve.

[2] Lieutenant Hamer, who had just taken over the Adjutant's duties from Captain Dawes, invalided, was killed, as were also Second Lieutenants Fletcher, Miller-Hallett and Salathiel. Captains Monteith, Browning and Second Lieutenants Ackerley, Lowe, Whittaker and Woodcock were wounded. Of the men about 50 were killed or missing.

fire on the Southern edge and making skilful use of a smoke barrage, he succeeded in distracting the German attention from the main attack, which advanced in splendid style over the 500 yards of open and penetrated into the wood. Here there was stubborn opposition and savage fighting, but the troops pressed on and eventually established an East and West line across the wood about north of Wood Support Trench.[1] All day the fighting continued with fluctuating fortunes. In the thickness of the wood it was hard to see what was happening, or to keep touch, while the superior officers found it almost impossible to exercise any control. Gradually the attacking brigades used up their reserves, and about midday the 10th S.W.B. were ordered forward.[2] Moving off about 1 p.m. the 10th reached the Eastern edge of Mametz Wood without many casualties, despite the heavy shelling which greeted them. Here Major Harvey had just deployed his men when he received orders to postpone his attack in order to allow of a fresh bombardment. At 4 p.m. he was to advance in conjunction with other troops on his left and was to clear the Eastern corner of the wood.[3]

Attacking with great vigour and dash the 10th made excellent progress at first, taking several prisoners and driving the surviving defenders out into the open, where in bolting towards Sabot and Flatiron Copses they gave targets to the rifles and machine guns of the 11th S.W.B. holding Caterpillar and Marlborough Woods. But opposition became more serious as the advance progressed: much trouble was experienced in dealing with machine guns,[4] bombers who tried to work along a trench on the edge of the wood met stubborn resistance and had many casualties, and the 10th were held up a little short of their objective, though two bombing attacks which Sergeant Edwards led with much courage and initiative gained not a little ground. Elsewhere the attack was less successful. Detachments fought their way forward despite savage opposition to within about three hundred yards of the Northern edge, but the portion of the wood West of the railway remained untaken. In the end an irregular line was formed, the 10th S.W.B. lining the Eastern edge S.W. of Flatiron Copse with their left thrown back at right angles towards the middle ride.[5]

[1] On map J—F—D.
[2] The battalion had before this moved up to Pommiers Redoubt and been placed under the B.G.C. 114th Brigade. A party with two Lewis guns had been sent to Caterpillar Wood to bring enfilade fire to bear on Germans in position between Flatiron Copse and the wood, and other detachments had been detailed for various fatigues.
[3] The battalion was to secure the line X—W—V—Y.
[4] Notably one at X.
[5] Approximately along the line running E. and W. through X towards Y.

Before this the 115th Brigade had received orders to relieve the other brigades, now quite exhausted. Half of it was already in action in the wood and the two companies of the 11th S.W.B. could not be moved from Caterpillar and Marlborough Woods, but the relief was at length carried out and the other half-battalion of the 11th came in between the 10th and the central ride, with the 17th R.W.F. and 16th Welch beyond it. The night was disturbed by much firing and many alarms, but no real counter-attack developed, though the 10th beat off one sharp little attack. Shortly before dawn Major Harvey made a fresh effort to secure his objectives, attacking them simultaneously from both flanks. This was most successful and by 5 a.m. the disputed points were in the hands of the 10th, who captured several more prisoners and in clearing up the captured position took possession of several guns and howitzers; Sergeant J. H. Williams, who distinguished himself by his courage and skill, led his men with great dash and good work was done by many others. General Watts meanwhile had given orders for a fresh effort to clear the untaken portion. This eventually got going at 3.15 p.m., an earlier start having been delayed by a barrage which our guns put down. The R.W.F. and Welch met very stubborn resistance and could make little progress, but the 11th S.W.B.[1] fared better and fought their way to the N.E. corner of the wood, despite heavy machine-gun fire and strong opposition, only to find their left completely "in the air." This was about 5.30 p.m. and for some time Colonel Gaussen and his men managed to maintain their ground, though German reinforcements prevented them from pushing West along the Northern edge. The Brigadier called on the other battalions to advance again and reduce the pressure on the 11th, but after gaining a little ground they were again driven back and about 9 p.m. the 11th had to fall back to a line about three hundred yards short of the Northern edge. Here they remained till early next morning (July 12th), when the Twenty-First Division took over the greater part of Mametz Wood, the Seventh coming in on their right and relieving the 11th S.W.B. in Caterpillar and Marlborough Woods.

Mametz Wood had been an exhausting and searching trial for the two "Gwent" battalions. In their six months of trench-warfare neither had had to "go over the top" and it was hard to have to carry out their first attack in a wood of such thickness and magnitude, in bad weather, when rains had made communication-trenches impassable and going over the open difficult. There was much delay over getting and directing artillery

[1] Two companies of the 10th moved forward in support of the 11th, the others remaining in the positions captured.

assistance, communication between Headquarters and the units in action was more than usually uncertain and slow, and little time was given to reconnoitre or to prepare for each successive operation. Still both 10th and 11th came out of their ordeal with much credit.[1] Neither battalion had, all things considered, suffered very heavily. The 10th, in addition to Colonel Wilkinson, had Second Lieutenants M. J. Everton and R. P. Taylor and 29 men killed and missing, while 9 officers[2] were wounded with 140 men. As against these losses the 10th could set the capture of three field-guns and two heavier pieces and the infliction of substantial punishment on the enemy. The 11th had been harder hit, the later stages of the fighting had cost it Captain L. R. Lewis killed and had brought its total of killed up to 36, as many more men were " missing," which almost always meant " dead," and the wounded came to over 150, including ten officers.[3] It too had acquitted itself well: with adequate support on its left its last attack would have made good the Northern edge of the wood.

The Thirty-Eighth Division's relief did not bring the 10th and 11th a prolonged rest or even a move from the Somme area, for after two days out of the line their brigade relieved one of the Forty-Eighth Division in front of Colincamps, facing the German lines between Hebuterne and Serre. They were thus still within sound of the fighting, if their sector was no longer included in the reduced frontage to which "active" operations were restricted in the second stage of the great offensive, now just opening.

[1] The following were brought to notice by the Brigadier for good work: 10th S.W.B., Captains E. T. Rees and A. Galsworthy; Lieutenant and Adjutant E. F. Orford; Sergeants J. H. Williams, R. Edwards, Corporal W. G. Woodhouse, Lance Corporal S. J. Woodhall, Private D. J. Owen. 11th S.W.B., Colonel J. R. Gaussen, Captain E. F. Browning, Second Lieutenants T. H. Davies and R. M. Heppel, Company Sergeant Major Davies, Sergeants Edwardes, Rees and P. Harris, Corporals Morgan and Witts, Privates Preston, D. J. Davies, Pashley, Dadey, P. S. Davies and Tilley. Captain E. Evans, M.O. of the 11th S.W.B., received the M.C. for his gallantry and devotion to duty in this action: he did splendid work and ran repeated risks in getting to the wounded and succouring them.

[2] Major Harvey, Captain Galsworthy, Lieutenants Gill and Parry, and Second Lieutenants Davenport, D. C. Davies, Yonge, Hillbourne and H. C. Williams.

[3] Besides those already mentioned Second Lieutenants Carrington, Heppel and Travis had been hit.

CHAPTER XVI

THE SOMME

II : *The Middle Period*

THE struggle for Mametz Wood belongs to an intermediate stage in the Somme battles, in which the gains made on July 1st were consolidated and extended in preparation for an advance against the German second position along the Southern crest of the main ridge. In this new attack, launched on July 14th from South of Delville Wood to the Albert–Bapaume road, the TWENTY-FOURTH had only one battalion engaged, for though the Twenty-Fifth Division just beyond the road profited by the attack to continue its pressure on the Germans near Ovillers, its front lay outside the " active " area. In like manner the Twenty-Ninth Division, still facing the Beaumont Hamel defences, was much too weak for any but a defensive rôle, while the Thirty-Eighth, as already mentioned, had been transferred to a quarter formerly part of the " active " frontage but now relegated to the " quiet " category. Thus only the 1st Battalion, recently arrived on the Somme, represented the Regiment in this stage of the struggle.

In the support trenches of the North Maroc sector the 1st Battalion had listened, on July 1st and 2nd, with intense interest to the sounds of the great battle raging miles away to the South. July 2nd brought orders for its Division's relief by the Fortieth and, this completed, the battalion entrained on the 6th at Chocques, reaching Doullens that evening and moving to a bivouac at Bonnyville, seven miles S.W. The next stage, a long and trying march in pouring rain which the men stood splendidly, finished at Coisy, whence a night march (July 8th/9th) brought it to Franvillers, half-way between Amiens and Albert. On the 10th the battalion moved forward to Albert in weather so hot and oppressive that a violent thunderstorm came as a positive relief. On the way the battalion met the Commander-in-Chief, who stopped to watch it go past and told the men of the capture of Mametz Wood; further on it passed through Baizeux Wood where the 5th S.W.B. were resting, while on reaching Albert it found the 6th Battalion billeted in the town.

The billets allotted to the 1st Battalion were thoroughly insanitary and provided the main occupation of the next three days, though the enemy tried to make things lively by shelling the town vigorously. The Welch and the Munsters caught it badly, but the S.W.B. were luckier and escaped without casualties. Officers had meanwhile been up to investigate the front trenches near Contalmaison which the 1st Brigade had taken over from the Twenty-Third Division on July 11th/12th. These were on the extreme left of the frontage to be included in the next attack, in which the First Division was to form a defensive flank to cover the Twenty-First, which was attacking from Mametz Wood Northward.

The 1st Brigade had had some sharp fighting, beating off a counter-attack and clearing the wood North of Contalmaison before, in the " big push " of July 14th, it advanced to and captured Contalmaison Villa, thereby covering the Twenty-First Division's flank. That evening the 3rd Brigade relieved the 1st, the S.W.B. being placed in Lozenge Wood North of Fricourt, in reserve. In moving up it had been heavily bombarded with gas shell while passing through Bécourt, but had been lucky in getting through safely and reached its assigned position about 2.30 a.m. on the 15th. Here the battalion was occupying some deep dug-outs in the reserve trenches of the German front system and examined with interest the elaborate accommodation with which the Germans had provided themselves. Nearly all that day it was carrying ammunition up to Mametz Wood, in preparation for an attack on some trenches running N.W. from Bazentin-le-Petit Wood towards Pozières. The Welch were to attack and the S.W.B. to support, so at 11.30 p.m. the battalion started for Mametz Wood. Here C and D Companies established themselves 300 yards from the Northern edge, which B lined, A occupying some shell holes running towards Bazentin-le-Petit Wood.

The attack was stoutly opposed and failed, but the Welch renewed the effort in the afternoon with more success, capturing most of their objective without having to use A Company, which had moved forward to support them, though its commander, Second Lieutenant Ward Jones, was unfortunately killed in gallantly reconnoitring for a bombing attack he was intending to make. The 3rd Brigade followed up this success by a night attack in which the S.W.B. were again in support, taking up a position in the open West of Mametz Wood. This move proved happily inspired, as the enemy's counter-barrage came down heavily but ineffectually on Mametz Wood, while the battalion escaped almost without casualties. The attack was a prompt and brilliant success, over 1200 yards of frontage being captured without using the battalion, though C Company was sent up to occupy Black Watch Alley, a communication trench running back from the left of the captured line.[1] The Germans shelled the positions freely, but without interfering seriously with their consolidation, and the battalion's luck continued in as, though kept busy all through the 17th, carrying bombs and

---

[1] This company " bought " a German prisoner from another unit for 700 sandbags.

stores up to the new line, it only suffered another ten casualties. Late on the 18th it was relieved by the 2nd Brigade and went back to Lozenge Wood, where it remained for twenty-four hours, sending up large working-parties on the night of the 19th/20th to construct two "keeps" near Contalmaison. These parties were heavily shelled and had several casualties, but they finished their work nevertheless, while Second Lieutenant Garnons-Williams distinguished himself by going out under heavy fire and bringing a wounded man in to shelter. Their task completed, the working-parties rejoined their main body which had gone back to Bécourt to rest.[1]

July 14th had resulted in a substantial advance, but some time passed before the British efforts to extend and improve their lodgment on the main ridge met with a similar success. The Germans brought up large reserves, counter-attacked in force, succeeded at several points in recovering ground they had lost and put up a determined resistance which was only overcome after desperate fighting and at a heavy price in casualties. Gradually the most bitterly contested points of vantage like Delville Wood, Ginchy and Guillemont, Mouquet Farm and Pozières were wrested from German keeping and the way thereby prepared for another attack on a wide front, while in the aggregate the gains were substantial, though hardly commensurate with their cost. It was a stubborn and often disappointing struggle; many Divisions were fought to a standstill with little to show for their efforts and losses, while whole battalions were often used up to win some minor tactical point.

In this stubborn fighting and slow progress from mid-July to mid-September the TWENTY-FOURTH was mainly represented by the 1st and 6th Battalions, though the 5th had ten hectic days at the end of July, in which hard fighting figured almost as largely as its normal work of pioneering, and losses were heavy. The 2nd, 10th and 11th all departed for Flanders before the end of July, though the 2nd were to return to the Somme in October.

The 1st Battalion's spell of rest had been but brief. By July 21st it was back at Lozenge Wood, prior to relieving the Northamptonshires of the 2nd Brigade in the front line near Contalmaison Villa in the small hours of July 24th. Here the battalion was confronted with Munster Alley, a trench South of the Bapaume road, which had already repulsed several attempts. Undeterred by this, at 2 a.m. on July 25th, A and D Companies, in two lines of platoons at fifty paces interval and thirty paces distance, began climbing out of our front line, here called

---

[1] Up to this time the battalion had only lost one officer and 7 men killed, 20 men wounded and 4 missing.

Sussex Trench, and advanced, only to be met by a heavy fire from machine guns which our bombardment had failed to silence. However, Captain Walshe led his company forward with great courage and resolution and was magnificently backed up by the young subalterns on whom the leading of companies and platoons had now devolved. Second Lieutenant Garnons-Williams, who remained at duty though wounded, set a fine example and kept his men in hand splendidly, Second Lieutenant N. Evans fell heading a charge, and close up to the German trench, Second Lieutenant Welsh led a party of bombers with great dash, refusing to go back even when wounded, while Second Lieutenant Skinner was hit when leading his platoon of B Company up to support some of A who had reached a shallow trench on the left just short of the objective. Among this party was Private Wannell, who managed to bring his Lewis gun into action and did splendid work, knocking out a hostile machine gun only a little distance away and being mainly instrumental, along with Company Sergeant Major Power, in repulsing a counter-attack. Elsewhere, no one could get anywhere near the German line and nearly all the other officers had fallen. Realizing the failure of the attack, Colonel Collier ordered the companies to withdraw at once and to concentrate on getting in the wounded before dawn. Many were brought in, Company Sergeant Major Power going out fifty yards to the front to rescue one man, but Second Lieutenant Skinner, who was last seen lying in a shell-hole, could not be reached, and besides him Second Lieutenants Evans, D. A. Williams[1] and R. H. Cole were missing, and Second Lieutenants Coghill, W. Cole, Bayliss, Farnall, L. M. Webb and Welsh were all wounded, while casualties among the rank and file came to nearly 80.[2]

That evening the battalion was relieved, as the First Division was going out of the line. It went back through Albert to Meillencourt, being on the way most hospitably entertained by Colonel Trower and the 5th Battalion, who were then at Albert. The drums of the 5th met the 1st outside Albert and played them through the town to a field where the 5th had prepared a meal for them, that battalion having forfeited two days' issue of rum and a proportion of rations to provide for the 1st's entertainment. There were many old hands among the W.O.'s and N.C.O.'s of the 5th and the meeting between the two battalions was altogether a very pleasant episode.

[1] His body was afterwards found: the others were never heard of again.
[2] For their gallantry in these operations the M.M. was awarded to Sergeants Wright, Winn and Jones, and Privates Cahill, Darwent, Hanford, Laughor and Williams. Company Sergeant Major Power and Private Wannell received the D.C.M. and Captain Walshe and Second Lieutenant Welsh the M.C.

The First Division remained " out " for nearly three weeks, the S.W.B. being at Millencourt nearly all the time. Here several drafts joined, though, with the drafting authorities' usual disregard for the *esprit de corps* regiments were officially directed to foster, most of them came from any other unit but the TWENTY-FOURTH, the culminating thing being the posting to it of 177 of the Welch who, after much correspondence, were ultimately transferred to their own 2nd Battalion.

While the 1st Battalion had been tackling Munster Alley the 5th had returned to the fighting zone just on its right, the Nineteenth Division having come into line between the First and the Fifty-First, which was facing High Wood. The 5th S.W.B. had moved up into Mametz Wood on July 22nd to find it most " unhealthy," as it was promptly subjected to an intense bombardment, first with shells of the heaviest calibre and then with gas. Great damage was done, trees being blown down, torn asunder and stripped of their branches, the trenches were in places quite obliterated and casualties were heavy. Colonel Trower's coolness and gallantry were never more conspicuous than during this shelling : he walked calmly up and down with heavy stuff bursting all round him, directing the stretcher-bearers, and by his fearlessness doing much to steady and encourage the men. This unpleasant experience did not, however, prevent the battalion putting in some exceedingly useful work, for during that night new front-line trenches were constructed to connect up their Division with the Fifty-First. This was accomplished under considerable shell fire, but fortunately without many casualties, though on subsequent days Mametz Wood was again so heavily shelled that to avoid further loss the battalion shifted into the open and dug in there.

On July 23rd the 56th and 57th Brigades attacked the " Switch Line " which ran between Bazentin-le-Petit and Martinpuich. This attack, though gallantly pressed, ended in failure. The Germans, by throwing forward an advanced line[1] somewhat nearer the British trenches, had virtually escaped the preliminary bombardment, and the attack found them practically intact in numbers and morale. Its repulse left the 5th with no gains to consolidate, but busy enough with bringing in the wounded and repairing the havoc wrought by the counter-bombardment. For several days the Division continued in line, the 5th lying up by day in Fricourt Wood, a mile further back than Mametz and rather less " unhealthy," though by no means immune from shelling, but coming forward at night to assist in digging a fresh front line N.E. of Bazentin-le-Petit and con-

[1] Later known as the Intermediate Trench.

necting it up with the Fifty-First Division nearer High Wood. Being quite close to the enemy large covering parties were necessary, and these had some difficulty in keeping the German patrols at a distance. Several sharp encounters occurred and involved many casualties, the wounded including Captains Newmarch, Rebsch and Parry-Jones. Captain Croft, who was in charge, did splendid service, and Captain Agate, R.A.M.C., the battalion's M.O., was conspicuous for his devotion and courage in attending to the numerous wounded. The main end before the Division was still to capture the "Intermediate" line, and on July 30th a fresh attempt was made. Launched an hour before dark this attack, though a failure on the left, was successful on the right, where the 7th King's Own and 10th Royal Warwickshires secured their objectives. On this Captain Rose took A Company forward to help them consolidate. This involved some fighting also, for the Germans were counter-attacking, but A did splendid work, Captain Rose displaying great gallantry and handling his men most skilfully, while Second Lieutenant D. L. Evans not only directed the wiring of the captured line, but assisted to clear part of it by leading a bombing party. D Company, who had to link up the new line with that of the Fifty-First Division, came in for several barrages and lost heavily. However, they reached the line assigned to them, encountering and driving back the enemy and securing several prisoners. They then started work, but the accurate and heavy German shell fire compelled them before long to withdraw. Losses were severe, indeed the Division was immediately afterwards withdrawn from the line prior to being transferred to Flanders. It had had a difficult and a trying time. With High Wood untaken on the right, the position had been peculiarly hard to attack and to retain when taken. The 5th S.W.B. in particular had worked splendidly, and though between July 18th and 31st they had had 36 men killed and missing and 4 officers and 179 men wounded, these losses were not disproportionate to the work they had got through and the fire to which they had been exposed.

About the same time as the 5th three other battalions of the Regiment which were due for a turn in some comparatively peaceful quarter also quitted the Somme area. Of these the 2nd preceded the 10th and 11th. Despite its disastrous experiences on July 1st, three weeks passed before it proved possible to relieve the Twenty-Ninth Division; indeed on the evening of July 2nd the weary survivors of the 2nd S.W.B.,[1] reorganized in two companies under Lieutenants Ross and B. J. Davies, had taken

[1] The battalion had already been over a week in the front line, right through our bombardment, and the men were very short of sleep and badly in need of rest.

over 300 yards of front-line trenches opposite Beaumont Hamel, rather to the right of Mary Redan. The trenches were poor and dirty, the communication and support trenches far too shallow, and much work was needed. Quantities of equipment littered No Man's Land, and much was brought in, with some bodies, for which a deep grave was dug behind our support line. There was little fighting on the battalion's own front, though South of the Ancre things were very active, and the 2nd tried to assist the British efforts there by long-range Lewis gun fire. On the night of July 5th/6th a new trench was begun by the 2nd Monmouthshires 300 yards out to the front, and the battalion started sapping out in that direction. From July 7th to 10th it was in support, during which time the Corps commander visited it and congratulated the officers and men warmly on their splendid conduct on July 1st. On this day the numbers on parade had risen to 232, including 15 officers, Captain Garnett, Lieutenant Cousmaker and Second Lieutenants E. G. Jones, Wardle and W. M. Evans having rejoined from schools and courses, and before the end of July some substantial drafts brought the battalion's strength up to over 600 men, though, as nearly a fifth were employed away from the battalion, its "trench strength" was much lower than the nominal figure.

It had gone back into the front line on July 17th for six days, mainly devoted to repairing the trenches, salvaging equipment and rifles from No Man's Land, and improving communication trenches. Its patrols were active, but found the enemy on the alert and were unable to bring off any minor successes such as directing our artillery on to hostile working parties. On July 24th the Twenty-Fifth Division arrived to relieve the Twenty-Ninth and the 2nd S.W.B. went back to Doullens, whence it travelled Northward to Proven on July 27th.

The 10th and 11th had found the Hebuterne–Serre front a great change from Mametz Wood. The enemy was concentrating his attention on his second line, though at the same time attempting to repair his much-damaged front line and to strengthen his wire which was decidedly thin. Those employed on these tasks afforded frequent opportunities to our machine gunners and snipers, and the 11th's patrols several times located parties, on which effective fire was then opened. But they were not to see much of this sector. After both 10th and 11th had done two tours of four days in the line, orders were received for their Division's transfer to Flanders, to which area General Hunter-Weston's whole Eighth Corps was being shifted. July 30th therefore found the 10th and 11th entraining for what was

THE HINDENBURG TRENCH

to prove a protracted acquaintance with the Ypres Salient. This left the 6th as for the moment the only battalion of the Regiment actively employed on the Somme front.

Even the 6th was hardly in the "active" area, for North of the Ancre, where its Division had, as already mentioned, relieved the Twenty-Ninth, things had become "quiet," and during its three weeks in this quarter nothing occurred to disturb the ordinary routine of trench-warfare. Much of its work, however, in constructing assembly trenches and dug-outs and generally preparing for another attack was eventually to prove very useful when, months later, the final and successful attack on Beaumont Hamel was delivered. Casualties were low, a bare dozen wounded between July 24th and August 9th, while some small drafts appeared and 8 new officers, among them Major G. A. Renwick of the 17th Northumberland Fusiliers who became second in command, and Captain Reid-Kellett. From August 9th to 18th the battalion was resting at Authie and then the Division moved back to the line, D.H.Q. being established at Hedauville and the frontage taken over being from the Leipzig Salient to the Ancre. This meant the usual variety of work for the Pioneer battalion, which had no sooner finished a job of road-making or repairing than newly captured trenches had to be put into a state of defence or parapets damaged by counter-bombardment to be rebuilt. A successful attack by the 1st Wiltshire on the 21st gave the 6th plenty of work in consolidating and cost them several casualties. Another success on August 24th, this time the capture of the Hindenburg Trench by the Wiltshire and 3rd Worcestershire, meant more consolidating and more casualties. Altogether the 6th had about 60 casualties in August, the great majority of them wounded. The officers were particularly unfortunate in getting hit, Captains Choinier and Mumford, Lieutenants C. M. Ede and Seden, and Second Lieutenants R. Jones and March all being wounded at this time. But the good defences the 6th had constructed proved most useful when a German Guard Division counter-attacked the Hindenburg Trench and was repulsed, and then on September 6th the Eleventh Division took over and the 6th S.W.B. went right back to Longvillers, where it arrived on September 12th for a fortnight's real rest. *En route* 100 men from the temporarily broken-up 2nd Monmouthshire (T.F.) had joined.

Meanwhile the 1st Battalion had been in the thick of things again. The First Division had moved back into line in the middle of August, relieving the Twenty-Third opposite and West of High Wood. High Wood had been reached on July 14th by the

Seventh Division, but the position had had to be evacuated, as being too much of a salient to be tenable. Ever since then it had been the scene of bitter and incessant fighting and was still in dispute. The 1st and 2nd Brigades, who took up the struggle on August 15th, met with the stubbornest resistance and could make little progress in the wood itself, though in the open to the West they gained some ground. Till August 20th the 3rd Brigade remained at Becourt Wood in reserve, then moving up to the front. The 1st S.W.B. acted at first as Brigade reserve, being busily employed in carrying up ammunition and stores to the front line, while large digging parties had also to be found. The enemy's guns were active and low-flying aeroplanes inconveniently prominent, but once again casualties were few, though on August 17th Second Lieutenant Bancroft, who had only joined a few days earlier, was wounded in reconnoitring the line of approach to the front trenches.

By this time the chief bone of contention was the Intermediate Trench N.E. of Bazentin-le-Petit. Its Eastern portion had been captured as well as another line beyond it, known as Clark's Trench, but to the West the Germans were still hanging on and the configuration of the ground made accurate observation of artillery fire difficult, while the trench was overlooked from the Northern end of High Wood. On August 24th the R.M.F. made a gallant but unsuccessful assault on this position, losing very heavily, and that evening the battalion replaced them with urgent orders to complete the capture of the trench. Attacking on the following afternoon A Company under Captain Walshe carried the barrier separating them from the Germans, capturing eight prisoners and causing about 30 Germans to quit the trench and retire Northwards across the open. Most of these were shot down, and the bombing party was pushing on down the trench when several more Germans came forward apparently to surrender. One of these, pretending to hand over his rifle, treacherously fired and killed Captain Walshe, whereupon, taking advantage of the confusion which naturally followed, the enemy counter-attacked and drove A Company back, only about thirty yards being retained.

Next afternoon (August 25th), however, A, now under Captain Inglis, renewed their attack, this time successfully. A heavy barrage had been put down at intervals with the object of driving the enemy back from the barricade and so clearing the Eastern half of the trench, and at 6.30 p.m. A Company pushed past the barrier and advanced nearly 300 yards, bombing the Germans back. Serious opposition was offered at a strong point, containing a machine gun which had been largely responsible for the non-success of the earlier attacks. It was captured, however, several prisoners being taken, one of whom, being recognized as the man who had shot Captain Walshe, was given a very short shrift. The attackers then pushed on, Privates Fitzpatrick and Murphy leading the way with the bayonet. Coming to a block of wire mixed up with bayonets which formed a *chevaux de frise* they climbed up on to the parapet and removed the obstacle, thus enabling the attack to get forward. C Company had simultaneously attempted to advance across the open against the Western portion of the trench, but this effort failed. A Company, however, captured another 80 yards and consolidated their gains, a trench being dug back from the Westernmost point reached to the old front line. In this fighting the example and leadership of Captain Inglis were conspicuous, and he was ably seconded by Private E. Williams who helped him to capture several Germans, while Sergeant Sheehan engaged successfully in a sniping duel with a German officer who had already shot two sergeants but was now picked off. Sergeant Geary too did fine work in charge of a party bringing up ammunition and rifle grenades, making several journeys from the support line to A Company's trenches when A was being hard pressed, and organized his men with great gallantry and skill, exposing himself freely and remaining at his post though wounded. Specially good work was also done by the battalion signallers who were constantly out repairing the repeatedly severed telephone wires between Headquarters and companies. Despite heavy shelling and machine gun fire they stuck to their work and succeeded in maintaining communications, Sergeants Pratten and Sanders and Corporal Melham being specially conspicuous. Second Lieutenant Vanderpump also distinguished himself: he had brought up a bomb-carrying party and volunteered to remain and take charge of the leading party, which he handled with great skill and coolness, while the bombs his men had brought were the more welcome because it was raining hard and mud had put all the Lewis guns and many rifles out of action. Altogether it was a useful success, and though the completion of the capture of the Intermediate Trench fell to the Fifteenth Division, who relieved the First two days later, the battalion's services were warmly acknowledged by a Brigade Order of September 3rd, which spoke of its attacks " by which nearly the whole of the Intermediate Line has come into our possession."[1]

High Wood, however, still remained untaken, and the First Division had not yet finished with that bitterly contested

---

[1] Captain Inglis, who had already won the M.C. in Gallipoli, was awarded the D.S.O. while Second Lieutenant Vanderpump received the M.C. and Sergeants Sheehan and Geary and Privates Fitzpatrick, Murphy and Williams the D.C.M. The total casualties, including Captain Walshe killed, came to nearly 60.

position. By September 2nd the Division was again in line and in front of the wood, and next day the 1st Brigade effected a lodgment in it, and captured 40 prisoners, though counter-attacks recovered most of the gains. The 3rd Brigade had accordingly to undertake yet another assault, and on September 8th the 1st S.W.B.[1] found themselves in position to support the Gloucestershire, who were attacking from the West while the Welch co-operated from the South. The attack started well enough, both battalions secured their objectives and started to consolidate. But very soon the Germans poured a deluge of shells upon the wood, inflicting many casualties, and then counter-attacked in force under cover of this hurricane bombardment. A, C and D Companies of the S.W.B. were thrown into the fight, but even so the position could not be maintained; the brigade was forced back to its original line and the tremendous shell fire[2] to which the Germans continued to subject the wood put a renewal of the attack out of the question. Casualties had been heavy; the battalion's were over 100, including Second Lieutenants Wileman and Pugh killed,[3] and Second Lieutenants Vanderpump and Pierce wounded. Three days later the Division was relieved, the S.W.B. going back to Henencourt for a week's rest[4] and thereby missing the big attack of September 15th, when the "tanks" were first used. The 6th, the only other battalion in the area, were also out of the line, so that the Regiment was unrepresented in this attack, one of the pivotal points in the Somme offensive, as it saw Flers and Martinpuich taken and High Wood finally mastered.[5] With this, on the Eastern half of the battlefield the British at last completed the capture of the main ridge and could now begin pushing forward down its slopes and on towards the next ridge which runs N.W. from Le Transloy and in front of Bapaume.

[1] The battalion after four days' rest near Albert had gone back into line on September 2nd, being at first in Mametz Wood and then in line opposite High Wood.
[2] At the height of the bombardment a runner was observed doggedly making his way across the open. He actually reached the C.O. unhit and his missive was promptly opened. It was a memorandum from Divisional Headquarters requesting that more care should be exercised in the construction of incinerators in back areas. An almost equally urgent message was received about the same time to say that soldiers were to be instructed in weaving into mats the old straw they slept on.
[3] The last-named had only just joined along with some 12 other new subalterns and over 220 men who had turned up while the battalion was at Albert.
[4] Here Major Addison joined with Lieutenant Bodley and half a dozen new Second Lieutenants, so that as regards officers the battalion was well up to strength.
[5] Even then it had to be attacked from the flanks before it could be taken.

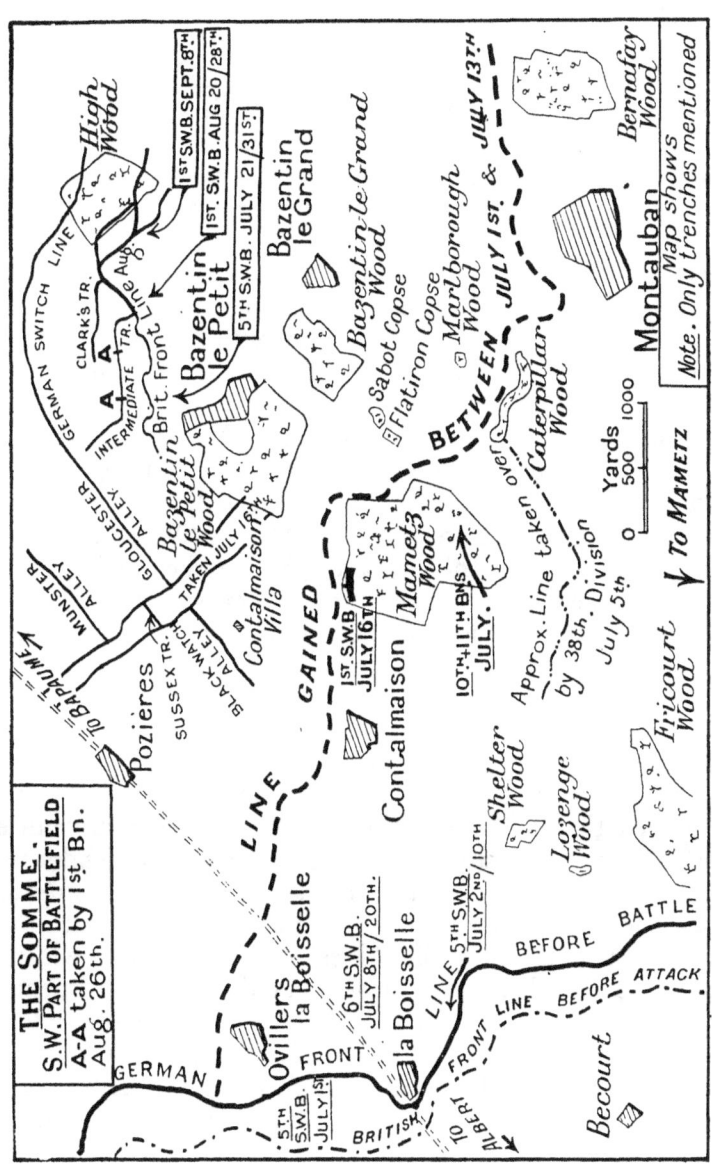

CHAPTER XVII

THE SOMME

III : *The Final Stage*

WITH the attack delivered on September 15th a third phase in "the Somme" began. The two months of hard fighting immediately preceding it had finally given the British the forward crest of the main ridge from Delville Wood to Mouquet Farm : September 15th, supplemented and completed on September 25th and 26th, dislodged the enemy from the main ridge but for a small area North of Thiepval, on which he still maintained a precarious grip. At the end of September it really looked as though the devotion, determination and tenacity of the Allies was at last going to be fully rewarded and as if substantial success was within their reach. The obstacles still to be encountered on the further slopes, on which his last prepared defensive positions ran, were nothing like as formidable as those already overcome : no more "Wunderwerks" and Contalmaisons and Leipzig Salients remained to be mastered, the Le Transloy line was not the elaborate network of fortifications which the 1st S.W.B. had faced between Contalmaison and Pozières, no new Mametz Wood awaited the attackers. Unluckily the break in the weather which the first days of October brought was to last several weeks and to rob Sir Douglas Haig and his men of nearly all they had seemed on the point of securing. The mud not only prevented rapid movement in actual attacks ; it aggravated the difficulties of keeping the men in front supplied with food, stores and ammunition ; it presented a nearly insuperable obstacle to getting proper artillery support for attacks ; when battered trenches were at last captured it impeded their reconstruction and doubled the difficulties of consolidating. The rain no doubt fell upon the defender no less than on the assailant ; it made life in trenches no less unpleasant for the Germans, except that their positions were partially prepared, whereas those of the Allies were improvised, while they had not behind them an area devastated by bombardments and pitted with shell-craters which the rains turned into pools or, what was almost worse, stretches of oozy and bottomless mud. Both sides alike were hideously uncomfortable, horribly impeded in their movements and delayed, but to the defence delay was a boon, not a drawback. "All time that is not turned to account falls into the scale on the side of the defence," a well-known German military writer has somewhat ponderously remarked, and there is no better example than the Somme of an attacker being robbed by weather-imposed delays of the legitimate fruits of his exertions.

The troops who shared in the closing stages of the Somme found themselves therefore involved in operations almost as disappointing and disheartening as in that middle stage when the German resistance had been at its stubbornest, exacting so stiff a price for every painfully won square yard. On September 15th no single battalion of the TWENTY-FOURTH was engaged, but by September 25th the First Division had returned to the line. After the fight for High Wood on September 8th the 1st Battalion had had three days in Mametz Wood in support, followed by a week at Franvillers and Henencourt Wood before moving up into line on September 16th near Bazentin-le-Grand. The battalion had been brought more or less up to decent strength again by some more drafts, coming largely from broken-up second-line Yeomanry units, the Welsh Horse and Montgomery Yeomanry both supplying parties, with some from the 2/1st Brecknockshire. The Division was taking over a position just N.W. of Flers, and confronted the Flers system of trenches where it crossed a low spur between Flers and Eaucourt l'Abbaye. Here another trench, known as far as Flers Trench as Drop Alley and beyond it as Goose Alley, intersected the Flers trenches, and the point of intersection, to which the Germans were still holding on, was the scene of strenuous fighting. Both the Munsters and the Black Watch were hotly engaged, repelling vigorous counter-attacks and eventually securing part of the coveted position. The S.W.B.'s activities, however, were confined to providing carrying parties to take bombs and S.A.A. up to the front line and to digging out a trench which the bad weather had almost filled. On the 23rd A Company and the battalion bombers were sent up to support another battalion which was making an attack, but a false alarm of a counter-attack caused great confusion and the attack fizzled out, the S.W.B. bombers narrowly escaping getting shot by their friends behind. A Company then took charge of the trenches, subsequently handing over to the Black Watch.

September 24th passed quietly enough and next day came the big attack, mainly directed against the German positions further East in front of Gueudecourt and Morval. On the First Division's front only a small advance was attempted, which the Black Watch carried out successfully, pushing some way down the Flers Support Line and capturing several prisoners. Their Regimental History speaks warmly of the "invaluable work" of the S.W.B. in bringing up bombs, and a party under Second Lieutenant Zacharias gave timely help to some hard-pressed Black Watch who were covering the erection of a barricade to secure the captured portion of trench. Aided by Sergeant Gawler, Second Lieutenant Zacharias headed the surviving Black Watch bombers and drove the enemy back, the advance being led by Private Crossland as leading bomber and Private W. Vaughan as bayonet man. By their efforts the Germans were kept at bay till the barricade had been completed and the covering party could come back. In covering the withdrawal Second Lieutenant Zacharias was killed and Sergeant Gawler wounded, while Private David Jones, whose gallantry had been conspicuous on many previous occasions, was killed after handling his Lewis gun most effectively till it was disabled. But they had not fallen in vain; the position had been made good and was handed over that evening to the New Zealanders who relieved the First Division, the battalion going back to Albert.

October 1st brought orders to proceed to Aigneville, 15 miles from Abbeville and so well away from the fighting area that the bus journey thither took nearly twelve hours. The long-promised month's rest was at last a fact, and the battalion was the more fortunate to be in comfortable billets, as this particular October proved no month to spend under canvas. It was marked by relentless and drenching rains, which seemed almost continuous and speedily converted the shell-torn ground into a morass of mud and slime. Good billets were therefore doubly welcome, while the abominable weather interfered considerably both with the training and with the programme of sports which had been arranged. Leave was given fairly generously, and the month passed only too quickly. October 31st saw the battalion "embussing" for its return journey to the Somme; its immediate destination being Baisieux, ten miles S.W. of Amiens. It had not received many drafts or new officers while at rest, though Major Addison left it to take over an appointment as Town Major.

Rather before this two other battalions of the TWENTY-FOURTH had returned to the area of active hostilities. These were the 2nd and the 5th, who had both had a chance of recovering from their experiences in the opening phases, having spent two months in comparative rest with the Second Army, the 2nd in the Ypres Salient, the 5th opposite Messines.

The Ypres Salient, the scene of bitter fighting in every other year of the war, was a "quiet" area in 1916, except in June, when the Canadian line was driven back near Hooge. When the 2nd S.W.B. arrived there the Salient was quiet again, and they found their ten weeks at Ypres extremely restful and the enemy most inactive. The British enjoyed an almost undisputed ascendency in the air, the German guns fired but little, seeming to lack ammunition; at night their machine guns blazed away freely, but by day even they were but little in evidence. The Twenty-Ninth

THE 2ND IN THE SALIENT

Division was not favourably impressed with its new surroundings when it relieved the Sixth in the Northern portion of the Salient, the 2nd S.W.B. taking over the line along the canal bank half a mile North of Ypres on the evening of July 31st. It found the trenches very bad, and, as the battalion diary feelingly observes, "the work to be done is limitless." Some of the reasons for this the S.W.B. were soon to realize. Water being so near the surface it was impossible to dig deeper than two feet, so the defences consisted of breastworks, not continuous, so that one could not go round the whole trench system by day. The flatness of the ground was a further disadvantage, while the battalion was so near the point of the Salient that its trenches were under observation from front and flanks. However, though occasionally the intermittent shelling developed into a bombardment, the German artillery generally abstained from provoking our guns to a duel, and what firing they did was mainly in retaliation for bombardments. The British guns were more aggressive, having usually five shells to send over in reply to every round the Germans fired. Gas alarms were frequent but mostly false, and early in September the issue of a more satisfactory respirator, the "small box" type, improved the battalion's equipment for dealing with gas, though all these false alarms tended to make men grow careless. Constant wet weather greatly increased the difficulty of keeping the trenches in good repair and reasonably habitable, while the battalion's patrols sought persistently but vainly to force on an encounter with the enemy in No Man's Land and obtain an identification. With things so "quiet" casualties were few, but drafts were also infrequent and the battalion's strength rose slowly. Rumours of a return to the Somme were persistent, and early in October came definite orders for a move South, the battalion finally entraining at Hopoutre on October 7th and proceeding by way of Cardonette (October 7th to 10th) and Buire (October 10th to 13th) to a camp S.W. of Fricourt, where it spent nearly a week in reserve. Just before leaving Flanders it had been again inspected by Sir A. Hunter-Weston. On this occasion (October 5th) the four officers and 125 men who had been present at the original landing at Gallipoli were formed up separately. After all the 2nd had been through it was really remarkable to find so many survivors of April 25th, 1915, still with it.

Meanwhile the 6th Battalion also was back in the fighting line again. The 6th had thoroughly enjoyed its rest, a rare experience with Pioneers, and it had welcomed the chance of assimilating its drafts. On September 24th the Division had started back for the line. After four days in reserve at Acheux

Wood it took over the sector South of the Ancre on September 30th, but soon shifted slightly to its right to take up a line across the Thiepval spur. Thiepval itself had been taken on September 26th and the chief bone of contention was now the Stuff Redoubt. At first the 6th S.W.B. were mainly employed on improving the communications with the front line, which cost them 30 casualties, including Second Lieutenant Cox wounded

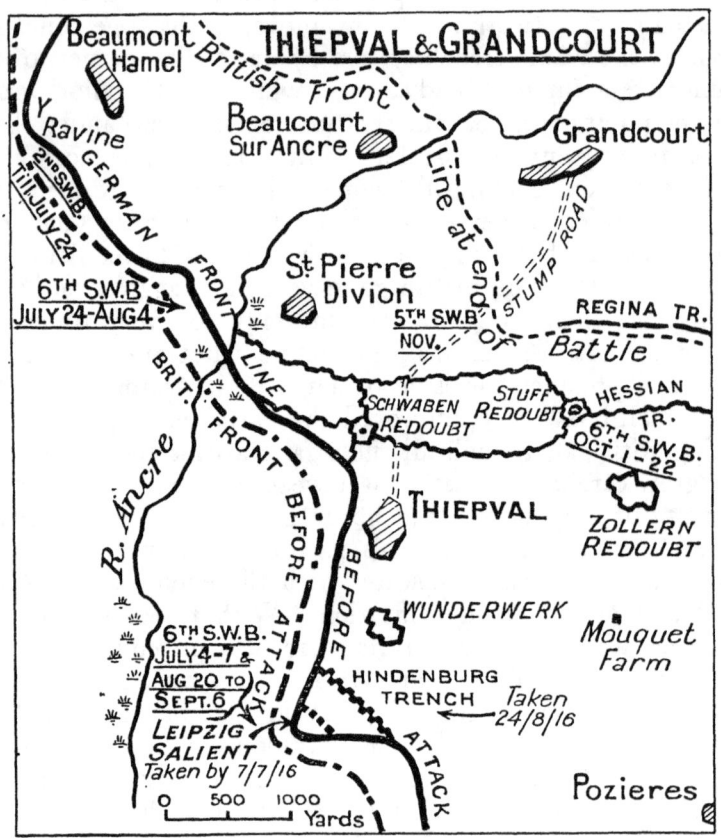

and 4 men killed, and then on October 10th to 11th two companies were detailed to dig a new fire-trench connecting Hessian Trench and the Stuff Redoubt. A working party of 800 had been collected, but the Germans put down so heavy a barrage that after nearly 80 casualties had been suffered, among them a dozen S.W.B., the attempt had to be abandoned. However, next night Captain Mumford took D Company forward and tackled an awkward situation with such skill that the previous night's task was accomplished without a casualty.[1] The following night the work was continued and progressed well despite heavy

---

[1] Captain Mumford was subsequently awarded the M.C.

bombardments. Private Berry displayed great courage and coolness in mending a gap in the line between the Stuff and Schwaben Redoubts. The position was under heavy fire, but he volunteered to build up the gap, and not only did fine work himself but inspired others by his example. Sergeants Sherman and Brooke were equally conspicuous for their gallantry and Private Paddock distinguished himself greatly : a gallant man, always cool and brave, he went out under heavy fire to help a wounded officer and had brought him almost into safety when he was himself killed. Sergeant Goodman also handled a detached platoon with great coolness and skill. Coming under a heavy bombardment he placed his men under cover and proceeded to walk quietly across the open to report to his company commander. But the outstanding episode was on October 21st when, after Regina Trench had been taken, three companies, A, C and D, were detailed to dig a communication trench to the new line. The Germans did their utmost to impede the work and their persistent shelling at one time drove a number of men from their posts. Company Sergeant Major O'Neil, however, collected these men and led them back to their work. His gallantry and determination were largely responsible for the completion of the trench, on which the battalion was deservedly complimented.[1] Next day the 6th was relieved by its own 5th Battalion, which had just been drawn back again into the vortex of the Somme from the comparative quiet of Wytschaete and Ploegsteert. The 6th's casualties during October, 11 killed and nearly 60 wounded, were really quite remarkably light, but the officers hit included the C.O., who after remaining at duty for four days after being hit retired to hospital on October 16th.

The 5th Battalion had found Wytschaete quite a rest-cure after the Somme. No active operations were in progress, though the Second Army was already maturing its plans for the successful Messines offensive of June, 1917, and the 5th were confined to the ordinary routine of trench maintenance, road-making and the supervision of working parties. A move to the right in September brought the Division to Ploegsteert, but the general situation remained unchanged. Its character may be gathered from the casualties, 1 killed and 4 wounded, but the battalion's work is rather to be judged by a specially complimentary Order of the Day in which General Bridges praised it warmly for its excellent work. At the end of September the 5th moved to Vieux Berquin

[1] Company Sergeant Major O'Neil, who was wounded, and Sergeants Sherman and Brooke received the D.C.M., Private Berry and Sergeant Goodman the M.M., which was also awarded to 18 other members of the battalion for deeds of bravery during October.

for training, and here at last ample drafts were forthcoming, amounting in all to nearly 350 men. On October 3rd it was inspected by the King of the Belgians and warmly complimented on its turn out. Three days later it entrained for the South. Here it had a fortnight on the still quiet Hèbuterne frontage, but on October 22nd the Division was transferred across the Ancre to relieve the Twenty-Fifth and prosecute the attack on Grandcourt, now coming within the range of probabilities.[1]

Shortly before the 5th Battalion's move across the Ancre the 2nd also had returned to the line, but to the extreme other end of the battlefield, the 87th Brigade going into line at Gueudecourt on October 19th. In this quarter the spur running N.W. from Sailly-Saillisel past Le Transloy was still being vigorously contested: its capture was essential to the launching of an Allied attack upon the last of the enemy's defensive systems, and despite the wet weather and all the consequent handicaps the pressure on the Germans was being maintained. The 88th Brigade had already carried out two successful local attacks, the second resulting in the capture of the appropriately named Grease Trench, which the 2nd S.W.B. took over on October 19th. This relief was an arduous business. Owing to the roads being completely congested the battalion which had left Fricourt at 10.30 a.m. only reached Bernafay Wood, 4 miles away, late in the afternoon. Bernafay Wood offered little shelter from the persistent rain, but it was possible to give the men a meal, and after dark the battalion set off again, along a road so deep in mud that many men soon became utterly exhausted by their efforts to drag themselves through it. Matters were not much improved when the guides left the road for a communication trench, Cocoa Alley, especially as the guides were none too certain of their way, while the German shelling was extremely heavy and inflicted many casualties. Dawn found the relief incomplete, barely half the men having reached the firing-line. It took nearly all day to ascertain the precise situation and the whereabouts of every detachment, and the relief could not be finally reported complete till after dark (October 20th). The next two days in Grease Trench were about the worst the 2nd ever experienced. The weather was bitterly cold, the temperature falling to 10 degrees below freezing; the men were without greatcoats, had arrived in the trenches wet through, and found no cover and no chance of getting dry. The position had been so heavily bombarded that the trenches were too much knocked about to afford much protection against the practically

---

[1] Major H. C. Oxley joined on October 20th from the 17th Northumberland Fusiliers (N.E.R. Pioneers).

continuous shell fire, and before the battalion was relieved it had suffered almost as much as an attack might have cost it, having had no less than 3 officers and 20 men killed and 6 officers and 58 men wounded.[1] Four more officers and over 180 men had to be admitted to hospital during the next three days, mostly suffering from trench feet, though every effort had been made to check the trouble by giving the men dry socks and whale oil on leaving the line; and when on October 25th the battalion had again to take over the front line, this time the right half of Grease Trench with a frontage of over 300 yards, it could only parade 16 officers and 330 other ranks, of whom two companies were required as supports. The weather was again of the vilest and the trenches in dreadful condition, with no shelter from rain or cold: admissions to hospital naturally continued numerous, including Captain Kelly and Second Lieutenant W. M. Evans. The shelling was heavy, for the enemy seemed apprehensive of an attack, but battle casualties were fortunately much lower than on the previous trip, though unluckily Lieutenant Harford, when out reconnoitring the enemy's wire, was fired upon and killed. All ranks naturally welcomed their relief on the night of October 29th/30th by an Australian battalion and after a miserable night under canvas in a sea of mud near Pommiers Redoubt, were glad to get back to real shelter in huts near Fricourt. Here many recovered sick rejoined and by the end of the month the battalion's strength had risen again to 13 officers and 416 men. There was no regret, however, when on November 3rd the battalion was ordered to entrain at Albert for Airaisnes, a village 14 miles from Abbeville, where it was to spend ten days. Airaisnes provided the best billets the battalion had as yet met and the rest did wonders for the men. The chance was taken to repair their clothing, which was in a terrible state, boots being particularly bad, and some useful drill and training smartened them up wonderfully.

Meanwhile, before the 2nd returned to the line the Somme had reached its official end with the Fifth Army's successful attack of November 13th astride the Ancre when Beaumont Hamel was at last taken, along with Beaucourt sur Ancre, St. Pierre Divion, and the enemy's last foothold on the ridge North of Thiepval. In this substantial success the 5th Battalion alone represented the TWENTY-FOURTH. It was not to be the Twenty-Ninth Division's fortune to avenge July 1st by capturing Beaumont Hamel, but the Nineteenth Division formed the right of

---

[1] The officers killed were Second Lieutenants Beardshaw, Bricknell and Wilton; Those wounded were Captain B. J. Davies, Lieutenant Coussmaker, Second Lieutenants Batty, W. F. Davies, Rhys Jones and Webb.

the attacking force and captured its objectives with great rapidity and an equally satisfactory absence of heavy casualties.

The 5th S.W.B.'s share in this attack did not present any unusual features. It may fairly be said that a Pioneer battalion's normal part in any big attack is played quite as much before as in the attack, and for three weeks before the assault the 5th had been strenuously preparing for it despite great hardships and difficulties. Tramways had to be constructed behind the lines, assembly and communication trenches had to be dug, routes marked out, dug-outs prepared for headquarters of units, for the reception of casualties, for advance depots of stores and ammunition: all sorts and kinds of work had to be done, often under shell fire and always under adverse weather conditions. The construction of a "tank track" was a new task and proved particularly difficult, the enemy's guns getting at least one direct hit on it a day, and the days preceding the assault cost the 5th over 20 casualties, including Second Lieutenant R. C. M. Jones mortally wounded on November 10th.

In the actual assault the 56th Brigade attacked and took the Division's objectives West of Grandcourt, completely surprising the enemy and taking over 100 prisoners. Two companies of the 5th had been detailed to help consolidate, and C, under Captain Simons, were employed to connect Lucky Way up with the left of the 7th East Lancashire in Desire Trench. This was a fine achievement, the trench being dug to a depth of 6 feet on a length of over 150 yards. Captain Simons, whose skill and fine example contributed greatly to this successful performance, was subsequently awarded the M.C., which was also given to Second Lieutenant Day, who superintended the digging of a new front trench under heavy fire. The various communication trenches leading forward from the captured position had to be blocked and posts established 100 yards to the front in them, so that the companies were kept busy. Luckily the success of the attack had clearly shaken up the Germans and their retaliatory shelling was not very severe, the 5th's casualties for the period November 13th to 15th amounting to 8 men killed and missing with Second Lieutenant E. S. Evans and 32 men wounded.

On November 15th the Nineteenth Division side-slipped to its left, relieving the Thirty-Ninth, and two days later attacked again in conjunction with the Eighteenth on the right who were attacking South of Grandcourt. This attack, though fairly successful on the left, met with misfortune on the right, the troops overshooting their objectives and getting cut off. An effort was made to consolidate a line just West of Grandcourt, but it could not be maintained, and a new line was dug a little further back, from the railway bridge over the Ancre near Beaucourt to a point on Stump Road about 1400 yards South of Grandcourt. To this line, which the battalion had dug, the troops were recalled on November 20th, and General Bridges called specially at Battalion Headquarters to congratulate the 5th on what he described as the best bit of Pioneer work he had ever seen. For several days longer the 5th continued hard at work helping to consolidate the position; nor were they allowed to withdraw when on November 23rd their Division was relieved by the Eleventh. Their retention gave a chance to Lieutenant Alisopp and 25 men to distinguish themselves on November 24th, by fetching in a German gun that was lying abandoned in No Man's Land about 200 yards down Grandcourt Road. The "road" hardly merited the name, but the detachment, though under heavy fire throughout, stuck to its task and succeeded in bringing the gun in. On November 27th the battalion was at last relieved. Though no opportunities of achieving anything outstanding had come its way, it had once again won high praise, and Colonel Trower and his men could withdraw to billets at Forceville feeling that they had thoroughly earned a rest.

CHAPTER XVIII

SALONICA 1915–1916

THE two battalions of the Regiment which had sailed from Marseilles in October, 1915, nominally for Alexandria, had had a fairly shrewd guess that their ultimate goal was the Balkans, nor had their surmise been at fault. With policy and high strategy a regimental history is not primarily concerned : and there is no need here to discuss the Allies' rather belated decision to sent 150,000 men from France to assist the Servians against the combined attacks of the Bulgarians from the East and of Mackensen's Austro-Germans from the North. Against such overwhelming forces even the Servians' desperate resistance was unavailing, and although General Sarrail, the Allied C. in C., hurried three French divisions up the Vardar directly they arrived, they were too late and too few to do more than distract some Bulgarians from pursuing the beaten Servians towards the Adriatic. When the S.W.B. battalions reached Salonica—the 8th arrived on November 9th, the 7th a few days later[1]—the situation was very serious. The Tenth Division from Gallipoli had already pushed a brigade forward to the Servian frontier N.W. of Lake Doiran to cover the French right, but to reinforce the advanced troops was very difficult. With the scarcely veiled hostility of the Greeks who opposed every possible obstruction to our using the very limited railway facilities, the lack of even decent roads and the dearth of available animals and vehicles, the Allied troops were virtually immobile. Moreover the Twenty-Second Division's disembarkation and move to a camp at Samli on the Galiko river, 8 miles from the Salonica quayside, was hampered by the late arrival of the first-line transport which had mostly gone in separate ships. Thus the 7th and 8th S.W.B. were first employed in Macedonia as navvies rather than as soldiers. Life was a succession of " fatigues," performed on half-rations and punctuated towards the end of the month with blizzards. The troops were very uncomfortable, though a rum ration, first issued on November 21st, was greatly appreciated. There were several shifts of camp, unending work to make the camps habitable, even more required on the roads, and scanty time for training.

The general situation, moreover, was most unsatisfactory. The Allies were on neutral territory, as King Constantine had vetoed M. Venizelos' proposal to join the Allies, there was a large Greek force in the neighbourhood, whose intentions were doubtful, and by the beginning of December all chance of

---

[1] There was a rumour that the 7th had been torpedoed. The *Lake Manitoba* was very slow and had no escort.

achieving the expedition's original purpose was clearly gone. The surviving Servians were in full retreat towards the Adriatic, the advanced French and British troops were hard pressed to extricate themselves. On December 7th indeed the Twenty-Second Division received orders to dispatch a brigade to Doiran to help the Tenth Division. The 65th Brigade, however, was detailed for this, so the 7th and 8th S.W.B. had no opportunity of trying conclusions with the Bulgarians, who halted after driving the Allies back over the Greek frontier[1] and showed no disposition to interfere with their occupation of a defensive position a little distance North of Salonica.

In this position, which roughly followed an East to West line from the Gulf of Stavros to the Vardar, the British took the right, having the Tenth Division next the sea, then the Twenty-Sixth from Langaza Westward, the Twenty-Eighth continuing the line to the Gnoigna Ridge and the Twenty-Second thence to Daudli. The 67th Brigade, which had been ordered forward on December 11th, held the right section of their Divisional front in front of Pirnar, and here for the next four months the two S.W.B. battalions were busy enough, though the Bulgarians' inaction denied them the satisfaction of profiting by the splendid work they put into their section of the defences.

The move up to Daudli gave the two battalions a fair foretaste of what was in store. They had to bivouac in what seemed a dry river-bed near Ajoxtli without either blankets or waterproof sheets, and during the night water oozed up through the sand and soaked everyone to the skin; the track was everything a road should not be, to get the transport forward was extraordinarily difficult, for when not blocked by boulders it stuck in the mud, and the weather was abominable. The proper positions once reached things gradually improved, though at first transport difficulties delayed the issue of the necessary R.E. stores for rock-blasting and constructing defences and kept the troops on very restricted rations, only bully-beef and biscuits being available for nearly two months. The line assigned to the 67th Brigade was difficult both to site and to construct. Continual mist hampered reconnaissance; it was hard to say whether the existing maps or roads were the worst travesty. To prevent the French positions beyond the Galiko from being enfiladed, a hill called the Matterhorn had to be included in our line, which entailed taking up a tactically unsatisfactory forward position S.E. of it, on some turtle-back spurs divided by deep ravines. The ground was mainly rocky and constant bad weather greatly hampered trench construction.

---

[1] According to an authoritative Bulgarian account (Nedeff) this was done by German orders.

However, both battalions contained plenty of men to whom rock-blasting and digging were no novelty. "The N.C.O.'s and men are in their element," writes the 7th's diary, they are "thoroughly happy and industrious and do splendid work." They reaped the rewards of their labours in that, as the roads gradually took on the semblance of a proper highway, supplies of all sorts reached the front more easily, rations became more varied and plentiful, and R.E. stores readily obtainable, so that the construction of defences was less like making bricks without straw. As the defences improved more time could be devoted to "soldiering," ranges were constructed, field-firing was practised and training resumed.

All this time (December, 1915–March, 1916), almost the only sign of the enemy was occasional bomb-dropping by aeroplanes, but if there were no battle casualties, the sick-rate was already appreciable. There were various changes in both battalions, mainly due to invalidings. Major Yatman was transferred from the 7th to command the 11th R.W.F., on which Captain Royle was promoted to Major. Lieutenant Martin was invalided in March, Regimental Quartermaster Sergeant Dunne being appointed Quartermaster in his place. From the 8th Major Hamilton-Jones went to hospital in December, and in February Captain Thorp followed, the Adjutant's duties being taken over by Lieutenant Franklin. Regimental Quartermaster Sergeant Lichfield proved another victim to the climate, Sergeant Glynn succeeding him, while though some new subalterns joined both battalions in April no drafts were forthcoming for either of them.

The first important development came in April when the Allies at length began advancing towards the Struma valley and Lake Doiran. One brigade only of the Twenty-Second Division got as far forward as Irikli in April, and May was far spent before the 67th Brigade moved up by Sarigol (May 22nd) and Janes (24th) to the new front 8 miles South of Doiran. Even then, too, the 8th S.W.B., who had been on duty in Salonica, remained at Pirnar till June 6th. On June 8th it also came forward and joined the 7th in constructing defences. But the two battalions did not stay long in the front area, for on the 19th their Division was drawn back into Army Reserve, occupying the Akbunar area. Here the two battalions spent six weeks, mainly occupied in training specialists and in musketry. The weather was almost tropical, flies were a fearful nuisance and, despite the assiduous work of the Medical Officers and their staffs, the sick-rate soared high. Diarrhœa, fever, malaria and dysentery all contributed; at the end of June the 7th had 150 men in hospital and another 100 sick in camp. Doses of quinine given every morning and evening did something to improve matters and the alteration of the chief meal from midday to the evening proved beneficial, the average number sick going down in the latter part of July. Many of the sick, however, had to be invalided, including Major Ward, Lieutenant C. B. Morgan and Regimental Sergeant Major Cashman from the 8th, and Lieutenant Wingard from the 7th.[1] Both battalions therefore were much below establishment[2] when, on July 30th, the brigade started for the front again.

This advance was due to the Division's having been ordered to relieve a French Division N.W. of Kilindir and so set it free for an attack on the advanced Bulgarian position S.W. of Lake Doiran. This was designed to assist French and Servian operations to the Westward in the Monastir direction and was to be supported[3] by the British Twelfth Corps,[4] the Twenty-Second Division on the right occupying at first a line from North of Vladaja to a hill known as "420." As the French advanced it was to occupy fresh positions in support. The French attack, launched on August 10th, met with fair success and resulted, after heavy fighting, in their consolidating a line running S.W. from Lake Doiran across the lower end of the Jumeaux Ravine, one of the chief gullies draining into the lake from the tangle of rocky hills West of it. Some battalions of the Twenty-Sixth Division co-operated by capturing Kidney and Horseshoe Hills, two outlying features S. and S.W. of Doldzeli, on the left of the French attack, but the Twenty-Second had no share in the fighting. Thus though the two S.W.B. battalions had reached Kukus on August 1st, after a toilsome march over bad and slippery roads, to the pleasures of which the new transport mules and their equally intractable Greek drivers contributed substantially, neither of them entered the front line till the end of the month. Then their Division received orders to relieve a French Division whose left rested on the Vardar opposite Macukovo village, as the British were now taking over the whole line from the Vardar to Doldzeli. The 67th Brigade was allotted the left sector and on the night of August 29th/30th the two S.W.B. battalions relieved respectively the 2nd and 3rd Battalions of the 84me

---

[1] Lieutenant Sellicks joined the 8th as Quartermaster in November and Company Sergeant Major Martin took over duty as Regimental Sergeant Major.

[2] The 7th moved out with 29 officers and 610 men, but as the transport section, now completed with pack mules, absorbed 2 officers and 93 men and the machine gun section took another 2 and 25, its rifle strength, after deducting signallers, pioneers, sanitary section and headquarters staff, was very low indeed.

[3] Lack of heavy artillery and the limited supply of ammunition available were the main reasons for the restricted part taken by the British in these operations.

[4] The Twenty-Second and Twenty-Sixth Divisions.

Regiment, the 7th being on the left next the Vardar, the 8th in the right, or Ardzan, sub-sector of the brigade's line.

At this point a No Man's Land nearly a mile wide separated the hostile positions. The British line, which followed a rocky ridge running from S.W. to N.E. and from 150 to 300 feet above the valley in front, was everywhere commanded by the Bulgarian positions opposite it. The rocky ground made trench digging difficult and the task of making the position really defensible was formidable enough, especially as both battalions were terribly weak. But with the enemy so far away there was little hostile interference, practically no sniping, not much machine-gun fire and little artillery activity, though his guns seemed to have all the chief ranging points in our line registered and were quick to open fire if targets presented themselves. Both battalions worked vigorously to improve the line and were also active in patrolling No Man's Land with a view to mastering its topography and to impressing on the enemy's patrols the unwisdom of approaching our lines. This led to several nocturnal encounters in which a vigorous offensive soon secured the British the upper hand. Lieutenant Dick and Second Lieutenants Parry and Davis of the 7th did particularly well and an identification obtained off a dead German in Macukovo proved very welcome to the Intelligence authorities. The 7th at first saw more of the line than the 8th, which was out of the line from September 4th to 15th, suffering severely from sand-fly fever, a particularly bad outbreak in A Company being traced to the occupation of some infected dug-outs at Ardzan when moving into line.

The only operation undertaken at this time was an attack on the Piton des Mitrailleuses, a prominent salient N.E. of Macukovo, for which the 7th S.W.B. was originally detailed. In the end, however, two battalions of the 65th Brigade attacked it on the night of September 13th/14th from the trenches held by the 67th. The attackers, though successful in capturing their objective, were subjected to a tremendous shelling and constant counter-attacks and found consolidation in the rocky ground extremely difficult. After a stubborn resistance they were eventually dislodged. The 7th S.W.B. suffered several casualties from the artillery retaliation, but its chief work was in sending out parties to bring in the wounded. Private Vine got the M.M. for excellent work in mending telephone wires, the only wire by which communication was maintained with Brigade Headquarters being that in his charge.

This attack had shown clearly how difficult it was to consolidate captured positions in that soil and in face of the command which the Bulgarian main positions enjoyed over the lower ground along which the Allied front ran. Orders were therefore issued to the Twelfth Corps to change its rôle, confining itself to the defensive and strengthening its positions so that they could be held with smaller garrisons and troops thus set free for more active operations elsewhere. The 7th and 8th S.W.B. therefore, instead of participating in even a local offensive of a serious character, found themselves committed to a monotonous but exhausting existence, in which labours were incessant, active encounters with the enemy infrequent, the conditions in which they existed uncomfortable and unhealthy, their sick-rate high, their opportunities for rest and recreation very limited, and all this with no visible result. From time to time they shifted from one set of trenches to another,[1] everywhere they confronted the same formidable and forbidding positions. That the two battalions should nevertheless have maintained a high standard of discipline and efficiency was greatly to the credit of officers and men.

Monotonous and strategically uneventful as were the months between October 1916 and April 1917, neither 7th or 8th S.W.B. found them a time of inactivity: indeed, with the sick-rate so high and drafts none too plentiful, both battalions were usually so weak that when in the line men were fairly worked off their legs. In November, for example, the 7th could find barely 200 rifles in a trench strength of 450 and the men in consequence were more often than not on night duty and had little chance of sleep or rest. Only about 30 men were available for a counter-attack, and as men came in from day outposts or patrolling they had at once to be detailed for other duties. Fortunately the enemy was torpid and seldom bestirred himself to interfere with our troops, even his artillery doing but little shooting after the end of October, when the serious fighting till then in progress further West,[2] had died down. Offensive action by Bulgarian infantry was quite the exception, only infrequently were they met in any force in No Man's Land, and such raids as were attempted were usually made by the British.

Of the two battalions the 7th had perhaps the more active time. They were twice detailed to carry out a big raid, and as it chanced, their patrols encountered the enemy rather more often. Both raids took place at Macukovo. In the first, on the

---

[1] The most important move was in March, 1917, when the whole Division shifted to the right on relief by the Sixtieth and took over from the Twenty-Sixth the frontage between Kidney Hill and Berks Hill opposite the famous "Pip" ridge.

[2] This resulted in the recapture of Monastir by the French, Italians and Servians, but failed to assist the Roumanians materially.

night of October 18th/19th, the objective was the vineyard on the river bank, N.W. of Macukovo.[1] The raiders, 4 officers and 80 men under Captain Villar, were drawn from B Company, while A and C provided five flanking parties to block gullies running into the Macukovo Ravine from the N.E. down which counter-attacks might be delivered to cut off the raiders' retreat. In all, including a supporting party on One Tree Hill, 250 officers and men were employed outside our wire. After reaching the vineyard the raiders were to lie up for a time in the hope of trapping hostile patrols. Unluckily, though Captain Villar's well-laid plans worked admirably, the wood proved so heavily wired that the raiders could not close with the enemy, who bolted after a short burst of fire and could not be caught. The wood was thoroughly searched and, much useful information being obtained, the whole force returned in good order, having only suffered two casualties, while the flankers under Captain Harris had the satisfaction of beating off some hostile patrols. The second raid, just a month later (November 17th/18th) virtually repeated the first. This time Captain Gottwaltz was in charge, the actual raiders being under Captain Burn, while Captain Taylor commanded a strong left flank-guard, the right being protected by a party from the 11th Welch, as owing to the battalion's low strength practically every man except the transport was already employed.[2] Once again the objective was the vineyard and a trench running N.E. to Cardiff Ravine, and once again the enemy unfortunately took the alarm just in time to get away before the raiders could close with them, though in retiring they must have run into the barrage. The vineyard was systematically cleared, much damage was done to the defences, and the R.E., besides carrying out demolitions, laid a mine which, according to reports from deserters, subsequently exploded with highly satisfactory results. Though unsuccessful in obtaining contact with the enemy and capturing prisoners these raids certainly served to alarm the enemy and caused German units to take over the hostile front between the Vardar and the Nose,[3] which line was systematically shelled by our guns.

Apart from these raids the 7th's energies found scope in vigorous and systematic patrolling directed by Captain Burn,

[1] The vineyard was approximately 1900 yards from the British front line and the route to be followed had had to be very carefully reconnoitred, while touch between the different detachments was maintained by means of ropes.

[2] Fourteen officers and 328 men of the 7th were employed in the raid with 4 officers and 119 men of other units.

[3] Four German deserters gave themselves up to the battalion on December 6th and proved communicative.

in which that officer and Captain Taylor along with several subalterns and N.C.O's did excellent work, Sergeant Arnold in particular distinguishing himself. Once Captain Burn and seven men ran into a Bulgarian patrol over 30 strong, but Captain Burn's skill and coolness extricated the party without casualties. In January the 7th had the misfortune to lose Major Royle and its M.O., Captain Jarman, R.A.M.C., who were both killed[1] by a stray shell along with an artillery observing officer when standing just outside the Officers' Mess. In February the battalion had a nasty experience. About 7 a.m. on the 17th a heavy bombardment began which went on with one short break till 7 p.m., was resumed at midnight with gas shells and continued for $4\frac{1}{2}$ hours. H.E. were then turned on for another hour, followed all next day (18th) by intermittent bursts of H.E. or gas shell and by another two hours' dose of gas during that night. It was a trying time, but the men stood it splendidly, and their behaviour earned warm praises from the Brigadier and the Divisional Commander, Major General Duncan. Despite the shelling and the gas they were on the alert when the enemy attempted to advance, and several men distinguished themselves greatly. Company Sergeant Major Hall, who was acting as Regimental Sergeant Major, was conspicuous for his good example and gallantry, Private A. W. Lewis did fine work as an observer, Private Heath brought in a wounded man under heavy fire, Captain E. L. Lloyd,[2] whose company, C, got the worst of the bombardment, went forward accompanied by a company cook over 200 yards of open to carry their dinners to a party in an advanced trench. The battalion was lucky to escape with no more than 5 killed and 37 wounded, though 80 more were slightly gassed, the symptoms generally not showing up till 48 hours later.

Apart from this losses in action were very few, and the battalion's health improved considerably in the colder months, though half a dozen officers were invalided between October and March: in December "rejoined from hospital" actually equalled the entry "to hospital." However, the sick-rate continued high, and even with several drafts[3] the battalion remained much below establishment, much too low for offensive purposes. At the end of February it only mustered 26 officers and 606 other ranks. March, however, saw large drafts, and when early in April the 67th Brigade was withdrawn into Corps

---

[1] Captain Gottwaltz was promoted to fill the vacancy as Major.
[2] He had recently joined, having served previously with the 6th Battalion.
[3] The largest was one of 100 which appeared in September, while in October 30 men transferred from Yeomanry units were posted to the battalion for transport duties.

Reserve at Galavanci for a month's training the 7th was nearly up to 800 all told.

During these months the 7th had seen a good many changes in personnel. Major Wakefield had left in October to become Assistant Commandant of a Base Camp at Stavros, and in his place Major Bradbury of the Welch Regiment was posted to the battalion and commanded while Colonel Grimwood was home on sick leave from the end of November till the end of January. The New Year Honours of 1917 brought Colonel Grimwood the D.S.O., and he, Lieutenant C. E. Williams and Sergeant Arnold were mentioned in Dispatches.

The 8th Battalion meanwhile had not actually carried out a raid on its own, though it had several times provided covering-parties or stretcher-bearers to assist other units engaged in raids. Gallantry while in charge of stretcher-bearers attached to the 11th Welch for a raid earned Lance Corporal Wetter the D.C.M. in December, and the battalion's assistance was gratefully acknowledged on several occasions. In patrolling it was extremely enterprising, though its efforts to collect prisoners were rendered fruitless by the enemy's lack of venturesomeness. In the Smol sector, which the 8th most often occupied, the Bulgarian lines were a long way off, and the battalion's patrols could do little more than acquire useful information, especially for the guidance of the artillery. On one occasion patrols led by Second Lieutenants Kenny and Cardwell reconnoitred the Bulgarian lines on the Dorsale ridge and at Petit Clou and successfully directed the fire of our guns by means of Very lights. Second Lieutenant Cardwell's party ran into a much larger hostile patrol but managed to get away. In crossing a ravine, however, Corporal Williams sprained his ankle and fell behind; Second Lieutenant Cardwell, discovering this, went back with Private George and succeeded in bringing him in.[1] In March, just before the Division's shift to its right, a standing post on Double Hill under Second Lieutenant Curling was attacked by superior force and was driven back toward our wire just as Second Lieutenant G. S. Evans was bringing its relief out. On the arrival of this reinforcement a stand was made and the Bulgarians were driven off in disorder.

Like the 7th, the 8th underwent many changes during the winter months. In September it lost Colonel Sword, who was invalided home, his place being taken first by Major Currall of the Lancashire Fusiliers, and then by Major Bruce of the 11th R.W.F., who took over command on October 17th. On Major

---

[1] Private George was awarded the M.M.: Second Lieutenant Cardwell for this and other services received the M.C.

Hamilton-Jones being definitely struck off the battalion's establishment, Captain Sharp was promoted Major, while in September Captain Thorp rejoined after several months' absence and took over A Company but was wounded in November and ultimately struck off in February. Of the officers who had gone overseas with the 8th Captains Percival and Casey, Lieutenants Haydon, Kaye, T. N. B. Jones and Lakin were all invalided and Captain Dawn wounded. On Regimental Sergeant Major Cashman's being finally struck off in December Company Sergeant Major Andrews replaced him. A very few officers and men had the privilege of 14 days' leave in England, and the honours conferred on the battalion included the Silver Medal of the Crown of Italy for Lieutenant Cardwell, the Bronze Medal of that Order for Private T. Williams, the M.M. for Private Crisp, and the M.S.M. for Sergeant Clevey, while Colonel Sword and Company Sergeant Major E. Williams were " mentioned."

As regards drafts the 8th was fortunate, getting some good batches of well-trained men with previous service in France or Gallipoli. The most substantial reinforcements were one of 66 which arrived in January and another of 80 which followed in February. But its drafts could hardly keep pace with the wastage from sickness, and the 8th was considerably under establishment when the move into Corps Reserve brought this long period of front line duty to an end. It had been a testing time for both battalions. There had been little to cheer or to encourage the B.S.F., either in the strategical situation or in the conditions and surroundings under which regimental officers and men had to exist. That the two battalions of the TWENTY-FOURTH should have maintained so high a standard of discipline and efficiency in these discouraging and disadvantageous circumstances was enormously to the credit of officers and men alike.

CHAPTER XIX

THE THIRD WINTER

From the Somme to Arras

FOUR months separated the Fifth Army's capture of Beaumont Hamel from the next event of any strategical importance, the start on March 16th of the German retirement to the Hindenburg Line. To regimental officers and men these months were mainly notable for the weather, always unpleasant and at times very severe, with much snow, hard frosts and bitter piercing winds. These conditions naturally prevented major operations, though several actions were fought which in any previous war would have ranked as important. From the standpoint of the higher strategy these months may be passed over lightly since they left the strategical situation virtually unchanged, but to those battalions of the TWENTY-FOURTH who held trenches in the more " lively " quarters they were quite strenuous enough, while even holding a " quiet " sector entailed the endurance of many hardships and great discomfort. Even in the strategical sphere the time was one of great importance, for decisions were taken which were to have far-reaching effects.

As already explained, the unusually wet autumn of 1916 had robbed the British Armies of the full fruits of their exertions in the earlier stages of the Somme. When that great struggle ended its results may well have appeared disappointing, especially to those who took a short view and were disposed to overlook its effects on the enemy's man-power and will-power. They saw the terrible British casualty lists but not the enemy's; they could measure the British advance on the map and found it insignificant, but they could not appreciate the threat to the German lines from the Ancre to Arras which that advance implied, or see that the tactical situation on the Somme promised very well if a big offensive could be developed early in the year from the front reached after the Beaumont Hamel operations. The British position on the Ancre was, moreover, substantially improved during January and February, when the 5th S.W.B., then under the Seventh Division, did excellent work; and at the other end of the line gains of ground were made, notably by the Twenty-Ninth Division. These months seemed to augur well for the prospects of an attack in force : for one thing indications were not wanting that in some German units something approaching to demoralization was setting in. Desertions were not uncommon, attacks met with less stubborn resistance, prisoners were more easily taken.

A British offensive, launched before the Germans had

completed their elaborate preparations for their retreat to the Hindenburg Line, might indeed have achieved much. That it would not have suited the German book may be confidently asserted, and 1917 might well have yielded much less disappointing results had the Allies kept to the plan arranged by Marshal Joffre and Sir Douglas Haig at the Chantilly conference. Actually this plan was completely changed: for a main offensive by the British on the Somme-Scarpe front was substituted General Nivelle's plan of a French offensive on the Aisne. This involved the British taking over a considerable stretch of frontage to their right, to let the French concentrate a sufficient force for their offensive.

Regimental officers and men were naturally quite unaware of the importance to them of these deliberations on strategy and of the consequent changes in plan. Their business was to get on with the war, even under conditions more unpleasant than usual. If troops did not have to remain in the trenches for the interminable periods of the winter of 1914–1915, and if periods of relief and rest were far more frequent and longer, if the administrative arrangements for feeding, housing, washing, doctoring, amusing and supplying the troops had reached an elaboration and a perfection undreamt of in the bad days of the first winter, the weather passed all records for severity, and the alternations of frost and thaw were peculiarly trying.

The 1st Battalion endured these hard times mainly on the Somme battlefield or in the new line to the South, recently taken over from the French. Early in November the battalion had been encamped in Mametz Wood for ten days of almost continuous rain and almost as continuous making of roads up to Bazentin and beyond. On the 10th it went back to Millencourt, being hospitably entertained in passing through Albert by Colonel Trower and the 5th Battalion, then at rest close by. After a week's rest it returned to Mametz Wood and the interminable fatigues with which that area was now associated in everybody's mind. On the 27th it took over front line trenches well to the North of Flers, with Battalion Headquarters at Factory Corner. The mud was terrible, several men stuck in it and were extricated with much difficulty, and in the morning a gap of 200 yards was discovered between the battalion and the R.M.F. in which five of the K.R.R.C. were embogged. These unfortunates were promptly rescued and succoured, but the incident gives some indication of the appalling conditions.

The battalion was to spend all December in these trenches or in camp behind them, generally at Mametz Wood or near Bazentin-le-Petit. Both trenches and camps were occasionally shelled, but, except that an excellent N.C.O. was lost when on

THE HISTORY OF THE SOUTH WALES BORDERERS

December 19th Company Quartermaster Sergeant Rickards was killed, the battalion got off fairly lightly.[1] On December 12th to the general regret Colonel Collier was invalided home. He had had fourteen months in command and had led the battalion through some strenuous encounters. In his place the 1st were so fortunate as to get another officer of the Regiment in Major C. L. Taylor, who had arrived a few days earlier. About this time conditions reached their worst; what with rain, mud and German shell fire the trenches were inconceivably bad. Half the shelters had collapsed; hard as the men worked it seemed impossible to make the least improvement, and all ranks welcomed their relief on New Year's Eve by the Fiftieth Division. This was followed by a move to Bécourt and three weeks' rest. A draft of 108 men which arrived on January 6th did something to make good the wastage caused by the recent tours in trenches —over 40 men had had to be sent down to the Base as unfit on arrival at Bécourt—but still the battalion was considerably under establishment.

From Bécourt the battalion moved on January 23rd to Baisieux, about the worst camp it had yet sampled. The accommodation consisted of tents so sited as to get the full benefit of the North wind—with the temperature 15° below freezing that was something to be remembered—and hardly any fuel was available. Here ten days were spent in training, while Captain Ramsden rejoined and became second in command. One one occasion the training was varied by marching companies out to various spots half an hour's march from camp and then telling the men to run home, the first home in each platoon being promised a tot of rum. The buried talent as runners which this incentive unearthed was really remarkable.

The training period over, the whole 3rd Brigade started for the new line which was being taken over from the French. Its route lay by Mericourt l'Abbé, Cerisy, where three nights were spent, and Marly to Flaucourt, about three miles S.W. of Peronne. On the way 150 men had joined, but even so the battalion was barely 700 strong, and as this draft needed training in musketry and could not be taken into the line, only 370 men were available for trench duty. After four days in support the battalion took over the front line in the Bois de Boulogne. Things were quiet at first except for a minenwerfer, most of whose missiles fell short, and a sharp bombardment by 5.9 inch shells on the 13th. The weather was as atrocious as ever and the mud so bad that once whilst going round the line Captain Ramsden actually lost his boots. After two tours in the front

---

[1] The casualties recorded come to about 30, including Second Lieutenant Davidson wounded.

line the battalion went back on February 23rd to Chuignolles, where parties of the Forty-Second Division, which had just arrived from Egypt, were attached to it for training. March 3rd brought a return to the front line. Greater liveliness prevailed now : a new 150 lb. heavy trench mortar was used for the first time and provoked some retaliation, further North considerable progress was being made, and there were some indications that the Germans were contemplating a retirement. Accordingly the Division attempted some raids to discover what the enemy were doing. A German patrol retaliated by trying to raid B Company but was beaten off.

March 17th saw the expected German retirement become a definite fact South of the Somme. The battalion was in support, but moved into the old German front line that afternoon and was soon busy searching for concealed mines and other " booby traps." Remarkable ingenuity had been lavished on their construction but casualties were successfully avoided, though there were several narrow escapes. The road to the Somme was clear now, and March 18th found the battalion assisting the R.E. to throw a bridge across near Brie, over which cavalry, cyclists and motor machine guns crossed next day to take up the pursuit. But the 1st's anticipations of open order warfare were to be disappointed, as its Division was drawn back to Chuignolles, round which it was concentrated for further training from March 21st on. It was still out of the line, varying instructional parades by much needed improvement of the roads, when on April 9th Sir Douglas Haig's attack at Arras opened the main offensive operations of the year.

The 2nd Battalion, on returning to the line on November 16th, had found itself back in the Les Boeufs quarter in which it had undergone such hardships in October. The weather at first was bitterly cold, with ten degrees of frost, but this had the compensation of drying up the mud so that movement was easier and the men were at least not wet through. A change to milder weather was not appreciated, for the mud promptly reasserted itself as the predominant partner and trebled the labours of carrying parties. The trenches too were in dreadful condition, and a new supply of boots was warmly welcomed. Waterproof capes and gum-boots were also issued, and this tour in the trenches produced less sickness than its predecessor, nor were casualties numerous, though shelling, if intermittent, was fairly heavy. Nine fresh subalterns appeared during November, while Major Raikes assumed command on Colonel Going being invalided. One of the chief incidents was a visit from the Prince of Wales, who called at Battalion Headquarters on November 19th.

THE HISTORY OF THE SOUTH WALES BORDERERS

The end of the month found the battalion again in front line trenches near Les Boeufs, on the extreme British right: indeed, on November 30th it took over 1000 yards of line from the French and was interested to notice the differences between French and British methods of trench construction. This tour was uneventful, the weather if cold was dry, and allowed of fair progress in improving the trenches and pushing saps forward. From December 2nd to 9th the battalion was in reserve at Carnoy, busy with fatigues, and then its Division was withdrawn from the line to rest.

The Division remained "out" till well into January.[1] It then moved back to relieve the Seventeenth Division in the Le Transloy sector (January 15th). Conditions here were awful: the mud was very bad, a communication trench completed before the Division left the line in December had ceased to exist, the front line (so-called) consisted of disconnected small posts without any wire in front. Hard frost and several inches of snow made matters little easier; if the mud dried, the ground was slippery, especially the duckboard paths. The German artillery was not active, though there was some sniping and their aeroplanes were much on the alert. However, on January 27th the 87th Brigade delivered a highly successful attack just South of Le Transloy. The Inniskillings and Borders were the attacking battalions, but the S.W.B. provided nearly 150 "moppers-up," divided into parties of one N.C.O. and eight men each, with orders to clear the trenches to the left directly they got in, each party marking its portion by sticking a flag into the parapet. The attack was a brilliant success, nearly 400 prisoners being taken at a cost of under 150 casualties. 1000 yards of trenches were captured and quickly consolidated, and though the Germans shelled the position vigorously they never ventured on a counter-attack. The S.W.B. did their "mopping up" well: only on the left did they meet any serious resistance, in overcoming which Second Lieutenant Webber was wounded. Second Lieutenant Lowe also did good service. When a machine gun held up the attack he led his party to the point, bombed the gun team, and by putting the gun out of action enabled the attack to get on, besides capturing half a dozen prisoners. He was well backed up by Lance Corporals Griffiths and Stevens and Privates W. H. Davies and Salt.[2] These parties remained in the captured position for another two days, the rest of the battalion, barely 300 strong, moving up meanwhile to relieve the Newfoundland Regiment

---

[1] The New Year Honours brought "mentions" to Major Raikes and Sergeant Press, D.C.M.'s to Company Sergeant Majors Chaplin and Tring and the M.S.M. to Corporal Moore, while Captain Garnett was promoted to Major.

[2] Second Lieutenant Lowe got the M.C. and the four men the M.M.

to the left of the captured line. It was heavily shelled here and had some 16 casualties on the 29th alone, which with the 30 odd suffered by the mopping-up parties on the 27th brought the month's total up to nearly 90.[1]

The Division continued in the Le Transloy sector till February 9th, when it had ten days' rest near Meaulté. Just before this the battalion had had rather a bad time from snipers, who succeeded in killing Second Lieutenant Sandys Thomas and wounding Captain Mundy[2] while they were superintending the building of a strong point in the position captured on January 27th. The frosty ground was particularly hard to dig and a bright moon added to the difficulties. After this rest the battalion took over the Sailly Saillisel sector to the right of its previous trenches on February 18th. It did two tours in front line here, in the second a small party under Second Lieutenant J. L. Morgan successfully entered the enemy's trenches and occupied a section which he found clear. He held on to this all day, and only withdrew because the German line was about to be bombarded prior to an attack by the 86th Brigade, which proved highly successful.

A longish period in reserve followed after this: the Battalion being first at Bronfay, then at Bonnay (March 3rd to 19th) and then at Le Quesnoy, where it found good billets in the pleasant country of the lower valley of the Somme. Open warfare was now assiduously practised, the instruction working up from that of platoons to a Divisional field-day. Some drafts joined, the more welcome because the battalion was much below establishment—it had only 580 men on its strength on March 15th and of the 30 officers nominally with it many were away on courses or various employments; earlier in the month indeed, after finding a fatigue party of 130 men for Brigade Headquarters, it had been unable to produce a single unemployed man for duty. The 2nd, like the 1st, thus missed the pursuit to the Hindenburg Line, the advance towards which had virtually ended before on March 29th it left its rest billets for Arras.

During a period like the winter of 1916–1917, when the maintenance of the trenches and even more of roads and communications generally made even greater demands than usual, no Pioneer battalion was likely to be idle long, and neither the 5th or the 6th S.W.B. could complain of wanting work. When

---

[1] 13 men killed, 5 missing, 66 and 5 officers wounded. These included Captain Matthews, who had joined on January 21st after serving with the West African Regiment in the Cameroons campaign and was wounded within a week of his arrival.

[2] Second Lieutenant Weeks took over the Adjutant's duties.

the Nineteenth Division was relieved after the "Battle of the Ancre" the 5th S.W.B. were left behind to assist the incoming Division, and did not follow their own to the back areas till December 1st, only to find themselves kept busy erecting hutments, repairing roads and preparing trench stores. On December 10th the battalion was recalled to the front to assist the Seventh Division, now in line East of Beaumont Hamel, and not a little of the credit for the successful attacks which that Division delivered early in January," models of quick hard blows " they have been called, was due to the splendid preparatory work of the 5th S.W.B., as General Watts of the Seventh Division warmly acknowledged on parting with it.[1]

Rejoining their own Division on January 12th the 5th found it on the old Hebuterne front, preparing for an attack. The preparations included the opening up of some extensive chalk caves under Hebuterne in which it was hoped the assaulting infantry might assemble under cover.[2] Apart from this, roads, trench-tramways, advanced dumps and all the other things to which the Pioneers had to attend provided ample occupation.[3] The break-up of the frost towards the end of February greatly aggravated the difficulties, but the arrangements for the attack on Hebuterne were on the verge of completion when, on February 25th, patrols discovered that the Germans had evacuated their front line. Stronger parties were at once thrust forward to find that it was not only the front line which had been evacuated, and soon the Division was pushing forward in pursuit as fast as the ground would allow.

The state of the ground was such that " fast " was an aspiration rather than an actuality; indeed the pace of the pursuit depended largely on the pace at which the 5th S.W.B. could reconstruct what had once been the Serre road and push on the trench-tramway. D Company was detailed to the tramway: the other three concentrated their energies on the road. The thaw had effectively broken up the surface of all the roads, turning them into rivers of liquid mud, and the retreating Germans had improved on this by exploding mines at intervals, leaving yawning craters into which vast quantities of road metal were

[1] In the New Year's Honours Colonel Trower, to the general satisfaction, got the C.M.G., and Captain Rebsch received the M.C. Colonel Trower, Lieutenants Lochner and I. T. Evans, the Quartermaster, Lieutenant Bryant, and Company Sergeant Major Mitchener were all " mentioned " in Dispatches about the same time.

[2] Eventually this scheme had to be abandoned owing to the constant falling of chalk from the roofs of the caves, due to the action of fresh air which the opening up of the caves admitted.

[3] Casualties were fairly heavy, 14 wounded in January, 8 killed and 27 wounded in February.

ROAD REPAIRING

poured without apparently producing the least result. It was an unending work; hard as the 5th toiled away progress was infinitesimal, but pressure on the retreating Germans could not possibly be maintained unless food and ammunition and field guns, not to mention heavier pieces, could be got across the old fighting zone, which the constant bombardments had churned up into a regular morass. Thus the chances of reaping a real advantage from the German retreat came to hinge on the thews and sinews of the 5th S.W.B. and other Pioneers.

The 5th worked splendidly. In five days D Company had constructed some 3000 yards of tram-line, including some twenty bridges and many long stretches of piling, which stretched right across the belt of crater-pitted and waterlogged devastation and connected up beyond it with a little-damaged German line. Thanks to this tram-line the guns of some five Divisions were transported across the morass and deposited on the unbroken ground beyond, followed by great quantities of ammunition and supplies. With guns to help them the infantry could get forward, and though much delayed, the pursuit could be effectively pressed.

March 10th saw the whole Nineteenth Division out of the line and starting on a long march to Belgium. This was quite enjoyable. The weather had taken a change for the better and the line followed took the troops into country untouched by war and off the normal track of its traffic. Eggs, fresh bread, butter and vegetables were plentiful and cheap. Billets were good and the men enjoyed comforts to which they had long been strangers in the over-crowded "rest areas" close behind the Somme fighting front. The Staff arrangements were admirable and the marches were not long, 10 to 12 miles as a rule, so that no great exertions were demanded of the men. They had had a long spell on the Somme, and if their losses had not been heavy[1] all ranks welcomed a change. The Ypres Salient was not then the name of ill-omen it was soon to become, and when the 5th S.W.B. arrived at Caestre on March 20th and found themselves faced with completing the preparations for the long-projected offensive against the Messines Ridge, they were not prepared to quarrel seriously with their lot.

---

[1] They came to 1 officer and 28 men killed, 1 officer and 83 men wounded since the battalion's return to the Somme in October. Major Lochner had left in February to join the 1st Battalion, Majors Crawford and Deacon had both been struck off the establishment, Captain Curtis had been transferred to Base duty, and at the end of March Lieutenant C. B. Lochner left to join the Indian Army. Lieutenant E. B. Trower now became Adjutant and several new officers appeared, while Lieutenant Rose, who had been wounded on the Somme, rejoined in March.

The Regiment's other Pioneer battalion had been in the Messines neighbourhood since the end of October. After the capture of Regina Trench the Twenty-Fifth Division had been sent up to Flanders and had taken over the Ploegsteert sector on October 31st, holding it with slight modifications till the end of February. It was low-lying country with a breastwork trench system, but while the ever-present water problem provided ample occupation the sector was quiet and remained so during the Division's stay. With 6000 yards of frontage, units reduced much below establishment and containing many raw recruits, little was to be gained by too offensive a policy in a quarter where no important tactical objective invited even a minor operation. From November 1st till the middle of February the 6th had under 30 casualties: invaliding accounted for many more, but as 16 officers, mainly new Second Lieutenants, and over 100 other ranks arrived as reinforcements the wastage was about balanced.[1] The battalion was confronted with a very varied assortment of jobs—on one typical day in December A Company was employed improving the defences of the Le Touquet Salient, B was at work on the "subsidiary line," C ballasting and repairing a light railway which rejoiced in the name of the "C.P.R.," while D spent the day putting up stables and huts for baths. The New Year's Honours brought Captain Choinier and Lieutenants Deane and Rumsey the M.C., well-deserved awards all three, and Colonel Hewett, Lieutenants Cox and Neale, Regimental Sergeant Major Casey and Company Sergeant Major O'Neil were mentioned in Dispatches.

March found the 6th in reserve near Thieushoek, moving later to Neuve Eglise, prior to relieving the New Zealanders in the Wulverghem sector. Their Division was eventually to assault from these trenches, and though the date of that attack was not yet fixed preparations were already well advanced. Plenty still remained to be done, however, and April saw the 6th hard at work. Casualties were few, for the Germans were inactive and apparently inattentive, but it was a strenuous time nevertheless, and the battalion's capacity for hard work was fully tested.

While the two Pioneer battalions found themselves fairly near neighbours on the right of the Second Army's frontage, at the other end, at the Northern angle of the Ypres Salient, the 10th and 11th Battalions seemed to have almost taken root. Unlike most Divisions transferred to Ypres after the July fighting on the Somme, the Thirty-Eighth had been left undisturbed.

[1] Major Renwick was struck off the strength in December and Captain Choinier was invalided in March, but in January Major A. H. J. Ellis joined while Lieutenants Deane and J. C. Owen were promoted to Captains.

THE 10TH AND 11TH IN THE SALIENT

After a fortnight's rest near Bollezeele it had relieved the Fourth Division in the St. Julien sector in the middle of August, and, but for three weeks in December and January, remained in line till the end of April, holding one or other of the Eighth Corps' sectors. There was little to choose between them, though those further to the left, the Elverdinghe and Boesinghe sectors, were less exposed to enfilade and reverse fire than the Irish Farm or Hill Top sectors on the right. In the left sector, moreover, the tactical situation had the distinctive feature that the Yser Canal divided the opposing lines, the British trenches running along its Western bank, while the enemy held the Eastern. Except when the canal was frozen, raiding and patrolling of No Man's Land were impossible, and when fairly solid ice covered the canal in January it was broken up by bombs. Nearly all the sectors wanted constant work to keep the defences in repair. The soil of the Salient was in many places sandy and the heavy autumn rains did much damage to the trenches, which collapsed wholesale, while drainage and sanitation were always troublesome.

The eleven months from the beginning of the Somme to the attack on Messines form the least eventful period in the story of the Ypres Salient. One major offensive was all the artillery and ammunition situation would allow the British Armies to maintain, and minor offensives, other than raids, required more guns and consumed more shells than even success would justify. Small raids, activity in patrolling, occasional bombardments, harassing fire by artillery and machine guns, therefore constituted the offensive activities of the troops in the Salient when they found themselves able to indulge in such departures from the daily routine. Divisions sent to a " quiet " area, as Ypres was at this time reckoned, usually arrived there too weak or too full of drafts, often only very imperfectly trained, to allow of even minor activities. Moreover, the heavy demands of the Somme fighting on the available reinforcements tended to divert drafts from quiet sectors. Thus though their battle wastage was not high[1] and careful attention to the men's health kept the sick-rate well down,[2] both 10th and 11th remained much below establishment. On December 27th Colonel Harvey had to report that the 10th was so weak that he could not find the garrisons for the front

---

[1] From August 19th to December 31st, 1916, the 10th S.W.B. lost one officer (Captain Charlton) and 8 men killed and missing and 1 officer (Second Lieutenant Taylor) and 49 men wounded: the 11th's battalion diary does not record casualties as regularly, but they do not appear to have been even as heavy. It had Second Lieutenant E. H. Williams killed and Second Lieutenant Moore wounded.

[2] In two tours in the line in November, when the weather was at its worst and the trenches waist-deep in mud, the 11th record respectively no admissions for "trench feet," and one only.

and support trenches required by the Divisional defence scheme and must utilize his reserves. The 11th got a draft of nearly 100 " Bantams " in January, 1917, but it was March before the 10th received any substantial reinforcements, 136 men turning up on the 1st, another 47 a few days later, followed by 61 more on the 21st. Officer reinforcements arrived rather more promptly: the 10th had some 15 new subalterns before the end of 1916, besides getting back several of those wounded at Mametz Wood, and the 11th was joined by nearly as many. Captain Long was promoted Major and second in command on Major Harvey taking over command, but was invalided and struck off in November. Major Gibson-Watt joined in October and Captain Rees was also promoted to Major, while in September Lieutenant Kenslade joined as Quartermaster in place of Lieutenant Ingledew, who had been invalided earlier on. The 11th were joined among others by Captain R. H. Evans, the only 1914 Regular officer who served with them, by one of its own old members in Captain Marle, and by Captain I. A. Morgan, while Captain Monteith rejoined in November and was shortly afterwards promoted to Major. Lieutenant W. T. Harris became Adjutant in place of Lieutenant Hamer and first Regimental Quartermaster Sergeant Rees and then Regimental Sergeant Major Pearson acted for some time as Quartermaster, owing to Lieutenant Barry being away ill. Eventually Lieutenant Barry was invalided out and replaced by Lieutenant G. Norton from the R.W.F.

Of incidents of note this long period was singularly barren. The Division carried out some big raids, in none of which either 10th or 11th S.W.B. took an active part, though when the 114th Brigade raided the High Command Redoubt in November, the 11th co-operated with rifle and machine gun fire. On October 6th a patrol of the 10th under Captain Charlton rushed a sap and disposed of its garrison of six men, but had to retire on the arrival of large reinforcements. Noticing that Captain Charlton and Private Spanwick were missing, Second Lieutenant Taylor and Sergeant P. F. Evans went back despite the heavy machine gun fire to look for them. Of Private Spanwick no trace could be found, but Captain Charlton was seen being carried away on a stretcher by the enemy.[1] Second Lieutenant Taylor, who was wounded in getting back to our lines, received the M.C. for his gallantry and Sergeant Evans was awarded the M.M. The 11th carried out two small raids, inflicting several casualties on the enemy but without obtaining any identifications. Sergeant W. T. Edwards distinguished himself in this work by conspicuous gallantry and resourcefulness, more particularly by bringing in Second Lieutenant Moore who was wounded in a raid on Canadian

---

[1] He was afterwards reported by the Germans as having been killed.

dug-outs. Patrolling was actively carried on wherever possible, but rarely led to encounters with the enemy: " as usual the Huns kept to their own side of the parapet " is the complaint of the 11th's diary for December, and the 10th write " our fighting patrols have undisputed possession of No Man's Land." With the enemy thus quiescent it was possible to repair and extend the wire, to improve the trenches and to obtain ample information about the enemy's defences.

The end of the year brought a welcome respite from the trenches, lasting over three weeks. The 10th spent these in Bollezeele Camp, but the 11th were sent back for duty at St. Omer and greatly appreciated the change. Both battalions figured in the New Year Honours: of the 10th Colonel Harvey and Sergeant Woodall were " mentioned," Major Rees got the M.C., and Sergeants R. Edwards and J. H. Williams the D.C.M. The 11th had Colonel Gaussen and Captain Browning " mentioned," Sergeant W. T. Edwards got the D.C.M., and the M.O., Captain E. Evans, R.A.M.C., was awarded the M.C. for his good work at Mametz Wood. Changes in personnel were fairly frequent, notably Colonel Gaussen's recall to India in February. Like other Indian Army officers who had been invaluable in raising, training and commanding " Service " battalions he could no longer be spared by the Indian Army which urgently required its British officers to help with the expansion of its establishment and the raising of new regiments and battalions. Colonel A. H. Radice of the Gloucestershire Regiment succeeded him in command of the 11th, having Major Monteith as second in command[1] till Major E. de P. O'Kelly of the R.W.F. joined in April. Both battalions suffered not a little from having to send some of their best Warrant Officers and N.C.O.'s to Cadet Battalions to be trained for commissions; the 11th losing several Warrant Officers in quick succession. To the 10th the chief change was the arrival in April of Major A. L. Bowen of the Monmouthshire, who was subsequently to command the battalion very successfully.

Towards the end of January the two battalions found themselves back in the Elverdinghe–Boesinghe sector next the Belgians and separated from the enemy by the frozen canal. They remained in this sector till the end of April, four-day tours in the front line alternating with periods in support, usually at Bluett or Roussel Farms, or in reserve in the Elverdinghe defences or nearer Poperinghe, where the 11th speak warmly of X Camp, " a model camp, the best in the area." Though somewhat uneventful the period saw increasing artillery activity on both sides, which was naturally reflected in the

[1] Major Morgan had been appointed Instructor at the Second Army School.

casualty lists. On February 15th for example one company of the 11th at Roussel Farm was heavily shelled and had over 20 casualties. For the first four months of 1917 the 10th had 8 killed and 33 wounded; the 11th, who were unluckier as regards getting bombarded, had 13 killed and 25 wounded in February alone. Towards the end of the time plans were being discussed for an operation by the Thirty-Eighth Division and the Belgians, with the idea of improving the local tactical situation and so facilitating the projected big attack, but the Division's turn for a month's rest came without anything being attempted.

The 12th Battalion meanwhile had been steadily acquiring experience and learning all the tricks of their trade. As the last " New Army " Division to come out to France the Fortieth had not been put into the Somme offensive, but had served a long apprenticeship to war in the neighbourhood of Loos. It shifted about between the Calonne, the Loos and the Maroc sectors. Things were on the whole fairly lively, though Loos proved quieter than Calonne; the enemy's snipers were active and their trench mortars much in evidence, so that casualties soon began to mount up. The 12th were unlucky: early in July a working party repairing the front line at Doughty's Post had a dozen casualties, including Captain Murphy wounded; on August 5th it lost a valuable and popular officer in Captain Rees, who was killed by an " aerial torpedo "; a week later it suffered another heavy loss when Captain Pritchard died of wounds received in leading a successful raid. In his time a mainstay of the Welsh Fifteen, Captain Pritchard had shown himself a fine officer and was very much regretted.

This enterprise was otherwise a distinct success, as it resulted in the Division's first prisoner and the inflicting of several casualties on the enemy, and the 12th were warmly commended by their Corps commander on their dash and enterprise. The battalion had already carried out some successful minor enterprises, Lance Corporal Hathaway and two privates had bombed a German sap-head, while Captain Pritchard and a party had reconnoitred the German wire on the night of August 11th/12th and obtained useful information for the next night's raid. This was carried out by three parties under Captain Pritchard and Second Lieutenants Enright and Wood. They crept out from a sap-head and were in a position to rush the enemy's trenches directly the barrage came down. All three effected an entrance and engaged the enemy with success. Directly a prisoner had been secured the order to withdraw was given, Lieutenant Enright, assisted by Private Pickett, bringing in Captain Pritchard, who had been badly wounded. Good work was also done by Lance Corporals

Lancaster and Willan and by Private Bullen,[1] while Lieutenant Wood, who went back to bring in wounded men, received the M.C. Shortly after this, the Germans having fired a mine, Captain Murphy and Lieutenants Lewis and Wingard retaliated by going out with a party of bombers, who entered the enemy's sap and bombed them, successfully preventing them from profiting by the explosion.

A shift in September to the Maroc sector brought the 12th face to face with the famous Double Crassier.[2] The opposing lines were quite close together and great alertness was needed; while, as the Germans opposite had not been identified, the Division was most anxious for a prisoner. This was none too easy, as the German wire was extremely strong, in places as much as 45 feet across, but the 12th did their best to effect a capture, sending out frequent patrols. Very good work was done in this, Captain Page, Lieutenant Wingard and Second Lieutenant H. J. Brown all being much to the fore. Eventually on September 28th Lieutenant Wingard and Second Lieutenant H. J. Brown and 30 men tried a raid. The party had just got through the German wire, and the leaders, Lieutenant Wingard and Sergeants Tanner and Pickett, had entered the trench and shot a couple of men, when a small mine was exploded and Lieutenant Wingard was mortally wounded. Some of those on the parapet, taking the smoke for a gas-cloud, retired, and the raiders had to come back, though Sergeant Tanner bombed two dug-outs before withdrawing. Second Lieutenant Brown did excellent work: taking command of the party and directing its withdrawal most successfully. Later on, finding that Lieutenant Wingard and two men were missing, he went out to fetch them in, actually bringing Private James back from quite close to the enemy's wire.[3] Lieutenant Wingard was a great loss: he had already served with the 7th S.W.B. at Salonica and in his few weeks with the 12th his dash and fearless keenness when patrolling had made a great impression. Things were rather quieter in October: the bad weather kept all ranks busy repairing the trenches. Major Hore left on the 27th to command the 10th R.W.F., which led to the promotion to Major of Captain Murphy who had rejoined from hospital, while Lieutenants Morris, H. C. Lloyd and T. O. Jones all went up to Captain.

---

[1] Privates Pickett and Bullen received the M.M., as did Private R. Jones who, though himself wounded, had brought Lieutenant Harrison safely in when wounded on patrol some days earlier.

[2] A good many officers had joined, in fact 28 were posted to the battalion before the end of October, but as against that several were transferred to the R.F.C. or M.G.C., and others taken away for duty with trench mortars or for Divisional employments, so what with casualties and invalidings the battalion had none too many officers.   [3] He subsequently received the M.C.

November brought the 12th a change from the Loos area. The battalion moved South by easy stages, reaching Pont Remy on the 25th. Here it spent a fortnight and then moved to a camp near Chipilly which the French had just vacated. This was found to be highly insanitary, and the 12th had to turn to and dig vigorously to improve matters. After another fortnight the 12th went back to the trenches again, as their Division was relieving the Thirty-Third in the Rancourt sector, just East of Combles, which had recently been handed over to us by the French. The 12th took over an apology for a front line here on December 27th. The line consisted of shell holes, more or less joined up, and the ground was in awful condition. All ranks found their four days' tour here most exhausting and "trench-feet" made its appearance, while the conditions to be endured were reflected by a rise in invalidings, nearly 60 being recorded in December, among them Captain Page. But when they were next in line, in the Bouchavesnes sector just to the South, from January 8th to 12th, they came to the conclusion that even Rancourt could be surpassed in vileness. They were to have ample opportunities of comparing these two sectors, as they held one or other of them till the end of February. Casualties were low, for the bad conditions curtailed the activities of both sides, but the sick-rate continued high, though less in the colder periods than when the weather was mild and the ground wetter. Major Murphy left for the 18th Welch in January and Captain Godwin-Austen was transferred to the R.E. for survey work, several new subalterns appearing, though drafts were none too frequent. March brought a shift to the right again, into the newly taken over South Clary sector, but from the 18th onward the battalion and the 19th Welch were set to work under the direction of the Corps on railway construction. A line had to be pushed forward to Péronne, and while others were pursuing the Germans Eastward the 12th S.W.B. were for the moment doing navvies' work. Not till April 8th were they to revert to the fighting rôle.

CHAPTER XX

ARRAS AND MESSINES

WITH five of its seven battalions in France already in or on their way to join the Second Army, it was not wonderful that the TWENTY-FOURTH should have been unrepresented in the highly successful attack of April 9th with which the Arras offensive began. On that day the 2nd S.W.B., the only battalion near the active front, were waiting in reserve at Monchiet, West of Arras. The Twenty-Ninth Division had been allotted to the Eighteenth Corps, which was detailed to be ready to take up the pursuit, and the men and the first-line transport were loaded up with extra ammunition and rations in readiness. However, substantial as was the success achieved, a break-through was just not effected: the Germans rushed up large reserves to the danger spot and managed to close the half-open door.

When the Twenty-Ninth got into action it was for the old familiar task, " consolidate and, if possible, extend your gains." On the 12th it relieved the troops holding Monchy le Preux, a village on the high ground between the Scarpe and the Cojeul. The 87th Brigade took over the right of the new line, from Monchy Southward to the Cojeul, having the 2nd S.W.B. on its left, facing the village of Guemappe. It was a difficult relief after a long march over roads packed with transport and troops: the outgoing battalion had just made an unsuccessful attack and lost heavily, its exact positions were hard to locate, and the Germans were plastering the area with gas shells. Eventually companies managed somehow to find their positions and patrols were promptly pushed out to locate the enemy and obtain touch with the flanking units. Monchy was the most advanced point reached in the right centre of the attack, and, having considerable tactical importance, was hardly likely to be left in the undisturbed possession of the British. On April 14th the Germans counter-attacked in force, advancing against the left of the Divisional frontage from the Bois de Sart, N.E. of Infantry Hill, the Eastward continuation of the hill on which Monchy stands. This attack practically overwhelmed the 1st Essex and the Newfoundland Regiment, but was eventually repulsed by the survivors of those units, who offered determined resistance and were effectively supported on the right by the 4th Worcestershire. The 87th Brigade was heavily shelled meanwhile, but as the infantry attacks did not extend as far as its frontage the S.W.B. were denied the satisfaction of helping their Worcestershire neighbours to shoot down the advancing Germans. That evening, however, owing to the 88th Brigade's heavy losses, their support companies had to come up into line to relieve the Worcestershire.

The battalion remained in the front line till April 17th, being mainly occupied in digging a "jumping-off" trench in front of its line. The weather was wet; greatcoats and blankets had been left at Arras: there was no shelter, scarcely enough fuel even to make tea, and the tour left the battalion very exhausted. It was heavily shelled most of the time and had some 80 casualties, including Captain C. P. Owen killed and Second Lieutenants A. T. Lewis and J. H. Davis wounded by the same shell which hit D Company's headquarters dug-out. Six days in support and reserve followed, and then on the evening of April 22nd it came back to the line to take part in a new attack. This attack had not formed part of Sir Douglas Haig's original intentions for the Battle of Arras: April 9th had secured him nearly all the ground he actually needed, but the fresh attack had to be improvised because the great French attack of April 16th on the Aisne had altogether failed to realize the confident expectations of General Nivelle and his backers. It was essential to divert the German reserves to Arras and so prevent them from taking advantage of the shattered state of Nivelle's troops to counter-attack on the Aisne, but the attack of April 23rd inevitably started under less favourable conditions than had its carefully prepared predecessor a fortnight earlier.

This time the 87th Brigade was on the left, attacking N.E. from Monchy against the Bois des Aubespines on the Northern slopes of Infantry Hill. The K.O.S.B. formed its right and the 2nd S.W.B. its left. A, B and C Companies were in line from right to left, their immediate objective lying along the Eastern edge of two copses, known as Twin Copses, just short of the Bois des Aubespines. "Zero" was at 4.45 a.m., and punctually to the moment the battalion went "over the top." The jumping-off trench had been full of water, so the dispositions had to be altered, with the result that a gap soon developed between A and B which had to be filled from the reserve company, D. The barrage, though effective in reducing opposition, was ragged and caused not a few casualties among our men, but all companies advanced with great dash and promptly secured nearly all their objectives. On the left, C, under Captain Dickinson, carried a German trench[1] running N.N.W. from Arrowhead Copse towards a sunken road which marked the left flank, though the battalion of the Seventeenth Division which should have covered that flank was nowhere to be seen. In the centre B, passing through Arrowhead Copse, cleared the Twin Copses, disposing of a good many Germans and taking a few prisoners. A (Captain P. A. Hill) established themselves level with B, S.E. of the Twin

[1] This was subsequently known as Snaffle Trench. North of the portion of this trench which C had taken Germans were still holding on,

Copses, and dug in, being reinforced by a platoon of D. Losses had been heavy, little more than 40 men of B under Second Lieutenant Woolveridge had reached the final objective; and although the K.O.S.B. and the 88th Brigade had also gained their objectives, the Divisions on either flank had been less successful, so that the position presented a salient. This put any further advance out of the question and consolidation was the order of the day, the Border Regiment coming up to the S.W.B.'s left rear and digging in to cover that flank. Consolidation, however, was much impeded by considerable sniping and shell fire: Captain Hill, who though wounded in the advance had remained

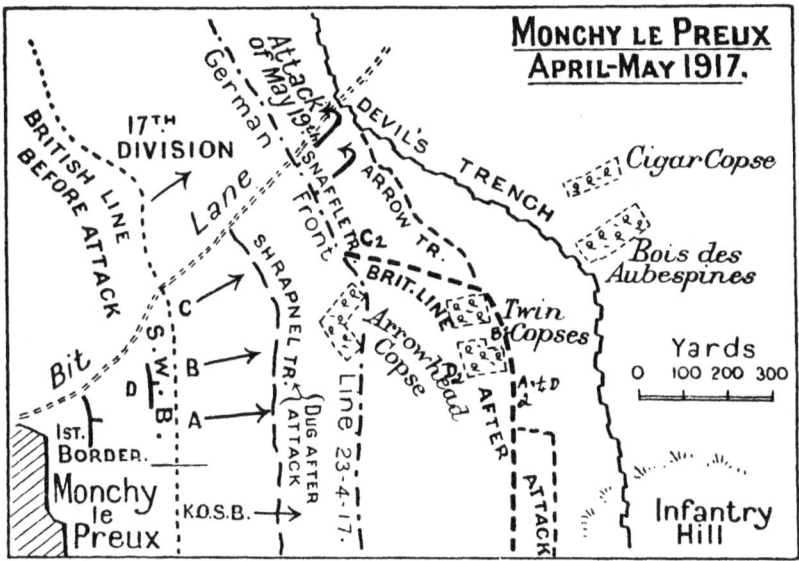

with his company, was now shot by a sniper and killed, and many other casualties occurred.

It was well that consolidation had been put in hand so promptly, for before long B sent back word that the enemy were collecting North of the Bois des Aubespines. About midday some Germans began working forward through the narrow wood known as Cigar Copse, and covered by their fire, a much larger party advanced against Twin Copses from between Cigar Copse and the Bois des Aubespines. But reduced in numbers as B were they held their ground stoutly, Second Lieutenant Woolveridge setting a fine example, and C's Lewis guns caught one party coming over the crest, knocking many over. Then when the counter-attackers had been brought to a standstill our guns, which Colonel Raikes had ranged most accurately upon the target, got well into them and sent the survivors running back.

Several times after this Germans appeared on the crest near the Bois des Aubespines and endeavoured to advance, but were prevented by our fire, Private Scott handling a Lewis gun with great audacity and ability; there was also much movement on the high ground South of the wood, and our Lewis guns got so many opportunities that before long they ran short of ammunition. There was intermittent shelling, the German snipers on the high ground were very active, and, with barely 150 rifles available to hold a terribly long line, the position was none too secure.[1] In the evening, however, the Borders pushed forward a company to relieve C, which could thus be used to fill gaps elsewhere. Before dawn, however, the 86th Brigade took over and the survivors began withdrawing to Arras, whence the battalion moved back to St. Amand. Casualties had been heavy, 7 officers and 69 men killed and missing, 2 officers and 159 men wounded,[2] so the arrival on April 28th of a draft of 220 men was extremely welcome. Even so the 2nd's "strength" on April 30th was only 20 officers and 602 other ranks.

The Twenty-Ninth Division's rest was not to be long. Attention had still to be diverted from the French, so yet another British attack was ordered, and the Division was detailed to be in readiness to exploit success. The 87th Brigade therefore moved up as far as Observation Ridge, two miles East of Arras, but so little success attended the attack that the Twenty-Ninth Division was never put in, and returned to Duisans for another week's training. During this Captain B. J. Davies joined with Second Lieutenants Angell, Netherclift, Newman and W. Williams and 96 men, which with the previous draft brought the battalion up to a respectable strength again. On May 14th it was back in the Monchy defences, C Company in the front line in Snaffle Trench along with the K.O.S.B., the others being in support in Orchard and East Trenches. The trenches were in bad condition and needed unlimited work, being full of rubbish, lacking proper fire-steps, waterlogged in places, too shallow in others, none too sanitary and unprotected by wire. Much good work was put in, but this tour of duty was made memorable by the great gallantry of one of D Company on May 19th when D was assisting the Border Regiment and the Inniskillings in an attack.

D, who were on the left of the Borders, had as objective the

---

[1] Captain A. J. Blake, the battalion's M.O., did splendid service here: after working hard at his "first aid" post for hours he was out all through the night searching for the wounded who were often lying in shell holes and were extremely hard to find. Always indefatigable, he never did better work.

[2] Captain Hill, Second Lieutenants H. Y. C. Clarke, J. E. Harries, D. J. Hopkins, W. B. Nightingale, R. Phillips and B. L. Shaw were killed or missing, and Lieutenant M. Thomas and Second Lieutenant W. C. Beynon wounded.

portion of Devil's Trench just astride of Bit Lane.[1] To protect D's left a rifle grenade section was to halt near the Northern end of a disused and waterlogged trench, half-way across No Man's Land, and give covering fire, while directly Devil's Trench was reached bombers were to work Northward along it and so cover the erection of a strong point. A and B were to move up into Snaffle and Shrapnel Trenches when D went forward, A providing a carrying party to take wire, bombs and other supplies across to D.

Directly the British barrage started German machine guns opened from behind some wire on our left of Bit Lane, and despite the barrage they maintained a destructive fire. Men fell fast, especially as they neared the waterlogged Arrow Trench. Captain Davies led the advance with the utmost courage, running forward well ahead to give the right direction. He was well backed up by Second Lieutenant V. Jones, but they were both shot down. Sergeant White, seeing that all depended on putting these machine guns out of action, promptly made for the nearest one which seemed to be doing most of the damage. Followed by Corporal Nowel he dashed at the party covering it, shot three and bayoneted a fourth, and was within a few yards of the gun when he caught its full discharge and went down riddled with bullets. His self-sacrifice, subsequently recognized by a posthumous V.C., diverted the fire from the other attackers for a moment, but even so it was impossible for them to reach their objective. The attack came to a standstill, the survivors sheltering in shell holes until darkness let them crawl back. Four officers and 112 men had gone over the top; only 61 got back, nearly half of whom were wounded. Further to the right some Inniskillings had got into the German trenches only to be cut off by a tremendous barrage and all killed or taken. There was reason to think that the enemy were expecting an attack; certainly it was so received as to put success out of the question

The 2nd S.W.B., though relieved next day (May 20th), had not finished with Monchy yet. After a week in reserve they were in trenches again from May 29th to June 2nd,[2] a time mainly occupied with constructing a strong point and a bombing post to cover a 250-yard gap between their right and the next battalion. However, this was the last of Monchy. June 5th saw the 2nd taking train for Candas, where it was to spend the next three weeks. A systematic programme of training was

[1] Where it crosses Bit Lane Devil's Trench bends from N.W. to N., forming a sharp angle.
[2] On June 1st the battalion's strength was down to 20 officers and 502 men, the company commanders being Lieutenant the Hon. E. A. French (A); Captain W. H. M. Pierson (B); Captain F. G. Dickinson (C); and Lieutenant W. Ross (D).

THE HISTORY OF THE SOUTH WALES BORDERERS

followed and several drafts, amounting in all to 227 men, filled up the depleted ranks.[1] Several officers also joined,[2] and at the end of the month the 2nd entrained at Doullens for Flanders, strong, rested and generally in good trim.

If the 2nd had been the only battalion of the TWENTY-FOURTH engaged in actual Arras offensive, the 12th had during this period been active enough in a quarter only just outside the area of the main operations. After nearly three weeks of road and railway work the 12th had come forward again just as the Arras offensive opened, its Division being now under the Fifteenth Corps which was confronting the outworks of the Hindenburg Line near Gonnelieu and Villers-Plouich. Partly to improve its tactical situation by gaining ground, partly to keep the enemy occupied, the Fifteenth Corps was making an attack on a fairly substantial scale on April 21st, in which the 12th S.W.B. were to have their first experience of anything that could be called a battle. In this attack the Eighth Division was tackling Gonnelieu, and on its left the Fortieth continued the line N.W., using the 119th Brigade on the right and the 120th on the left. The 12th S.W.B., being the left battalion of the 119th Brigade, had as its objective part of the nullah known as Fifteen Ravine, which the Germans had converted into a quite formidable position, well protected by wire and with several cleverly placed strong points, both in front and on the flanks of the main position.

The 12th's attack was to be made by A Company (Captain Whitworth) on the right and B (Captain H. C. Lloyd) on the left, two platoons of C (Captain O. D. Morris) acting as moppers-up, the rest of that company and D (Captain T. O. Jones) forming the supports. Starting off at 4.20 a.m. (April 21st), the 12th advanced to their first attack with great steadiness: they encountered a heavy fire from guns, rifles and machine guns, but pushed ahead nevertheless. B Company had some difficulty in disposing of snipers whom the barrage had missed, in some skilfully chosen posts in front of the objective, and did not reach the ravine till after A had dashed into it, driving out the survivors of the garrison. A indeed overshot the mark and went too far, but Captain Whitworth, whose skill and gallantry were alike conspicuous, brought them back to their proper line and started consolidating. By this time B had dealt with the troublesome strong points, bombers and Lewis guns co-operating effectively,

---

[1] It had 34 officers and 831 other ranks on its strength at the end of June.
[2] Lieutenants G. M. Haydon, G. D. O. Lloyd, who became Adjutant, and W. F. Page, Second Lieutenants G. T. Baggallay, N. V. Evans, G. F. Gibson, G. C. B. James, C. Lewis and R. R. Rees.

and had also reached its objective. Even then three posts on the left continued to give trouble but these also were tackled and taken, several more prisoners being added to the couple of score already taken. Captain Whitworth, though wounded, refused to go back till the consolidation had been completed, which it was despite some German shelling. Casualties, considering the strength of the position, were not high, Captain Morris, Second Lieutenants D. R. Williams and Green and 12 men killed or died of wounds, 11 men missing, Captains

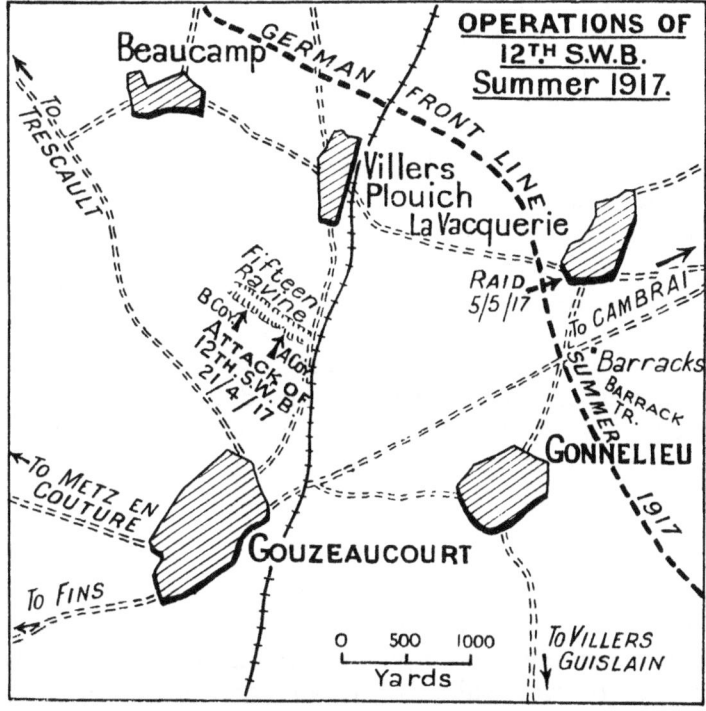

Whitworth and Jones, Second Lieutenant J. S. Lewis and 45 men wounded. As against this there were nearly 40 German dead in the position taken and many more were lying further out, having been shot down as they retired. The other attacking troops had also secured their objectives, so altogether the attack had been a distinct success and the 12th had good reason to be satisfied with their first " battle," which earned Captain Whitworth the M.C.

The 12th were to see a good deal of the Gouzeaucourt-Gonnelieu quarter; indeed they were to spend the whole summer in one or other of the neighbouring sectors. They were in brigade reserve on April 24th when Villers-Plouich was taken, but were not put in. The beginning of May found them in front line opposite La Vacquerie. Here the enemy were fairly quiet, although the British guns were systematically cutting wire and our patrols were extremely enterprising, obtaining much useful information and some identifications. On May 5th a raid of some magnitude was undertaken against La Vacquerie by the battalion in co-operation with the 17th Welch on its left, the Eighth Division simultaneously making a similar raid some way further South. The plan was that the attack should start at 11 p.m. and should hold the village till 1 a.m., in order to give ample time for the demolition of its defences. Once again the 12th were able to congratulate themselves on the successful attainment of their objectives. The right company ran into uncut wire short of the village and was much delayed, though it eventually got through, but the left company rushed the village up to time, capturing several prisoners. The attached R.E. parties then started their work of demolition under cover of the screen formed by the attacking companies and eventually the withdrawal was satisfactorily accomplished "according to plan," the supporting companies taking up a line to cover the movement. Second Lieutenant F. E. Morgan distinguished himself greatly in this raid: he took command on the fall of his company commander, Lieutenant Osborn, and led the men well, besides doing fine work later on in getting in wounded.[1] Casualties had been fairly severe, Lieutenant Osborn and a dozen men being killed and three men missing, while the wounded included Second Lieutenant Pollock.

Apart from this raid, May was a fairly quiet month for the 12th. Major Benzie, who had joined from the Scottish Rifles in April as second in command, now became C.O. as Colonel Pope, who had gone to hospital as the result of an accident, was unable to return, while Lieutenant Francis joined and took command of C in place of Captain Morris. By this time with the "stabilization" of the Arras front the neighbouring sectors also were tending to become "quiet," and though the 12th were far from inactive during the summer months they spent them outside the main area of active operations.

The 1st Battalion meanwhile had found its way to Flanders. It had remained at Chuignolles till April 7th, when it was turned on for ten days to work on the main Amiens road between Brie and Villers-Carbonnel. With a big offensive in progress it was strange employment for troops with the First Division's fine

[1] Second Lieutenant Morgan received the M.C. while the M.M. was awarded to Lance Corporals Freeman, Mason, and Quinn, and to Privates Jacques, Prince, Thorpe, Witherall and Wood.

fighting record, but road repairs were of paramount importance just then and the organization and strength of the Labour Corps only as yet partially developed. The weather was atrocious all the time, and the battalion was not sorry to hand over its road-making equipment to the Forty-Second Division and to move Southward to Mesnil near Nesle. However, it was not yet free of road-making. Large " fatigues " for this purpose were still required and took up more time than the training which was its other occupation. The surrounding villages were still inhabited and good billets were obtainable, while the weather showed some improvement. The end of April brought a move to Roisel, seven miles East of Peronne, and for a week the battalion was encamped in pleasant surroundings at Villers-Faucon, still working on the roads with some railway reconstruction thrown in. To escape the German airmen the work was done at night, though Lewis guns mounted as an anti-aircraft battery dealt quite successfully with these unwelcome visitors.

On May 7th the battalion shifted back to Peronne and encamped in a ruined suburb on the river bank. Water had been none too plentiful of late and a good bathe was very welcome. Next day brought a move to Eclusier, near Bray, " the worst camp we have seen, little more than a manure dump," the battalion diary calls it, and for the next few days the 1st had the task, very repulsive in hot weather, of burying and burning rubbish, though the excellent bathing was some compensation. Next, on May 19th, the battalion moved to much pleasanter quarters at Warfusée-Abancourt, 12 miles East of Amiens, where there were few fatigues to interfere with the programme of training that had been arranged. On May 26th the 1st entrained at Guillencourt and after a night journey through Abbeville, detrained at Caestre and marched to billets near Fletre, moving four days later to the Dickebusch neighbourhood.

By this time the French situation had improved enough for Sir Douglas Haig to break off at last the offensive on the Arras front, and with the delivery on June 7th of the long-prepared attack on the Messines Ridge the centre of activity shifted to Flanders. This was such a complete success that the Divisions in reserve were not required, so the 1st S.W.B., though in close proximity to the battle-area, having returned on June 5th to Fletre, were denied the chance of earning distinction for the Regiment. On the 11th they moved to scattered billets in farms round Staple (5 miles N.W. of Hazebrouck). A draft of 83 men, mostly transfers from the A.S.C., joined on June 14th and the battalion was gratified to hear on June 7th that

Major G. C. Thomas had been awarded the D.S.O. and Sergeant Melham the D.C.M. Then on June 21st it started off for the Dunkirk neighbourhood, as the Division had been posted to the Fifteenth Corps, which had just relieved the French in the sector of the Allied line next the coast.

But if the 1st S.W.B. missed the Battle of Messines the TWENTY-FOURTH was very well represented in it. The 5th Battalion had had a shift into the actual Ypres Salient during May. Its Division was now astride the Ypres–Comines railway and canal from in front of Armagh Wood on the left to just South of Verbranden Molen. The 5th's main employment in this area was upon the roads and trenches opposite "Hill Sixty," which was in German hands, while C Company had to look after the tramway from Zillebeke. For billets the battalion used some not yet destroyed barracks in Ypres. These had their disadvantages, for on May 6th the Germans concentrated their fire on them, with disastrous results. The three-foot thick walls of the Infantry Barracks offered enough resistance to enable the men to be evacuated in time to avoid serious losses, but B Company in the less solid Cavalry Barracks suffered heavily,[1] as a salvo of heavy shell burst right inside the barrack rooms. The 5th were hardly sorry to return on May 10th to their old hunting grounds opposite Wytschaete where June 7th found them. Between that time and the assault they had little rest; dug-outs had to be constructed for brigade and battalion headquarters, overland tracks put down for infantry, bridges laid by which guns might cross over the trenches, and up to the last minute the 5th was kept busy. The entry in the battalion diary for May 18th may be quoted as typical of its activities. "A Company, sandbagging and draining Stuart Trench. B Company, sandbagging parados Vierstraat Switch. C Company, 150 yards ballasted and camouflage erected Poppy Lane; old trench tramway taken up and new 16 pound rails laid instead of old; three breaks in trench tramway repaired, 190 yards of track laid and banked up. D Company, strengthening trenches and erecting head cover Poppy Lane."

Apart from the losses on May 6th casualties were not heavy, 5 killed and 16, including Captain Croft and Second Lieutenant Gwynne, wounded, while at the end of May a big draft brought the battalion nearly up to establishment again. Eight new subalterns joined during April and May and one or two others had rejoined. The battalion's fighting strength on June 7th was 27 officers and 856 other ranks in addition to details

[1] Second Lieutenant Raymond and 19 men were killed, Second Lieutenant Heppel and 20 men wounded.

amounting to 7 officers and 84 men, including those on leave, on courses and in various employments.

The 6th, like the 5th, were busy up to the last moment over the preparations for the assault. Through April, May and June they were hard at work, save for a ten days' rest early in May. Drafts amounting to 230 men joined and casualties up to June 7th were low, a bare dozen in May. Their main work was on communication trenches, tramways and roads, and included a bridge over the Douve for tanks. Regimental Sergeant Casey left in May to become Quartermaster of the 12th Royal Fusiliers, and was succeeded by Company Sergeant Major Shermer, and in the June "Honours" List Captain J. C. Owen was awarded a well-merited M.C.

In the assault the Nineteenth Division, the second from the left of those engaged, was attacking from N.W. of Wytschaete through the Grand Bois. It had five successive objectives to capture, known as the Red, Blue, Green, Black and Mauve Lines, the last running along the Eastern edges of Oosttaverne Wood, about 2500 yards from the existing British front. Beyond this yet a sixth line East of Oosttaverne village was to be tackled by a brigade of the Eleventh Division. The Red Line, running N.E. through the Grand Bois, was to be consolidated as a reserve line, the Black Line from Estaminet Cross-roads to In der Sterkle Cabaret as the main line of resistance, and the Mauve Line as an outpost line. Of the 5th, D Company was attached to the 56th and 58th Brigades, who were to take the first three objectives, and A to the 57th to which was allotted the capture of the Black and Mauve Lines. Their special duties were to assist in consolidating the positions captured, B and C meanwhile being told off to the less exciting but essential work of making it possible for the guns to follow hard on the heels of the assaulting infantry. The Twenty-Fifth Division further to the right was separated from the Nineteenth by the Sixteenth and Thirty-Sixth. It was to advance across the Steenbeck through L'Enfer Wood and past the Northern end of Messines. Of the 6th S.W.B. A and C Companies under Major Ellis and Captain Owen were to clear the Messines road for guns and wheeled traffic, B (Captain Cox) and D (Captain Reid-Kellett) had to lay a trench tramway to Messines.

"Zero" on June 7th was at 3.10 a.m. Before the smoke and dust from the explosion of mines had begun to clear the assaulting infantry were well into No Man's Land. Opposite the Nineteenth Division enough Germans survived to give the assailants some real fighting as they swept up and over the crest of the ridge. This gave both Company Sergeant Major Hooper of A

Company and Sergeant Rees of D a chance of distinguishing themselves. The former took charge of his platoon when its commander was wounded, directed consolidation in the open under heavy fire and persistent sniping, showing complete disregard of danger and much power of command. Sergeant Rees led a party against a strong point which was holding out and captured it by skilful tactics, taking or killing its garrison of 20 men

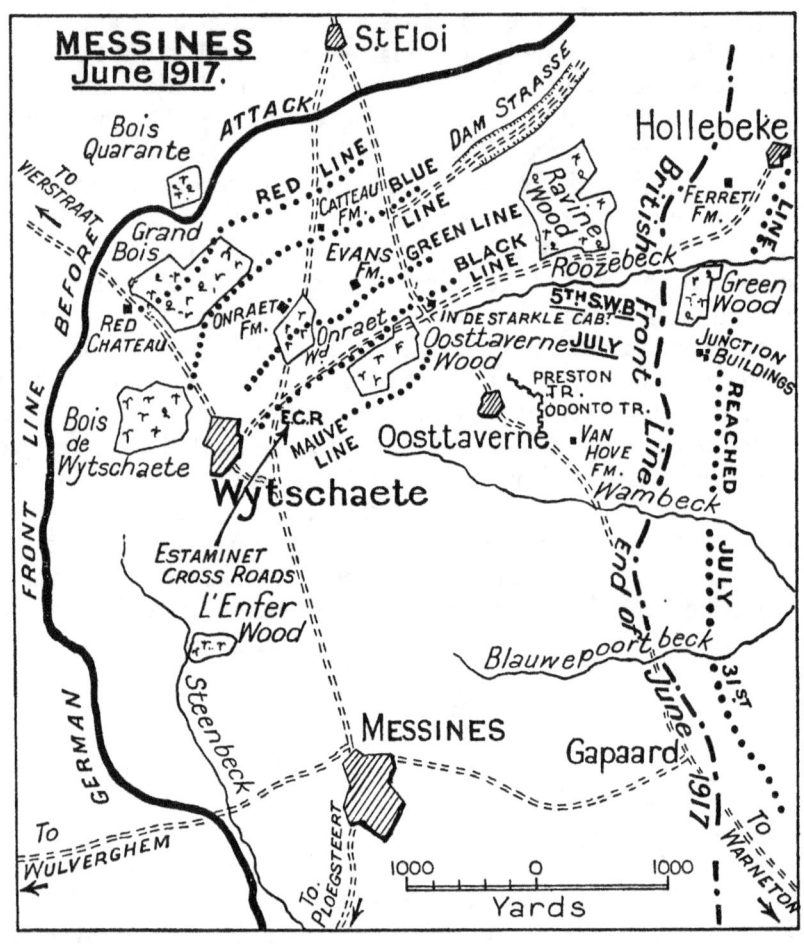

and securing a machine gun. The German resistance did not, however, avail to prevent the Nineteenth reaching the Mauve Line well up to time. Directly the Red Line was taken D began constructing "strong points," two in the Grand Bois, one N.W. of Catteau Farm, but after getting these properly started the Pioneers handed them over to the infantry to complete and pushed on to the Green Line, which was to serve as a support line. Here also it had three strong points to construct, near

Estaminet Cross-roads, in Onraet Wood, and at Evans Farm. A Company, who had followed the 57th Brigade to the Black Line, worked on that till the infantry advanced again and secured the Oosttaverne Line.[1] Parties then went forward and started work on two strong points East of Oosttaverne. Captain Simons showed great gallantry and skill in this attack: his clever leading saved his company many casualties and his resourcefulness and initiative were most marked.[2] B and C meanwhile were busily employed in helping the guns forward, bridging trenches, clearing away obstructions, filling in shell holes and craters and laying down fascines. Two tracks were made, one on the left through the Bois Quarante to Evans Farm, the other through the Grand Bois towards Estaminet Cross-roads. Good progress was made with both, Second Lieutenant Pink[3] doing splendid service in pushing on the work. The complete success of the attack had evidently staggered and upset the Germans, who not only failed to develop any counter-attacks, but at first hardly even shelled the captured positions.[4]

The Twenty-Fifth Division meanwhile had been equally successful and within an hour of " Zero " the 6th had their tasks well in hand. So vigorously and efficiently did they labour that by evening B and D had constructed 400 yards of trench tramway, Captain Cox showing great gallantry and resourcefulness in pushing on the work despite much hostile fire and many difficulties.[5] A and C meanwhile had their road open to within 300 yards of Messines, despite almost continuous shelling.

" Messines " was notable because for once practically all the objectives were secured on the first day. It was fought with a definite object—to secure the Second Army's right flank as a preliminary to the main attack at Ypres, and that limited object once obtained nothing was to be gained by trying to exploit it further. This did not mean, however, that the battle frontage became quiescent immediately. For several days the Germans tried to impede the consolidation by all means in their power short of a really big counter-attack. This meant strenuous times for the Pioneers in very uncomfortable conditions, for the weather had broken soon after the battle, while the German shell fire and machine guns made the work

---

[1] The Nineteenth Division, having lost but little, had ample troops in hand for this, so the Eleventh's help was not needed.

[2] He received a bar to the M.C.

[3] He received the M.C., while Sergeant Apsden and Private Butcher, who had done fine work, were awarded the M.M. Company Sergeant Major Hooper and Sergeant Rees got D.C.M.'s.

[4] The 5th had less than 40 casualties in all, including Second Lieutenant Lush wounded and 5 men killed.

[5] He received the M.C.

dangerous: the 5th, for example, had Second Lieutenant D. C. Roberts and several men wounded on June 8th, when A Company was wiring Odonto Trench East of Oosttaverne under constant fire from snipers and machine guns. Despite these difficulties, the work progressed well, B and C pushing on their tracks and tramways at a remarkable rate, an average of 200 yards being ballasted and sleepered a day, though innumerable shell holes and craters had to be filled in.

The 5th were the first of the two battalions to be relieved, Battalion Headquarters with A and D going out—somewhat to their surprise—with their Division on June 21st, though B and C remained behind to work on their tramways; the others, however, got twelve days' well-earned rest before returning to the Oosttaverne sector on July 3rd. The Nineteenth Division's line now extended some way to the North of Oosttaverne, nearly to Hollebeke. It was quite a lively quarter, the British making several attempts to advance their line to get a better "jumping off" place for the next attack, for which preparations were now in progress, the Pioneers being kept fully occupied.[1] In this the Division was to be on the extreme right, charged with advancing its line on a longish front but only to quite a short distance.

The 6th had to remain in the line till June 27th before they were relieved. On the 15th their Division shared in a fresh advance which carried the line about 800 yards forward on the front from the Warnave river to Klein Zillebeke, thereby considerably improving the tactical position. This brought the 6th more work and added another 20 casualties to the 50 it had already incurred, while the subsequent consolidation of the new line increased the month's total to nearly 100.[2] Relief, however, took the 6th no further back than Ouderdom, where they remained until July 20th, being mainly employed in improving the roads between Kruisstraat and Zillebeke.[3] This was much more costly than any previous spell of duty out in the actual front line. The Germans had changed their tactics and, instead of shelling the front trenches, devoted themselves rather to increasing fire on back areas, shelling camps and road junctions and searching for the British guns—the artillery had never before suffered casualties like those of the summer of 1917.

---

[1] During July, but exclusive of the attack of July 31st, the 5th had about 20 casualties, including Second Lieutenants Dunham and T. O. Jones wounded.

[2] The figures were: killed, 19 men; wounded, Major Renwick, who had recently rejoined, Captain Reid-Kellett, Lieutenant Petts, Second Lieutenants Hanna, Hill, Jacobs, Kite, Pierce, A. D. Roberts and 64 men.

[3] The Twenty-Fifth Division, now in the Second Corps, was holding the left sector of its line, North of Hooge.

German aeroplanes were also active, night bombing had become unpleasantly common, and the 6th, with 15 men killed and Captain Mumford and Lieutenant J. H. Davies and 72 men wounded, lost nearly as much in the first three weeks of July as in capturing and consolidating the Messines Ridge.[1]

To the Thirty-Eighth Division the middle of 1917 had proved a time of rest and preparation rather than of actual achievement. The repeated postponements of the Flanders offensive were mainly responsible for this: the effort to oust the Germans from the Belgian coast-lands and deprive them of the submarine bases which were just then so serious a menace to the Allied cause should have been started much earlier. Unfortunately, the changes and delays occasioned by the Nivelle fiasco were to prejudice the chances of the Flanders offensive by postponing it until an abnormally wet late summer and autumn. Still the 10th and 11th S.W.B. were far from idle during these months. After being in rest at Bollezeele for the first three weeks of May their brigade had spent nearly all June in the Boesinghe sector. The main work was digging a new front trench about 300 yards forward and within 200 of the enemy's line. This was accomplished without much interruption, as the Germans apparently took its construction as a feint to divert attention from the Messines direction, and casualties were fortunately low. For May and June together the 10th got off with 3 men killed and Captain Orford[2] and 15 men wounded, despite a destructive bombardment on June 3rd. The 11th, with 3 killed and 29 wounded, could also be considered fortunate. Both battalions received substantial drafts, 112 men joining the 10th during June and 136 turning up for the 11th. These reinforcements were more welcome because both battalions were much below establishment: on June 1st the 11th only had 632 " other ranks " on its strength, but by July 1st it had risen to 25 officers and 744 men. Captain Orford of the 10th received the M.C. in the June "Honours List" and Captains Havard (C.F.), Charlton and J. A. Jones were mentioned in Dispatches, while Lance Corporal Allen and Private Hancock were awarded the M.M., and Regimental Sergeant Major Lockie the Italian Bronze Medal for Valour. Lieutenant Norton

---

[1] About this time Major Ellis was invalided home and Captain Caldwell was transferred to the 5th Battalion, while Captain Mumford, who rejoined from sick leave on July 5th, was wounded within 10 days. The battalion being thus rather short of seniors, Major G. S. Crawford was posted to it from the 5th Battalion, joining on July 22nd. Regimental Quartermaster Sergeant Segers also left to become Quartermaster of the 11th Cheshires and was replaced by the promotion of Company Quartermaster Sergeant Kearns.

[2] Captain Kenward, who had joined in March, now became Adjutant.

having rejoined the R.W.F., Lieutenant A. Cox joined the 11th for duty as Quartermaster.

Towards the end of June the Division was taken right back to the St. Hilaire area for special training. A replica of the sector to be attacked had been laid out and brigades were systematically practised in their precise tasks. Opportunities for field-firing were now available and the 10th's keenness over this received special commendation from the Divisional commander, Major General Blackader. July 16th saw the two battalions starting their return march to the front, four days later the Division was again in line, finding many working parties to complete the preparations for the assault. The German artillery was very active now, shelling back areas more assiduously even than the front line, and the 10th fared rather badly. On July 23rd one working party alone had 7 men wounded and 16 gassed.

The Division which the Thirty-Eighth had just relieved was the Twenty-Ninth, though neither 10th nor 11th S.W.B. had the luck to relieve their 2nd Battalion. The Twenty-Ninth, on arriving in Flanders at the end of June, had taken over the Zwaanhof sector. The Division was here three weeks, during which large carrying parties were needed almost every night, while the recently dug new front line still needed much work. Raids were fairly frequent, though the 2nd S.W.B. did not happen to be detailed to carry one out nor was any German raid directed against it. The German guns were active, but the 2nd was luckier than most units in the Division inasmuch as it escaped with few casualties, though a patrol encounter on July 5th cost it Second Lieutenant J. H. Davies killed, and one man missing. Several drafts arrived, including a good proportion of experienced men who had been out before, while Major Garnett rejoined from a course at Aldershot and resumed duty as second in command: Captain Robertson also rejoined and took over the Adjutant's duties from Lieutenant G. D. O. Lloyd, and the battalion was much gratified to hear that Sergeant White's gallantry and self-sacrifice on May 19th had won him a posthumous V.C. The award of ten M.M.'s and five Long Service and Good Conduct Medals was also announced about this time. On July 20th the Division went back to a reserve area to train, being now in reserve to the Fourteenth Corps.[1]

Thus when the time for the attack drew near six of the Regiment's seven battalions on the Western Front were in or near to the active area. Of these only the 5th, 10th and 11th

---

[1] This also included the Thirty-Eighth Division and the Guards.

Battalions were to be in action on the opening day, as the Twenty-Fifth and Twenty-Ninth Divisions both happened to be in Corps Reserve. The First Division meanwhile had been detailed for a task of peculiar interest and importance. If the main attack made sufficient progress it was hoped to develop offensive operations along the coast also, partly from the Lombartzyde bridgehead, which the First and Thirty-Second Divisions were holding beyond the Yser, and partly by a landing further East. It was probably with a view of forestalling some such operation that the Germans had on July 10th developed a tremendous bombardment of our bridge-head defences, which they followed up by an assault in force. This, though repulsed on the right, succeeded in capturing the almost completely demolished defences then held by the 2nd Brigade, who had recently relieved the 1st S.W.B. The destruction of all communications across the Yser made it impossible to reinforce or to withdraw the garrison of the bombarded area, which was virtually annihilated. The 1st S.W.B. being in reserve came in for a share of the shelling but escaped with trifling casualties. A week later the whole Division was transferred to a camp at Le Clipon some miles West of Dunkirk. Here it was to spend the next three months, carrying out special training for the disembarkation on the Belgian coast for which it had been selected. Most elaborate precautions were taken to preserve secrecy. Le Clipon camp was carefully wired and all communications with it closely restricted on the plea that, as a dangerous epidemic had broken out in the Division, a rigid quarantine must be enforced. Actually the troops in the " hush hush camp," like Napoleon's Grand Army at Boulogne over a century earlier, were assiduously practising embarking and disembarking for an operation that was never to come off. Special pontoons had been prepared : the Cape Helles and Suvla landings had been carefully studied and plans drawn up in the light of their lessons, but the opportunity for launching the First Division upon the enterprise never arrived. It would have been remarkable had it fallen to both the Regular battalions of the TWENTY-FOURTH to share in an opposed landing on a hostile shore :[1] still, with Germans to hold shore defences constructed with German thoroughness and efficiency, the 1st Battalion would have been confronted with a task even more difficult and formidable than the 2nd had faced at Morto Bay.

[1] The Munsters were also represented both in the First and in the Twenty-Ninth Divisions, so that the honour would not have been confined to the TWENTY-FOURTH only.

CHAPTER XXI

MESOPOTAMIA : 1917

BETWEEN the fall of Kut and the resumption of active operations in December, 1916, one important tactical change had taken place on the Tigris front. Just before the 4th S.W.B. moved to Sheik Saad in May the Turks had retired some distance upstream on the right bank, thereby allowing the British to occupy the Sinn banks. They still retained the Sannaiyat position, and even with the British able to bombard it from the rear showed no signs of shifting. They had merely constructed entrenchments along the left bank to cover their communications and prevent a landing above Sannaiyat. General Maude, however, had no intention of attacking by the left bank: he meant to work round to the South, crossing the Hai and eventually establishing himself on the Tigris above Kut, where he would be favourably placed to strike at the Turkish communications. This scheme promised to be a more economical method of breaking down the Sannaiyat defences than direct attack. Being now adequately supplied with transport both by land and by water he was no longer as restricted in his movements as his predecessors had been. His force was not only more mobile but better equipped with artillery; the troops had been rested, reorganized and reinforced, and the resumption of active operations found them in excellent health and spirits.

The campaign opened with an advance on December 14th by the cavalry[1] and the Third Corps from the forward British position South of Magasis. The cavalry were to cross the Hai and make for the Shumran Bend, four miles upstream from Kut, where the Turks had a bridge, while the infantry secured a position on the Hai, prior to dealing with the Turkish positions in the Khudhaira Bend, N.E. of Kut, and in the so-called "Hai Salient" just S.W. of Kut. The main share in this was assigned to the Thirteenth Division, which had concentrated overnight at Imam al Mansur, a conspicuous tomb two and a half miles S.W. of the Dujaila Redoubt. The 40th Brigade was detailed as advanced-guard, so that the S.W.B. found themselves taking a leading part in starting the campaign.

The battalion had not stayed long at Sheikh Saad, arriving there on December 6th and moving on next day to Twin Canals, eleven miles away. It had been joined at Sheikh Saad by Lieutenant Griffiths with 125 men, mainly so-called "Bantams," men under the standard height but otherwise fit. These poor fellows were sorely tried next day when the battalion, fairly heavily laden although it had dumped its heavy baggage at Twin Canals,

---

[1] "Force D" now included a Cavalry Division.

had to plough its way to Sinn Abtar over a road which heavy rain was converting under their feet into a bog, sometimes a foot deep in mud. It took eight hours to cover eleven miles, and the camping ground, when reached, proved to be flooded and needed draining before tents could be pitched. Next day a warm sun soon dried things up, and even the " Bantams " forgot their troubles. From the Sinn banks, in places thirty feet high, a distant view of Kut could be obtained and forty miles to the North could be seen the Persian mountains, glistening with snow. Then at 11.45 p.m. on the 13th the battalion moved off to Imam al Mansur, whence after an hour's rest the move to the Hai started.

The 4th were heading the main body of the advanced-guard and had orders to force the crossing at all costs should the van and flank-guards, found by the R.W.F. and Wiltshire, be held up. Actually the Hai was reached at Atab, eight miles from the starting-point, without any opposition, just before dawn. Contrary to expectation it proved fordable, and the 4th and Wiltshire pushed across and took up a semicircular position forming a bridge-head with the battalion's left resting on the Hai just above Atab. Connection was soon established with the Fourteenth Indian Division, who were picqueting a line from the Dujaila Redoubt to the Hai to protect the rear against Arab raids. The 39th Brigade meanwhile advanced along the Eastern bank, parallel with the cavalry on the far side, and drove the Turkish advanced posts back to Umm es Saad, a ford two miles from the Hai Salient. Covered by this the 38th Brigade and another from the Fourteenth Division began entrenching a line from the Wiltshire's right back to the Dujaila depression S.W. of Magasis.

There had been scarcely any fighting but General Maude's operations could hardly have started better. The 4th's only excitement had been some brushes with mounted Arabs who hovered about in their front, taking cover in the very broken ground. Patrols went out to reconnoitre these nullahs and this gave Captain Philpotts a narrow escape. Going out just before dusk to look for one of his patrols he suddenly found himself within twenty yards of some twenty Arabs, who promptly dashed at him, firing. Luckily for him a timely shot from one of his men 400 yards away bowled over the leading Arab, whereupon the others turned and bolted, and Captain Philpotts rode in untouched. Next day (December 15th) the Arabs proved much more enterprising, but when they ventured within reasonable range of the battalion they were promptly dealt with by its picquets, who used their Lewis guns effectively. One party nearly 500 strong tried to charge home, but could not face the rifle fire and wheeled off, having had many saddles emptied. These Arabs seemed to have their headquarters at an old fort some 2000 yards downstream, so Lieutenant Griffiths took out a strong patrol from C Company with two Lewis guns and had got within 800 yards of the fort when by arrangement our guns opened fire, bursting their first salvo right in the fort. This brought a crowd of Arabs streaming out in confusion, affording splendid targets to C and the guns, and thereafter the Arabs gave the 4th no further trouble. That evening (December 16th) the 36th Brigade relieved the S.W.B., who rejoined their brigade at Umm es Saad. The Third Corps had now advanced much closer to the Hai Salient and was establishing itself opposite the portion West of the river. To assist in this work the 40th Brigade crossed the Hai at midnight and proceeded to entrench a line of posts running roughly parallel to the Hai and over a mile West of it. To take up this line correctly in the dark guided only by compass bearings and in a featureless country was not easy, and the accuracy with which the battalion accomplished it spoke well for its recent careful training. After three days on this line the 40th Brigade assembled three miles West of Umm es Saad for a stroke which General Maude had projected against the Turkish communications. The 40th Brigade, accompanied by the 7th Cavalry Brigade, two batteries and some R.E., including the Bridging Train, was to march to the " Brick Kilns " fifteen miles away, where the Husaini Canal joins the Tigris, effect a crossing and establish a bridge-head in the Husaini Bend.

Starting about 5 a.m. (December 20th) the column at first made good going but, as it changed direction from West to N.N.W. and approached the river, a series of water-cuts caused delays to the transport. After covering twelve miles the canal was reached and the column profited by the covered approach to the river which its dry bed provided. The march had been quite unopposed, but as the troops neared the river heavy rifle and machine gun fire opened, to which the Brigade Machine Gun Company under Captain Marr replied effectively.

The Tigris was 250 yards wide, the canal bed and a dam at its river end afforded the only cover near its banks, and from the top of the dam there was a sheer drop of six feet to the water. However, it was decided to attempt a crossing by using the pontoons as ferry boats; and Lieutenant Light with 13 volunteers from B Company and some men from the Bridging Train started to launch a pontoon. To carry it down to the bank in full view of the enemy and under fire was not easy, but launched it was nevertheless. Some Indians should have served as rowers but could not face the fire, and Lieutenant Light and his men started to row across. Just as they got off, the column commander, deeming the attempt hopeless, recalled the party, who had some difficulty and several casualties in getting back.[1] The R.W.F. then tried to cross further upstream, but with the Turks on the alert and well entrenched it was useless to persevere, so at dusk the column started back for the Hai. It was a tiring march, the men were short of water and had to bivouac at night in the desert as the exhausted mules could go no further. Not until 5 p.m. on the 21st did the S.W.B. get back to Umm es Saad ford.[2]

The next week, spent in bivouac at Umm es Saad, was a

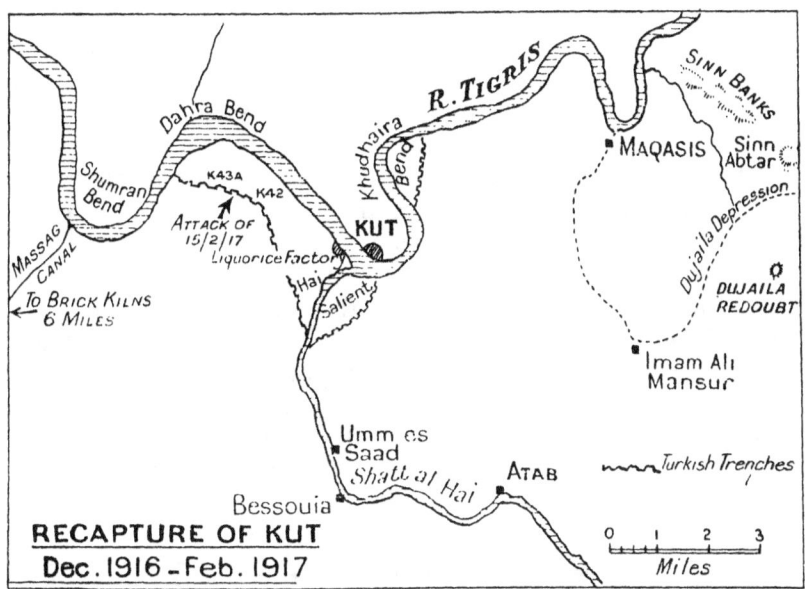

RECAPTURE OF KUT
Dec. 1916 – Feb. 1917

wretched time. It rained heavily, the men had no shelter and only one blanket apiece, and as all wheeled transport was withdrawn to help the Supply department, only the barest rations were available. On December 29th the 4th moved to a standing camp at Bessouia Ford where conditions were better. Here ten days were spent in training and road-making, the liquorice bushes, which grow in profusion along the Hai, making quite a fair road-bed when thickly strewn and covered with soil well rammed down.

Meanwhile the British were consolidating and improving their new position astride the Hai, and pushing their advanced

---

[1] Lieutenant Light was awarded the M.C. and Lance Corporal Mirey and Private Loxton the M.M. for their gallantry on this occasion.

[2] The battalion had had Lieutenant Gould and 2 men killed and 8 men wounded.

trenches steadily nearer the Turkish lines in the Khudhaira Bend and East of the Hai. Our artillery pounded away systematically, evidently producing considerable effect, and on January 8th General Maude started to oust the Turks from the Khudaira Bend. This operation, completed ten days later, involved stubborn fighting for the Lahore Division, but the S.W.B. were not directly engaged, as the Thirteenth Division was merely pushing forward its trenches, besides distracting the enemy by bombardments and demonstrations The 38th Brigade held the front East of the Hai, nearly three miles in length, the 39th the mile-long front West of it, the 40th being in reserve at first and then taking over the left of the 38th's line. On the evening of January 11th, the 4th S.W.B. were sent up to dig a new trench 250 yards further forward. It was bright moonlight and the working parties were clearly visible to the Turks, who maintained a steady fire, but, to the Divisional Commander's great satisfaction, this did not prevent the 4th from having the trenches fit for occupation by morning, though the night cost the battalion a dozen casualties, including Second Lieutenant R. Evans killed and Second Lieutenant Lewis wounded. For the next week the work went on, the trenches being steadily pushed forward despite all the Turks' efforts to interfere. If these failed to stop the work they inflicted many casualties, and the 4th was particularly unlucky. On January 14th it lost Major Fairweather, now second in command, a very popular and efficient officer of long service with the battalion; on the 17th Colonel Kitchin, exposing himself as usual with complete disregard for danger, was severely wounded; a week later Captain Blaxland, who as next senior to Major Fairweather was now in command, was also killed, the command being taken over by Major Gransmore from the 8th Welch, who was relieved early in February by Major Crocker from the 8th Cheshire. By this time the line was within 150 yards of the Turkish trenches, but the battalion had had to pay dearly for this progress.

January 25th saw the definite attack on the Hai Salient begun, when the R.W.F. and Wiltshire successfully assaulted the front trenches facing the 40th Brigade. The S.W.B. were in support and A Company went up to assist in consolidating. For the next few days the 40th Brigade continued to extend its gains, beating off some small counter-attacks, and by the end of the month had cleared both the first and second lines East of the Hai, the battalion escaping with only one officer (Second Lieutenant R. Smith) killed and a dozen men wounded. West of the Hai more strenuous opposition had been offered, the counter-attacks were more vigorous and progress slower and more costly. On February 1st the Cheshire carried nearly all the remaining positions East of the Hai, and that night the 40th Brigade was relieved. It was not to rest, however; next evening it was sent across the Hai to cover the extension of the picquet line North-Westward to the Tigris, thus enclosing the Turks in the Dahra Bend. In moving out to its assigned line the brigade encountered considerable opposition; the battalion advanced to within close range of the Turks but to dig in as ordered proved quite impossible, it had therefore had to retire level with the rest, the retreat being skilfully conducted with but few casualties, while the operations had diverted Turkish attention Westward and certainly contributed to a distinct advance against the Western portion of the Hai Salient. On this the Turks evacuated their last foothold East of the Hai, retreating to a line running West across the Dahra Bend from the Liquorice Factory just opposite Kut. To bring the British front line within assaulting distance of this position took nearly ten days—or rather nights—of strenuous digging, in which the S.W.B. took their full share.

The attack on the Dahra Bend began on February 9th; by February 13th the Turks after severe fighting had been pressed back to its Northern extremity, and that evening the 40th Brigade, till then in Divisional reserve, relieved the 38th opposite the centre of the hostile position.[1] The S.W.B., who took over the left of the brigade's frontage, found themselves in shallow trenches, indifferently sited and exposed to enfilade fire, so suffered severely on the 14th when waiting for the order to assault, Second Lieutenants F. H. Best[2] and F. F. Evans and 6 men being killed, while Captain Buchanan,[3] Second Lieutenant W. L. Jones and 16 men were wounded. It was a real relief therefore when at 8.45 a.m. next day (February 15th) the time came for the assault.

The Turks had been induced to expect an attack further to their left and the 40th Brigade's attack on their centre caught them by surprise. Advancing in four waves, after fifteen minutes' intensive bombardment, the battalion and the R.W.F. on its right rapidly mastered the front line, capturing many prisoners and promptly extending their gains on both flanks. The Turks made several counter-attacks but without success, and by midday the assaulting battalions—now reinforced by the Cheshire—had secured a foothold in the second line. Profiting by the 40th Brigade's success the 35th then attacked from the S.E., catching the Turks on the left flank. This attack was

---

[1] The brigade's line ran approximately opposite the point marked K42 to K43 A.

[2] This officer had only joined on February 7th, together with Second Lieutenant S. W. Best and 140 men, mostly from the Brecknocks.

[3] He was shot through both eyes and, though he ultimately recovered, lost his sight.

equally successful, hundreds of Turks surrendered, and the 35th Brigade, pushing on, joined up with the 40th. This virtually ended organized resistance in the Dahra Bend; a few Turks still held out in the extreme N.W. corner but were mopped up during the night, and daylight (February 16th) found the right bank of the Tigris from the Shumran Bend downwards clear of Turks. They had fought obstinately, the assailants had required to exert both skill and determination to oust them from their position, and the 4th had good reason to be proud of their share. The last attack had cost them Second Lieutenant G. L. Davies, Regimental Sergeant Major Solomon and 31 other ranks killed, and Captain and Adjutant Bickford-Smith, Lieutenant S. H. Griffiths, Second Lieutenants Usher, Herbert, Hind and Barker and 72 men wounded.

The next task before General Maude and his troops was the passage of the Tigris, which was achieved at Shumran by the Norfolk and two battalions of Gurkhas on February 23rd, the Meerut Division co-operating by attacking and having the satisfaction this time of taking the Sannaiyat position, which had so long defied them. The 4th S.W.B. meanwhile had been forming part of an outpost line along the Shumran Bend and had been busy strengthening the bunds to keep back the river, now in full flood.[1] On the evening of February 24th it crossed the Tigris by the newly established pontoon bridge, bivouacking that night on the Shumran Peninsula. The Turks were now in full retreat, even their rear-guard had at last withdrawn, and next morning the Thirteenth Division and the cavalry started the pursuit towards Baghdad. The Thirteenth Division was stoutly opposed by the Turkish rear-guard, but dislodged it without employing the 40th Brigade, and the pursuit reached Azizieh without further serious fighting. Here a halt proved necessary to allow of the reorganization of the transport and supply services, but on March 5th the advance was resumed, the Third Corps taking the left bank of the Tigris and the First the right. The chief fighting took place on the River Diala, where the Turks put up a stiff resistance to the 38th Brigade (March 7th–9th), but once again the S.W.B. had no fighting. On March 10th the passage of the Diala was at last effected, and before evening the 40th Brigade had followed the 38th across, and by moving against the left flank of the line from Qarara to Tel Muhammad contributed to make the Turks decamp hurriedly during the night. Next morning (March 11th), the Thirteenth Division's patrols found the enemy gone, whereupon a prompt

[1] Major Crocker having rejoined his own battalion, Captain Woosnam was in command of the 4th till March 1st when Major Crake (K.O.S.B.) joined and took command.

advance was made on Baghdad, and C and D Companies of the 4th S.W.B. had the distinction of being the first British infantry to march through the main city.[1]

Baghdad did not impress the 4th very favourably: few of its buildings were of any size or attractiveness and the city was no less squalid than other Eastern towns. The inhabitants, however, welcomed the British warmly, they had little love for the departing Turk and were only too anxious for protection from marauding Arabs and Kurds. But the 4th were to see little of the beauties of Baghdad; that evening their Division concentrated three miles upstream, whence it advanced to Yahudiya twenty miles further North. Arriving there on March 15th it set to work to entrench an outpost line between the Tigris and the Diala to protect Baghdad against a possible counter-attack. But, while the consolidation of his position at Baghdad was General Maude's immediate object, he was also anxious to clinch his success by smashing up any Turkish forces within his reach, and the next six weeks were spent in a series of efforts to bring them to action, which involved the 4th S.W.B. in much strenuous marching and counter-marching and not a little hard fighting.

Of these forces the most important was their XIIIth Army Corps, now retiring from the Persian mountains, where it had been in contact with General Baratoff's Russians, part of the Army of the Caucasus. Part of the Lahore Division was sent forward by Shahraban towards the Jebel Hamrin range to intercept this Corps, and on March 24th the 40th Brigade group[2] was ordered forward to co-operate with this column and protect its left rear. Reaching Diltawa next day the 40th Brigade was soon in touch with the Turks, for their XVIIIth Corps which had retired upstream from Baghdad was now advancing down the left bank of the Tigris to assist the XIIIth. This offered General Maude an opportunity of another blow at the XVIIIth Corps, and the Thirteenth Division pushed forward with that object, the 40th Brigade acting as advanced-guard. On March 27th it reached a line from Abu Tamar to the Tigris, and on the 29th the Division moved forward to attack the Turkish position.

The right of this rested on the Tigris near Mara, its left, which was slightly "refused," extending Northwards into an open plain. The main attack was aimed at the left centre and was delivered by the 40th Brigade, the Wiltshire leading with the S.W.B. supporting them, while the 39th moving wide on the right tried to outflank the Turkish left. The 40th Brigade had

---

[1] The 5th Buffs had previously occupied the suburb on the right bank but were delayed by having to be ferried across the Tigris.
[2] The 40th Brigade and attached artillery and R.E.

to cross quite bare ground in face of considerable shelling and rifle fire, and the 4th had soon to come up on the Wiltshire's left to drive the enemy from some rifle-pits which formed their advanced line. From here the advance had pushed to within a few hundred yards of the main position, when, about 10 a.m., as the mirage made it hard to locate the enemy or to give the infantry adequate artillery support, the 40th Brigade was instructed to suspend the attack till the 39th's advance made

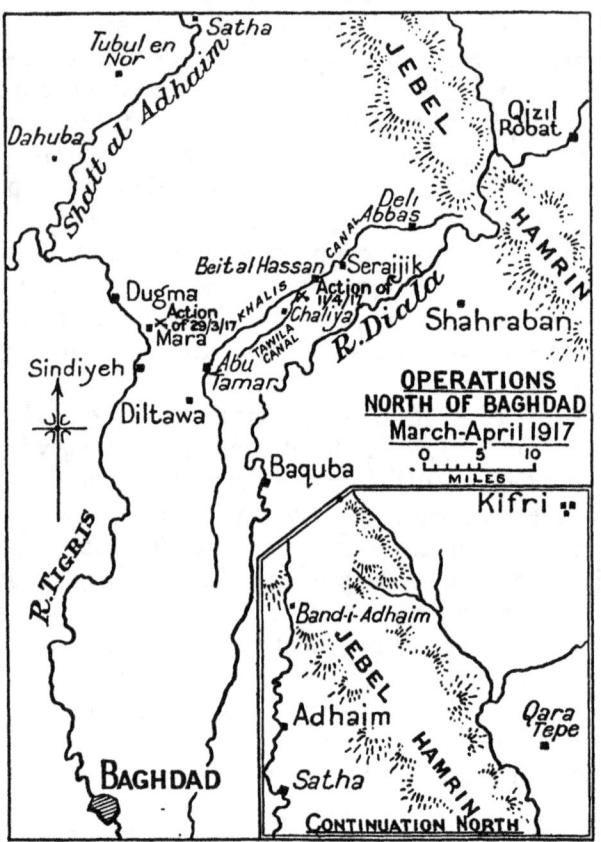

itself felt. The 4th had therefore to hang on under a heavy fire. Eventually the 39th Brigade delivered their attack with some success, but up to nightfall the 40th's efforts to advance met with steady resistance. Then, however, the Turks evacuated their position, managing to slip away, though they left behind nearly 200 prisoners and as many dead. The 4th came off quite lightly, having only 6 men killed and 36 with 3 officers, Second Lieutenants S. W. Best, D. L. Jones and H. J. Griffiths, wounded; but the great heat and the lack of water had made the day very trying. However, while the XVIIIth Corps' advance had been successfully stemmed and heavily punished, their XIIIth Corps succeeded in evading interception, partly because the Russians failed to pursue vigorously, largely because transport difficulties prevented the British from operating in force at any distance from Baghdad.

These operations over, the Thirteenth Division withdrew to Diltawa but was soon on the move again. The progress of the Russian revolution had now put an end to any prospect of effective assistance from the Russians, but General Maude was anxious to deal the Turks another blow, to which end two columns were organized to operate simultaneously on both banks of the Tigris, the Thirteenth Division forming the main part of that on the left. On April 6th, therefore, the 4th started Northward towards the Shatt el Adhaim, behind which river the Turkish XVIIIth Corps was now standing. However, before the British attack across the Adhaim could be developed, the Turkish XIIIth Corps from Deli Abbas, profiting by the Russians' inactivity, counter-attacked down the Khalis Canal, which runs parallel to the Diala, driving back the cavalry who were covering the Thirteenth's right flank. The bulk of the Division had therefore to move East to meet this thrust, and after dark on April 10th the 39th and 40th Brigades left Dugma for Chaliya, fifteen miles away.

The night march took them across broken and unreconnoitred ground which caused many delays, but by 5 a.m. the column was within five miles of Chaliya and halted for breakfast. Meanwhile the Turks had developed their attack between the Khalis and Tawila canals and were pressing the Cavalry Division back, thus bringing themselves within reach of a counter-stroke by the Thirteenth Division. This was promptly delivered and began with a race for a low ridge West of Chaliya, which the 40th Brigade succeeded in reaching just before the Turks. The S.W.B., following in second line behind the R.W.F. and Cheshire, reinforced the leading line and helped to drive back the Turks, who were heavily punished in retiring, both by the infantry and by the LXVIth Brigade R.F.A., which pushed its guns right forward into the firing line, coming into action at quite close range. The retreating Turks, however, were not pursued. The weather was extremely hot, water was scarce, and the British infantry, still clothed in thick serge, suffered considerably, indeed heatstroke accounted for almost as many as wounds. The Turks accordingly could face about and re-form, while the Thirteenth Division had to wait for a detachment of the Fourteenth to come up and relieve the cavalry, who were then to pass round the Thirteenth's rear and make a wide turning movement on its left. This took time and could not be completed before dusk, and during the night the Turks seized the chance to slip back several miles to Bint el Hassan on the Khalis Canal.

Next day (April 12th) the infantry moved forward, but the necessity for thorough reconnoitring delayed their start and the heat proved most oppressive, so that by dark the advanced troops were hardly beyond the junction of the Tawila and Khalis canals. The 40th Brigade, which was on the left with the battalion and the Wiltshire in front line, had come under some shell fire, but had very few casualties. Under cover of darkness the two leading battalions pushed forward another 1000 yards and dug in, so that morning found them entrenched within long range of the Turks. Here they had to hold on all day (April 13th), under heavy shell fire and suffering greatly from the heat and lack of water, while the 35th Brigade came up level on the right and the Cavalry Division worked forward on the left, trying to outflank the thrown back Turkish right. They had also to retain their position through another hot and oppressive day (April 14th) while the guns were bombarding the Turkish line, but the Turks once more retired under cover of darkness, and though cavalry patrols followed almost to Deli Abbas there was no overtaking them before they reached the Jebel Hamrin.

The 4th S.W.B. were glad to be spared the pursuit; they moved into bivouac near Seraijik for a little welcome rest, for while the fighting had not been severe and casualties had been few the operations had been most exhausting. However, General Maude was not yet satisfied and wished to secure the remaining portion of the Baghdad railway.[1] But before he could advance up the right bank the Turks must be forced back from the Shatt al Adhaim; accordingly General Cayley's portion of the Thirteenth Division, which had been fighting the XIIIth Corps between April 10th and 14th, entrenched a position astride the Khalis Canal to act as covering force to the column under General Marshall engaged in this operation. This brought the 4th S.W.B. several days of hard digging, during which time the passage of the Adhaim was forced near its mouth (April 18th), while the right bank column routed the XVIIIth Corps at Istabulat (April 21st and 22nd), its remnants retiring hastily upstream to Tikrit. Meanwhile the XIIIth Corps had begun moving West from Deli Abbas towards the Adhaim, part of General Marshall's column was pushing up the Adhaim to intercept it and the 4th S.W.B. were ordered to the Tigris to hold the Adhaim bridge-head. This involved some strenuous exertions. Starting on the 22nd the battalion had already done a thirteen-mile march to Abu Tamar when, about nightfall, it received an

[1] This ended at Samarra on the right bank of the Tigris nearly 70 miles N.N.W. of Baghdad.

urgent summons to push forward to the Kewar reach of the Tigris, twenty-one miles away. This meant a forced march, only completed at 6 a.m. on the 23rd, the men being much exhausted and not even then at an end of their exertions, having to reach the bridge-head that evening.

Further exertions awaited them, however. Next morning (24th) came orders for two companies to escort some artillery reinforcements for General Marshall up the Eastern bank of the Adhaim. These came up with his column just after the 38th Brigade had taken the Turkish advanced position near Dakuba but were not actually in action that day, nor on the 25th when, the Turks having retired up the Adhaim, General Marshall advanced to Tubul en Nor. The remaining companies, having been relieved in the Adhaim defences, followed the others North, and the rest of the 40th Brigade was also on its way to reinforce General Marshall.

April 28th saw General Marshall reach the ruins of Satha on the Adhaim, where the second half of the S.W.B. overtook him after marching thirty-one miles in great heat. All ranks, however, were anxious to be up in time and had responded splendidly to the calls upon them. Next day (27th) the 40th Brigade arrived, and on the 28th, after the Turkish position had been carefully reconnoitred, the troops moved forward to a bivouac four miles from Satha. Dust-storms, however, impeded aeroplane observation and artillery preparation and thereby postponed the attack till April 30th. The Turkish position extended for some distance astride the Adhaim, which here ran in a wide depression bounded by steep cliffs. On the left they were holding two lines from about four hundred yards in front of Adhaim village to some mounds a mile to the East, with another line

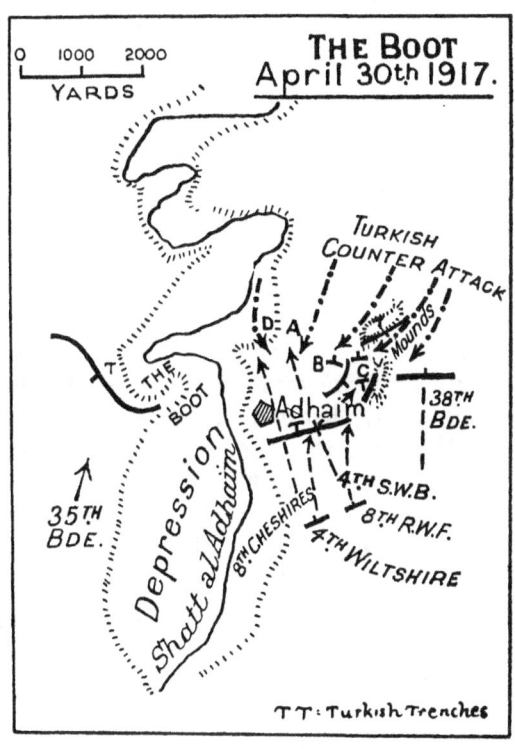

thrown back on their left behind the mounds. West of the river their line ran roughly N.W. from "the Boot"—a curiously shaped piece of high ground which projected into the river valley just opposite Adhaim. The main attack was being made by the 38th and 40th Brigades East of the river. On the other bank the 35th was to capture the Boot, if this could be done without very heavy loss, and to cover the main attack against a possible counter-stroke across the river. Ample artillery support was available, and though the infantry units were weak—the S.W.B. had only 340 rifles present and other battalions were no stronger—they were in good condition and full of confidence.

The 40th Brigade had its left flank resting on the edge of the valley. The Cheshire formed the left of the front line with the S.W.B. on the right, the Wiltshire and R.W.F. supporting. Punctually at 5 a.m. the leading battalions advanced behind an excellent creeping barrage, thanks to which and to the cover given by the smoke and dust they reached and carried the front line with little loss. The second line was quickly mastered, and then with the Turks bolting before them the Cheshire pressed forward in pursuit, though Brigade orders had directed them to halt at the enemy's second line. Within 45 minutes of the attack beginning they had swept into and through Adhaim village, taking many prisoners, and only stopped at the edge of the depression, where they captured six guns. The leading companies of the 4th, A and D, under Captain Staples, seeing the Cheshire forging ahead, pushed on also. The Brigade orders had not apparently reached Captain Staples, and certainly no recognizable second line had been encountered.[1]

Soon after 6 a.m., therefore, A and D found themselves nearly a mile beyond their original objective. In their victorious advance they had captured many prisoners, inflicted considerable casualties on the enemy, and taken a mountain gun. But in overshooting their mark they had quite lost touch with their supports, which, finding no trace of A and D in the captured position, had swung to the right and advanced half a mile N.E., capturing a camel gun, before they halted just about N.W. of the mounds, C Company (Captain Philpott) being on the right and B (Captain Usher) echeloned on its left rear. They got good targets in the Turks retreating Northwards, and before long runners from Captain Staples brought back news of his position. He had moved N.E. and had A Company lining a ridge about 1200 yards North of B's position, with D on his left overlooking the depression and in touch with the Cheshire. Unluckily telephone wire had run short and it was difficult to

---

[1] There was apparently a gap in the Turkish second line.

report the exact position promptly to Brigade Headquarters and to the artillery, who were further hampered in getting information by the dust-storms. There was therefore an inevitable delay in bringing up the other battalions to make good the ground gained, and though the 38th Brigade had captured the mounds it had been held up by the line in rear and by the threat of a counter-attack on its outer flank.

The advanced troops therefore were precariously situated. A battery South of Ahmadliyia was shelling them from the North, machine guns from the Boot enfiladed them from the left, and, to crown all, about 7 a.m. a tremendous dust-storm obscured everything completely. When it cleared away B and C found Turks advancing in great strength from the N.E. and already within 100 yards. Blazing away for all they were worth they kept the attackers at bay till ammunition failed and there was nothing for it but to fall back. This they did at a walk, the Turks following at a distance which suggested reluctance to come to close quarters. Captain Usher showed conspicuous skill and gallantry in conducting this retirement, and it was largely due to his coolness and resource that it was successfully effected, while Private Colley handled a Lewis gun with great effect, keeping it in action though all the rest of its team had been hit. Sergeant Smith was also conspicuous for his able handling of his platoon during this withdrawal, and Company Sergeant Major Moss rallied a detached party, and showed marked ability and coolness in controlling his men.[1]

By this time the Wiltshire and R.W.F. had occupied the original objective, on reaching which B and C halted and, with their pouches refilled, assisted to check the Turks. Company Sergeant Major D. T. Jones did good service by bringing up ammunition at this critical juncture under heavy fire; he and his party were attacked but beat off their assailants and prevented their precious ammunition from falling into the enemy's hands.[2] Splendid work was also done at this stage by the Brigade Machine Gun Company, still commanded by Captain Marr, and about ten o'clock the Turks began to fall back, being heavily punished by the British guns as they did so.

Of A and D however little was known. Some few of D and about half the Cheshire had regained the position held by the supporting battalions, having been thrust back by a counter-attack delivered from the Adhaim depression, but practically all A Company were missing. Not till long afterwards was

[1] Captain Usher received the M.C. and Company Sergeant Major Moss, Sergeant Smith and Private Colley the D.C.M., which was also given to Private Roberts for gallant and resourceful work as a stretcher-bearer.
[2] He received the D.C.M.

their exact fate ascertained. The Turks, taking advantage of the dust-storm, had penetrated into the gap between the companies and practically surrounded A, whose attention had meanwhile been engaged by Turks advancing against its front. Captain Staples now tried to get away along the river-bed but was intercepted by more Turks. His men had fired away their last round in keeping the frontal attack at bay, and realizing that an attempt to force a way through with the bayonet would only end in a massacre, Captain Staples ordered them to lay down their arms. This did not prevent the Turks from promptly bayoneting many of the badly wounded, and their treatment of the prisoners was discreditable in the extreme. They were deprived of most of their clothing and forced to take in exchange the filthy rags worn by their captors, and then had to march, most of them barefoot, nearly 200 miles to their destined place of captivity. Several tried to escape, only to be recaptured or murdered by Kurds, many others perished on the march. About 100 were taken : only a handful survived to be released after the Armistice.

Though the retreating Turks had not been pursued they had had quite enough, their casualties had been extremely heavy and nearly 400 prisoners remained in British hands, and that night they made off towards the Jebel Hamrin pursued by British aeroplanes. General Maude had by now accomplished his main object, both Turkish Corps had been rendered incapable of resuming the offensive, and with the hot weather beginning active operations would be impossible, and the sooner the troops got into summer quarters the better. On May 4th therefore, once more under Colonel Kitchin, who had just rejoined, the battalion[1] moved back to Adhaim bridge-head, but had only been there a week when a column was sent up the Adhaim as a demonstration to assist a Russian advance on Kifri. But the Russian move fizzled out completely, and the demonstration was abandoned, to the relief of the troops, who had no shelter from the scorching sun and were finding the little water in the Adhaim brackish and virtually undrinkable. On May 15th the column started back for the Sindiyeh line, now the advanced position to be held by the Division, and on the 17th found itself established beside the Tigris at Saliyeh, where its summer camp was fixed. After their strenuous exertions during the last five months the 4th welcomed the prospect of rest cordially.

· · · · · ·

[1] The casualties on April 30th came to over 200 : Second Lieutenants S. W. Best and Mitchell were killed with 50 men, Lieutenant Peel and 50 men were wounded, Captains Staples and Jenkins, Lieutenant Napier and 105 men were missing and the battalion was reduced to barely 140 rifles.

THE BRECKNOCKS IN INDIA

While the 4th Battalion had been having a very varied experience in Mesopotamia, both in regard to the country it saw and the occupations in which it was engaged, the 1st Brecknockshires at Mhow had had no such changes. The duties which fell to a British battalion at an Indian station in the plains proved to differ but little from the normal routine of peace: there were perhaps more guards and duties to be found, several drafts went off to active service—many of the Brecknocks went to the 4th in Mesopotamia and were well reported on by Colonel Kitchin as well trained and disciplined—men were constantly being wanted for various specialist employments or for commissions, parties had to be found to look after prisoners of war camps, and in the hot weather detachments were sent up to the hills. One company at a time was usually at Indore, and during the cold weather the battalion was usually in camp. To replace the drafts, the occasional invalidings, and the other drains on the battalion's strength substantial reinforcements were from time to time dispatched from the battalion's Reserve unit at home. The first draft of 5 officers and 260 " other ranks " appeared in May, 1916, and others arrived at intervals.

During this period the Brecknocks saw many changes among their officers, the most notable being that in July, 1916, Lord Glanuck vacated command and proceeded home. He had been a pillar of strength to the battalion, and had the satisfaction of leaving it in excellent order, as was evident from the report of the G.O.C., Mhow District, who had recently inspected it. Major D. W. E. Thomas succeeded him in command but was appointed in August, 1917, to be Commandant at Pachmari, and left the battalion after serving with it for 32 years. Major Hamilton of the Connaught Rangers then took command, which he retained till September, 1918, when he vacated and was replaced by Major Wigley of the Royal Sussex, while about the same time Captain M. F. Thomas handed over to Lieutenant H. B. Griffith the Adjutant's duties which he had discharged for nearly four years. Though repeatedly reported upon as in every way fit for active service the battalion was denied any further opportunity of showing its efficiency, and had to content itself with winning a large number of athletic contests and trials.

CHAPTER XXII

THIRD YPRES

I: *July and August*

THE many postponements of Sir Douglas Haig's Flanders offensive had inevitably prejudiced its chances appreciably. Starting as late as the last day of July, with the summer already far advanced, much depended on the autumn proving reasonably dry. As fine an August, September and October as those of 1914 and 1918 might have brought "Third Ypres" much nearer to achieving its objects, and would have spared the troops the awful struggles against those appalling expanses of mud and slime which make its memory such a nightmare. The character of the Ypres Salient, its loose soil, its drainage, never more than indifferent and now, owing to the constant trench digging and bombardments, almost incredibly worse, made dry weather indispensable to success. Actually the worst possible happened: with the start of the offensive the heavens opened their sluice-gates, and continued almost uninterruptedly to deluge the already waterlogged ground until the whole Salient became one vast morass in which occasional spurs of relatively dry ground afforded some approach to the possibility of progress. Urgent strategical and political reasons doubtless demanded the continuation of the offensive despite these virtually prohibitive tactical and administrative conditions, but the critical state of affairs on—and more especially behind—the French front could not be divulged at the time; regimental officers and men, therefore, found themselves repeatedly required to attempt the impossible with no idea why they must be thus sacrificed. The imperative need for not relaxing the pressure on the Germans might almost have been inferred from its mere maintenance despite these appalling difficulties, the terrible exertions it was exacting and the fearful losses it was entailing. To the troops from whom these exertions and these losses had to be required, "Third Ypres" must always be all the more honourable because they could not be told the why and the wherefore. Of those sufferings and exertions the TWENTY-FOURTH was to have its full share: few stages in the battle failed to see one of its battalions in action, and their labours and losses were alike heavy, for if the Pioneers lost less than those who went "over the top" in front of them they had to labour longer.

The frontage attacked on July 31st extended for some 15 miles, from North of Steenstraat to near Deulemont, but only on half, from Hollebeke to the Boesinghe sector, was more than a subsidiary advance intended. Thus of the three battalions of

PILCKEM

the TWENTY-FOURTH in action, the 5th were outside the area of the main thrust, but the 10th and 11th had as ambitious a programme as any unit engaged. Lord Cavan's Corps, with the Guards as its left Division and the Thirty-Eighth as its right, was attacking astride the Ypres–Staden railway, the Pilckem Ridge being its main objective, with the crossings of the Steenbeck as a further goal. On its left it had French troops; on its right the Fifty-First Division of the Eighteenth Corps. Four days before the attack it looked as if the Germans opposite the British left had evacuated their trenches, and investigation confirmed the impression. Opposite the Guards in the Boesinghe sector the enemy had actually retired over 3000 yards,[1] but in the Pilckem sector only the front line had been abandoned.

General Blackader's plan of attack was that the 113th (left) and 114th (right) Brigades should capture the first three objectives, the Blue, Black (just East of Pilckem) and Green Lines. This last ran along Iron Cross Ridge, from which the 115th Brigade, till then in reserve, was to push forward to the Steenbeek and secure its crossings. In the 115th Brigade the 11th S.W.B. (right) and 17th R.W.F. (left) were the attacking battalions, the 10th S.W.B. and 16th Welch being in Divisional reserve.

Both 10th and 11th had moved up to the Corps concentration area on July 29th and started for the assembly position soon after dark next day.[2] The 10th left one company at the Canal to help lay bridges, but the other companies reached their assembly position before midnight. The 11th, though later in getting into position, still had an hour to spare before " Zero."

This was at 3.50 a.m. (July 31st), and the leading brigades advancing with great dash, carried the Blue Line with little difficulty. Pressing on they met more opposition, especially from " pill-boxes," but captured the Black Line well up to time. The supporting battalions took up the running here, but the Green Line proved a tougher nut to crack. There was hard fighting round Iron Cross, while a farm on the right, which the Fifty-First Division had not yet reached, gave considerable trouble. On nearing Iron Cross Ridge, therefore, about 9 a.m., the 11th S.W.B., who had started their advance 100 minutes after " Zero " and had till then had an easy passage, suffering slightly from long-range shelling, found themselves under machine gun fire

[1] This meant an unopposed passage of the Canal.
[2] The 10th took into action 18 officers and 509 other ranks, Major Rees commanding: 10 officers and 60 men (half of them a new draft) were left at the transport lines, 3 officers and 65 men had been sent back to the Divisional Reinforcement Camp, 1 officer and 50 men were detailed to keep an infantry track in repair, and 35 men were on leave, making a total of 32 officers and 719 other ranks.

from some still untaken " pill-boxes." Two company commanders, Captain Jenkins of C and Lieutenant Sayce of D, were hit, but the 11th had soon completed the capture of Iron Cross Ridge and were sweeping down the slopes leading to the Steenbeek, beyond which stream ran their objective, the Green Dotted Line. They encountered considerable opposition, several machine guns were in action, many riflemen were about, and casualties were numerous. However, the 11th were not to be stopped, though they were behind the barrage now and therefore had to fight hard to gain ground. At one moment the left was held up by machine gun fire, but Second Lieutenant Vizer promptly led his platoon against the spot from which the fire was coming, rushed and captured the machine gun, taking an officer and over 50 men prisoners, and enabling the advance to get on. Thus before long the survivors of the attackers had reached the Steenbeek. The worst trouble came from machine guns in concrete shelters, in houses, or on the sites of what had once been houses. However, special attention had been paid during training to the tactical problem of these " pill-boxes " and the 11th were ready to tackle them. One of these machine guns opened fire at close range and was inflicting many casualties, so Sergeant I. Rees led his platoon forward by short rushes till he had worked round to the rear of its position. Then, having got within 20 yards, he rushed the gun, shot one of its team, bayoneted another, and silenced it. Then he bombed the adjacent " pill-box " so effectually that, after he had killed five of its occupants, the rest, 2 officers and 30 men, surrendered.[1] Others were dealt with in the same way, a good haul of prisoners being made. The Steenbeek was crossed without real difficulty and about 12.30 p.m. A and C Companies reached Au Bon Gite, a party of D crossing to their left with the 17th R.W.F. beyond them. All three detachments promptly set to work to establish bridge-heads, although considerably hampered by snipers and machine guns from the direction of Langemarck.

The 10th meanwhile had moved up to the old German front line, and though suffering some casualties from shell fire, including Second Lieutenant W. H. Evans wounded, arrived at Kiel Cottage at 6.50 a.m., the scheduled time. The men were then placed in such shelter as Caddy Lane afforded, to await further orders. They were to wait for some time, for, although Germans began to collect for a counter-attack within two hours of the passage of the Steenbeek, communication between the troops in front and their supports was proving hard to maintain: heavy shelling made the work of runners very dangerous besides

---

[1] He was subsequently awarded the V.C.

cutting the wires which the signallers had managed to lay. Accordingly, when about 3 p.m. the expected counter-attack developed, two large bodies of Germans advancing from nearer Langemarck, the 11th's "S.O.S." remained unanswered and the battalion had to rely on itself to repulse the attack. This, however, it accomplished, rifles and Lewis guns bowling over the enemy freely. The 17th R.W.F., however, were forced back across the Steenbeek and when, a little later, the Germans renewed their attack they managed to seize some concreted buildings on the 11th's now exposed left. From there, machine guns enfiladed the Au Bon Gite post and soon rendered it untenable. There was nothing for it but to withdraw to the Steenbeek, but the Germans' efforts to occupy the bridge-head were frustrated. Casualties had been fairly heavy, Colonel Radice had been wounded[1] and the firing line was very thin.

The arrival about 5 p.m. of D Company of the 10th under Lieutenant Cottam was therefore very welcome. This company had been sent forward to reinforce shortly after its battalion had reached Iron Cross Ridge, to which the 10th had just moved up, while the other companies started digging in 300 yards in front of the road running S.E. from Iron Cross, thus forming a support line behind that held by the 11th along the Steenbeek. Touch had by now been established with the artillery and a second counter-attack was greeted by an excellent barrage. The enemy had collected for this in shell holes in front of Langemarck but could make but little progress in face of the barrage and of the rifle and Lewis gun fire.[2] Lieutenant Cottam did splendid work in repulsing this counter-attack, taking command of men who had lost their officers, reorganizing them and directing their fire. Though badly wounded he refused to go back until he had established a well-consolidated line. Rain had set in during the afternoon, and was falling heavily so that mud soon made it difficult to keep rifles and Lewis guns in action. The 10th adopted the plan of sending back the Lewis guns from the line to Rudolphe Farm, where Battalion Headquarters were now established, to be cleaned, by which means the teams in the line were kept supplied with effective weapons.

That night the rain and the German shell fire both continued, the former being the more troublesome. Between them, however, they failed to prevent Second Lieutenant George, the Transport Officer of the 10th, from getting rations up to the front. Second Lieutenant George, when the pack animals were

---

[1] Captain B. E. S. Davies had taken over command.
[2] These counter-attacks were carried out by the 9th Grenadiers who suffered very heavily.

hit, helped to carry the rations himself and later worked for hours to get the wounded away and to rescue mules which had fallen into shell holes. But the situation was none too satisfactory. The 11th had lost heavily, its front line was but weakly held, Lieutenant B. H. Jones and Second Lieutenants Treloar and Vizer being the only officers left with the main body of the battalion opposite Au Bon Gite, while touch had been lost with A Company on the right.[1] The enemy were now established about 100 yards from the Steenbeek, having machine guns and snipers in shell holes. These hindered communications between the front line and its supports, but the Germans never tried to advance and during the early part of August 1st their shell fire was only intermittent. Indeed the Brigadier issued orders for the 11th to re-establish the Au Bon Gite bridge-head, but Captain Davies was killed by a sniper in going forward to see if an attack was really practicable, and Captain King, the Brigade Major, who had accompanied him, realized that the 11th was much too weak to advance, and therefore cancelled the orders. Shortly afterwards a terrific barrage opened, both along the Steenbeek and on Iron Cross Ridge, which seemed to herald a counterattack. Accordingly, as Lieutenant Cottam had reported that he had many casualties, Second Lieutenant Cobb took B Company of the 10th forward to reinforce, while Captain Galsworthy and A began consolidating a support position in the German wire and machine gun posts forward of the Ings. A little later, as the front line was running out of ammunition, some of C Company of the 10th took a fresh supply and some bombs forward. Captain Kenward, now Adjutant of the 10th, not only went forward under heavy fire to collect information, but himself brought up a party with ammunition to the front line and was also largely responsible for keeping the troops in front fed with hot food. The German shelling along the Steenbeek was so heavy that about 6 p.m. Lieutenant B. H. Jones, now the senior officer of the 11th in the front line, withdrew about 200 yards to where shell holes clear of the barrage provided shelter. About 9 p.m. the shelling slackened off and the original line was re-occupied, while later on Second Lieutenant Lancaster brought up a platoon of B Company of the 11th from reserve. Excellent work was done by Second Lieutenant Cobb in reorganizing the front line, posting the men skilfully in well-sited strong posts, covered by battle-outposts, and his dispositions proved very effective, while Second Lieutenant L. G. Williams managed to establish touch with the units on the flanks and was very

[1] It afterwards appeared that this company had had to fall back about 200 yards from the Steenbeek but had maintained itself there successfully, keeping the enemy at bay.

helpful in organizing the defences. He was hit but refused to go back until a satisfactory line had been established. Some good patrolling was done, and in consolidating the position the German wire, which was available in profusion, proved notably useful.

Early on August 2nd orders were received that the 113th Brigade should relieve the 115th, but owing to the 11th's scattered situation this took a long time. Battalion Headquarters, now under Captain W. T. Harris, and part of B Company started for Mauser Cottage about 5 a.m., but not till evening could most of the battalion be relieved, C Company indeed only rejoined headquarters early on August 4th. This was because the relieving battalions had been ordered to consolidate a line 250 yards back from the Steenbeek and did not apparently realize that there were troops to be relieved down by the stream.

The 10th's relief was accomplished simultaneously with the 11th's, the battalion taking post in support in Candle and Cancer Trenches (S.W. of Pilckem), where it remained till the evening of the 5th, when the Twentieth Division relieved the Thirty-Eighth. On this both 10th and 11th proceeded to Elverdinghe Château, where a hot meal awaited them, while baths, or at any rate clean socks, were available. Both battalions were very weary and terribly dirty: the rain had hardly ceased since the attack, everybody was wet through and covered with mud, so that a withdrawal to the Proven area for a real rest was warmly welcomed. The 10th, with 41 men killed and missing and 6 officers[1] and 159 men wounded, had not escaped very lightly: the 11th had naturally been harder hit. Four officers[2] and 116 men had been killed or were missing; 10 officers[3] and 220 men wounded, more than half those in action. Still the two battalions had reason to be proud of a memorable achievement.[4] If the Division's first big attack at Mametz Wood had fallen short of complete success, " Pilckem " had been a very different story.

[1] Captain Galsworthy, Lieutenant Cottam and Second Lieutenants L. G. Williams, W. H. Evans, H. O. Jones and Davenport.

[2] Captain B. E. S. Davies, Second Lieutenants L. R. Lloyd, G. C. Owen and Bullock.

[3] Colonel Radice, Captain Jenkins, Lieutenants B. H. Jones and Sayce; Second Lieutenants H. Roberts, T. G. Williams, Vizer, Ellis, Mathews and Humphries. Captain Jenkins subsequently died of his wounds after several operations. Company Sergeant Majors Dorchester and Darcy were also among those wounded.

[4] The following honours were awarded to the two battalions for this battle: 10th S.W.B., Captain Kenward, Lieutenant Cottam, Second Lieutenants L. G. Williams and George, M.C.'s; Sergeants H. J. Williams, Bull and Hulbert, Corporals J. James, D. J. Morgan, Pleese, Lance Corporal R. Baker, Drummer Hales and Privates J. Bevan, T. Watkins, Hiscock and Foote, M.M.'s. 11th S.W.B., Sergeant I. Rees, V.C.; Second Lieutenants Bryant and Vizer, M.C.'s; Privates O. Evans and P. Mahoney, M.M.'s.

The Division had gone straight through to its ultimate objective, had consolidated a good line only just short of the farthest point reached, had captured over 700 prisoners, besides inflicting heavy casualties on the enemy, and had incidentally had the satisfaction of smashing up a highly reputed German Division, the 3rd Guards, included in which was the famous Guards Fusilier Regiment nicknamed the "Cockchafers," from which alone 400 prisoners had been taken.[1]

As already explained, the Nineteenth Division had a much smaller part on July 31st than in the attack on Messines. It was attacking S.W. and S. of Hollebeke on a frontage of 2000 yards, but was only required to push its attack to a depth of about 500 yards. The 56th Brigade was detailed for the attack, A and C Companies of the 5th S.W.B. being attached to it. C's particular task was to establish communication with the new line, the company having to continue Preston Trench across No Man's Land, but when it started work it came under such a heavy shell fire that it could not continue. A Company meanwhile went forward to assist in consolidation, but though the 56th Brigade had taken its objectives it was having some difficulty in maintaining them against vigorous counter-attacks, which succeeded in pushing back the right, though a defensive flank was eventually formed. The 5th did good work in this and were extremely fortunate to escape with only 20 casualties, mostly in A Company, though these included Second Lieutenant L. V. Kent and 9 men killed, Captain Caldwell, who had joined on July 3rd, being slightly wounded. For the next ten days the Nineteenth Division continued in the line, the 5th doing all the awful weather would permit to render it defensible, and having several more casualties. The Thirty-Seventh Division then took over the frontage South of the Canal and the Nineteenth departed for the Lumbres training area, even the Pioneers for once getting away from the line and entraining on August 10th for Wizernes, whence they marched to Lotinghem. They were to have four weeks' respite from their labours, and certainly deserved their holiday.

The 6th was the next battalion to represent the TWENTY-FOURTH in the great offensive. On July 31st the Twenty-Fifth Division had been in reserve to General Jacob's Second Corps, then in line between the Menin Road and the Ypres–Roulers railway, and, had all gone well here, it should have passed through the Eighth Division to capture the Corps' final objective, North of Polygon Wood. Unluckily the next division on the right was

[1] It was afterwards learnt that the 3rd Guards Division had had to be withdrawn to reserve immediately after the battle.

checked, and this neutralized the Eighth's early successes, the advance being held up short of the Westhoek Ridge. The 6th S.W.B., therefore, though busy enough working under the Corps' C.R.E. at roads, mule-tracks and communication trenches, never went forward. However, the Eighth Division had lost heavily and needed relief, so the Twenty-Fifth took over its gains and found its hands full. The combination of bombardments and rain had reduced the trenches to a fearful state: in place the mud was thigh deep, and movement along them was virtually impossible. To add to the difficulties German aircraft were persistent in their attentions, attacking working parties with bombs and machine guns besides ranging guns upon them. More than once parties were driven from their tasks and casualties were numerous. But the 6th stuck grimly to their work: Major Reid-Kellett superintended his working parties with great skill and coolness, by dividing up the men when under heavy fire he was able to keep the casualties down and yet get on with the work, while Second Lieutenants D. Jenkins and J. H. Richards distinguished themselves by bringing up convoys of stores and ammunition through a gas bombardment and a barrage. Eventually, on August 10th the Twenty-Fifth Division completed the capture of Westhoek Ridge and held the position against repeated counter-attacks. On this occasion B Company did splendidly in assisting to consolidate, though its commander, Major G. S. Crawford, was mortally wounded. Private Frayne was conspicuous for his gallantry: though hit in one eye and blinded, besides being thrice buried when taking a message back, he persisted in duly delivering his message before getting his wounds attended to. Private Reecher, a stretcher-bearer, was equally conspicuous, staying with the wounded under a heavy fire until himself hit and killed.[1]

The 6th remained in line till August 13th, was then " out " at or near Ouderdom till the 22nd, when it returned to the old headquarters at Belgian Château for work under the C.R.E. Second Corps, although the Division remained " out " till early in September when it had another week on the Westhoek Ridge. Its main work was to construct a timber-road in full view of the enemy and under intermittent shelling: it was lucky that only another 30 casualties were added to those sustained earlier in the month.[2]

[1] Sergeant Sheppard, Corporal A. Williams and Privates Carter, Horrobin, Lipyeart, Price, Reecher and Sargent received the M.M., while Sergeant Quinton got a bar to the M.M., and Private Frayne the D.C.M.

[2] Its casualties for August came to 2 officers (Major Crawford, Second Lieutenant H. Kent) and 11 men killed, 1 officer (Lieutenant Hanna) and 94 men wounded. September contributed Second Lieutenant Kerley and 1 man killed. Major Reid-Kellett, who had been promoted Major in July and had become second in command and 6 men wounded.

THE HISTORY OF THE SOUTH WALES BORDERERS

The completion of the capture of Westhoek Ridge was among the chief operations undertaken between July 31st and the next big blow. This had been delayed by the persistent rains, which transformed the depressions between the ridges into stretches of bog, resisting not only any advance, but such ordinary routine movements as ration-parties and reliefs; the delay was the more regrettable because it allowed the defence time to recover from its disorganization, to readjust the line, bring up reinforcements, relieve demoralized troops, and generally to offer a more formidable resistance to the second attack on August 16th than would have been possible had it followed immediately after the first. Among the troops who carried out this second attack[1] was the Twenty-Ninth Division, which had relieved the Guards on the extreme British left on August 8th. Immediately in front flowed the Steenbeek, now swollen with rains and overflown and only passable on bridges. Before the attack the 86th Brigade had effected a passage, and cleared the enemy away from the near neighbourhood, thereby allowing bridges to be laid.

The 2nd S.W.B. had moved up into the front line on the evening of August 14th. There was some German shelling on the 15th, but a good dose of gas shell from the British guns discouraged the hostile batteries and the day passed uneventfully. After dusk covering parties of a platoon each from A and B Companies advanced across the Steenbeek and at 9.30 p.m. the battalion followed. The advance and the forming up lines had already been marked by tapes, and the battalion took up its position[2] on the extreme British left without incident. A and B Companies,[3] who formed the first wave, had as objective a line half-way between the hamlet of Wijendrift and Montmirail Farm, C and D in second line being allotted an objective just beyond Craonne Farm. The Border Regiment was then to pass through and take the third objective, just short of the Broombeek. To deal with Montmirail and Craonne Farms, where special trouble was anticipated, a Stokes gun detachment was to follow behind the first wave. Careful arrangements were made to secure liaison with the French, and nothing was omitted that forethought and careful preparation could devise to secure a success.

[1] It extended from the Menin Road to the junction with the French near Bixschoote.
[2] Battalion Headquarters were established at Sentier Farm where Colonel Raikes was to remain, Major Garnett commanding the actual attack.
[3] Each company took 4 officers only into action, the commanders being Lieutenant French (A), Captain Pierson (B), Lieutenant Haydon (C) and Captain Ross (D).

ACROSS THE STEENBEEK [AUG. 16TH, 1917

Shortly before "Zero" (4.45 a.m.) the Germans started shelling, their barrage falling along the Steenbeek. Casualties were avoided by closing the rear companies up to the first wave so that at "Zero" the whole battalion advanced together. The going was awful, in places men sank over their knees in the swamps, and in the centre some completely flooded ground forced A and B to diverge. However, the barrage, which was splendidly accurate, had been timed to suit the going and the leading companies reached the first objective close on the barrage. With the ground so muddy and so cut up the main

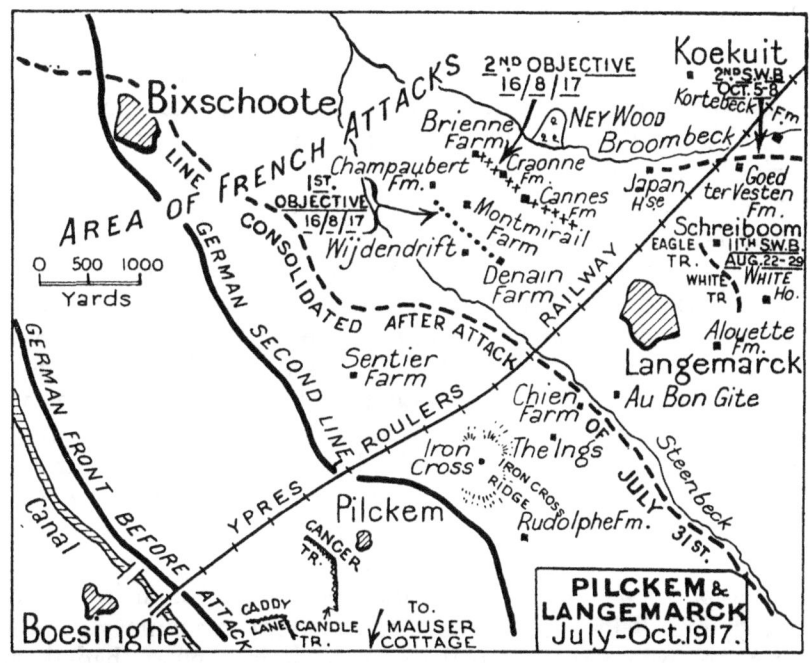

difficulty was to recognize the objective, both companies overshot the mark and were only stopped by the barrage halting. What opposition was offered was easily overcome, some Germans who emerged from dug-outs being promptly disposed of. Just ahead of B's objective was a "strong point" from which a sharp fire was being maintained, Captain Pierson and Lieutenant Gibbon accordingly collected a small party and started working round to its rear. In the marshy ground the two officers outdistanced their men but, nothing daunted, they pushed ahead and rushing the point from the rear captured it and its garrison, thereby disposing of an obstacle that might have seriously impeded the advance to the second objective. Lieutenant Mayger also, seeing that a blockhouse just ahead was still holding out, led a party forward and captured the blockhouse, which cleared the way for the supports to go through.[1] Touch had been maintained with the K.O.S.B., but on the left the marshy ground and machine guns in some concrete dug-outs near Champaubert Farm had caused the French to fall behind. C and D found these machine guns troublesome when they started their advance, and being also fired upon from two strong points at Montmirail Farm they were held up. However, the French brought their barrage down again on Champaubert Farm with satisfactory results, whereupon C and D advanced again, clearing the Montmirail Farm strong points, where 25 prisoners were taken with two machine guns, and eventually reaching their objective. Patrols which were promptly pushed ahead towards the Broombeek[2] could discover no enemy except a few riflemen in Ney Wood and a machine gun and some snipers opposite the French. There was nothing therefore to interfere seriously with consolidation. Strong points were dug on both objectives and a Lewis gun post advantageously established on a rise 150 yards from the Broombeek.

C and D had reached the second objective about 10 a.m. : the afternoon was well on before Germans began working forward in small parties towards the Broombeek. More could be seen moving in the woods and farms further back, and about 4 p.m. a real counter-attack was launched. Advancing in two lines the Germans presented good targets to rifles and machine guns, while the "S.O.S." brought down a most effective barrage. The counter-attack crumpled up completely, most of the enemy seemed to be knocked out and a scanty few regained the shelter of the woods behind, well content to leave the 2nd in undisputed possession of its gains. These included two 5.9-inch howitzers, one 77mm. field gun, a trench mortar, two machine guns and over 50 prisoners. Casualties, considering what had been achieved, had not been heavy, but unfortunately the seven officers killed or died of wounds (Captains Robertson, Ross and Haydon, Lieutenant French and Second Lieutenants N. V. Evans, D. C. Philipps and Reid) included the Adjutant and three company commanders, all experienced and much regretted officers.[3] Of men, 36 were killed and missing and 127 wounded.

[1] Captain Pierson and Second Lieutenant Gibbon received the M.C., and Lieutenant Mayger a bar.

[2] On the battalion's front the final objective, slanting back North-Westward, practically coincided with the second ; so the Border Regiment only went through the K.O.S.B.

[3] Lieutenant G. D. O. Lloyd now resumed the Adjutant's duties but left soon after to join the Indian Army, whereupon Captain Mumford, who had just rejoined, replaced him.

As the K.O.S.B. and the 88th Brigade had been equally successful, securing the final objective, August 16th had been a red-letter day for the Division, which had not only achieved a substantial initial success but had subsequently exploited it most skilfully.

The 2nd S.W.B., though relieved on the night of August 16th/17th, were soon back in the front line, holding the left of the British line, from August 22nd to 27th. During this time they established several posts across the Broombeek, getting into Ney Wood. On the 27th an attack on Langemarck provoked a retaliatory heavy bombardment followed by a German counter-attack which was repulsed, the 2nd escaping with but few casualties. That night the 2nd Scots Guards turned up to relieve the battalion, which went right back at once, entraining on the 28th for the Proven area.

For the last week the 2nd had had the 10th and 11th Battalions as near neighbours. The Thirty-Eighth Division after a fortnight's rest at Proven had relieved the Twentieth, which had meanwhile captured Langemarck, on August 16th. During this interval the 10th had one draft of 85 men and the 11th in all received 136 reinforcements with 3 officers, Major C. D. Philips, Captain G. D. Page and Second Lieutenant Jeffcoat, while on August 6th, Major Angus from the 16th Welch joined to take command in Colonel Radice's absence.[1]

The 115th Brigade was in reserve at first, being placed between Pilckem and the canal. Here there was ample work in improving the position and keeping the tracks to the front in repair, while parties were in constant request for work on intermediate lines and for carrying. The Germans were quite on the alert and their guns and aeroplanes did their utmost to interfere, the back areas being almost more vigorously harassed than the front line. Both 10th and 11th had their share of casualties. One of the 11th's working parties had 20 men hit at Chien Farm on August 19th, and the 10th had in all 4 men killed and 20 wounded before moving forward on the evening of the 22nd. Early on the 19th the pack-mules bringing up the 10th's rations were caught and destroyed, rations and all, but the Quartermaster was not to be beaten and by 10 a.m. a second supply had been safely delivered.

The 10th's new position was near Au Bon Gite, already familiar to the 11th. Here it was in support, the 11th, who came up next day, being in front, with Battalion Headquarters at Alouette Farm near Langemarck. Two companies, B and D,

---

[1] Major O'Kelly who had been second in command since April had been invalided early in July.

were in front line East of Langemarck, holding part of White Trench, with their left thrown back to connect with the 17th R.W.F., who continued the line past Langemarck towards the railway. As far as the rainfall would allow both sides were active enough, alike with artillery and in the air, and on the 26th the 10th had the satisfaction of seeing two German aeroplanes brought down. C Company was so unlucky as to have its headquarters hit on the 25th and to lose a valuable W.O. in Company Sergeant Major Clissold, who was killed, but Battalion Headquarters were more fortunate in that the German concrete of the pill-box in which it was located proved proof against their 4.2cm. shells. The tactical situation meanwhile was most uncertain. Eagle Trench, which continued White Trench to the N.W., was in German keeping, though on the night of August 24th/25th a patrol of the 11th under Second Lieutenant Pembridge found it badly damaged and unoccupied save for many dead, victims of a heavy bombardment earlier in the day. Two days later (August 27th) the 16th Welch attempted to secure possession of Eagle Trench and the cemetery behind it. The weather, after clearing up quite hopefully in the morning, broke before the attack started in the afternoon and the men could hardly get forward out of their waterlogged shell holes, let alone keep pace with the barrage. A platoon of the 11th S.W.B. went forward on the right to maintain touch with the Eleventh Division, which was also attacking, and this platoon managed to reach and capture White House. B and C Companies of the 10th had meanwhile been ordered up to be ready to support the Welch, but did not attack as the Welch had failed to reach their objectives; though, later on, when the Welch withdrew these companies took over their line. Meanwhile, as the 11th were being heavily shelled and suffering severely, the Brigadier told Colonel Harvey to be ready to reinforce. Communication by wire with them had long been cut, but two runners, Privates Park and J. C. Williams,[1] gallantly made their way through a tremendous barrage to the 11th's headquarters to find out if help were needed and brought back a request for two platoons. On this, Second Lieutenant Silby took A Company forward, and reached his destination with surprisingly little loss, though rain had made the ground a regular quagmire. The 11th, moreover, maintained their grip on White House, and did not relinquish what was about the only ground gained. On the 28th and 29th, although the enemy's infantry and machine guns were active, his artillery quieted down, and casualties were lower. On the evening of the 29th the 113th Brigade relieved the 115th and both S.W.B. battalions went back to reserve,

[1] They were awarded the M.M., which was given to Sergeant Patrick also.

the 10th at Elverdinghe, and the 11th at Leipzig Farm. Both were pretty well exhausted; conditions had been exceptionally trying, and the weather as bad as ever, while the 10th had had over 100 casualties. Major W. O. Jones had been killed on the 26th when B's headquarters caught a bad dose of gas shelling, Captains Hornsby and Fearby and Second Lieutenant Taylor had been wounded. In all, this period saw 28 men killed and 89 wounded, 50 more including Regimental Sergeant Major Lockie were evacuated sick, mostly suffering from shell-shock. The 10th came out with only 10 officers and 302 men and though on September 9th they were up on the Canal bank they escaped another turn in front line. The 11th, who had had 20 men killed and 40 with Second Lieutenant H. H. Morris wounded, went as far forward as Iron Cross Ridge in the first week of September,[1] but did not revisit the front line, and on September 11th the Twentieth Division again relieved the Thirty-Eighth, which now bade a final farewell to the Ypres Salient, being sent down to the Armentières district.

The abominable weather of the last half of August had done more than merely make conditions in the line unpleasant. The attack of August 16th, usually termed the "battle of Langemarck," had resulted in substantial gains on the British left, though South of St. Julien little had been achieved. But the success on the Northern half of the battlefield could not be exploited, for the deluges which promptly set in with renewed vigour prevented any major operation. Indeed a full month elapsed before another big attack was possible; for such an effort the ground must have dried to some extent, but with the naturally poor drainage system completely disorganized by the digging of trenches and the blocking of ditches and streams by the debris of battle this took abnormally long, even though the first half of September brought a distinct improvement in the weather. This five weeks' pause, a longer interval than had elapsed between any two major attacks on the Somme, was naturally all to the advantage of the defence.

[1] They had a few casualties here, among them Regimental Sergeant Major Davies wounded.

CHAPTER XXIII

THIRD YPRES

II : *The Later Phases*

WHEN by September 20th conditions in the Salient had at last improved enough for another big attack, only one battalion of the TWENTY-FOURTH happened to be in the battle-area. The 1st was in its seaside "internment camp," the 2nd was moving from near Proven to De Hippe, the 6th had recently left the Salient for Bethune, the 10th and 11th were settling down to what was to prove a long stay in the Lys valley, the 12th was still in the Gouzeaucourt country of which it had seen so much.

Thus only the 5th Battalion saw anything of the fierce fighting of September 20th and the days which followed, when the Germans, counter-attacking in force, strove ineffectually to recover the tactically important ground wrested from them by that day's attack. Even the 5th was only on the fringe of the fighting, for the Nineteenth Division had the strictly limited objectives of protecting the right flank of the main attack and preventing the formation of too abrupt a salient. Its right rested on the Ypres–Comines Canal just South of Lock 6, whence its line ran N.E. past Klein Zillebeke to Shrewsbury Forest. Its objective passed through Hessian Wood and East of Potsdam and Moat Farms to Belgian Wood, forming a frontage of 2000 yards. Its attack proved a great success, all the objectives were captured with 400 prisoners, and consolidation was promptly started, the 5th sending up large parties to assist in the work and dig communication trenches forward to the new line. In this quarter the Germans never ventured on a counter-attack, and though their shell fire inflicted several casualties, the 5th having a dozen, including Second Lieutenant Settle wounded, it did not stop the consolidation. Eight of the 5th's Lewis guns under Lieutenant Runham, which were posted in Battle Wood, Ravine Wood and near the Canal for anti-aircraft work, proved most useful : not merely did they drive off the persistent German aeroplanes, but they had the satisfaction of bringing a couple down, the successful marksmen, Privates Hitchings and Brown, being rewarded with the M.M.

The attack of September 20th was repeated six days later, but on a still narrower frontage which extended only slightly South of the Menin Road. The Nineteenth Division, therefore, though it had extended its line to the left on September 23rd, taking in Bulgar Wood, merely came in for the retaliatory bombardment which the Germans developed. This meant as usual more work for the Pioneers in repairing damages to trenches, tracks and communications, and the 5th S.W.B. were kept busy enough. They were fairly lucky as regards casualties, the total for September amounting to 4 men killed and 4 officers[1] and 30 men wounded. Captain Evans, who was wounded on September 20th, was then temporarily attached to the 9th Welch and distinguished himself greatly in the attack; he led his company forward in face of heavy machine-gun fire and although wounded, refused to go back till consolidation was complete.[2] Captain Rose was similarly lent to the 9th Cheshire to command a company and did good service. Lieutenant Runham, whose Lewis gun teams had been so effective against the German aeroplanes, received the M.C., which was also awarded to Lieutenant R. S. Griffiths for the good work he had done in constructing the trench tramways which had proved so useful, especially in evacuating the wounded.

Not having suffered severely in the September fighting the Nineteenth Division could hardly expect to be relieved immediately. Still, it was even longer in the line[3] than it had expected, for not till November 9th did it quit the Klein Zillebeke area. October saw much hard fighting astride the Menin Road, but between that and the Canal there was nothing more than "normal" activity. Occasionally the German guns bombarded the front line, itself a mere series of disconnected posts in shell holes. As a rule the ground and the weather gave more trouble than the enemy, especially to the 5th S.W.B., whose energies were concentrated mainly on the communication trenches. These needed improving and extending, though merely to keep them in repair taxed the battalion's resources and ingenuity. Revetting, duckboarding, draining—a peculiarly disheartening task—filling in shell holes, laying fascines over bottomless bogs, these were labours which seemed unending. The more the 5th did the more work the rain and the enemy's shelling provided for it. But if the battalion could barely keep pace with the needs of the situation its work earned warm praise from the Division's new G.O.C., General Jeffreys, and its Lewis gun teams were highly successful in discouraging the hostile air-craft. October cost the battalion nearly 50 casualties, including seven men killed, but its strength was fairly well maintained by drafts and by men returning from hospital.[4]

[1] Captain I. T. Evans, Second Lieutenants E. S. J. Evans, Rogers and Settle.
[2] He was awarded the D.S.O.
[3] It held the frontage just N.E. of the Canal.
[4] Captain Copner left in October to join the 1st Battalion but Captain Maynard and five new subalterns joined, followed by half a dozen more early in November.

The front had hardly become "stabilized" again after September 26th when the 2nd S.W.B. found their way back to the fighting zone after spending nearly all September out of the line. During this time the French General La Cappelle had inspected the 87th Brigade and presented the Croix de Guerre to Major Garnett, Captain Pierson, Sergeant Mason and Private Swift, while the Divisional Commander had also inspected the battalion, presented the decorations won on August 16th,[1] and congratulated it warmly on its good work. The 2nd had received substantial reinforcements, had had a good rest, in which training and recreation had been judiciously mingled, and come back to the line in good condition, relieving the Newfoundland Regiment in the left sub-sector of the Divisional front[2] on September 29th. This was familiar ground; the recent attacks had not extended much beyond Langemarck, and the British line ran along the left of the Broembeek. Of the front line two companies, C, on the left, was round Craonne Farm, B just N.E. of Cannes Farm, D and A, the supports, being near Montmirail and Denain Farms respectively.

The 2nd had four days in front line: the hostile artillery was intermittently active, especially about daybreak, and inflicted several casualties, including Second Lieutenant Joyce killed. However, this did not prevent the battalion from putting up an almost complete belt of wire along its front or from digging several hundreds of yards of communication trenches. Patrols were active, bringing in useful information about the state of the Broembeek and locating accurately the enemy's posts on the far bank; but the battalion, having been relieved on the previous evening, was "out" when, on October 4th, the Twenty-Ninth Division once again shared in a successful attack. The main thrust was being made in the centre, nearer Zonnebeke and Polygon Wood, and only a short advance was required of the Twenty-Ninth to cover the flank of the Fourth Division N.E. of Langemarck. This advance brought the Division's right forward almost to Kortebeck Farm;[3] and it was this new front line, stretching from Japan House on the left, past Goed ter Vesten Farm nearly to 19-Metre Hill, a total of 1800 yards, that the 2nd S.W.B. took over on October 5th. It was a difficult relief; the country was unknown, two of the officers sent ahead to reconnoitre had been hit, Second Lieutenant Lowe being killed and Second Lieutenant Gibson wounded, the guides did not know the way, the going was bad and the enemy's shelling was

[1] Captain Mayger bar to M.C., Captain Pierson and Second Lieutenant Gibbon, M.C., nine "other ranks" M.M.
[2] The battalion had the French on its left.
[3] Between Koekuit and Poelcappelle.

steady and caused several casualties. It continued to be fairly troublesome throughout the next four days (October 5th–8th), and the casualties for the tour totalled nearly 50,[1] while on October 7th B Company lost its rations, owing to five of the transport mules being hit when bringing them up to the ration dump.

Good work was done in patrolling, especially by Corporal Smith of D Company and Lance Corporal Bentley of A, but having been relieved on the evening of October 8th the battalion was not engaged in the battle of Poelcappelle next day. The Twenty-Ninth Division again achieved a substantial success, for it took over 500 prisoners and secured practically all its objectives, a fine finale to its efforts in " Third Ypres," of which it was to see no more. After a week in reserve at Proven the 2nd S.W.B. entrained on October 15th for Bellacourt, some six miles South of Arras, to which area the whole Division was bound. Since coming out of the line the battalion had received a draft of 27 men, as many men had rejoined from hospital and several officers had joined, including several transferred from the A.S.C.,[2] while Captain Somerville, who had been wounded on July 1st, 1916, rejoined on October 12th and resumed his duties as Adjutant, Captain Mumford taking over C Company.

Nearly three weeks after the 2nd Battalion quitted the Salient, the 1st was at last drawn into the vortex of the Ypres struggle. Since its confinement within the barbed wire of Le Clipon the 1st S.W.B. had had experiences which only their novelty kept from becoming monotonous. The elaborate preparations for throwing the First Division ashore required of the men much that was new. The German coast defences included a sea wall several feet in height and extremely difficult to scale. An exact replica of this had been built and all ranks were systematically practised in scaling it. At first only the more conspicuously agile could climb it, and that only when empty-handed, but the 1st was not going to be baffled, and after six weeks practically every man could negotiate it in fighting order with a load of bombs or barbed wire into the bargain.[3] Landing from rafts was also practised, together with siting and consolidating trenches at night, outpost schemes and other more ordinary exercises, which yet bore directly on situations which might arise if the attacking columns were successfully landed from their armoured pontoons

---

[1] In all the 2nd had 2 officers and 12 men killed or missing, and 1 officer and 50 men wounded during October.

[2] In all twelve joined in October and November.

[3] It was discovered that boots with new nails in them greatly simplified the task.

and succeeded by the aid of their specially constructed tanks in breaking through the sea wall and advancing inland.

To combat the monotony of isolation all sorts of recreations were devised, in addition to the usual football, boxing and athletics. One speciality of the S.W.B. was catching fish in the shallows with nets, which proved most popular, besides adding variety to the daily menu. Occasional visits to the monitors which were to assist in the operations proved pleasant as well as instructive: the Adjutant with those of other battalions spent three most interesting days in the estuary of the Thames with the pontoons specially constructed for the enterprise, and parties of sailors who came ashore for short attachments to different units proved welcome guests.[1]

However, as the summer wore on doubts began to be expressed about the great enterprise. The season at which gales might be expected to prohibit it was drawing near much faster than the Ypres offensive was progressing; and unless that offensive made really substantial progress, even a successful landing could achieve little. August gave place to September, September in turn faded into October, and the long-expected moment never came, but in its place on October 20th the news that the enterprise had been abandoned. Thus the departure from Le Clipon took the humdrum shape of a 17-mile march to the Eringhem area. This the men stood very well, profiting by the unlimited exercise and "P.T." of their "Hush, Hush" camp. Next day (October 21st) brought the battalion to Bruxeele, whence it moved five days later to Houtkerque. Here, when the weather allowed, it continued its training, while Major H. G. C. Fowler[2] joined with two new subalterns. After nearly a fortnight the battalion moved again, and this time to Ypres.

The Ypres offensive had now degenerated into a struggle for the high ground near Passchendaele, the possession of which would complete the capture of the main ridge East of Ypres, and the First Division was to relieve Canadian troops N.W. of Passchendaele village. This had been captured on November 6th, when a line had been established on the Goudberg Spur facing North towards another spur on which stood the strong points known as Vocation and Vox Farms and Vat Cottages. The capture of this spur was regarded as essential to the rounding-off

---

[1] In July the battalion lost Major Ramsden, transferred to command the 15th H.L.I. In his place Major Baillie-Hamilton of the Black Watch was attached to the battalion as second in command.

[2] He became second in command, Major Baillie-Hamilton being transferred to the 1st Gloucestershire. Another "pre-war" officer, Captain Copner, joined about the same time on transfer from the 5th Battalion.

of the position, so the 3rd Brigade was to attack on November 10th in co-operation with the Canadians on its right nearer Passchendaele village. The S.W.B. and R.M.F. were detailed to attack and accordingly moved up to Irish Farm on November 8th, and on the following evening set out for the front. The night was pitch dark, with rain at intervals, the country was a mixture of glue and water, churned up indescribably by the bombardments so that off the duck-board tracks a footing was hard to obtain. In places the duck-boards themselves were under water, and if a man slipped off he usually fell into a deep shell hole full of water and would be lucky to escape alive. Lightly equipped men would have found the move toilsome, but for men burdened with three days' rations, extra ammunition, two bombs apiece, steel helmets and other trifles such as packs, it was indeed a searching test of fitness and endurance. German shell fire increased the troubles of the move. The enemy had the duck-board tracks accurately registered and the battalion was fortunate to suffer only a few casualties during its approach-march. It fared less well, however, while waiting for "Zero" on the taped line which served as assembly position, both A and B Companies suffering heavily.

This taped line ran due West from Valour Farm for about 200 yards. A Company with a platoon of C was on the right, its objective being a line from Vocation Farm N.W. through Vox Farm. B was to attack on A's left, C being in reserve, and D detailed as counter-attack company. Zero was at 5 a.m. (November 10th) and for an hour before that a barrage was put down on and just behind the German front line. But the difficulties against which the artillery had to contend in that sea of featureless mud almost surpassed those of the infantry; it was hardly wonderful if the barrage was irregular, so that our own men ran into it when the advance started. This caused several casualties and resulted in the battalion edging off to the right, so that a gap developed on the left between B Company and the Munsters, while Virile Farm and Goudberg Copse were never taken. On the right the men got forward better, establishing a post close to Vocation Farm and obtaining touch with the Canadians, while D Company dug in near Virtue Farm. Vox Farm, however, they could not reach, so heavy was the machine gun fire and sniping. Before long, too, hostile counter-attacks developed.

The first of these, about 7.15 a.m., was successfully repulsed by D's Lewis guns and the Vocation Farm post, but on the left the gap proved a weak spot and the enemy succeeded in gaining ground. The battalion, or rather its remnants, for casualties had been heavy, clung on tenaciously, though pestered by

German aeroplanes and under heavy shell fire, which was the more effective because it caught the battalion on the flank and enfiladed the line. Colonel Taylor was wounded early on, but Captain Lochner took command and set a fine example: he was well backed up by the other officers, Second Lieutenant Nott, for example, though twice wounded, refused to go back but rallied and encouraged the men and helped them to beat off the counter-attacks. To hold on was the more difficult because the mud had put so many rifles and Lewis guns out of action, the bombs had been largely used up in capturing various pill-boxes

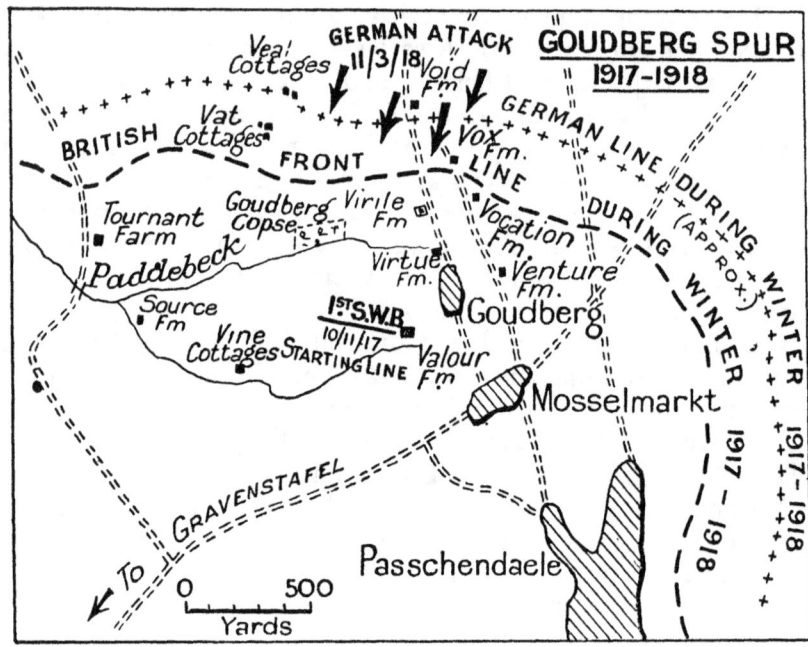

and the hostile barrage impeded the fetching of fresh supplies from the rear. Nevertheless, the S.W.B. maintained their position till, about 1 p.m., the enemy succeeded in working round the left of the Vocation Farm post and rendered it untenable. Covered by a party from Battalion Headquarters, which Captain Lochner had collected and dug in, the survivors of the advanced parties fell back to a line from near Venture Farm on the right to Valour Farm and thence along the original starting-off line. On this line they rallied, Captain Manley and Second Lieutenant Massy doing great work: the latter not only rallied and reorganized his men but walked across 300 yards of open to take charge of a post on the flank where there was no officer left. Largely thanks to their efforts, and to the tenacity of Captain Lochner's party the counter-attacks were held up.

Later on two companies of the Gloucestershire came up in support and helped to make good the position, touch being obtained also with the Munsters near Source Farm. German aeroplanes and guns continued to be troublesome next day, but the battalion's trials were nearing their end; that evening the Loyal North Lancashire arrived to relieve it, and before daylight the exhausted survivors were struggling back to rest. Losses had been heavy: Lieutenant C. G. Philips and Second Lieutenant H. H. Davies killed, Second Lieutenant Mason missing, Colonel Taylor, Captain Piggott, Lieutenants Deacon and J. R. T. Edwards, Second Lieutenants Giles, W. A. Thomas and Nott wounded, with 372 casualties among the men, well over two-thirds of those in action. If the objectives had not been secured, the endurance and good discipline of the troops had been conspicuous, and the failure may fairly be ascribed to the appalling conditions. The men had gone into action after an exhausting march, the ground was as difficult to consolidate as to cross, adequate artillery support had been hard to assure. Special credit attached to the stretcher-bearers, whose disregard of difficulties and dangers was beyond all praise, many wounded being rescued who must otherwise have perished. Captain Campbell, R.A.M.C., the battalion's M.O., deserved enormous credit for his careful training of them. Privates Burgess and Lomas were specially conspicuous for their gallantry and resource in helping the wounded, the former going on with the work though himself wounded.[1]

On reaching Hospital Farm, near Brielen, the battalion, now under Major Fowler, who had been with the rear echelon during the action, started to clean up. This last was difficult, the mud was more than usually clinging, and clothes, equipment and weapons were literally caked in it. At this camp the 1st remained for ten days, finding stretcher and working parties for the forward areas, and then moved to Poperinghe and thence (November 27th) to Proven. Eighty-three men had joined at Poperinghe, but the battalion was still much below establishment when, on December 5th, the Division returned to the line, taking over the sector South of Houthulst Forest. If it was still in the Salient active hostilities there had ended with the attack of November 10th and the centre of interest had shifted elsewhere: indeed, before the 1st S.W.B. went into the front line again the Cambrai fighting also, in which a big success

[1] Captains Lochner and Manley and Second Lieutenants Massy and Nott received the M.C., while Lieutenant Wales, who had done splendid work as Brigade Intelligence Officer, sending back a series of excellent reports, received a bar to the M.C. Private Burgess was awarded the D.C.M. and Private Lomas a bar to his D.C.M.

had at one time really seemed to have been achieved, had come to its disappointing end. In that battle both the 2nd and the 12th S.W.B. had been actively engaged and had added greatly to the laurels of the TWENTY-FOURTH, if the contribution to its casualty list had been proportionately considerable.

CHAPTER XXIV

CAMBRAI

SOME weeks before the heavy fighting in the Salient died down preparations had been begun for a fresh offensive at a point where the German garrison had been weakened to provide reinforcements for Flanders. Of all such quarters the Cambrai front offered the most promising prospects both strategically, as regards the possibilities of exploiting success, and tactically, through its being favourable for using tanks. By employing a mass of tanks it might be possible to dispense entirely with any previous artillery preparation and thereby to effect a complete surprise. The tanks, it was hoped, would smash through the wire, though here it was specially deep and strong, and so open a road to the infantry.

The German defences in this quarter were extremely formidable. The main Hindenburg Line, the first obstacle to be carried, was not a line which had been hastily taken up as the result of fighting at close quarters. It had been constructed deliberately in the winter of 1916-1917, and had been carefully sited to take full advantage of the topographical features. During the summer the Germans had added greatly to its strength, at certain places they had constructed strong forward positions as outposts to it, immediately in its rear they had a second line, the Hindenburg Support, which was nearly as strong, while about half-way between the front line and Cambrai ran a third defensive system, known as the Beaurevoir-Masnières Line. On the right of the front to be attacked the Scheldt Canal provided yet another obstacle which must be negotiated before the Beaurevoir-Masnières Line could be attacked, while on the Western part of the battlefield the unfinished Canal du Nord also complicated matters considerably.

For the actual attack the Third Army was using two Corps, the Third and Fifth. The Third Corps, to which the Twenty-Ninth Division had been assigned, was using three of its four Divisions to carry the Hindenburg Line itself and the Support Line, after which the Twenty-Ninth was to go through to the Scheldt Canal, 4000 yards farther on, capture the villages of Masnières and Marcoing and breach the Beaurevoir Line beyond the canal. The cavalry were then to push on through the gap and isolate Cambrai on the East, while the Fifth Corps exploited the success in a Northerly direction towards the Sensée. If it could make substantial progress the German defences nearer Arras, on the Bullecourt–Croisilles–Henin sur Cojeul front, would be turned and taken in rear Unluckily, the Italian collapse at Caporetto had necessitated the dispatch to Italy of substantial reinforcements, both British and French, and therefore at the critical moment Sir Douglas Haig found himself short of the urgently needed reserves. The five Divisions already in or on their way to Italy did invaluable service on that front, but their absence from the Cambrai battlefield was none the less to be deplored.[1]

Since coming out of the line at Ypres the Twenty-Ninth Division had enjoyed nearly a month's rest in a training area six miles South of Arras, the 2nd S.W.B. being in fairly comfortable billets at Bellacourt. With a full month available for training a systematic and carefully planned programme could be drawn up, working up from platoon and company work, with special classes for signallers, machine gunners and other specialists, to battalion, brigade and Divisional training. Leave was freely granted and opportunities for recreation were not overlooked, special attention being paid to getting the men as fit as possible for the exertions expected of them. It was impressed upon Divisional Headquarters that the troops would have to consolidate the ground won and must be prepared to hold on to it, though no one ever contemplated how long they would actually have to go without relief. The 2nd had come out of the Salient none too strong and at first drafts were not plentiful; not till November 14th indeed did any substantial draft appear, 107 men joining on that date, while another 50 also rejoined from hospital.[2]

Orders to move came on November 17th, when the battalion entrained at Boisleux for Peronne, arriving there about 2.30 a.m. next day and marching to a camp near Moislains. Here it spent the day under cover, as every effort was being made to conceal the concentration of troops and thereby preserve secrecy as long as possible. Movements therefore were restricted to the hours of darkness, which meant three sleepless nights with only disturbed rest by day, not too good a preparation for an attack. On November 18th a five-mile advance was made to Fins, where the final preparations were completed. Captain Gibbon and Second Lieutenant Netherclift had remained with the 10 per cent reinforcements at the Divisional reinforcement camp, and the transport under Lieutenant Williams was also left behind with orders to follow the battalion to Villers-Plouich as soon as it was safe.

"Zero" was at 6.10 a.m. on November 20th, at which hour the tanks went forward. It was an inspiring sight to the battalion

---

[1] No battalion of the TWENTY-FOURTH was included in any of these Divisions and the Regiment does not therefore include "Italy" among its battle-honours.

[2] The battalion took into action 18 officers and 596 other ranks, with 3 officers and 147 men at the transport lines, and 3 officers and 61 men at the Corps reinforcement camp.

to see them move forward in the semi-darkness, each with a large faggot on its top for use in crossing the trenches. Ten minutes later the guns opened fire. A complete surprise had been achieved, and the attacking infantry, following hard in the wake of the tanks, were quickly on top of the defenders. In places there was hard fighting, but all three Divisions of the Third Corps, the Twelfth on the right, the Twentieth in the centre and the Sixth on the left, captured their objectives well up to time, though on their left the Fifty-First Division was held up by a particularly stout resistance at Flesquières. The Twenty-Ninth Division, which had been formed up in its assembly position before 4 a.m., started forward at 6.30 a.m., the battalion moving in column of fours, companies at 50 yards distance. There was a little shelling, which increased after the battalion passed Villers-Plouich, but did not do much damage, barely a dozen casualties being incurred,[1] nor did it prevent the battalion establishing itself in the Hindenburg Line by 7.15 a.m.

Here the 2nd had a long wait. A thick fog made it difficult to see what was happening, but all reports from the front were encouraging. The hostile shelling had died down directly the leading troops reached and captured the German batteries, and prisoners soon appeared in numbers. Eventually orders to advance were received and before 10.30 a.m. the battalion was moving forward again behind some tanks, in artillery formation with a line of scouts in front. A (right) and D (left) were the leading companies, with C and B in support.

The 87th Brigade had the battalion (right) and the K.O.S.B in front line, followed respectively by the Inniskillings and the Border Regiment, its objective being Marcoing, a village situated on the Western bank of the Scheldt Canal. It was to cross the canal—there were three bridges on its frontage —and secure the Beaurevoir Line from the canal bank near Marcoing to the Cambrai road just beyond Masnières. The 88th Brigade on the right was to capture Masnières, on the left the 86th was to secure Nine Wood and the trenches behind it. The battalion's special objectives were Marcoing Copse and the lock N.E. of it, and after securing the passage it and the K.O.S.B were to form a bridge-head across the bend in the canal from the Marcoing Copse Lock to that opposite Château Talma. The supporting battalions would then go through and attack the Beaurevoir Line.

The advance from the Hindenburg Line met with little opposition, though the remains of the wire and the many broad and deep trenches to be crossed made formations difficult to

[1] These included Company Sergeant Major Irons, whose death was a great loss.

keep, and the right line of advance was hard to follow in the smoke and mist. Machine guns were still in action in an untaken strong point in the 86th Brigade's area, but neither they nor such snipers as were encountered could interfere seriously with the battalion's advance, though there was harder fighting just S.W. of Marcoing Copse, where two guns were taken. D Company soon cleared the Copse of its defenders, they were not very numerous, and a selected party pushed on as ordered to reconnoitre the crossing at the lock. Really serious opposition was now offered, machine guns and rifles opening fire from houses on the canal bank, especially West of the lock, and A Company in trying to reach the lock suffered heavily. To get there they had first to cross the river, which ran parallel to the canal, and turn to the left towards the lock 60 yards away. The space between the two bridges was swept by machine gun fire, and A's efforts to cross this narrow space resulted in heavy casualties, Lieutenant Weeks, the company commander, being badly wounded and many men shot down. On the left, however, Captain Mayger and D Company crossed the river by a footbridge at Marcoing Copse, and finding a barge on the canal used it to cross that obstacle. Directly he was across Captain Mayger sent a platoon to work to its right towards the lock and assist A. Almost simultaneously a tank arrived and opened fire with its 6-pounder on the houses near the lock.

The defence was already shaken when Captain Mumford without waiting for orders brought C Company up to reinforce A. He worked his men round to the flank under heavy machine gun fire till they could enfilade the guns and give covering fire. His initiative was successful, the obstructing position was rushed, and C pushed forward up the slope to where, about 250 yards from the canal, it was studded with pits, believed to have been dug as receptacles for ammunition. A stout barbed wire fence ran in front of these pits and the enemy were in some force. C, however, were not to be denied and rushed the pits, capturing many prisoners and a machine gun, though Captain Mumford was seriously wounded. D meanwhile had taken up a position 250 yards beyond the canal, and B, the reserve company, had arrived at Marcoing Copse. Touch was established both with the 86th Brigade and with the K.O.S.B., and about 2 p.m. the Inniskillings came through and advanced up the slope towards the Beaurevoir Line, C Company going forward with them. By this time the Germans had managed to man the Beaurevoir Line in some force and most unluckily a tank, which had tried to cross at Masnières, had merely completed the destruction of the half-ruined bridge, while the advance of the guns had been seriously delayed by the many trenches and sunken roads to be crossed. Thus neither the Inniskillings nor C Company could reach the final objective, though they established themselves about 1100 yards ahead up the slope. Meanwhile A and B and Battalion Headquarters had come across, and night found the battalion holding a line running from the lock towards Masnières Station, C being dug in where its advance had halted, nearly 1100 yards ahead. Casualties had been light, under 80, but included no less than seven officers: Captain Mumford, Lieutenants Baggallay and Weeks, Second Lieutenants H. E. Evans, H. T. Edwards, G. C. B. James and Woolveridge all being wounded, three of them, Lieutenant Weeks and Second Lieutenants Edwards and James, mortally. As against that over 60 prisoners had been taken with two field guns and several machine guns.

Substantial as had been the success achieved, all objectives had not been attained, and the failure to break through the Beaurevoir Line, coupled with the check to the Fifty-First Division, had prevented the cavalry from exploiting the opportunity. The Beaurevoir Line, moreover, was to prove a serious stumbling block when the attack was continued next day.

The 2nd S.W.B. actually received orders about 11 p.m. to renew the attack at dawn, but these were cancelled and the time changed to 11 a.m. Tanks were to co-operate and the K.O.S.B. to advance at the same time. The three companies holding the main line were to advance 200 yards behind the tanks, and when they passed through C's line, that company was to join in as supports. There was considerable delay over getting touch with the tanks and collecting them for the attack, and actually it was nearly noon before the advance got started, while even then the artillery support was almost negligible, for touch had not been established with the artillery and very few guns had come forward. One of the tanks went on ahead to tackle a machine gun located on the Cambrai road some way North of Masnières, but the German position was extremely formidable: the ground to be crossed formed a regular glacis sloping up to their trenches and was swept by machine gun fire from the right flank. The centre and left had a little cover from view at first, but this would cease after they topped the crest of a low spur running West from Rumilly. Indeed the troops had hardly covered 200 yards before heavy fire was opened, both from front and flanks. The ammunition pits, of which there were several rows, gave fair cover, but after they were left behind there was no more cover and casualties were heavy. In addition to the machine guns in the trench line the Germans had others echeloned back on the high ground behind who developed a concentrated fire over the ground the battalion had to cross. With hardly any artillery support these machine guns could not be silenced and could fire unimpeded by any reply.

Despite this, B Company, under Captain Pierson, forced their way into the German line where it crossed the Cambrai road North of Masnières. The line proved in places to be spit-locked only, with dug-outs at intervals containing machine guns. This was but a poor position to consolidate, and the Germans, who had taken refuge in the dug-outs when the tanks approached, emerged again when they passed on. In the centre, Captain Mayger and some of D got through a gap in the wire which a tank had made, but he himself was wounded, as was also Lieutenant Cooke, who had shown a splendid example of leadership and determination throughout the 1500 yards advance, eventually entering the enemy's trenches. On his officers being hit Company Quartermaster Sergeant Ruffle took command and led the men splendidly, and a few other men managed to force a way into the German position, but they were not numerous, and on the left uncut wire had made it impossible to effect an entrance. Little support was forthcoming on the flanks: the 88th Brigade's energies were absorbed in mastering the rest of Masnières, while the K.O.S.B. had met equally severe opposition and could not get on. Thus the few S.W.B. who had gained their objective were too weak to withstand the counter-attacks which developed before long. The tanks were out of action by now—one had come back bringing with it two wounded officers, Captain Mayger and Lieutenant Cooke, who were lying inside the wire—and the counter-attack at once drove the left back. Company Quartermaster Sergeant Ruffle's party put up a stout fight, but attacks on both flanks forced it also to withdraw, its commander being last seen tackling some Germans with the bayonet to cover his men's retreat. Second Lieutenant Rowlands, too, was last seen in the German trenches fighting fiercely and trying to keep the enemy at bay. Of Captain Pierson's party no more was heard after the first messages reporting that it had reached its objective, and before long the Germans began advancing over the crest and down the slope. By this time Colonel Raikes and Captain Somerville, who had only three very junior subalterns left to help them, had rallied the men who had fallen back and reorganized them on a line about level with C Company's overnight position. Thanks largely to the fine work of the Commanding Officer and Adjutant a successful stand was made here. A steady fire checked the German advance, whereupon a sharp fire-fight followed, ending eventually in the Germans retreating and leaving the battalion to consolidate its line. Orders were actually received from the brigade to withdraw to the position held in the morning, but these were cancelled when the battalion's actual line became known and its importance as covering Masnières fully realized.

This line the 2nd was to hold for another 48 hours. By night it dug vigorously, making good progress despite its much diminished numbers,[1] and establishing satisfactory touch with the 86th Brigade in Masnières. German snipers were active enough to make movement by day risky, and there was some shell fire, but casualties were not numerous and by 7 p.m. on November 23rd, when the battalion was relieved by the K.O.S.B., quite satisfactory trenches had been dug. Relief, however merely meant a move to the Marcoing bridge-head, very much the position originally taken up by the battalion across the canal. Here cookers met the men, who enjoyed a good hot meal before occupying their new positions, A and C Companies being in trenches, B and D in deep dug-outs.

Though by this time the fighting had quite died down on the right of the battlefield, from Noyelles and Marcoing Eastward, on its other flank desperate struggles were still in progress. The capture of Flesquières early on November 21st had been followed by that of Anneux, Cantaing and Fontaine-Notre-Dame, which straightened out the re-entrant in the British line which had existed on the previous evening. These positions, however, were dominated by the high ground of the Bourlon Ridge North of them, and this ridge also gave its possessors considerable advantages of observation over the ground sloping Northwards to the Sensée. If the British could secure it they might hope to render untenable the enemy's defensive lines as far as the Sensée, if not to the Scarpe, and Sir Douglas Haig accordingly determined to prosecute his offensive in the Bourlon direction and to employ all the available reserves in that effort. For the Third Corps this meant having to remain in line, holding the positions captured, although few reinforcements had arrived to fill the gaps in its ranks,[2] and the length of its line was out of all proportion to its strength, especially as the line was newly dug and in consequence very incomplete. The Twenty-Ninth Division, whose G.O.C., a devoted advocate of the gospel of " Dig, dig, dig," had instilled into them the essential importance of consolidating immediately any position they might capture, had gone far to make their line defensible, but much work was required to render so long a front secure.

---

[1] The day had cost it Captain Pierson, Lieutenant Cooper and Second Lieutenant Rowlands and 87 men killed or missing, Captain Mayger and Second Lieutenants Cooke and J. E. Lloyd and 64 men wounded. Only about 360 men now remained, including the Headquarters personnel and the stretcher-bearers.

[2] The 2nd S.W.B., who had lost over 250 all told, had merely been joined by 1 officer, Second Lieutenant Jordan, and 26 men from the transport lines.

The reserves detailed to carry on the operations on the Bourlon front included the Fortieth Division, so that the 12th S.W.B. at last found themselves called upon to show their mettle in a big action.

The 12th S.W.B. must have felt as if they had positively taken route in the Gonnelieu–Villers Plouich area. All through the summer they remained here, holding one or another of the sectors facing the Hindenburg Line, nor when autumn arrived did it bring them any change. Other Divisions were shifted Northward to struggle through the swamps and slime of the Ypres Salient; that long-drawn-out agony was nearing its close before the Fortieth was taken out of the line and sent back to Gouy en Artois for a long rest. Still there had been little inactivity for the 12th S.W.B. The battalion had generally had a long front to hold, and not too many men to put into line, for if its casualties were low,[1] units in " quiet " sectors got comparatively few drafts. The losses incurred in April and May were hardly made good till July, and thereafter only one small draft joined until the very end of September, when nearly 90 men appeared. Despite this the 12th were very active in patrolling and had several successful encounters in No Man's Land. In one of these in June a party under Second Lieutenant W. J. Williams surprised and dispersed a hostile patrol, killing five of them at a cost of one killed and one wounded. Second Lieutenant Williams, who, as on other occasions when out patrolling, handled the situation most skilfully, displaying much dash and initiative, received the M.C. and Private Creighton, who backed him up well, was sent up for the M.M. There was more sharp fighting in July in which Second Lieutenant Snelson, who had only just joined, was killed, but the 12th had much the best of these encounters. They also carried out two very successful raids. On July 4th Second Lieutenants H. R. Hill and E. Edwards and 32 men raided Barrack Trench and Barrack Support. The " Bangalore torpedo " having failed to explode, Second Lieutenant Hill himself cut a gap in the wire and led his men through. Finding the front trench lightly held he pushed on to the second, which was more stoutly defended, forced a way in, and eventually extricated his party after a sharp fight with only two casualties, a heavy loss having been inflicted on the enemy.[2] The other raid, in August, was on a rather larger scale: Lieutenant Welford and Second Lieutenant Price and 60 men blew a gap in the enemy's wire with a " Bangalore torpedo " and got well into the German trenches, where they separated into two parties and worked some way along the

---

[1] From June 1st to October 7th less than fifty all told are recorded.
[2] Second Lieutenant Hill received the M.C.

trenches to left and right, bombing dug-outs and inflicting many casualties. The right party captured a machine gun emplacement, taking the gun and disposing of its crew, and the Lewis gun team did some effective shooting at Germans who were trying to escape. Finally the raiders withdrew most successfully, having lost only 3 killed and 10 wounded.[1]

Casualties among the officers were higher in proportion in this period than among the men. Major Murphy, who had rejoined in July, was wounded within a few days. Captain W. E. Brown was then promoted Major and handed over the Adjutancy to Second Lieutenant J. M. W. Barker. In September Second Lieutenant D. Powell was killed by a sniper, and in July Second Lieutenant A. D. Jones was wounded when in charge of a working party, the day after he had joined. Several officers who had been away sick or wounded rejoined, among them Captains J. E. Jenkins and H. C. Lloyd and Lieutenant Howell, and in October eight new officers joined, mainly Second Lieutenants, but including Captain W. G. L. Foster and Lieutenant Goodman.

By this time the battalion was out of the line, resting and training, first at Gouy en Artois and then in the first half of November at Humbercourt where it was billeted in some exceedingly draughty and leaky barns. The great incident of this time was a football match against the 2nd Battalion, who were quartered not so very far away, a great struggle ending in a victory for the senior battalion by two tries to a dropped goal. The 12th consoled themselves for their defeat by winning several other matches, and after their long spell in the line the rest was greatly appreciated. However, with the middle of November came orders for a move, and on November 16th the battalion marched from Humbercourt to Gouy, thence to Gommecourt (17th), Barastre (19th) and Doignies (21st). Here warning was received from the Fourth Corps, to which the Fortieth Division had been posted, that the Division would be shortly required for an attack on Bourlon Wood. This was a dominating feature on the Northern portion of the Cambrai battlefield, lying just North of the Bapaume–Cambrai road, and its capture was essential to secure a good flanking position prior to exploiting the advantages gained by breaking through the Hindenburg Line.

On the second day of the battle the Fifty-First and Sixty-Second Divisions had endeavoured to extend the previous day's gains in a Northerly direction, but the Sixty-Second had only succeeded in establishing itself on the Southern outskirts of Bourlon Wood. Accordingly orders were issued to the Fortieth Division to relieve it, and on the evening of November 22nd

---

[1] Sergeant Nelson, Corporal Goodship and Privates Crossdale and Potter were awarded the M.M. for good work on these raids.

the 12th S.W.B. found themselves moving up through Graincourt to do so. The relief was effected before midnight, and the battalion settled down to get what rest it could before the attack, which was to start at 10.30 a.m. (November 23rd). The plan was that the Fortieth Division, with the 119th Brigade on the right and the 121st on the left, should attack Bourlon Wood and village, the Fifty-First simultaneously renewing the effort to secure Fontaine-Notre-Dame, East of the wood, and the Thirty-Sixth trying to improve the position on the left in the direction of Moeuvres. The 12th S.W.B. were on the left of their brigade, having the 19th R.W.F. on their right, and had as objective the Eastern end of Bourlon village and the Northern edge of the wood East of the village. Tanks were to precede the left company, but that on the right had no such assistance.

At the start the attack went very well. The first line of German trenches was crossed within a quarter of an hour of "Zero," almost without any opposition. Then, as the troops plunged forward into the wood, resistance stiffened. The right company was the first to meet the enemy in strength, but went for the Germans with the bayonet and drove them back. About midway through the wood the advance crossed a sunken road, where it had sharp fighting, taking several machine guns and some prisoners. After this the German defence grew more stubborn and progress became more difficult, especially on the left where heavy machine gun fire delayed the advance. The supporting companies had been put in by now and by their aid the attack gained ground. Second Lieutenant Eames and R. Thomas were both conspicuous for their gallantry and good leadership: the latter showing great dash and setting a fine example till very badly wounded. Private Plummer, on the advance of his platoon being checked, went forward alone to a "strong point" and cleared it, taking 8 prisoners, and then pushing on repeated the performance twice, capturing a machine gun and 5 prisoners in one and an officer and 10 men in the other. By noon the Northern edge of the wood had been reached on the right, but casualties had been heavy and the attackers were much disorganized. However, the R.W.F. reinforced the left and eventually the village also was reached, Captain Symes and a party overcoming all resistance and establishing themselves on the final objective, while No. 4 Platoon, which for a time was held up by a small factory, took it in the end by the aid of a tank. The 121st Brigade had also made a lodgment in the village, and for a time it looked as though the objective would be secured. But away to the right the Fifty-First Division was meeting very stubborn opposition, and the right of the battalion, which had reached the outskirts of the village, found itself out of touch on both flanks, and could get no further.

It was now about 1 p.m., and Major Brown, hearing that there had been heavy casualties especially among the officers, went forward to reorganize. Shortly after his arrival at the front line a heavy counter-attack developed which before long pushed the right of the battalion back to the sunken road. Here a stand was successfully made, and a tank, which appeared most opportunely, managed to extricate and bring back Captain Symes' party which had held on to the village with both its flanks in the air and was in danger of being cut off. The arrival of this tank was largely due to Sergeant Hampton who had made his way back through the enemy and guided it to the spot. The brigade was now holding a line some way short of the village but more advanced on the right than on the left. All units were now much mixed up and all the officers of the 12th who had started the attack had been hit, though Lieutenant W. M. Evans had come forward to help Major Brown. It was all the more creditable, therefore, that when about 4 p.m. a fresh counter-attack developed the 12th should have held on stoutly, though both flanks were unsupported and the pressure was very heavy. In the nick of time two companies of the 18th Welch reinforced and a little ground was actually won back by a counter-attack, in which Lieutenant Evans was much to the fore, his gallantry and resource being alike conspicuous, while Lance Corporal Prescott led a party forward to tackle a couple of strong points and managed to consolidate a position well forward of his starting point. In this emergency several of the surviving N.C.O.'s and men showed great capacity for leadership, notably Private Hewett, who rallied a party whose officers and N.C.O.'s were all hit and led them forward successfully. Company Sergeant Major Stone was also prominent in encouraging the men to hold on and resist the counter-attacks. Company Sergeant Major T. Jones, who had already distinguished himself by going forward to reconnoitre a strong point which was holding up the attack, now took charge of a company and did splendid work in defence. Eventually some high ground inside the wood was made good and some advanced posts established on the edge. During the night efforts were made to reorganize the troops and consolidate the position. Colonel Benzie had now been put in charge of the front area, and aided by Major Brown and Lieutenant Evans he contrived to collect the 12th and establish them in a fairly good position, but the work was not made easier by several small counter-attacks which were, however, repulsed. Excellent work was done about this time by Corporal Haywood who distinguished himself by his courage and assiduity in attending to the wounded.

The regimental aid-post having been blown in, not once but three times, he found a new place of shelter and carried on his work. Corporal James was also responsible for splendid and devoted work in keeping open communications and transmitting messages under heavy fire.

Morning brought a renewal of heavy fighting. About 8.30 a.m. the enemy came forward in great force, advancing, as one account says, "in droves without any particular formation." This attack drove in the advanced posts, but it never reached the main line, for the 12th withheld their fire by order till the enemy were about 150 yards away and then let fly with tremendous effect, the attack melting away completely under the fire poured into it. However, almost immediately afterwards the Germans put down so heavy and accurate a barrage that there was nothing for it but to fall back to the sunken road, 300 yards or so behind. Here two companies of the 14th Argyll and Sutherlands reinforced, and on the barrage lifting about 10 a.m. they and the remnants of the 119th Brigade, assisted by the 15th Hussars acting dismounted, pushed forward and recovered the former line. Colonel Benzie was largely responsible for this success and was ably supported by Major Brown. Counter-attacks continued, however, and were the more difficult to repulse because the heavy shelling to which the wood and the approaches to it were subjected greatly impeded the supply of ammunition. In the afternoon came a renewed advance against the 119th Brigade and the units helping it, which also was repulsed after heavy fighting, the net result of the day being that our troops were left in possession of the high ground in the centre of the wood with posts on the Northern edge, while on the left most of Bourlon village was in our hands, the 121st Brigade and some dismounted cavalry having established a fresh lodgment there. In the evening the remnants of the 12th S.W.B., still further reduced by the day's fighting, in the course of which Major Brown had been wounded when a German bombing party tried to drive in one of our posts, were collected with other details of the 119th Brigade and placed between the King's Own of the 121st Brigade and the 2nd Scots Guards, who had come up on the right, the Guards Division having now replaced the Fifty-First.

The morning of November 25th brought something of a lull in the fighting, though German snipers and machine guns were fairly brisk. On the left there was greater activity, the most advanced troops of the 121st Brigade had reached the railway line North of Bourlon village but had been cut off by Germans getting into the village behind them, and confused fighting was going on there. About 2 p.m. a fresh attempt at an advance was made, in which the battalion concentrated its efforts on giving covering fire to help the Scots Guards who were advancing on its flank. Private Stockton handled his Lewis gun most effectively to assist this advance, standing up so that it could be fired resting on his hip. This fresh advance seems to have coincided with a new counter-attack, which it drove back, but the situation was still rather confused when the Sixty-Second Division came forward again to relieve the Fortieth. About 10 p.m., just before the 2/6th Duke of Wellington's arrived to relieve what was left of the 12th S.W.B., the Germans tried a fresh advance. This was met with a great burst of fire, in the face of which it faded away, and thereafter things were quiet and the relief was fairly easily accomplished.

Not many of the 12th S.W.B. were left to be relieved. Ten officers[1] and 123 men were killed and missing, 12 officers[2] and 243 men wounded; and Colonel Benzie had only a handful to take back with him to Ytres, where the battalion entrained on November 27th for Beaumetz. From Beaumetz it moved to Berles aux Bois, where it was to be given a few days to refit. If they had suffered heavily in Bourlon Wood the 12th S.W.B., in common with the whole Fortieth Division, had fought splendidly there and earned great credit. The adoption of an acorn as the Divisional badge was a fitting token of the stout fight the Fortieth Division had put up among the oak trees in Bourlon Wood; and the 12th S.W.B.'s share in that struggle was rewarded by the award of two D.S.O.'s,[3] six M.C.'s,[4] six D.C.M.'s,[5] and eleven M.M.'s.[6]

The 12th Battalion's part in the Cambrai struggle had been brief if creditable; the 2nd, in the battle before them, were still in the fighting area when the 12th left it and had by no means seen the fiercest of their fighting yet. After the Fortieth Division withdrew heavy fighting continued in the Bourlon region until November 27th, without the British objectives being

[1] Captain Sharpe, Lieutenants E. Edwards, G. W. B. Price, Goodman, Reed and Yorath, and Second Lieutenants E. O. Davies, Hooper, F. E. Morgan and R. I. Thomas.
[2] Major Brown, Captains H. C. A. Davies, J. E. Jenkins and Symes, Lieutenants W. M. Evans and Hartley and Second Lieutenants F. A. Stephenson, Shawcross, G. Simpson, W. T. Powell, L. Thomas and E. Jones.
[3] To Colonel Benzie and Lieutenant Evans.
[4] To Major Brown, Captain Symes, Second Lieutenants Eames and J. R. Thomas and Company Sergeant Majors Jones and Stone.
[5] To Sergeant Hampton, Corporal Haywood, Lance Corporals Prescott and Stockton, Privates Hewitt and Plummer.
[6] To Sergeant Carroll, Lance Corporal Boobyer, Privates Cochrane, Forsythe, Lockwood, Moffatt, Mollison, McCormick, Pace, Smith and Townsend.

completely attained. Another effort was therefore being prepared, but was anticipated by the Germans delivering the tremendous counter-attack which quite altered the aspect of affairs. For some days previously various symptoms of activity had been noticed on their front, increased movement of troops and transport, more guns being registered. So far as the weak effectives in the line would allow all possible preparations were made against a counter-attack, but with no reserves available to rein-

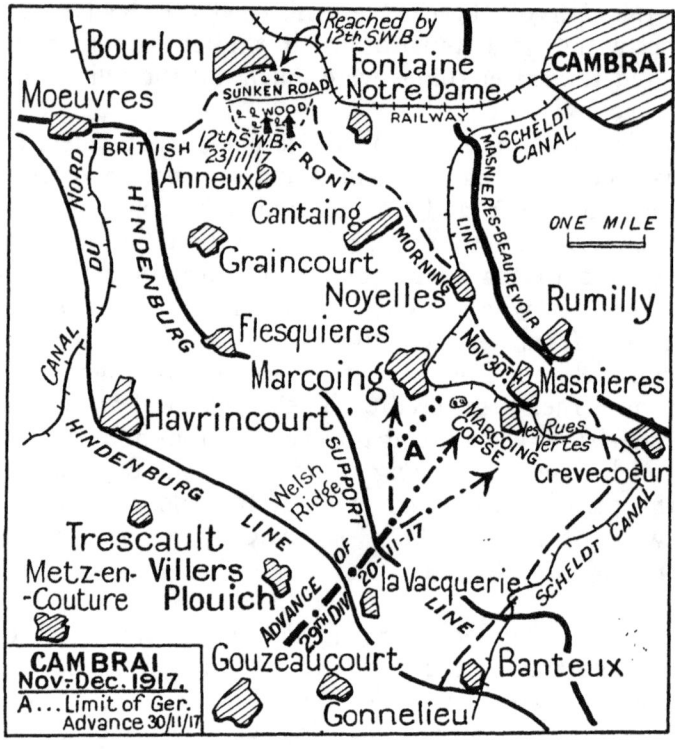

force the weak and tired Divisions of the Third Corps the prospect was not encouraging.

The 2nd S.W.B. had spent three days in improving the bridge-head, in particular digging over 400 yards of communication trench towards the front line. Then for 48 hours they were in reserve at Marcoing, still under shell fire but in billets and able to get a little much-needed rest and to do something to clean up, complete equipment and refit. At 8.30 p.m. on November 28th the battalion moved back into the bridge-head defences and was holding them on the morning of the 30th, when between 7 a.m. and 8 a.m. the Germans opened a tremendous bombardment and followed it up with an attack in great force. This came with special vigour against the flanks of

THE COUNTER-ATTACK

the new salient; on the British right, from Vendhuille to Masnières, five fresh German Divisions assailed three British, all weak and very weary, while against Bourlon Wood and Moeuvres even greater forces were employed.

At the moment the Twenty-Ninth Division had the 86th Brigade on the right, holding Masnières, and the 87th across the bend of the canal between that village and Marcoing, with the Borders and Inniskillings in front, the S.W.B. in support[1] and the K.O.S.B. in reserve in Marcoing along with the 88th Brigade. The main German attack just extended to the 86th Brigade's front, on which they were quite unable to make any serious impression; against the 87th Brigade there was no real attack, though its positions were heavily shelled. General Lucas could therefore employ not only his reserve but his support battalion at the point of real danger. This lay South of the canal and in rear of the Masnières–Marcoing front, for the German attack striking Westward from Les Rues des Vignes had not merely broken through the Twentieth Division's thinly held line, but had taken the defences of Gonnelieu, Banteux and Villers Guislains in flank and rear. Indeed soon after 8 a.m. German infantry were swarming over Welsh Ridge, right in among the Twenty-Ninth's battery positions, and its Headquarters staff had evacuated Gouzeaucourt in precipitate haste. All the British troops in the salient were in dire peril, the Twenty-Ninth Division in particular seemed in a hopeless position, and a really big disaster was staring the Third Army in the face. By dint of desperate efforts some sort of line was patched up along Welsh Ridge, not a little assisted by various isolated parties in the front line whose stubborn resistance delayed the Germans enough to let the Guards Division and some tanks come up and counter-attack, recovering Gouzeaucourt and most of the St. Quentin Ridge just East of it. But the real pivot of the British defence was the Twenty-Ninth Division. Had it given way it is hard to see what could have prevented the Germans from pushing on right across the salient and taking in rear the defenders of the Bourlon front, already sufficiently hard pressed by the main attack. Of all the Division's achievements hardly any other comes up to its stand on November 30th, when, with the enemy right in its rear and many of its guns in German hands, it not only maintained its positions but counter-attacked most successfully, driving the enemy back and re-establishing a line running S.W. from Masnières to join up with the Guards.

When the firing first started there was nothing to indicate to the 2nd S.W.B. that a really big attack was beginning. It was foggy and some time elapsed before any idea of what was

[1] The battalion was under orders to relieve the Border Regiment that evening.

happening could be obtained. Indeed it was not realized that things had gone seriously wrong till, about 10 a.m., the enemy were reported to be advancing in force across the 86th's rear and well over the Les Rues Vertes–La Vacquerie road.[1] Almost simultaneously rifle and machine gun fire was opened on Battalion Headquarters[2] from the rear. Colonel Raikes promptly turned out his Battalion Headquarters, lined the near bank of the canal and opened enfilade fire on the enemy who could be seen advancing in several lines South of the copse. This fire was efficacious: the enemy checked, lay down and opened fire in reply. While this fire-fight was being maintained Colonel Raikes collected another party and posted it North of the lock, where its fire could sweep the ground between Marcoing Copse and Les Rues Vertes. One company (D) had already reinforced the front line, and shortly afterwards, on an urgent appeal from the 86th Brigade, half B with two Lewis guns was dispatched to help that brigade, whose reserves, the Guernsey L.I. and the 2nd Royal Fusiliers, were making desperate efforts to recover Les Rues Vertes, into which the Germans had penetrated. However, the right of the German advance was effectively checked and this materially assisted the counter-attack from Marcoing which General Lucas and General Nelson of the 88th Brigade proceeded to launch. This was most successful. Aided by the battalion's fire from North of the canal, the K.O.S.B. and the 88th Brigade swept right forward, driving the Germans back over 2000 yards from the outskirts of Marcoing nearly to the Les Rues Vertes–La Vacquerie road. This success went far to secure the Welsh Ridge position, and the battalion, who had taken full advantage of the good targets afforded by the retreating Germans, contributed substantially to it.

The counter-attack had been delivered about 11 a.m., and shortly afterwards Colonel Raikes received orders to send two companies across the canal to dig in East of Marcoing Copse and facing Les Rues Vertes. C and the remaining half of B accordingly started digging in on the left of the 88th Brigade. A little later, A Company having also been brought across, it and C swung forward to face South instead of East, A connecting up with the 86th Brigade at Les Rues Vertes.[3] The German attacks were not renewed and the men were able to dig in well. That evening Captains Gibbon and Tragett brought up 64 men from the Corps Reinforcement camp, each of whom carried 250 rounds

---

[1] The first report was brought by the Master Cook, who was on the canal bank with the cookers, and so little did the situation seem to suggest any disaster that he was told not to spread rumours.

[2] On the canal bank North of Marcoing Copse.

[3] The battalion, though so weak, was holding a front of 1000 yards.

of extra ammunition besides his ordinary pouch allowance. Captain Gibbon took over C Company and Captain Tragett B.

The night (November 30th/December 1st) passed quietly enough. Rations were got up and issued and good progress was made with the trenches, but soon after dawn the enemy began bombarding Les Rues Vertes and Masnières and followed this up with renewed attacks in force. A Company was just on the edge of these attacks, which succeeded in penetrating into Les Rues Vertes. D, which had remained North of the canal, had to be thrown into the desperate fight for Masnières, while the enemy's attacks now extended to the bridge-head defences and Marcoing. These, however, held, and the 86th Brigade, fighting very stubbornly, retained its grip on Masnières and on the Western half of Les Rues Vertes. The situation here was obscure, so after dark the battalion sent two patrols to explore. That from A Company got touch with the 86th Brigade on the Western edge of the village, but C's ran into the enemy S.W. of it and was driven back, Second Lieutenant Windsor being missing. Masnières, however, now formed so pronounced and indefensible a salient that orders were issued for its evacuation during the night of December 1st/2nd, a new line about 650 yards in length being taken up West of Masnières and connecting at the lock with the bridge-head defences beyond the canal. This meant a readjustment of the battalion's position, A Company being drawn back into reserve but finding posts at the lock and at the river bridge near it. C threw back its left to face East parallel with the track leading from La Vacquerie to the lock, the half company of B continued the line to its left with a company of the Hampshire Regiment and some details beyond it and reaching down to the lock. Amongst other things this readjustment involved bringing the battalion cookers back across the canal by the lock bridge, which was now the most advanced and exposed post held by the battalion. During the night the exhausted remnants of the 86th Brigade[1] retired through the battalion's new line.

December 2nd proved fairly quiet. The battalion worked away at its defences under intermittent trench mortar fire, digging more trenches round Battalion Headquarters and reinforcing its post near the lock. But this quiet did not mean that the enemy had shot his bolt. Fairly early on December 3rd his guns started off again, maintaining a heavy bombardment of the battalion's front line and shelling the canal and Marcoing Copse. The battalion's position was a marked salient,[2] both flanks being

[1] With them were a few survivors of D Company and of the two platoons of B.
[2] The line held by the Newfoundland Regiment on the right swung back at right angles.

much exposed, and hard as the men had dug their hastily constructed trenches lacked dug-outs and wire. The defenders of the front line did their best, but about 11 a.m. the bombardment became intense and the enemy, advancing in great force under cover of the barrage, managed to rush the front trench, only a few of its garrison getting back to the support line 250 yards behind. Here, however, Battalion Headquarters and A Company, aided by the few survivors of B and C, put up a splendid fight. All the enemy's efforts to press on were successfully foiled by their steady fire, and on the right the Newfoundland Regiment, though its left company had been overwhelmed, held on stubbornly. Captain Somerville's coolness and leadership did

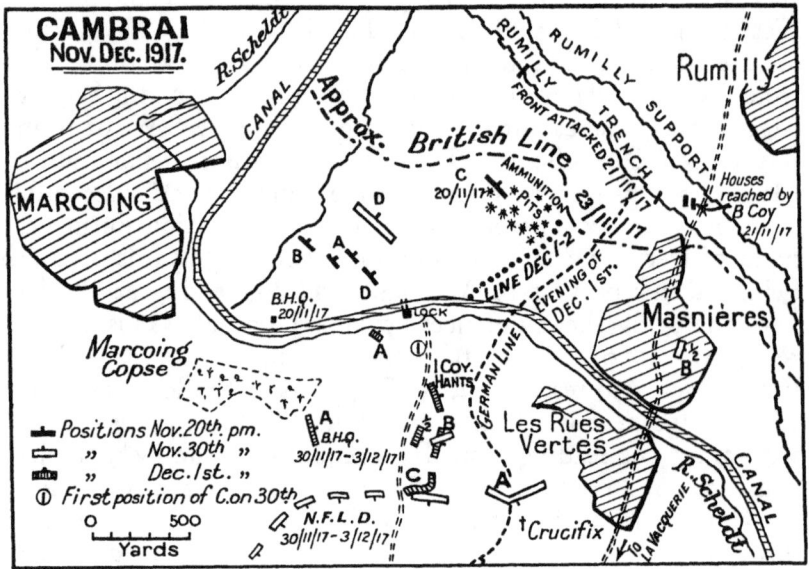

much to keep the defence going, and though the bursting shells threw up such dense clouds of dust that rifles positively jammed with it the Germans were somehow kept at bay. Unfortunately North of the canal, where the Sixth Division had relieved the 87th Brigade, the Germans managed to capture the front line of the bridge-head defences and, advancing in force into the loop of the canal, brought flanking machine gun fire to bear on the trenches to which the S.W.B. were clinging so tenaciously.[1] This fire was most damaging, inflicting many casualties, among those killed being Major Garnett, who had just arrived back off leave and had hurried up to rejoin the fighting line. However, the

[1] A message was received from Brigade Headquarters saying that the enemy had got into Marcoing well in rear of the battalion and asking if the S.W.B. could withdraw. Colonel Raikes, however, regarding this as quite impossible in daylight, preferred to hang on where he was.

THE END OF CAMBRAI

2nd, inspired by the splendid fearlessness of their C.O., who exposed himself continuously and set a magnificent example, stuck grimly to their position: counter-attacks by the Sixth Division recovered some ground North of the canal, and the German advance South of it was successfully checked.[1] Towards dusk the hostile fire died down, and then about 7 p.m. the Hampshires arrived to relieve the remnant of the 2nd S W.B. It was small enough; the C.O. and Adjutant, Second Lieutenant Hearder, and 73 men, with Captain Blake, the M.O.

On reaching the reserve trenches no ambulances were available to evacuate the wounded from the battalion aid post, so Captain Blake and some 50 men went right back to the aid post and removed seven stretcher-cases who must otherwise have been left behind, carrying them the whole way back to Ribecourt, to which the battalion now moved. At Ribecourt the men found a hot meal awaiting them with their blankets and were able to get a real rest. Next day came orders to march back to Sorel as the Division was being withdrawn from the fighting line. When orders arrived most of the exhausted men were still asleep, but they were roused in time to get their dinners before marching off at 2 p.m. Sorel was reached at 5.30 p.m., but it was not their ultimate destination. By 11 a.m. on December 5th the 87th Brigade was entraining at Etricourt for the familiar Arras " rest area," so terribly reduced that one train only was needed. That evening saw the 2nd S.W.B. established in billets at Liencourt, a battered and exhausted remnant.

"Cambrai" had indeed hit the 2nd hard. The last stage had added 200 names to its casualty list. Captain Tragett and Second Lieutenants Jordan, H. J. Edwards and Windsor were missing, Captain Gibbon and Second Lieutenants Cain and Netherclift[2] had been wounded: 12 men were known to be killed, 71 were wounded, 108 missing.[3] Major Garnett's loss was specially regretted. One of the first to join up in 1914, he had received his first wound with the 1st Battalion at Givenchy in December, 1914, had joined the 2nd just after Gallipoli, had served with it continuously, and had led it successfully on more than one occasion. A fine athlete and an "International" cricketer, he had proved himself a fine officer and had been one of the mainstays of the 2nd, while many of the N.C.O.'s who had fallen had been with the battalion some time and were also badly missed. Indeed, Colonel Raikes and his Adjutant found

---

[1] So much so that after dark Captain Gibbon, who had been lying wounded close to the trench taken by the Germans, was able to get away to the support trench.

[2] Second Lieutenant Netherclift subsequently died of his wounds.

[3] This made the total casualties 11 officers and 233 men killed and missing, 10 officers and 181 men wounded.

themselves confronted with the task of practically rebuilding the battalion all over again. Even so " Cambrai " is an " honour " of which the TWENTY-FOURTH may well be proud.[1] Both in the original attack and still more in its stubborn and protracted resistance to the German counter-attack the Twenty-Ninth Division had earned great praise. The Army and Corps commanders were warm in their recognition of its splendid work, and the defence of Masnières elicited special commendation from Sir Douglas Haig. In this the 2nd S.W.B. had taken their full share if they had had also its full share of losses, and the award of a bar to the D.S.O. to Colonel Raikes, of bars to the M.C. to Captains Somerville, Blake and Mumford, of the M.C. to Lieutenant Cooke, and of M.M.'s to Sergeants Key and Shaw, Corporal Richards, Lance Corporals Ackerman and Knight, and Privates Starr and Taylor was no more than their gallantry and endurance deserved. Nor must the 12th's contribution to the honour of " Cambrai " be forgotten. As it happened the Bourlon Wood fighting was that battalion's one " pitched battle " : it had certainly showed there conduct fully worthy of the Regiment and in keeping with its great traditions.

[1] It is among the ten selected to be borne on the King's Colour.

CHAPTER XXV

SALONICA IN 1917

WHILE 1917 had brought to the 4th Battalion the opportunity to get its own back after the previous year's disappointment and to share in a conspicuous success, no such chance had come to the 7th and 8th. Macedonia indeed had seen no such dramatic reversal of fortunes as had Mesopotamia, only renewed disappointment and heavy losses with nothing to show for them.

Into the complicated details of the abortive Allied offensive of 1917 in Macedonia a regimental chronicle cannot enter, especially as, where General Sarrail was concerned, political considerations and intrigues played so considerable a part. With so long a front, such formidable positions to attack, no real superiority in heavy artillery or in effective strength, no Allied offensive could have stood much chance of success at that time; certainly the piecemeal attacks to which General Sarrail committed first the French and Italians near Monastir (March), and then the British S.W. of Lake Doiran (April), were merely calculated to expend resources uselessly, while even what should have been a combined attack by Italians, Servians, French and British in May resolved itself into more or less simultaneous but uncoordinated efforts by the different contingents, all too deficient in weight and too ill-supported by artillery to be justifiable.

Being in Corps Reserve in April the 7th and 8th S.W.B. missed sharing in the Twelfth Corps' first abortive attack on the formidable Bulgarian positions between Lake Doiran and the Vardar, and though both were employed in May both only undertook minor diversions. Both therefore escaped the heavy losses suffered in the main operations, but the non-success of these attacks and the subsequent relapse into inactivity inevitably brought in their train depression and disappointment. Salonica was never an attractive or encouraging front, the difficult conditions, the want of facilities for rest and recreation, the virtual impossibility of getting leave to England, certainly not on any settled system, all combined to ensure that; "No one could feel chirpy in that climate," one officer writes. When to these hardships was added the sense of failure the monotony of the daily routine became increasingly felt, the more so because officers and men had always the feeling that given anything like equal conditions they could push the Bulgarians anywhere. But to expect them to capture positions like the Pip Ridge or Grand Couronné without an overwhelming artillery superiority, such as the B.S.F. never enjoyed, was demanding the impossible. Regimental officers and men do not usually concern themselves much with strategic considerations, but it was difficult at times to avoid wondering what useful purpose the B.S.F. was serving, whether any return was being secured for its labours and its losses in action and from the climate. There was certainly enough hard work to take men's minds off the strategical situation; when in the line units had their hands full with keeping their defences in order, being usually much below establishment and having so long a line to hold; when out of the line training took up what little time could be spared from camp sanitation and road-repairing. Still month after month crept past without any change in the strategical or tactical situation; even the occasional shifts from one sector to another usually seemed only to mean that other units entered into the fruits of the battalion's labours, while they themselves took over trenches and camps far below their standards of defensibility and sanitation, which had toilsomely to be brought up to those requirements before the next move to another equally unsatisfactory sector.

When the 67th Brigade came forward again after its long spell in Corps Reserve, the situation was that in the Doldzeli–Krastali sector Hill 380 and the position known as " P. $4\frac{1}{2}$ " had been captured and retained, though counter-attacks had wrested from the Twenty-Sixth Division the positions it had carried nearer Lake Doiran. The Twenty-Second Division now held the centre of the Twelfth Corps' line, having previously extended its line to include the Whaleback, a spur running West from the great " Pip " Ridge, on whose lower end the British had effected a lodgment. It was on this spur that the 7th S.W.B. relieved a battalion of the 65th Brigade on the night of May 1st/2nd, the 8th coming into line next evening further to the right and relieving a battalion of the Twenty-Sixth Division on the hump-like hill known as La Tortue. Things were fairly lively, not having quieted down again after the attack of April 24th; the Bulgarian guns and machine guns blazed away vigorously whenever any target presented itself; the British artillery retaliated readily and patrols were energetically trying to recover equipment and weapons from No Man's Land and to obtain information about the enemy's defences. Both battalions were actively employed on preparations for the renewed attack, timed for May 8th, and were lucky, considering the disturbed condition of affairs, to escape with only trifling casualties.

The main attack on May 8th was to be again delivered by the Twenty-Sixth Division between the Jumeaux Ravine and the lake, but the Twenty-Second and the Sixtieth on its left were both to push forward into the wide No Man's Land S.W. of Doldzeli, partly to divert attention from the main attack, partly to secure a more advanced line. Both battalions of the S.W.B. were to be employed; the 7th having orders to seize the Roach

THE ATTACK AT DOIRAN

Back, a spur running S.W. from P. 5 towards the Krastali nullah roughly parallel to the Whaleback: the 8th, the right battalion of the Division, were to raid the trenches confronting them across Claw Ravine so as to distract attention from the 7th Oxfordshire's attack on the Petit Couronné.

The heavy preliminary bombardment had damaged the Bulgarian wire and trenches considerably, but at the cost of warning the defence, and the 8th's raiders, 60 men under Captain Dickie and Second Lieutenant Cardwell, met a heavy barrage directly they left our lines—at 9.25 p.m. on May 8th. Though losing

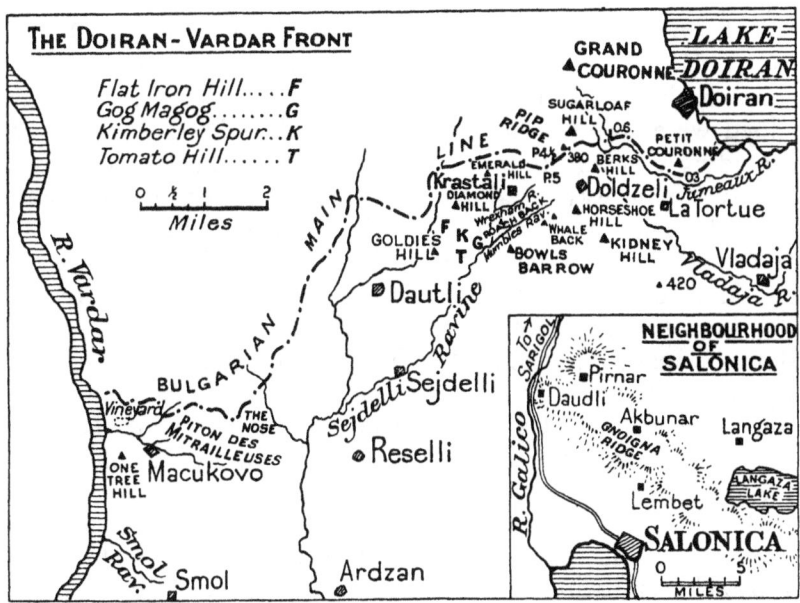

several men they pushed on, crossed Claw Ravine, and, finding the wire well cut, forced their way into the trenches at the point known as O. 6. Bombing parties promptly pushed out to right and left, and though the N.C.O.'s detailed to lead them were both hit two privates took charge, with such good results that a considerable distance was cleared on each flank. After waiting the prescribed time in the hostile trenches Captain Dickie gave the order to withdraw and the whole party got away successfully, the withdrawal being very effectively covered by the flanking fire of a Lewis gun detachment under Second Lieutenant Shearman. This, though in a very exposed position, maintained a rapid and effective fire, Second Lieutenant Shearman carrying on though twice wounded and directing the fire most skilfully. Then as the enemy crowded into their evacuated trenches our barrage crashed down, driving them out again. The raid thus achieved its purpose, and the Corps commander commented favourably on the " great determination " with which it had been carried out. The Oxfordshire had meanwhile taken the Petit Couronné and though repeatedly counter-attacked stubbornly maintained their hold; the rest of the attackers, however, had been ousted from the positions carried and the retention of the Petit Couronné was not worth the inevitable losses. Accordingly the 8th S.W.B. sent off D Company to assist the Oxfordshire to withdraw, which task was successfully accomplished, the 8th's total casualties, Second Lieutenant Montague and 4 men killed, Second Lieutenant Shearman and 17 men wounded, being remarkably light.[1]

The 7th meanwhile had had a more elaborate task. D Company (Major Gottwaltz) was to raid Krastali to distract attention from the Roach Back, which B and C under Captains Villar and Lloyd were to seize and entrench, A (Captain L. V. Williams) providing a strong covering party South of the Krastali nullah and Wrexham Ravine, along with a wiring party, the Whaleback being held in the meantime by the 11th R.W.F. Moving out at 8.30 p.m. the troops had reached the Roach Back by 9 p.m. and started work, dummy trenches being dug on the forward slope and the main position taken up some way down the reverse slope. Meanwhile the raiders had reached the wire in front of Krastali only to find the enemy fully on the alert. Searchlights were turned on and a heavy barrage brought down. Realizing that as all chance of surprise was gone to push on would involve very heavy casualties, Major Gottwaltz decided to retire, his withdrawal being covered by our guns who concentrated their fire on Krastali, apparently with good effect. Meanwhile spade and pick were being vigorously plied on the Roach Back, despite the shelling, being admirably organized by Captain Lloyd, while by moving the covering party slightly forward Captain Williams successfully avoided the barrage. By 3.15 a.m. the work had been so far completed, three lines of wire over 1000 feet long having been put up, that A and B could withdraw, leaving C in occupation. The steadiness of the troops was most creditable, especially as nearly half the men were under serious fire for the first time, and the battalion was warmly congratulated by the Divisional commander. It remained in the line for several days, completing the consolidation. There was some shelling and a few more casualties, the total rising to 4 men killed and 1 officer (Second Lieutenant G. E. P. Williams) and 31 men wounded.

For the rest of May " a certain liveliness " prevailed on the Doiran–Vardar front. The consolidation of the advanced line

---

[1] For good conduct in this raid a man under a " suspended " sentence by court martial had his punishment remitted.

was completed, to the accompaniment of intermittent Bulgarian shelling, and the Twenty-Second Division had both to extend to the left, relieving the Sixtieth, and to push forward on the new frontage. This was begun (May 14th to 15th) when both S.W.B. battalions were out of the line, but on May 19th the 8th took over the so-called " Tomato " sector, where advanced positions had been occupied along Kimberley Spur and the hills known as Gog and Magog and Anvil, 600 yards nearer to the Bulgarian trenches than our main line of resistance, here some 1200 yards from the enemy's front. The Bulgarians were doing much night firing to hamper the consolidation and the 8th had a memorable and strenuous week, being persistently shelled or swept by machine gun fire. However, the Bulgarians did not venture on any infantry attacks, and when the 8th got back to Paliasse Camp, they had the satisfaction of leaving the Tomato Hill–Gog and Magog line reasonably secure; good trenches had been dug despite the rocky soil and much wire put up. They were luckier too as regards casualties[1] than the 7th who, after holding the Bowls Barrow trenches, S.W. of the Whaleback, for four nights, shifted on to that ridge on the 25th/26th and came in for a fearful shelling next day which cost them over 50 casualties, including Captain L. V. Williams and Lieutenant C. E. Williams, who were killed by the same shell. Both officers had gone overseas with the battalion in September, 1915, and were very much regretted.[2] Company Sergeant Major Probert did splendid work on this occasion, helping the surviving officers with the company to carry on.

By this time all idea of continuing the Allied offensive had been abandoned; indeed it had been decided to transfer the Tenth and Sixtieth Divisions to Palestine to assist in breaking through the Gaza–Beersheba Line. This meant for the Divisions remaining in Macedonia more line to hold and in consequence more work in maintaining it, without any chances of distinction in active operations. The Bulgarians made no attempt to profit by the departure of a third of the B.S.F., and beyond intermittent bombardments and occasional small raids remained inactive. For the rest of 1917 the 7th S.W.B.'s battle casualties were under 60, those of the 8th being scarcely heavier. Unfortunately the same did not apply to the sick-rate. Despite unceasing attention to the sanitation of camps and trenches and the assiduity of the Medical Officers the sick-rate was hard to keep down. In July the 7th could boast the lowest figures in the Division for malaria, but early in August a tour in " D "

---

[1] Their losses were 5 killed and 18 wounded.
[2] Lieutenant Dick, who had become Adjutant in April, was now promoted to Captain.

sector, the advanced line taken up in May, where there was practically no protection against the fierce rays of the sun, sent the sick-rate jumping up. The daily average of sick reached 340, 160 men went to hospital, barely half that number returned. In September things were even worse, the daily average rose to 540, over 300 men went to hospital, and the battalion, which had had nearly 800 effectives at the end of July, was down below 400,[1] many of them quite unfit for heavy duty. Matters improved somewhat with the advent of colder weather. In October over three times as many were returned from hospital as were sent down to it. November and December saw this improvement continued, and the 7th ended the year with a daily sick-rate of little over 200 and with 26 officers and 770 men—nominally—effective.

With the 8th things went on much the same. July and August saw the effectives dwindling as the great heat and the mosquitoes sent man after man to hospital. In September, however, things improved, and thanks to two substantial drafts, totalling 121 men, the battalion had nearly 700 effectives. In November the return of cold weather brought on attacks of fever in many who had previously suffered from malaria, and on December 31st the 8th mustered only 21 officers and 622 men.

Both battalions had suffered many changes. The 7th had lost Colonel Grimwood in July, when he returned to England for a special appointment, his health being unequal to the Macedonian climate. He had done great work for the battalion, had identified himself with its interests in every way and had been invaluable in training it. His successor, Lieutenant Colonel A. D. Macpherson of the Cameron Highlanders, proved only a bird of passage. After being in charge of the brigade most of the two months of his nominal command, he received substantive command of it on September 5th, on General Cooke leaving for India. In his place Lieutenant Colonel D. Burges of the Gloucestershire Regiment was appointed. Major Bradbury soon afterwards went on medical leave and did not return, and several subalterns, among them two of the officers who had originally gone overseas with it, Lieutenants J. N. Taylor and Gilmore-Ellis, transferred to the Flying Corps or to the Indian Army, so that the commissioned ranks changed considerably. Two other " originals " received recognition for their constant good work, Captain Burn[2] and Lieutenant Dick being awarded the M.C. in the June Honours List, Major Gottwaltz and Captain Mills obtained that reward in the 1918 New Year's distribution, when

[1] D Company had to hold 1200 yards of front within 300 yards of the Bulgarian line with 47 men, including cooks and sanitary men.
[2] Captain Burn was appointed Staff Captain of the 78th Brigade.

Company Sergeant Majors Hall and Probert got D.C.M.'s, while Sergeants Page, O'Neill and Thain got the M.M., and Major Gottwaltz, Captain Dick, Sergeants Doran, Elliott and Thomas, Corporals McDonald and Norman and Private Moore were all " mentioned."

The 8th also had a change of C.O. In June Colonel Bruce went to hospital with a bad knee, Major Sharp officiating in his absence. Colonel Bruce returned on July 23rd, but was transferred to the 9th Border on September 30th, when Major Sharp succeeded to the command. He, however, went to hospital early in October, and Major Dobbs of the R. Irish Fusiliers joined on the 11th and took command, Major Sharp being invalided to England shortly afterwards. In August Captain Franklin was promoted to be Major and second in command, while Captain F. T. Williams had taken over the Adjutancy.[1] Lieutenants Dickie, Laurie, Harvey, Wood and Woolley all went up a step in rank, apart from acting-promotions. Several new officers arrived, including a new Quartermaster, Lieutenant A. Carter (August), as Lieutenant Sellicks had been invalided, but what with sickness and transfers there were never more than enough for the work.

Both 7th and 8th found the second half of 1917 singularly uneventful. During their tours in the line they both usually found their opponents very quiet and disinclined to leave their trenches even to patrol No Man's Land. They on their part were precluded from undertaking anything more than mere patrolling by their numerical weakness. This did not, however, prevent them from developing great activity in this work. In August Lieutenant Woolley and four men of the 8th, Corporal James and Privates Martin, Skeath and Joyce, earned the Brigadier's praise by daring work in Jumeaux Ravine, and in September Lieutenant Woolley with Second Lieutenant Cardwell and Corporal J. Williams carried out a daylight reconnaissance of Krastali. They were seen and shelled, but escaped by crawling through some thick undergrowth and eventually reached the enemy's wire. This they were about to cut when bombs were thrown at them; however, they managed to give the artillery a prearranged signal and got away under cover of the promptly put down barrage. Obtaining information for the artillery was an important function of these patrols and much useful work was accomplished, while several of the " mentions "[2]

---

[1] He was Gazetted to that post in June but had been officiating for some months before that.

[2] These included Lieutenant Colonel Bruce, Major Sharp, Captain Dickie, Lieutenants Woolley and Bodenham, Sergeants Cooper, McPherson, Sherman, Tarrant and Corporal J. Williams. Five M.M.'s were also awarded to N.C.O.'s and men.

which the 8th obtained in Sir G. Milne's Dispatch of November 13th, 1917, were earned by good patrolling, while Lieutenant Woolley got an M.C. and Corporal Williams the M.M. The 8th also distinguished itself by winning the trophy offered by General Duncan at the Divisional Sports for the most successful unit competing, the 7th being the runners-up, but its story, like that of the 7th, was marked by a few outstanding incidents, though a high-explosive shell which completely demolished the officers' mess in Bude Camp in August nearly added a sad page to the battalion's history as several officers, the C.O. and Quartermaster in particular, had very narrow escapes.

CHAPTER XXVI

THE LAST WINTER

THE close of the Cambrai fighting, marked by the British withdrawal from Marcoing and Bourlon to the Flesquières Ridge, was followed for the British forces in France by some gloomy months. The high hopes with which 1917 had opened had not been fulfilled. The collapse of Russia had been the first thing to go wrong, then had come the French failure in April, and the disproportionate share in the fighting in which this had involved the British Armies. Add to these the tremendous exertions and losses which this fighting had entailed, particularly in the long struggle against the all-engulfing mud of "Third Ypres," the disappointing results which those exertions had achieved despite the terrible casualties, and then on top of all Caporetto and the bitter disappointment over Cambrai. The large forces available for the German counter-attack were a nasty revelation of what Russia's retirement from the war had involved, and the enforced evacuation of so much of the ground won had put a very different complexion on what had once promised to provide the year's vicissitudes with a hopeful ending. True, millions of men were getting ready in America, but America was far away, and the American forces, whatever their as yet unproved value might turn out, were a potential rather than a practical assistance. It was not certain that they would arrive in time. Worst of all was the situation with regard to British " man power," a problem which presented itself to British regimental officers and men in the shape of the unsatisfactory situation with regard to drafts. Drafts had been none too plentiful in 1917, particularly in the later stages. Battalions had rarely found their "trench strength" anywhere near a satisfactory figure, particularly in the "quiet" sectors: attacking battalions had often "gone over the top" with no more than 500 bayonets, casualties had been but slowly replaced, and when drafts did appear a large proportion had been produced by "combing out" the A.S.C. and other "departmental" units. Returned wounded seemed to be coming back rather sooner than of old, after less time for recovery and rest, medical standards seemed to be growing less severe, to judge by some of the reinforcements received, and it was evident that the authorities were finding it increasingly difficult to keep units anywhere near establishment.

Another feature of the situation that could not help striking those who gave heed to anything beyond purely personal and immediate considerations was the work required when "out of the line" in preparing rear defences. "Army Lines," "Corps Lines," and other fortifications were being constructed in places well back behind the fighting zone, a very laudable precaution, but hardly calculated to inspire confidence or promising a speedy advance in the spring. Periods in the line, too, tended to be more prolonged, even though the line was rather more thinly held, continuous trenches being abandoned in favour of systems of mutually supporting " posts," with wire between them, while a battalion in the line usually found the frontage assigned to it longer than heretofore. Spells in the line and the frontages to be held increased again in January, when some 28 miles of front were taken over from the French. But the most disturbing factor was the reduction of every infantry brigade by one battalion. This was not only a confession of the inadequacy of our means, but involved a considerable disturbance of the tactical principles on which our troops had been working. Clearly the dispositions appropriate to brigades of four battalions did not apply equally well to brigades of three; and though the disbanded units provided drafts to bring other depleted battalions up to establishment the scattering of officers and men who had got accustomed to work together was in itself a disadvantage. As a rule officers and men found their way to another battalion of the same regiment, but even so they took some time to settle down and become completely assimilated.

After their unpleasant experiences on the Passchendaele Ridge the 1st S.W.B. had had, as already mentioned, over three weeks "out of the line," before returning to the Salient. From December 5th to 12th the battalion was in reserve or support to its brigade, N.E. of Woesten, and then in the front line South of Houthulst Forest till December 16th. This was a shocking bit of line, no trenches, merely shell holes " in a state of defence," and the men were extremely uncomfortable. Fortunately the enemy were quiet and the four days in the line brought only four casualties. Turns in support and in the Eikhoek reserve area followed, and then the battalion moved up to the canal bank for work under a Tunnelling Company R.E. The end of 1917 found it again in support near Woesten. Colonel Fowler was evacuated sick on December 21st and was replaced by Major D. G. Johnson, who joined on the 26th, having vacated a Staff appointment.

January was not much more eventful than December. The New Year Honours brought Sergeant Dare a D.C.M. for excellent work on patrols, he was always going out and bringing back useful information. The battalion did eight days in the line (Jan. 5th to 12th), "a quiet time though the hostile artillery showed increased activity" is the description in the war diary; it was then "out" till the 25th, during which time 10 officers and 25 N.C.O.'s of the 2nd Battalion came over to pay it a most enjoyable visit, a performance by the Divisional theatrical troupe and a smoking concert in the Sergeants' Mess being prominent features.

From January 25th to February 8th the 1st was on the canal bank, working on roads and drainage and on salvage, followed by ten days at Hospital Farm, training. Several drafts appeared: one of 102 on the 18th, mostly boys but containing 20 recovered wounded of the November fighting, another of 32 on the 16th, five officers[1] and 177 other ranks from the recently disbanded 12th Battalion on January 31st, and then on February 8th five officers and 83 men, while on February 17th Colonel Taylor resumed command.[2] Casualties had been few and admissions to hospital not specially high, so the battalion was up to a quite respectable figure again. The last days of February were spent in reserve in the Hill Top Farm area working on the back lines, and on March 6th it went up into the front line, having Battalion Headquarters at Hubner Farm. Here the 1st for the only time in the war found themselves alongside their own 2nd Battalion who were holding the next sector to the right. It was the first time the two battalions had met since the Zulu War. Things proved fairly quiet, though alarms that the Germans were going to attack put our patrols on the alert to discover the hostile intentions, in which Lieutenants Wales and R. G. Evans were conspicuous. Actually the battalion's defence was never tested, though on March 11th the Germans attacked the Twenty-Ninth Division, thereby giving the 2nd S.W.B. the chance of distinguishing themselves greatly.

The 1st was in line till March 12th, in support for two days, then in line again for 48 hours in the next sub-sector to the left, with two platoons at Poelcappelle. This sub-sector included a post known as Meunier House, which for some reason attracted the enemy's special attention. It was constantly shelled and two Lewis gun teams were knocked out. Otherwise the time was quiet and casualties were low. This spell over the battalion was back at Hill Top Farm for the next twelve days, working on the Army Line. The end of the month brought another turn in the front line, which ended early in April when the Thirty-Sixth Division arrived to relieve it. On relief (April 6th) the battalion moved back to Hospital Farm Camp, where it found eleven officers from the disbanded 11th Battalion who had been posted to it, among them Major C. D. Phillips and Captain W. T.

[1] Captain Francis, Lieutenant Pozzi, Second Lieutenants Dilloway, T. O. Phillips and Woodward.
[2] Major Johnson then reverted to second in command but was transferred in March to command the 2nd Royal Sussex in the 2nd Brigade. Captain Copner also left to join the R.F.C. and Captain Manley transferred to the Indian Army.

Harris. Here the 1st spent a busy day, completing its kit and generally getting ready for a move to an unspecified destination. After four months of relative quiet it was about to be plunged into the hottest of the fighting again.

Like the 1st Battalion the 2nd had spent a fairly uneventful winter. After Cambrai it had been given ten days' welcome rest at Liencourt in excellent billets, most of them actually having wire beds. Some reorganization and training had proved possible and nine new officers[1] and 73 men joined. On December 17th the battalion started in very cold weather on a three days' march to Embry, in the Wizernes training area. Part of the way lay over hilly country, and deep snowdrifts made marching difficult and greatly delayed the transport of most of the brigade. The 2nd S.W.B. had an old campaigner as Transport Officer in Lieutenant T. R. Williams, and as he had taken the precaution to pursue a more circuitous route over flatter ground its transport arrived up to time. At Embry the battalion remained until December 31st, being visited by its old Divisional Commander, General Hunter-Weston, under whom it found itself once more, and being joined by a draft of 137 men under Second Lieutenants Pratt and G. F. Smith. On the 31st it started on a four days' march to the Proven neighbourhood. January 5th found it encamped at Boesinghe and busily employed on the Army Line West of the Steenbeek, mainly wiring and making machine gun emplacements. The 1st Battalion being nearby the opportunity was taken, as already related, to visit it. News was now received that Colonel Raikes had been given a Brevet-Majority,[2] that the Quartermaster's constant good work had won him an M.C., and that Company Sergeant Major Hillier had been awarded the D.C.M. Colonel Raikes, Lieutenant T. R. Williams and Sergeants Blair and Duckin were also mentioned in Dispatches.

On January 18th the battalion moved forward to Brandhoek on the Division taking over the Passchendaele sector. After a week in reserve it went forward to Abraham Heights, and put in some solid work on the Divisional line. On February 3rd it took over support positions near Bellevue,[3] being heavily shelled on the Gravenstafel road when moving up and having

---

[1] Second Lieutenants P. H. Franks, H. G. Arnold, G. P. Davies, J. E. A. Gibbs, W. S. Parry, W. H. Morris, A. Rees, E. F. Russell and J. E. Seager.
[2] Substantively he was only a Captain.
[3] Another ten officers had been posted to the battalion during January, all except Lieutenant Holyoake being new-comers. Captain Somerville had been promoted temporary Major and had become second in command, Captain Page succeeding him as Adjutant.

15 casualties, while directly it reached Bellevue two officers were hit by the same shell, Second Lieutenant W. H. Morris being killed and Second Lieutenant Parry wounded. Two days later it relieved the Border Regiment in the front "line," a series of small posts and short lengths of trench.

This sector was hardly an encouraging specimen to sample as one's first experience of "the line," which this was for four-fifths of the 500 men with the companies.[1] It had hardly any wire, communication trenches did not exist, the ground was pitted with shell holes full of water, there were too many unburied dead about to be sanitary, and the scattered posts and short trenches needed linking up. The 2nd accomplished something towards this end, but the tour was not altogether satisfactory, for largely through the inexperience of the majority of the men one of D Company's posts was surprised and bombed, and next day No. 13 Post, held by C Company, was rushed and the garrison killed or taken, though the posts on either side managed to bring fire to bear on the retiring raiders and knocked over several. Altogether the 2nd had nearly 40 casualties while in line, and was not sorry to be "out" in the Watou area most of the rest of February. Five officers[2] and 152 men, mostly from the 12th Battalion, joined on the 12th. On February 26th the battalion moved to Poperinghe for work on the Army line, and then on March 9th it took over the front line on the Goudberg Spur.

Here it was on the ground over which the 1st Battalion had attacked in November, the two companies in the line having their headquarters at Virile Farm, and facing Vat Cottages on the left and Void and Velox Farms on the right. The line still consisted of scattered posts and, though these were fairly dry, the wire was indifferent and no communication trenches existed. The company in reserve was kept very busy "carrying," as rations had to be brought up by hand from 3000 yards away. Two days passed quietly with a little hostile shelling, and then, about 7 a.m. on March 11th, the enemy suddenly put down a barrage on the front and support trenches and advanced in force to the attack. They came on in two lines and probably amounted to a whole battalion, as the lowest estimate put them at 400 strong. Fortunately their barrage was not very accurate, the shells mostly falling behind the front line, and B and C Companies met the attack with a heavy and

[1] The recent drafts had consisted mainly of boys from the "graduated battalions" though there was a fair proportion of recovered wounded. On this occasion only two officers had been in the line with the battalion before.

[2] Second Lieutenants Hardwick, H. Jones, L. R. Jones, W. H. Morgan and Pemberton. Second Lieutenant Parry also rejoined on recovery from wounds.

effective fire from rifles and Lewis guns, in face of which the enemy tended to bunch, affording better targets than ever. At one point, where the ruins of Vox Farm slightly impeded B's field of fire, the advance made better progress, but Lewis guns from the right caught and stopped the Germans here also, and the whole attack was quickly brought to a standstill. Second Lieutenant Seager, who had hurried forward to his company's front line position directly the attack began, did splendid work, moving across the open from post to post under a heavy fire, directing the men's fire most effectively and inspiring them by his magnificent example. Captain Bennett in the same way went along his line, which also consisted of detached posts, and Lance Corporal Turton did capital work in indicating targets, besides shooting down several men himself. Two subsequent efforts to renew the attack were also frustrated and when, twenty minutes later, reinforcements attempted to come forward past Void Farm it was not long before the S.W.B.'s steady fire sent their survivors running back. Colonel Raikes promptly sent forward a fresh supply of ammunition, which was running short, but it was not needed; the reception of the attack had evidently discouraged its repetition, though from the battalion observation post at Goudberg the German front line could be seen to be crowded. Indeed, instead of reinforcements stretcher-bearers came forward under the Red Cross and proceeded to carry away the wounded. Their journeys made it possible to estimate with fair accuracy the German casualties. At least 100 men were carried back, besides many "walking wounded." As the S.W.B.'s casualties only amounted to 17, including Second Lieutenant Seager wounded, the battalion had good cause for satisfaction over the episode.[1] Young and quite inexperienced as most of its men were their steadiness and spirit had been admirable, and their musketry, if not quite up to 1914 standards, most effective, while excellent use was made of Lewis guns.

After this the battalion was "out" for three days (March 13th to 15th) and then had another week in front line, just to the left of its last position. This was marked by unusual activity on the part of the German guns, while on the 19th some raiding parties attempted to bomb the posts at a salient in A Company's line North of Tournant Farm but were repulsed, a useful identification being obtained off a German killed just in front of our wire. Casualties for this tour came to nearly 30, including several men gassed,[2] but the battalion had the satisfaction of

[1] Captain Bennett and Second Lieutenant Seager received the M.C. and Lance Corporal Turton the D.C.M.

[2] For March the battalion had 12 men killed, 13 gassed and 30 with 1 officer wounded.

doing some very effective sniping and effecting considerable improvements in the wire and trenches.

Twelve days in reserve followed, during which the battalion "bathed and deloused," as the war diary puts it, worked on the Divisional reserve line and received a draft of 33 men, including a C.S.M. and several N.C.O.'s in exchange for "war-worn" men posted to the Home establishment for temporary duty. It was well up to establishment on paper now, mustering 38 officers and 1027 men on March 31st, though effectively it was considerably weaker, the 29 officers and 887 "O.R." of the April 1st return being a much more correct approximation to its available fighting force. On April 2nd it went back into the line again, holding a series of posts covering the ruins of Passchendaele. This was a horrid piece of line, the ground was waterlogged, several posts were so shallow that by day it was impossible to stand up in them and the wire was very bad. However, the enemy was quiet, apart from some heavy shelling on the 5th, which cost the company in the intermediate line 3 killed and 5 wounded, and the battalion's patrols, which were active despite the swampiness of No Man's Land, encountered no opposition. On the night of April 8th/9th a battalion of the Forty-First Division, much reduced by heavy fighting on the Somme, arrived to relieve the 2nd whom the next evening found at St. Jan ter Biezen,[1] in readiness to be thrown into the battle which had just opened with the German break through the Portuguese at Neuve Chapelle.

While the 1st and 2nd Battalions had spent the winter in the Ypres Salient the 5th, after its long spell in Flanders, had found its way to the other end of the British front in the middle of December and for the next three months was busily engaged on rear defences near Havrincourt. Detachments were occasionally employed nearer the front and it was among these that the casualties mostly occurred. January cost the battalion nearly 50 men and February another dozen. Hostile aeroplanes were now a serious trouble in back areas, and on the night of January 27th they bombed the 5th's transport lines and killed or damaged twenty horses and mules. Major Croft and Captain B. O. Jones rejoined in January and took over D and A Companies respectively. Captain Caldwell was wounded and evacuated to hospital in that month, and two officers[2] and 50 men joined from the 12th Battalion on February 8th. This was the only reinforcement received, and early in March, in accordance with

[1] Nine officers from the 11th Battalion joined here, among them Captains I. A. Morgan and Dendy.
[2] Second Lieutenants Chapman and Hart.

the revision of establishments of Pioneer battalions, A Company was broken up and its men distributed among the other companies, one of the many discouraging signs of the shortage of available reinforcements. In the Dispatches published in December Major Oxley, Captains Caldwell, I. T. Evans and B. O. Jones, Lieutenant and Quartermaster Bryant, Second Lieutenants White and J. R. L. Jones, Regimental Sergeant Major Francis, Company Sergeant Major Searle and Sergeant Winston were " mentioned," and the New Year " Honours " brought Captain Bence Trower a well merited M.C. and the D.C.M. to C.S.M. Searle. But on the whole these months were uneventful, almost monotonous. But if the battalion's work lacked variety, it did not lack difficulty. One entry in the January diary, " no impression could be made on mud and water and some time was spent in digging men out," about epitomizes the obstacles against which the 5th had to struggle. What they accomplished despite these difficulties may be gathered from the warm praises received from those in authority: " magnificent work; the men must have worked like Trojans " was one message from the Brigadier, and both in wiring and in trench digging it accomplished a portentous amount before, on March 21st, the storm broke on the Third Army's frontage.

Like the 5th the 6th were busy during the winter of 1917-1918, if their experiences also were lacking in excitement and variety. From the beginning of October till the end of November its Division held the Givenchy sector. Things were quiet here and casualties infrequent, only eight in all in October. This was fortunate, as drafts were scarce and small, though several officers joined, among them Captains Hitchcock and N. G. Pearson and Lieutenant Amos, who had been wounded in May, 1916. In October Colonel Hewett, who had successfully commanded the battalion for so long, returned to England, Major T. N. Fitzpatrick, R.E., taking over the command.

In December the Twenty-Fifth Division moved farther South, taking over the Bullecourt sector, some 6000 yards in length. The battalion's main work in this sector was to construct an intermediate line, a task which kept it well employed all through the winter months. A draft of 100 " B 1 " men joined on December 29th, but in exchange the same number of " A " category were transferred to the 12th Battalion, and after that only some driblets were received. Major Reid-Kellett proceeded home on a tour of duty in January, Captain Deane being promoted to Major and becoming second in command in his place, and Sergeant Glenister became R.S.M. on Regimental Sergeant Major Cox being given six months home duty. February brought orders for the reorganization of the battalion in three companies, B being the company to be sacrificed.[1] That same month Battalion Headquarters were transferred from Fremicourt to Achiet-le-Grand, where they were still established on March 21st.

As already mentioned the Thirty-Eighth Division had found its way to the Lys valley after its second turn in " Third Ypres," and till the middle of April it remained in that area, shifting at times from one sector to another between Laventie and Armentières, but never quitting the low-lying and usually waterlogged flats. The Lys valley had long enjoyed the reputation of being " quiet," indeed between Armentières and Fauquissart the line had scarcely changed since October, 1914, and during the Thirty-Eighth Division's long sojourn nothing happened to change its character. The worst feature of this quarter was its wetness. To keep the country drained even in fairly fine weather was difficult, and the natural drainage had been completely disarranged by the digging of trenches, which tended to fill with water and become themselves little better than drains. The line, therefore, was largely breastworks, which needed far more work to keep them in repair than trenches did. As some compensation there were many trees and hedges still standing quite close up to the line, the country had not been mangled out of all recognition by shell fire, and in places one could get up to the front line under cover.

Both 10th and 11th had come out of " Third Ypres " considerably below establishment, and as a rule the battalion nominally " out of the line " had to leave two companies behind to provide supports for the battalion " in," whereby its rest was very much curtailed. The Division was holding a longish stretch and in consequence the demands on the battalions were pretty heavy, while the line consisted mainly of detached posts often some distance apart. This offered opportunities to an enterprising enemy, and the Germans were fairly energetic about raiding. On September 19th, shortly after the 10th had taken over the L'Epinette sub-sector, a party variously estimated at 40 and 200 attacked one of the right company's posts. The attack was preceded by ten minutes' heavy bombardment, but Second Lieutenant Sibly, hearing that the N.C.O. in charge of the post had been killed, hurried forward from the main trench and took command. His coolness and resource encouraged the men greatly and they received the raiders with so effective a fire from rifles and machine guns that the party was broken up and on our barrage coming down fell back, leaving a prisoner

[1] This meant the transfer of 180 men to the three surviving companies.

behind.¹ This was by no means an isolated incident, but the British more often delivered than received these attacks. The Division was determined to establish a firm control over No Man's Land and patrolled with great vigour. Both 10th and 11th sent out many fighting patrols and frequently encountered the enemy. More than one " scrap " ended in the capture of prisoners and useful identifications: thus one near Pear Tree Farm on November 22nd established the presence of the 2nd Guards Reserve Division opposite the Thirty-Eighth, on another occasion in October Corporal Rogers and Private Evans of D Company of the 11th received certificates for distinguished service from the Divisional Commander for capturing two Germans on patrol, and in December a German patrol was met and defeated by one from the 10th, two Germans being killed and one taken, whereby the presence of a division recently arrived from Russia was discovered. The 11th again beat off several small raids. Once, when a very dark night had enabled the Germans to get into a post, Sergeant Brice dashed at them and single-handed expelled them, taking a prisoner, for which he was deservedly awarded the M.M.

The main event of the autumn months was the 10th's great raid. This, carried out on the night of November 7th/8th, was quite a big affair, ten officers and 270 men, virtually all available from A, B and C Companies,² being employed under Captain W. T. Cobb with Captain Davenport as his second in command. Incandescent Trench, the frontage attacked, had been systematically bombarded for some days and the wire effectively cut on a frontage of 300 yards. It presented no obstacle and the raiders penetrated to the support line 200 yards farther back. One detachment missed its way but Captain Davenport went back and guided it to the right spot and so enabled it to carry out its tasks. The party remained in the German trenches over an hour, during which time it blew up three concrete dug-outs, accounted for at least 50 Germans and brought back 15 more as prisoners. An admirably accurate box barrage round the section attacked contributed greatly to the success of the raid, and though the casualties amounted to nearly fifty, most of these were but lightly wounded and only five men were killed. Captain Davenport again did excellent work organizing the removal of the wounded and himself returned to the enemy's lines to fetch in two men who had been left behind. It was easily one of the Division's most successful raids and reflected

---

¹ Second Lieutenant Sibly received the M.C. and Lance Corporals T. Edwards and J. Taylor and Private G. G. Dover the M.M. for their gallantry on this occasion.

² Companies were so weak that they were all organized as two platoons.

THE LAST WINTER

considerable credit on Captain Cobb's organization and training of the raiding party.[1]

The 11th had been so unlucky as to lose their new C.O., Colonel Angus, by accident : he was drowned when bathing in the Lys on September 17th. Major J. E. C. Partridge, of the Welch Regiment, a well-known Army Rugby football player, succeeded him, but left the battalion in October for the 10th Welch, when the command passed to Major T. H. Morgan, who had just rejoined, Major O'Kelly leaving shortly afterwards to rejoin the R.W.F. Major E. T. Rees was promoted from the 10th to command the 7th Norfolk and Major Gibson Watt was invalided, Major Bowen now becoming second in command. Captain Orford rejoined in December but had to go to hospital again at the end of March, while on February 1st Lieutenant W. Whitworth joined as Quartermaster in place of Lieutenant Kenslade who had been invalided. On the whole neither battalion suffered heavily, although the Germans at times went in rather extensively for gas shelling. Exclusive of their raid casualties the 10th had only four men killed and 17 wounded in November, and that was a month of rather greater activity. One notable incident of the autumn was the attachment of the Portuguese to the Division for instructional purposes. The men, many of whom were fishermen and very decent fellows, proved a good hard-working lot, when under British supervision, and got on quite well with their instructors.

The middle of January[2] saw the whole Division out of the line for a spell of nearly a month, one of the longest rests it had ever enjoyed. Unluckily bad weather interfered greatly with the training, some of the farms in which the troops were billeted were islands in a sea of flood water, and the rest was badly cut into by demands for working parties to help with the construction of the new rear lines on the far bank of the Lys, a task on which battalions in reserve found themselves increasingly employed. By the middle of February the Division was back in the line, having taken over the Wez Macquart sector, but by this time the 10th was the only representative of the TWENTY-FOURTH in the Division. The order already mentioned had gone out for the reduction of all brigades by one battalion, and as the junior battalion of the Regiment in the Division the 11th S.W.B. was among those to be broken up.

---

[1] Captains Cobb and Davenport received the M.C. for this raid.
[2] The New Year Honours included among other things a D.C.M. for Regimental Sergeant Major Davies of the 11th Battalion, whose constant good work and devotion to duty had thoroughly earned a reward. Regimental Sergeant Major Lockie, who had been a pillar of strength to the 10th as R.S.M. for over two years, also received the M.C.

Its disbandment took place in February, seven officers and 150 men being transferred to the 10th on February 16th. Detachments were also dispatched to join the 1st and 2nd S.W.B., 15 officers being posted to the former battalion and nine to the latter, but the bulk of the battalion was kept together for some little time longer under the title of the 2nd Entrenching Battalion and was not finally dispersed till early in April.[1] In its two years of active service overseas the 11th had borne itself well and had earned an excellent reputation: the attack of July 31st, 1917, on the Pilckem Ridge stands out as its most conspicuous and notable achievement, but even apart from that great day it had done steady work in the face of hardships and difficulties.

The 10th continued in the same part of the line for some weeks after the disbanding of the 11th. Things were quiet on the whole, but as March wore on the enemy's artillery became decidedly more active, and as our guns retaliated in proportion "a certain liveliness" soon prevailed. "The enemy continued his unpleasant industry," runs the entry in the battalion diary for March 19th, "and got two directs on Battalion H.Q., one on the mess, one on the cook-house." On this day the battalion was fortunate in escaping without casualties, but the toll mounted up. However, a successful raid by B and D Companies in the early hours of March 28th did a good deal to redress the balance. Admirably led by Captain Cottam they assaulted and carried Include Trench which faced a salient in our lines. Second Lieutenant A. Morgan was well to the fore; forcing his way through the wire despite heavy fire from machine guns, he rushed a post, killing five of the garrison and taking two prisoners. He then pushed on to a dug-out and bombed and killed its occupants. Sergeant Hughes and Lance Corporal Lane were also to the fore and the net result of the raid[2] was the capture of six prisoners and the killing of some 25 more enemy at a cost of eight wounded. Next day came orders for the battalion's relief by the 2/5th King's Own of the Fifty-Seventh Division, and the end of March found the 10th at Haverskerque, preparing for sterner work. A draft of 144 men had just arrived and had brought the 10th's strength up to a respectable figure again.

---

[1] Of about 750 men still on the 11th's strength at the end of February about 200 were posted to the 5th Battalion early in April, but a party who had not been posted to any unit were actually thrown into the fighting on the Lys and nearly 70 of them were "struck off" in May as missing. Their defence of Merville (cf. pp. 411–412) may be regarded as the last fight of the 11th.

[2] Captain Cottam got a bar to the M.C. for this raid, Second Lieutenant Morgan receiving the M.C. and the two N.C.O.'s the D.C.M.

THE 11TH AND 12TH DISBANDED

The 11th was not the only victim contributed by the TWENTY-FOURTH to the reduction of battalions. The 12th S.W.B. had not escaped the fate which had befallen their next ahead. Since Bourlon Wood the 12th had been quite busy. Less than a week after coming out of that struggle the Fortieth Division had been sent into line at Bullecourt, relieving the Sixteenth Division. Ground had been gained here recently by a subsidiary operation which had coincided with the attack at Cambrai, and the sector was quite lively. The 12th had been so fortunate as to get Captains H. J. Brown and H. C. Lloyd back from courses, but only one small draft had joined, and it was still very weak when it took over the front line on December 8th. There was a heavy bombardment on the 13th, when the Germans counter-attacked the Third Division in the next sector to the right, but the 12th escaped with only one casualty. They remained in the Bullecourt sector for the remainder of their days, doing alternately six days in the line and six out. Fairly substantial drafts joined early in January and nearly 20 new subalterns, while the New Year's Honours List brought Colonel Benzie a bar to the D.S.O. and Major Brown a bar to the M.C. Casualties were few, though Second Lieutenant Brewer was mortally wounded on patrol on January 12th, and on the 31st a dozen men were hit during a heavy bombardment of the support line. Against that the battalion carried out some useful patrols, capturing a prisoner and getting a helpful identification. At first the weather was cold but dry, but in January a thaw reduced the trenches to an awful state. The communication trenches became so bad that the front line could only be reached over the top and at night. This postponed a raid on Dog Trench, which the battalion was preparing, until the night of February 4th/5th, when Second Lieutenants Dilloway, Little and Loxton and 30 men attempted it. One belt of wire was negotiated quite successfully, but, just as they reached a second they were detected and fired upon, so, seeing that surprise was hopeless, Second Lieutenant Dilloway wisely withdrew his party, bringing it back without any casualties. Two nights later the 12th left the trenches for the last time and went back to Mory. On February 8th the breaking up of the battalion started with the departure of Second Lieutenants Hart and Chapman with 50 of C Company to join the 5th S.W.B. The handing in of equipment followed and the end came on the 10th, when parties of five officers and 100 men each went off to the 1st and 2nd Battalions respectively, ten officers and the remaining N.C.O.'s and men being formed into a 9th Entrenching Battalion along with the remnants of the 11th King's Own and 19th Welch, the other two battalions which the Fortieth Division had to sacrifice.[1]

The 12th had had the shortest career of any of the battalions of the TWENTY-FOURTH who went overseas. Cambrai was the one big battle of its twenty months in France, and apart from that it only " went over the top " once—at Fifteen Ravine in April, 1917. But its career was none the less creditable : in the minor activities of trench warfare it had done very well, it had made several highly successful raids, and its patrols had been energetic and effective. It was on the score of its junior standing alone that the 12th was marked down for reduction, and in parting with it General Ponsonby, G.O.C. Fortieth Division, expressed emphatically his regret at losing so efficient and well-conducted a battalion.

[1] The officers who went to the 1st and 2nd Battalions have already been named (cf. pp. 381 and 385); the ten sent to the 9th " E.B." were Captains Barker, W. M. Evans, Foster and H. C. Lloyd, Lieutenants Greaves and E. R. Taylor, Second Lieutenants Eames, Little, Pitten and Reeve. Colonel Benzie was transferred to command the 14th Argyll and Sutherland, Major Brown went to the 18th Welch and subsequently distinguished himself greatly in command of it, Regimental Quartermaster Sergeant Westhorpe became R.Q.M.S. of the newly formed Divisional M.G. Battalion. The remaining officers proceeded to the Base, but several of them were later on posted to other battalions of the S.W.B. Of the men, of whom there were over 500 still on the strength on March 31st, most went eventually to the 4th Bedford and 14th Worcestershire and a smaller draft to the 28th London (Artists) in the Sixty-Third Division.

CHAPTER XXVII

THE GREAT GERMAN "PUSH"

AFTER the Cambrai counter-stroke a German attack in force on the Western Front had become almost a certainty. The men and guns set free by the collapse of Russia had now reached the Western Front and their arrival had transferred the initiative to the Germans. It was obviously to their interest to force a decision before the United States could send over from the New World forces sufficient to redress the balance of the Old, and, as already explained, the British troops' main occupation during the winter had been the preparation of rear defensive lines. Lines, however, possess little value without men to man them adequately, and all the digging and wiring put in by the 5th and 6th S.W.B. and all the other Pioneer battalions and the working parties of units nominally "resting" was largely thrown away owing to the extension of the British front and the inability of the authorities at home to keep the British infantry brigades up to four battalions. It is not the province of a Regimental History to go into strategical controversies at length, but the effect of important decisions of policy on the fortunes of individual battalions must not be overlooked. Undoubtedly the fog which prevailed on March 21st, 1918, contributed most substantially to the German success. It provided the conditions most unfavourable to the system on which the British defences had been designed, as by virtually blinding the defence it neutralized the arrangements for sweeping the gaps between the different posts and strong points with rifle and machine gun fire. Still the story of March, 1918, might have been very different, even with the fog, had the British Commander-in-Chief had at his disposal all the reinforcements who had to be hurried out from England on the news of the break-through, and all the units which were ultimately brought back to France from the minor theatres of war. With more men to man the rear defences of the front system, more men to complete the half-finished Corps and Army Lines, more Divisions in reserve to be pushed up into the gaps in the thinly held fronts of the Third and Fifth Armies, would the German offensive of March 21st have penetrated much deeper than did their effort against the Arras front on March 28th?

When the German attack was launched the TWENTY-FOURTH had in the battle zone only the two Pioneer battalions, and as it happened both were in the Third Army and at no great distance apart. Both curiously enough were with Divisions in reserve, the Nineteenth Division being about Bertincourt in support to the Fifth Corps and the Twenty-Fifth round Bapaume, behind the

Fourth Corps. Both these Corps were vigorously assailed in great force, and at more than one place the Germans succeeded by dint of numbers in forcing their way through, despite desperate resistance and at the cost of colossal casualties. Before evening both these Divisions had been involved in the struggle, and the two Pioneer battalions of the TWENTY-FOURTH were getting ready for much harder fighting than had yet come their way.

It was at 6.30 a.m. on March 21st that warning orders reached the 5th to " stand by," in readiness to move at half an hour's notice. At noon it was ordered to an assembly position on the Bertincourt–Haplincourt road, where it arrived at 3.30 p.m. B Company was promptly sent off to the 57th Brigade to dig a line between Beaumetz and Hermies, C reported to the 58th, also near Hermies, D meanwhile digging short lengths of trench in the so-called " Green Line," an aspiration rather than a real " line," near the Fremicourt–Beugny road. These positions were well in rear of the points to which the Germans penetrated either on that day or the next. The third day of the battle (March 23rd) found the 5th S.W.B. still labouring on defences without having come into action, though the rest of their Division had already been thrown into the fighting. On that day D were working at the " Green Line " East of Fremicourt, B, subsequently relieved by C, digging in between the Fremicourt–Bapaume and Beugnatre–Bapaume roads, where the " Red Line " ran. Though the Germans had maintained a most vigorous pressure on the Third Army they had as yet achieved but little against its left and centre, but on its right and further South against the Fifth Army they had made more progress.

By this time the 6th S.W.B. had already come under fire. On March 21st that battalion was at Favreuil Wood; it was sent up in the afternoon to man the Army Line N.E. of Favreuil, but as the ground was unfamiliar and the fog still dense the wrong position was taken up North of the Beugnatre–Longatte road and entrenched, so next morning when the fog cleared away and the true position of the Army Line was ascertained the battalion had to go forward 800 yards. The trench it then occupied was continuous but only three feet deep. This it started to improve under intermittent shell fire. After working at this line nearly all day the 6th were relieved by some of the Forty-First Division and ordered back to Sapignies, which they reached about 8 p.m. Their night's rest was somewhat disturbed by shelling, but casualties were not numerous, and at 7 a.m. the battalion was placed under the B.G.C. 75th Brigade and was ordered to entrench a position East of Sapignies to prepare for an attack from the direction of Mory. This was done and

THE GERMAN ATTACK BEGINS

the battalion spent March 23rd entrenching the new line. There was no perceptible movement in front, though both sides seemed to be shelling Mory. Actually the line from Beugny past Vaulx-Vraucourt and Mory to St. Leger was maintained nearly all day, the Nineteenth, Forty-First, Fortieth and Thirty-First Divisions all putting up a most determined resistance and keeping the enemy at bay. The 6th had a few casualties from shell fire but could work on undisturbed.

As yet the offensive had not gone too badly for the Third Army: if it had had to give ground it had exacted a high price for every yard. Further South, however, the Germans had achieved much greater success, and by March 24th with its right turned the Third Army's centre could no longer maintain its position astride the Bapaume–Cambrai road.

The first indication of what lay before the 5th S.W.B. came when, early in the morning, C Company was sent off to support the 56th Brigade near Bancourt, the other two companies being placed behind the 58th further to the left, East of Fremicourt. C, though on the more exposed flank, did not at first get involved in heavy fighting. It was told off to dig a defensive flank South of Fremicourt and worked on this till nearly 3 p.m. when the 56th Brigade fell back through it. On this C also withdrew, but halted at Bancourt where a stand was being made. The Germans came on in great force both in front and in flank, giving C splendid targets, of which, while its ammunition lasted, it took full advantage, inflicting heavy casualties, until, having fired away nearly all its cartridges, it had to fall back through Bapaume, ultimately rejoining the rest of the battalion on the Bapaume–Thilloy road.

B and D meanwhile had dug in N.E. of Fremicourt, B being on the right. All through the morning the 58th Brigade which was holding the "Green Line" in their front was repeatedly attacked, but till nearly 2 p.m. the front held and the Germans were kept back. Then the right flank suddenly gave and the troops came streaming back. To help the 58th Brigade to withdraw two platoons of B pushed across the main road to counter-attack, D simultaneously being brought across West of Fremicourt to cover the right of this stroke. The Germans were coming on in strength, and just as D neared the top of a rise the Germans appeared in mass over the crest. Major Croft was not to be caught napping: before the enemy had realized the situation he had opened so heavy and accurate a fire that despite their superiority in numbers the Germans were checked and driven back, while the 9th R.W.F. came up on D's left and helped to secure the position. For another two hours the fight raged, the Germans making repeated efforts to advance but being successfully beaten off. However, the position could not be maintained indefinitely. " The right kept on going," writes one account, and to avoid being surrounded Major Croft's party had to fall back. Luckily there was dead ground just behind and this helped the retirement, which was further assisted by machine guns and B's other two platoons, which had meanwhile been holding on well on a ridge covering the railway embankment. After retiring under heavy fire for over 1800 yards they rallied at the " Red Line " they had dug on the previous day beside the 9th Royal Warwickshire of the 57th Brigade. This stand allowed most of the wounded—the casualties already amounted to over 50—to be got safely away to Bapaume. D even attempted a counter-attack towards Fremicourt, but found the Germans coming on in great force and was pushed back. By 6 p.m. the Germans were already half a mile beyond the " Red Line " South of the road, so a fresh retirement was necessary. In Bapaume some of B helped the 9th Welch to make another brief stand, but that position in turn proved untenable and the troops fell back to the Grevillers line West of Bapaume.

It was really wonderful that the bulk of the 5th managed to reunite that evening. Considering the severity of the fighting losses had not been heavy, somewhere under 150 all told, the wounded including Captain B. O. Jones and Lieutenants Fraser, A. L. Richards and C. W. H. White. The missing amounted to over a third, but the 5th had reason to congratulate themselves. Attacking in force in the open the Germans had given good targets and must have suffered much heavier casualties than they had inflicted, for in each case it had been the situation on the flank, not in front, that had compelled retirement.

The 6th meanwhile had had a much easier day. The battalion, which was still under the B.G.C. 75th Brigade, was holding the line it had dug on the previous day, having the 11th Cheshire on its right, the 8th Border and 2nd South Lancashire being on the left and extending in front of Behagnies. Heavy fighting was in progress further to the right, at and beyond Beugnatre, but no advance was attempted against the 75th Brigade, and only towards evening, when men were seen to be retiring from Favreuil, did any unfavourable developments occur. It then proved necessary to throw back the right S.W. of Sapignies to form a defensive flank and to withdraw West of the Sapignies-Bapaume road South of the village to avoid enfilade machine gun fire from near Monument Corner. After dark, some of the Forty-First Division came up to relieve the 6th, and two companies, A and C, went back to Sapignies to rest, leaving a machine gun detachment under Lieutenant Pearce to cover a gap in the line.

Daylight on March 25th found Sapignies quite untenable. Fire was being brought to bear on it from North, East and South, and though Lieutenant Pearce's detachment did admirable work, especially Private Holliday who fought his gun till the Germans were on three sides of him, a retirement could not be postponed long. Accordingly A and C Companies were sent back to take up a new line in rear of the village, the move being effectively covered by Lieutenant Pearce's machine guns. This they held for some time, repulsing an attack, but it was the old story again—the right went and a retirement Westward became necessary. However, some of the Forty-Second Division were found in position West of Biefvillers and a fresh stand was made, the machine guns doing most successful shooting and silencing two German machine guns before they were located and knocked out by the German guns, and even then their teams took to their rifles and carried on. The C.O. now went off to Ablainzeville to get orders, and in his absence orders were received for A and C to go right back to Puisieux where they were to entrench a position facing S.E. towards Miraumont. D Company, meanwhile, under Major Deane had been in position between Sapignies and Behagnies. Up till 10 a.m. the enemy had made no impression on this position, but they then entered Sapignies and worked some way forward along the ridge West of that village. Major Deane's party now came under heavy shell fire and, partly to avoid this, partly to get a better field of fire, he shifted his ground twice, eventually taking up quite a good line N.W. of Bihucourt. Here a battalion commander of the Forty-Second Division requested his co-operation in attacking Bihucourt Wood from which his trenches were being enfiladed. To this Major Deane agreed, and D Company by a splendid rush reached a line of posts a little way from the wood, where they reorganized for the final advance. This, covered by Lewis gun fire and assisted by some tanks, was fairly successful, and when the Germans attacked, which they did twice, they were so decisively repulsed that they abandoned further efforts to advance. Reinforcements then arrived and relieved the 6th, now quite exhausted from want of food and sleep, so as the line was quite strongly held Major Deane decided to withdraw and rejoin the battalion. D had certainly earned their relief; they had fought stubbornly and successfully, thanks largely to Major Deane's good leadership and skilful handling of the situation, and their stand had helped appreciably to check the enemy's advance.

To find the battalion was no easy matter. The C.O.,

returning from Ablainzeville with orders to take the battalion into Divisional reserve, could only find a few of C Company, but eventually came across the transport and Battalion Headquarters near Hebuterne, so set off to Sailly au Bois, which was reached about 3 a.m. on the 26th, everyone being dead beat. About 7 a.m. the rest of A and C turned up from Puisieux, and a little later the battalion had to turn out and man a defensive position in front of Bayencourt. No attack developed against this line—actually the German advance in this quarter was successfully stopped some way further East, not penetrating beyond Hebuterne, and that evening the 6th was sent off towards Hannescamps to entrench another new position. This was done—it took the battalion from 5 p.m. to 9 p.m. to dig it—and the men then settled down to a night's rest, only to be interrupted at 2 a.m. (March 27th) by orders to march to Rossignol near Coigneux. Here the relics of D Company rejoined, after hunting for the battalion for over 36 hours, and after a long halt the 6th moved on to Puschevillers, where it bivouacked, proceeding next day to Pernois, which it reached late in the evening. Since March 21st the 6th had marched 60 miles, D Company had done nearer 90, each company had dug and manned at least five different positions, no man had had more than 18 hours' sleep, the majority much less, or more than three real meals. Nevertheless the men were in good spirits, only three went sick and less than 30 fell out when marching; and the condition of the transport animals, which if tired were all quite serviceable, reflected tremendous credit on those in charge of them. Casualties had been remarkably low, the total losses among the men being under 60, though on March 25th Second Lieutenant Hillier had been killed and Lieutenants Pearce, H. L. Thomas and Hanna wounded. Major Deane, whose leadership, gallantry and endurance had been alike conspicuous, received the D.S.O.: he had shown wonderful disregard of personal safety and had handled the counter-attack on the 25th admirably. Private Holliday, who in addition to his splendid work with his Lewis gun had gone out under heavy fire to rescue a wounded man, was given the D.C.M. Lieutenant Pearce's good service with his machine guns was rewarded by the M.C., which was also awarded to Lieutenants H. Davis and Petts and to Captain Mann, R.A.M.C., the battalion's M.O., who, besides doing splendid and devoted work in succouring the wounded, had organized the battalion stretcher-bearers admirably and been largely responsible for most of the wounded being got away. M.M.'s were awarded to 14 men, Private Horrobin receiving a bar.

The 5th had come out of the battle just before the 6th,

having finished up with a very hard day's fighting and heavy casualties. After reuniting West of Bapaume the battalion had soon become split up again, the transport being sent back next morning (March 25th) to Fonquevillers, B Company being attached to the 58th Brigade which was trying to form a defensive flank and cover the Bapaume–Albert road, C and D joining the 57th Brigade East of Grevillers, facing N.E. on the outskirts of that village.

The German attack was not slow to develop, beginning on the right. From 7 a.m. on the 58th Brigade was vigorously assailed, but for a long time held its own, not letting the Germans get nearer than 200 yards and inflicting heavy casualties on them. About 11 a.m., however, the 57th Brigade on the left were forced to give ground, which made the 58th's position quite untenable. The attack had spread to the 57th's frontage about 8 a.m.: some troops further to the left gave way quite early, and to make matters worse the ammunition and rations for C and D had gone astray. By 9 a.m. the position was so serious that a counter-attack was attempted. C joined in this, D and the machine guns giving covering fire. Advancing some 600 yards to a railway embankment which afforded a good position the counter-attackers not only checked the enemy, but forced them to give ground. But the Germans were too strong to be stopped for long, and the survivors of the counter-attack, their left " in the air," their ammunition exhausted, and their right under heavy fire, had to fall back, covered by D and by C's Lewis guns. D hung on to Grevillers for another half-hour till the enemy were right into it, when they also went back, the 58th Brigade on the right conforming, for further to the right the enemy could be seen pressing on and already some way West of the Nineteenth Division's position.

A retreat over nearly a mile to the next defensible ridge followed. The fighting had now reached the area of the Somme battles of 1916, and old trenches often afforded covered lines of retreat or ready-made positions for a stand. Units were now greatly mixed up, which added to the difficulty of rallying men and organizing a stand. More than one, however, was attempted: B held on for nearly two hours at Loupart Wood, C and D and the 57th Brigade tried to rally S.W. of Grevillers, but were pushed back, stood again near Loupart Wood in a position the enemy did not venture to attack directly, preferring to turn it by working round to the Southward. This compelled another retirement, in which B standing East of Irles were all but surrounded and cut off. However, Major Croft, Captain I. T. Evans and Second Lieutenant J. R. L. Jones organized a stand of C and D on a reverse slope, and, linking up with B, fought

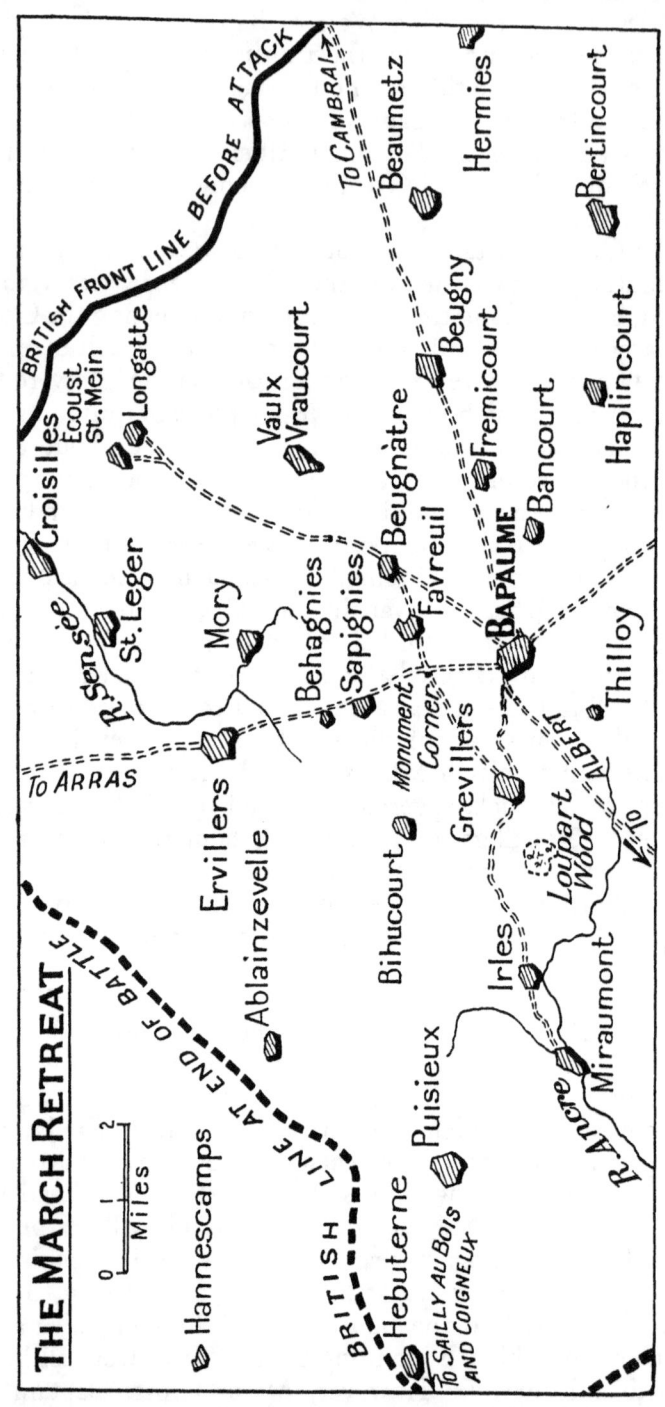

most resolutely. Here for a while the Germans were checked, time being thus given for the New Zealand Division, which had been hurried down from the North, to get into position further back nearer Hebuterne. However, the pressure continued, and about 5.30 p.m. the line had to go back, to rally yet again 800 yards N.W. of Irles. Heavy shell fire and the outflanking of the position from the South ended this stand also, but it was dark now, and as the exhausted troops fell back they stumbled into the outposts of the reinforcing Division, now in position and ready to take over. The 5th were then directed to Hebuterne, where rations were awaiting them.

A brief rest was all the wearied men could be given, however. A composite company was formed from B and D and attached to the 10th R. Warwickshire, while part of C was placed N.E. of Hebuterne to defend that flank, the company also finding parties to search for stray Germans who might have penetrated Hebuterne, and later to clear a wood East of the village. This last lot rounded up and destroyed a machine gun team, but the party searching Hebuterne had the misfortune to lose Lieutenant Moore, who was shot by a sniper after carrying out his task most successfully. Actually no attack developed, too much had been taken out of the Germans for them to do more than feel the new line with occasional patrols, and in the evening the 5th were ordered back to Bayencourt to reorganize, moving two days later to Candas, whence they entrained for Flanders on March 30th.[1]

" The " March retreat " had given the 5th more hard fighting compressed into a few days than they had yet experienced. On the Somme, at Messines and in Third Ypres individual members of the battalion had had sharp fighting, but in the main it had been kept at Pioneering work, and March, 1918, saw it employed as infantry for the first time. The 5th, and the 6th too, could claim that they had shown that good Pioneers could also be good infantry, that they could shoot and march as well as dig and wire, and could handle rifle and bayonet no less effectively than pick and shovel and axe. Both battalions had fought splendidly and earned great credit. Most flattering messages reached Colonel Trower about his battalion's splendid conduct, and the " honours " awarded to the 6th speak for themselves. Both battalions scored no doubt from the fact that as Pioneers they had escaped the heavy casualties incurred by ordinary infantry when engaged in a big attack. Not an infantry battalion but had not at one time or other been virtually wiped out and

[1] Besides those already mentioned, Second Lieutenant White was conspicuous for good work during these days, as were also Sergeant Crum and Lance Corporal Rolls who fought their Lewis guns most effectively.

completely reconstructed. Indeed a battalion might be reckoned lucky if this had not happened to it several times. Pioneers had their share of casualties, but as a rule the drain on them was fairly steady, regular not cataclysmic. Well on into 1918 the 5th had still with it many men and several officers who had joined it at Park House Camp and been with it right through. Such a nucleus naturally imparted a solidarity and cohesion unknown to the ordinary infantry battalion, which was more frequently renewed and usually included only a few officers and men who had been with it any length of time. It was a great asset to the 5th to be still commanded by its orginal O.C. after nearly three years at the front, especially when he happened to be Colonel Trower; and the fine performance of the two Pioneer battalions was due in part to the same officers and men having been long enough together to get to know each other.

By the time that the Nineteenth and Twenty-Fifth Divisions were taken out of the line the fighting front North of the Somme was, if not already stabilized, in a fair way to be. After March 27th there was little change of importance along the line on which the Germans had then been checked, though South of the river the situation continued critical for some days longer. The " quiet " parts of the front had been called on to release their reserves and battered Divisions were being sent to them to set fresher units free. Among these was the Thirty-Eighth, whose infantry, as already mentioned, had been hauled out of the line at the end of March and were then hurried down to the neighbourhood of Albert, being placed in Army Reserve. The first ten days of April brought the 10th S.W.B. various orders and counter-orders with moves to and fro, but it did not actually go into the line until April 12th when its Division relieved the Twelfth on the frontage opposite Albert. By then the Germans had opened a new offensive elsewhere, and had for the time abandoned their efforts to press the British on the Somme front.

CHAPTER XXVIII

THE LYS

THE quarter to which the enemy's main offensive had now been transferred was the Lys valley, so long the specially "quiet" portion of the British front, to which Divisions thinned and exhausted by participation in offensive operations had long been wont to be sent to recuperate. Indeed, when the Germans attacked there on April 9th, all five British Divisions holding the line from Neuve Chapelle Northward had just been through the furnace of the "March retreat," and their depleted ranks were full of young drafts they had not yet had time to assimilate. The prospect of having to deal with Divisions thus unfavourably situated may have helped the Germans to select this locality for their fresh offensive, but, whatever their motives and their original objectives, their attack brought back into the fighting the two Pioneer Battalions of the TWENTY-FOURTH which had just been moved up to Flanders. The 5th were back on the Messines front, so familiar to them in 1917, with the 6th on their immediate right in the Ploegsteert area.

Both battalions had had scanty time in which to refit and reorganize. The 5th had entrained at Candas on March 30th for Caestre and had taken up quarters at Spy and Gable Farms. They had promptly got to work on the defences and communications and had been kept busy. Several men who had got separated from the battalion during the fighting now rejoined, and on April 9th 400 nineteen-year-olds from a Graduated Battalion brought the companies up to full strength again. The 6th had followed them over the same route a day later, moving to Romarin, where they remained till April 9th, partly in training —drafts amounting to 160 men had joined and needed much instruction—partly in working on reserve lines. Both their Divisions had extensive frontages, the Twenty-Fifth holding 7000 yards from the Lys to the Douve, and the Nineteenth, whose line ran from the Douve to Hollebeke, having over 5000 With their reduced establishments and the high proportion of recent drafts in all battalions their prospects of defending these long fronts against a serious attack were hardly promising.

On the opening day of the offensive, however, neither Nineteenth nor Twenty-Fifth Division was attacked. The Germans concentrated their efforts against the Portuguese at Neuve Chapelle and the Fortieth and Fifty-Fifth Divisions on their left and right respectively. These two held, but the Portuguese defence collapsed completely, and the Germans quickly penetrated to the Lys at Estaires. This advantage they promptly exploited by outflanking the Divisions on either side of the gap, both of which suffered severely and had to give ground. The Fifty-Fifth's right held firm at Givenchy and its left was flung back to form a defensive flank past Festubert to Loisne, a line to prove of special interest to the 1st S.W.B. before many days were past; the Fortieth likewise threw back its right from Bois Grenier to the Lys but could not prevent the Germans establishing themselves across the river, while the depth to which the attack had penetrated made the

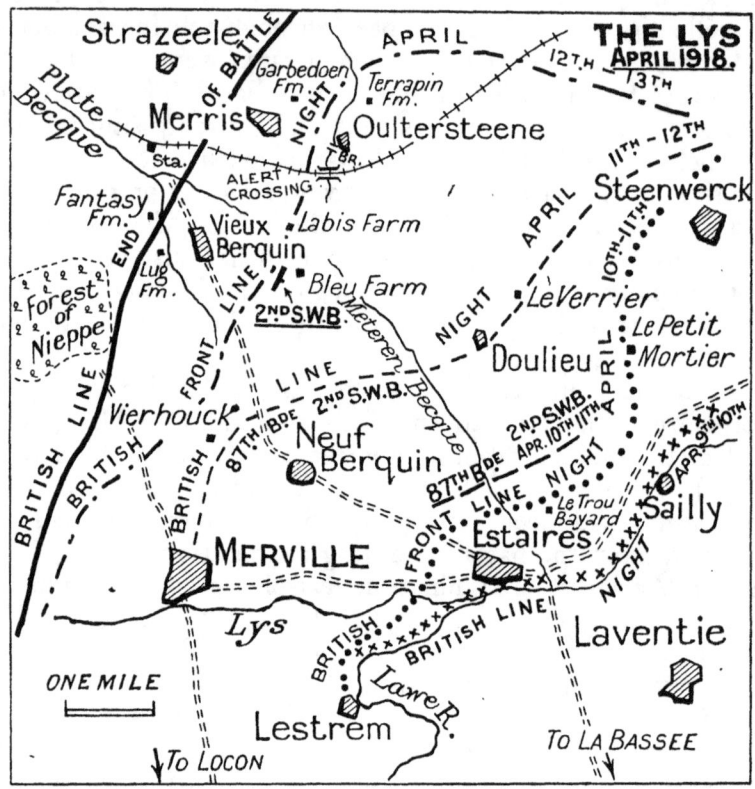

defensive flanks very long and seriously endangered both Divisions. Moreover, having ample reserves at hand, the Germans could not only press home the success already achieved, but could extend considerably the frontage of their attack.

Directly the attack began all troops in the neighbourhood had stood to arms. The Twenty-Fifth Division sent off soon its reserve brigade towards Estaires, which left the 6th S.W.B. and the three Field Companies as its only available reserve; and about 10 p.m. the battalion was ordered to take up a defensive flank along the Lys near Le Bizet. This was done and patrols pushed out upstream as far as Pont de Nieppe, without, however, encountering any enemy. The German advance had not as yet passed Croix de Bac, and the Thirty-Fourth Division, in the Armentières sector on the Fortieth's left, had not been attacked.

The 5th S.W.B. meanwhile had passed an uneventful day, having merely concentrated and stood by, but evening found a third battalion of the Regiment on its way to the fighting zone. This was the 2nd, which had only just reached some hutments at St. Jan Ter Biezen (West of Poperinghe) at 6.30 a.m. that day. At 5.20 p.m. orders were received for its brigade to " embus " and proceed to Merville. Before it could start, however, its destination was changed to Neuf Berquin, where it arrived after an all-night journey about 8 a.m. on April 10th. Sixteen officers and 170 men had been left behind as " battle nucleus," the battalion taking into action 20 officers and 704 men. Colonel Raikes being on leave, Major Somerville was in command.

When the 87th Brigade reached Neuf Berquin the situation was none too satisfactory. The enemy was attacking in force above Sailly, where he was already over the river, and despite stubborn resistance was making headway and enlarging his bridgehead over the Lys. He had also extended the scope of his attack and was pressing in upon the Twenty-Fifth, Nineteenth and Ninth Divisions from the Lys Northward. The Border Regiment was at once pushed forward to occupy a line West of Estaires with its right on the road to Neuf Berquin, and in the afternoon the other two battalions were sent to advance on its left, with their right directed on Sailly. They moved off about 5 p.m., the 2nd S.W.B. on the left, and eventually took up a position S.E. of Doulieu, about a quarter of a mile behind the front to which the Fortieth and Fiftieth Divisions[1] were still clinging about Trou Bayard. Beyond the 87th Brigade's left the front line turned rather abruptly Northward through Le Petit Mortier, so that the brigade was in a salient with the S.W.B. on the more exposed flank. On reaching the position the battalion at once dug in, B Company on the right, then D, then C in touch with a mixed battalion of the Fortieth Division, A being retained by Major Somerville in reserve close to Battalion Headquarters. The battalion had a long line to cover and was accordingly disposed of in a series of posts, sited as far as possible to afford each other support.

So far the 2nd S.W.B. had not come into contact with enemy. The 5th and 6th, however, had both been heavily engaged, more particularly the 6th. The attack on the Twenty-Fifth Division had developed quite early, and under cover of a mist the Germans soon succeeded in breaking through the 75th Brigade, though

[1] The Fiftieth Division had reinforced the Fortieth.

on its left East of Ploegsteert Wood the 7th kept them at bay. Orders were promptly sent to the 6th S.W.B. and the R.E. to move to Chapelle Rompue and counter-attack towards Le Touquet. The move was carried out under shell fire, but when Colonel Fitzpatrick pushed forward with C Company to reconnoitre he found the situation already restored. However, with so long a line to hold and such superiority in numbers on the attacking side, another break through was soon made, and about 10 a.m. the enemy were in Ploegsteert village and threatening Romarin: Major Deane with A and D Companies was thereupon ordered back to the Army Line nearer Romarin. In moving back the troops were again shelled and had several casualties, but the position was duly occupied, and later, as the enemy were not advancing, the two companies moved forward and dug in on a line running South from Regina Camp. The C.O. had rejoined the main body, as did C Company also rather later, and eventually the battalion was ordered to attempt to recover Ploegsteert village in co-operation with the 2nd South Lancashire and 9th Cheshire. This started at 8.10 p.m., but at once encountered strong opposition, machine guns away to the right developing an effective and destructive fire. Captains J. C. Owen and D. Jenkins, commanding C and D Companies respectively, were both wounded, but Company Sergeant Major Pearson now took command of his company and handled it admirably, eventually carrying his wounded company commander back to safety though the enemy were close about.[1] Eventually when within 200 yards of its objective the attack came to a halt. For a time it did actually hold up the enemy, but towards nightfall the Germans began to press on, and the whole brigade had to go back, a stand being made on a line running from Regina Camp past Doudou Farm by a switch which joined the Army Line some way South and nearer Nieppe. Here A Company was on the left, C and D on the right. Casualties had been heavy, nearly 80 killed and missing, nearly 100 wounded including 7 officers. On the left the 7th Brigade was still hanging on to Ploegsteert Wood, but to the right the Thirty-Fourth Division had had to evacuate Armentières and retire across the Lys towards Nieppe. Beyond that again the enemy had made a substantial advance, having penetrated to Steenwerck, and the position was far from satisfactory.

Further to the left also the Germans had pushed in the Nineteenth Division's outpost line from East of Oosttaverne to the West of the Messines Ridge. This had brought the 5th S.W.B. into action. That battalion had stood to on the 9th, Headquarters and C Company near Lindenhoek, B and D close to

---

[1] He received the D.C.M.

Wulverghem. Early on the 10th heavy shell fire was opened and two platoons of B were promptly ordered forward to their allotted position in the Corps Line on the crest of the ridge at Lumm Farm. On arriving here no infantry were to be found in front,[1] the enemy seemed to be pressing on and to have entered Messines, so the detachment fell back to Earl Farm in the Corps Support Line where the other half company reinforced. It was not long before the enemy attacked in strength and the company was soon hard pressed. It was ably handled, however, by Captain I. T. Evans, whose leadership and gallantry had a most inspiring effect on the young soldiers of whom it was mainly composed. There was a field battery near by which was blazing away at the enemy, doing much execution, so B extended its front to cover these guns, and the enemy were held at bay long enough for the South African Brigade of the Ninth Division to counter-attack across B's front, which drove the enemy back and greatly improved the situation. C was retained in reserve all day, but D under Major Croft, which originally moved up to Maedelstede Farm, was put in platoon by platoon into the 58th Brigade's line in front of Wytschaete. Here also the enemy were attacking in force, but D held on well. Second Lieutenant I. D. Jones set a magnificent example, standing up on the parapet regardless of danger to encourage his raw hands. He was killed, but the men stuck to their ground till after 7 p.m. when, as the enemy were advancing on the left and two Lewis gun teams had been knocked out, a retirement to the Bois de Wytschaete became necessary to avoid envelopment. Both companies had fared astonishingly well as regards casualties, the total was under 50, which included Major Croft, Lieutenant H. C. Williams and Second Lieutenants Edmonds and White wounded. Though the Nineteenth Division's front line had gone and Messines had for a time been lost the South Africans' counter-attack had recovered that village and the British still retained possession of the ridge, though it was none too strongly held.

Early on April 11th heavy fighting was resumed all along the British front. Whatever their original intentions the success the Germans had already achieved had apparently encouraged them to entertain hopes of penetrating to Hazebrouck and securing that all-important railway junction, second only to Amiens itself. They had therefore brought up large reserves and threw them in vigorously, almost recklessly, advancing at times in masses which offered splendid targets to the British rifles and machine guns, so that if by sheer weight of numbers they bore down the

[1] The enemy had attacked in overwhelming force and the meagre garrisons of the front system of trenches had been virtually annihilated after a desperate defence.

British resistance they had to pay dearly for their gains. The main weight of their attack on April 11th fell upon the Southern portion of the British line, from Estaires to Givenchy. Here the right of the defence held firm, but from Locon Northward the attack made substantial progress and evening found the Germans already into Merville. Soon after daybreak a heavy trench mortar barrage was put down on the Trou Bayard–Le Petit Mortier line in front of the 2nd S.W.B. For a time the line held, but the troops on this frontage mostly belonged to Divisions already exhausted and terribly depleted and so were by now at their last gasp; the pressure was too heavy for them and by 9 a.m. men were beginning to fall back through the S.W.B. whose front companies were soon busy in keeping the pursuing Germans at bay, while Major Somerville was trying to rally the stragglers of the Fortieth Division at Battalion Headquarters. It was the more urgent to do this because the retirement of the troops on the left nearer Le Petit Mortier had uncovered the battalion's flank, and though Captain Bennett promptly threw back C Company's left and formed a defensive flank this could not avail to keep the enemy back for long. To prolong this line Major Somerville sent up part of A Company with such stragglers as he had rallied, and for a time the enemy were checked here as well as in front. The situation had been reported to Brigade and Divisional Headquarters and a battalion of the 86th Brigade was being pushed across towards the 2nd's left rear, but the situation was changing too fast for Divisional commanders or even Brigadiers to keep abreast of it and the orders they issued were usually out of date almost before they had been given.

The fight which the Twenty-Ninth Division put up on April 11th was well worthy of its record. Over-matched and out-flanked, it held on long enough to give time for other units to come up and take post on a more defensible line in rear, the Thirty-First Division on its left rear near Vieux Berquin and Merris, the Fifth further to the right and nearer Merville. In this stand the 2nd S.W.B. played their full share. It was difficult in that enclosed country to cover much ground to the flank, and after nearly two hours' fighting the enemy, taking advantage of the cover of the hedges, managed to work round the battalion's left and roll it up. Captain Bennett and his men were rushed from behind, while successfully keeping the enemy in their front at bay. Battalion Headquarters, taken in flank and rear by the German advance, put up a desperate fight, Major Somerville and his men being last seen defending a trench with the enemy right round their flank on top of them. Their resistance enabled a substantial portion of B and C Companies on the right to get

THE 2ND OVERWHELMED

away, though their casualties were heavy and it was only in small and disorganized parties that they extricated themselves. These appear to have mostly joined up with other units and fought alongside them in the stubborn rear-guard action which the Division maintained for the rest of the day, giving ground gradually to the N.W. Evening found the Twenty-Ninth established on a line from East of Vierhouck across the Neuf Berquin–Vieux Berquin road towards Doulieu, joining up with the Thirty-First on the left. The 87th Brigade held the right of this, all that could be collected of the 2nd S.W.B., barely 150 men with three officers, of whom Captain W. Davies was the senior, being placed on its left about Le Ferme Prince. Three-quarters of the battalion were gone, but the time its resistance had gained was invaluable.

Though in this direction the Germans had made considerable progress their efforts on the Armentières frontage had hardly achieved as much. Their guns had blazed away freely during the night, and by 9 a.m. (April 11th) the troops on the 6th S.W.B.'s left were moving back. This, coupled with enfilade machine gun fire from the right, forced Colonel Fitzpatrick to withdraw, first to the Army Line East of Romarin and then, when that in turn proved untenable, to a line half a mile further West, North of Rue du Sac. Here a stand was made with success, and about 2 p.m., some of the Thirty-Third Division having come up, an effort was actually made to retake Romarin. It was vigorously pressed: Major Pearson, who behaved magnificently, setting a splendid example and handling his men most skilfully: on the right A, led by Captain Stickler, who showed great gallantry and quickness in decision, and C, now under Lieutenant Amos, whose grasp of the situation and determined leadership were alike conspicuous, actually reached the village, while D on the left reached the road junction North of it but were held up there by machine guns. Second·Lieutenant Potts, who did some fine work, silenced one of them by concentrating rifle fire upon it and led his men splendidly until he was hit. About 4 p.m. Colonel Fitzpatrick came forward and tried to organize a fresh advance, but no support was forthcoming on the right and no progress could be made. However, the ground gained was held till after dusk, when the battalion was ordered back to a new line running North from Pont d'Achelles through Neuve Eglise, to which it had been decided to retire. This was being done to blunt the salient held by the Thirty-Fourth Division and to shorten the line, but unfortunately it involved also evacuating Hill 63 North of Ploegsteert Wood and the Messines Ridge South of Wytschaete.[1]

[1] The 6th's casualties on this day were 31 men killed and missing, 5 officers (Lieutenants Richards and Taylor, Second Lieutenants Jakeway, Potts and Fraser) and 31 men wounded.

On that Messines Ridge B Company of the 5th S.W.B. had been heavily engaged nearly all day, assisting in the gallant defence which the South Africans maintained between Messines and Wytschaete. Till nearly 4 p.m. the attacks continued, but finally the Germans were driven back across the Messines–Wytschaete road by a counter-attack in which Captain I. T. Evans distinguished himself. He had earlier on rallied some officerless South Africans and led them back into the fight, besides sending out patrols which had recovered touch with the units on the flanks. C had by this time come up to reinforce, and when, a couple of hours later, the Germans advanced again they were again stopped on the line Guy Farm–Four Huns Farm, the guns putting down a most effective barrage. Finally, however, as the position on the right had had to be evacuated the defenders had to withdraw to Spanbroekmolen, B going back in small parties through a terrific barrage. The work these companies had done in maintaining their advanced position for so long was of the greatest value to the Division. They had held the enemy up for several hours and had inflicted heavy casualties on them, while thanks to Captain Evans' skilful handling they got away with remarkably small loss. Lieutenant J. R. L. Jones had backed him up well, rallying stragglers and holding on to the position with his platoon to the last possible minute and directing its fire most effectively.

D Company also had been engaged, though less heavily. They had been in support to a battalion of the Northumberland Fusiliers near Wytschaete and had been called up about 5 p.m. to assist them beat off an attack, after which D had again withdrawn to reserve. Captain Runham, now in command of the company, handled his men admirably and did splendid service. During the night, owing to the retirement further South, the line near Wytschaete had to be drawn back, and a defensive flank formed along the Kemmel road. Casualties, considering the severity of the fighting, had not been heavy, under 40 in all, including Captain Littleton-Geach wounded.

Meanwhile in quite another part of the battle front a small party of the Regiment had come in for heavy fighting. When the 11th Battalion was disbanded the bulk of its officers and men were formed into a " 2nd Entrenching Battalion," and under that description were employed in constructing rear lines of defence in the La Bassèe–Armentières area, their work earning warm congratulations from the G.O.C. Fifteenth Corps. Early in April the battalion was broken up and the officers and men sent off, mainly to battalions of the TWENTY-FOURTH; over 200 men, for example, were posted, as already mentioned, to the 5th on

April 4th. Some 60 to 70 men, all of whom had belonged to C Company, had apparently been overlooked and a like fate had befallen Second Lieutenant H. E. Griffith, formerly second in command of that company. This party had remained at Steenwerck until April 10th, when with other detachments it was hastily formed into a Corps Composite Battalion and dispatched to Merville. This town was in considerable danger as the Germans were already close to it, despite the gallant efforts of

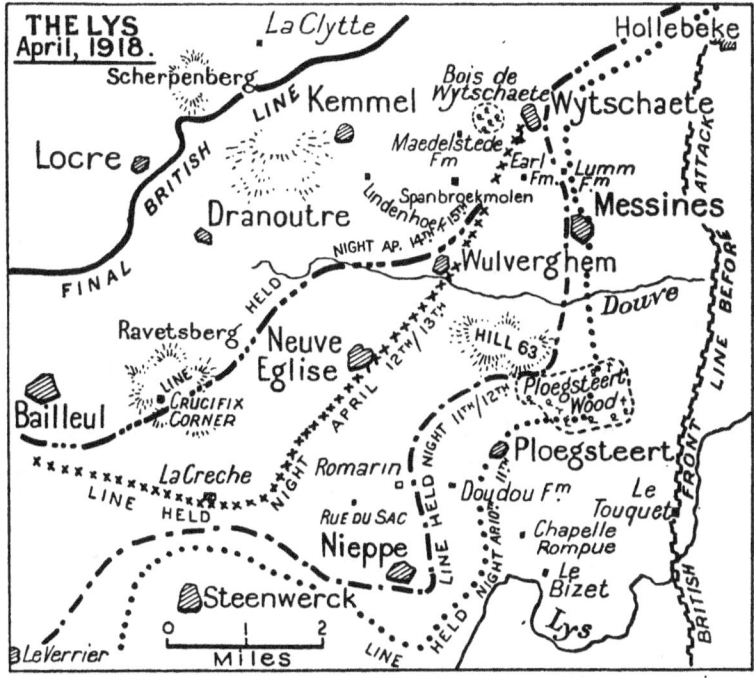

the Fiftieth Division who had been thrown in to close the gap created by the collapse of the Portuguese.

On arriving at Merville Colonel Scott of the Royal Sussex, who was commanding the Composite Battalion, ordered Second Lieutenant Griffith to take the party of the S.W.B., as being the only portion of his command still under an officer who knew them, while they were also the most experienced in fighting, forward down the Locon road to occupy an outpost position in some houses, the remainder of the battalion lining the railway embankment East of Merville. In the course of the 11th considerable German pressure began to develop on the position, but the S.W.B. managed to keep the enemy at bay, inflicting many casualties. They had taken over some Lewis guns from a party of the Fifty-First Division who retired through them and used these with great effect. However, about 5 p.m. sounds of heavy machine gun fire in rear showed that the position was becoming untenable and with some difficulty a retirement was effected behind the canal which runs West of Merville. The town was in flames and had been almost demolished already by shell fire, but it was reported that some wounded men of the Durham L.I. had been left behind, so Colonel Scott called for volunteers to rescue them. Second Lieutenant Griffith and twenty of his men promptly came forward, and despite the difficulties of burning houses, falling timber and the enemy's fire, managed to fetch the men out. They were then posted West of the canal on the right of a party of the Fiftieth Division and dug in behind a hedge, utilizing some shell holes. There was much shelling during the night and when morning came on April 12th the situation proved to be most unpleasant. The houses along the canal were occupied in force by the enemy, who had brought up several trench mortars, with which they did some extremely good shooting. However, the S.W.B. gave a good account of themselves, concentrating their fire first on one target, then on another. " Each N.C.O. passed on his fire orders," writes one account, " and we did some almost regimental fire-drill. First a machine gun on a house-top, then one coming down the railway, then window after window we sniped, while the Hun did all he knew to hit us in our holes. Our results were splendid and we simply could hold out till the artillery found itself. But we hadn't heard our guns for three days and this awful though sunny morning they never barked once."

What made the situation worse was that quite early on the troops on both flanks of the S.W.B. detachment had been shelled out of their positions and had retired, losing heavily as they went, and leaving the party isolated. By 7 a.m. over a third of the detachment had been hit, and though two gallant runners tried to get back and obtain help no assistance was forthcoming. Casualties continued to mount up, by 8.30 less than 20 were left to fight, and though they stuck gallantly to their posts ammunition was beginning to fail. Soon after 9 o'clock the end came, and the Germans, coming forward in swarms, overpowered the eight survivors. They had the satisfaction as they were marched as prisoners of seeing how effective their fire had been and of realizing that their little handful had held up overwhelming numbers of the enemy for several hours. The stand they had made would have been highly creditable in any case, but for a party of " nobody's children," detached from their old unit, it was doubly so. But what had helped them to put up so good a fight was the feeling that they were still South Wales Borderers and that they must live up to the traditions and reputation of their Regiment.

THE PRESSURE MAINTAINED

April 12th meanwhile had brought the 5th S.W.B. some relief from heavy fighting, though heavy shelling added another 30 to its already high casualty list. D remained near Wytschaete to which the Ninth Division had now extended its line. B and C moved back to the Army Line between the Douve and the Wulverghem road. There was heavy shelling, but no renewal of infantry attacks in force, the German efforts not extending North of Neuve Eglise. Here the 6th were again sharply engaged, and in the afternoon, the troops on their right having given way, a retirement was made to the road running South from Neuve Eglise to La Crèche where with the help of the 2nd Worcestershire[1] a successful stand was made. The day had cost the 6th another 30 casualties and all ranks were now becoming extremely weary.

As on April 11th, so on the 12th the Germans made their chief efforts against the Bailleul–Merville front. Success here would have brought them close to Hazebrouck, so it was vital that a stout defence should be offered. The remnant of the 2nd S.W.B. thus found itself again involved in a desperate struggle. The enemy started his attacks soon after 7 a.m., pressing hard along and West of the Neuf Berquin–Vieux Berquin road. The 87th Brigade had dug in well, and for some time its line remained firm. But the enemy gained ground on both flanks, especially on the left in the direction of Merris, and early in the afternoon a retirement became inevitable. Units were completely mixed up by this time and the fighting, which was practically continuous, was very confused: its precise course is therefore very hard to ascertain, but it seems that about 4 p.m. a stand was made round Bleu Farm, East of Vieux Berquin. The Border Regiment, which had been in reserve at first and was still respectably strong, provided the nucleus of this stand and parties of other regiments attached themselves to it. However, the left gave again and the Borders and those who had rallied round them had to retire yet another 700 yards to Labis Farm.[2] Here the German advance was so successfully resisted that they relaxed their efforts and left the remnants of the 87th Brigade to themselves for the night. Colonel Raikes, who had arrived back from leave, had now taken charge of the remnants of the brigade, now including only about 30 survivors of his own battalion, but such was their spirit that he was able to report that the men were confident and " seemed pretty comfortable." If they had been forced back they had at least seen ample evidence of how

---

[1] This was the " battle reserve " of that battalion, which belonged to the Thirty-Third Division.
[2] Between Vieux Berquin and Merris.

heavily the Germans had had to pay for their advance. Reinforcements were arriving, the Fifth Division, just back from Italy and with four battalions in each brigade, had come up behind the right and the situation was to that extent improved.

Hard fighting, however, still awaited the remnant of the 2nd S.W.B. About 9 a.m. (April 13th) the enemy came on in force under cover of machine guns and trench mortars. During the night Colonel Raikes had contrived to sort his men out by battalions, and they were well dug in and received the attack steadily and successfully. Against the 87th Brigade's front it was held up, and though on the left the Germans gained ground by taking advantage of the cover provided by hedges and houses, here also they were caught and checked by Lewis guns and by well-directed artillery fire. At a critical moment an explosion of ammunition occurred in the enemy's lines, causing something of a panic, and in bolting back the Germans gave good targets and many were bowled over. This caused a welcome respite of nearly two hours. Early in the afternoon, however, the troops on the right were pushed back and the enemy pressing on penetrated into Vieux Berquin. Even this did not shift the 87th Brigade party. Inspired by the determination and gallantry which Colonel Raikes displayed, they held on even with both flanks " in the air " and the enemy pressing them hard.[1] A defensive flank was thrown back on the right and the position was maintained till dusk, despite renewed advances against the left, all of which were beaten off. Then, however, the Thirty-First Division fell back by orders to a new line West of Vieux Berquin and Merris, and the remnants of the 87th Brigade, with both flanks left in the air, could do nothing but retire also. The retirement was most skilfully effected: at a fixed moment the whole party rose together, turned to the left, and in single file, piloted by Colonel Raikes, filed across a country swarming with the enemy and reached the British lines in safety to find that for the moment its troubles were over. Orders had been issued for the Twenty-Ninth Division's relief, and behind the front it had been holding an Australian Division was now dug in, fresh and ready to take on unlimited Germans.

By midnight the remnants of the battalion were moving back to a camp near Borre, transferring next day (April 14th) to St. Sylvester Cappel. Besides the party Colonel Raikes brought out with him many men who had got detached and had joined other units reported themselves sooner or later, but of the 20 officers who had gone into the fight all but three, Second Lieutenants

[1] Colonel Raikes was subsequently awarded a second bar to his D.S.O. for his gallantry and leadership on this occasion.

T. Roberts, W. S. Parry and H. Jones, who had been wounded early on, were either dead or prisoners.[1] In the end 146 wounded men proved to have reached our ambulances, 18 were known to be killed, the missing coming to nearly 350. Luckily the reinforcement camp contained a substantial nucleus on whom the battalion might be reconstructed, the 17 officers including several of some experience, if new-comers to the 2nd Battalion, like Captains I. A. Morgan, Whitworth, Dendy and Crowder. With this nucleus, the transport party, and men returning off leave, the battalion's "ration strength" on April 14th was returned as 413,[2] and two days later it was able to contribute 200 men in two companies under Captains Morgan and Dendy to an 87th Brigade Composite Battalion which was being sent up to support the line near Merris.

Before this the 6th had also been withdrawn from the fighting line. It had been hardly tried again on April 13th, as about 6 a.m. the Germans, profiting by a fog, broke through on the right and drove the Twenty-Fifth Division back. Near Neuve Eglise a long stand was made in which some of the 6th shared, while others withdrew with the 75th Brigade to Crucifix Corner near Ravelsberg on the Neuve Eglise–Bailleul road. Here a fairly good line was taken up, on which eventually the detachment from nearer Neuve Eglise fell back, when that village had at last to be evacuated. Major Pearson, though wounded on this day, remained at duty, continuing to set a splendid example of courage, cheerfulness and resource. By this time much of the sting had been taken out of the enemy's attacks, and though completely exhausted the remnants of the Twenty-Fifth Division managed to retain their ground next day (April 14th) despite heavy shelling. So heavy was the shelling that at one point some men began to fall back. Sergeant Green, however, ran forward, rallied the retiring men and led them back to their places. Later on he moved his men to another line to avoid casualties, but promptly advanced again and filled up the gap in the line directly the barrage lifted. Unluckily this day's casualties included the C.O., who was wounded when reconnoitring the point in the line where an attack seemed imminent. Major Deane thereupon took command and early next morning had the satisfaction of leading the battalion back to a concentration area near Dranoutre where the Division was being collected on relief by French

[1] Second Lieutenants Malins and E. D. Thomas died of wounds, those missing were Major Somerville, Captains W. Davies, Page and Bennett, Second Lieutenants Arnold, Bees, Hearder, E. A. Lloyd, J. S. Lewis, W. H. Morgan, Pemberton, W. Parry, G. F. Smith and F. T. Williams.   [2] Drafts amounting to nearly 280 men joined the battalion on April 17th and 18th.

troops.¹ The 6th were at the end of their tether when relieved, they had been hard at it for six days on end with little rest or sleep, and irregular rations, having to dig position after position and to repel any number of assaults. Their casualties were nearly 400, nearly half of them killed and missing. One officer only, Lieutenant W. T. Davies, was killed and one, Second Lieutenant A. Jenkins, missing, but 14, including, besides the C.O., Captains J. C. Owen and D. Jenkins, were wounded.²

The 5th, like the 6th, had had another day of hard fighting before quitting the line for a time. This was on April 14th when, owing to the loss of Neuve Eglise, a defensive flank had to be formed across the road thence to Kemmel, and B and C Companies were put in to make a local counter-attack. This was well led by Captain I. T. Evans, who was commanding both companies as Captain Rose had been hit, and proved successful, though casualties were rather heavy, over 40 all told. Next day B and C were sent back to dig a new defensive position at the Scherpenberg, part of the line on which the German offensive in this quarter was eventually stayed. D, which had been resting at La Clytte since the evening of April 12th, returned to the front line East of Kemmel on the 16th, and remained there till the 19th, when the French completed the relief of the Division. These last days had added several casualties to the already long roll of the battalion's losses,³ among them Major Oxley, who was mortally wounded on the 18th, during a heavy shelling of the rear lines. Joining the battalion in October, 1916, Major Oxley had served it well for 18 months: he was succeeded as second in command by Captain Bence Trower, in whose place Captain Runham became Adjutant.

By April 19th then the 2nd, 5th and 6th Battalions were all out of the fight and resting, so far as anyone in that strenuous and critical season could be allowed to rest. Both 5th and 6th indeed spent most of the last ten days of April digging away hard at new rear defences. They were not otherwise engaged in the heavy fighting round Kemmel, with which the German offensive in this region ended. But meanwhile, at the other end

¹ Major Pearson was awarded the D.S.O. for this battle, Captain Stickler and Lieutenant Amos getting the M.C., Company Sergeant Major Pearson the D.C.M., Sergeant Green and Corporal Elsdon a bar to the M.M. and 11 men the M.M.
² Lieutenant J. H. Richards died of wounds later.
³ The battalion's casualties between April 9th and 19th amounted to 11 officers and 205 men, Major Oxley, Second Lieutenants I. D. Jones and Rumbelow and 64 men being killed. Captains I. T. Evans and Runham received a bar to the M.C., Lieutenant J. R. L. Jones and Second Lieutenant O. Hart the M.C., Company Sergeant Major Morris, Corporal Smithey, and Lance-Corporal Rowles the D.C.M., and Private Handcock a bar to the M.M.

of the battle area, the 1st Battalion had been heavily engaged and had been earning notable laurels by a stubborn and skilful defence of a key position.

The 1st had actually entrained at Poezelhoek on April 8th, the day before the offensive opened, and after five uncomfortable hours in the train had reached Beuvry that evening. It had been rudely awakened from its slumbers early next morning by heavy shell falling in the village. Everyone turned out and the battalion spent most of the day "standing to" and awaiting information, most of which was inaccurate when it came, and orders. Ultimately D Company and half A were ordered up to hold various bridge-heads on the La Bassée Canal, in the course of which Lieutenant Ackerley was wounded. For two days nothing much happened: "details" under Captain Lochner were sent off to Burbure, but for the rest of the battalion still "stood by" till, on the afternoon of the 11th, it received orders to man the canal defences East of Bethune. Here it spent three days of relative quiet, though the attentions of some 8-inch howitzers caused Battalion Headquarters to shift from their original quarters. Then on April 15th the First Division relieved the Fifty-Fifth, who had put up so fine a defence of their all-important sector, and the battalion found itself responsible for the line to the left of Festubert and East of Loisne,[1] with headquarters in Loisne Château.[2] Nearly three years had passed since the 1st had been in this part of the front and few who had shared in the successful defence of Givenchy in January, 1915, were present to make an equally creditable fight for Loisne.

The line which the 1st took over was extremely weak. The so-called "Tuning Fork Line" which ran in rear of Festubert and in front of Loisne Château, was a mere bank of mud breastworks about five feet high with no parados or dug-outs. It was held by two and a half companies, C on the right and in rear of Festubert, which the Gloucestershire were holding, half B in the centre S.E. of the château, D on the left nearly 400 yards from B. In front of this gap was an advanced post known as Route A Keep, trenches disposed in a square round a concrete pill-box, which served as Headquarters for the two platoons of B which formed its garrison. A was in reserve in a "Switch Line," some distance in rear of B. There had been some savage fighting

---

[1] The Fifty-Fifth had had to throw back its left flank towards Loisne but had held the enemy there.
[2] A quantity of old liqueur brandy and some excellent red wine was found in the cellars of the château. Some of the former it was found possible to utilize, but the wine it was considered prudent to destroy, though it went to the hearts of Battalion Headquarters to see this excellent liquid pouring down the gutters.

already for Route A Keep; it had been taken by the Germans and retaken by the Liverpool Scottish, many of whom were lying dead about it. For two days the 1st S.W.B. did what they could to improve a far from satisfactory position. Except for snipers and occasional shelling and machine gun fire things were fairly quiet.

About 4 a.m. on the 18th, however, there developed an

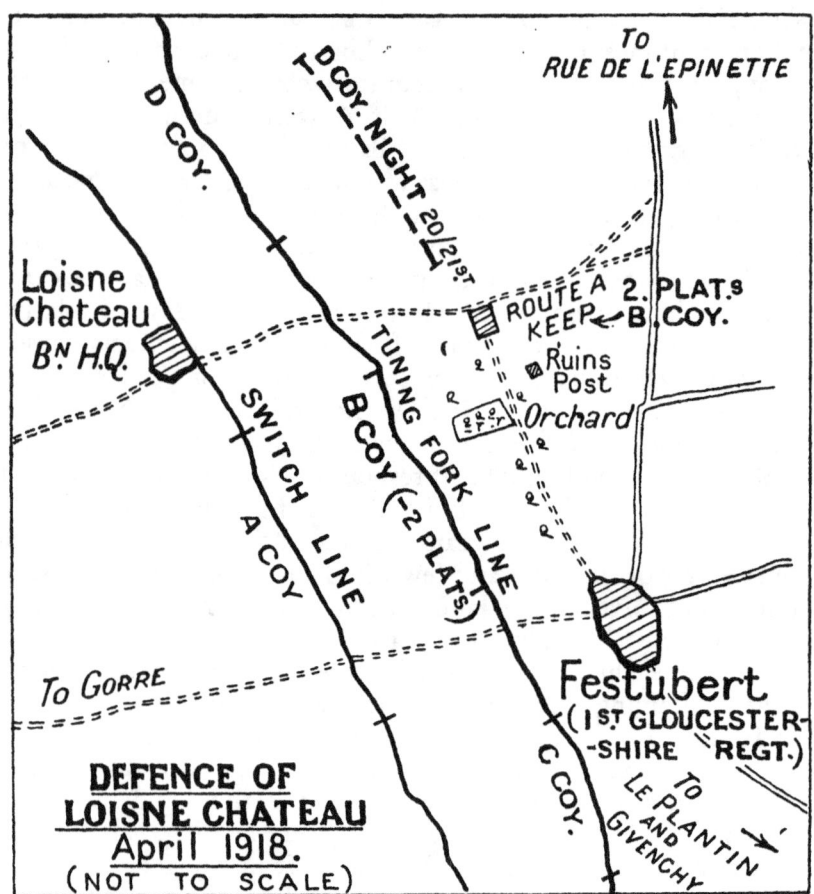

intense bombardment not only of the front area but of the back line also, in which gas shell was freely used. A Company indeed in the "Switch Line" suffered fully as much as those in front. This lasted till after 8.30 a.m., and then under cover of a thick mist the Germans attacked in force. Route A Keep had already had a tremendous shelling and the garrison had been reduced to little over 20 men before the attack broke over them. They put up a fine fight; when the Keep was recovered most of the two platoons were lying dead among its ruins with many

THE ATTACK REPULSED

Germans heaped around them, but the enemy were in overwhelming force and soon overpowered the survivors. The Keep once taken the Germans began to push on towards the Tuning Fork Line. On the left about 300 men advanced against D Company, but the rifle and machine gun fire which they encountered soon quenched their ardour. A few, however, got down into an old trench and pushed along it till within a short distance of our line, only to be shot down. Captain Fowkes did splendid work in directing the defence: though wounded he carried on, and his example was a great encouragement to his men. Second Lieutenant Dilloway was also prominent in his efforts to encourage the men to endure the bombardment. Sergeant Dare, when his Lewis guns and their crews were buried, not only dug out the men and guns but remounted the guns and maintained a steady fire and later on pushed out to the front, establishing a Lewis gun post in a shell hole so as to enfilade the line and inflicting many casualties. Sergeant Jeremiah and Corporal Chapman were also conspicuous for good work, setting a splendid example. The half of B Company in the Tuning Fork Line under Lieutenant Ainsworth were equally successful in maintaining their line. They could see figures moving about in the orchard in front, but at first the mist made it impossible to distinguish who these were. Thinking they might be his own men who been driven out of the Keep Lieutenant Ainsworth sent a small patrol forward to investigate. This came back quickly to report that the figures were German in full marching order. "From that moment," writes one account, "we had them stone cold"; a heavy fire was promptly opened upon them with great effect. Though the Germans attempted to advance, urged on by two officers who displayed wonderful courage and enterprise, one of them reaching our parapet before being hit, they were shot down in numbers, the Lewis guns being most effectively handled, and the attack was completely broken up. By 11 a.m. things were quite quiet again, though Route A Keep had gone the Tuning Fork Line had been held without having to call up the company in reserve.

Battalion Headquarters meanwhile had been subjected to a tremendous shelling which set fire to an ammunition dump and destroyed all means of communicating with the companies. The ammunition dump gave a wonderful pyrotechnic display as hundreds of Very lights caught fire, and as a high wall surrounded the château it was very hard to discover what had happened. Colonel Taylor, thinking from the sounds of firing coming nearer that the enemy must have got through, turned out every available man at Headquarters, batmen, signallers, sanitary men and others, and disposed them along a line of shell holes and other cover ready to resist attack, but none came and, as already stated, before long the attackers abandoned their efforts and the firing died down.

The subsiding of the attack had left some parties of Germans established fairly close to the British line; machine guns were located at two points about 300 yards from Loisne Keep, while there were other parties in front of B. Some of these points, however, were rather refuges from the British fire than bases for a renewed attack and, shortly after things quietened down, Second Lieutenant Parfitt noticed some Germans in a shell hole on the left of B's position in the Tuning Fork Line and worked his way out with a small party, intending to rush them, when an officer and half a dozen men with a machine gun jumped out of the shell hole and " Kameraded." They at any rate had had quite enough. Another party of about the same strength was mopped up a little later by a patrol which Sergeant Jeremiah took out, and from prisoners and dead several identifications were obtained.

However, Colonel Taylor was not content to have held the German attack, despite the very flattering messages he received from the higher authorities, Brigadier, Divisional Commander, Corps and Army, on his battalion's fine defence. He meant to get back Route A Keep and set to work to plan an attack. B Company, though down to less than 50 men, was ready to tackle the job, but being too weak alone was reinforced by two platoons of C, while a company of the Welch took over their bit of the Tuning Fork Line. Good work had been done in reconnoitring the position by Second Lieutenants Dilloway and Parfitt and by Second Lieutenant Tunnicliffe, who was acting as Brigade Intelligence Officer. Indeed the German dispositions were fairly accurately discovered before, early on April 20th, B led by Lieutenant Ainsworth filed out of their defences and lined up South of Route A Keep, with a platoon of C on either flank to cover them. There was a short but accurate bombardment,[1] in which trench mortars in the Tuning Fork Line took the lion's share, and then the attackers rushed the Keep. They had crept up as close to the barrage as they could and their attack was a complete surprise. The Germans had no time to man two machine guns which commanded the line by which the attack came before B were on top of them, had bayoneted the sentries and were bombing the dug-outs. Sergeant Jeremiah was much to the fore, leading his men round traverses and into dug-outs and accounting single-handed for several of the enemy. One officer alone made any real fight and less than 15 minutes from

[1] Only one 18 pounder was available but it proved enough to force the enemy under cover.

the start of the bombardment the Keep was again in British hands. Two machine guns and 19 prisoners were taken and D Company could now bring its line forward on the left and establish itself level with the Keep. Lieutenant Ainsworth and his men received warm congratulations from the Brigadier and Divisional Commander and the whole affair earned the battalion several well-deserved honours.[1] Its casualties had amounted to 150 of all ranks, including Second Lieutenant D. F. Watkins killed, Lieutenant Fowkes and Second Lieutenants T. H. Morgan Griffiths and Pozzi wounded,[2] but those inflicted on the Germans were certainly very much heavier.

Two days later (April 21st/22nd) the battalion was relieved and went back to Annequin for a short rest. As far as it was concerned the battle of the Lys was over, for the Germans proved to have been too much discouraged by their reception in the Givenchy–Loisne sector to try another effort there. Farther North, however, they had not yet finished, and a mass attack wrested Kemmel from the French on April 25th. Heavy fighting continued for several days, but the Germans could make no further advance, and the heavy losses with which their attempts were flung back led to their accepting the situation on this front also.

As already mentioned neither of the Pioneer battalions of the Regiment had any share in the Kemmel fighting. The 2nd, who came into the line again before the end of April, when the Twenty-Ninth Division took over the line from the Forest of Nieppe to the Hazebrouck–Bailleul railway, also missed this last phase of the battle. The German offensive in that quarter died down after the withdrawal of the Division from the line and was not renewed, though the party of the 2nd S.W.B. in the 87th Brigade's composite battalion which was in support on April 16th–18th was heavily shelled and had 20 casualties, including Captain I. A. Morgan killed and Second Lieutenants Russell and Garner wounded. The Loisne fight therefore marks the end of the TWENTY-FOURTH's active participation in the second of the German offensives of 1908. All four battalions who shared in it had been heavily tried, and all had done well. The 2nd had been the hardest hit, none of the others needed quite so much rebuilding, but all could congratulate themselves on having played important parts in bringing to a standstill what

[1] Lieutenants Ainsworth and Fowkes, Second Lieutenants Dilloway, Parfitt and Tunnicliffe got the M.C., Sergeant Dare a bar to the D.C.M., Sergeant Jeremiah and Lance Corporal Chapman the D.C.M. and 15 men the M.M.
[2] Colonel Taylor, Lieutenant Ainsworth and Second Lieutenant Parfitt were also wounded but continued at duty.

THE HISTORY OF THE SOUTH WALES BORDERERS

was in a way the most dangerous of the German offensives, seeing that it had in the main to be met by tired or young troops, at a point where there was little margin of ground that could be safely yielded. What ground the Germans had gained was reluctantly surrendered, especially at Ypres, where the hard-won gains of 1917 had to be evacuated, but nothing vital had been lost and, situated as the Germans were, nothing short of a really decisive success was quite worth the casualties the defence had inflicted on them.

CHAPTER XXIX

THE AISNE, 1918

AFTER the holding-up of the German offensive in Flanders and the simultaneous defeat at Villers Brettonneux of their last advance against Amiens, relative quiet prevailed on the British front for some weeks. Both sides were for the moment too exhausted for another big effort. The British had enough to do in converting into a properly defensible front the improvised line on which they had contrived to make their successful stand, while hardly a Division but had been heavily engaged once, if not twice, and was either much below strength or full of recently arrived drafts.

For three battalions of the Regiment in France, May, 1918, was not specially eventful. The 1st, after a short rest at Verquin, took over the Hohenzollern sector on April 24th and held it for four days and again from May 2nd to 12th. Their main occupation was to put the defences in order in accordance with a new defence scheme, but several attempts were made to liberate gas, which after fickle winds had caused several failures was at last brought off on the night of May 9th/10th. A turn in reserve was followed by one in the Cambrin defences. Things were quiet here; the enemy's guns fired occasionally but did little damage and the casualties were low, while the weather was mostly fine.

The 2nd Battalion found May more eventful. It had been reorganized as two companies, A and D forming one, B and C the other. This was more due to lack of trained N.C.O.'s[1] and specialists than to numerical weakness, for even when two more drafts amounting to 81 in all had joined the two-company organization was retained.[2] The battalion remained in billets near Hazebrouck till April 27th, and then went into line again opposite Vieux Berquin. The outpost line here consisted of posts only and was but lightly held, but the main line behind was continuous, a shallow trench with a breastwork and well wired. The country here had been but little shelled and the hedges afforded plenty of cover, which was increased as the crops which had been planted during the winter and early spring grew up. Patrols were active and some advanced posts were pushed forward without any interference by the enemy. From

---

[1] On April 18th there were only 8 Sergeants and 12 Corporals in the battalion.
[2] Captain A. B. Cowburn (Border Regiment) joined on May 6th and became second in command vice Major Somerville, while Captain A. E. Crowder was now Adjutant, but was replaced in June by Captain W. V. D. Dickinson, who had been serving with the King's African Rifles since August, 1914.

May 5th to 13th the battalion was out of the line, during which time the arrival of 143 men with ten subalterns allowed of its reorganization in four companies commanded respectively by Second Lieutenants Hall (A) and Pratt (B), and Captains Whitworth (C) and Dendy (D). The day after it returned to the line the battalion, being then in support, came in for a tremendous bombardment with gas shell, the gas, a mixture of phosgene and mustard oil, having a delayed effect and putting four officers and nearly 100 men out of action. However, it was not slow to get some of its own back. The Germans had some advanced machine gun posts in enclosures round Lug Farm West of Vieux Berquin, and as Divisional Headquarters were most anxious to identify their "opposite number" by capturing a prisoner the battalion was ordered to raid them.

The British front curved sharply back S.W. at this point and the attack, on the night of May 21st/22nd, had to be delivered almost diagonally, the right having much farther to go than the left. Little time for preparation was available, but the raiders, three officers and 67 men under Second Lieutenant Esmond, who were divided into five groups, were just able to keep up with an excellent barrage. A machine gun at the N.W. corner of the first enclosure opened fire on the left group, and its leader, Corporal Connolly, was seriously wounded, but the next group rushed the position from the flank, though its leader, Second Lieutenant Dixon, was killed just as he had forced his way in. This enclosure was speedily cleared, the enemy retiring hastily. Meanwhile, Second Lieutenant Esmond with the centre group had cleared a second enclosure, and the other groups under Second Lieutenant W. H. Morris and Sergeant Richards had been equally successful. A machine gun opened fire at Second Lieutenant Morris' party at about 40 yards range, but he promptly brought a Lewis gun into action against it. Covered by its fire he worked round to the flank and rushed the machine gun, capturing it and half its crew and killing the others with the bayonet. He then led his men on to the final objective nearer the farm. All objectives were duly gained and the different groups then took up their allotted positions on the farther edges of the enclosures. However, finding that prisoners had been taken and his main objective therefore achieved, Second Lieutenant Esmond decided to withdraw. Before he did so a strong party was seen approaching from Vieux Berquin. It was allowed to come within about 50 yards before fire was opened with telling effect and, covered by this, the withdrawal was safely accomplished, all the wounded, six in all, being brought away. The success of the raid was largely due to the excellence of the barrage, but it reflected special credit on those concerned, as the raiders were nearly all young " unblooded " soldiers recently out from home, who had never seen a barrage before.[1]

The 2nd remained in front line for another week, the chief incident being that on the evening of the 25th a platoon of D Company, under Second Lieutenant C. L. Thomas, pushed quietly out into No Man's Land and dug themselves in well in advance of our line. Just before the relief a small draft arrived, which brought the battalion's strength up to 750 again, and five officers joined, including Captain Givons, who took over A Company, and Lieutenant T. R. Williams, who resumed his duties as Transport Officer.

The 10th S.W.B. also had had quite a satisfactory time since being hurried down to the Ancre to hold the Germans back. It did not go into the front line till the last week of April, though being in support proved anything but a time of idleness, as many carrying parties were called for and the back positions needed much improving and consolidating. When in the line its snipers were extremely active, the Germans, who also were consolidating their positions, giving them many chances. Still the 10th did not escape lightly, its casualties for April coming to nearly 60, including Second Lieutenant A. Morgan and 8 men killed. Things continued fairly " lively " along the Ancre during May. On the night of May 8th/9th a party of A Company under Second Lieutenant Howarth successfully rushed a post near Lone Tree, though the Germans returned in force and reoccupied the post, driving out the garrison left to hold it. A little later the battalion's Lewis guns did some effective shooting at Germans who had been dislodged from their trenches by a bombardment and exposed themselves in running back to shelter. On the last ten days of the month the 10th was at Herrisart training; though it had had 80 casualties[2] since May 1st, it was nearly 850 strong. Several new officers appeared, including some old members of the 11th and 12th Battalions, among them Major Monteith, who joined early in May. But for the time the battalion lost Colonel Harvey's guidance, as he was invalided home at the end of May, and Regimental Sergeant Major Lockie, after a long period of excellent service, was also invalided in May, Company Sergeant Major F. C. Williams becoming R.S.M. in his place.

But if three battalions of the S.W.B. had no special reason

---

[1] Second Lieutenant Esmond received the M.C.
[2] Seven killed, 3 missing, 2 officers (Second Lieutenants Rayner and F. F. Williams) and 68 men wounded.

to remember May, 1918, to the 5th and 6th that month has very particular significance. The Nineteenth and Twenty-Fifth were among the dozen British Divisions who had been engaged in both the big German offensives, and both were now badly in need of an easy time. The Twenty-Fifth had had 3500 casualties in March and over 7500 in April, and the Nineteenth's losses had been on the same scale. Both were among the five Divisions allotted to the Ninth Corps, which, by arrangement between Marshal Foch and Sir Douglas Haig, was sent to the Aisne in May to replace the French Divisions who had been sent up to Flanders and had been engaged round Kemmel. The Aisne had long been one of the French "rest cure" sectors. Except for General Nivelle's ill-fated offensive in the spring of 1917 there had been no serious fighting there since early in 1915, and the British Divisions which took over the sector were not as favourably impressed with its defences as with the general surroundings. The country was a most agreeable change on Flanders, and the French from whom the Ninth Corps took over scouted the idea of a German offensive on that front. They promised a very peaceful kind of war, and at first it seemed as if their prophecies would prove correct.

The 6th were the first of the two S.W.B. battalions to reach the new front. After working away at new second line defences till May 5th it had moved back to near Steenvoorde and entrained on the 9th for Soissons. Thirty hours in the train brought it to Vezilly on the 11th, where it remained nearly a fortnight training its last batches of recruits. Like the rest of the Division it had been mainly filled up with young soldiers from Graduated Battalions, good material but very immature, along with some men over 35, mostly "combings" from protected industries or from "departmental" Corps. A dozen new officers had arrived, including Major T. H. Morgan, formerly of the 11th Battalion, who became second in command to Colonel Deane, whose promotion was announced on May 13th. Major Reid-Kellett, who had been away wounded since September, also rejoined. On May 23rd the battalion shifted to Mayneux[1], where at 8 p.m. on the 26th it received warning orders to be ready to move at once. The attack which the French had declared to be quite out of the question was about to be delivered.

The 5th had been a week later in moving to the Aisne. The battalion had been kept at work on the Vlamertinghe line till May 13th, coming in for some long range shelling and having

---

[1] The Twenty-Fifth Division had not yet gone into line, being in Corps Reserve.

THE ATTACK ON THE AISNE

over 30 casualties[1] while on this task. It had left Flanders on May 17th, had arrived at Vitry La Ville on the 19th, and moved to Francheville, where it remained till the German attack started.[2] Like the 6th it had been filled up with recruits, mostly very young soldiers, and had received several new subalterns.

When the fighting began, therefore, neither the Nineteenth nor the Twenty-Fifth Division was actually in the line, so both 5th and 6th S.W.B. escaped the first brunt of the attack. Both had very similar parts to play, they were hurried up in turn to endeavour to stop the German advance which was being vigorously pushed towards the Marne, but rather to the Eastward of the area over which the 1st Battalion had pursued the Germans in September, 1914.

The 6th was the first to come into action. Its Division was sent up to hold a second line 12 miles long along the heights South of the Maizy-Cormicy road and thence S. to Trigny. The 6th, who had started off at 10.30 p.m. and reached Vaulx-Varennes at 3 a.m. (May 27th), were placed under the B.G.C. 7th Brigade, who sent them to prolong his right in front of Hermonville. Two companies, C (Lieutenant Amos) and D (Lieutenant H. Davies), took up their position here N. and N.E. of Hermonville, while A (Captain Stickler) was in reserve on high ground N. of Trigny. By this time the German attack had already made considerable progress. It had begun about 1 a.m. with one of the heaviest bombardments of the war, which was kept up for over three hours and did tremendous damage to the defences of the battle-zone, besides inflicting heavy casualties, and put many of the defenders' guns out of action.[3] At 4.30 a.m. the infantry attack had followed and had thrust back across the Aisne the survivors of the left and centre Divisions, the Fiftieth and Eighth. On the right, to which the 6th S.W.B. had been sent, the Twenty-First Division, rather more fortunately placed, had held its own fairly well, but the driving in of the troops on its flank rendered its position insecure, and before long its outflanked left had to be brought back to avoid being cut off. The Twenty-Fifth Division had barely reached its assigned position before it was hotly engaged on the left and centre. The scanty few of the Eighth and Fiftieth Divisions who had survived the attack on the front system rallied on them,

[1] Three killed, Second Lieutenant E. S. J. Evans and 28 men wounded.
[2] The Nineteenth Division, like the Twenty-Fifth, had remained in reserve.
[3] The French scheme of defence had not found favour with the Ninth Corps, more particularly the dangerously advanced positions of the batteries and the too high proportion of infantry exposed to the original bombardment. The experience of May 27th proved that the British misgivings were only too well founded.

but the Twenty-Fifth's task proved too much for one Division, especially as further to the left the French were being pushed back fast and the Germans were thus threatening that flank.

The 6th, who had a long line to hold but were so fortunate as to find a good trench, well wired and traversed, ready for them, were not seriously engaged till, in the afternoon, the Twenty-First Division had to wheel back in conformity with the troops on its left. The Germans followed them up, and before long C and D found themselves sharply engaged. The pressure was heavy enough: at one moment some Germans got within 100 yards, whereupon some gunners just in rear of the 6th abandoned their guns and went back, but so accurately and steadily did the 6th shoot that the Germans recoiled, on which the gunners, returning to their battery position, reopened fire. It was now about 7 p.m., and for a time the Germans seemed to have been stopped, though about 8.30 p.m. they came on again but were beaten off. Shortly afterwards the Twenty-First Division retired, C Company going with them, though D, having received no orders, remained in position. For some hours D held on, a few stragglers being collected and put into line, while Second Lieutenant Parry formed a defensive flank on the left with about 60 men and held on well, delaying the German advance effectively. Eventually, however, scouts discovered that the Germans were already in the left rear and swarming in the woods around. Lieutenant Davies therefore decided to retire and, evacuating his position under cover of Lewis guns, which did great execution when the enemy emerged from the woods, he led his men round S.E. of Hermonville and ultimately, after some fighting in which two officers and about 40 men got cut off, the rest rejoined the other two companies next morning (May 28th) between Prouilly and Trigny. Company Sergeant Major Ricketts did great work in this retirement, taking command of a party who had lost their officers and handling them coolly and skilfully, while Second Lieutenant Bowen, who had already done good work in rallying and reorganizing scattered parties and assisting to hold on by using Lewis guns effectively, was most successful in extricating his men when the position proved quite untenable.

A, on whom C had fallen back during the night, had made a stout stand near Château Hervelon. They had had various details on their left, and some Zouaves came up and joined them, but in the end the Germans had got round the left and made a retirement necessary. This had been successfully covered by A, who had held on after the rest had gone, but had eventually to conform. Captain Mann, the battalion's M.O., was again most energetic and resourceful in seeing to the evacuation of the wounded, organizing parties to go back under heavy fire to a dressing-station in which several men had been and rescuing the majority. He well earned the bar to the M.C. which he received.

On the Prouilly–Trigny line the Twenty-First Division with the assistance of the 7th Brigade held the Germans up for some time, but eventually this line also had to be given up and a fresh stand attempted along the railway line in the valley of the Vesle. Here the 6th took post near the tile works East of Jonchery, but was soon ordered back again, this time to Hill 202, West of Rosnay.[1] On the way it was heavily shelled, and though it escaped with fairly light losses, these included the C.O., who was killed near Rosnay Church. The third C.O. of a battalion of the Twenty-fourth killed in action during the war, Colonel Deane was much missed by his battalion. Joining it as a subaltern in October, 1914, he had served with it practically continuously, had done excellent work in many capacities, and his promotion to command it had been well deserved and popular. A mining engineer by profession he was well qualified to command Pioneers, and he had shown himself a fine fighting man, resourceful, daring, quick to appreciate a tactical situation and possessed of the qualities of a true leader.

On reaching its destination the 6th, now under Major Reid-Kellett, found French troops in occupation and was placed in a wood half a mile in rear for the night. Early next morning (May 19th) it was ordered back again, as support was no longer needed at this point. Proceeding through Marfaux, where it had the good luck to encounter a lorry laden with rations, the 6th made its way across country, thereby escaping both the press of traffic and the dust, to Damary, where it bivouacked, much exhausted by the heat and long marching. Two days more marching followed, bringing it on May 31st to Loisy en Brie, where the remnants of the Division were being collected. It had in all covered 84 kilometres in five days, with constant fighting thrown in, and all ranks were thoroughly tired. At Loisy the companies rejoined the transport, which had been forced by shell fire to quit its bivouac at Vaulx-Varennes on the night of May 26/27th and had had a long march Southward through Jonchery, much hampered by terribly crowded roads and harassed by machine gun fire from German aeroplanes, which inflicted several casualties, the Quartermaster, Captain Case, being wounded.

The 6th had not been engaged in the "Second Aisne" for nearly as long as in the Lys and their casualties were not as heavy. Still they were bad enough, Colonel Deane, Regimental Sergeant Major Glenister, and 18 men killed, Lieutenant H. Davies,

[1] As a result of the greater success of the Germans on the left of the line attacked, the British front was now tending to run N.E. to S.W. rather than East to West.

THE HISTORY OF THE SOUTH WALES BORDERERS

Second Lieutenants Carlyle, Kitchen and Murray and 111 men missing;[1] Captain Case, Lieutenant Kendrick, Second Lieutenant Parry and 110 men wounded, in all nearly 250. To have to withstand three successive German offensives and go through three fighting retreats had been a sore trial, and in the last two the 6th had been largely composed of new-comers to its ranks who knew little of each other and their officers. Its performance in the Second Aisne, the last fight of the Twenty-Fifth Division as originally constituted,[2] certainly ranks high among its achievements.

As the 6th S.W.B. were quitting the battle-zone the 5th were entering it. The Nineteenth Division, though not originally in the Ninth Corps, had been placed at his disposal on May 28th and had been moved up in motor omnibuses from near Chalons to Chaumuzy, North of Epernay. The Germans were now pressing up the Ardre valley against the left of the line on which the remnants of the Ninth Corps and the French who had reinforced them were trying to stand, and the Nineteenth Division had to be put in to counter-attack down the valley. The 5th S.W.B., who had started off for Chaumuzy at 10 p.m. on May 28th, arrived there at 6.30 p.m. next day and were retained as a Divisional reserve along with the three R.E. companies. Early next morning they were moved forward to Chambreçy, and while B Company started work on a new line in rear of Romigny C and D moved into a gap in the front line, astride the Romigny–Chatillon road, B later on coming up into line on the left with a platoon thrown forward to cover some dangerous dead ground. The enemy were soon attacking this line but, thanks to having a good field of fire, the 5th punished its opponents heavily. B's advanced platoon caught them in enfilade and did great execution, but D was in turn enfiladed and forced back by the intensity of the machine gun fire. Behind the Romigny–Ville en Tardenois road C, who had been in support, reinforced them and a stand was successfully made against repeated attacks. Casualties had been heavy, Captain W. H. Williams and Second Lieutenant L. T. Morris and 18 men killed,[3] Major Bence Trower and 18 men missing, Second Lieutenants T. H. Kent and

---

[1] A dozen men rejoined about a fortnight later, having become detached and joined other units. All 4 officers were subsequently reported as prisoners of war.

[2] The Division was broken up, the Service battalions being disbanded and the three Regular units transferred to other Divisions. It was later on (September) reconstituted with battalions withdrawn from Italy, but by that time the 6th S.W.B. had been transferred to the Thirtieth Division.

[3] These included Company Sergeant Major Mitchener, who was awarded a posthumous M.C. for his gallantry and resourcefulness.

Smeathers and 95 men wounded, but the Germans had been really checked and their gains had been unimportant.

Major Trower, to the general regret, proved to have been killed. He had gone forward to reconnoitre a position before sending men to occupy it and must have run into the enemy. His body was never found and as one account says, " It is impossible to say how he met his end. That it was a brave one no one can doubt." He had been a mainstay of the 5th. A most efficient platoon commander, for over a year a most competent Adjutant, he had just become second in command. "Everyone loved him," it has been said. " He was quite fearless: he put the performance of duty above all questions of personal safety and comfort. 'I'll do anything or go anywhere for Mr. Trower,' said a sergeant on one occasion, and it represented the feelings of all."

That evening the 5th was relieved and withdrew to the Bois de Courtin, where it rested on May 31st, moving up next day in close support to the 57th Brigade and digging a support line from the Bois d'Eclisse to the Chaumuzy–La Neuville road. That evening a determined German attack pushed the front line back from the Bois de Courmont but could not penetrate any further, part of B Company doing fine service on a spur near Boujacourt. For the next four days the 5th continued in close support; there were no actual attacks but consistent shelling, at times very heavy, and every day brought some casualties. This did not prevent the battalion from digging away steadily at a series of defensive lines. On June 6th came a big attack which captured the Mont de Bligny, a point of vital importance. An immediate counter-attack was necessary and this the 56th Brigade carried out successfully, the 4th K.S.L.I. winning the Croix de Guerre. But losses had been heavy, and that evening the 5th S.W.B. had to turn from Pioneering and take over the front line West of the Bois d'Eclisse. Here it was severely shelled at times but dealt very effectively with various patrols and other small parties of enemy who showed up on its front. After holding this position with only one day's rest until June 15th it was then relieved by an Italian Division. This relief was remarkable. Every other Italian soldier seemed to be accompanied by a dog; the relieving battalion had many more men than the trenches could accommodate. Nobody knew the other people's language—least of all the interpreters—and the confusion was complete. However, the Germans did not take advantage of it to attack and the 5th got away safely to Hautvillers (North of Epernay) not a little glad of the prospect of a rest after three weeks in the line. It had had 15 men killed and missing since June 1st and over 70 wounded.

From Hautvillers it moved on June 20th to Le Mesnil where General Pellé of the French Vth Corps, under whom it had been fighting, inspected it, congratulated it on its achievements and presented the Croix de Guerre to Company Sergeant Major Hooper and Sergeant Vaughan. Its Division was now out of the line but remained in the French zone till the first week in July, when it returned to the British area, reaching Mazinghen on the 9th. It was to have a long spell, though not exactly one of rest, before it was to be in the fighting line again.

The third great German "push" had had much the same results as its predecessors. Substantial as were its gains of ground, a line had in the end been patched up beyond which it could not penetrate. In bringing this advance to a standstill the Ninth British Corps had played an important part. A French General has spoken of the tenacity with which its decimated Divisions had fought on, re-forming new units which served as the basis of the dike against which the tide of the German advance had finally spent itself. Moreover, the deep re-entrant in the Allied line which was the result of the May "push" was to prove peculiarly disadvantageous to the Germans when, two months later, the tide at last turned against them. The 5th and 6th had deserved well of the TWENTY-FOURTH in adding to its laurels the " honour " of " Aisne, 1918."

CHAPTER XXX

THE SUMMER OF 1918

THE German attack on the Aisne, though making a substantial gain of ground, had been held up, like its predecessors of March and April, before it could produce really decisive results. The Allies had once again patched up a defensible line and the Germans had relapsed into virtual inactivity on the British front. Thus with more and more Americans landing weekly in France—their arrival was in itself convincing proof of the waning efficiency of unlimited submarine warfare—and the return from Salonica and Palestine of the many British units which, better late than never, had been recalled to the theatre of critical operations, the situation seemed to be taking a welcome turn for the better. The hastily taken up positions along which the German advance had been arrested were gradually consolidated. The many lost guns were soon replaced, despite all the vast dumps that had been captured there was no stint of munitions, and several successful minor enterprises straightened out and improved the line. This happier state of affairs was a relief after the dark days of the March retreat and of April. If it was felt that there might yet be more to come, that the Germans were probably preparing for a supreme and final effort, there was fair reason for confidence as to its probable result. Among those in authority anxiety might still prevail; regimental officers and men who were in the line during June and July usually found themselves securing an ascendency over their "opposite numbers" which augured favourably for the future. It may not have been obvious to them that the exertions and sacrifices which had brought the Germans to the outskirts of Amiens and Hazebrouck had really been out of proportion to the results achieved and had left many German units quite unfit for further efforts, but they certainly did not find it difficult to gain the upper hand locally, and as the weeks passed by it was the British who were usually the more aggressive and active.

The 1st Battalion spent this period in the near neighbourhood of the sector in which it had so greatly distinguished itself in April. The beginning of June found it in line in the Cambrin sector, things being unusually active owing to a projected raid by the battalion on its right, which was preceded by shelling and wire-cutting. The raid, carried out on the evening of June 4th, provoked heavy retaliation, which fortunately did not cause the 1st any casualties. From June 5th to 13th the battalion was at rest at Noeux les Mines, a period marked by a most successful Divisional Gymkhana and Horse Show and an inspection of the brigade by the Corps Commander, who was very much pleased with the smartness of the Guard of Honour produced by the battalion. Shortly before the battalion returned to the trenches several cases of an ill-defined feverish nature had shown themselves, Captain Baker, the Adjutant, being among the earliest victims; this soon attained to the dimensions of an epidemic, which received the nickname of "creeping barrage." Three officers in quick succession took over the Adjutant's duties and went down sick; and, despite all the M.O.'s efforts to check the epidemic, cases proved so numerous that after an inter-company relief one of the relieved companies had to be retained in support to keep the trench garrison up to its proper strength. Fortunately the epidemic abated after about ten days, though many of its victims were away from duty for some time: Captain Baker, for example, only rejoined on July 15th.[1]

The battalion was in the Hohenzollern sector from June 13th to 21st and again from June 25th to July 2nd, during which Second Lieutenant Dilloway and Sergeant Moore earned warm congratulations from the Brigadier by admirable work in patrolling. From July 2nd to 11th it was "out," mainly training in the Houchin area, and then did two turns in the Cambrin sub-sector.[2]. Two raids were carried out in hopes of obtaining identifications, but without success. In the first Second Lieutenant Hall and his platoon reached their objective, three German posts, but found them unoccupied. In the second Second Lieutenant Treloar and his party had just reached the wire in front of these posts and were crawling through the gaps, when the Germans, discovering them, opened a heavy fire and threw bombs. Second Lieutenant Treloar, though wounded in no less than twenty-seven places, succeeded in getting his party away, removing all the casualties and thereby preventing the enemy from obtaining any identifications, for which he was subsequently awarded the M.C. On July 31st the battalion went back to Noeux les Mines for ten days, then had a fairly quiet week in the Hohenzollern sector, though a daylight patrol cost it Second Lieutenant W. M. Llewellin, who was reported "missing." The last ten days of August were spent in training at Pressy les Pernes, and then on August 31st the Division entrained for Arras and a share in greater activities than had been its lot for the last four months. Though far from inactive since its hard fight in April, the 1st had had few casualties and had had a good chance of assimilating

---

[1] He was then attached to the Brigade Staff as a "learner," Captain Wales continuing to discharge the Adjutant's duties which he had taken over in Captain Baker's absence.

[2] July 11th to 15th and 19th to 27th.

its drafts. Major Lochner had left in July to take command of the 10th K.S.L.I., but otherwise changes had not been numerous.

The 2nd S.W.B. had had a rather more eventful summer than had the 1st. Returning to the old front line opposite Vieux Berquin on June 14th it found things very lively.[1] Warnings had been received that an attack on Hazebrouck by at least four Divisions was highly probable, and everyone was much on the alert in consequence. Actually no attack in force came, though early on June 15th heavy shelling developed, lasting over one and a half hours, while the left platoon of the front line company[2] saw enemy extending in its front in some force. Rifles and Lewis guns promptly opened fire, and proved sufficient to prevent any advance, while the German barrage cost the battalion a bare dozen casualties. Two days later orders were issued for the Division to carry out an attack in conjunction with the Fifth on its right, but these were cancelled, and on June 21st the Twenty-Ninth Division was relieved and given a full month's rest. This was the more welcome because it afforded an opportunity for the systematic training of the substantial drafts which had replenished the Division's depleted ranks[3] but consisted mainly of recruits of rather limited training, especially in open warfare. Indeed this month was most beneficial in every respect, though the epidemic of " P.U.O." which afflicted the whole British Army at this time did not spare the Twenty-Ninth Division.

Early in August the Twenty-Ninth Division took over the Merris sector,[4] and on August 15th the 2nd S.W.B. were back in front line again. This consisted of platoon posts about 150 yards apart, lying South-West of Merris and astride the Armentières-Hazebrouck railway. Facing the battalion and on the far side of the Meteren Becque was the Oultersteene ridge, the last piece of higher ground between Merris and the Lys. For some time past small British advances in this quarter had been winning back bit by bit the ground lost in April, and another of these operations was now in preparation. In this the Ninth Division, now in line on the Twenty-Ninth's left, was to co-operate, and vigorous patrolling and scouting were necessary to obtain exact

[1] Just before this Captain N. Roberts had joined and taken over C Company, Captain Whitworth, who had returned from hospital, taking over B, while Captain Crowder and Regimental Sergeant Major Vatcher, who had been transferred from the 12th Battalion, had been awarded the M.C. in the June Honours List.
[2] The company was holding Fantasy Farm.
[3] The 2nd was up to 30 officers and 835 men by the end of June.
[4] Shortly before this Captain Laman had left for the well-earned relief of six months' duty at home and had been replaced as Quartermaster by Lieutenant Waldron.

information about the hostile positions. In this the 2nd did excellent work, the enemy's line being accurately located. The plan of attack was rather complicated: the Meteren Becque would have proved an awkward obstacle to an advance from the West, but on the left the Ninth Division's recent capture of Meteren (July 19th) had advanced the British line well to the Eastward of the frontage held by the Twenty-Ninth, and it was possible to attack astride the Becque from North to South. As a start the Ninth Division, assisted by the 1st K.O.S.B. on their right, were to secure a line from Garbedoen Farm (just North-East of Merris) across the Becque to Terrapin House and thence roughly back Northwards to Gaza Cross-roads. The 2nd S.W.B. were to keep touch with the K.O.S.B. during this stage and on their establishing themselves on their objectives, known as the "Blue Line," A and C Companies, being then in front line just South-East of Merris, would push patrols forward to see if the success could be extended by capturing Oultersteene.

The Ninth Division and K.O.S.B. were rapidly and completely successful; by 12.10 p.m. (August 18th) the Blue Line had been made good and 150 prisoners captured with 40 machine guns. A and C then pushed their patrols forward, with a platoon of each company in close support and the rest following behind. The advance was vigorously and skilfully conducted, so much dash and initiative being shown by individuals and junior commanders that opposition was quickly overcome. Machine guns were rapidly located and outflanked, excellent use being made of rifle grenades; while the careful training the battalion had just been through bore ample fruit in the admirable co-operation between the platoons, one keeping a machine gun engaged and occupied, while another rushed it from the flank.

On the right C Company soon secured the line of the railway from Alert Crossing Eastward as far as the railway bridge over the Becque. The company was admirably handled by Lieutenant Glover,[1] who took charge when the company commander was hit, and led it on to its objectives. His right flank was exposed, but he showed great judgment and initiative in disposing his men to protect it and beat off a counter-attack. A strayed too much to the right but eventually crossed the Becque at the railway bridge and at the Oultersteene Road bridge, and got touch with the K.O.S.B. who had penetrated into Oultersteene. B had meanwhile manned C Company's old front line posts and D had occupied a support position North-West of Oultersteene.

The success was so complete and so quickly achieved that the Germans never attempted any serious counter-attack and did not even interfere seriously with consolidation, only starting to

---

[1] Lieutenant Glover subsequently received the M.C.

OULTERSTEENE RETAKEN

shell Oultersteene vigorously after the attacking companies were well dug in. Nearly 140 prisoners, including 5 officers, were taken, with 16 machine guns and 3 trench mortars, while substantial casualties were inflicted on the Germans. Considering the sharpness of the fighting the losses were not heavy, Second Lieutenants D. C. Dickinson and C. R. Thomas having been killed with 9 men, while Captain Roberts and 11 men were wounded.

On the battalion's right, South of the railway, the 86th Brigade had been less successful, but next afternoon it attacked again and secured all its objectives, thereby improving the position materially. However, the German shell fire had increased in intensity and accuracy, and before the 2nd were relieved, which was not till the night of August 20th/21st, casualties had mounted up to well over 60, more than a third being killed or missing.[1] Even at this cost the success had been useful enough. The fighting in the Lys valley indeed, though overshadowed in importance and influence by that in progress further South, which had started on August 8th with the smashing defeat of the Germans in the battle of Amiens, had brought the British left centre into a good position for profiting by victories elsewhere to deliver Lille and thrust the Germans back from the outskirts of Ypres. Before long it would not be local successes only which this quarter would produce, but a more sustained and substantial contribution to the German overthrow.

After all they had gone through the two Pioneer battalions were, naturally enough, given a good rest during the summer months. The Nineteenth Division on returning from the French zone was placed in G.H.Q. Reserve, near Hazebrouck, and the 5th S.W.B., who had left Fère-Champenoise on July 1st, were at Mazinghien from July 9th onwards, mainly occupied in constructing rear defences, known as the "B.B." line, in readiness for an expected German offensive. By the first week in August its Division had been sufficiently rested and recruited[2] to return to the line, taking over the centre section of the Thirteenth Corps[3] front, opposite Locon and Hinges. This meant for the 5th a march by Norrent-Fontes, St. Hilaire and Lillers to Burbure, where it found itself concerned rather with preparing for an offensive. It was now employed mainly on the roads, removing obstructions, filling in shell holes, levelling

---

[1] The wounded included Second Lieutenant J. Davies.
[2] Captain I. T. Evans had been promoted Major in Major E. B. Trower's place and Major T. H. Morgan joined from the 6th Battalion in June, while 10 new subalterns had joined.   [3] This Corps was in the Fifth Army.

and smoothing, besides clearing ditches and streams and improving the drainage. Immediately the Division took over its line the enemy began withdrawing from their advanced positions, evacuating Locon and Le Vertbois; on August 19th our outposts pushed forward another 1000 yards, and ten days later a fresh advance carried the line past Vieille Chapelle and Zelobes and over the Lawe Canal. This meant additional work on roads for the Pioneers, whose headquarters now moved to Bethune, familiar country to such few survivors of 1915 as still maintained with the battalion. As yet the successive advances had been largely due to the enemy retiring of his own volition, but now the repercussion of events elsewhere began to affect even "quiet" quarters like the Bethune–La Bassée area, and on September 3rd the Nineteenth Division took the offensive successfully, pushing forward across the Estaires–La Bassée road and regaining approximately the old British line of April 9th, 1918. Beyond this, however, it did not for the moment advance. The Fifth Army consisted largely of troops from whom too much could not be expected, so-called "Garrison Guard" battalions, "B.1" men and the like, and its offensive capacities were limited. To the 5th S.W.B. the advance merely meant more work; roads, trench tramways and railways had to be carried forward to the new front, the damage done by the retreating Germans to roads and bridges had to be repaired as quickly and effectively as possible, craters made by mine-explosions—for choice at road junctions—had to be filled in, or deviations made round them, and the way sufficiently cleared of obstructions for guns, ambulances, ammunition wagons and lorries with stores and supplies to follow hard on the heels of the evading enemy.

The 6th Battalion meanwhile had spent most of June in reorganizing. It was at Loisy en Brie till the 9th, moved thence to St. Loup, worked there for ten days on roads and rifle-ranges, and then shifted to Vindey. Here it came under the Fiftieth Division, but was soon afterwards transferred to the Thirtieth, which had just been reconstructed out of battalions withdrawn from Palestine and Salonica and had been allotted to the Second Army. On July 1st it left Vindey, and after a varied journey by road and rail joined its new formation at Clairmaris, near St. Omer, on the 7th. Major W. L. Crawford, of the Lancashire Fusiliers, had joined on June 2nd to succeed to the vacancy created by Colonel Deane's death, Major Reid-Kellett being second in command, Major T. H. Morgan having been transferred to the 5th Battalion, while a dozen new subalterns had joined.

MINOR ADVANCES

Until early in August the 6th was kept busy working on an "Army Line," being quartered either at Boeschepe or at Oxelaere. On August 9th it moved to a "forward area" at Westoutre and transferred its activities to constructing and clearing roads and communication trenches. On the night of August 20th/21st A Company, under Captain Stickler, assisted the 2nd London Scottish in a successful local attack on the Dranoutre Ridge, supervising the consolidation of the captured position and digging in to the East of the ridge while C dug a communication trench and sent up two platoons to wire the line to the left, D meanwhile digging a support line. Good progress was made with all these tasks, and as companies were withdrawn before daybreak heavy casualties were successfully avoided. For the next two nights consolidation was continued under considerable difficulties. On the night of the 21st/22nd, for example, a heavy barrage drove A Company from its work, forcing it to shelter in a sunken road till, the counter-attack having been beaten off, the shelling subsided and the company could resume work. Altogether the 6th had over a dozen casualties, among them Lieutenant W. L. Bowen, who died of wounds on September 1st.

The 10th Battalion, after a fortnight's rest at Herissart at the end of May, had returned to the line on June 3rd, its Division then relieving the Sixty-Third in the Aveluy Wood sector. The battalion was at first in the support trenches of the Mesnil sub-sector on the right. Things were fairly lively, the enemy's artillery being extremely active; on June 9th, for example, reserve dumps, the canteen, the regimental aid post and the officers' mess all suffered severely, the officers' kitchen being completely destroyed. That evening the Germans tried to rush some of the battalion's advanced posts but were repulsed with several casualties, but all efforts to reach the German corpses and obtain identifications were frustrated by machine gun fire, while next night the Germans repeated the attempt, rushed a post and captured a prisoner. This was the more galling because never before had the 10th been raided successfully.[1]

However, the 10th gave as good as they got, and in the exchanges between snipers and patrols they scored heavily on several occasions. Private Bassett was particularly successful as a sniper; on one occasion when he and three other snipers were watching a hostile post seven enemy emerged from it; he

[1] The total casualties for June came to 9 killed and missing, and 1 officer and 42 men wounded, several casualties being incurred by carrying and wiring-parties while the battalion was in reserve from June 12th to 27th.

opened fire, bringing the leading man down and putting the rest to flight; he then rushed to the body and searched it for identifications, getting back safely. The battalion owed its control of No Man's Land very largely to his energy and activity.

The Thirty-Eighth Division continued to hold the Aveluy Wood–Hamel Line till the middle of July. The battalion was in the front line from June 27th to July 1st and from July 9th to 19th. On July 2nd a direct hit caught the headquarters house and killed Captains A. J. Evans and W. G. L. Foster, while Lieutenant Travers and the Quartermaster, Lieutenant Whitworth,[1] were wounded, and the casualties for July, two officers and 11 men killed and missing, four officers and 36 men wounded, were rather high. Colonel Bowen,[2] who had rejoined from hospital on the 5th and taken over command from Major Monteith, was among the wounded. He was hit on July 17th, being succeeded by Major Sykes of the King's, who arrived on July 28th. From July 19th to 30th the 10th was " out " at Herissart, the whole Division having come back for special training, which was not so strenuous but to allow of such relaxations as a Divisional horse show, a race meeting and athletic sports. The gaps in its ranks were fairly well filled up by the arrival of drafts and fresh officers, eight subalterns being posted to the 10th in July, while Captain E. Lloyd and ten subalterns were posted in August. This period over, the Thirty-Eighth resumed charge of the Aveluy Wood sector. It came back to the line expecting to attack the German positions South of Aveluy Wood, but in its absence at Herissart an important change had taken place: the Germans had evacuated their positions West of the Ancre, mainly owing to the success of the Fourth Army in minor operations farther South. The 10th, who had a tiring march to Acheux on July 30th in very hot weather, were therefore not called on to deliver the attack for which they had been practising, and for the next few days had a quiet time, being in reserve. By this time, however, things were on the verge of becoming active and the 10th's period of quiet was not to last long.

[1] Lieutenant Cottrell from the 10th Welch was appointed Quartermaster in his place.
[2] Promoted Lieutenant Colonel while commanding a battalion, June 21st.

CHAPTER XXXI

THE TURN OF THE TIDE

FEW operations in the four years of war were more startling or surprising than the Fourth Army's successful attack to the Eastward of Amiens on August 8th. "The black day of the war for Germany," as Ludendorff has described it, began that victorious advance for which three months earlier no one on the Allied side could have dared even to hope. In that day's actual attack, carried out mainly by Australians and Canadians who had escaped the March retreat and some of whom only had shared in the Lys battle, no battalion of the TWENTY-FOURTH took part, though the 10th were near enough to be able to watch the Eighteenth Division on their immediate right advancing successfully just North of the Somme. For several days the fighting on this front continued, but before long opposition began to stiffen: German reserves had been rushed to the threatened spot, and, realizing that the limits of profitable exploitation of the success of August 8th had been reached, Sir Douglas Haig broke off this battle and sprang upon the Germans a second surprise elsewhere. This new attack was delivered North of the Somme by the Third Army, and brought the Thirty-Eighth Division into action. The 10th S.W.B. were thus the first battalion of the TWENTY-FOURTH engaged in the decisive movement of the war, though before many days the 1st Battalion also came into the thick of things.

The new offensive opened on August 21st on a short front North of the Ancre from Miraumont to Moyenneville. It was a brilliant success, and the British gains allowed them to threaten the Germans between Ancre and Somme, already endangered by our advance South of the latter river. A day was spent in readjusting the line and bringing up more troops and guns, and then (August 23rd) the Third Army struck again, the Fourth chiming in on its right. The main thrust was delivered at Bapaume well to the North of the old Somme battlefield of 1916. This was now a wilderness of shell holes and derelict trenches, covered with rough self-sown vegetation and crossed in all directions by half-destroyed wire entanglements, and presented no small obstacle to progress. It was essential, however, for the Fourth Army to cross this area, in order to cover the right flank of the main advance, so the Thirty-Eighth Division had to be launched across the Ancre against some extremely awkward positions.

The first obstacle to be negotiated was the Ancre, which had overflowed its banks and extended over a width of 300 yards. There were no bridges and though the water-covered area was not very deeply flooded no one could tell where there might lurk an unfordable ditch or a dip in the ground. The 10th S.W.B. were not detailed, however, for the difficult preliminary task of establishing bridge-heads across the Ancre. This was successfully accomplished between August 21st and 23rd by the 113th and 114th Brigades, the 115th being back in reserve at Bouzincourt. On the evening of August 23rd it moved forward to Aveluy, where the 151st Field Company R.E. had just laid a bridge, after the troops already across had cleared the enemy away from some posts which commanded the site of the crossing.

In crossing the river the 10th came under shell fire and had several casualties, B Company's whole Lewis gun team being knocked out and Lieutenant R. P. Thomas killed, but it was in position well up to time, nevertheless, with the 17th R.W.F. on its right. Its brigade's objective was La Boisselle, the 113th on its right advancing South of that village, the 114th on its left facing Thiepval.

"Zero" on August 24th was at 1 a.m., and despite the darkness the advance went very well, A and D Companies leading, with B and C in support. Considerable opposition was encountered but successfully overcome, and long before daylight the 10th was established on what was believed to be its objective. Daylight, however, revealing that the line reached was over half a mile short of the true objective, an attempt was made to push on, only for machine guns on the La Boisselle ridge to show that a direct advance was out of the question. Manœuvre had therefore to be tried, so the 10th withdrew a little and started working round to the North of La Boisselle, while the 113th Brigade did the same to the South. This was quite successful, the position being turned and the enemy forced to evacuate La Boisselle in haste. That evening found the Division established on the line Contalmaison–Pozières. It had suffered fairly severely but had captured 600 prisoners and over 100 machine guns, while during the evening, more bridges having been constructed by the indefatigable Field Companies, its artillery crossed the Ancre and came forward to give close support to the next day's attack.

The Germans were now standing on a line running South from High Wood by Bazentin le Petit to Mametz Wood, and it was against Bazentin le Petit and the adjacent wood that the 10th S.W.B. were to advance on the 25th.[1] To launch its attack the battalion had to march by compass over very intricate and difficult ground, but it managed it and reached the assembly position in good time. The advance met stubborn resistance and in places there was quite stiff fighting, but the 10th were not to be denied and eventually established themselves in Bazentin le Petit.

[1] The Division had all three Brigades in line, the 115th being in the centre.

Farther to the right the 2nd R.W.F. and the 113th Brigade had done equally well; but on the left High Wood, that perennial thorn in the British side, had once again proved a formidable obstacle and the 114th Brigade had been held up some way back. The 10th's casualties had been quite light, though its transport had come in for heavy shelling, in which Second Lieutenant W. P. Hughes and Company Quartermaster Sergeant Pembrey had been killed and two other C.Q.M.S.'s wounded. Second Lieutenant Haworth, who now took over the Transport Officer's duties, contrived nevertheless to reach the battalion in its forward position with a welcome supply of water.

To maintain the pressure was essential, so, despite the hard work and sharp fighting of the preceding days, August 26th saw the Thirty-Eighth Division attacking again: on its right the 113th Brigade pushed on as far as Longueval and the Western outskirts of Delville Wood, where a stubborn resistance developed and held it up; on the left the 114th again tackled High Wood. Again determined opposition was offered, and the frontal attack's chances of success seemed far from promising. However, A and C Companies of the 10th S.W.B., under Captains Hornsby and Hoffmeister, were acting as a left flank guard to the 113th Brigade, and these, when advancing along the shallow valley South of High Wood, were diverted against that position. The two companies were admirably handled; working forward with much skill and dash they soon outflanked High Wood and were thus largely responsible for its enforced evacuation and the capture in it of 15 machine guns, while A Company itself took another four machine guns with 30 men. B and D then came forward and continued the advance with such vigour that evening found the battalion only just short of Longueval: it had had 50 casualties but had covered nearly 3000 yards in the day.

August 27th saw the Division arrested by the formidable and strongly held position Delville Wood–Longueval–Flers. This foiled all attempts to get forward; indeed, the Germans proceeded to develop counter-attacks, one of which enfiladed C Company of the 10th and forced it back. The formation of a defensive flank on the right checked the counter-attack, and next day, after a systematic bombardment by our artillery, the 113th Brigade, feeling the enemy's resistance weakening, attacked and cleared Longueval, but was then checked by heavy artillery fire. The 10th, who were moving forward in support, were caught in the open by this barrage, and C and D had hastily to take refuge in shell holes. A and B meanwhile pressed on so close after the 113th Brigade as to be practically in its front line at dusk. Then, however, they were extricated and the whole battalion reassembled near High Wood, where its brigade spent the 29th in well-earned rest, while the other two cleared Delville Wood and captured the Ginchy Ridge East of it.

Next day (August 30th) saw the 10th S.W.B. on the move early. Advancing at 3.30 a.m. from its position East of High Wood the battalion covered nearly 3000 yards, eventually reaching and capturing Les Boeufs. Machine guns on a ridge farther East then checked its further advance, and Second Lieutenant Loxton, who was leading a battle-patrol, ran into an ambush and was killed. The capture of Les Boeufs was the more welcome because the 113th Brigade had been held up at Morval. But if the Division's victorious progress was for the moment checked, the men, though tired, were in great form, much elated at sweeping so rapidly forward over ground which had only been won in 1916 inch by inch at the cost of terrible casualties. The arrival that evening of a draft of 120 men with six officers was a great encouragement, though it hardly filled all the gaps made by the recent fighting.

By this time the battle-frontage had been extended further North and the British line was going forward East of Arras, while their advance North of the Somme had caused the Germans to relinquish their remaining positions West of that river above Peronne. The French also were advancing, and Roye and Noyon had fallen into their hands. On August 29th the Germans evacuated Bapaume and three days later quitted Peronne also. Thus ten days' fighting had sufficed to push the Germans back approximately to the line they had held just before their March retreat of 1917, this being continued Northward by the formidable Drocourt–Quéant Line. This line it was Sir Douglas Haig's intention to attack on September 2nd, and to divert attention and to keep the Germans further South fully occupied vigorous pressure was maintained on the Somme front. September 1st therefore found the 10th S.W.B. attacking again, and for four days it had neither rest nor pause in the fighting.

The Thirty-Eighth Division's advance towards Sailly-Saillisel and Morval had brought it well ahead of the Seventeenth on its left, and as a gap had also developed between its right and the Eighteenth Division its task for September 1st with both its flanks exposed was one of some difficulty. The 114th Brigade began the attack by assaulting and taking Morval, after a stubborn fight: the 115th then started about 5.30 a.m. to attack Sailly-Saillisel, the 2nd and 17th R.W.F. leading and the 10th S.W.B. following in support. Almost at once effective enfilade fire developed from the left, the Germans being advantageously posted on ground which the Seventeenth Division were not yet ready to attack, and the 2nd R.W.F. lost heavily and were held up. The 10th were therefore thrown in to assist them and intervened most effectively, advancing just as the enemy began a counter-attack. A and B Companies, who led, did splendidly, pushing the enemy back and restoring the line at a critical moment. Second Lieutenant Excell was conspicuous for his gallantry, and it was largely due to his grasp of the situation that the counter-attack was checked, the enemy driven off, and the flank secured. Second Lieutenant Ashe also headed a handful of men in a most successful charge, completely routing five times their number of Germans, whom he caught in flank, and taking 60 prisoners with 8 machine guns. Second Lieutenant Ellis, too, seeing the leading companies in danger of being cut off, dashed forward with his platoon and made a most timely charge, taking 6 men himself and completely demoralizing the enemy. The diversion of the battalion to the flank had, however, left the 17th R.W.F. without the support needed to carry Sailly-Saillisel, but the 113th Brigade reinforced and swept into and over the ruins of that village, securing the day's objective.

The Germans had now been thrust back almost to the Tortille and next afternoon the 115th Brigade formed up in hollow ground East of Sailly-Saillisel, covered by the 113th Brigade on the ridge in front, and about 5 p.m. started to advance through the 113th against Mesnil, the 10th S.W.B. having A and C leading, B and D in rear. Previous reconnaissance had failed to induce the enemy to disclose his positions, but immediately the battalion neared its objective machine guns opened a heavy fire. Captain Hornsby, who had done so well at High Wood, was killed, Captain Lloyd and Lieutenants Anderson, D. T. Davies and Franey were wounded and over 50 men were hit. However, Second Lieutenant Simpson rose to the occasion and by his promptitude and fine example rallied the men and prevented them from becoming disorganized, while Second Lieutenants Ashe and Ellis again distinguished themselves by taking command of their companies, rallying them under heavy fire from machine guns and led them on, showing great courage and skilful leadership. Sergeant Power also took command of his company on all its officers being hit, rallied the men, got them into line, afterwards controlling their fire effectively and getting touch with the troops on his flanks. Similar good work was done by Private Norris who brought his platoon forward to reinforce in face of a very heavy fire and gave timely help. However, to push on in face of the opposition which had been disclosed was clearly useless without better artillery support, so the 10th could only hold their ground, pushing patrols forward under

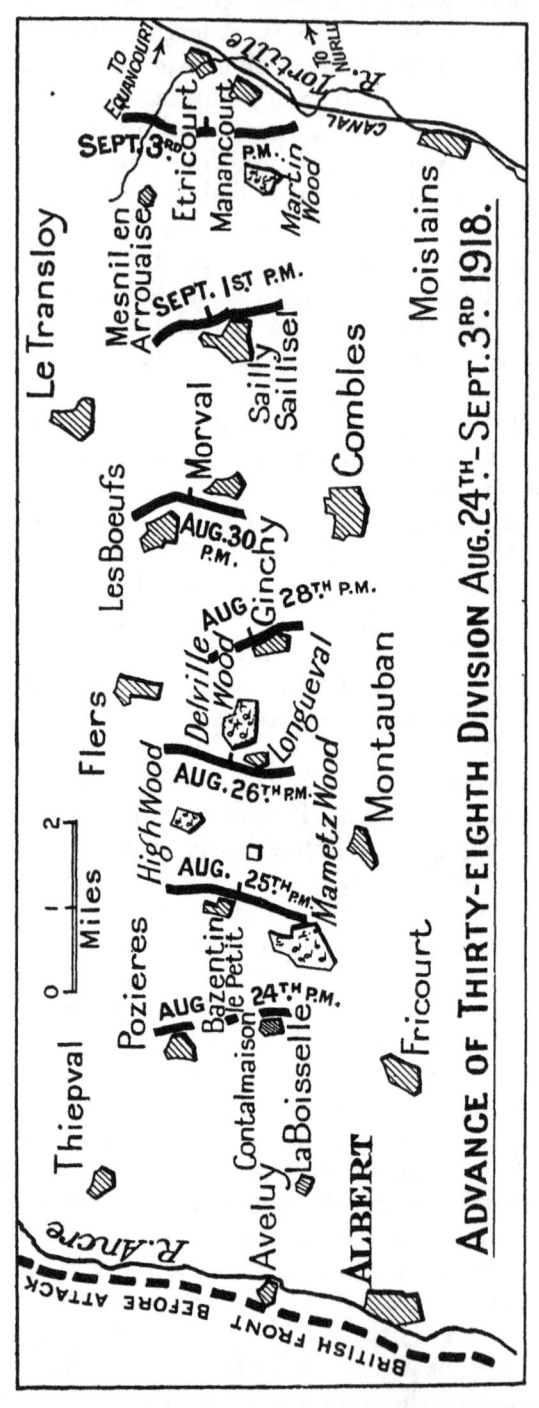

cover of darkness to locate the enemy more accurately and to observe his movements.

Everyone was very much on the alert all night as information had come in that German reinforcements were coming up for a counter-attack. It never developed, however; indeed, early next morning (Sept. 2nd) our patrols found the Germans gone, whereupon the 113th and 115th Brigades promptly occupied a line of trenches running Southward from Mesnil en Arrouaise to Martin Wood with nothing more than a few casualties from a feeble barrage the Germans put down to cover their retirement. The 114th Brigade then went through the leading troops and pushed on to the Canal du Nord, beyond which the enemy were standing, well posted behind an impassable obstacle, all the bridges having been destroyed. For the next two days the 115th Brigade remained in the position occupied on September 3rd, while the 114th Brigade endeavoured to force the passage of the Canal and secure the Equancourt-Nurlu line beyond. This the 114th could not achieve, and for the 10th S.W.B. the main incident of these days was a severe dose of gas shelling by 5·9 cm. howitzers on the evening of September 4th, which caused 30 casualties, mainly in B Company. Private Mansbridge, one of the battalion runners, did good service by locating a platoon which had got cut off, and his devotion to duty in carrying messages was really remarkable. Next day orders came for its Division's relief by the Twenty-First and the 320 men to which the previous fortnight's fighting had reduced the battalion tramped back to a camp at Les Boeufs, where a brief rest was to be enjoyed. Since the battle began the 10th S.W.B. had advanced 24 kilometres, had been in action for nearly a fortnight and had had 12 officers[1] and 294 men casualties. But it had inflicted more loss than it had suffered; the Division's prisoners alone came to more than half its 3600 casualties, while it had taken 6 guns, with many machine guns and trench mortars, and had forced its way through many strong and well-defended positions. A high standard of tactical skill and ability had been shown and the 10th's share in these brilliant achievements could stand comparison with that of any other unit in the Division.[2]

Despite its exertions and losses, however, only the briefest rest could be granted to the Thirty-Eighth Division, and September 10th saw the 10th S.W.B., now again under Lieutenant Colonel Bowen, who had just rejoined, moving up to the front. The

---

[1] Besides those mentioned Lieutenant Jewell had been killed on September 1st, Second Lieutenant Schofield gassed and Second Lieutenant Excell wounded.

[2] Second Lieutenants Ashe, Ellis, Excell and Simpson all received the M.C., Sergeant Power and Privates Mansbridge and Norris the D.C.M.

Germans had in the interval been pushed back to the trenches dug by the British in 1917 when our Eastward advance had ended at the Hindenburg Line: what they were now holding had been the old British front line, and the Seventeenth Division, whom the Thirty-Eighth were relieving, had their front line in the old support system. The British had therefore to clear the Germans out of their own old trenches before they could assault the actual Hindenburg Line, for on no less daring a venture than this Sir Douglas Haig had now determined.

The 10th S.W.B. on relieving the 6th Dorset in the Gouzeaucourt sector on September 11th, found themselves in an active and disturbed quarter. The German position had much tactical value as overlooking the Scheldt Canal, and they were determined to hold on to it as long as they could: indeed they tried several local counter-attacks in hopes of recovering parts of the old support system, while their guns swept our positions with constant bombardments. The British also made several small attacks, hoping thereby to secure a more advantageous line from which to launch a bigger attack. Thus the day after the 10th went into line C Company assisted by half a platoon of A was put in against African Trench, in conjunction with an attack on the left by the New Zealand Division. The position was strong in itself, and was stoutly defended by a Jäger Division, picked troops whose presence testified clearly to the importance of the position, and the attackers found the task beyond them. Second Lieutenant Simpson, who was commanding C, was killed, and though a small party under Second Lieutenant Bundy forced their way into the German trenches, a vigorous counter-attack hurled them out again before they could consolidate their position, Second Lieutenant Bundy being wounded. Later in the day the attack was unsuccessfully renewed, and after dark C was ordered back to the line held before the attack.[1] Three uneventful days followed, the chief incident being a heavy barrage on our trenches on the 16th; the attack which was expected to follow this did not develop, and that evening the 113th and 114th Brigades relieved the 115th, who withdrew into reserve. Two days later the Third and Fourth Armies simultaneously attacked the positions covering the Hindenburg Line; in this the 115th Brigade was in support and the 10th S.W.B., advancing behind the 114th Brigade on the right, reached a line of captured trenches South of the Fins–Gouzeaucourt road practically without loss. Here a pause followed. Though the 114th Brigade had gained its final objective, its left was exposed as the 113th had been held

---

[1] The total casualties were well over 80, Lieutenant Silby and Second Lieutenant W. F. Williams being also among the killed.

up. However, the 10th S.W.B. were not put in, but merely moved up into close support and that night relieved the 113th Brigade in Rue d'Enfer, B Company being used to form a defensive flank. This line they retained next day, despite heavy shell fire, and then on September 20th the Seventeenth Division came forward again and took over from the Thirty-Eighth, who went back to Le Transloy for something really worthy of being called " rest."

The 10th had not been the only battalion of the TWENTY-FOURTH engaged against the outworks of the Hindenburg Line. The 1st Battalion, after spending the last ten days of August at Pressy-lez-Pernes, had been warned on the 31st to be ready to move at two hours' notice. Notice came that evening; at 8.30 p.m. the battalion was entraining, early on September 1st it detrained at Arras and moved forward in the evening to Wancourt, in readiness to support the Canadians in the next day's attack on the Drocourt–Quéant Line. This attack, delivered by the right of the First Army and the left of the Third, was a great success; there was no need to put in the supports, and the 1st S.W.B. saw no fighting in this quarter. On September 6th it withdrew to a back area again, as its Division was about to be transferred to the Ninth Corps,[1] and on the 10th the battalion entrained at Aubigny, detraining that afternoon at Villers-Bretonneux. Here the 1st " embussed " two days later for the front and relieved the 15th Lancashire Fusiliers of the Thirty-Second Division in front line at Caulaincourt on the Omignon river, North-West of St. Quentin. The Ninth Corps had just taken over the right sector of the Fourth Army's line, from Holnon Wood to opposite Vermand, and was thus on the extreme British right and next to the French.

The 1st S.W.B. were no sooner in front line than they began to push forward patrols, under cover of which they advanced during the night of September 12th/13th to a line East of Vermand. Next day the advance was continued, through Villecholes, over the Peronne–St. Quentin road to some quarries further East. Some opposition was encountered, but not more than vigorous action by our fighting patrols could overcome, though the battalion had over 20 casualties, including Second Lieutenant David killed and Second Lieutenants King (Monmouthshire Regiment attached) and Giles wounded. Continuing the move next day, with the 3rd Brigade as advanced-guard, the Division made a little progress towards the Maissemy Ridge, three miles North-East of Vermand, but found that position too

[1] The other divisions in the Ninth Corps were the Sixth, Thirty-Second, and Forty-Sixth.

strongly held to be rushed. More guns were therefore pushed forward, and on 5.30 a.m. on September 15th the Division advanced behind an excellent barrage which moved at the rate of 100 yards in three minutes. The 1st S.W.B. had the task of tackling Maissemy itself and put in D Company under Captain E. R. Taylor to attack the village from West and South, while C (Captain Harris) secured a sunken road from which D might have been enfiladed. The attack was completely successful, not without stubborn fighting. D indeed followed the barrage so closely that they had to halt within a few yards of the village and wait for it to lift. Thereupon a German machine gun opened fire at short range and was causing casualties when Private Ryan engaged it with a Lewis gun and rapidly knocked out three of the team. Then, dashing forward, he disposed of the others with the bayonet and captured the gun, whereupon the company, inspired by his example, dashed into the village and soon made themselves masters of it. A then came up on C's right and cleared some rising ground, Sergeant Manning being greatly to the fore, leading his platoon very skilfully and twice rushing machine guns that threatened to hold up the advance. Eventually A obtained touch with the Gloucestershire, while B, prolonging the line to the left, secured the passages over the Omignon North of the village and formed a defensive flank. The fighting had been quite sharp and the casualties amounted to 100 all told, Captain Harris and Second Lieutenant Hall being wounded. As against that over 20 prisoners were taken with 4 machine guns, and the battalion earned warm praise from the Corps Commander, General Braithwaite, while Captains Harris and Taylor and Lieutenant Carpendale were subsequently awarded the M.C., Sergeant Manning and Private Ryan got D.C.M.'s, Private J. Thomas a bar to the M.M., and ten N.C.O.'s and privates[1] the M.M.

After holding its gains till the evening of September 16th the battalion was drawn back into reserve and so missed the big fight of September 18th. The Ninth Corps' objectives on this day included Holnon village, Selency, Fresnoy le Petit, Pontruet and Ste Helene, its frontage of attack being nearly 7000 yards. It encountered stubborn opposition and, though in the main successful, did not secure all its objectives. The 3rd Brigade was not put into the fight, however, and the S.W.B. did no more than occupy a support position on Maissemy Ridge, where they remained till the night of September 20th/21st, when they moved forward to relieve part of the Sixth Division just West of Fresnoy le Petit. This village had defied capture on September

---

[1] Among these was Private Macaulay who had won the D.C.M. at Loos in October, 1915, and a bar to it on the Somme in 1916.

18th, further efforts against it had also failed and it was a lively corner, bombing encounters being frequent and casualties quite numerous. On September 24th the Ninth Corps made a fresh attempt to secure the still untaken portions of its objective of September 18th. In this the 3rd Brigade tackled Fresnoy le Petit, the Gloucestershire and the Welch, to whom D and C Companies respectively were attached, attacking from the line held by the battalion. The attack not only carried Fresnoy but was skilfully exploited, Marronnières Wood being cleared, some troublesome machine guns outflanked and nearly 150 prisoners taken. Not content with this, the Brigadier, Sir

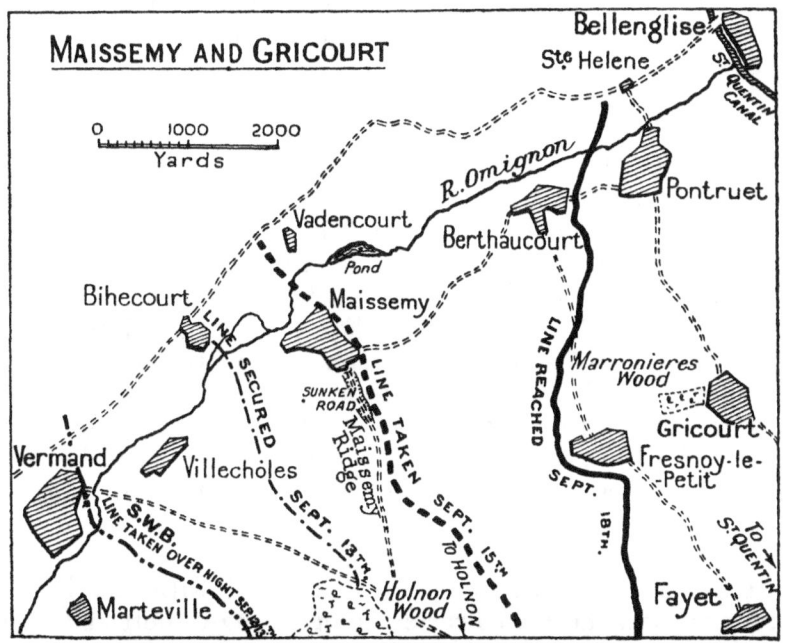

In map, for "taken over night Sep. 12/13th" read "reached."

W. A. Kay, determined to push on against Gricourt; and before evening that village had also fallen to the 3rd Brigade, whose success materially assisted the 2nd Brigade on its left to capture its final objectives. In all this C and D had had a full share, while A and B did good service in the humbler but essential rôle of carrying parties. After the attack the battalion took over the front line East of Gricourt and held this position despite shell fire till the 28th, when the First Division was relieved and drawn back to Vermand for a brief rest before the main attack on the Hindenburg Line, the outworks of which had now been captured all along the British line.[1]

[1] The battalion had by no means escaped scot-free during this period, having a dozen men killed, while Captain Fowkes and Second Lieutenants Hulbert and Pembridge were among the wounded.

THE HISTORY OF THE SOUTH WALES BORDERERS

The success which Sir Douglas Haig's plans had achieved on the right of the British line had by this time become so pronounced as to exert a considerable influence over other quarters. Instead of being able, as they had intended, to renew their attacks in Flanders the Germans found themselves compelled to draw troops off from that quarter to meet the main attack; and September saw the British Fifth and Second Armies gradually regaining much of their April losses in the Lys valley. None of the battalions of the S.W.B. serving in these Armies, the 5th on the La Bassèe front, the 2nd near Merris and Meteren, and the 6th opposite the Messines Ridge, were called upon to undertake any major operation during August and September, but September 30th found practically every Division on the British front further forward than August 1st had found it and ready for a more pronounced advance.

Of these three the 2nd had been the most actively engaged. The attack on the Oultersteene Ridge had not provoked any counter-stroke, though examination of the captured positions had revealed elaborate and extensive preparations for an attack, such as large forward dumps of ammunition. Indeed the Twenty-Ninth Division had been left in undisturbed possession of its gains, though towards the end of August the German guns blazed away unusually freely and on the 27th the 2nd S.W.B., now back in the front line North of Oultersteene after a few days' rest,[1] had Lieutenant R. G. Evans and five men killed by shell fire. Large fires too were frequently noticed behind the German lines, and on August 30th our morning patrols discovered that the enemy were no longer holding their old positions. Orders were promptly issued for an advance, and with the Border Regiment and the 86th Brigade co-operating on left and right the battalion began pushing Eastward. The platoon of C Company and two of D, who formed the leading line, encountered only the feeblest opposition, and by 10 a.m. they had reached a line running from Bailleul Railway Station to Noote Boom. A brief pause followed and then the advance was resumed, once again without meeting any serious opposition, and by evening its advanced posts were over two miles East of Bailleul. Officers and men alike were new to open warfare, and the delayed action mines and other booby-traps which the Germans had left behind contributed to slow down the pace of the advance, but all ranks were greatly encouraged by the new experience and by the many signs of the bad time which the British guns had of late been giving the Germans. On August 31st and September 1st, when the 87th Brigade pushed forward to La Creche and

---

[1] During this half a dozen officers and about 60 men had joined.

Steenwerck, the S.W.B. were not engaged, but their turn came again on September 2nd when, having relieved the Borders in front line over night, they started off at 9 a.m. for Nieppe, while on their left the 88th Brigade made for Neuve Eglise. Opposition was stiffer now, more than once guns had to be brought up to help the infantry to deal with machine guns well posted in farm-houses and cottages, and progress, though steady, was not rapid. However, by evening the battalion had reached the line Murder Farm–Trois Arbres–Pont d'Achelles, at the cost of less than twenty casualties. On the 4th the Division's advance culminated in a successful attack on Ploegsteert and Hill 63, in which nearly 400 prisoners were taken. The S.W.B., however, had no share in this, having gone back to Oultersteene for a rest, prior to a shift of the whole Twenty-Ninth Division to Ypres.

This by September 17th brought the Division into line between the Menin road and Zillebeke Lake, the frontage assigned to it in the projected offensive by the Second Army which the successes further South had now rendered not only practicable but desirable. The prospects of success in the main attack would be substantially improved by giving the Germans ample occupation on other parts of the front, so that no further reinforcements could be found by the once " quiet " sectors to try to stem the main attack. Moreover, there were now good chances of local success and of winning back from German keeping substantial portions of French and Belgian territory.

To the 5th S.W.B. September was marked by Colonel Trower's resignation of the command he had held so long and with so much distinction. He left the battalion at his own request because he felt no longer equal to discharging his duties in command of his battalion through the strain of another winter as he had done and as he would wish to do. When Colonel Trower took the 5th S.W.B. to France he had already close on forty years' membership of the Regiment behind him : that he should have stuck out three and a half years of active service speaks for itself. As has been well said by one of his officers, " The fact of this splendid continuity of command being broken just before the end emphasizes the effort and the struggle. . . . Had Colonel Trower led his battalion home to Brecon the achievement might have seemed less difficult by the fact that it was done."

What Colonel Trower had done for and had meant to the 5th S.W.B. only those who served under him can fully appreciate. He was loved and respected and trusted, he was feared by those who had occasion to fear him : he never spared himself for the good of those under him and he taught his officers to do the same. He was instantly down on any sign of negligence or carelessness, but an officer who was doing his work well was given ample opportunity to do it without fussy or unnecessary intervention. He set the highest standards in every respect. He was fearless as well as untiring: "his visits to the trenches," it has been said, "were often unwelcome, for he would select the most exposed position in order to share with his officers and men in all their duties. To those who had to accompany him and dawdle at a corner where they knew well, and the Colonel knew too, that men had been killed the day before, the proceedings sometimes appeared as a needless danger. But it was not. It was one of those risks which were necessary and justified that efficiency and esprit de corps might not languish."

Colonel Trower had embodied for the recruits out of whom he had to form the 5th Battalion the traditions and the standards that they would have to maintain. If he insisted upon efficiency, his fair-mindedness, his reasonableness in dealing with faults due to inexperience or excess of zeal, his patience, his friendliness, his wonderful knowledge of those under his command, were invaluable in converting that mob of raw hands into an efficient body of soldiers. If the 5th S.W.B. had a good reputation in their Division—and the Nineteenth prided itself that to stand high among its units was no easy thing—its officers and men would have ascribed that in the first place to Colonel Trower's work and influence. He himself in his farewell order spoke of "the splendid spirit animating all ranks," and thanked them warmly for their "loyalty, discipline and courage in face of the enemy." More particularly he spoke of the good work done by Majors Oxley, Croft and Bence-Trower, by Captains I. T. Evans, Littleton-Geach and Runham and by the Quartermaster, Captain Bryant. But one and all of those would have insisted that if the 5th had earned an honourable place in the records of the TWENTY-FOURTH it was as "Trower's battalion" that it should be remembered.

Shortly before Colonel Trower's departure things had become more active on the La Bassée front. Small advances were being made, at various places a footing was gained in the German line, and on September 20th, 25th and 30th successful local attacks were carried out. These were continued in the opening days of October, and the 5th, working harder than ever on making roads available for the pushing forward of guns and their ammunition and the necessary supplies for the fighting line, moved their Headquarters forward from Locon to Fiefs on October 1st, only to be ordered back a couple of days later—the line being then already East of Aubers. Its Division was being transferred to the Third Army and was to proceed to the area between Graincourt and Moeuvres.

To the 6th S.W.B. September had been uneventful. The German retreat from the Lys Salient had not involved the Thirtieth Division in any serious fighting, though it had come forward level with the troops on its flank and the 6th had found themselves once more upon the ground for which some few of them had fought so hard in April. On September 8th the main body moved forward to Kemmel Hill. It might change its location; however, it did not change its work. Wherever it was " work on roads as usual " is the normal entry in the battalion diary, and except for the arrival of a few small drafts, some convalescents and half a dozen new officers little else is recorded. Major Pearson had left early in the month to command the 2/19th London Regiment, Captain Stickler becoming second in command in his place.

CHAPTER XXXII

THROUGH THE HINDENBURG LINE AND FURTHER

THE successful attack on the Hindenburg Line delivered by the Third and Fourth Armies on September 29th ranks with the "bolt from the blue" of August 8th among the outstanding achievements of the closing stage of the war. So formidable was this line, so apparently insuperable the obstacles which its defences presented to the assailants, so doubtful in many people's eyes the chances of success, that it called for no little resolution and confidence to embark upon the attack. If complete success afforded ample justification for the courage and determination involved in risking the venture, this should not be allowed to obscure the risks or to leave the impression that success was a foregone conclusion. The German defences, carefully and skilfully sited so as to take full advantage of the obstacle provided by the St. Quentin Canal, formed a position as near to the impregnable as the skill of the military engineer with ample time, labour, and material resources at his command could contrive. Moreover, an attack could not enjoy that factor of surprise which had been so important an element in the success of August 8th. Still an attack on the Hindenburg Line was the only natural sequel of the Allied strategy since August 8th, since to suspend the offensive would have sacrificed the advantages already won. As to its precise time, locality and methods it might be possible to effect a surprise, but an assault could hardly hope to again find the defence quite unprepared.

In this attack the Fourth Army was operating on a front of twelve miles; on its left the Third Army[1] extended for another nine, from Vendhuille to Marcoing, while on its right the French First Army was to attack on a six-mile frontage. The Ninth Corps, still the right of the Fourth Army, was using the Forty-Sixth Division to deliver its main blow against Bellenglise, and the First to cover the Forty-Sixth's right and gain ground South of Bellenglise towards Thorigny and Le Tranquoy. It had the 1st Brigade on its left in touch with the Forty-Sixth Division and the 3rd on the right.

The 1st S.W.B., the left attacking battalion of the 3rd Brigade, were to form up on a 500-yards front about a quarter of a mile East of Pontruet and had as first objective Faucille Trench, which ran along the reverse slope of a spur projecting

---

[1] The First and Third Armies had already on September 27th begun attacking in the direction of Cambrai and these operations must be regarded as an essential part of the plan which culminated in the attack of September 29th. The Thirty-Eighth Division was in reserve to its Corps during these operations and thus the 10th S.W.B. took no active part in the battle.

SEPT. 1918] TACKLING THE HINDENBURG LINE

North from the high ground S.E. of Pontruet. The Gloucestershire on the right were attacking this high ground and the S.W.B. had orders to wait in Faucille Trench till they came up level. B Company, under Captain H. C. S. Davies, which started the 1st's attack, achieved a rapid and complete success, reaching and clearing Faucille Trench despite stubborn opposition and taking 30 prisoners and a couple of machine guns. However, on the right the Gloucestershire were held up West of Sycamore Wood by machine gun fire and could not get forward. Notwithstanding this Captain Davies, finding the Black Watch up level with his

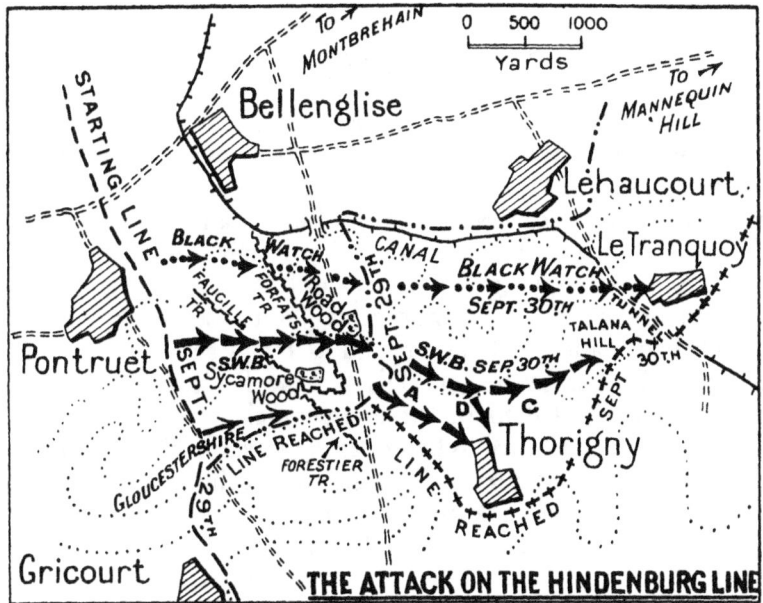

left, determined to press on towards the second objective, Forçats Trench, which ran just West of the Bellenglise–St. Quentin road, along the next spur to the Eastward. His initiative was rewarded with success. Making skilful use of the cover which the ground afforded, B Company not only reached Forçats Trench but cleared most of it by bombing to right and left and captured 150 prisoners. This not only effectively assisted the advance of the 1st Brigade, which was swinging round to its right South of the canal and meeting considerable opposition in the maze of trenches it encountered, but ultimately improved the situation on the right also. By swinging up his left and working forward to the high ground near Road Wood Captain Davies threatened the retreat of the defenders of Sycamore Wood, who promptly retired. The Black Watch had meanwhile secured the main road North of Road Wood, so C Company under Lieutenant Ackerley, which had come forward in close support of B, could be put in against the third objective, the village of Thorigny. C, however, promptly encountered heavy machine gun fire and very soon had to halt and dig in, just East of the St. Quentin road. The final position held by the battalion during the night formed the Eastern side of a sharp salient, the Gloucestershire continuing the line back about Westward towards Gricourt. If less spectacular than the Forty-Sixth Division's astonishing passage of the canal, the achievement of the First Division had been of great value and was successfully continued next day.

At 8 a.m. precisely the First Division resumed its advance against Thorigny and Talana Hill. Of the S.W.B. A Company under Second Lieutenant Napier advanced direct against the machine gun post on the ridge which had stopped the previous evening's attack, and thereby distracted its attention from C and D which, working forward on the left lower down the slope, got round to the rear of the post and captured it, guns and all. After this, little opposition was offered, and C pushing past Thorigny reached Talana Hill, where they proceeded to consolidate, D occupying Thorigny and A connecting with the Gloucestershire on the right rear. Simultaneously the Black Watch had made good the ground as far as the canal and linked up with the Thirty-Second Division at Le Tranquoy, thereby securing the right flank of the main attack.

This important success had been remarkably cheaply obtained. The battalion had taken 3 guns, 36 machine guns, 4 trench mortars and 2 anti-tank guns at a total cost of 7 killed[1] and 31 wounded. On September 30th the enemy's opposition had rather lacked determination, though on the previous day they had fought well enough, and the lightness of the casualty list had been due rather to skilful handling by company and platoon commanders and intelligent use of covering fire and ground. The warm praise of General Strickland, G.O.C. First Division, was certainly well deserved and Captain Davies fully earned the M.C. which was awarded him. Second Lieutenant Parfitt got a bar to his M.C., Company Sergeant Major House, Sergeant Rawlings and Lance Corporal E. J. Thomas the D.C.M., and seven men the M.M.

Active operations in and about the Hindenburg Line continued for several days, the British seeking to clinch the success achieved on September 29th and 30th by breaking through the Masnières–Beaurevoir Line, which ran about three miles in rear of the Hindenburg Line and was the last fully prepared German defensive position. To prevent this the Germans

[1] The killed included three officers, Second Lieutenants R. King, H. F. Martin and L. R. Parker.

delivered repeated counter-attacks, expending their reserves far more freely than at any period since August 8th. They occasionally won back villages or trenches for a time, but not only did they fail to stop the Fourth Army, which by October 5th had successfully effected a breach in the Beaurevoir Line, they were equally unable to hold up the Third, which in the course of these days had steadily exploited the success of September 27th and was now in the outskirts of Cambrai.

In the later stages of this great struggle the 1st S.W.B. had only a minor part. On the evening of October 1st they were relieved by French troops, who were now taking over the line up to the canal, and were back in reserve till the night of October 3rd/4th. The 3rd Brigade was then placed at the disposal of the Forty-Sixth Division, now in line about Montbrehain and Mannequin Hill, where it had encountered stubborn resistance and had very heavy fighting. The battalion, though not actually placed in front line, came in for some severe shelling while thus in support and had its M.O., Captain Dold, R.A.M.C., killed on the 5th, when Captain Davies, Lieutenant Whyte and Second Lieutenant E. C. Lloyd were all wounded, the latter mortally. It remained under the Forty-Sixth Division till October 8th, when it reverted to its own Division, now in Corps Reserve, so that it spent the next week near Bellenglise resting, refitting and training while the Fourth Army was pushing steadily Westward towards Le Cateau and the Selle, behind which river the Germans might hope to make more of a stand than was likely in the open and undulating country between it and the Hindenburg Line.

Meanwhile at the other end of the British line the Second Army had suddenly taken the offensive. The change in the general situation had been so complete that the time was now ripe for this, and both military and political reasons made it expedient to clear the Germans out of Belgium. The narrow gap between the Dutch frontier and the Ardennes through which the German communications ran was the natural objective of an advance in Flanders, and though many miles stretched between Ypres and Liége there was now nothing unreasonable in making this the ultimate goal of the Second Army and the Belgians, whose attack was to begin on September 28th. Two Corps of the Second Army were being used, the Second and the Nineteenth, and to the former the Twenty-Ninth Division had been posted on arriving for the last time in the Salient. The Division had the Ninth on its left next the Belgians, and the objectives assigned to these two Divisions included the capture of the line Broodseinde–Gheluvelt–Kruiseick. So ambitious a programme was in itself some indication of the change which had come over the situation since the desperate struggles over the same ground in the autumn of 1917. It was known that the Germans had already thinned out their troops in this quarter, and the Second Army's offensive aimed not only at preventing them carrying this process further, but by profiting by the extent to which it had already been carried.

In the attack the Twenty-Ninth Division was employing the 86th Brigade on the left and the 87th on the right, the latter detailing the S.W.B. to capture its first and second objectives. The first of these, to be taken by B and D Companies, ran from Maple Copse Northward, the second, for which A and C were detailed, was Jackdaw Switch road, just West of Stirling Castle. Here the Border Regiment was to "leap-frog" and to secure the high ground from Glencorse Wood Southward, the K.O.S.B. then going through to take Veldhoek and the Tower Hamlets Ridge. Zero was to be at 5.30 a.m., and except on the Belgian front there was to be no preliminary bombardment, though ample artillery assistance was provided, the barrage moving forward at the rate of 100 yards in three minutes.

It was still dark when the attack started, and heavy rain added to the difficulties; but the barrage was splendidly steady and accurate, and though direction was hard to keep the attack made rapid progress. Machine gun posts offered considerable resistance, but several of them were rushed by Second Lieutenant Bronham, who led his platoon with great dash. B and D under Lieutenant Newman and Captain Dendy reached their objective well up to time, whereupon Captain Givons and Lieutenant Dutton took A and C through them and continued the advance. Some casualties were caused by men in their eagerness running into our barrage, the ground actually being dry enough to allow of this, a thing almost incredible to survivors of attacks over the same ground in 1917, but the second objective was punctually secured. Then, after the Border Regiment had passed through, companies were reorganized—there had been but few casualties—and held in readiness to move forward again. Orders to advance were before long received, and by 2 p.m. the battalion was advancing in platoons at 100 yards interval down the Menin road towards Gheluvelt. By this time the 88th Brigade had gone through the 87th and was exploiting the success already achieved. Beyond Nieuwe Kruiseick, however, the 88th was checked; and as the Thirty-Fifth, the left Division of the Nineteenth Corps, was not up level on the right, the S.W.B. were diverted to the right to secure that flank. This move was carried out in artillery formation, and in face of some shell fire, but without much loss, a position being secured about dusk on the Western slopes of the Kruiseick knoll, nearly five miles from the battalion's assembly position of the morning. Second Lieutenant Bronham on his own initiative pushed forward some way with his platoon and secured some very valuable ground. Over a thousand prisoners had been taken by the Division with several guns and many machine guns, and even if the German resistance had not been distinguished for determination the success achieved had been really remarkable and the troops were greatly elated. They wanted some encouragement, for they had to spend a most miserable night; it was wet and cold, "cookers" had been left far behind, and the men were not carrying their greatcoats, while the length of the advance and the state of the road prevented any transport vehicles getting up anywhere near the front line.

With the morning of September 29th came a fresh attempt by the 88th Brigade to get forward, the battalion's orders being to advance in support of its right. To do this companies were echeloned back so as to cover the flank and given a line running S.W. from the Menin road past Kruiseick as objective. Directly the 88th Brigade started off A and C Companies began to advance, but the German resistance had stiffened by now and the advance met with heavy fire from machine guns and snipers. The 88th Brigade was soon held up and the battalion had to conform after it had reached a line just West of Kruiseick, capturing several Germans in the process. Here it remained stationary for a time, but in the afternoon under cover of a bombardment by Stokes guns an advance of nearly 200 yards was made, a troublesome machine gun post South of Kruiseick being rushed. This advanced position, however, proved to be enfiladed from the right, and as the German guns were ranged fairly accurately on it and were shelling it vigorously it was decided to fall back, though after dark the posts were reoccupied, to be handed over to the Border Regiment who arrived to relieve the battalion. Casualties this day had been much heavier than on the 28th, two company commanders, Captain Givons and Lieutenant Newman, being wounded, and twice as many men killed as on the previous day.

Relief did not mean more than going back to very uncomfortable quarters in an old trench just West of the site of Gheluvelt. Here the S.W.B. spent September 30th and most of October 1st, while the other brigades were advancing to the outskirts of Gheluwe, only to be held up by that strong position. Late on October 1st the 87th Brigade was sent forward to take over part of the new front line, and the S.W.B. found themselves holding a longish frontage N. and N.E. of Gheluwe running in the direction of the Menin-Roulers road. There were no trenches and the line consisted of platoon-posts in houses or blockhouses which needed much improvement, especially as hostile machine guns and snipers were very active. Much good work was done in making this line more defensible, but the 88th Brigade's efforts to secure Gheluwe were only partially successful and the village had not been completely taken before the Forty-First Division arrived to relieve the Twenty-Ninth. On October 4th the S.W.B. found themselves back in reserve at Westhoek. The total casualties had amounted to 2 officers, Second Lieutenants G. P. Davies and Sherer, and 33 men killed and missing, 7 officers[1] and 89 men wounded. For the moment they were to have a rest, but with the Germans being pressed back all along the line the days were past when any unit on the British front could expect any prolonged rest.

As already explained the Third Army had been almost as heavily engaged between September 27th and October 5th as the Fourth, but as it happened, the Thirty-Eighth Division, though in support to its Corps and in readiness to be put in, had not been employed. The front line Divisions had done all that was required, and not till the Third Army was virtually through the Hindenburg defences did the 10th S.W.B. come into action again. The Division had moved up on September 28th to Sorel-le-Grand and waited there till October 3rd, in readiness to move and spending the time in training. It was none too comfortable, the villages around were completely ruined and the men had to bivouac in old trenches; and the orders to advance which were received on October 3rd were a welcome relief. With good news coming in from all quarters spirits were high, and it was encouraging, as the troops went forward, to see how formidable were the obstacles which had not sufficed to check the British advance.

The situation on the right of the Third Army which confronted the Thirty-Eighth Division was that after heavy fighting, in the course of which it had repulsed several vigorous counter-attacks, the Fiftieth Division had established a line running from Prospect Hill on the right North of Gouy and Le Catelet towards Vendhuille. The Thirty-Eighth was to relieve its left brigade and advance Northward, thereby turning the portion of the Hindenburg Line facing Vendhuille. To carry this out the 115th Brigade left Sorel-le-Grand on the morning of October 4th, the battalion moving in platoons 150 yards apart, and reached Bony about midday. Here it passed through the defences which had been stormed a few days earlier and had a chance to estimate both them and the achievement involved in overcoming them. Officers now went forward to reconnoitre the positions to be taken over,

[1] Besides those mentioned already Second Lieutenants Garner, Griffiths, Hartley, Smith and Nicholas were hit. Second Lieutenant Bronham received the M.C.

and in the evening the relief of the Fiftieth Division was effected, the 10th taking over from the 2nd Royal Munster Fusiliers, in readiness to advance Northward early next morning with the object of ultimately swinging to its right and pushing East. The advance, which was led by C and D Companies with A and B in close support, made good progress at first; and on reaching Basket Wood (N.E. of Vendhuille) the 10th brought up their left shoulders and swung Eastwards towards Aubencheuil aux Bois.

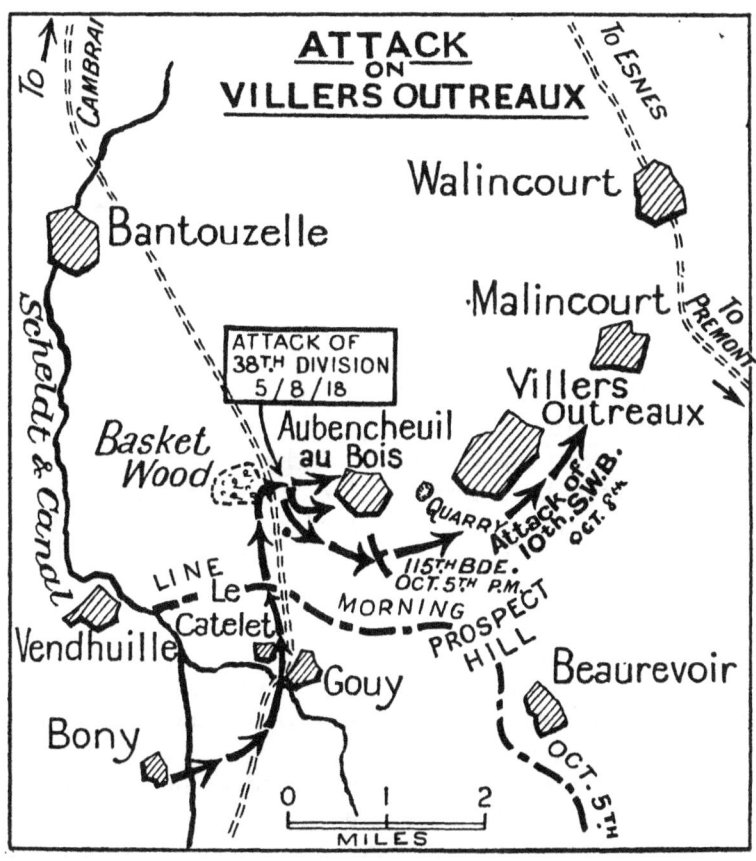

Opposition now began to stiffen: snipers, machine guns and field guns all came into action; and as it was no part of the day's programme to become heavily engaged the 10th dug in with the rest of the brigade S.E. of Aubencheuil and in touch on the right with the Fiftieth Division. Elsewhere the Fourth Army had completed the capture of the Beaurevoir Line in its front, and the defenders of the Hindenburg Line from Vendhuille Northward had been compelled to retire to avoid being completely cut off.

The way was now open for further advance into the open country between the Hindenburg Line and the Selle. But before this could start there was much to be done in bringing forward the heavy guns, in getting up ammunition and supplies, in reconnaissance and in improving the line by minor advances. On October 6th, the 17th R.W.F.'s patrols having entered Aubencheul and found its defenders gone, the 10th pushed two platoons forward past the village towards Villers-Outreaux. It was rather a reconnaissance in force than a definite attack, but a useful advance was made, one platoon seizing a quarry some way East of Aubencheul while the other established itself in a sunken road S.W. of Villers-Outreaux. During the night another platoon pushed out to the right and got touch with the Fiftieth Division, and patrols obtained useful information about the hostile defences, which proved to be strongly held with many machine guns and covered in front by a thick belt of uncut wire. Evidently Villers-Outreaux was not going to be evacuated without a fight; and all through the next day the Germans maintained a heavy fire on the battalion's position, besides repulsing an attempt of the Fiftieth Division to get forward.

When the advance towards the Selle started on October 8th the task before the Thirty-Eighth Division was both complicated and difficult: it had a formidable position to attack, the co-ordination of its movements with those of the units on its flanks was not easy, and the short time available between the issue of orders at 7 p.m. October 7th and the Zero hour of 1 a.m. 8th did not make things easier. The part the 10th S.W.B. had to play was peculiarly difficult, involving an advance N.E. in the dark to the East of Villers-Outreaux with the idea of cutting that village off. The 17th R.W.F. on the left were in the same way to move past the village, so that it might be left isolated for the brigade reserve, the 2nd R.W.F., to deal with at daybreak with the assistance of two tanks.

Punctually at 1 a.m. the attack started, A and B Companies leading. Almost at once thick and uncut wire was encountered, and as the battalion was struggling through this machine gun fire opened. In the dark there was some confusion and loss of direction. Part of the battalion under Major Monteith, however, persisted in their attack and established themselves on their objective. This they were able to do largely owing to the courage and initiative of Company Sergeant Major Williams of B Company: finding his men held up by a machine gun post he engaged it with a Lewis gun, while he and Private R. Evans worked forward round the flank till they could rush the post, surprising and capturing the entire garrison of 11 men.[1] The

---

[1] For this and subsequent acts of gallantry he was awarded the V.C. Private Evans got the D.C.M. and Captain England the M.C.

rest of the battalion, however, got very much scattered, and the 17th R.W.F. also had been held up and had lost heavily, so the 115th Brigade came to a standstill, while efforts were made to reorganize the attacking battalions. On the left the 113th Brigade had fared rather better, and on the arrival of the 2nd R.W.F. and their tanks the attack on Villers-Outreaux was resumed. This time things went better: the tanks got into the village and assisted the 2nd R.W.F. to clear it. The 113th Brigade supported by the 114th pushed forward further to the left across the road to Lesdain, and the scattered parties of the 10th, having been rallied, forced their way forward to rejoin Major Monteith's detachment which was clinging to its lodgment in its first objective. By 11 a.m. Villers-Outreaux was ours, and the 114th Brigade, thrusting forward, made rapid progress thanks largely to a splendid artillery barrage, ultimately securing the final objective near Walincourt along the Premont–Esnes road. The 10th, who had been reorganized, came forward behind them, digging in for the night just S.E. of Walincourt: losses had been heavy,[1] but the battalion had the satisfaction of knowing that it had in the end, despite opposition and set-backs, accomplished the difficult task assigned to it.

For the next three days little was demanded of the 10th. On October 9th the Thirty-Third Division passed through and continued the advance N.E., the Thirty-Eighth moving forward in its support and reaching Clary on the afternoon of October 11th. Here the troops met with the most enthusiastic reception from the civilian population, whose rejoicings at delivery after four years from German rule were a thing to be remembered. How they had kept their tricolour flags hidden all this time it was hard to say, but hardly a house failed to produce one, and the battalion found itself surrounded by mobs of old men, women and children, cheering vociferously and embarrassing their deliverers by embracing them freely.

The Third Army had by this time reached the left bank of the Selle, on the far side of which the Germans were strongly posted, and for the moment there was a pause in its advance, while preparations were being made to force the passage. In the meantime the Fourth Army had also pushed forward successfully on the Third's right and now found itself confronted West of the Selle above Le Cateau with a strong but incomplete line of defences. Against this it was decided to launch an attack

[1] Captain J. A. Jones, Lieutenant R. H. Jones and Second Lieutenant D. Jones were killed. Captain England, Second Lieutenants W. J. Roberts, Rayner, Cupp, Swanson and J. G. Williams wounded: casualties among the rank and file coming to 200.

on October 17th, to be followed by a fresh effort by the Third Army lower down the river; and the First Division, its rest being over, was brought forward to share in this attack. In this the Ninth Corps, still forming the British right, was attacking on a front of 7000 yards from the junction with the French to Vaux-Andigny and was using the Sixth and Forty-Sixth Divisions to take its first objective along the Northern and Western edges of Andigny Forest. The First Division was then to go through and take the final objective, which included the villages of La Vallée Mulâtre and Wassigny. The 1st S.W.B., who had moved forward to Bohain on October 16th, were not actually engaged in the first day of the battle in which the line was carried forward to La Vallée Mulâtre, approximately the second of the day's objectives. The enemy's resistance had been determined, but it was successfully overcome by all three Corps of the Fourth Army, which established themselves on the ridge between the Upper Selle and the Sambre et Oise Canal, in readiness to push on again next day.

On October 18th the 1st S.W.B. therefore got their chance. They had moved up during the night to just West of La Vallée Mulâtre, and at 10.30 a.m. advanced under cover of a smoke barrage to a starting-off line North of the village. Morning fog had prevented a reconnaissance, but the line was reached up to time, despite considerable hostile shelling, and at 11 a.m. the advance started, A and D leading with C in support and B in reserve. A met but little resistance, but D had a sharper fight. Bellevue sheltered a nest of machine guns which opened a heavy fire, and though when D pressed its attack many enemy surrendered, a party of about 30 men held out and was only disposed of when D worked up quite close and rushed them with the bayonet, killing a dozen and capturing the rest. By 2 p.m. the 3rd Brigade had secured the road from Ribeauville to Wassigny and proceeded to consolidate it. On the right the Black Watch had secured Wassigny, but on the left D Company found its flank in the air, so half C had to form a defensive flank. The Scots Greys then tried to push patrols forward but were soon held up by machine gun fire. However, the enemy, if still able to make a stand, were not inclined to counter-attack, and during the evening C Company established touch with the Americans, who had at last succeeded in clearing Ribeauville, but were still slightly in rear of the S.W.B. Farther North the Thirteenth Corps, which had taken Le Cateau on October 17th, had penetrated as far as Bazuel, and to complete the success already achieved a fresh advance was attempted on the 19th between that point and Oisy, with the American IInd Corps on the left and the Ninth Corps on the right. In this the battalion's objective was the hamlet of Rejet de Beaulieu lying in a dip in the ground just West of the Sambre et Oise Canal.

The attack was carried out by B and C Companies who, screened by a thick mist, met little opposition till practically into the hamlet. Here machine gunners put up a fight but were soon overpowered, and patrols, pushing up the ridge beyond, established an outpost line 200 yards farther on and proceeded to consolidate. Efforts to get on to the canal bank were held up by machine gun fire, but the main objective had been secured and a good position obtained for the crossing of the canal, an indispensable preliminary to the advance against the main line of railway running South from Maubeuge on which the enemy's armies farther South depended. For the moment this advance had to be postponed until the Fourth Army could bring its left up level with its right and till the Third and First Armies beyond it could come also into line, and the next attack of any size was to be made lower down the Selle. The 1st S.W.B., though left for the next two days in occupation of the position reached on October 19th, were not required to make any special effort. Patrols were active, but could not capture any of the enemy's machine guns, which were now proving troublesome, though Lewis guns, trench mortars and rifle grenades retaliated effectively. On the evening of October 21st the battalion was relieved, and went back to Wassigny where it found quite comfortable billets. It had had in all one officer (Lieutenant H. S. Bennett) and 29 men killed[1] or died of wounds, and three officers and 60 men wounded, so that its captures alone, one officer and 76 men, nearly equalled its casualties, while its trophies included five field guns and eleven machine guns.[2]

During this first stage of the battle of the Selle the 10th S.W.B., though not inactive, had not had to make an attack. Their Division had after dark on October 13th relieved the Thirty-Third along the Selle, N.E. of Troisvilles. The 115th Brigade was employed to hold the front line, and thus the 10th, now under Major Sykes, found themselves holding a couple of bridgeheads which the Thirty-Third had established across the river. Some rather lively days followed, the enemy's artillery doing their best by vigorous bombardments to interfere with the preparations for the next attack, while the 10th's patrols were extremely active, locating the enemy's position along the railway

---

[1] These included that hero of many adventures, Private Macaulay, who had just added a M.M. for the capture of Maissemy to his D.C.M. and bar.

[2] Second Lieutenants J. J. O'Neil, V. J. L. Napier and T. C. Phillips received the M.C. for gallantry in action on October 18th and 19th, while the M.M. was awarded to 17 N.C.O.'s and men in connection with these operations.

embankment North of the river and obtaining much valuable information. In the course of this several sharp encounters occurred. In one of these Second Lieutenant Hicks and a fighting patrol of 20 men put a German patrol to flight, obtaining useful identifications. On the 18th Second Lieutenant Ruther and a party of 24 men going forward to establish an advanced post in a quarry found the enemy in occupation with several machine guns. Nothing daunted, Second Lieutenant Ruther and his men rushed the post, cleared the Germans out with bombs and proceeded to consolidate. But they were interrupted in this by the enemy returning in force, whereupon, finding his party in danger of being cut off, Second Lieutenant Ruther decided to withdraw and extricated his men successfully, with no more loss than six wounded, he himself being one. That evening the 115th Brigade was relieved and the 10th went back to Troisvilles, where it remained until the evening of October 21st. It was thus in reserve on October 20th when the Third Army followed up the success already gained by the Fourth by driving the enemy out of his positions along the Selle. On October 21st the 10th relieved a battalion of the 113th Brigade in front line, but was itself relieved 24 hours later, when the Thirty-Third Division again replaced the Thirty-Eighth. Thus when, on October 25th, the Third and Fourth Armies renewed their attacks both 10th and 1st S.W.B. were for the moment in reserve; and as the Nineteenth Division, now in the Third Army, was also out of the line the TWENTY-FOURTH had no share in that attack which clinched and confirmed the two earlier successes and carried the British line right forward almost to the Western outskirts of the Forest of Mormal. This placed the British in a good position for the next big operation which Sir Douglas Haig had in mind, but before which a short pause was essential, owing mainly to administrative reasons and the great difficulty of enabling supplies and ammunition to keep pace with the rapidity of the advance.

In the attack of October 20th the Nineteenth Division had had its first share in the main offensive since joining the Third Army. After concentrating round Graincourt and Moeuvres it had advanced in support to the Seventeenth Corps without being put into the fighting, and the 5th had been fully occupied on their usual but unending task of removing obstructions to traffic, filling in shell holes and generally making the roads fit for use.[1] Arrival at the Selle brought it a change from this. The Division's task was to capture the high ground beyond, between Saulzoir and

---

[1] Lieutenant Colonel R. R. Rayner joined from the Cheshire Regiment and took command while the battalion was at Graincourt.

Haussy, and on the evening of the 19th B and C Companies were sent forward to assist the R.E. in bridging the river prior to the passage of the infantry. The river here was unfordable and the laying of the bridges was an indispensable preliminary. It was a really difficult task, but was accomplished to the great satisfaction of the G.O.C. Division, each company laying no less than ten light bridges for the brigade to which it was attached.

The Nineteenth Division's attack was a complete success, and its leading troops pushed on well beyond the Selle, so that the 5th soon found themselves back at the old familiar job of improving the roads in the forward area. Three days of hard work followed and then, on the Division being relieved by the Sixty-First, the 5th went back, first to Avesnes lez Aubert and then to Rieux, for the usual mixture of " rest " and " training " that was the lot of those " out of the line." For once it obtained some welcome relief from its perennial road repairing.

While the Armies engaged on the main British battle-front had been delivering their rapid succession of hammer-strokes the Second Army in Flanders had also been exploiting its earlier successes. The period of rest which the 2nd S.W.B. had enjoyed after its successful advance from Zillebeke to Gheluvelt had ended on October 11th, when it had returned to its old position North of Gheluwe, for a two days' spell in the line. On the evening of October 13th it was relieved by the 2nd Royal Fusiliers and moved to the left to some old trenches North of Dadizeele, prior to a fresh attack in which the Ninth and Thirty-Sixth Divisions were co-operating on the left and right respectively. The advance had first to cross the Menin–Roulers road and then to tackle the considerable and still undamaged town of Ledeghem. At the start the 87th Brigade was in reserve, and as the other two brigades were immediately and conspicuously successful, advancing nearly 6000 yards and capturing 1000 prisoners with many guns, the S.W.B.'s part in the day's operations was confined to an advance in a thick fog, artificially increased by the use of smoke shells and by the dust created by the barrage. Direction was exceedingly hard to keep, and the men pushed forward, hardly able to see where they were going. About midday there was a long halt while the situation was being cleared up, and eventually the brigade went into billets close behind the front line in readiness to continue the attack at an early hour next day. One advantage of having passed out of the old fighting zone was that in the undevastated country to which the British advance had now penetrated most houses were intact, so that to be in billets meant having a roof over one's head. This was some set-off against the trouble caused by the presence in large numbers of civilians, whom the Allies were anxious to spare from injury but for whose safety and comfort. the Germans naturally took no thought, shelling them and their houses indiscriminately.

Rousing from their rest by 5 a.m. on October 15th the 2nd had time to get a good breakfast and yet reach their assembly position well up to time. At 9 a.m. the barrage started and the battalion moved forward. It was on the left of the Division and had as its objective the village of Salines. However, as it approached this point heavy machine gun fire developed from the left flank from the direction of Heule Wood, which was on the Ninth Division's frontage, and had been reported captured by them. Actually the Ninth had diverged to the left to attack Steenbeek and Heule Wood from the North, and B and D Companies found themselves being fired into from the rear. Luckily the officers on the spot proved fully equal to the emergency, and D Company, promptly swerving aside, attacked the wood at its S.E. corner. Captain Dendy was killed, but B Company, which was following D, gave vigorous and effective support, Second Lieutenants Pritchard and Glover with the leading platoons having very sharp fighting. Second Lieutenant Glover's men rushed and captured some machine gun posts, disposing of their defenders in a hand-to-hand struggle, and Second Lieutenant Pritchard, though stubbornly opposed along the near edge of the wood, overcame the resistance and also forced his way forward through the wood. Second Lieutenant C. J. Hardy also brought up the supporting platoons in the nick of time and with their assistance the wood, though strongly held, was soon cleared and the dangerous situation on the left flank made secure, so that when, a little later on, the Ninth Division came up the wood could be handed over to it.

Meanwhile D's diversion to the flank had created a gap in the front line and C had been checked. Captain Dutton, however, brought up the supporting platoons of C to reinforce and, handling his men very skilfully, soon broke down all opposition. Second Lieutenant F. W. Hardy did splendid service at this point; when the leading platoons were checked, he rallied and collected the scattered men and dashing forward at the machine gun post which was holding up the advance, rushed it, killing several of the enemy. A Company also came forward and filled the gap and the advance swept on again, the battalion's final objective, the Courtrai–Ingleminster railway, being reached well before midday.[1] Our troops had suffered several casualties

[1] Captain Dutton and Lieutenant Glover received bars to the M.C., Second Lieutenants C. J. Hardy, F. W. Hardy, Mayou and Pritchard being awarded the M.C.

through running into our own barrage, and the enemy's shell fire had been heavy, while in places his machine gunners put up a stiff defence. This was overcome, however, and in the early afternoon C and D Companies established an outpost line some way farther East, while later on the K.O.S.B. pushed through and continued the line towards the Lys, the passage of which

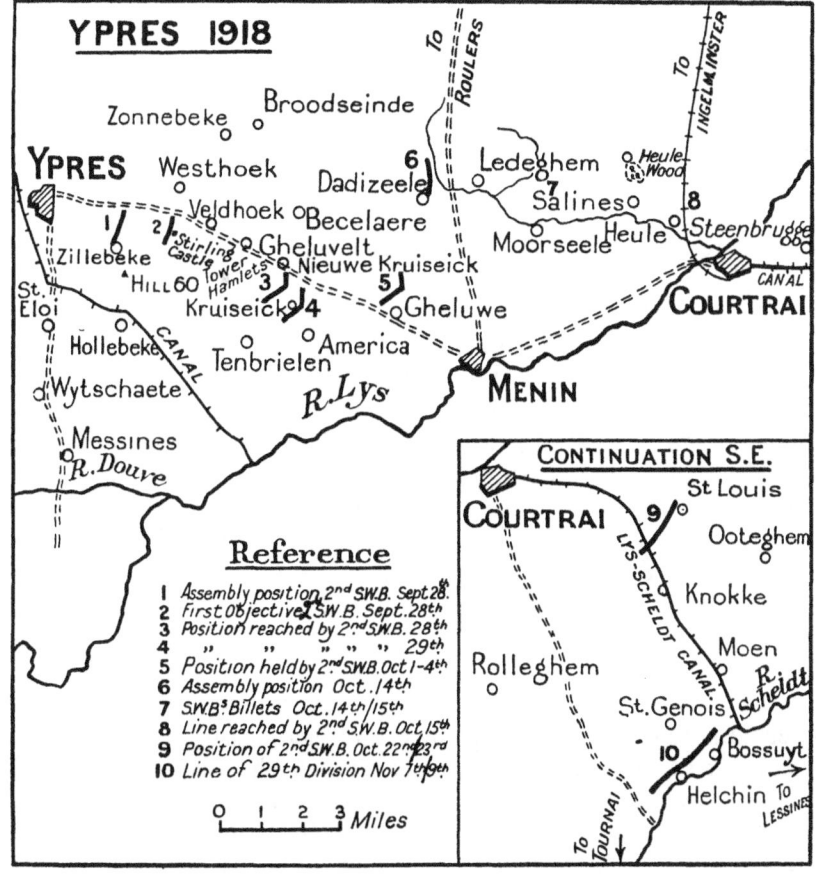

it was now the object of the Division to secure. This, however, took some time and was not finally accomplished till October 20th, when the 86th and 88th Brigades not only forced the passage of the river but advanced nearly five miles in all, capturing 300 prisoners and many guns. The 2nd S.W.B., however, took no active part in this operation. They had been relieved early on October 16th,[1] and were at rest until the 20th, being in reserve on

---

[1] Casualties, though otherwise very light, included Captain Dendy killed, and Second Lieutenants H. Jones and G. Smith wounded.

that day, and merely crossed the Lys peacefully late in the afternoon with no more difficulties than those presented by the congestion of the traffic. Going into billets that evening at Stageghem the 2nd had a quiet day on October 21st, while the 86th Brigade pushed ahead, and then on the 22nd a big advance was made towards the Scheldt by the whole Second Army. In this the 87th Brigade was leading the Twenty-Ninth Division, but the S.W.B., having been detailed as the Brigade reserve, were not actually engaged, only coming forward after dark to relieve the other two battalions which had been held up. They found the enemy active with machine guns, and came in next day for considerable shell fire, but no counter-attack developed, and in the evening of October 23rd the Forty-First Division relieved the battalion, which went back to billets near Steenbrugge, moving a few days later to St. André, near Roubaix, to get a rather longer rest than it had recently enjoyed.

To the 6th S.W.B. meanwhile the Second Army's resumption of the offensive had meant a change not of work but of locality. The Thirtieth Division, though not engaged in the main attack of September 28th, had worked forward on the right flank of the main advance, assisting to clear the Messines ridge and linking up with the Nineteenth Corps at Hollebeke. When the attack was resumed on October 14th its frontage was extended to include the line held by the Tenth Corps, in which the Thirtieth Division was serving, South of the Ypres–Comines Canal. But in neither operation was the 6th called on to do any fighting; what the advance meant for it was incessant labour on the roads, the repair and improvement of which was indispensable to the maintenance of the pressure on the retreating army. As the Germans fell back the 6th pushed on: the beginning of October found it at Wytschaete, by October 7th the plank-road it was making had reached Tenbrielen, four days later it was at "America," and the 6th was becoming actually acquainted with names long familiar to it on the map only. When the Second Army made its way across the Lys bridge-building was added to the 6th's labours, but in the main road-making remained its chief occupation. By October 21st it was at Rolleghem, five days later at Holchin, and the first week of November found it almost half-way between Knokke and Moen, still at its old job of filling in craters, clearing away obstructions, and generally making roads fit for the flood of traffic that was waiting to use them, guns, ambulances, ammunition and supply lorries. If it had no fighting the battalion did not escape without some casualties; its labours often took it well into the forward area and brought the working parties under shell fire. On October

22nd, for example, parties working near St. Genois had 15 casualties, and its ranks were further depleted towards the end of the month by an outbreak of influenza. But the 6th's work, if somewhat monotonous and not in the limelight, was of the utmost value and importance.

CHAPTER XXXIII

THE LAST GREAT BATTLE IN THE WEST

BY November 3rd Sir Douglas Haig had completed all the preliminary operations needed to enable him to deliver his final blow. From S.E. of Le Cateau to N.E. of Valenciennes, a thirty-mile front, seventeen British Divisions were lined up for the attack with half a dozen more in close support. The series of defeats already inflicted on them had produced in the Germans something not far removed from demoralization, here and there individuals and even whole units still fought with bitter tenacity and dogged determination, but the rank and file were mostly weary of the war, unwilling to continue the now hopeless struggle or to sacrifice themselves for their country. The British troops, though exhausted by their continued exertions, were buoyed up by the hopes, now rising high, of speedy victory and an assured peace, and were braced up to the one more effort that should bring about that much desired end. They had taken the measure of their opponents by now, were justly confident in their own superiority, and went forward to their last battle feeling final victory well within their grasp.

Three battalions of the TWENTY-FOURTH were to be engaged in this final effort; the 1st, on the extreme right of the Fourth Army, had the Sambre et Oise Canal to cross at Catillon; the 10th, on the right of the Third Army, faced the great Forest of Mormal; the 5th, whose Division was the left-most of the Third Army, had in its front the undulating country West of Bavai. All three had serious natural obstacles to overcome: the passage of the canal was far from an easy undertaking; the forest, though thinned by the saws and axes of German wood-cutting parties, was still thick enough to delay progress: the rolling downs opposite our left were traversed by streams which would have provided a determined defence with many advantageous positions. But the British were not in the mood to be checked by natural obstacles, even had their opponents been in the frame of mind to profit by these opportunities.

Since the battle of the Selle the 1st S.W.B. had had little fighting, though D Company had been attached to the 2nd Welch for the attack of October 23rd when the First Division had reached the outskirts of Ors and Catillon. D had the misfortune to be caught in the German barrage and had lost its commander, Captain E. R. Taylor, and five men killed and 19 wounded.[1] From October 24th to 30th the battalion had enjoyed a rest at Vaux Andigny, after which it had relieved the 2nd Royal Sussex[2] in front of Catillon and spent five rather

---

[1] The other companies had been in support and were not engaged.
[2] Now commanded by a S.W.B. officer, Lieutenant Colonel D. G. Johnson.

uneventful days there, while the preparations for the attack were being completed. Lieutenant F. James was killed on November 1st, but otherwise casualties were few.

In the attack of November 4th the First Division was drawn up on a 7000 yard front from Oisy to Catillon. Its first task was to force the passage of the Sambre et Oise Canal, here 20 yards wide and more difficult to approach because the low ground on its banks was either inundated or swampy. The 1st and 2nd Brigades were attacking on left and right respectively, starting from the line which the 3rd were holding, but, as a subsidiary operation, that brigade was to clear Catillon village and establish a bridge-head beyond the canal. The battalion's function was to distract the defenders by attacking Catillon from the West and thereby enable the Gloucestershire to enter the town from the South and take the defenders of its Western edge in rear. As a preliminary D Company was to clear the way by driving the Germans out of some orchards. It should have had the help of a tank, which owing to fog did not appear so D had to tackle the orchards alone: this task D accomplished most successfully and then the Gloucestershire worked their way into Catillon, while the frontal attack by B and C Companies of the S.W.B. kept the defenders fully occupied. Many Germans who had been sheltering in cellars to avoid the barrage,[1] emerged from them when it lifted, to walk straight into the hands of the Gloucestershire, who quickly mopped up the village and established a bridge-head beyond the canal. B and C meanwhile pressing forward collected over 120 prisoners with seven machine guns. Altogether it was a neat and most successful operation, especially satisfactory because success was so cheaply achieved, only five men being killed, and Second Lieutenant Rees and 15 men wounded. Elsewhere the Division had been most successful, at the cost of 500 casualties it not only crossed the canal and penetrated to a depth of 4000 yards beyond, but captured 20 guns and over 1700 prisoners, besides inflicting heavy casualties on the enemy. In forcing the passage near Fesmy Lieutenant Colonel D. G. Johnson's courage and tactical skill had been alike conspicuous and had been largely responsible for the 2nd Brigade's success. The V.C. which he received was certainly well earned, and it gave great pleasure to the 1st S.W.B. that one of its officers should have won this high distinction when fighting almost alongside it. Catillon was indeed to be that battalion's farewell to the war. That same evening its First Division was relieved by the Forty-Sixth and sent back into reserve; the 1st Battalion being actually at Fresnoy le Grand

---

[1] This had been put down on the Western part of the town and lifted right over the Eastern part.

when on November 11th it received the news of the Armistice. The battalion diary's entry for the day is simple but effective: "Training was washed out and the battalion washed its feet."

Like the 1st Battalion the 10th S.W.B. were in reserve when the fighting ended, after having had a brief but quite satisfactory share in the final battle. From October 23rd to November 2nd it had been out of the front line, either resting at Forest or in

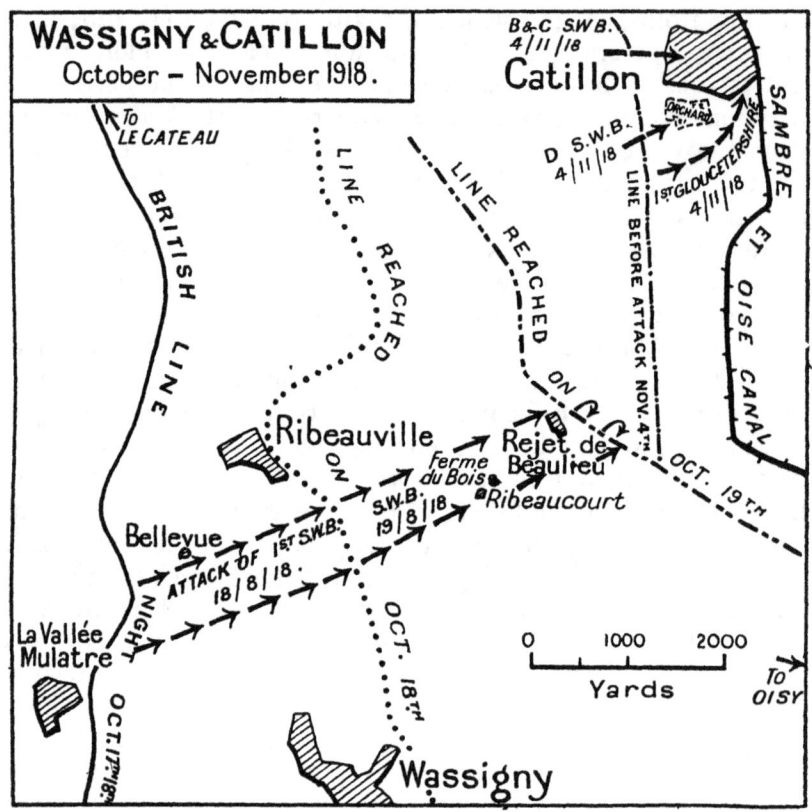

Brigade reserve. It then went into the front line at Englefontaine on the Western outskirts of the Forest of Mormal. The enemy's artillery were intermittently active, and on November 3rd the battalion had nearly a dozen casualties, including Second Lieutenant Shawson wounded, but though the Germans had just previously counter-attacked another battalion of the Division, they did not try an advance against its line.

On November 4th the Thirty-Eighth Division was putting in the 115th Brigade to take its first objective. The 10th S.W.B. were in the centre, with the 2nd and 17th R.W.F. on right and left respectively, and were to have the assistance of two tanks.

These were specially useful as the country was both thickly wooded and enclosed and the hedges, which were close and high, presented troublesome obstacles to an infantry advance. Tanks could smash a way through, and were also useful in dealing with the numerous machine gun posts, in tackling which the junior officers and N.C.O.'s had ample opportunities for showing their capacity to use ground and take advantage of the cover which hedges and enclosures offered.

Starting off in a dense fog at 6.15 a.m. the 10th met fairly vigorous opposition at first but were not to be denied, and by 7.15 a.m. had established themselves 800 yards inside the forest. Particularly good work was done by Corporals Dover and Parker and by Lance Corporal Apps, who were prominent in dealing with the machine gun posts, and the capture of the objective cost the battalion only about 40 casualties. The killed, however, included Second Lieutenant H. T. Jones and the M.O., Lieutenant Cassell, of the U.S.A. Medical Corps, while Captain W. G. Williams was wounded. The other battalions had been equally successful, and the other brigades passing through in turn carried on the attack to a depth of 11 miles before they halted and let the Thirty-Third Division come through. For the next two days the Thirty-Eighth Division was in reserve, but on November 7th it came forward again to take over from the Thirty-Third, which had pushed well beyond the Sambre and had nearly reached the Avesnes–Maubeuge road. But it was the 113th Brigade which was put in to lead, and the Armistice came before the 115th had another chance at the enemy; so that for the 10th S.W.B. as for the 1st Battalion November 4th had been the last day of battle.

The other battalion of the TWENTY-FOURTH engaged in the main advance of the British Armies, the 5th, had come forward with its Division on November 1st to a position South of Valenciennes, and on November 4th the Nineteenth Division attacked with great success, taking Jenlain and Bry, and pushing on across the Wargnies-le-Grand–Bry road. On the following day it resumed the advance and was again successful, but was shortly afterwards squeezed out of the line by other Divisions converging on Mons. It had had some hard fighting, but had not needed to take the 5th S.W.B. off their proper work as Pioneers, for which the rapidity of the advance gave every opportunity. From November 2nd to 11th the 5th were continually at work, usually close up to the front line, repairing roads and bridges. This brought them under shell fire most of the time and they were lucky to escape with only about a dozen casualties. Armistice Day, which found the 5th at Hergies, not far from Bavai, meant no cessation of its labours. Though its Division went back to Cambrai to rest there was as much need as ever for Pioneers to work on roads and railways, and the 5th were retained in the forward area.

In the other portion of the Western Front in which other battalions of the TWENTY-FOURTH were serving there had been heavy fighting before the Armistice stopped hostilities, but as it happened neither the 2nd nor the 6th S.W.B. were very actively engaged. After its prominent part in the hard fighting in the middle of October, the Twenty-Ninth Division had been given a rest near Roubaix. This period, which lasted ten days, was much appreciated, for the towns in this area had been but little damaged and afforded the troops really comfortable quarters. By November 7th, when the Division returned to the fighting line, it found that the British advance had reached the Scheldt and that the next operation before it was the passage of that river. About Bossuyt, where the Twenty-Ninth were now established, the Scheldt was over sixty yards wide and too deep to ford, and the right bank, which the enemy were holding, was considerably higher than the left. It looked therefore as if the operation might be one of some difficulty. However, on November 9th, the very day before the attempt to force the passage was to have been made, the Germans evacuated their positions and fell back. The 88th Brigade promptly pushed across by any means available and started in pursuit, and orders were issued to the 87th to come forward to St. Sauveur in readiness to relieve the 88th. But before this could be done the news of the Armistice had come round, and instead of advancing Eastward the 2nd found themselves halting in the neighbourhood of Lessines, where they were most enthusiastically received by the populace, who could hardly believe that their long subjection to German rule was at an end.

The last weeks of the war had been singularly uneventful for the 6th S.W.B. Road-repairing was now of such paramount importance that a Pioneer battalion was not likely to be taken off that work for any other task, and November 11th found the 6th " navvying," not fighting. It was actually at Amongies, whither it had just moved from Avelghem, and was commanded for the time by Major A. J. Ellis (3rd Battalion) who had recently joined. The Armistice brought no change in its labours and it continued to ply pick and shovel on the roads almost to the end of the month, though latterly this was varied by a little training. On November 20th Colonel Crawford rejoined from leave and resumed command, the battalion being then at Aelbeke.

CHAPTER XXXIV

THE LAST YEAR IN THE BALKANS

JUST before the end of 1917 a change had taken place in Macedonia which made for increased efficiency on that front and more sincere and effective co-operation between the Allies. This was General Sarrail's departure, and with him went that atmosphere of intrigue and its consequence, distrust, till then so unfortunately prominent a factor. In his place came General Guillaumat, a capable soldier and a man of high character, under whom the organization and general effectiveness of the " Allied Armies in the Orient " soon improved enormously. This change and its happy consequences were the more welcome because the collapse of Russia, the disaster at Caporetto, the consequent dispatch to Italy of French and British troops and the generally unfavourable situation on the Western Front naturally reacted on the less important theatres of war. No reinforcements could be spared for Macedonia, except that some thousands of Slav prisoners taken from the Austrians found their way to Salonica to reinforce the Servians, while the definite triumph of M. Venizelos over King Constantine placed the whole Greek Army at the disposal of the Allies, and in the spring of 1918 various portions of the front were entrusted to Greek Divisions. As a set-off both the French and the British contingents were considerably reduced, one battalion being withdrawn in May from each brigade of the B.S.F., and this coupled with the previous transfer of the two Divisions to Palestine reduced the infantry strength of the B.S.F. by July, 1918, to just about half of what it had been in April, 1917.

In these circumstances, with a successful Allied offensive in the Balkans seeming hopelessly improbable—indeed it looked rather as if the B.S.F. might have to withstand an attack in force—the 7th and 8th S.W.B. found the first half of 1918 anything but lively. The sick-rate, though fairly low early in the year, rose steadily with the temperature, and whereas in February the 7th averaged 187 sick per diem, in April the number rose to 230 and in July to 340: invalidings and admissions to hospital increased correspondingly; the 7th sent only 26 to hospital in January, but 110 in May, 84 in June and 107 in July, and though the 8th's figures did not go up quite so fast they also showed a steady rise. A few drafts appeared early in the year, mainly transfers from the A.S.C. and R.A.M.C., but from March on the only set-off against wastage consisted of the trickle of men discharged from hospital. For the four months April to July barely one-fourth of those sent to hospital rejoined the 8th. Battle casualties fortunately were not numerous; the 7th had 17 men killed and 89 wounded from January 1st to August 31st, and the 8th got off even more lightly, though a big raid in July swelled its casualties. Even so "effectives" dwindled steadily, the 7th, nearly 850 strong at the end of March, could only produce 580 by July 31st and the 8th were little better off. Moreover both battalions contained many men only nominally effective whose health had been seriously affected by a long sojourn in that unhealthy climate and who had malaria in them, liable to assert itself under any prolonged strain or extra exertion.[1] It says all the more, therefore, for their spirit and discipline that the two battalions should have maintained so high a standard of efficiency and accomplished so much. In February, for instance, the Brigadier sent a most appreciative message to the 8th, saying how impressed he had been by the quantity and quality of its work in digging and wiring; it was the more satisfactory and creditable, he declared, as showing how well the battalion had maintained its keenness and efficiency unimpaired despite its long service in the country and the absence of all things which could dispel the monotony of existence in Macedonia.

Certainly during the first half of 1918 the normal round was little varied. On both sides the guns were intermittently active, occasionally indulging in regular bombardment, more often endeavouring to worry the enemy by harassing fire. Even if bombardments failed to damage the trenches seriously the weather usually kept the trench garrisons too absorbed in repairs and maintenance to find time for systematic training; indeed, even when in Corps reserve, as both battalions were for most of January, road-making and work on rearward defences competed with training. With so long a line and so small a force it was impossible to relieve a whole Division at a time; however, during April a valuable period was spent in reserve at Irikli and Moravea, special attention being paid to musketry, the importance of which recent events in France had emphasized.

For the 7th the chief incidents were a small Bulgarian raid near Snake Ravine early in February, which was successfully repulsed, and some good patrol work in March, when a small party worked through the enemy's wire near the Sugar Loaf, here of special thickness, and lay up near a trench which was obviously used as a sentry post. It was misty and the party remained in hiding for several hours, ultimately ambushing and shooting down a Bulgarian patrol. Then in May No. 13 platoon under Second Lieutenant Lucas raided O. 3 with conspicuous success. The Bulgarian trenches were entered despite opposition, two dug-outs full of men were bombed and several other casualties inflicted on the defenders, at a cost of only one killed and

[1] Some of those affected with malaria were transferred to France, where it was hoped the climate would allow of their being effective.

a dozen wounded, mostly slightly. Sergeant Rowlands distinguished himself particularly in this raid and gave great help to his officer who led his men splendidly. The enemy seemed very nervous just then, our harassing fire had apparently made them jumpy and they were constantly putting down barrages, usually without cause or provocation; indeed the Bulgarian account gives the impression of much more serious activity on the part of the B.S.F. than British sources convey. The B.S.F., if severely limited as regard enterprises, certainly seems to have fulfilled its orders to worry the Bulgarians near Doiran and thereby distract their attention from Franco-Greek activities further West, which culminated in June in a successful attack on the Skra di Legen in the sector West of the Vardar when the Bulgarian defences were broken through to the depth of one mile on a front of seven, nearly 1700 prisoners being taken.

To the 8th this period had brought an important change, as in June the battalion was transferred from the 67th Brigade to the 65th,[1] from which two battalions had just been withdrawn for service in France. At the end of June it moved into trenches to the left of the line it had recently been holding, and shortly afterwards it was detailed to raid the Bulgarian outpost on Flat Iron Hill, S.W. of Krastali. Flat Iron Hill was about 1000 yards distant from the British front line and was protected by two substantial belts of wire. For several days before the raid No Man's Land between Kimberley Spur and Flat Iron Hill was systematically patrolled: most officers and N.C.O.'s selected for the raid got an opportunity to familiarize themselves with the ground to be crossed and ample information was collected about the Bulgarian defences. The raiders, six officers and 100 other ranks[2] under Major Browning,[3] were divided into two wire-cutting parties of eleven each, who carried four Bangalore torpedoes, two assault parties, each of one officer and 16 men, a blocking party (one officer and 15 men), a demolition party (one officer and 20 men) and a reserve. There was no preliminary bombardment and the raiders, leaving Bowls Barrow at 9.35 p.m., (July 12th) reached the foot of Flat Iron Hill undetected. Then the wire-cutting parties crept forward and had fixed their Bangalores successfully before the enemy, becoming suspicious, sent up Very lights. This revealed what was afoot and immediately the Bulgarians began blazing freely away and hurling bombs.

---

[1] The other remaining battalions of the 65th were the 9th King's Own and 9th East Lancashire.

[2] To make up the required strength, Second Lieutenant Lightfoot and 20 men from C Company had to be attached to A which provided the main body.

[3] He had been promoted in May to be Major and second in command, in place of Major Franklin, invalided.

The Bangalores were promptly exploded, cutting gaps through which the raiders rushed just as the Bulgarian barrage came down. Only a minute later the British guns opened, for Colonel Dobbs from his observation post on Bowls Barrow had called for the British barrage directly the Very lights went up. The second belt of wire proved in bad condition and the raiders rushed the post without being for a moment checked. Lieutenant Benfield's blocking party quickly made its way to the Northern end of the work, bombing two dug-outs *en route*, both full of men, and started building a block. The assault parties, working right and left as ordered, met and disposed of several small groups while Second Lieutenant Ptolemy's demolition party carried out its prescribed tasks, blowing up several dug-outs. After spending 20 minutes in the enemy's position the party withdrew according to its programme, regaining its own lines with the trifling loss of two killed and one officer (Lieutenant Benfield) and eight men wounded. The Bulgarian casualties were hard to estimate accurately, 30 was a conservative estimate, and as satisfactory identifications were obtained the raid fully deserved the warm congratulations which it elicited from the higher authorities.[1]

This raid was for the 8th the chief incident of the summer, but it seemed to have rendered the Bulgarians extremely nervous, for their guns were very active for some time afterwards, while on July 28th/29th they tried to revenge themselves by raiding our small outpost at Gog Post. About 30 enemy reached the wire and started to cut it, but Sergeant G. Clark, the N.C.O. in charge, met them with well-directed rifle fire, and when they shifted along the wire, hoping to effect an entrance elsewhere, he moved his party along the trench to the same spot and drove the Bulgarians off. Three of the little garrison were wounded, but the Bulgarian losses must have been heavier, and Sergeant Clark's gallantry and resource richly merited the M.M. which he received.

Apart from these incidents the summer was chiefly noticeable for changes in company commands and other appointments. Leave to England had at last been opened and several officers took advantage of it, while others transferred to the Indian Army and invalidings were only too numerous, among them Captain Kaye. Thus D Company, which was under Captain Harvey earlier in the year, went to Lieutenant Mellsopp in May: he was wounded by shrapnel on July 6th and sent home; Second Lieutenant Matthias then took charge till August, when Captain

---

[1] The following awards were made on account of this raid: D.S.O., Major Browning; M.C., Lieutenant Benfield; a bar to the M.M., Sergeant Cheyne; M.M's., Sergeant Cox and Private Morgan.

R. N. Caldwell joined, and other companies changed hands almost as frequently. In Captain Williams' absence on U.K. leave Second Lieutenant Fairs acted as Adjutant and Lieutenant Kenny officiated as Quartermaster while Lieutenant Carter was in hospital. Besides the " immediate awards " already mentioned, several " honours " came to the battalion : in the New Year's List Lieutenant Woolley had received the M.C., in the June awards Major Franklin got the D.S.O., Captain F. T. Williams the M.C., Company Sergeant Major Martin the D.C.M. and acting Regimental Sergeant Major Andrews the M.M., while besides these four, Colonel Dobbs, Captains Dickie and Brown, Sergeants Dunn and L. Lewis and Corporal Martin were mentioned.

The 7th also had experienced many changes and received several awards. When Major Bradbury was " struck off " (December, 1917), Major Humphreys joined from the 8th D.C.L.I. as second in command. In May Captain E. L. Lloyd, who had commanded C Company most successfully for over a year, was invalided home and the battalion lost two of the few remaining officers who had joined it on its formation, Major Gottwaltz and Captain Villar, transferred respectively to the 9th East Lancashire and 11th R.W.F. as second in command. Other officers also left for the Machine Gun Corps, the R.F.C. or the Indian Army. In the June " Honours " list, Colonel Burges got a bar to the D.S.O. and Company Quartermaster Sergeant A. Dix received the M.S.M., and " mentions " in the Salonica dispatches of March, 1918, included the C.O., Lieutenant and Quartermaster Dunne, Corporal Arthur and Lance Corporals Driscoll and Heath. Of the officers who joined the most noteworthy was Captain Mundy, who had already served with the 4th Battalion at Gallipoli and with the 1st in France.

Meanwhile things were at last beginning to move in Macedonia. Before the Skra di Legen fighting nearly all the few Germans in the country had been recalled to the Western Front, and after the tide in that quarter had definitely turned with the failure of the German attack on the Rheims front in July, Bulgarian deserters had been coming over with increasing frequency. From them and from other sources ample information was received of the despondency now spreading through Bulgaria. Her peasant soldiery were weary of their long absence from their homes : men returning from leave brought back bad accounts of conditions at home, and Bulgaria had no intention of sacrificing herself for Germany, whose side she had originally taken not from affection or gratitude, but from mere greed, and whose catspaw she now felt herself in danger of becoming. Could the Allies have induced the Servians to make concessions in

Macedonia to the Bulgarians, accepting compensation elsewhere, Bulgaria would probably have been out of the war before the end of August. No such arrangement proved practicable, but none the less Bulgarian war-weariness helped to induce the Allies to attempt another offensive in Macedonia.

The scheme adopted by General Franchet d'Espéry, who had replaced General Guillaumat as C. in C. in the Balkans in June, demanded from the British yet one more assault upon the forbidding defences between Lake Doiran and the Vardar. Success here would, if promptly exploited, intercept the retreat of the Bulgarian forces farther West, and the Bulgarians, realizing this, had not only gone on elaborating their defences but had increased the force holding this sector to two complete Divisions.[1] They had also substantially revised their defensive scheme in the light of the lessons learned in the 1917 attacks. Success was therefore hardly to be confidently expected, especially with the diminished establishments and scanty effectives of the four British Divisions remaining in Macedonia, which had just been still further reduced by a sudden epidemic of influenza. This swept right through the B.S.F., and though fortunately fairly mild in character literally prostrated thousands. The 8th S.W.B. started with 20 cases on September 2nd, rose to 54 two days later and had in all nearly 300. The 7th fared nearly as badly, and the eve of the offensive found few British battalions equal to putting into the field half their established number of bayonets.

The Allies' main blow was to be delivered well West of the Vardar towards Demir Kapu and Gradsko. Should the Franco-Servians in this quarter succeed in penetrating to the Middle Vardar the Bulgarian game would be up and their communications endangered. Besides this subsidiary attacks both East and West were aimed at distracting the Bulgarian attention and detaining troops who might have reinforced the threatened sector, but it was also hoped to effect a double or even treble break through.

Thus once again the Twenty-Second Division found itself required to assault the positions against which the British attacks had been so terribly shattered in 1917. The Twelfth Corps now included the Greek Seres Division[2] and had that unit on its right, the Twenty-Second Division continuing the line

---

[1] A Bulgarian Division at this period was more than twice as strong as a British Division at its full establishment. That holding the Doiran sector mustered 34,000, including nearly 4000 machine gunners and 6000 artillerymen and was supported by 136 guns, 188 machine guns and over 200 trench mortars and similar weapons (cf. Nedeff, p. 196).

[2] This belonged to the Venizelist "National Defence Army" which had joined the Allies in March, 1918.

Westward to Krastali with the Twenty-Sixth beyond again. The Twenty-Seventh was just West of the Vardar, the Sixteenth Corps, now comprising the Twenty-Eighth Division and the Greek Cretan Division, was East of Lake Doiran with more Greeks in its old haunts lower down the Struma.

The Twelfth Corps' attack was to be begun by the Seres Division, which after storming the " advanced Doiran position," as the Bulgarians called it, North and East of the Jumeaux Ravine, would push on against the Grand Couronné and co-operate from the S.E. with the 67th Brigade, which was attacking that stronghold from the South, with O. 6 as its first objective, the line of the Hilt, the Knot and the Tassel as its second, and Grand Couronné as final goal. The 7th S.W.B. were its left

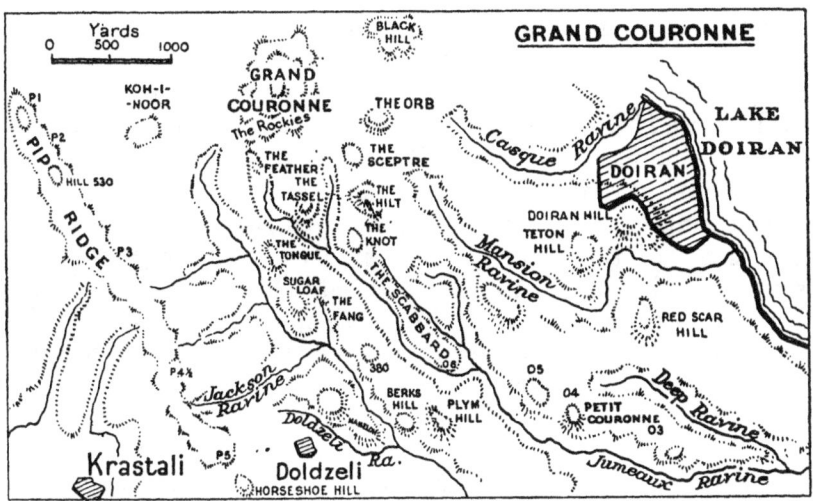

battalion and had first to link up the attack on the second objective with the 3rd Greek Regiment on the left which had the Sugar Loaf and Tongue as objectives; these taken, it would press on up the Feather Ridge towards Grand Couronné. Further to the left again the 66th Brigade was tackling the famous P Ridge. The 65th Brigade being absent in an influenza isolation camp the 77th Brigade (Twenty-Sixth Division) acted as Divisional reserve. To the left the Twenty-Sixth Division, strung out thinly from Horseshoe Hill to the Vardar, was to demonstrate and if possible to secure the line Emerald Hill–Flat Iron Hill.

The Bulgarians' advantages in observation made concealing preparations impossible, and with their lines rising on terraces one behind the other, well provided with dug-outs and protected by thick belts of wire, which the bombardment had only managed to cut in places, the prospects were hardly promising. Though most of the German and Austrian artillery had recently quitted the Macedonian front the Bulgarians still had an advantage in heavy guns and were about as well off in machine guns, and in the actual Doiran sector were superior in all respects, more especially as the recent epidemic had left the British battalions extremely weak. The 7th S.W.B. could only produce 17 officers and 436 men and the 8th had to reorganize its four companies as two, A and B forming the new A, C and D the new C.

The day selected for the attack was September 18th. For three days previously the Bulgarian positions had been vigorously bombarded, the trenches being much damaged, though according to the Bulgarian account the splendid shelter of their well-built dug-outs kept their casualties down. A gas bombardment on the evening of the 17th caused them much discomfort and more losses, but their artillery, though heavily shelled and well gassed, stuck to their guns, and did excellent work both in counter-battery and in barraging assembly positions. On September 17th the 7th were severely shelled while waiting on the Southern slopes of Tortoise Hill for the signal to attack, and had nearly 30 casualties, including Captain F. J. T. Dickinson killed.

"Zero" was at 5.15 a.m. and both Greeks and British started to the minute. Largely because the 67th Brigade had taken the opponents of the Seres Division in flank and rear,[1] that unit swept quickly over the "advanced Doiran position" and pressed on towards its second objective, while the 11th R.W.F. and 11th Welch penetrated to the Hilt–Knot–Tassel line. The 7th S.W.B. meanwhile had by orders let the 3rd Greeks get a start before advancing on a two-company front against the Sugar Loaf. This the Greeks should have cleared, but the 7th found Bulgarians still in these trenches, having presumably emerged from dug-outs after the Greeks had pushed on. This opposition the battalion overcame after sharp fighting and several casualties and then pressed on to the Tongue trenches, cleared them and began advancing up the Feather.

The advance was one of no little difficulty: the ground was rough and rocky, much intersected by wire, and in places precipitous. The darkness and the clouds of smoke and dust made direction hard to keep. The objectives were so far from our gun positions that only a few gaps in the wire could be cut, while the machine guns had been hard to locate and silence, and as the 7th pushed forward their fire grew steadily more intense. The battalion struggled on nevertheless, though losing heavily, till the wire in front of the Rockies trenches, nearly a mile from the position of deployment, was reached. Here a short halt was necessary to wait for our barrage to lift. Casualties had been heavy and the battalion was ahead of the troops on its flanks.

[1] cf. Nedeff p. 236.

GRAND COURONNÉ

The 11th R.W.F. and 11th Welch, very stubbornly opposed, had not got beyond the line of the Hilt and the Tassel and most of the 3rd Greeks, though that regiment had passed the Tongue, had fallen behind. Thus from both flanks machine gun fire concentrated upon the 7th, and though, when the barrage lifted, the men dashed at the gaps in the wire, they were bowled over in numbers by the stream of bullets, more deadly now because on the barrage lifting the dust and smoke cleared away and the machine gunners could see their targets clearly. A mere handful struggled through the wire and entered the trenches, but far too few to effect anything in face of the strong trench garrisons.

Such Greeks as had accompanied the battalion seem now to have fallen back and there was nothing left for the few remaining men of the 7th but to retire also. Two officers, both wounded, rallied these survivors on the Tongue and held on for some time, though the Greeks had all retired and they were unsupported on either flank. To the left the 66th Brigade's desperate attacks against the P Ridge, after penetrating to the Bulgarian third line, had resulted in the virtual annihilation of the leading battalion, and not even the trenches first captured could be retained. On the right the Bulgarians had retaken both the Hilt and the Knot, though despite counter-attacks O. 6 was held and the Greeks retained Doiran town and all South of it. The survivors of the 7th had finally to retire to our own trenches. Only the merest fragment of a battalion remained, and of the 50 odd survivors whom Captain Donald, the M.O. and Lieutenant Stephenson could collect more than half were suffering so badly from gas that they had to be evacuated to hospital next day. Of 17 officers engaged in the attack only Captain Donald remained unhit. Captains Mundy and Treglown with Lieutenants Round and Stephenson, though wounded, had got back to our lines, the others, including Colonel Burges who was known to be wounded, were missing, and not till some days later, when the Bulgarians retired, could their fate be cleared up by the discovery of their dead bodies, that of Captain Dick being found farther forward up the Grand Couronné than any other officer's or man's. He and Captain Mills, who was also killed, were almost the last survivors of the 7th's " original " officers and were much regretted. Another splendid officer who fell on Grand Couronné was Lieutenant Lucas, originally a Sergeant in the 2nd Battalion, who had distinguished himself at Gallipoli and had subsequently been given a commission for gallantry in the field.[1] Of the missing a terribly high proportion had been killed, the deadly

[1] Others killed were Captain Gotelee, Second Lieutenants C. A. Davies, P. C. Hughes, E. G. Jones, W. Roberts, W. J. Whitehorne and W. L. Woolley.

hail from the machine guns had not spared the wounded, and though most of those hit in the earlier stages crawled back to our lines[1] not many of the 7th subsequently turned up among released prisoners. Still, disastrous as the day had been, the desperate and enduring gallantry with which the 7th had pressed its attack and the skill and leadership of Colonel Burges had been outstanding, even on a day on which every British unit engaged had fought so splendidly. It says volumes for the 7th that after three years spent in the monotonous and discouraging conditions of the Salonica front, with probably more than half of them absolutely saturated with malaria, they should have shown such dash, devotion and determination in the face of odds they so well knew to be heavily against them. The signal honour of the award of the Croix de Guerre speaks for itself—the 7th was the only battalion in the B.S.F. so honoured and but four were given to British units on the whole Western Front. Colonel Burges, whom all ranks were rejoiced to recover a few days later in a Bulgarian hospital, received a well-merited V.C., Captain Donald, who had been simply magnificent, might well have been as highly rewarded: no man ever deserved the V.C. better, but the D.S.O. awarded to Captain Mundy, three M.C.'s given to Captains Treglown and Donald and Lieutenant Round, three D.C.M.'s to Sergeant Torney, Lance Corporal D. Davies and Private Berry, and six M.M.'s to Sergeants Edmunds and Price, Corporals Regan, Griffith and Evans and Private Brunker, formed a goodly list. General Duncan, too, issued a special order of appreciation. "The manner," he wrote, "in which this battalion carried out the assault in face of almost impossible difficulties is an example of extreme self-sacrifice and worthy of the highest praise."

The ill-success of the attack notwithstanding, if the Bulgarians were to be prevented from dispatching reinforcements from Doiran to the quarters where their line looked like giving way, pressure must be maintained, and General Milne had no option but to renew the assault next day, using Greeks and the 77th Brigade on the right and a regiment of Zouaves in the centre West of the Vladaja Ravine, while beyond them again the 65th Brigade was to attack the P Ridge, the 9th King's Own leading. The 8th S.W.B., who had come up from their isolation camp to Shelter Ravine Camp on September 18th, accordingly assembled in Jackson's Ravine before dawn on the 19th. They had some casualties from shell fire on the way up past Doldzeli and were heavily shelled while waiting for orders to advance, but the men took cover cleverly, and considering the intensity of the bombardment casualties were not numerous. Meanwhile the

---

[1] About 160 are recorded as "wounded."

King's Own had taken "P. 4½" after heavy fighting, but the Zouaves never went forward, being stopped in the Doldzeli Ravine by a barrage they would not rush. Consequently about 7.30 a.m. the King's Own, having been scourged by a devastating fire and then counter-attacked in force, were dislodged from their isolated position. They rallied in Jackson Ravine on the supporting 8th, their sixty survivors being ultimately posted on that battalion's left. About 11 a.m. Colonel Dobbs received orders to retire, but feeling that to retreat under that heavy shelling would mean more casualties than sticking it out, he got the order cancelled and held on till after dark, when he withdrew safely to Gun Ravine, having had 50 casualties, including only three killed. Lieutenant Benfield, who was wounded, was the only officer hit.

September 19th, like its predecessor, had been a bad day. The Scots of the 77th Brigade, attacking with great dash, had swept over the front line defences and carried the Fang, the Sugar Loaf, the Tongue and the Knot, but being unsupported on either flank had been dislodged by vigorous, well-executed counter-attacks. That evening the situation was gloomy in the extreme. Once again the Twelfth Corps had been shattered to pieces against the same old impregnable obstacles. Had the Bulgarians counter-attacked, its sadly depleted battalions would have had the utmost difficulty to keep them out. Even the fragment of the 7th S.W.B. had to remain in the line till the evening of September 20th, so urgent was the need for men to defend the position. But the Twelfth Corps had not made its sacrifices in vain. Further West French, Servians and Italians had all broken through and the whole Bulgarian line was crumpling up.

Actually September 20th passed quietly on the Doiran front, though the Bulgarian guns blazed away unaccountably freely. Next day, however, frequent explosions were heard and fires seen behind the Grand Couronné, our aeroplanes reported great movements Northward of transport from the Doiran front, and battalions were warned to look out for a Bulgarian retreat. On the 22nd a suspicious quiet prevailed, and before long the patrols which had gone out before daybreak reported that the enemy's front line from Doiran Westward was unoccupied. Orders were promptly issued for an advance, and the 7th, now 100 strong under Major Humphreys, who had brought up every available man from the transport lines, moved forward and occupied the Grand Couronné. To tread that fatal and long-coveted ridge at last seemed incredible, covered as it was with British dead, but there was no doubt about it, the Bulgarians were in full retreat, they had abandoned trench equipment and weapons of every description, and had also left behind several wounded prisoners taken on the 18th and 19th, among them Colonel Burges.

Next day (September 23rd) the regular pursuit began. The 67th Brigade with the 7th S.W.B. as advanced-guard started at 7.30 a.m. for Volovec, arrived there at 9 a.m. and after a five-hours' halt, pushed on to Cernisté, getting in at 9 p.m. The 65th Brigade moved by Doldzeli to Kara Ogular, the 83rd Brigade, now under General Duncan's orders, reaching Pazarli and establishing an outpost line. There was little opposition, though seven guns were taken, and the 7th and 8th were greatly interested to examine the positions that had so long defied them. It was easier now to understand why our attacks had fared no better.

The orders for September 24th were that the 65th Brigade with the 8th S.W.B. leading should push through the outpost line and make for Zeus Junction, North of the lake, the 67th meanwhile coming forward to Hasanli. After passing through the outposts the 8th forged ahead, encountering some opposition though not enough to delay its advance seriously. It was brought to a halt, however, about Zeus Junction because the Greeks on the left had fallen behind, and though two platoons of C Company under Major Caldwell[1] secured Asser Junction, a strong patrol which was sent forward later towards Point 1472 in the Belashitza range encountered opposition in the foothills and had to come back. However, by this time ample information had been collected, on the strength of which the 65th Brigade was ordered to attack Point 1472 next day with the 67th in support. At 8 a.m. on September 25th therefore the 8th moved out, the 9th King's Own, now reduced to one company, being placed under Colonel Dobbs' orders. Almost at once the battalion came under shell fire but pressed on undeterred. After following the main road for nearly 1000 yards, the 8th started working across country towards the foot of Boundary Spur. In the mountainous and scrub-covered country frequent halts were needed to let those in rear keep up, but if progress was slow the scrub and the undulations afforded good cover and casualties were low. About 1 p.m. the ascent of the spur began. The slopes were steep and thickly wooded, but this helped to conceal the move and eventually Lieutenant Greaves and the battalion scouts rushed a rocky knoll, which was believed to be Point 1472 but was nearly 1000 yards N.W. of it. This position was quickly made good, despite considerable opposition from riflemen and machine guns, which Lieutenant Greaves' skilful handling of his Lewis guns soon overcame.[2] Here the battalion put out outposts and settled down for

---

[1] Promoted to that rank in Major Franklin's vacancy.
[2] Second Lieutenant Greaves was awarded the M.C.

PURSUING THE BULGARIANS

a disturbed night, the King's Own occupying a flanking position on the left. Intermittent rifle fire and bomb throwing continued all night, but an attempt to rush one of our posts was repulsed, and though cold, hungry and short of both water and ammunition the 8th successfully maintained its advanced position.

Actually the 65th Brigade had issued orders which never reached Colonel Dobbs to stop the attack and withdraw the battalion: the Cretans had not come up on the right, so the Corps

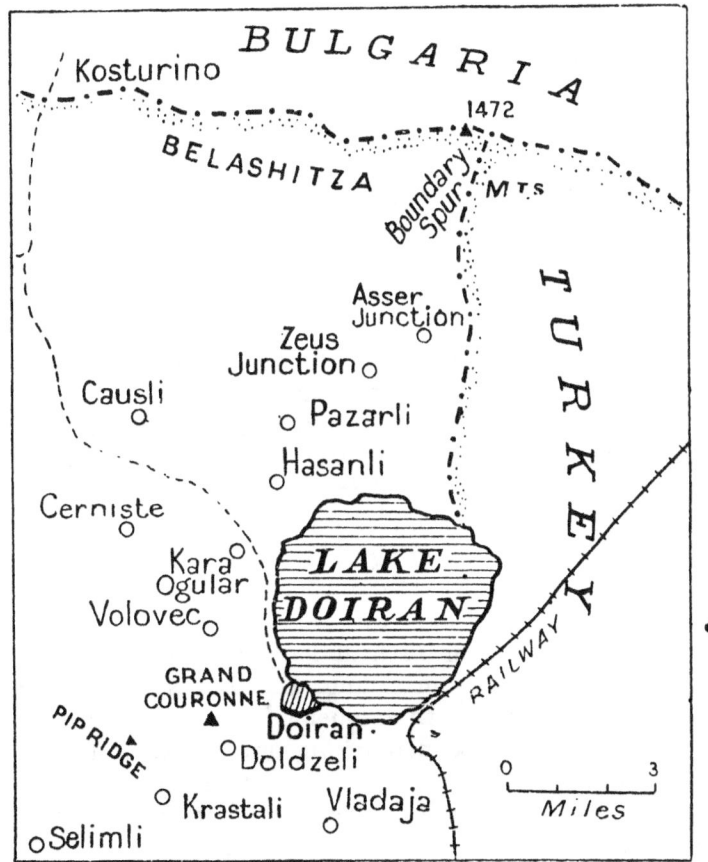

intended to postpone the attack till the 27th when the Twenty-Eighth Division and the Cretans would co-operate. Thus Colonel Dobbs' force, little over 300 all told, found itself completely isolated, but held its ground nevertheless throughout the 26th, though subjected to much sniping and artillery fire. After dark the Bulgarians attempted an attack but were easily beaten off, and next morning the battalion reaped the reward of its tenacity, when its patrols found Point 1472 unoccupied. The 8th thus had the satisfaction of anticipating the Zouaves who were to have attacked that point. During the day touch was established with the Cretans to the East and in the afternoon the Division received orders to withdraw to the Kara Ogular–Volovec area, leaving to others the continued pursuit of the Bulgarians whose retreat, harassed by Allied airmen, was fast degenerating into a rout. Already on September 25th troops of the Sixteenth Corps had entered Bulgarian territory by the Kosturino road, further West the French and Servians had severed the hostile line and rendered it unlikely that the Bulgarian right would regain their homeland. The Twenty-Second Division could therefore be allowed the rest it needed so urgently: its ten battalions, Pioneers included, only mustered 110 officers and 2950 other ranks, the 9th Border, the Pioneers, producing nearly a fifth of the total, while the 8th S.W.B., though down to 13 officers and 330 men,[1] were well above the average, the 7th, now 7 officers and 201 men, being nearly the weakest. That battalion, after advancing on the 25th to West of the Blaga Planina range, had remained in position there, being somewhat innocuously shelled by mountain guns, but now moved down to Hasanli to refit.

Actually neither 7th or 8th was to fire another shot. They were still enjoying their rest when on September 30th the surrender of Bulgaria was announced, and in the month which elapsed before the Turks followed this example the Twenty-Second Division never came into conflict with them. After spending a fortnight in the Hasanli area, a period devoted by the 7th and 8th partly to salvaging the P Ridge, partly to work on the Doiran–Dedeli road, the Division marched to Stavros, there to embark for the Thracian port of Dedeagatch. The move, which was started on October 12th and completed by the 18th, involved some strenuous marching, the longest stage being the 17 miles from Tomba to Gomenicil, but both 7th and 8th marched well, hardly a man falling out. A week was spent at Stavros, affording an opportunity for much enjoyed sea bathing, and then on October 25th the troops embarked for Dedeagatch, only to have to return to Stavros as the weather was too rough to let them land. A second effort was more successful, and the Division was taking up a position on the Maritza to cover the B.S.F.'s concentration to the Westward in readiness for an advance on Constantinople when, on October 31st, the Turks also capitulated.

The immediate effect of this on the 7th and 8th S.W.B. was that after a fortnight's stay at Dedeagatch they were transferred by rail and motor lorry first to Drama and then to Kavalla, whence a five days' march of 62 miles over bad roads

---

[1] Its casualties in the pursuit were under 20 all told.

and in worse weather brought them back to Stavros before the end of November. Both were stronger now, the 8th reaching 26 officers and 609 other ranks by October 31st, mainly owing to the discharge from hospital of recovered victims of the influenza epidemic. The 7th had also recovered many of their sick, over 160 returned in October and 50 more in November, while a draft of 146 men from the Base, some of them released prisoners of war, which arrived on November 28th raised the battalion over the 600 mark. Several officers had rejoined from leave or from hospital, some new subalterns arrived from home, but various officers departed on different errands, half a dozen from the 8th, including Major Caldwell and Captain Laurie, being detailed for attachment to the Indian Army units which were now arriving to reinforce the B.S.F.

The two battalions were still at Stavros when on December 6th orders were received for their amalgamation, prior to employment in the Army of Occupation now being formed out of the Allied "Army of the Orient" for the countries bordering on the Black Sea. The command of this combined battalion was given to Colonel Dobbs, in whose absence on leave Major Humphreys officiated as C.O., Major Caldwell becoming second in command, Captain F. T. Williams Adjutant, and Lieutenant Carter Quartermaster. Of the company commanders, Captains Harris[1] (A), Parry (B), and Cochrane[2] (C) came from the 7th, Captain Wood (D) from the 8th.[3] A dozen officers surplus after amalgamation were sent to the Base, while 130 men of the 8th not needed to complete the combined battalion up to establishment were transferred to the 2nd Gloucestershire in the Twenty-Seventh Division.

It was not the fortune of the two battalions who represented the TWENTY-FOURTH in Macedonia to go through anything like the hard fighting or to have the same chances of winning laurels for the Regiment that fell to the other Service battalions, but the 7th and 8th are entitled nevertheless to be remembered with no little pride. The Regiment's reputation never suffered at their hands, despite the depressing conditions under which they were called upon to serve. If battalions on the Salonica front escaped fairly lightly in casualties, of the discomforts of active service they had even more than their share; they had to face a climate that taken all round compared unfavourably

---

[1] Captain Harris was the only "original" officer of the 7th posted to the combined battalion, which also included four of the 8th's, Captains Wood and Dickie and Lieutenants W. W. Thomas and Cardwell.
[2] He had just arrived from home.
[3] Regimental Sergeant Major Andrews from the 7th became Regimental Sergeant Major of the amalgamated battalion.

with Gallipoli, Egypt and Palestine, to say nothing of France. Mesopotamia in its hot weather may perhaps have surpassed even Macedonia, but there were seasons when Mesopotamia was not too bad and even the Shamal must yield pride of place to the Vardar wind, too bleak and bitter for any words to express it adequately, that penetrated the thickest clothing. For dust, for dirt, for flies, for mosquitoes, Macedonia was hard to beat. Devotedly as the medical staff strove to reduce the sick-rate and despite all the efforts of regimental officers and men to keep trenches and bivouacs and camps sanitary, malaria and fevers of every kind slew many, sent ten times as many to hospital and sapped the strength of those nominally fit. Moreover, in the rare periods when troops were behind our own guns, and able to get anything recognizable as " rest," only the scantiest opportunities for recreation were available. Leave was practically non-existent, only in the last summer was it opened on a very limited scale, and quite apart from all these material disadvantages the situation had immaterial aspects which must not be overlooked in trying to appreciate all that was involved in keeping up a high level of efficiency in units serving at Salonica.

Hard work, discomforts, losses in action and by disease, would one and all have been less felt had there been any visible and appreciable return for all the troops had to endure. But this was lacking. Units might shift from one sector to another, they could not escape the " shut in feeling," as one officer has described it, that one had when one looked up at the enemy's positions, everywhere formidable, everywhere overlooking ours. It was difficult to avoid feeling that our line was far too long for our numbers, especially after the summer of 1917, that if the Germans really liked to make a big effort in Macedonia there was nothing behind the Allies, except the sea; there was the feeling also that nobody in England knew or cared much about the B.S.F., stranded as it was in a backwater of the war where it could not hope to achieve anything definite, still less decisive. The majority of the rank and file may not have bothered much about strategical possibilities, they could not fail to realize that their lot had fallen to them in a stony and far from salubrious place, for nearly three years their share in the war consisted merely of moving from one damp and smelly dug-out to another, with unending toil, malaria and constant shelling thrown in. That they should have risen as splendidly and devotedly as they did to their great ordeal on Grand Couronné is all the more to their credit and secures for them a place of honour in the Regiment's record.

CHAPTER XXXV

MESOPOTAMIA

The Final Stages

WITH the consolidation of the British position at Baghdad in the early summer of 1917 operations in Mesopotamia had reached a turning point; the British attained their main objects, they had recovered their ascendency, had effectively countered the first Turkish efforts to penetrate into Persia, and had freed India from serious anxiety on the score of the fomentation from that quarter of Frontier troubles. The now complete collapse of Russia made any further substantial extension of our holdings inadvisable: the urgent demands of other theatres of war both on our man-power and on our supplies of every kind flatly forbade any offensive which would require additional troops and transport facilities. From May, 1917, on, therefore, " Force D " had merely to maintain and consolidate its gains, only extending them so far as practicable without additional calls on the Empire's resources. For some time substantial Turkish operations for the recovery of Baghdad seemed likely: their German masters certainly favoured such an effort, hoping no doubt thereby to detain in Mesopotamia troops who might otherwise have been transferred elsewhere. This prospect prevented any substantial reduction of the British forces in Mesopotamia, and though in 1918 the project gave place to plans for extending Turkish power North-Eastward into the countries bordering on the Caspian, such as Russian Armenia and North-West Persia, the change necessitated the dispatch to those regions of " Dunsterforce " as a counterstroke. Subsequently nearly a whole Division followed " Dunsterforce," and as in the winter of 1917–1918 the Lahore and Meerut Divisions had been transferred to Palestine, and newly formed Indian Divisions substituted for them, the idea of withdrawing the Thirteenth Division from Mesopotamia was dropped and the 4th S.W.B. finished out the war in that country. They were kept busy enough and saw plenty of fighting, though none equal in intensity or importance to the operations round Kut and Baghdad.

Compared with the summer of 1916 the 4th found that of 1917 quite endurable. Conditions were in every way better: the country round Baghdad was pleasanter and more productive than Amara and Sheikh Saad, the transport services were working well, and therefore the supply of provisions and comforts was infinitely better, the reorganized medical arrangements were excellent, leave to India had been opened, and the experience of 1916 could guide them in such things as pitching the camp so as best to avoid the dust storms caused by the Shamal, the strong N.W. wind which usually sets in about June. The weather was certainly oppressively hot, the Baghdadis declared it was the hottest season ever known, the shade temperature for July averaged 117.5 degrees and reached 130.5 degrees, and the sick-rate was high enough, though nothing like that of 1916. Drafts appeared at intervals, largely recovered sick and wounded, though in May 150 men arrived, mainly, however, coming from North Country units. Various changes occurred among the officers: Major Crake was transferred to the 8th Cheshire in June, Captain Bloxham, who had succeeded Captain Bickford-Smith as Adjutant, received a Staff appointment in July, on which Lieutenant Usher took over the Adjutancy. Captain Hooper rejoined in June; Captain Crewe-Reed, who had served with the 1st Battalion at Ypres in 1914, had arrived on May 18th, and Lieutenant Colonel Whitmore-Jones joined in August as second in command. By the end of July the battalion's attenuated ranks had been partly filled up, 16 officers and 466 men being present.

In August the 40th Brigade relieved the 35th (Indian) at Baquba, thereby enabling the Fourteenth Division to occupy Shahraban. The move was completed on August 17th, but no sooner had the 4th reached Baquba than they were sent forward to hold Qalat al Mufti on the Diala as an advanced post, half a squadron of cavalry, a section of field guns and some R.E. being also placed under Colonel Kitchin's command. Starting at 9.30 p.m. the column encountered serious difficulties in the numerous irrigation ditches and canals to be crossed, the majority of them unbridged. Delays were frequent, the transport carts were constantly upsetting; finally they had to be left behind under an escort, while the rest of the column, pushing on, reached Qalat al Mufti before it became unbearably hot. The camp here was situated on a peninsula formed by a bend in the river, the bed of which was some 1500 yards wide and covered with tamarisk scrub, the actual stream being only 100 yards across. For its protection a line of picquet-posts had to be constructed and a large mound 1600 yards N.W. of the camp, known as the "Beacon," to be occupied. The troops found ample occupation in constructing defences and road-making, but except that on one occasion A Company went out as escort to some guns which shelled a village from which our cavalry patrols had been sniped, August and September passed away quite peaceably. Sandfly fever was prevalent at first; but the most memorable incident was the capture of nearly half a ton of fish by the unorthodox method of exploding gun-cotton in the river. The current being very rapid, swimmers had to jump in and bring the fish to shore, and as some of them were very much alive and ran to 110 lbs. the swimmers' struggles with the larger and livelier of the prizes greatly amused the spectators, while the fish gave a welcome variety to the menu.

October brought cooler weather and greater activity. The anticipated Turkish offensive had not developed, but General Maude intended to forestall it. Already General Brooking's Fifteenth Indian Division had smashed up the Turkish force on the Euphrates at Ramadi (September 27th–29th), and operations were now to be undertaken in the Jebel Hamrin range, mainly to drive the Turks away from a line of advance into Persia, but also to prevent them interfering with the supply of water from the Diala for irrigation purposes. The plan involved an advance by the Fourteenth Division East of the Diala and by the greater part of the Thirteenth, including the 40th Brigade, past Deli Abbas against the hills just N.W. of the river.

Operations really started with the move on October 17th of Colonel Kitchin's detachment, acting as advanced-guard to the Division, from Qalat al Mufti to Sulaimaniyeh, five miles nearer Deli Abbas, and next day the battalion[1] pushed forward against Deli Abbas, making a holding attack while the rest of its brigade tried to turn the Turkish right. As the attack developed it came under considerable shell fire, but good use of ground avoided casualties; before long opposition ceased and the 4th, crossing the canal by a partially destroyed native bridge, occupied Deli Abbas. The Turks had gone right back, evacuating also a well entrenched line between two high mounds North of the village. The 40th Brigade now took up a position to cover the left of the 38th, which pushed on next day to Mansuriyeh, a large village on the river bank where the canals take off from the Diala. This was followed by the Turks retreating Northward; and as the Fourteenth Division had also achieved its purpose operations were suspended, the 4th S.W.B. being withdrawn to the line Qalat al Mufti–Saraijik, which was now entrenched. Here a programme of training was started, while those who were lucky enough to possess shot guns had some quite good shooting, black partridges and Blue Rock pigeons being the most abundant game. A pause of some weeks followed on the Diala front, though on the Tigris an advance was made in which the First Corps had sharp fighting at Daur and Tikrit, resulting in a fresh Turkish retreat upstream. Then on November 18th came the tragic news of General Maude's sudden death from cholera. His loss was naturally keenly regretted by the 4th S.W.B.; as

[1] Three drafts had joined since the battalion's arrival at Qalat al Mufti, amounting to 5 officers and 302 men.

Divisional Commander he had won their confidence at a discouraging time when great hardships and exertions had to be faced, under his guidance and inspiration the Thirteenth Division had weathered some bad times both in Gallipoli and on the Tigris, and to his patience, skill and leadership officers and men mainly ascribed the great successes of 1917.

General Marshall, who succeeded to the command, had no intention of letting the Turks alone, and December found the 4th on the move again. The battalion was actually up to establishment for the first time since leaving England and was in good fighting trim. It left camp after dark on December 1st for the brigade rendezvous in a deep nullah 5 miles N.E. of Saraijik, remained concealed there next day and started off at 10 p.m. towards the foothills through which the Qara Tepe road begins to ascend the Sakaltutan Pass. The Turkish forces West of the Diala were simultaneously to be attacked by the Fourteenth Division, advancing across the Diala from the S.E., and by the 38th and 40th Brigades attacking the Jebel Hamrin. The 38th was advancing from the South towards Suhaniyeh, and the 40th hoped to cut off its opponents by anticipating them at the Sakaltutan Pass, while the Cavalry Division was crossing the range further N.W. on a similar errand.

About 2.30 a.m. on December 3rd the 40th Brigade reached an Arab village, 3½ miles from the foothills. Here it changed direction from North to East and advanced towards the hills, with the 4th and the Cheshire leading. Just before dawn some trenches were reached and found empty, whereupon strong patrols were thrust out to investigate. One under Captain Fountaine made its way undiscovered to within 400 yards of Suhaniyeh and located the enemy in force. Thereupon A and C Companies, profiting by the patrol's information, succeeded in surprising the Turks, capturing two guns and over 50 prisoners, while the remainder fled in disorder. This enabled the brigade to make considerable progress, but the road was difficult and the foot of the pass was not reached till too late in the day to attack, especially as only two mountain guns were up at the front. The 4th had to bivouac therefore high up on the range without food or blankets, very cold and with little water. The transport was held up back in the plains; and though Colonel Whitmore-Jones, who was in charge of it, by great exertions pushed some water mules up, the 80 gallons they brought did not go far among 800 men. Directly it was light (December 4th) the 40th Brigade prepared to assault; but the Turks had gone, the pass was clear and the brigade could push on down its further slope, making for the bridge over the Nahrin river at Nahrin Kopri, 10 miles along the Qara Tepe road. The

35th Indian Brigade was also advancing on Qara Tepe from the S.E., moving East of the Nahrin, but was still some way off when the 40th reached the bridge, to find it destroyed. The bad road surface and the steep gradient had left ration carts far behind, so that the troops passed another comfortless and hungry night. However, they moved forward briskly enough at 5 a.m. next day (December 5th), and after about 6 miles deployed to assault the hills covering Qara Tepe from the West. The Wiltshires formed the left of the front line with the 4th on their right, both in lines of platoons on a 600-yards front with one platoon with two Lewis guns well ahead. The advance was admirably carried out, despite heavy Turkish shelling and long range rifle fire. Some 800 yards from their line a deep water-cut with steep banks and a strong stream presented an awkward obstacle, the Turks had clearly ranged on it and their fire was heavy. Nothing daunted, A and D dashed forward, plunged down into it, climbed out and began scrambling up the slope beyond. The Lewis guns covered the advance splendidly, and with hardly any casualties the position was rushed, over 20 prisoners, including a battalion commander, being taken. The 40th Brigade's success was decisive, the opposition to the 35th, till then quite determined, crumpled away and the Turks were soon in full retreat on Kifri. Luckily for them the cavalry had been held up and did not succeed in intercepting their retreat, but heavy casualties had been inflicted, and the chances of their pushing parties into Persia by the Kermanshah–Hamadan roure much reduced.

Thanks to Colonel Whitmore-Jones's energy in urging forward his transport carts and mules, the 4th got both blankets and rations that night; but the problem which was now arising was that of boots. " Up to the time when we set foot on the Jebel Hamrin," writes one account, " the battalion had not seen a stone in Mesopotamia "; but its " roads " were covered with small pebbles which produced a crop of sore feet and tested boot-leather severely. However, there was no intention of occupying permanently the country beyond the Jebel Hamrin. On December 6th the 4th started their return journey, re-crossed the Sakaltutan next day, and reached Qalat al Mufti by midday on the 8th, having covered 90 miles and fought two actions since December 1st. They had had a strenuous time, though casualties had fortunately been low, only a dozen, including Lieutenant Light, wounded.

Two days later the brigade received orders to return to Saraijik, where it was to be encamped beside the Khalis Canal for over four months, a period mainly devoted to training; though heavy rains early in January did great damage to roads and defences, sweeping away a bridge and giving the battalion a fortnight's hard work to get things straight. Most of the time the climate was quite pleasant: warm days but cold nights, and recreation was not neglected. At the invitation of the local Sheikh the officers joined in a jackal hunt, for which 50 of the queerest dogs had been collected, most of whom preferred fighting each other to pursuing their proper quarry. A little later the 4th swept the board at a brigade boxing tournament and also became brigade champions in Association football. Another notable incident was the starting of a brigade canteen, when after many months beer was again obtainable. The arrival of 102 men under Captain Barraclough and Regimental Sergeant Major Murray (March 8th) kept the battalion well up to strength, while in January Lieutenant Usher relinquished the Adjutancy to Captain Purves.

All through April rumours of another move became persistent. "Dunsterforce" was already in Persia, General Brooking had achieved another striking success on the Euphrates at Khan Baghdadi (March 26th); and although the Lahore and Meerut Divisions had been transferred to Palestine the situation fully justified General Marshall in taking the offensive in Southern Kurdistan. To clear the Turks from the Tuz Khurmatli–Kifri–Qara Tepe area, thereby securing communications with "Dunsterforce" by the Hamadan road, would be the most effective parry to Turkish designs on Persia. Four columns were accordingly organized for this purpose from the Third Corps, now under General Egerton, that in which the S.W.B. were included being directed on Umr Maidan, N.W. of Qara Tepe, to block that line of retreat to the Turkish forces S.E. of Tuz Khurmatli.

Operations began for the 4th at 7 a.m. on April 24th, when they started Northward in heavy rain and, passing East of Deli Abbas, crossed the Jebel Hamrin next day (25th) by the Abu Hajar Pass and reached the Nahrin river by 10 a.m. On the 26th the column moved up the Nahrin to Nahrin Kopri, whence it set out again the same evening for the Lesser Naft, 18 miles away. The night march was not made easier by a thunderstorm, but bad as the going was not a man in the brigade fell out. As yet no enemy had been encountered: the Turks, alarmed by the converging movement of three British infantry columns, the 38th Brigade being N.W. and the 37th (Indian) S.E. of the 40th, had mostly quitted Kifri and were making for Tuz Khurmatli with all possible haste. On the 27th the 6th Cavalry Brigade defeated their rear-guard at Kulawand, and to clinch that success the 40th Brigade was put in motion for Tuz. A fourteen-mile night march over ground intersected by nullahs, followed by another five-hour advance on the following afternoon, brought it to Kulawand in readiness to attack Tuz early on April 29th.

Tuz lies on the right of the Aq Su river, which here debouches from the Naft Dagh hills. The cavalry and the 38th Brigade were to ford it four miles West of Tuz and work round to the North while the 40th attacked Northward from Kulawand. The 40th started its move about 1.30 a.m., the R.W.F. leading. They were held up South of the river, and though the Wiltshire were put in to climb the ridge of the Naft Dagh on their right and outflank their opponents, they too were checked. It was now getting light, the Turkish guns had come into action, and before long the battalion also had to be thrown in, No. 1 Platoon under Lieutenant Jamieson being sent up the ridge to tackle a strong point which was the main obstacle to progress. Covered by Lewis guns No. 1 worked steadily forward till close to the strong point, and then springing up rushed it, taking an officer and 14 men. This was the decisive incident on this flank, and with the S.W.B. pushing forward along the foot of the hills on the Wiltshire's left, the 40th Brigade had soon cleared the left bank of the Aq Su. The 38th were now across, and the Turks were in full retreat, giving the cavalry fine opportunities for effective action. Hundreds of prisoners were taken, with several guns; and General Marshall decided to follow up this success by continuing the move to Kirkuk, 40 miles further North.

The next move was to secure the bridge at Tauq, 21 miles away, and early on May 2nd B Company under Lieutenant Everett was sent on ahead in Ford cars and reached the bridge, a massive brick and stone structure of thirteen arches, before the Turks could demolish it. The other companies, starting the same day, did the distance in two marches, although much delayed by having to make the road fit for transport. The country here was hilly and rugged, and the difficulties of keeping the troops supplied so far from rail-head were enormous; and for the 40th Brigade the operations degenerated into mere road-making. The battalion had a trying night march in abominable weather to Taza Khurmatli, 20 miles from Tauq Bridge. It poured with rain, the road became a river of mud, through which carts and guns could not move; and the column had to remain halted till dawn, soaked to the skin and with only their thin khaki drill clothing. Luckily a ration of rum was available and was issued, along with some hot tea from the ever-invaluable cookers, with excellent effect, though, even so, several men collapsed from exhaustion and cold. Ultimately the column had to bivouac and remained there till May 10th, improving the road on very short rations, though the scanty supplies were augmented by procuring a few sheep locally. Meanwhile the 38th

Brigade had reached Kirkuk, capturing many prisoners, while the Turks had hastened to retire behind the Little Zab. Further pursuit was impossible; indeed Kirkuk proved too advanced a position to maintain, so the troops were drawn back, Tuz Khurmatli and Kifri being the most forward positions retained.

The 4th were allotted Kifri as summer quarters. They were

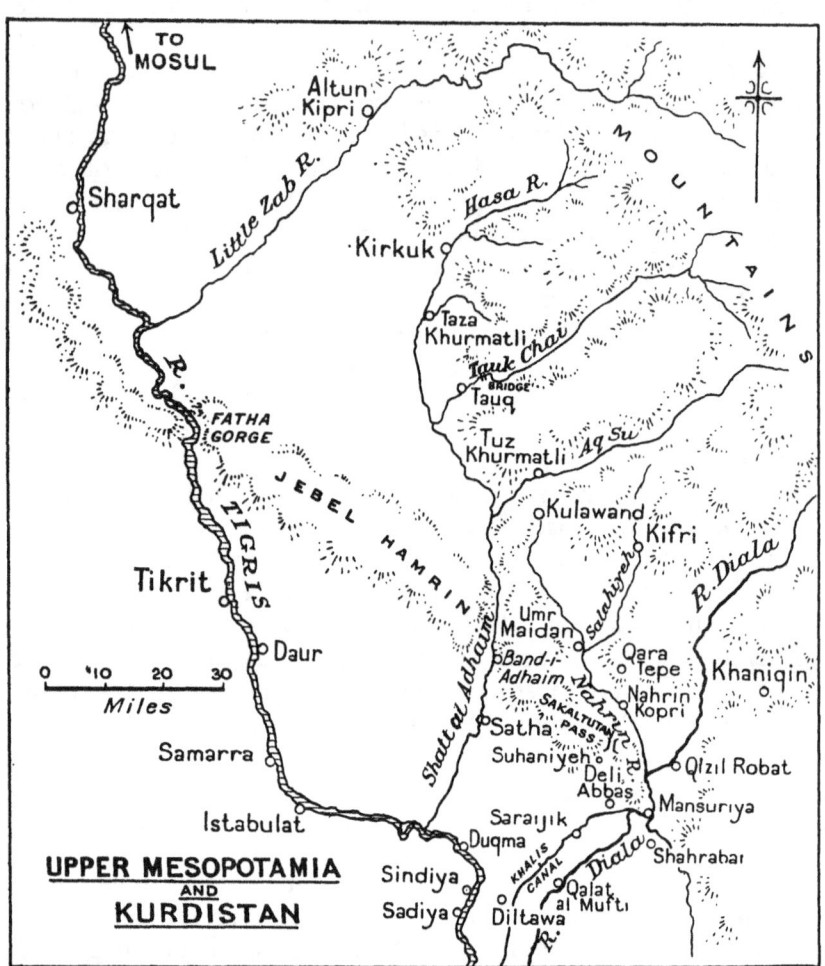

accommodated in the serai, a large walled-in enclosure with buildings round the sides. Though well built this building was indescribably filthy and verminous and required unlimited libations of disinfectant and whitewash, while the sanitary condition of the town was scarcely improved by a great influx of starving Armenian refugees. Lieutenant Everett, who was appointed Town Major and given a special staff of Military Police, rose to the occasion splendidly; and, thanks largely to his work and to the weather being less hot than in 1917, the battalion passed through the summer months with a satisfactory bill of health, though in September an influenza epidemic prostrated one man in four. The authorities spared no effort to make the troops comfortable, a canteen and an ice-factory being established, while local supplies were fairly abundant—there are worse and less fertile countries than Southern Kurdistan. In September leave to England was for the first time opened, and the C.O. and the Quartermaster accordingly left for Basra on the 27th. Except for about three months in hospital in 1917 Colonel Kitchin had served uninterruptedly with the 4th since September 1914, while Captain Mellsopp had discharged his duties without any break since the battalion's formation. Colonel Whitmore-Jones now assumed command, Lieutenant Miller officiating as Quartermaster.

The summer months, though full of incident and importance in other theatres of war, had been very uneventful in Mesopotamia. A dozen Indian battalions had been withdrawn for service at Salonica, trained officers and men had been drafted to Egypt to assist in forming the new battalions needed for the "Indianization" of General Allenby's army,[1] the increased force in Persia was absorbing so much transport that any other offensive in the country seemed most unlikely. Early in October, however, General Marshall received instructions from Home to resume the offensive.[2] With this object he decided upon an advance by General Cobbe's First Corps up the Tigris from Tikrit, now "rail-head," on Mosul, and to cover its right flank a column under General Lewin was to advance by Tauq, Kirkuk and Altun Kopri and prevent the Turks on the Lesser Zab reinforcing those holding the Fatha Gorge on the Tigris. This column was to include the 4th S.W.B., their old friends the Wiltshire, a cavalry regiment, a battery and details. October 18th, therefore, saw the 4th moving out for their last round in the great struggle. The battalion had been much reduced by the influenza epidemic, many men were still sick, others, though nominally recovered, were hardly fit for severe exertions; but everyone wanted to be "in at the death" and they faced the task before them gamely. A night march from Tuz Khurmatli to Tauq enabled the column to surprise the Turkish garrison, who retired in haste, leaving 30 prisoners behind. Pushing on, General Lewin occupied Taza Khurmatli also (October 23rd),

---

[1] It was actually intended to convert the Thirteenth Division into three new mixed Divisions, utilizing the battalions remaining in Mesopotamia after the 39th Brigade's departure to the Caspian as the British battalions of the infantry brigades, but the rapid change in the situation caused the plan to be dropped.

[2] The object was to wrest as much territory as possible from the Turks before negotiations should be begun.

and then next day advanced to Kirkuk. Here the enemy showed themselves in strength, and as General Lewin's orders were merely to keep the Turks employed he contented himself with demonstrations and reconnaissances. In one of these the 4th fired their last shots in action and suffered their last casualties; D Company, who were carrying it out, drew heavy shell fire, but the leading platoons under Lieutenants Paterson and Picton pressed on nevertheless till within 1200 yards of the town, which forced the Turks to unmask a battery of machine guns. Captain Hooper thereupon stopped any further advance and withdrew his company under cover of darkness, having had three men killed and as many wounded.

Next evening, however (October 25th), the Turks evacuated Kirkuk. Things were going badly with them on the Tigris and they were afraid of being cut off. General Lewin's advance was accordingly continued[1] and on October 31st he entered Altun Kopri without further opposition, to receive the news next day (November 1st) of the conclusion of the armistice with Turkey.

Thus the 4th's active career ended over 500 miles up the Tigris valley, in a remote country to which no British troops had ever before penetrated. Its few remaining " originals "—few indeed after Gallipoli and the Kut relief operations—had been through wanderings and adventures they had hardly contemplated when they had responded to the call to enlist " for three years or the duration of the war." " Duration " had certainly exceeded everybody's expectations, but the 4th were not to have their service prolonged by being detailed for the Army of Occupation. By November 24th the battalion was back on the Diala and demobilization soon began, Captain Hooper and Lieutenants Picton and D. T. Jones being dispatched to Salonica with 250 men not entitled to discharge.

[1] Colonel Whitmore-Jones having gone down with heat-stroke, Major Crewe-Read was now in command.

CHAPTER XXXVI

AFTER THE ARMISTICE

THE terms of the Armistice had included the occupation by the Allied Armies of the left bank of the Rhine, and as soon as the necessary administrative arrangements could be completed the Second Army, which had been detailed to occupy the zone assigned to the British, started on its march. As it happened both the First and Twenty-Ninth Divisions were now included in that Army, so that it fell to both the Regular battalions of the TWENTY-FOURTH to take part in the historic march to the Rhine. It was an interesting and impressive conclusion to all they had gone through.

The actual march did not begin till December 1st, though before that the troops of the Army of Occupation had moved up to the German frontier in readiness. The 1st S.W.B., whom the Armistice had found at Fresnoy-le-Grand, started Eastward on November 13th, moving by Bazuel, Marbaix (November 15th), Beugnies (16th) and Beaumont (18th) to Walcourt (19th). After four days there it advanced to Florennes, where it remained another week, moving on December 1st to Corennes, thence to Oulaye (2nd) and through Dinant to a château near Celles (3rd). It was here nearly a week and eventually started the final march to the Rhine on December 9th, crossing the German frontier S.E. of Malmedy on the 18th, and having its first quarters on German soil at Breitfeld. Six days later it reached its destination at Kircheim, some way above Cologne. Snow fell freely during the later stages of the march, and the weather was on the whole stormy with frequent rain, but the men marched well and every effort was made to reach a high standard of appearance as well as of march discipline in order to make as much impression as possible on the inhabitants of Germany. The Germans, who seem to have expected the worst from the Allies, were agreeably surprised by the good discipline and order maintained, and their demeanour, if sullen and gloomy, indicated no little relief that the war was over and that they had escaped experiencing invasion. The troops had been enthusiastically welcomed in the liberated districts West of the frontier, and in Germany they found good quarters and very efficient local administration; while, if in the uplands of the Ardennes there was no superabundance of supplies, in the actual Rhine valley there was plenty of everything to be had at reasonable rates.

Thus the end of 1918 found the 1st S.W.B. comfortably settled in on German soil for its six months' stay in the Rhineland. It was on the whole an uneventful time, though in one way and another the men were kept well occupied. Athletics played no small part in this period, a notable feature being an exchange of visits with the 2nd Battalion, which was no great distance away, Rugby football matches being played, of which each battalion won one, followed by smoking concerts, while in the various brigade and Divisional contests the 1st Battalion did very well and Captain Baker was picked to represent the British Army at Rugby football. Only very few of the 1st S.W.B. by this time were serving soldiers; the great majority both of officers and men were looking forward to demobilization and their return to civil life. Some had jobs awaiting them and were urgently wanted back, others were as anxious to get back lest the available jobs should all be snapped up before they could return. But the Army of Occupation had to be kept up and the British Army as a whole to be got ready for the resumption of its normal activities. India, Egypt, the Mediterranean and Far Eastern stations needed their normal Regular garrisons, to say nothing of all the new calls on the Army created in Palestine, Mesopotamia and other quarters. As soon as possible therefore the Regular units had to be reconstituted on a peace basis with serving soldiers. To this demobilization and the discharge of all those entitled to return to civil life was an essential preliminary.

The 1st S.W.B. were not among the earliest Regular units to be reduced to cadre on relief by Young Soldier battalions or other units available for duty with the Armies of Occupation. June came before its cadre found itself on the homeward road. It had transferred all men liable for retention in the service to Young Soldier units, mainly to the 51st, 52nd and 53rd Battalions of the Regiment which now formed part of the Army of the Rhine,[1] and the cadre consisted of five officers, Colonel Taylor, Captains Baker, Shipley and Ainsworth, and Lieutenant Cobb, with Regimental Sergeant Major Shirley and 39 N.C.O.'s and men. Of these Captain Baker, Regimental Sergeant Major Shirley, Company Sergeant Major Saunders and Sergeants Gibb and Ravenhill were the only representatives of the original 1st Battalion that had landed in France in August, 1914.[2]

Landing at Tilbury Docks on June 12th the cadre first proceeded to Thannington near Canterbury, whence a week later it went on to Brecon, where it was most enthusiastically received. Its arrival at its permanent headquarters may be taken as a fitting end to the story of its experiences in the war of 1914–1919. Its reconstitution under the command of Colonel Reddie by the

---

[1] These were battalions formerly known as "Graduated Battalions," and the 52nd was the unit which had started life as the 9th S.W.B., which thus eventually found its way overseas.

[2] Of the 25 officers who had gone overseas with the 1st Batalion in 1914 11 had been killed.

THE 1st RETURNS HOME

incorporation of the bulk of those officers and men serving with the 3rd Battalion is rather to be regarded as the opening of the "post-war chapter" in its history. Since going overseas in August, 1914, the battalion had had no less than 50 officers and 1174 men killed and 70 officers and 2400 men wounded. In all 258 officers and 6201 other ranks had served in the 1st Battalion during the war, and in addition to many foreign orders and decorations it had won 1 V.C., 2 C.M.G.'s, 10 D.S.O.'s, 32 M.C.'s, 44 D.C.M.'s, 2 M.S.M.'s and 136 M.M.'s. Of its performances and experiences, as of those of the other battalions of the Regiment, these pages have been able to give little more than some bare record of the main features, but the 1st Battalion had added some notable names to the Regimental record. If any one of its battles is to be picked out for special mention its stand at Gheluvelt on October 31st, 1914, has perhaps the strongest claims to that distinction, but there are others that run it close; September 26th, 1914, on the Aisne, the defence of Givenchy in January, 1915, its stand at Festubert in April, 1918, are all outstanding episodes; but it was not only on the great occasions to which it never failed to rise that the battalion had done well. It was often as hardly tried on more ordinary occasions, in the strain of "normal trench warfare," and there too it had shown itself steady, tenacious, resourceful and enduring. When it had had its chance in attack also it had done well. It had not always been successful. May 9th, 1915, is an outstanding example of the inability even of great devotion and determination to ensure success in the conditions of modern war, but in the "Advance to Victory" of the autumn of 1918 the 1st's chance had come and it had shown itself dashing, skilful and enterprising.

The 2nd S.W.B. had preceded the 1st both in entering Germany and in leaving that country. Immediately after the Armistice it had moved forward to the neighbourhood of Steenkirk, remained there long enough to send a detachment to share in the formal state entry of the King of the Belgians into his capital on November 22nd, and next day started its Eastward move across Belgium. Its march took it past two famous battlefields of the past, Waterloo and Ramillies, over the Meuse at Huy and through the almost mountainous country of the Ardennes to Stavelot on the frontier. It was a hard march; the roads were pavé and in bad condition, the country was hilly, the marches were long, the men were carrying full packs and equipment, and there had been no time to issue fresh boots before the march started. But the men marched splendidly, and despite hardships and occasional lack of rations were wonderfully cheerful. March discipline was excellent and there was hardly any falling out.

The German frontier was crossed by the Twenty-Ninth Division near Malmedy on December 4th, and nine days later the 2nd S.W.B. had the privilege of sharing in the formal entry of the British into Cologne,[1] and of crossing the Rhine by the famous Hohenzollern Bridge. As they crossed the bridge General Plumer, G.O.C. Army of Occupation, was standing by the Kaiser's statue to take the salute, and though the rain was doing its best to spoil the occasion the spectacle was one to be remembered, and the 2nd S.W.B. might well be pleased to have a share in so remarkable an incident. After all the Regiment had been through in the war, it had well earned the right to be represented in what may fairly be regarded as its closing incident.

The quarters assigned to the Twenty-Ninth Division were not in Cologne itself, but on the perimeter of the bridge-head, 20 miles N.E., the 2nd S.W.B. being assigned quarters at Burchied. The battalion was not, however, destined to make a very long stay in the Rhineland. It was due for foreign service as soon as it could be reconstructed with serving soldiers, as its normal tour had still several years to run, and before the end of December demobilization had been begun by the dispatch home of nearly all the miners in the battalion's ranks. Students, " pivotal men," and others quickly followed, and those who re-enlisted for service in the Regular Army were for the most part sent home on leave. Up to the end of February a substantial number of officers and men remained with the colours, enough to make a fine show on parade on January 8th when, after the Colour party had rejoined from the Depot, a great ceremonial parade was held and about 20 officers and men were presented with the various decorations won in the last engagements. The visits exchanged with the 1st Battalion were much enjoyed, and though the attitude of the inhabitants was naturally hardly cordial and conditions were none too easy as regards food, fuel and other necessaries, the troops were fairly comfortable. A substantial detachment from the 10th Battalion joined on March 8th and swelled the battalion's ranks for the moment, but shortly afterwards all " retainable " officers and men, mainly those most recently called up for service who were not yet entitled to their discharge, were sent off to the three Young Soldier battalions, 6 officers and 60 men joining the 51st, 7 officers and 120 men the 52nd and the same number the 53rd. This brought the battalion down to little over 200 of all ranks, a number still further reduced by the departure for home on March 14th of 120 men due for

---

[1] The TWENTY-FOURTH had been at Cologne once before, on their way down the Rhine in 1704, after Blenheim.

demobilization. A few days later the relieving battalion, the 51st Devons, arrived, whereupon what was left of the battalion, 7 officers and 80 men, moved to Mulheim. Here it was finally reduced to a cadre, which eventually embarked at Dunkirk on April 4th, 1919, arriving at Brecon on the following evening, to be enthusiastically received. Colonel Raikes, who brought the cadre home in person, had with him Lieutenant Green and Second Lieutenants Hardwick and McPherson, with Regimental Sergeant Major Tring, Regimental Quartermaster Sergeant Russell, Company Sergeant Majors Barker and Hipkiss, Company Quartermaster Sergeant Theobald and 42 others.

The 2nd Battalion's record in the war is in certain respects more varied than that of the 1st. It has the distinction of having served in four theatres of war, though in one, Egypt, it was never in action. What is the peculiar and distinguishing feature in its record is its share in the reduction of Tsingtao, though what it went through there cannot compare with what it endured in the long strain of the Gallipoli campaign and with its experiences in France. Its record in both those countries is a proud one, its losses in both were heavy indeed: actually the 2nd with 1400 names in the Roll of Honour lost more killed than any other battalion of the Regiment. Cambrai stands out in its story somewhat in the same way that Gheluvelt does in the 1st Battalion's, but its great fight on the Lys in April, 1918, its gallant attempt to achieve the impossible at Beaumont Hamel on the opening day of the Somme, its dash and enterprise in attack at Ypres in August, 1917, are all worthy of being remembered with pride. It was in a Division which had a great record and acquired an abiding reputation, and in that Division it ranked as high as any battalion.

Of the three Service battalions still in France at the time of the Armistice none was selected for the Army of Occupation, but, as Pioneers, both 5th and 6th found themselves in considerable demand during the early months of 1919. Roads and railways were in urgent need of them, a start had to be made, albeit on a very limited scale, to repair the ravages of war and to clear things up, and there was plenty for skilled workmen to occupy themselves with. The 5th were at Valheureux during January and February, during which time the battalion's strength sank from over 800 on January 1st to less than 200 on February 28th. This was largely because of the large proportion of coal-miners in its ranks, one of the occupations given precedence in demobilization. Over 50 of these men were demobilized in December and another 150 early in January. A holiday to celebrate the 40th anniversary of the defence of Rorke's Drift and the presentation of the King's Colour to the battalion on January 29th were the chief incidents of the time. Major General Jeffreys in inspecting the battalion when he presented the Colour was most complimentary both in his appreciation of the good services it had rendered in the past and of its turn-out and bearing, but the beginning of the end came early in February when Major I. T. Evans and 7 other officers were transferred to the 6th Battalion along with 200 men. This with the demobilization of another hundred left the 5th a mere skeleton, but the final disbandment of the battalion did not take place till June. By this time the 5th had moved to the Amiens neighbourhood and was at Glisy when its final reduction to a cadre took place on June 7th. Next day Captains Morris, now Adjutant, and Bryant with the remaining men entrained at Longeau for Havre, crossed thence to Southampton six days later and there dispersed to their homes. The 5th left a fine record behind them of devotion to duty, hard work, constant helpfulness and self-sacrifice. They had shown themselves sturdy and successful fighters when they had had to exchange their Pioneering work for active conflict with the enemy, and their share in resisting three successive German "pushes" in 1918 did them great honour. All those who had served with the 5th will think of it in connection with the fine old veteran who raised and trained it, impressed upon it the stamp of his own high standards, commanded it so long with such distinction and success and was largely responsible for the splendid spirit by which the battalion was always imbued. "The 5th was always a happy family," one of its members has said; those who had served with it always wanted to get back again.

The 6th outlasted the 5th some months. From the beginning of January till nearly the end of March the battalion was at Dunkirk, mainly occupied in preparing and improving camps. It then shifted to Ecault and was there till early in June when it moved to Henriville Camp near Boulogne. By this time it had ceased to bear any real relation to the 6th of war-time. Most of its own officers and men had been demobilized and in their places there had been posted to the battalion drafts from the 9th Welch, from the Welsh Yeomanry battalions in the Seventy-Fourth Division and from other units: the big draft from the 5th S.W.B. being the only one from another battalion of the TWENTY-FOURTH. Colonel Crawford had been demobilized at the end of February; Major Ellis then commanded for a time, but in April Colonel H. W. Dakeyne of the Royal Warwickshire was posted to the 6th and commanded it during the closing stages of its career. It was not till the autumn that the final dissolution of the 6th took place, about 200 men being posted on October 4th to the "Details, S.W.B.," on the disbanding of the 6th. Like the other Pioneer Battalion the 6th had had a mixed experience of working and fighting; with 380 names on the Roll of Honour against the 5th's 470, the 6th had perhaps had a little less fighting or been more fortunate in the day-to-day losses of "trench warfare." Like the 5th it had had a great reputation for hard work, for being able to get through an enormous amount and being unwearying, resourceful and skilful. If Pioneer battalions were not often "in the limelight" they proved their usefulness over and over again, and among Pioneer battalions those of the TWENTY-FOURTH were certainly not lacking. Many of those who joined them brought to their work in the war no little skill and experience acquired in their civil occupations, and both the Nineteenth and the Twenty-Fifth Divisions had good reason to congratulate themselves that their Pioneers came from the TWENTY-FOURTH.

The 10th Battalion had ceased to exist some time before the 5th was disbanded. The Thirty-Eighth Division had not been included in the Army of Occupation, and after remaining round Aulnoye till the end of Deceember moved to quarters round Amiens, prior to disbandment. With so many miners in the Division the strength of its units diminished rapidly and by the end of February most of its battalions were reduced to little more than cadres. The 10th S.W.B., for example, sent off about 125 officers and men to the 1st and 2nd Battalions during February and was down below 100 of all ranks by the end of the month, many men having re-enlisted for Regular service. Prior to that two events of importance had taken place: the presentation of a King's Colour, received on January 16th, and a visit from the Prince of Wales on February 7th. The Prince stayed at Divisional Headquarters for several days and in turn visited every unit in the Division. His visit was virtually the last event in the Division's career, after that nearly all units were down virtually to cadre strength, though with so much administrative work needing to be accomplished before disbandment could take place a couple of months elapsed before the final reduction to cadres and their departure for Home. May saw the remnant of the 10th, still under Colonel Harvey, embarking at Havre for Southampton, from which place its members dispersed.

Considering the amount of fighting the 10th had seen, especially in the final advance of 1918, it is rather astonishing that its killed, 455 in all, were almost identical in numbers with those of the 5th Battalion. The 10th, however, had missed the German offensives of 1918 and its battles had nearly all been offensive battles with a considerable weight of artillery to support them. Success had been less costly than checks and failures, the 10th had not had large parties cut off and wiped out in trying to hold up hostile advances. Something, however, must be allowed for the skilful leadership, good use of ground and vigorous handling of situations which had characterized its fighting during the great advance and had contributed materially to keep down casualties. But the 1918 advance is not the only fine contribution of the 10th to the Regimental record: it had won its spurs at Mametz Wood and had proved itself notably at Pilckem, and it has to its credit much good work in " trench warfare." It had notably upheld the reputation of that Gwent from which it took its name as the home of a fighting race.

Of the four battalions serving in the other theatres of war the 8th, as already explained had been absorbed into the 7th before the end of 1918. The fortunes of the 7th S.W.B. after the Armistice were varied but not particularly exciting. The battalion remained at Stavros till the middle of December, moved then to Gugunci and was there nearly two months, during which period 15 officers, mostly " students," were demobilized and over 450 men, including 250 miners. A draft from the 4th Battalion joined, but by the end of February the battalion was cut down to two companies, as its total strength was under 400. Just before leaving Gugunci, the C. in C. of the Army of the Black Sea, General Milne, presented the battalion with the Croix de Guerre, so well won at Grand Couronné, and on March 9th it left for Salonica, where it embarked on March 16th for the Dardanelles, landing at Chanak, but shortly afterwards transferring to the Gallipoli Peninsula. Here it took over from the 1st Suffolk, four officers and 150 men of that battalion being attached to it. On March 27th it re-embarked for Constantinople, and went into camp at Feneraki, near Haidar Pasha, shifting to Chanak in June. From time to time its ranks were replenished by drafting in officers and men from other units, notably the Norfolk, the Wiltshire and the Welch, while gradually more and more of the S.W.B. element departed to be demobilized. Colonel Dobbs stayed with the battalion till October, but some time before November 29th, when its disbandment was finally completed, it had ceased to be in more than name the 7th S.W.B. of the war years.

As already mentioned, the 4th S.W.B. had started demobilizing in November and at first it had looked as if its return home would not be long delayed. January saw 8 officers and nearly 350 men demobilized, and by the end of the month the 4th could only muster 14 officers and just over 200 men. Early in February came orders to proceed to Amara, the battalion going by rail to Kut and there taking a steamer to Amara. Here it encamped 6 miles below the town and remained for a time, while the process of demobilization continued till the 4th was down to cadre. In its homeward journey the cadre was not very lucky; on reaching Karachi it was hurried up country to Rawalpindi, owing to the troubles on the Frontier, and was retained there for several weeks. Not till July 26th, 1919, could it start for home, only to come in for a bad outbreak of influenza on the voyage. This prevented its being publicly received on its arrival at Brecon (August 19th),[1] as the troops were in quarantine; but next day quarantine restrictions were withdrawn, and it proved possible after all for the 4th to be publicly welcomed home after their long wanderings. The first "Service" battalion of the TWENTY-FOURTH formed, almost the last disbanded, the 4th had had a distinguished career and had added some remarkable pages to the Regiment's records. General Lewin in his farewell speech had told the battalion that he was always glad to have the 4th South Wales Borderers with him; whenever there was a nasty show they were in it, and they had lost more than any other battalion in the brigade. In a hard-fighting brigade like the 40th that was no small distinction, and may well serve as an epitome of the 4th's career. Of its debt to its first commander, Colonel Gillespie, something has already been said, but all who served with it in Mesopotamia will testify to the great debt which it owed to the officer who led it during the greater part of its service in that country. Colonel Kitchin indeed had shown himself a splendid C.O. Always calm, conspicuously, almost recklessly, brave, he was always cheerful and helpful, far-seeing and ready to grapple with any difficulty that might arise, not only in fighting but in administration. Climate, lack of water or rations, anything that might lower the efficiency or vitality of the men, he faced all troubles with energy and resource, and the fine record of the 4th is in no small degree a tribute to his gifts of leadership.

The other battalion on service in the East was even later in returning home than the 4th. The Brecknocks had remained at Mhow for several months after the Armistice. Things were far from settled in India: trouble was brewing on the North-West Frontier which eventually developed into definite hostilities against Afghanistan, and the services of an effective British unit

---

[1] Major Crewe-Read was in command and with him were Captain Usher, Lieutenant Hind, Regimental Sergeant Majors Staite and Hales, Regimental Quartermaster Sergeant Spence and 40 men.

could not be spared. Its strength was, however, substantially reduced by the demobilization of the coal-miners in its ranks; before the end of January two large batches amounting in all to 220 men had gone off and 30 more followed in February, so that by the end of March the battalion was down to a total strength of 19 officers and 456 men. The return of men from various employments brought it up over 500 again, but in August it was called upon to find large drafts for service on the Frontier and 12 officers and 300 men went off to join the 1st South Lancashire and the 25th London, whereupon the remainder of the battalion, barely a full company in strength, left Mhow for Calcutta. Here it was quartered at Fort William, where it spent another couple of months before at last receiving the welcome and long-expected order to return home. It eventually arrived back in England early in November, almost exactly five years after its departure for foreign service. Not many of those who had quitted England with it were still with the battalion on its return; of its original officers Major Cockcroft was the senior remaining.

. . . . . .

With the return home of the 1st Brecknocks this record of the experiences of the TWENTY-FOURTH in the war of 1914–1919 finds its natural termination. The reconstitution of the Regular battalions and the departure overseas of the 2nd Battalion to resume its tour of foreign service belong to another period in the Regiment's experiences. The fifty-nine battle honours earned by the Regiment epitomize those experiences effectively and bring out the very varied nature of the wanderings and services of its many battalions. Though it did not fall to its lot to be represented in either Italy or Palestine, there was scarcely a single major operation on the Western Front in which one or other of its battalions did not take part, and the record of decorations awarded to its officers and men speaks for itself. The 5777 names included in the Roll of Honour afford another testimony to what the members of the Regiment had to endure. They are inscribed in the book deposited in the Chapel in the Cathedral at Brecon which forms the tangible memorial erected to commemorate the sufferings and sacrifices of which this account can only claim to have tried to give a summary. There were many deeds fully deserving of record of which no proper accounts have been preserved, many individuals to whose work less than justice has inevitably been done, many episodes for which adequate space could not be spared. To have told the TWENTY-FOURTH's story during the four years and a half of war at the length its variety and its interest deserves would have required not one volume but several.

APPENDICES

APPENDIX

HONOURS AND AWARDS

[This list is only approximately accurate. It has been extremely difficult to trace awards made to officers serving on the Staff, as neither the Battalion War Diaries nor the Part II's of the Daily Orders notice them, and to search for individuals through the *London Gazette* is a fallible and uncertain process. Occasionally awards mentioned in a Diary are not recorded in the Part II's or the initials and number are not given : occasionally also the Diary and the Part II's disagree as to these particulars. Information as to ex-officers has also been very difficult to obtain and there are probably many omissions in this category. As a rule the rank given is that held by an officer at the time of the Armistice, of N.C.O.'s and men that at the time of the award. Awards to officers attached from other corps (e.g. R.A.M.C.) or regiments, or gained by them with some other unit before transfer to the Regiment, are not included, but awards to officers of the Regiment serving with other regiments are included.]

Victoria Cross

Capt. A. Buchanan.
Pte. J. H. Fynn.
Lieut.-Colonel D. G. Johnson.
Sgt. I. Rees.
Sgt. A. White.
C.S.M. J. H. Williams.

K.C.B.

Lieut.-General Sir A. S. Cobbe, V.C.

K.C.S.I.

Lieut.-General Sir A. S. Cobbe, V.C.

C.B.

Colonel H. G. Casson.
Lieut.-Colonel J. Grimwood.
Major-General W. E. B. Smith.
Brigadier-General J. H. du B. Travers.

C.M.G.

Major A. G. Board.
Lieut.-Colonel R. W. Bradley.
Colonel H. G. Casson.
Lieut.-Colonel E. V. O. Hewett.
Brigadier-General H. E. B. Leach.
Lieut.-Colonel L. I. G. Morgan-Owen.
Colonel C. W. Pearless.
Brigadier-General A. J. Reddie.
Major-General W. E. B. Smith.
Lieut.-Colonel C. L. Taylor.
Brigadier-General J. H. du B. Travers.
Colonel C. V. Trower.

C.B.E.

Lieut.-Colonel H. Cleeve.
Lieut.-Colonel L. I. G. Morgan-Owen.

O.B.E.

Capt. G. H. Buchanan.
Capt. and Q^{r}Mr A. Case.
Lieut.-Colonel R. P. Crawley.
Capt. C. M. D. Curtis.
Capt. W. B. Drake.
Major A. R. Godwin-Austen.
Lieut.-Colonel J. Grimwood.
Major F. St. J. Hughes.
Lieut.-Colonel F. G. Lawrence.
Major H. Marr.
Lieut. G. S. Mellsopp.
Capt. J. A. Mellsopp.
Major T. H. Morgan.
Lieut.-Colonel G. C. Thomas.
Lieut.-Colonel L. H. Tudor.

M.B.E.

Lieut. R. T. Everett.
Lieut. L. H. Green.
Capt. E. K. Laman.
Capt. S. C. Morgan.

2nd Lieut. A. J. Morris.
Capt. A. P. Percival.
Capt. W. B. Wilson.

D.S.O.

Lieut.-Colonel R. Benzie (bar).
Lieut.-Colonel M. J. B. de la P. Beresford.
Major G. H. Birkett.
Major A. G. Bond.
Lieut.-Colonel R. W. Bradley.
Major C. E. Browning.
Lieut.-Colonel B. W. Collier.
Lieut.-Colonel S. F. Cooke.
Lieut.-Colonel R. P. Crawley.
Capt. R. O. Crewe-Read.
Major D. W. Croft.
Lieut.-Colonel L. C. W. Deane.
Major I. T. Evans.
Lieut. W. M. Evans.
Major H. G. C. Fowler.
Major W. V. Franklin.
Lieut.-Colonel J. Going.
Lieut.-Colonel T. C. Greenway.
Lieut.-Colonel J. Grimwood.
Lieut.-Colonel R. F. Gross.
Lieut.-Colonel R. S. d'Arcy Gwynn.
Lieut.-Colonel E. V. O. Hewett.
Major H. J. Inglis.
Lieut.-Colonel D. G. Johnson (bar).

Lieut.-Colonel C. E. Kitchin.
Major W. L. Lawrence.
Capt. A. A. F. Loch.
Capt. A. G. Masters.
Lieut.-Colonel T. P. Melvill.
Lieut.-Colonel L. I. G. Morgan-Owen.
Capt. P. R. M. Mundy.
Colonel C. W. Pearless.
Major N. G. Pearson.
Major R. L. Petre.
Capt. D. T. Raikes.
Lieut.-Colonel G. T. Raikes (2 bars).
Capt. W. T. Raikes.
Major B. V. Ramsden (bar).
Brigadier-General A. J. Reddie.
Major A. Reid-Kellett.
Capt. H. M. B. Salmon.
Capt. C. K. Steward.
Colonel C. L. Taylor.
Major G. C. Thomas.
Lieut.-Colonel G. B. C. Ward.
Major A. E. Williams.
Lieut.-Colonel C. V. R. Wright.
Lieut.-Colonel H. P. Yates.

M.C.

Lieut. R. O. Ackerley.
Lieut. B. L. Ainsworth.
Capt. T. R. Allaway.
Capt. E. C. Amos.
Lieut. C. V. Ashe.

Capt. C. A. Baker.
2nd Lieut. W. G. Baker.
2nd Lieut. W. R. Barker.
Lieut. W. T. Benfield.
Capt. J. B. S. Bennett.
2nd Lieut. G. E. Berry.
Capt. W. N. V. Bickford-Smith.
Capt. W. V. Bloxham.
Capt. J. Bradstock.
Lieut. T. C. R. Bronham.
Lieut. H. J. Brown.
Capt. W. E. Brown (bar).
2nd Lieut. J. H. Bryant.

Capt. A. Buchanan.
Capt. W. A. Burn.

Capt. A. N. Cahusac.
Major R. N. Caldwell.
Capt. A. J. Canton.
Lieut. H. St. J. M. Carpendale.
2nd Lieut. G. Cardwell.
Lieut. J. Chamberlain.
Capt. E. C. Choinier.
Capt. W. T. Cobb.
Lieut. E. S. W. Cooke.
Lieut. W. E. Cooper.
Lieut. H. Cottam (bar).
Lieut. G. St. J. Coventry.
Capt. R. M. Cox.
Major D. W. Croft.
Capt. A. E. Crowder.

HONOURS AND AWARDS

Lieut. H. H. Davenport.
Capt. H. C. S. Davies.
Lieut. W. H. Day.
Lieut.-Colonel L. C. W. Deane.
Capt. R. Dendy.
Capt. W. T. Dick.
Capt. W. V. D. Dickinson.
2nd Lieut. W. Dilloway.
Capt. C. F. Dutton (bar).

Lieut. S. Eames.
Lieut. W. G. T. Edwards.
2nd Lieut. J. Ellis.
Capt. J. R. England.
Lieut. J. P. Enright.
2nd Lieut. G. Esmond.
Lieut. D. L. Evans.
Major I. T. Evans (bar).
Lieut. S. Evans.
2nd Lieut. C. B. Excell.

Lieut. A. E. Fairs.
Capt. K. Ffrench.
Capt. P. G. Fountain.
Capt. C. C. Fowkes (bar).
C.S.M. H. Franklin.

Capt. A. A. C. Garnons-Williams.
Lieut. S. H. Gelderd.
Lieut. D. F. George.
Lieut. E. M. Gibbon.
Lieut. E. Gill.
2nd Lieut. A. N. Glover (bar).
Major A. R. Godwin-Austen.
Capt. P. Gottwaltz.
Lieut. L. B. Greaves.
Lieut. C. H. Griffiths.
Lieut. R. S. Griffiths.

C.S.M. F. Haberfield.
Lieut. C. E. L. Hall.
Lieut. A. C. Harding.
Lieut. C. J. Hardy.
Lieut. T. W. Hardy.
Capt. T. B. Harris.
Capt. W. T. Harris.
Lieut. O. Hart.
Lieut. E. O. Hill (bar).
Lieut. H. R. Hill.
Lieut. W. E. Hind.
Capt. A. W. Hooper.

Major H. J. Inglis.

Lieut. D. Jenkins.

Lieut. S. B. Johns.
Lieut.-Colonel D. G. Johnson.
Capt. J. R. L. Jones.
C.S.M. T. Jones.

2nd Lieut. T. W. Keighley.
2nd Lieut. W. Kelly.
Capt. R. F. E. Kenward.

Capt. E. K. Laman.
Lieut. M. W. H. Lancaster.
2nd Lieut. F. W. Light.
Capt. A. M. O. J. Lloyd.
Capt. J. C. Lloyd.
Lieut. C. B. Lochner.
Capt. R. G. Lochner.
Lieut. A. D. W. Lowe.

Lieut. W. J. Manley.
Major H. Marr.
Lieut. B. S. Marshall.
Lieut. G. W. Massey.
Capt. A. G. Masters.
Lieut. F. J. L. Mayger (bar).
Lieut. C. H. Mayou.
Capt. E. E. Mills.
Lieut. A. Morgan.
2nd Lieut. E. Morgan.
2nd Lieut. F. E. Morgan.
Capt. M. C. Morgan.
2nd Lieut. W. R. Morgan.
2nd Lieut. W. H. Morris.
Capt. P. R. M. Mundy.
Capt. C. L. Mumford (bar).

Lieut. V. J. L. Napier.
Lieut. C. W. Nott.
Lieut. D. M. Noyes-Lewis.

2nd Lieut. J. J. O'Neill.
Capt. J. C. Owen.
Capt. E. E. Orford.

2nd Lieut. N. H. Parfitt (bar).
Lieut. W. Parkes.
Lieut. C. Patteson.
Lieut. A. G. Pearce.
Major N. G. Pearson.
Capt. R. L. Petre.
2nd Lieut. L. Petts.
Lieut. T. C. Phillips.
Capt. F. O. Philpott.
Lieut. T. Picton (bar).
Capt. W. H. M. Pierson.
Lieut. S. T. Pink.

2nd Lieut. L. B. Potts.
Lieut. A. C. N. Prance.
2nd Lieut. H. L. Price.
Lieut. A. J. Pritchard.
Capt. A. G. Purves.

Capt. D. T. Raikes (bar).
Capt. W. T. Raikes.
Major V. B. Ramsden.
Lieut. T. F. Rawle.
Lieut. R. S. P. Rawlins.
Capt. R. F. W. Rebsch.
Capt. E. T. Rees.
Lieut. J. F. Rees.
Major A. Reid-Kellett.
2nd Lieut. J. H. Richards.
Capt. M. G. Richards.
2nd Lieut. W. J. Roberts.
Capt. L. Rose.
Lieut. C. J. Round.
Lieut. S. E. Rumsey.
Capt. W. K. Runham (bar).

Capt. O. D. Schreiner.
Lieut. J. E. Seager.
2nd Lieut. H. J. Shearman.
R.S.M. J. Shirley.
Lieut. T. S. Sibley.
Capt. E. Simons (bar).
2nd Lieut. G. Simpson.
Capt. D. H. S. Somerville (bar).
Lieut. F. A. Stephenson.
Capt. C. K. Steward.
Capt. D. H. Stickler.

C.S.M. H. H. Stone.
Capt. J. R. Symes.

Capt. E. R. Taylor.
2nd Lieut. T. T. Taylor.
Lieut. R. Thomas.
Lieut. P. Treloar.
Lieut. C. J. H. Treglown.
Major E. B. Trower.
2nd Lieut. H. E. Tunnicliffe.

Capt. C. G. Usher (bar).

Lieut. F. L. Vanderpump.
R.S.M. H. J. Vatcher.
Capt. P. L. Villar.
2nd Lieut. J. H. Vizer.

Lieut. O. M. Wales (bar).
Capt. R. K. B. Walker.
2nd Lieut. H. Wallace.
Capt. F. W. Walshe.
Lieut. F. V. Ward-Jones.
Capt. G. C. N. Webb.
Lieut. A. C. R. Welsh.
Capt. E. E. A. Whitworth.
Capt. W. H. H. Wilkins.
Major A. E. Williams.
Capt. F. T. Williams.
Lieut. L. G. Williams.
2nd Lieut. W. J. Williams.
R.Q.M.S. F. Wiltshire.
Lieut. J. S. Windsor.
Lieut. J. B. V. Wood.
Capt. C. C. Woolley.

Distinguished Conduct Medal

Where no rank is given the recipient was a Private.

13208 Adams, Corpl. W.
12281 Arthur, Sgt. R.

12762 Barrett, Corpl. J.
22143 Bassett, F.
8206 Bean, Sgt. S. D.
13102 Beary, M.
15403 Berry, F.
8725 Black, R.
17661 Brooke, C.S.M. H.
7065 Burgess, G.

9358 Chaplin, C.S.M. J.
15873 Chapman, L/Corpl. J.
18651 Clent, T.
22075 Cole, Sgt. A.

20131 Cole, Corpl. C. H.
27056 Colley, W.
22355 Cooper, C.S.M. A. E.
7473 Corbett, Sgt. H.
16065 Cox, C.S.M. C.
9180 Coxhead, Corpl. R. H.

10983 D'Arcy, C.S.M. W. H.
14727 Dare, Sgt. J. (bar).
18997 Davies, L/Corpl. D.
15429 Davies, R.S.M. W.
38025 Doyle, D.
6291 Duffy, Sgt. G. S.

8269 Edwards, Corpl. J.
20407 Edwards, Sgt. R.

HONOURS AND AWARDS

21561 Edwards, Sgt. W. T.
20315 Evans, R.

18734 Feast, Sgt. G.
13027 Fitzpatrick, J.
10629 Foley, L/Corpl. C. J.
34600 Foley, Sgt. W.
263109 Fordrey, W. H.
10729 Foster, A. W.
11153 Francis, Corpl. W. (bar).
17476 Frayne, L.

71921 Gask, Sgt. H. F.
11089 Geary, Sgt. R. J.
9580 Gibbs, Corpl. W. T.
9011 Green, A.
29403 Griffiths, D. I.
12935 Gronow, Corpl. N. J.
8238 Gunter, Sgt. H. C.

14077 Hall, C.S.M. D.
24115 Hampton, Sgt. H. A.
12757 Harcourt, L/Corpl. E. W. (bar).
23938 Haywood, Corpl. H.
17442 Heaton, F.
9929 Hendy, L/Corpl.
9524 Hewitt, J.
14312 Hibbert, Sgt. P.
210687 Hillier, C.S.M. F.
14829 Hollands, J.
16760 Holliday, W.
13829 Hooper, C.S.M. C. J.
9854 House, C.S.M. H. G.
17912 Hughes, Sgt. H. L.
10834 Hullah, A.

10521 Jackson, Sgt. W.
33308 James, H.
41242 James, Corpl. T. G.
11882 Jeremiah, Sgt. H.
9738 Jones, A/R.S.M. D. T.
29365 Jones, L/Corpl. J. M.

8584 Knott, L.

22297 Leclare, Sgt. W.
9178 Lewis, Corpl. R.
34647 Lister, C.S.M. F.
21340 Lockie, R.S.M. G.
11161 Lomas, L. (bar).

14952 Macaulay, D. M. (bar).
42112 Manning, Sgt. T. C.
40928 Mansbridge, P.
14821 Martin, C.S.M. W. J.

6201 Matthews, E.
14967 McCarthy, L.
8943 Melham, Sgt. H.
9223 Miller, C.S.M. A.
9500 Millward, J.
8652 Milton, Sgt. W. T.
13004 Mitchell, Sgt. H.
13906 Mitchener, C.S.M. W.
14508 Moore, C.Q.M.S. J. B.
27338 Morgan, Corpl. D.
14746 Morgan, W.
14369 Morris, C.S.M. G. J. (bar).
8119 Moss, C.S.M. M. C.
12517 Murray, A/R.S.M. W.
14496 Murphy, P.
13113 Myles, Sgt. W.

10458 Norman, C.S.M. C. A.
17537 Norris, W.

14537 O'Neill, C.S.M. P. J.
8192 O'Toole, Sgt. D. P.

24991 Page, N.
17090 Pearson, Sgt. T. (bar).
23484 Plummer, F.
15420 Power, Sgt. J.
20540 Power, Sgt. P.
16440 Prescott, L/Corpl. A.
13999 Probert, C.S.M. W. J.

15021 Quicke, P.

25028 Rawlings, Sgt. E.
14835 Rees, C.S.M. A. L. (bar).
17603 Ricketts, C.S.M. W. H. (bar)
22769 Riley, C. W.
14827 Robbins, Sgt. A. B.
12955 Roberts, W.
14769 Rowles, L/Corpl. L. J.
21654 Russell, Sgt. E.
11577 Ryan, L/Corpl. M.

10415 Scarborough, Sgt. F. E.
11230 Scarles, C.S.M. S.
6865 Sheehan, Sgt. T.
14547 Shermer, C.S.M. T.
14489 Silcox, Sgt. J.
13142 Simmons, L/Corpl. H. W.
12469 Smith, Sgt. J. S.
14855 Smithey, Corpl. G.
9977 Snow, G.
9121 Spink, L/Corpl. A. R.
22798 Stockton, L/Corpl. J. H.
13138 Sullivan, Sgt. W.
31852 Sweetman, L/Corpl. S.

THE HISTORY OF THE SOUTH WALES BORDERERS

15706 Terry, Sgt. J. H.
23762 Thomas, Sgt. H. G.
20928 Thomas, L/Corpl. E. J.
14649 Thoms, Sgt. R.
15706 Torney, Sgt. J. H.
 6296 Tring, C.S.M. H. F.
24821 Turton, L/Corpl. J.

11958 Wannell, Corpl. G.
10423 Ward, Sgt. J.
46561 Whelan, L/Corpl. F. J.
 9952 West, T.

 4961 Westlake, R.S.M. H.
17709 Wetter, Corpl. J. J.
 8893 White, Sgt. F.
 6384 Whitehouse, C.M.S. J.
 8836 Wilcox, Sgt. W.
22530 Williams, D.
15177 Williams, E.
11338 Williams, Corpl. E. J.
20408 Williams, Sgt. J. H.
13318 Williams, Sgt. T.
16330 Williams, T.
 9813 Woods, T.

Meritorious Service Medal

14364 Andrews, R.S.M. E. C.
200586 Bath, L/Corpl. H. A.
 9198 Belcher, Corpl. C. H.
 2164 Betterton, Sgt. J.
20489 Burgess, C.S.M. R. W.
16032 Clevey, Sgt. R. J.
13847 Cobner, Sgt. L.
46327 Coward, H.
15115 Cox, R.Q.M.S. J. E.
17128 Davies, Sgt. D.
23661 Davies, Sgt. W J.
14137 Dix, C.Q.M.S. A.
 9457 Ellis, Sgt. W. H.
 7011 Evans, C.Q.M.S. A.
26804 Evans, Sgt. T.
16775 Everson, Corpl. A.
17302 Ewing, C.Q.M.S. A.
13986 Francis, R.S.M. J.
200451 Fry, Sgt. F.
19374 Goldthorp, Sgt. W.

14492 Hadley, C.S.M. G.
16156 Hiley, Sgt. F. H.
15597 Hitchings, Sgt. W.
21667 Jackson, Sgt. J. E.
24772 Jenkins, J.
15968 Jones, L/Corpl. J. A.
15497 Jones, C.Q.M.S. R. H.
 9181 Kearns, R.Q.M.S. W.
10232 Kelly, Sergt. E. A.
24946 Lewis, L/Corpl. T.
12638 Maher, R.Q.M.S. U.
25157 Moore, Corpl. P. S.
15392 Pearson, R.S.M. P. J.
17417 Phillips, C.Q.M.S. M. T.
21341 Roberts, Sgt. R. W.
40263 Salt, R.Q.M.S. C. T.
39665 Swain, Corpl. W.
17403 Taylor, Sgt. W.
14409 Winston, R.Q.M.S. T. C.

Military Medal

19432 Ackerman, L/Corpl. J.
15927 Adams, A.
36599 Adams, A.
41152 Adderley, A.
38535 Ainsworth, E.
27623 Allen, Sgt. C. H.
23200 Allen, L/Corpl. J.
44354 Allen, J.
10897 Allison, C.
13527 Andrews, Sgt. G. E.
44289 Apps, Corpl. S. G.
26698 Arnold, O.
12281 Arthur, Sgt. R.
13441 Aspden, Sgt. J.
 1711 Atherton, J.

45416 Bagnall, W.
40583 Bailey, Sgt. J. T.
29657 Baker, L/Corpl. R.
22258 Barbour, C.Q.M.S. J.
 7970 Barker, C.S.M. A.
14310 Barnes, Sgt. H.
10337 Bartlett, C.
44361 Baxter, A. G.
21147 Beach, G.
17117 Beard, A.
10785 Beaver, Sgt. J. W.
 9721 Bell, C.Q.M.S. F.
19130 Bendorffe, S.
24930 Bentley, Corpl. W.
16739 Berry, A.

HONOURS AND AWARDS

19962 Berry, Corpl. S.
208461 Bevan, J.
9007 Bilton, L/Corpl. S. P.
17159 Bishop, Corpl. B.
9261 Blair, Sgt. T.
40951 Blythe, P.
263049 Bogard, I.
11603 Bolch, Corpl. L.
23431 Boobyer, L/Corpl. J.
9801 Bowen, Sgt. B.
16671 Bowen, G.
16585 Brewster, L. S.
22452 Brice, Sgt. F.
202426 Bridges, C.S.M. F.
44732 Brown, A.
17640 Brown, F.
39854 Brown, W.
12227 Brunker, J.
20236 Bull, Sgt. L. G.
23710 Buller, P.
20529 Bullock, Sgt. J. T.
14310 Burnes, Sgt. H.
37815 Burrows, W.
17458 Burston, F.
21801 Bush, Corpl. T.
18007 Butcher, D. J.
16639 Bywater, W.

9532 Cable, G.
19864 Cahill, M.
260137 Cahill, P.
17056 Capewell, L/Corpl. F.
18111 Carey, Corpl. W.
8272 Carroll, C.S.M. P.
16973 Carter, F. L.
15424 Casey, Sgt. P. (bar).
19225 Cassidy, J.
19102 Chappell, H.
16470 Chattington, Sgt. T. H.
17374 Cheyne, Sgt. J. D. (bar).
16551 Clarke, Sgt. G.
20031 Clarke, Corpl. W.
15534 Cleary, Sgt. P.
26204 Clissold, C. E.
20470 Clubb, R.
33847 Cochrane, H.
39470 Cockbill, A.
10975 Cole, Sgt. H. L.
13003 Coleman, Corpl. T.
39131 Colley, Sgt. A. H.
43064 Conroy, Corpl. J.
36126 Cook, F. H.
9666 Cook, C.Q.M.S. W. R.
17449 Coombs, Corpl. R.
22356 Cooper, C.S.M. A.

11112 Cooper, B.
53953 Cooper, Sgt. J.
25213 Cooper, Sgt. J. S.
17433 Corbett, H.
10943 Corcoran, Sgt. P.
36128 Cosh, E. H.
10205 Cottrell, Corpl. A.
16122 Cox, Sgt. C. F.
45173 Creighton, J. T.
10468 Crisp, W.
24218 Crossdale, G.
42070 Crossland, A.
18281 Crum, Sgt. T. J. (bar).
14078 Cunningham, J.
46902 Cuttell, W.

25905 Darwent, C.
12373 Davies, L/Corpl. A. A.
14186 Davies, Corpl. A. E.
11450 Davies, Sgt. E.
17152 Davies, L/Corpl. E.
38799 Davies, F.
18081 Davies, J.
16928 Davies, Sgt. W.
39578 Davies, W. H.
44220 Dawes, E.
17229 Dawson, Sgt. W.
48660 Deardon, W.
40419 Dover, G. G. (bar).
14562 Dowd, T.
44668 Downey, B.
18965 Drewitt, L/Corpl. R.
18091 Dunning, Corpl. C.

15013 Edmunds, Sgt. F.
21200 Edmunds, L/Corpl. T.
16666 Edwards, A.
11128 Edwards, Sgt. D.
40992 Edwards, H.
19764 Edwards, Corpl. J.
11894 Edwards, P.
39552 Edwards, R. W.
21200 Edwards, L/Corpl. T.
39139 Edwards, Sgt. W. H.
14526 Ellaway, Sgt. J.
7323 Ellis, L/Corpl. A. H.
17154 Elsdon, Corpl. J. (bar).
40851 Elvin, W.
13670 Evans, Sgt. A. J.
23156 Evans, Sgt. E.
228773 Evans, Corpl. F. J.
21514 Evans, H.
21069 Evans, H. J.
44172 Evans, O.
20400 Evans, Sgt. P. F.

THE HISTORY OF THE SOUTH WALES BORDERERS

49392 Evans, Sgt. W.
26937 Eyre, Sgt. E.

15470 Fawdon, Sgt. T. F.
17106 Fellows, Sgt. J. T.
21430 Foote, E.
19805 Ford, A. P.
16520 Ford, C.S.M. C. C.
41216 Forsythe, R.
48919 Franklin, A. T.
24275 Freeman, A.
8828 Freeman, Sgt. J. J.
40309 Fry, L/Corpl. A.

39058 Gardner, Sgt. A.
25481 Gardner, W.
11622 Garland, A.
11074 Gawler, Sgt. W. J.
11089 Geary, Sgt. R. J.
25650 George, W.
11305 Gibbin, Sgt. J.
6235 Gibbs, Sgt. G. (bar).
25818 Gilbert, Corpl. J. M.
20403 Gill, Sgt. H. J.
8546 Godwin, L/Corpl. C. J.
16463 Goodman, Sgt. W. H.
24202 Goodship, Corpl. W.
19383 Goth, Corpl. W.
24233 Greatholder, Corpl. G.
44495 Green, Sgt. T. (bar).
202431 Green, Corpl. W. J.
13675 Griffith, Sgt. F. (bar).
26801 Griffiths, L/Corpl. A. E.
10726 Griffiths, Corpl. H.
21707 Griffiths, Sgt. W.
16884 Griffiths, L/Corpl. W.
40962 Grindle, T.
42331 Guthrie, T.

44468 Hales, J.
44234 Hall, L.
33887 Halliwell, G.
39504 Hamlett, F.
260120 Hampson, G.
24115 Hampton, Sgt. H. A.
32658 Handcock, D. (bar).
13391 Hanford, T.
38671 Hardaker, L/Corpl. G.
46832 Hardman, C. E.
34773 Harris, G.
24439 Harris, Sgt. H.
9125 Harris, Sgt. W.
10660 Harrison, E. F.
18898 Harvey, G. (bar).
8303 Hatchard, A.

10499 Hatherton, Corpl. J.
17596 Heath, L/Corpl. P. T.
21423 Hemmings, L/Corpl. I.
31887 Hensley, W.
29802 Higgins, L/Corpl. W.
18187 Hill, C.
20975 Hill, L/Corpl. G.
30620 Hills, E. A.
23148 Hiscox, C.
18391 Hitchings, J.
26108 Hockley, L/Corpl. S.
14706 Hodges, Corpl. W. J.
44674 Hollis, W.
9240 Holloway, A.
17016 Horrobin, J. (bar).
19507 Horton, W.
13013 Howcroft, Sgt. C. E.
31131 Howells, D. U.
40526 Hudson, Corpl. C.
20014 Hughes, Sgt. C. B.
21822 Hughes, L/Corpl. J. (bar).
21346 Hughes, Sgt.
20847 Hulbert, Corpl. O.
25594 Hull, L/Corpl. J. A.
10425 Hutchings, L/Corpl. J.

13050 Ivins, D. J.

11663 Jackson, Sgt. J. E.
23772 Jacques, J.
33220 James, Sgt. D. J.
18400 James, Corpl. E.
20982 James, Corpl. J.
21090 James, J. M.
19956 James, W.
22188 Jay, Corpl. A.
20378 Jenkins, Sgt. H. C.
13107 Jenkins, W. J. (bar).
15620 Jenkins, W. S.
40200 Jennison, L/Corpl. G.
42240 Johnson, Sgt. A.
17285 Jones, Sgt. A. T.
27206 Jones, Corpl. D. O.
21963 Jones, F.
9625 Jones, L/Corpl. F. J.
9056 Jones, Sgt. J.
24330 Jones, J.
40040 Jones, J.
17059 Jones, Sgt. J. T.
24086 Jones, R.
19038 Jones, T.
25439 Jones, T.
9562 Jones, Sgt. T. W. A.
21296 Jones, W.
24744 Jones, W.

524

HONOURS AND AWARDS

13993 Jones, Sgt. W. J.
11623 Jones, W. L.
39091 Jordan, Corpl. C. J.
17074 Judkins, Corpl. W.

46893 Kay, J.
19445 Keigher, Corpl. J.
9338 Kelly, Sgt. B.
41026 Kelly, J.
8876 Kelly, L/Corpl. W. J.
30164 Kemp, W. J.
38586 Kennerley, H.
11016 Kennington, C.S.M. F.
16917 Keohane, D.
17246 Kew, G. A.
9346 Key, Sgt. A. R.
46838 Kinder, E. M.
10610 King, Corpl. F.
14677 Kitchener, G.
25902 Knight, L/Corpl. A.

17176 Lander, Sgt. W. C.
11194 Lane, H. C.
14016 Lane, Corpl. J.
10300 Lane, L/Corpl.
13690 Lawler, Sgt. S.
14688 Lawrence, Corpl. D. G. (bar).
11692 Lee, J.
25946 Lee, L/Corpl. J. T.
202517 Leuthwaite, J.
16794 Lewis, B. J.
21533 Lewis, H.
10436 Lewis, L/Corpl. J.
14787 Lewis, J.
17284 Lewis, Sgt. J.
17246 Lewis, L.
11215 Lewis, W.
18484 Lewis, W. J.
16327 Lihou, L/Corpl. G. C.
36091 Lipscombe, A.
25290 Lipyeart, F.
13724 Lister, S.
24043 Lockwood, J.
24612 Lomax, R. T.
11083 Lougher, O.
19443 Lovatt, Sgt. T.
14155 Loxton, W.

14952 Macaulay, D. M.
40606 Madden, A.
22538 Mahoney, L/Corpl. P.
21925 Mahoney, W.
17120 Maiden, Corpl. T.
22177 Mainwaring, M.
13171 Maloney, J.

39573 Marsh, L/Corpl. W. J.
41049 Marshall, S.
22917 Martin, W.
24263 Mason, L/Corpl. A.
45208 Mason, Sgt. H. E. (bar).
44425 Matthews, Sgt. A.
8602 Matthews, T.
17203 Maybury, R.
11319 McCarthy, T.
24261 McCormick, J.
10311 McFarlane, Corpl. A.
40205 McKee, S.
42076 McLoughlin, L/Corpl. C. J.
19416 Meese, A.
61261 Merchant, Sgt. S.
10169 Millward, W. C.
8562 Milton, Sgt. W.
10033 Mitchell, C.Q.M.S. H.
25236 Moffatt, C. W.
45154 Mohan, T.
42068 Moore, Sgt. A.
17188 Moore, F.
9581 Morgan, C.
14370 Morgan, Sgt. D.
21202 Morgan, Corpl. D. J.
15809 Morgan, G.
14738 Morgan, Sgt. T.
9615 Morgan, W. J.
13105 Morris, G.
8207 Morris, W.
24079 Morton, G.
34688 Mosey, L/Corpl. J. R.
23921 Mottram, J. A.
44586 Mulford, Corpl. C. H. C.

39342 Need, F.
21443 Nelmer, C.
23472 Nelson, Sgt. S.
17506 Nethercott, W.
13884 Newberry, P. T.
34626 Nicholls, H.
14329 Nolan, J.

15459 O'Neill, Sgt. H. C.
39997 Onions, Corpl. C.
10632 Osborne, F.

24309 Page, E.
45695 Page, G.
14923 Page, Sgt. W.
24967 Park, L/Corpl. M.
44464 Parker, Corpl. R. H.
45111 Parkinson, Corpl. R.
24697 Parle, L/Corpl. L.
20138 Pask, T.

25171 Pasquill, Sgt. J.
20926 Patrick, Corpl. S. W.
10342 Peacock, A.
17528 Pearce, Corpl. A. W.
16971 Pearce, J.
11669 Periam, R.
16409 Perrins, H. J.
14301 Phillips, W.
29801 Philpin, J.
23384 Pickett, H.
19834 Pike, Sgt. F. C.
9570 Pine, Sgt. F.
20308 Pleece, Corpl. E. W.
17179 Pollard, Sgt. I. D.
9598 Poole, Sgt. A.
9901 Porter, S.
24394 Potter, E. J.
24908 Potts, Sgt. A.
6459 Pratten, Sgt. B.
15614 Price, Sgt. A.
16334 Price, Corpl. A.
16946 Price, L/Corpl. E.
9250 Price, Sgt. F.
14433 Price, J.
16899 Price, J.
29040 Prince, I.
23606 Prince, J.
20756 Pritchard, G.
12611 Pritchard, Corpl. W.
14309 Probert, Sgt. W.
16341 Prout, J.
18758 Pullen, L/Corpl. D.

23918 Quinn, L/Corpl. J. D.
11820 Quinn, P.
17437 Quinton, Sgt. A. J. (bar).

36392 Rae, Sgt. J.
19223 Ransom, C.S.M. J.
9595 Ravenhill, A.
8329 Ravenhill, Corpl. A. E.
10910 Raynor, W.
42289 Reacher, F.
14391 Rees, Corpl. E. W.
16428 Rees, L/Corpl. J.
15566 Rees, Sgt. W.
14709 Reeves, Sgt. A. L.
24809 Regan, Corpl. J.
17529 Reynolds, W. T.
9962 Rice, L/Corpl. J. R.
18966 Richards, Sgt. J. C. F. (bar).
18905 Richards, Corpl. J.
19299 Richardson, J. R.
11125 Riding, S.
48124 Rigby, J. C.

48179 Rigby, W. H.
38690 Roberts, D.
33652 Roberts, R.
44126 Roberts, R. A.
41024 Robotham, W. C.
48992 Rogers, A. H.
10965 Rose, J.
11636 Rosser, Corpl. H.
14017 Rowlands, Sgt. J.
13416 Russell, Sgt. G.
22144 Ryall, Corpl. E.
18672 Ryan, Sgt. E.

10836 Sanders, Sgt. G.
16753 Sargeant, G. H.
19297 Scott, F.
27305 Scott, Corpl. G. W.
10581 Seabourne, R. H. G.
14320 Seager, A.
21807 Selway, C. S. W.
10040 Seth, W. R.
25148 Shant, J.
15428 Shaw, Sgt. J.
13062 Shea, L/Corpl. G. D.
16757 Shepherd, Sgt. W. J.
27816 Sims, J.
40929 Skelton, R. B.
14903 Slade, F.
10210 Slater, W.
19622 Small, J.
45862 Smith, A.
39947 Smith, C. E.
15497 Smith, F.
33342 Spears, C.
39251 Stanley, Corpl. E. J.
40760 Starr, H.
17120 Step, Corpl. F. A.
13000 Stevens, B.
      Stevens, L/Corpl. H.
9993 Stevens, L/Corpl. M.
13086 St. Ledger, B.
28626 Strange, T. L.
20899 Stride, A.
22804 Sullivan, E.
18507 Sullivan, T.
39315 Swattridge, L/Corpl. G.
45302 Swift, T. E. (bar).
11357 Suddick, J.

15183 Tamplin, W. E.
29143 Taylor, E. C.
40341 Taylor, L/Corpl. J.
19491 Tellwright, M. W.
9505 Terrett, Sgt. W. C.
15278 Thain, Sgt. O.

HONOURS AND AWARDS

17567 Thomas, L/Corpl. A. J.
14504 Thomas, L/Corpl. D.
20254 Thomas, Sgt. D. H.
46143 Thomas, D. L.
15833 Thomas, F.
21269 Thomas, G. A.
11511 Thomas, J. (bar).
20899 Thomas, J.
46916 Thomas, T. J.
14491 Thomas, Sgt. W.
14498 Thomas, Z. D.
11667 Thompson, S.
23714 Thorpe, Sgt. E.
46944 Thorpe, Sgt. G.
23804 Tibbs, A.
40004 Tildsley, L/Corpl. J. E.
17599 Tommy, Corpl. A.
9876 Toothill, R.Q.M.S. W.
27657 Townsend, F.
28600 Tucker, L/Corpl. G. B.
28489 Tulloch, W. H.
19414 Tweeny, L/Corpl. R. C.
20016 Tyrrell, A.

13568 Vaughan, W. J.
15549 Vine, H. T.

41147 Wall, F. J.
25653 Wallbank, R.
40572 Walmsley, E.
14386 Walsh, M.
25520 Walters, W. H.
11958 Wannell, Corpl. G.
42092 Warburton, Sgt. C. A.
9504 Wasley, B.
17050 Waters, S.
20444 Watkins, S.
17154 Watkins, T.
5719 Webber, Corpl. F. D.

13196 Wellington, C.
42291 Wells, W.
17436 Wheeler, Sgt. K. D.
19215 White, Corpl. H. V.
17169 Whitehouse, Sgt. J. S.
24187 Whiting, Sgt. W.
26065 Whittaker, T.
45716 Whyld, S. S.
27616 Wild, Corpl. A.
16329 Williams, Sgt. A.
17153 Williams, Corpl. A. H.
22530 Williams, D.
15177 Williams, E.
13760 Williams, G.
25993 Williams, G.
16243 Williams, Sgt. J.
20299 Williams, L/Corpl. J.
17649 Williams, J.
50807 Williams, J.
20408 Williams, Sgt. J. H.
12911 Williams, Sgt. J. R.
20346 Williams, T.
15134 Williams, W.
39228 Williams, W.
14682 Williams, W. H.
39195 Wilson, Sgt. J. T.
39850 Wiltshire, A. E.
9469 Winfield, Corpl. H. S.
10629 Winn, Sgt. W.
23404 Witherall, A.
23706 Wood, J.
11044 Wright, Sgt. H. J.
39404 Wright, Corpl. J.
21579 Wyatt, Sgt. J. G.
39188 Wyatt, W.

24848 Yalden, L.
17236 Yates, F.
17353 Young, L.

BREVET PROMOTIONS

To be Colonel

Lieut.-Colonels H. G. Casson.
           H. E. B. Leach.
C. W. Pearless.

To be Lieut.-Colonel

Majors R. W. Bradley.
     B. W. Collier.
     K. Ffrench.
     T. C. Greenway.
     R. F. Gross.
     D. G. Johnson.
     C. E. Kitchin.

C. W. Pearless.
G. T. Raikes.
A. J. Reddie.
W. H. Stanway
C. L. Taylor.
G. B. C. Ward.
H. P. Yates.

THE HISTORY OF THE SOUTH WALES BORDERERS

To be Major

Capts. M. A. M. Dickie.
J. F. Edwards.
K. D. F. Gattie.
A. R. Godwin-Austen.
C. B. Habershon.
C. E. Kitchin.
M. C. Morgan.
R. L. Petre.
G. T. Raikes.
V. B. Ramsden.
C. M. Tippetts.
G. B. C. Ward.
A. E. Williams.

FOREIGN ORDERS

Order of Leopold

Lieut.-Colonel C. L. Taylor.

Belgian. Croix de Guerre

22143 Bassett, Pte. F.
14826 Beard, Pte. W.
      Capt. F. W. Clarke.
22188 Day, L/Corpl. W.
      Capt. W. V. D. Dickinson.
20272 Jones, Corpl. T. C.
      Major F. G. Lawrence.

20156 Pembrey, C.Q.M.S. W.
19889 Pike, Pte. F. W.
 6459 Pratten, C.Q.M.S. B.
14705 Rees, Corpl. D. J.
 5616 Shirley, R.S.M. J.
17454 Whitehead, Sgt. R.
      Capt. W. H. A. Wilkins.

Egyptian. Order of the Nile, Second Class

Lieut.-Colonel C. W. Pearless.

Egyptian. Order of the Nile, Fourth Class

Captain R. K. B. Walker.

French. Legion of Honour

Commander. Lieut.-General Sir A. S. Cobbe, V.C.
Officer. Brigadier-General A. J. Reddie.
         Colonel C. V. Trower.

French. Croix de Guerre

14826 Andrews, R.S.M. E. C.
17177 Beard, Pte. A.
      Lieut. W. T. Benfield.
15403 Berry, Pte. F.
      Major C. E. Browning.
16065 Cox, C.S.M. C.
      Lieut. R. M. Ford.
      Major H. G. Garnett.
62206 Haddock, C.Q.M.S. J.
17442 Heaton, Pte. F.
13829 Hooper, C.S.M. C. J.
      Major F. G. Lawrence.
      Capt. A. M. O. J. Lloyd.
 8886 Lucas, C.S.M. E.
45208 Mason, Sgt. H. L.
14952 Macaulay, Pte. D. M.

15809 Morgan, Pte. C.
      Capt. M. C. Morgan.
      Capt. P. R. M. Mundy.
13884 Newberry, Pte. P.
14923 Page, Sgt. W.
17528 Pearce, Sgt. A. W.
      Capt. W. H. M. Pierson.
      Lieut.-Colonel G. T. Raikes.
      Capt. A. Reid-Kellett.
      Lieut. C. J. Round.
13416 Russell, Sgt. G.
13487 Steele, Sgt. W.
45303 Swift, Pte. T.
15706 Torney, Sgt. J. H.
18116 Vaughan, Sgt. A. C.
      Major A. E. Williams.

HONOURS AND AWARDS

French. Medaille Militaire

4670 Attwell, R.S.M. A.
17376 Cheyne, Sgt. J. D.
11699 Geary, C.S.M. R. J.
9580 Gibbs, Corpl. W. T.
21654 Russell, Sgt. E.
4961 Westlake, R.S.M. H.

Greek. Croix de Guerre

16675 Blackmore, Sgt. H.
18997 Davies, Pte. D.
Capt. M. A. M. Dickie.
15134 Williams, Pte. W.
Capt. C. C. Woolley.

Italian. Crown of Italy

Cavalier. Capt. M. C. Morgan.

Italian. St. Maurice and St. Lazarus

Commander. Lieut.-General Sir A. S. Cobbe, V.C.
Officer (Fourth Class). Brigadier-General H. E. B. Leach.

Italian. Silver Medal for Military Valour

Lieut. G. E. Cardwell.

Italian. Bronze Medal for Military Valour

13690 Lawlor, Sgt. S.
21340 Lockie, R.S.M. G.
16330 Williams, Pte. T.

Roumanian. Croix Virtute Militare

16520 Ford, C.S.M. C. C.

Roumanian. Medaille D'Honneur

14826 Martin, C.S.M. W. J.
14017 Rowlands, Sgt. J.
16443 Williams, Corpl. J.

Russian. Order of St. Anne, Second Class

Major V. Ferguson.

Russian. Order of St. Anne, Third Class

Lieut.-Colonel C. E. Kitchin.
Colonel C. V. Trower.
Lieut.-Colonel H. P. Yates.

Russian. Order of St. Anne, Fourth Class

Lieut. I. T. Lloyd.

Russian. Order of St. Stanislaus, Second Class

Major V. Ferguson.

Russian. Order of St. Stanislaus, Third Class

Brigadier-General A. J. Reddie.

Russian. Order of St. Vladimir, Fourth Class

Capt. A. Buchanan.

RUSSIAN. CROSS OF ST. GEORGE
8836 Wilcox, Sgt. W.

RUSSIAN. MEDAL OF ST. GEORGE

9238 Day, L/Corpl. W.   13221 Stevens, Pte. J.
9178 Lewis, L/Corpl. R.   6384 Whitehouse, C.S.M. J.
13171 Maloney, Pte. J.

SERVIAN. ORDER OF KARAGEORGE, THIRD CLASS
Casson, Brigadier-General H. G.

SERVIAN. CROSS OF KARAGEORGE

11220 Fynn, Pte. J. H.   11318 Sullivan, Sgt. W.

SERVIAN. GOLD MEDAL OF KARAGEORGE

10468 Crisp, Pte. W.   Price, L/Corpl. W.
12757 Harcourt, Pte. E. W.   24807 Regan, Corpl. J.

SERVIAN. ORDER OF THE WHITE EAGLE

Lieut. L. B. Crewes.   Capt. F. T. Williams.
Capt. C. B. Habershon.

MENTIONED IN DISPATCHES

Those " brought to notice by the Secretary of State for War for valuable service in connection with the war " have been included. The rank given in the case of those mentioned more than once is that held at the time of the last mention.

2nd Lieut. T. R. Allaway.
Capt. and Q^rM^r J. Allbutt (twice).
243892 L/Corpl. J. Allen.
14866 R.S.M. E. C. Andrews.
23387 Corpl. H. C. Anstice.
15272 Sgt. J. Arnold.
13441 C.Q.M.S. J. Aspden.
13915 Corpl. J. Arthur.
Capt. T. C. M. Austin.

7156 L/Corpl. J. Bailey.
Capt. C. A. Baker.
15554 Pte. J. F. Baker.
7122 Sgt. T. R. Baker.
12762 Corpl. J. Barrett.
Major J. Barrett-Lennard.
200586 Corpl. M. A. Bath.
13202 Pte. M. Beary.
Lieut.-Colonel R. Benzie (twice).
Lieut.-Colonel M. J. B. de la P. Beresford.
Lieut. S. W. Best.
Major G. H. Birkett (three times).

16675 Sgt. H. Blackmore.
9261 Sgt. T. Blair.
Lieut. A. Bodenham.
12253 L/Corpl. L. Borton.
16459 C.S.M. C. E. Bourne.
Major R. W. Bradley.
Capt. J. Bradstock (twice).
53258 Corpl. F. J. Bravery.
16119 Sgt. A. Brown.
Capt. M. W. Brown.
Major W. E. Brown (twice).
Major C. E. Browning (twice).
Lieut. and Q^rM^r J. Bryant (twice).
Capt. A. Buchanan (twice).
Major N. Burrows.

9352 Pte. G. Cable.
Capt. A. N. Cahusac.
Capt. R. N. Caldwell (twice).
Capt. J. A. Campling.
Capt. and Q^rM^r A. Case (twice).
14720 R.S.M. E. Casey (twice).

HONOURS AND AWARDS

Brigadier-General H. G. Casson (five times).
Capt. G. F. H. Charlton.
16470 C.S.M. T. H. Chattington.
6753 Pte. T. Claffey.
Capt. F. W. Clarke.
Lieut.-General A. S. Cobbe (seven times).
Lieut. C. J. Coker.
Lieut.-Colonel B. W. Collier (twice).
9666 Sgt. W. R. Cook.
Lieut.-Colonel S. Fitz W. Cooke.
16713 Sgt. W. R. Cooper.
Capt. C. J. P. Copner.
14513 R.Q.M.S. J. Corfield.
12752 R.S.M. W. Cornish.
Capt. R. M. Cox.
8536 L/Corpl. W. Cox.
Major R. O. Crewe-Read (twice).
Major D. W. Croft (twice).
42341 Sgt. H. A. Croker.
8785 Pte. H. Cudlipp.

2nd Lieut. H. J. Daniel.
9238 L/Corpl. W. Day.
Capt. W. H. Day.
Lieut. E. T. Deacon.
Lieut.-Colonel L. C. W. Deane (twice).
Capt. M. A. M. Dickie.
Capt. W. V. D. Dickinson (twice).
15701 Sgt. J. E. Doran.
Capt. W. B. Drake.
13188 L/Corpl. J. Driscoll.
13567 Sgt. A. Duckin.
6291 Sgt. C. Duffy.
17411 Sgt. J. H. Dunn.
Lieut. and Qr Mr A. Dunse.
Lieut. A. E. Durand.

Capt. J. F. Edwards (twice).
39139 Sgt. W. H. Edwards.
15685 Corpl. T. W. Elliot.
Capt. A. J. Ellis.
7011 C.Q.M.S. A. Evans (twice).
Lieut. G. S. W. Evans.
Major I. T. Evans (twice).
2nd Lieut. S. Evans.
14408 Pte. S. E. Evans.
Lieut. W. M. Evans.
Lieut. N. V. Everton.
17702 C.Q.M.S. D. A. Ewing.

Capt. J. Farrow (twice).
Major V. Ferguson.
Capt. K. Ffrench (three times).
15059 Sgt. T. Fitzgerald.
16520 C.S.M. C. C. Ford.
Capt. P. G. Fountain.
Major H. G. C. Fowler (twice).
13986 R.S.M. J. Francis.
9239 C.S.M. H. Franklin.
Major W. V. Franklin (twice).
8828 Sgt. J. J. Freeman.
Capt. Lord de Freyne.
11220 Pte. J. H. Fynn.

Capt. A. Galsworthy.
13842 Sgt. W. Gardner.
Capt. K. F. D. Gattie (three times).
Lieut. E. O. Gilbee.
Lieut.-Colonel F. M. Gillespie.
12278 Pte. H. Godfray.
Capt. A. R. Godwin-Austen.
Lieut.-Colonel J. Going.
20048 C.Q.M.S. J. Golightly.
Capt. P. Gottwaltz.
Major T. C. Greenway (three times).
182190 Sgt. E. Griffiths.
22569 Sgt. W. Griffiths.
Lieut.-Colonel J. Grimwood.
2395 Corpl. J. Gronow.
Lieut.-Colonel R. F. Gross (four times).
Lieut.-Colonel R. S. Gwynn (twice).

24115 Corpl. H. A. Hampton.
2nd Lieut. W. H. Hanna.
12737 Pte. E. W. Harcourt.
9125 L/Corpl. W. Harris.
Capt. W. T. Harris.
Lieut. G. A. Harrison.
17876 Corpl. P. T. Heath.
19227 Sgt. G. Hemmings.
Lieut. H. M. Herbert.
Lieut.-Colonel E. V. O. Hewett (twice).
5267 C.S.M. H. Hicks.
Lieut. W. E. Hind (three times).
12909 Sgt. C. Hiscox.
12790 Corpl. R. Hoba.
12640 Sgt. W. Holliday.

26903 Corpl. C. Iball.
38847 Pte. C. W. Iles.
Major H. J. Inglis (twice).

9761 L/Corpl. A. Jeffries.
6083 Corpl. T. C. Jenner.
2nd Lieut. A. E. Johnson.
Lieut.-Colonel D. G. Johnson (three times).
Capt. B. O. Jones.
Capt. J. A. Jones.
Capt. J. R. L. Jones.

2nd Lieut. T. W. Keighley.
2nd Lieut. S. Kelly.
11016 C.S.M. F. Kennington.
16098 Corpl. R. King.
Lieut.-Colonel C. E. Kitchin (five times).
34690 C.S.M. H. J. Kite.

12637 Sgt. D. Lamont.
Major F. G. Lawrence.
10792 Sgt. J. J. Lawrence.
Major W. L. Lawrence.
Brigadier-General H. E. B. Leach.
24042 Pte. W. Lerigo.
16024 Sgt. L. Lewis.
11215 Pte. W. Lewis.
Lieut. H. Littleton-Geach (twice).
Major A. M. O. J. Lloyd (twice).
Capt. A. A. F. Loch.
Lieut. C. B. Lochner (twice).
44627 Corpl. J. K. Loney.
Pte. E. Lowe.
Lieut. E. Lucas.

22177 Sgt. M. Mainwaring.
13171 Pte. J. Maloney.
14869 Corpl. H. Mannion.
Major H. Marr (four times).
48296 Corpl. D. Martin.
14826 C.S.M. W. J. Martin.
Capt. A. G. Masters.
20478 C.S.M. C. Mathews.
Lieut. S. A. Mawson.
Lieut. F. J. L. Mayger.
14697 Pte. L. McCarthy.
14952 Pte. D. M. Macaulay.
15066 Corpl. D. McDonald.
17384 Sgt. N. McPherson.
8943 Sgt. H. Melham.
Lieut. G. S. Mellsopp (twice).
Lieut. J. A. Mellsopp.
17092 Pte. G. Meredith.
Lieut. H. Miller (twice).
Capt. E. E. Mills.

10169 Pte. W. C. Millward.
915 Sgt. F. Milsom.
2nd Lieut. A. C. O. Mitchell.
13096 C.S.M. W. Mitchener.
Major J. H. I. Monteith.
14967 Pte. W. Moore.
Capt. M. C. Morgan (four times).
Major S. C. Morgan.
Major T. H. Morgan.
14726 Pte. W. Morgan.
9618 Pte. W. J. Morgan.
Lieut.-Colonel L. I. G. Morgan-Owen (five times).
Lieut. J. R. Morris.
6021 R.S.M. G. Moses.
Capt. P. R. M. Mundy (twice).
12517 C.S.M. W. Murray.
13113 Sgt. W. Myles (twice).

Capt. A. W. Newton.
Capt. F. J. Ney.
15625 L/Corpl. J. Norman.
Pte. W. Norman.

13274 Corpl. P. O'Grady.
14537 C.S.M. P. J. O'Neil.
Lieut. A. G. Osborn.
12368 C.Q.M.S. O. Ottley.
Lieut. G. M. Owen.
Capt. J. C. Owen (twice).
Capt. C. P. Owens.
Major H. C. Oxley.

14507 Pte. F. Parker.
17619 Sgt. J. Parker.
20057 Sgt. R. Parry.
Lieut.-Colonel C. W. Pearless (four times).
Major N. G. Pearson.
Major R. L. Petre (seven times).
Capt. L. Potts.
17413 Sgt. M. T. Philipps.
Capt. H. H. Philps.
10337 Sgt. T. Pickering.
Lieut. T. Picton (twice).
Capt. W. H. M. Pierson.
Capt. C. F. L. Piggott.
9598 Pte. R. Poole.
Lieut. L. B. Potts.
3692 Sgt. T. Press.
21750 Pte. P. Preston.
Capt. C. M. Pritchard.
Capt. W. O. Pritchard.
Lieut. W. H. Pugh.

HONOURS AND AWARDS

Lieut.-Colonel G. T. Raikes (five times).
Capt. W. T. Raikes (twice).
Capt. V. B. Ramsden (twice).
9595 Pte. A. Ravenhill.
8389 Pte. A. E. Ravenhill.
Brigadier-General A. J. Reddie (seven times).
24807 Corpl. J. Regan.
Major E. T. Rees.
Major A. Reid-Kellett.
9964 Pte. J. R. Rice.
48719 Pte. W. H. Rigby.
5604 C.S.M. W. E. Robinson.
Lieut. F. O. Rogers.
Capt. W. Ross.
Lieut. C. J. Round.
12708 Pte. R. Rowlands.
Capt. S. E. Rumsey (twice).
Capt. W. K. Runham.

Capt. H. M. B. Salmon.
8970 Pte. J. Scott.
8677 C.S.M. W. A. Scott.
11230 C.S.M. C. Searle.
Major C. H. C. Sharp.
16154 Sgt. D. Sherman.
5616 R.S.M. J. Shirley (twice).
13412 L/Corpl. H. W. Simmons.
12745 Pte. W. Simmons.
1010 Corpl. F. Smith.
2nd Lieut. J. Smith.
6215 L/Corpl. S. Smith.
Capt. D. H. S. Somerville (twice).
12596 Sgt. H. Spence.
Capt. W. H. Stanway (twice).
13222 Pte. J. Stevens.
Capt. C. K. Steward (four times).
Capt. D. H. Stickler.
11845 Corpl. C. Stowell.
8898 C.S.M. D. L. Stuart.
8738 C.S.M. H. W. Sudlow.

15183 Pte. H. Tamplin.
17397 Corpl. C. F. Tarrant.
Lieut.-Colonel C. L. Taylor (three times).
9505 R.S.M. W. C. Terrett.
14093 Sgt. B. Thomas.
20250 Sgt. D. H. Thomas.
Major G. C. Thomas.
Capt. H. F. Thomas.
22127 Pte. O. G. J. Thomas.

Major C. M. Tippett (twice).
9836 R.Q.M.S. W. Toothill.
13855 Pte. T. Townsend.
Lieut. H. H. Travers.
Colonel C. V. Trower (four times).
Major E. B. Trower.
12717 Sgt. J. Trumper.
2nd Lieut. S. F. Trusler.
Lieut.-Colonel L. H. Tudor (twice).
Lieut. P. H. Turner.
10582 Pte. J. Turrall.

23563 R.S.M. H. Vatcher.
13274 Corpl. H. Vernall.
Capt. P. L. Villar (twice).

Capt. R. K. B. Walker (twice).
Major G. B. C. Ward.
24563 C.Q.M.S. R. I. Ward.
19738 L/Corpl. J. T. Wardle.
8813 R.Q.M.S. G. Watkins.
15247 Pte. T. H. Watkins.
8957 C.Q.M.S. Weston.
Lieut. C. W. H. White.
20328 Sgt. D. White.
24811 Corpl. W. Whiting.
Capt. E. E. A. Whitworth (twice).
17058 Sgt. J. Wilkinson.
Major A. E. Williams (five times).
23429 O.R.S. C. Williams.
Capt. C. E. Williams.
16214 C.S.M. E. Williams.
2nd Lieut. J. Williams.
7230 Sgt. J. Williams.
16243 Corpl. J. Williams.
13741 Sgt. S. Williams.
18733 Corpl. T. Williams.
Lieut. T. R. Williams.
14801 Sgt. W. O. Williamson.
10685 R.Q.M.S. F. Wiltshire (twice).
Lieut. H. S. Wingard.
14409 Sgt. J. C. Winston.
Capt. T. G. Wood.
20304 Sgt. S. J. Woodall.
17318 L/Corpl. P. Wooldridge.
Capt. C. C. Woolley.
Capt. R. W. Woosnam.
12268 Sgt. H. Worthington.

Major H. P. Yates (twice).

THE ROLL OF HONOUR

(a) OFFICERS.

Addams-Williams, D. A., 2/Lt.
Allaway, T. R., Capt.
Allen, L. R. W., Lt.
Arnold, H. G., 2/Lt.
Austin, T. C. M., Capt.

Bailey, The Hon. J. L., Capt.
Beardshaw, R. D., 2/Lt.
Bedbrook, E. A. St. George, T/2/Lt. (Act. Major).
Behrens, R. P., Lt.
Bell, A. F., 2/Lt.
Bence-Trower, E., M.C., Major.
Bennett, H. S., Lt.
Best, F. H., Lt.
Best, S. W., Lt.
Bill, J. F., Capt.
Birch, F. W., Major.
Blackall-Simonds, G. P., Lt.
Blake, F. S., Capt. (King's Liverpool Regt.).
Blaxland, J. B., Capt.
Bowyer, G. H., 2/Lt.
Bradly, J. F., Lt.
Bricknell, E. T. S., 2/Lt.
Budd, W. J. C., Lt.
Bullock, G. F., 2/Lt.
Bunce, G., 2/Lt.
Burmester, C. M., Capt.
Burrell, P. E., 2/Lt.
Byrne, E. J. W., Capt.

Cass, H. L., 2/Lt.
Chamberlain, J., M.C., Capt.
Charlton, G. F. H., Capt.
Clarke, H. Y. C., 2/Lt.
Coker, C. J., Lt.
Cole, R. H., 2/Lt.
Cooper, F. N. N., Lt. (Royal Army Service Corps).
Cooper, L. G., 2/Lt.
Cracroft-Wilson, C. W., Lt.
Crawford, G. S., Major.
Cullimore, S., Capt.
Curgenven, W. C., Capt.

Darby, E., 2/Lt.
Davies, B. E. S., Capt.
Davies, B. J., Capt.
Davies, G. L., 2/Lt.
Davies, H. H., 2/Lt.
David, A. W., 2/Lt.

David, F. J. L., 2/Lt.
Davies, C. A., 2/Lt.
Davies, G. P., 2/Lt.
Davies, W., Capt.
Davies, W. T., Lt.
Davis, J. W. F. McNaught, Lt.
Deane, L. C. W., D.S.O., T/Major (A/Lt.-Col.).
De Freyne, A. R. F., Lord, Capt.
Dick, W. T., M.C., Capt. & Adjt.
Dickinson, D. C. C., 2/Lt.
Dickinson, F. J. T., Lt. (T/Capt.).
Dixon, L. F., 2/Lt.
Dodd, C. L., M.C., Capt. (Royal Army Medical Corps).
Don, D. F., 2/Lt. (Sherwood Foresters).

Earland, R. J., 2/Lt.
Edwards, E., 2/Lt. (T/Lt.).
Edwards, H., 2/Lt.
Elgee, H. F., Capt.
Evans, A. J., Lt. (A/Capt.).
Evans, F. F., 2/Lt.
Evans, H. P., Lt.
Evans, N., 2/Lt.
Evans, N. V., 2/Lt.
Evans, R., 2/Lt.
Evans, R. G., Lt.
Everton, M. J., 2/Lt.

Fairweather, J., Capt. (T/Major).
Farrier, A., 2/Lt.
Farrow, J., Capt.
Field, A. C. H., 2/Lt. (Royal Fusiliers).
Field, J. A. F., Lt.-Col.
Fletcher, A. S., 2/Lt.
Foster-Morris, H. G. F., 2/Lt.
French, The Hon. E. A., Lt.
French, Hon. G. P., Lt.

Garnett-Botfield, A. C. F., Lt.
Garnett, H. G., Capt. (A/Major).
Garnons-Williams, A. A. C., M.C., Capt.
Gillespie, F. M., Lt.-Col.
Gotelee, G. H., Lt. (A/Capt.).
Gould, R. B., 2/Lt.
Graham, E. M., Lt.
Green, H. S., 2/Lt.
Griffiths, E. A., Lt.
Griffiths, N., 2/Lt.

THE ROLL OF HONOUR

Hadley, R. B., 2/Lt.
Hall, C. E. L., Lt.
Hall, J. E. K., 2/Lt.
Hamer, T. P., Lt.
Harford, J. H., Lt.
Harmood-Banner, W., Capt.
Harries, J. E., 2/Lt.
Haydon, G. M., Lt. (A/Capt.).
Heal, C. H., 2/Lt.
Hemingway, S., Lt.
Heslop, W., Lt.
Hill, P. A., Capt.
Hillman-Miller, J., Lt.
Hillier, S. N., 2/Lt.
Holden, N., 2/Lt.
Homfray, J. R., Lt.
Hooper, E. J. J., Lt.
Hopkins, D. I., 2/Lt.
Hornsby, J. P. S., Capt.
Huggett, W. W., 2/Lt.
Hughes, A. A., Capt.
Hughes, P. C., 2/Lt. (Welch Regt.).
Hughes, W. P., 2/Lt.

Inglis, R. C., Lt.

Jackson, E. P., 2/Lt. (Royal Warwickshire Regt.).
James, F., Lt.
James, G. C. B., Lt.
Jenkins, A., 2/Lt.
Jenkins, C. F. B., Capt.
Jenkins, J. E., Capt.
Jenkins, R. B., 2/Lt.
Jewell, W. J., 2/Lt.
John, I. G., 2/Lt.
Johnson, M. T., Lt.
Jones, B. I. L., 2/Lt.
Jones, D., 2/Lt.
Jones, D., 2/Lt.
Jones, E. G., M.M., 2/Lt.
Jones, G. B., 2/Lt.
Jones, G. W., 2/Lt. (Cheshire Regt.).
Jones, H. T., 2/Lt.
Jones, I. D., T/Lt.
Jones, J. A., Capt.
Jones, R. H., T/Lt.
Jones, R. C. M., 2/Lt.
Jones, T. G., Revd. (Royal Army Chaplains Department).
Jones, T. W., 2/Lt.
Jones, W. O., Major.
Jordan, J., Lt.
Joyce, F. G., Lt.

Kane, A. K., 2/Lt.
Kane, J. G., 2/Lt.
Karran, J. B., 2/Lt.
Kent, H., 2/Lt.
Kent, L. V., 2/Lt. (T/Lt.).
Kerley, B. F., 2/Lt.
Keyzor, H. L. A., 2/Lt.
King, R., 2/Lt.
Kirk, A., 2/Lt.
Kitchen, F. T., 2/Lt.

Lake, J. S. R., Capt.
Langlands, A., 2/Lt.
Lawrence, W. L., D.S.O., Major.
Lee, J. W., 2/Lt.
Le Thicke, G. M., 2/Lt.
Lewis, A. G., 2/Lt.
Lewis, C. V., Lt.
Lewis, L. R., Capt.
Lewis, T. E., Capt.
Livesay, G. A. B., Lt.
Llewellin, W. M. J., 2/Lt.
Llewellyn, H. A., Lt.
Lloyd, E. C., 2/Lt.
Lloyd, L., 2/Lt.
Loch, A. A. F., Capt.
Lowe, A., Lt.
Lowe, A. D. W., M.C., 2/Lt.
Loxton, L. D'Estelle, 2/Lt.
Lucas, C. M., 2/Lt.
Lucas, E., Lt.

McCowan, J., 2/Lt.
MacGregor, C. R., Lt.
Malins, E. F., 2/Lt.
Margesson, E. C., Major.
Martin, H. F., 2/Lt.
Mason, D. C., 2/Lt.
Matthews, W. F., Capt.
Maxwell, I. B., Capt.
Maxwell, W., 2/Lt.
Mayne, V. C. M., Lt.
McLaren, R. J., Capt. (Cheshire Regt.)
McShane, V., Lt. (Northumberland Fusiliers).
Miller-Hallet, S. A., 2/Lt.
Mills, E. E., M.C., Capt.
Mitchell, A. C. O., Lt.
Montague, R. M., 2/Lt.
Moore, A. H., Lt.
Morgan, A., M.C., 2/Lt.
Morgan, F. E., M.C., 2/Lt.
Morgan, I. A., Capt.
Morgan, M., Lt.
Morgan, R. C. W., 2/Lt. (T/Lt.).

Morgan, W. H., 2/Lt.
Morgan, W. R., 2/Lt.
Morgan-Owen, J. G., 2/Lt.
Morris, E. A., 2/Lt.
Morris, O. D., Capt.
Morris, W. H., 2/Lt.
Moss, G. P., 2/Lt.
Moynan, H. O. W., 2/Lt.
Murray, J. C., 2/Lt.

Napier, Sir W. L. (Bart.), Major.
Nethercleft, H. K., 2/Lt.
Nevile, H. G., Lt.
Newman, A., Lt.
Nightingale, W. B., 2/Lt.
Nisbet, D. G., Lt.

Osborn, A. G., Capt.
Owen, E. H., 2/Lt. (Lincolnshire Regt.).
Owen, G. C., 2/Lt.
Owens, C. P., Capt.
Oxley, H. C., Major.

Palmer, R. G., Capt.
Parker, L. R., 2/Lt.
Parry-Davies, D. C., 2/Lt.
Paterson, C. J., Capt.
Peel, A. R., Capt.
Phillips, C. G., 2/Lt.
Phillips, O. S., 2/Lt.
Phillips, R., 2/Lt.
Pierson, W. H. M., M.C., Lt. (A/Capt.).
Platten, W. H., 2/Lt.
Playford, A. B., 2/Lt.
Pollock, M. V., Lt.
Powell, D. B., Lt.
Powell-Jones, P. M., Capt.
Prance, A. C. N., M.C., Lt.
Price, G. W. B., Lt.
Prickard, G. T., 2/Lt.
Pritchard, C. M., Capt.
Pryce-Jenkin, R. D., 2/Lt.
Pugh, H. L., 2/Lt.

Raikes, F. M., 2/Lt.
Reed, C. N., Lt.
Rees, H. C., Major.
Rees, J. O., 2/Lt.
Reid, J. S., 2/Lt.
Renwick, H. A., Lt.
Rice, F., 2/Lt.
Richards, J. H., M.C., Lt.
Roberts, D. C., 2/Lt.
Roberts, W., 2/Lt.

Robertson, G. A. N., Capt.
Robinson, C. G., 2/Lt.
Robinson, J., 2/Lt.
Ross, W., Lt. (A/Capt.).
Rowlands, F. T. R., 2/Lt.
Royle, J. B., Major
Rumbelow, A., 2/Lt.
Rundle, C. N., 2/Lt.

Salathiel, E. G., 2/Lt.
Sandys-Thomas, W. J., 2/Lt.
Saunders, L. D., 2/Lt.
Scott, W., 2/Lt.
Seager, W. H., 2/Lt.
Sharpe, S. A., Lt. (A/Capt.).
Sherer, S. F., 2/Lt.
Silby, T. S., M.C., Lt.
Silk, N. G., Lt.
Sills, C. C., 2/Lt.
Simpson, G., M.C., 2/Lt.
Skinner, H. F. C., 2/Lt.
Smith, R., 2/Lt.
Snelson, V. L., 2/Lt. (Welch Regt.).
Sparrow, G. L., Lt.
Spartali, M., 2/Lt.
Spence, G. S., 2/Lt.
Stanborough, W. T., 2/Lt.
Stephens, G. G. B., 2/Lt.

Talbot, A. A., Lt.
Taylor, E. R., M.C., Capt.
Taylor, R. P., 2/Lt. (Northamptonshire Regt.).
Thomas, C. R., 2/Lt.
Thomas, E. D., 2/Lt.
Thomas, R. I. V. C., 2/Lt.
Thomas, R. P., Lt.
Towler, F. S., 2/Lt.
Travers, H. H., Lt.
Turner, N. P. J., Lt.
Turner, P. H., 2/Lt.

Walshe, F. W., M.C., Capt.
Ward, T. P., 2/Lt.
Ward-Jones, F. V., M.C., 2/Lt.
Watkins, D. J. G., 2/Lt.
Watkins, H. H., 2/Lt.
Weeks, H. W. M., Lt.
Welby, G. E. E., Major.
Wells, T. W. M., 2/Lt.
Wernet, W. E., Capt.
Whitehorn, W. J., Lt.
Wileman, G. W. B., 2/Lt. (A/Capt.).
Wilkinson, S. J., D.S.O., Lt.-Col. (W. Yorkshire Regt.).

THE ROLL OF HONOUR

Williams, C. E., Lt. (T/Capt.).
Williams, D. A., 2/Lt.
Williams, E. H., 2/Lt.
Williams, I. P., 2/Lt. (King's (Shropshire Light Infantry).
Williams, L., Lt.
Williams, L. V., Capt.
Williams, W. F., 2/Lt.
Williams-Vaughan, J. C. A., 2/Lt.
Wilton, C. I., 2/Lt.

Wingard, H. S., 2/Lt.
Wood, C. H., 2/Lt.
Woodward, R., Capt.
Woolley, W. L., 2/Lt.

Yeatman, M. E., Capt.
Yorath, G. L., Lt.
Young, A. J., 2/Lt.

Zacharias, F. H., 2/Lt.

(b) Warrant Officers, Non-Commissioned Officers and Men.

1st Battalion.

Abell, J. C., 13025, Pte.
Abrahams, R., 7201, Pte.
Adams, C., 7272, Pte.
Ager, F., 36178, Pte.
Ainsworth, J., 25066, L/Cpl.
Akers, T., 10049, Sgt.
Alford, J., 29344, Pte.
Allen, J., 15110, Pte.
Allen, S., 48004, L/Cpl.
Allen, T. W., 7885, L/Cpl.
Allison, A., 25877, Pte.
Allman, J., 11489, L/Cpl.
Almond, J., 38934, Pte.
Amos, A. E., 8325, Pte.
Anders, J., 19975, Pte.
Andrews, J., 14205, Pte.
Aram, E., 8079, Pte.
Archer, H. S., 38998, Pte.
Armitage, C. F., 15405, Pte.
Armitt, E., 11160, L/Cpl.
Armstrong, E., 27088, Pte.
Armstrong, J., 19502, Pte.
Arnold, T., 39053, Pte.
Arthan, C., 39146, Pte.
Astley, T. F., 8346 L/Sgt.
Austin, H., 13278, Pte.
Austin, T. G., 11001, L/Cpl.
Atkins, J., 8687, Sgt.
Attewell, A., 19897, Pte.
Attwood, T., 9380, Pte.
Aylwin, F. J., 8111, Pte.

Badger, A., 6909, Pte.
Baggin, R., 8252, Pte.
Bailey, A. J., 10192, L/Cpl.
Bailey, C., 13669, Pte.
Bailey, F., 8287, Pte.
Bailey, J., 36147, Pte.
Bailey, T. E., 15109, Pte.
Bailey, W., 11316, Pte.

Baker, A. J. H., 29124, Pte.
Baker, E., 6174, Pte.
Baker, J., 25827, Pte.
Baker, J., 10174, Pte.
Baker, P., 27195, Pte.
Baker, T., 7090, L/Cpl.
Baker, W., 48008, Pte.
Baldwin, J., 25957, Pte.
Baldwin, W., 25955, Pte.
Banham, F., 18389, Pte.
Barkwell, J., 13819, Sgt.
Barnard, A. C., 8421, Pte.
Barnard, C., 46761, Pte.
Barrett, H. W., 19340, Pte.
Barton, J., 27360, Pte.
Banfield, G., 10109, Pte.
Bannan, P., 11132, Pte.
Barrell, W., 15013, Pte.
Barrett, F. W., 11438, Pte.
Barrett, R., 11058, Pte.
Barton, J., 7069, Pte.
Basnett, R., 33046, L/Cpl.
Bastian, W., 26394, Pte.
Bateman, T., 11010, Pte.
Bath, W., 10983, Pte.
Ball, E., 44364, Pte.
Baldwin, T. G., 44362, Pte.
Beaman, E., 46762, Pte.
Beaton, W., 18950, Pte.
Beatson, J., 11245, Pte.
Beckitt, H., 44371, Pte.
Beddoes, C., 10381, L/Cpl.
Bees, D. J., 11729, L/Cpl.
Belcher, A., 7815, Pte.
Bell, J. T., 11448, Pte.
Bell, W., 9334, A/Cpl.
Benjamin, G., 29118, Pte.
Bennellick, W., 15381, Pte.
Berry, A. E., 44660, Pte.
Berry, S., 7488, Pte.

537

Bessant, D., 15489, Pte.
Bethel, J., 11003, Pte.
Bevan, R., 18474, Pte.
Bevan, S., 15390, Pte.
Bevister, J., 15348, L/Cpl.
Bigwood, W., 11422, L/Cpl.
Binning, H., 10303, Pte.
Bird, T. E., 45704, Pte.
Birmingham, W., 36241, Pte.
Bishop, L. N., 9416, Pte.
Bisp, R., 13221, Pte.
Bland, J., 9119, Pte.
Blaney, W., 26233, Pte.
Blewitt, A. E., 11925, Pte.
Blundell, H., 11637, Pte.
Bradley, H. C., 8734, Pte.
Bradshaw, F., 6632, Pte.
Bradshaw, T., 7880, Pte.
Brain, G., 26122, Pte.
Breach, G., 39123, Pte.
Breddy, C. H., 8761, Pte.
Breeze, E., 11610, Pte.
Breeze, J., 10505, Pte.
Brewis, J. N. S., 11305, Pte.
Brewer, H. G., 36025, Pte.
Brewis, W. T., 13770, Pte.
Brewster, L. S., 16585, Pte. M.M.
Brickly, J., 14236, Pte.
Bridge, T., 38779, Pte.
Brinton, J., 11376, Pte.
Brockway, F., 6637, Pte.
Bromley, D., 13658, Sgt.
Bromley, N., 6380, Pte.
Brown, A., 9454, Pte.
Brown, E. J., 9197, Pte.
Brown, W., 9958, Pte.
Boit, P. E., 45658, Pte.
Booth, S., 25845, Pte.
Burrows, J., 42073, Pte.
Bourne, F. H., 6926, Sgt.
Bowditch, C., 12341, Pte.
Bowen, G. F., 42194, Pte.
Bowles, C., 7286, Pte.
Bowring, J., 48015, Pte.
Boyle, C. H., 11157, Pte.
Buckley, J., 8510, Pte.
Bufton, W. A., 8739, Sgt.
Burcher, H., 11350, Pte.
Burchett, W., 8255, Pte.
Burgess, J., 14635, Pte.
Burgess, S. H., 10002, Pte.
Burke, J., 10255, Pte.
Burke, P., 29683, Pte.
Burke, T., 7424, Pte.
Burling, C., 2281, Pte.

Burns, J. P., 10912, Pte.
Burns, P., 11495, Pte.
Burridge, W., 6492, Pte.
Burrows, R., 48011, Pte.
Burrup, A., 9420, Pte.
Bushell, H. R., 19259, Pte.
Butt, O., 9234, Pte.
Butt, T., 13195, Pte.
Bye, G. A., 44368, Pte.

Cadman, J., 11844, Pte.
Cain, J., 11887, Pte.
Cannell, H. R., 48045, Pte.
Cannon, G., 25380, Pte.
Carless, W., 19480, Pte.
Carson, T., 27599, Pte.
Carter, H., 36438, Pte.
Casson, T. J., 8966, Pte.
Catherall, T., 44497, Pte.
Catlow, S. W., 46490, Pte.
Cattell, W., 45655, Pte.
Caveill, J. C., 29158, Pte.
Chandler, E., 11692, Pte.
Chapman, C. H., 40224, L/Cpl.
Chapman, T., 15168, Pte.
Chapman, W., 15873, A/Cpl. D.C.M.
Charles, O., 14672, Pte.
Chinchen, F. W., 8315, Pte.
Chittock, A., 35186, Pte.
Churchill, T., 35541, Pte.
Clark, E., 8054, Pte.
Clark, J. A., 35648, Pte.
Clark, T., 8114, Pte.
Clarke, T., 44723, Pte.
Clarke, W., 14985, Pte.
Clarke, W. H., 11135, Pte.
Clarke, W., 45688, Pte.
Clifford, P., 6101, Pte.
Clifford, W. T., 7975, L/Sgt.
Clingo, W., 11803, Sgt.
Clutterbuck, J. E., 7420, L/Cpl.
Coan, T., 46774, Pte.
Cobham, L., 38781, Pte.
Cochrane, W., 9336, Pte.
Cocklin, J., 8811, Pte.
Colbert, B., 11421, Cpl.
Colclough, I., 10914, Pte.
Cole, H., 8669, L/Cpl.
Coleman, T., 13093, L/Cpl. M.M.
Coles, F., 11345, Pte.
Collin, H. G., 44308, Pte.
Collins, D., 15122, Pte.
Colston, A., 11476, Pte.
Coltman, A., 8429, Pte.
Colverson, F., 22813, Pte.

THE ROLL OF HONOUR

Compton, D., 13711, Pte.
Conibere, F. J., 25001, Pte.
Connor, P., 38921, Pte.
Connors, M., 14656, Pte.
Cooil, J. D., 25453, Pte.
Cook, J., 8161, Pte.
Cooke, A. J. W., 24735, Cpl.
Cooke, J., 8518, L/Cpl.
Cooksley, F. J., 15077, Pte.
Coombey, W., 13893, Pte.
Coomby, R., 26078, Pte.
Cooper, H., 39148, L/Cpl.
Corfield, H., 26136, Pte.
Corrin, T., 42102, Cpl.
Corse, F., 11123, Pte.
Coslett, D. J., 15108, Pte.
Costin, R., 13095, Pte.
Cotter, D., 17416, Pte.
Coulson, G., 8821, Cpl.
Cox, A., 12452, L/Cpl.
Cox, J., 14840, Pte.
Cox, J., 27705, Pte.
Craigie, J. W., 44375, Pte.
Cramer, A. H. L., 8960, Pte.
Craze, C., 36393, Pte.
Crimmins, J., 13758, Pte.
Croft, C., 8433, Pte.
Crook, H., 6747, Pte.
Crowe, P., 6100, Pte.
Cudlipp, H., 8785, L/Cpl.
Cullen, T., 46773, Pte.
Cunningham, W., 8700, Pte.
Curnick, G., 8835, Pte.
Curtis, W. J., 22864, Pte.
Cushen, D. W., 10940, Pte.

Danaher, B., 26266, Pte.
Daniels, G., 13733, Cpl.
Daniels, J., 13096, Pte.
Daniels, R., 7229, Pte.
Daniels, W., 18814, Pte.
Darbon, C., 5858, C.S.M.
Davidson, C. B., 23650, Pte.
Davies, B., 39072, Pte.
Davies, C. J., 10854, Pte.
Davies, D., 11654, Pte.
Davies, D., 8254, Cpl.
Davies, D. G., 29739, Pte.
Davies, E. J., 33608, Pte.
Davies, G., 11005, Pte.
Davies, H. E. G., 12006, Sgt.
Davies, I., 9414, Pte.
Davies, J., 12005, Pte.
Davies, J., 46777, Pte.
Davies, L., 19967, Cpl.

Davies, R., 36294, Pte.
Davies, R., 33009, Pte.
Davies, S., 11113, Pte.
Davies, T., 11851, Pte.
Davies, T., 10785, Pte.
Davies, T., 13243, Pte.
Davies, T., 29077, Pte.
Davies, T., 8852, Pte.
Davies, W., 11898, Pte.
Davies, W. D., 29742, Pte
Davies, W. R., 8311, Pte.
Davis, L., 36553, Pte.
Davis, R., 9724, L/Sgt.
Day, J., 13405, A/Cpl.
Day, R., 10137, Pte.
Deacon, H., 11907, Pte.
Deakin, T., 11690, Pte.
Deans, C., 11419, Pte.
Delan, E. L., 10827, Pte.
Denning, W. R., 29343, Pte.
Denny, J., 8470, Pte.
Dick, W. J., 14333, Pte.
Dilley, J., 8731, Pte.
Dickinson, H., 6396, Pte.
Dix, D., 31247, Pte.
Dix, F., 11630, Pte.
Dobbs, W. H., 25819, Pte.
Dobinson, J., 6304, Pte.
Dodd, G., 38658, Pte.
Doidge, J., 29734, Pte.
Donavon, D., 6434, Pte.
Donovan, E., 8457, Pte.
Doswell, C. E., 11085, Pte.
Dowding, H., 36484, Pte.
Downes, C. A., 18498, L/Cpl.
Doyle, J., 13591, Pte.
Drake, J., 46042, Pte.
Driscoll, J., 8352, A/Cpl.
Driscoll, J., 14707, Pte.
Driver, F., 36337, Pte.
Drury, G., 45652, Pte.
Duckworth, G., 11179, Sgt.
Dudman, T., 7248, Pte.
Dufty, H., 14213, Pte.
Duffus, J. V., 39125, Pte.
Dumper, F. H., 7887, Pte.
Duncan, J., 25660, Pte.
Dunk, A. L. S., 44667, L/Cpl.
Dunkley, S., 46342, Pte.
Dunn, T., 10869, Pte.
Durbin, A., 11526, Pte.
Durbin, J. A., 6515, Pte.
Dwane, W. J., 8209, Sgt.
Dyke, J., 13674, Pte.
Dykes, T., 7827, Pte.

THE HISTORY OF THE SOUTH WALES BORDERERS

Eagle, A. E., 10882, Pte.
Early, P., 7464, Pte.
East, C., 6316, Pte.
Ebdon, G. W., 12377, Pte.
Edmond, A. T., 11804, Pte.
Edmunds, J., 25593, Pte.
Edwards, A. J., 9514, Pte.
Edwards, A. E., 8013, L/Cpl.
Edwards, G., 35329, Pte.
Edwards, J., 13683, Pte.
Edwards, J. T., 39059, Sgt.
Edwards, L. J., 11537, L/Sgt.
Edwards, T., 11544, Pte.
Edwards, W., 11133, Pte.
Egan, J. J., 10931, L/Cpl.
Elliott, E. W., 13097, Pte.
Ellis, A., 39149, Pte.
Ellis, A. H., 7323, L/Cpl. M.M.
Ellis, R., 7932, Pte.
Elmore, A., 10905, Pte.
Elson, T., 6141, Pte.
England, C., 9112, L/Cpl.
Erney, W., 15148, Pte.
Evans, A., 11902, Pte.
Evans, A., 11242, Pte.
Evans, B., 13461, Pte.
Evans, D. M., 14878, Pte.
Evans, D., 14673, Pte.
Evans, E., 26310, L/Sgt.
Evans, E. G., 30380, Pte.
Evans, E., 26110, Pte.
Evans, E. I., 10539, L/Cpl.
Evans, F., 11061, Pte.
Evans, G. W., 9006, Pte.
Evans, H., 8137, Pte.
Evans, J., 7218, Pte.
Evans, J., 35435, Pte.
Evans, J. H., 15718, Pte.
Evans, J., 14654, Cpl.
Evans, J., 13423, Pte.
Evans, J., 11628, Pte.
Evans, L., 22018, Pte.
Evans, R., 13499, Pte.
Evans, R. J., 39120, Pte.
Evans, T., 15017, Sgt.
Evans, T., 11510, Pte.
Evans, W., 12008, Pte.
Evans, W. D., 33612, Pte.
Evans, W. J., 46926, Pte.
Eyres, J., 48055, Pte.

Fabian, A., 36527, Pte.
Fairclough, G. H., 15283, Pte.
Farquharson, W., 46978, Pte.
Farrow, T. R., 34507, L/Cpl.

Faulkner, R., 11617, Pte.
Fawdry, F., 11571, Pte.
Field, G. A., 10664, L/Cpl.
Fieldhouse, E., 34515, Pte.
Fielding, T., 8391, Pte.
Findlow, T., 29446, Pte.
Fish, R. J., 10995, Pte.
Fitchett, E. E., 11626, Pte.
Fitzmorris, R., 11831, Pte.
FitzPatrick, J., 13027, Pte. D.C.M.
Fitzpatrick, J., 41150, Pte.
Fitzpatrick, T., 14399, Pte.
Flertey, E., 8684, Pte.
Fletcher, H., 9217, C.S.M.
Flexney, F. W., 8548, Pte.
Forrest, A., 46352, Pte.
Forster, H., 48063, Pte.
Foster, A. W., 10729, Dmr. D.C.M.
Foweather, H., 10955, Sgt.
Francis, R., 13226, Pte.
Francis, W., 11153, Pte. D.C.M.
Franklin, E., 10696, L/Cpl.
Franklin, F., 19860, Pte.
Franklin, W. N., 8115, Pte.
Foley, J., 11165, Pte.
Forknall, J., 9114, Pte.
Foskett, J., 9339, Pte.
French, N. J., 19333, L/Cpl.
Friend, E., 9021, Sgt.
Frowd, H., 11644, Pte.
Fuller, F. J., 9369, Pte.

Gabb, A. J., 22228, Pte.
Gage, J. T., 10699, Cpl.
Gale, F., 13001, Pte.
Galozie, D., 18523, L/Cpl.
Gamlin, H., 12987, L/Cpl.
Gane, F., 10713, Pte.
Gardiner, J., 9483, A/Sgt.
Gardner, J., 7080, Pte.
Gardner, J., 36535, Pte.
Garner, J., 19966, Pte.
Gatsell, W. H., 7477, Pte.
Gayland, F. G., 46793, Pte.
Geoghan, W., 9003, Pte.
Gerrard, W., 8091, Pte.
Gettings, G., 11105, Pte.
Gibbins, W., 33479, Pte.
Gibbons, J., 12375, Pte.
Gibbs, F. H., 13202, Pte.
Gilbert, E. G., 25994, Pte.
Giles, B. J., 27306, L/Cpl.
Giles, J., 13988, Pte.
Gilfoil, E., 38000, Pte.
Gill, J. W., 8803, Pte.

THE ROLL OF HONOUR

Gimblett, T., 11919, Pte.
Gittins, J. H., 10838, Pte.
Goddard, H., 45707, Pte.
Godfrey, H., 12278, Pte.
Goldsmith, G., 9668, L/Cpl.
Goldstone, C. E., 10661, Pte.
Goodbody, F., 34524, Pte.
Goulding, G., 13798, Pte.
Goulding, T., 23416, L/Cpl.
Gorman, J., 13345, A/Cpl.
Gosney, H., 10644, Pte.
Grace, T., 11080, Pte.
Gradie, W., 11783, Pte.
Graham, W. H., 23876, Pte.
Gray, G. R., 19087, Pte.
Gray, W., 11193, Pte.
Green, E., 44730, Pte.
Green, H. D., 9055, A/C.S.M.
Green, J., 15276, Pte.
Green, M., 11252, Pte.
Greening, W. T., 8881, L/Cpl.
Greenham, W. H., 11733, Pte.
Grendon, W., 19268, L/Cpl.
Griffin, H., 7494, Pte.
Griffiths, D., 14233, Pte.
Griffiths, D., 44499, Pte.
Griffiths, E., 44133, Pte.
Griffiths, E., 14650, Pte.
Griffiths, T. C., 14927, Pte.
Griffiths, T. H., 34759, Pte.
Grimes, A., 7963, Pte.
Groom, A., 45677, Pte.
Gundy, E. C., 29126, Pte.
Gunnell, A. E., 11052, Pte.
Gunter, H. C., 8238, Sgt. D.C.M.
Guthrie, T., 42331, Pte. M.M.

Haines, J., 10127, Pte.
Hale, A., 13218, Pte.
Hall, G., 42087, L/Cpl.
Hall, S., 13643, Pte.
Ham, A., 13584, Pte.
Hamer, W. A., 46813, Pte.
Hamilton, H. W., 22833, Pte.
Hammond, A. J., 8692, Pte.
Hammond, W. J., 9160, L/Cpl.
Hanbury, W. G., 15237, Pte.
Hands, J., 6269, Pte.
Hanford, T., 13791, Pte. M.M.
Hanford, W., 14630, Pte.
Hannan, C., 15123, Pte.
Hard, W. J., 12895, Pte.
Harding, C. A. G., 7936, Pte.
Harding, J., 10561, Pte.
Harding, J., 11889, Pte.

Harding, W. G., 22979, Pte.
Hargeaves, J., 8112, Pte.
Harris, A. H., 10842, Pte.
Harris, E., 8380, Pte.
Harris, E. W., 44586, Pte.
Harris, E., 11970, Pte.
Harris, F., 38839, Pte.
Harris, H., 24439, Sgt. M.M.
Harris, H., 13257, Pte.
Harris, J., 12406, Pte.
Harris, W., 11722, Pte.
Harrod, A., 18871, Pte.
Harker, A., 46377, Pte.
Hardy, A., 7918, Pte.
Harvey, A. E., 11981, Pte.
Harvey, J., 10840, A/Cpl.
Harvey, J., 26256, Pte.
Hathaway, S. E. W., 8100, L/Cpl.
Haughton, F., 42047, A/Sgt.
Hawkins, F., 8147, Pte.
Haworth, F., 38829, Pte.
Haydon, W. B., 14924, Pte.
Hayes, H. F., 50136, Pte.
Hayes, R., 9408, Pte.
Haywood, A. J., 45725, Pte.
Hazel, T., 14982, Pte.
Heard, T. H., 24758, Pte.
Hearne, C., 11874, Pte.
Heathcote, E. G. B., 45697, Pte.
Hedford, T., 8180, Pte.
Hennessey, R., 15187, Pte.
Herbert, H., 13039, Pte.
Hern, I., 11403, Pte.
Herrington, H. W., 11116, L/Cpl.
Hicks, B., 36145, Pte.
Higgs, F. J., 5998, A/Cpl.
Higgins, W., 15124, A/Cpl.
Higham, G. S., 8073, Pte.
Hill, A., 10656, Pte.
Hill, H., 15831, Pte.
Hills, F. G., 6873, L/Sgt.
Hilton, S., 10832, Pte.
Hinton, S., 6627, Pte.
Hockley, S., 26108, L/Cpl. M.M.
Hodge, J. F., 8563, Pte.
Hodges, W. H., 10857, Pte.
Hodges, W., 33231, Pte.
Hodges, W. J., 14706, Cpl. M.M.
Hodkinson, J. W., 46370, Pte.
Hodgkinson, L., 48828, Pte.
Hoffman, J., 10235, Pte.
Hoffman, P. G., 25681, Pte.
Hole, W. G., 13715, Pte.
Holland, H., 11807, Pte.
Holland, W., 16359, Pte.

Holley, A., 5711, Pte.
Hollis, W. C., 7928, Sgt.
Holt, W., 11087, Pte.
Honeywell, A. E., 7907, Pte.
Hood, A., 14708, Pte.
Hooker, A. H., 44323, Pte.
Hooper, E. C., 6513, Pte.
Hopkins, A. E., 8635, Sgt.
Hornsby, W. E., 36260, Pte.
Horrigan, D., 14149, Pte.
Hoskins, T., 11881, Pte.
Hoskins, W., 10869, Pte.
Hough, T., 46385, Pte.
Houghton, A., 44618, Pte.
Houssein, L., 45730.
Howarth, A. P., 11182, L/Cpl.
Howcroft, H., 8740, Pte.
Howells, F., 13042, Pte.
Howells, J., 8878, Pte.
Howes, C., 11014, Pte.
Hucker, J. H., 8670, L/Cpl.
Hudson, E., 36464, Pte.
Hufton, B., 7836, Pte.
Hughes, B., 29136, Pte.
Hughes, H., 28943, Pte.
Hughes, I. B., 25381, Pte.
Hughes, J. E., 25402, Pte.
Hughes, O., 11688, Pte.
Hughes, T. H., 14851, L/Cpl.
Hughes, T. J., 39055, Pte.
Hulbert, L., 5748, R.Q.M.S.
Hull, J. A., 25594, L/Cpl. M.M.
Humphreys, M., 9056, A/Cpl.
Humphries, A. J., 3927, T/R.S.M.
Hunt, A., 10940, Pte.
Hunt, J. T., 11910, Pte.
Hunt, W., 11752, L/Cpl.
Hunter, J. W., 8084, Pte.
Hurley, T., 9619, Pte.
Hurley, T., 11298, Pte.
Hutchins, A., 8338, Pte.
Hutton, J. T., 48076, Pte.
Hyatt, W., 13747, Pte.
Hynes, F., 11148, Pte.

Ince, A., 18230, Pte.
Inker, T., 27686, Pte.
Inskip, R., 8061, Pte.
Ireland, H. A., 10794, Cpl.
Irvine, A. H., 46394, Pte.
Isaac, R., 35284, Pte.

Jackson, A., 25842, Pte.
Jagger, C., 24602, Pte.
James, A. T., 7450, Sgt.
James, D. T., 4804, Sgt.
James, J. P. A., 10266, A/Sgt.
Jarman, H., 9025, Pte.
Jayne, A., 7247, L/Cpl.
Jefferies, G. W., 11209, Pte.
Jenkins, B., 13730, Cpl.
Jenkins, D., 14124, Pte.
Jenkins, D. J., 10728, Sgt.
Jenkins, F., 15149, Pte.
Jenkins, L., 7814, L/Cpl.
Jenkins, W. J., 23141, Pte.
Jennings, H., 11773, Pte.
Johns, J., 13208, L/Cpl.
Johnson, W., 40967, Pte.
Johnson, W., 39050, Pte.
Jones, A., 10706, Sgt.
Jones, B., 13722, Pte.
Jones, C., 32079, Pte.
Jones, C., 11725, Pte.
Jones, C., 46819, Pte.
Jones, D., 25271, Pte.
Jones, D., 15586, Pte.
Jones, E., 6869, Pte.
Jones, E. T., 29280, Pte.
Jones, E., 11671, Pte.
Jones, E. J., 27180, Pte.
Jones, F., 46397, Pte.
Jones, F., 10210, Pte.
Jones, F., 8257, Pte.
Jones, G., 9793, Pte.
Jones, G. H., 15409, Pte.
Jones, H., 19180, Cpl.
Jones, H., 11030, Pte.
Jones, H. F., 44550, Pte.
Jones, J., 12700, Pte.
Jones, J., 8853, Pte.
Jones, J., 15270, Pte.
Jones, J., 39167, Pte.
Jones, J., 44493, Sgt.
Jones, J., 7974, Pte.
Jones, J., 9050, Sgt. M.M.
Jones, J., 13182, Pte.
Jones, J., 7093, Pte.
Jones, J. R., 33620, Pte.
Jones, P., 39154, Pte.
Jones, R., 8472, L/Cpl.
Jones, R., 26257, Pte.
Jones, S., 11352, Pte.
Jones, T., 8693, Pte.
Jones, T., 11957, Pte.
Jones, T., 11632, Pte.
Jones, W., 14072, Pte.
Jones, W., 10439, Pte.
Jones, W., 11833, Pte.
Jones, W. A., 29740, Pte.

THE ROLL OF HONOUR

Jones, W. H., 7322, Pte.
Jones, W. H., 8946, Pte.
Jones, W. O., 28985, Pte.
Johnson, G., 18829, L/Cpl.
Jordan, G. O., 8234, Pte.
Joy, J., 13064, Pte.

Keeffe, J., 10278, Pte.
Keevill, W. W., 24642, Cpl.
Kellett, J., 41153, Pte.
Kelly, J., 11830, Pte.
Kelly, R., 13888, Pte.
Kemp, E., 8749, Pte.
Kenton, E. J., 44683, Pte.
Kew, C., 7807, Pte.
Kew, J., 18924, Cpl.
Kiley, T., 11081, Pte.
King, J. H., 11354, Pte.
Kirkland, S. A., 7259, L/Cpl.
Knight, L., 45953, L/Cpl.
Kyle, A. W., 10046, Pte.

Lacey, H., 8817, L/Sgt.
Lake, F., 8579, Pte.
Lake, W. J., 11900, Pte.
Lane, J. H., 36591, Pte.
Lane, J. M., 9728, Pte.
Langman, E., 37808, Pte.
Lassen, J., 25731, Pte.
Lawman, G., 46843, Pte.
Lawrence, W., 10868, Pte.
Lawron, W. J., 8378, Pte.
Layland, J. A., 10986, Pte.
Layton, J., 25854, L/Cpl.
Leaker, J. H., 12022, Pte.
Leatherbarrow, E., 48709, Pte.
Leddington, C., 18995, Pte.
Lee, B. S., 46839, Pte.
Lee, E. P., 29159, Pte.
Lee, J., 10374, L/Cpl.
Lee, J. T., 25946, L/Cpl. M.M.
Lee, S., 10767, Pte.
Leek, W., 19541, Pte.
Leigh, E., 6828, Pte.
Lester, H.-A., 9906, L/Cpl.
Letton, A., 8198, C.S.M.
Levy, L., 36565, Pte.
Lewer, G. H., 26232, L/Cpl.
Lewis, A., 11384, Pte.
Lewis, A., 11128, Pte.
Lewis, A. E., 11408, Pte.
Lewis, A., 20786, Pte.
Lewis, D., 11562, Pte.
Lewis, D. J., 7904, Pte.
Lewis, E. J., 8553, L/Cpl.

Lewis, F., 13229, Pte.
Lewis, G. T., 44607, Pte.
Lewis, I., 12678, Pte.
Lewis, P., 9652, Pte.
Lewis, R., 9178, L/Cpl. D.C.M.
Lewis, T., 13181, Pte.
Lewis, W., 18547, Pte.
Lewis, W. T., 6465, Pte.
Lewtas, J. P., 46408, Cpl.
Lightwood, J. W., 10754, L/Cpl.
Linney, J., 13601, Pte.
Little, T., 44611, Pte.
Lixton, J. H., 8578, Pte.
Llanfear, C., 13779, Pte.
Lloyd, I., 28289, Pte.
Lloyd, J., 14700, Cpl.
Lloyd, J., 10463, L/Cpl.
Lloyd, T. F., 41143, Pte.
Lloyd, W., 9374, Pte.
Lloyd, W. J., 13849, Pte.
Long, J., 10413, Pte.
Longley, A., 9962, Cpl.
Loughlin, T., 10801, Pte.
Looney, W., 44629, Pte.
Lovegrove, A., 10840, Pte.
Lowe, J. H., 8159, Sgt.
Lowe, J., 19157, Pte.
Lynch, H., 8292, Pte.

Macaulay, D. M., 14952, Pte. D.C.M. and clasp, M.M.
Macey, L. F., 30080, Pte.
Madden, J., 44714, Pte.
Maher, P., 13291, Pte.
Mahon, W. H. J., 11015, Pte.
Mahoney, J., 11327, Pte.
Mahoney, N. P., 8897, Cpl.
Mahoney, T., 15268, Pte.
Maiden, A. J., 7818, A/Cpl.
Maidment, W., 15173, Pte.
Main, G. A., 11758, Pte.
Mancey, A. G., 9353, Pte.
Mandale, R. B., 40204, Pte.
Mann, F. C., 44326, Pte.
Mann, R. E., 11126, Pte.
Mansell, E., 36437, Pte.
Mansfield, W., 9194, L/Sgt.
Marshall, T., 8101, Pte.
Marston, G., 38943, Pte.
Martin, E. G., 44689, Pte.
Martin, E., 48966, Pte.
Martin, P., 10794, Pte.
Matthews, M., 11287, Pte.
Matthews, S. H., 14073, Pte.
Matthews, S., 13395, Pte.

Mattocks, W., 11280, L/Cpl.
Mayersbeth, R., 9857, L/Cpl.
Mayes, F., 7859, Pte.
Mazzei, L., 8673, Pte.
McCartney, H., 38862, Pte.
McDermott, G., 24593, Pte.
McHardy, H., 38865, Pte.
McKenzie, J. L., 44329, Pte.
McLeod, N., 9511, Sgt.
McNeill, J., 13058, Sgt.
Meek, G. E., 9847, A/Cpl.
Mercer, H., 41156, Pte.
Meredith, C., 11985, Pte.
Meredith, G., 8558, Pte.
Miles, T., 11974, Pte.
Miles, W., 13379, L/Cpl.
Miles, W. G., 23925, Sgt.
Miller, H. F., 24881, A/Cpl.
Mills, G. H. T., 8788, Pte.
Mills, T., 15109, Pte.
Mills, W., 13765, Pte.
Mills, W., 10911, Pte.
Mills, W., 10984, Pte.
Millward, A., 23848, Pte.
Milton, W. J., 8652, Sgt. D.C.M., M.M.
Minon, D., 8188, Pte.
Minshall, W. T., 41146, Pte.
Miskell, J., 13255, Pte.
Moffatt, C. W., 25236, Pte. M.M.
Mogford, G., 13242, Pte.
Monaghan, P., 11649, Pte.
Monks, T., 11297, Pte.
Morgan, C., 8014, Sgt.
Morgan, E., 13367, Pte.
Morgan, H., 13232, Pte.
Morgan, J., 11475, Pte.
Morgan, S. C., 8784, Pte.
Morgan, T., 14735, Sgt.
Morgan, W., 11741, Pte.
Morgan, W., 26089, Pte.
Morgan, W. J., 18300, Pte.
Morgan, W. J., 8039, Pte.
Morgans, D., 39052, Pte.
Morgans, M., 10994, Pte.
Morris, E., 18430, Pte.
Morris, F., 4622, Pte.
Morris, G., 13108, Pte.
Morris, G., 9404, Pte.
Morris, G., 22394, Cpl.
Morris, J., 9132, Sgt.
Morris, S. B., 10924, Pte.
Mortin, E., 6833, Pte.
Moss, C. H., 9255, L/Cpl.
Moss, E. G., 9318, Pte.

Moyle, G., 6426, Pte.
Mulchay, T. H., 15041, Pte.
Mulford, H. G., 44688, Cpl. M.M.
Murphy, J., 8012, Pte.
Murphy, J., 10318, Sgt.
Murphy, P., 14496, Pte. D.C.M.
Murphy, T., 15267, Pte.
Murphy, W., 36012, Pte.
Murray, M., 49977, Pte.
Musker, P., 11029, L/Cpl.

Naylor, F., 44729, Pte.
Nethercott, G., 10525, Pte.
Newell, A. J., 45696, Pte.
Newport, B. F., 42097, Pte.
Newman, W. J., 9351, Pte.
Nicholls, F., 8718, Pte.
Norton, S. H., 8880, Pte.
Norvil, H., 8343, Pte.
Nugent, M., 14271, A/Sgt.

O'Callaghan, M., 10892, Pte.
O'Connor, T., 8196, Pte.
O'Neil, J., 9386, Pte.
O'Neil, J., 11331, Pte.
O'Neil, P., 11091, Pte.
O'Sullivan, W., 11125, Pte.
O'Toole, D. P., 8192, Sgt. D.C.M.
Oliver, G. H., 10837, Pte.
Orman, R., 9311, A/Sgt.
Overend, H., 31618, Pte.
Owen, B., 25302, L/Cpl.
Owen, D. C., 11079, Pte.
Owen, J. L., 39046, Cpl.
Owen, T., 46866, Pte.
Owens, G., 26269, Pte.
Owens, J. W., 37797, Pte.
Owens, O., 10004, Pte.
Owens, W., 46864, Pte.

Packham, C. A., 9124, Pte.
Padgett, O., 6425, Pte.
Page, W., 11060, Pte.
Page, W., 8067, Pte.
Paget, H., 27179, Pte.
Pakes, D. H., 25894, L/Cpl.
Palmer, D., 18468, Pte.
Palmer, G., 6280, Pte.
Palmer, W., 14411, Pte.
Pargeter, W., 9860, Cpl.
Parker, E., 21214, Pte.
Parker, F., 13022, L/Cpl.
Parker, G., 8242, Pte.
Parker, W. H., 9382, Pte.
Parr, W., 7325, L/Cpl.

THE ROLL OF HONOUR

Parrish, W. H., 37688, Pte.
Parrott, A. J. W., 14203, Pte.
Parrott, F. C., 44333, Pte.
Parry, E., 42549, Pte.
Parry, G., 7767, Sgt.
Patton, D., 40916, Pte.
Payne, E., 25579, Pte.
Payne, P., 11264, Pte.
Payne, T. J., 24935, Pte.
Pearce, W. H., 7409, Pte.
Pearn, J. S., 11192, Pte.
Peerless, T. B., 44691, Pte.
Peploe, R., 11860, Pte.
Perkin, W. J., 7215, Pte.
Perks, W. E., 8189, Pte.
Pert, J. E., 13003, Pte.
Perry, A., 18477, L/Cpl.
Perry, F. J., 13219, Pte.
Peskett, F., 10926, Drmr.
Peters, H., 11344, A/Cpl.
Pettit, C. G., 9449, Pte.
Phillips, C., 11586, Pte.
Phillips, D. J., 11204, Pte.
Phillips, J., 13187, Pte.
Phillips, S., 11938, Pte.
Pickersgill, J., 44733, Pte.
Picking, C. F., 9126, Pte.
Picking, J., 12912, A/Cpl.
Pike, E. G., 22565, Pte.
Pitt, H., 7800, Sgt.
Porch, L. H., 11019, Pte.
Potts, C., 25409, Pte.
Powell, H., 13531, Pte.
Powell, J., 13412, Pte.
Powell, T., 26181, Pte.
Powell, T. W., 8534, Pte.
Power, E., 11219, Pte.
Power, J., 5402, Sgt. D.C.M.
Power, J., 8353, Pte.
Power, T., 14449, Pte.
Powis, J., 11104, Pte.
Pratt, H., 10440, Pte.
Preston, M. H., 46868, Pte.
Preston, P. H., 25604, L/Cpl.
Price, B., 8381, Pte.
Price, C., 13897, Pte.
Price, C., 11782, Pte.
Price, J., 15383, Pte.
Price, J., 7950, Pte.
Price, J., 11205, Pte.
Price, J. M., 10420, Pte.
Price, J. P., 7812, Pte.
Price, M., 18513, Sgt.
Price, P., 39140, Pte.
Price, R., 13921, Pte.

Price, T., 11687, Pte.
Price, T., 11744, Pte.
Price, W. A., 7924, Pte.
Probert, P., 11037, Pte.
Prouse, J., 11093, L/Cpl.
Prout, A. J., 9417, Sgt.
Prothero, D., 13610, Pte.
Pryce, S. M., 25555, L/Cpl.
Pygott, W. H., 24014, Pte.

Quill, D., 11913, Pte.
Quinn, W., 8403, Pte.

Rae, F. J., 44619, Pte.
Ranger, J., 13506, Pte.
Rappell, E. J., 11564, Pte.
Rawlinson, F., 9023, Pte.
Reade, B. J., 10889, L/Cpl.
Reardon, M., 11042, Pte.
Rees, E., 31436, Pte.
Rees, G., 15090, Sgt.
Rees, L., 16616, Pte.
Rees, S., 19856, Pte.
Rees, T., 30142, Pte.
Rees, W., 11576, Pte.
Rees, W. E., 8820, Pte.
Reddy, J., 18773, Pte.
Redfern, A. J., 42113, Pte.
Regan, M., 11998, Pte.
Reeves, W., 9963, Pte.
Reynolds, W., 10727, Cpl.
Rhodes, J. A., 9371, Pte.
Ribbon, F., 15081, Pte.
Richards, A., 11879, Pte.
Richards, D. L., 11043, Pte.
Richards, H., 14901, Pte.
Richards, M., 14769, Pte.
Richards, W. K., 29062, Pte.
Rickards, W. H., 6043, A/C.Q.M.S.
Rideout, F., 7979, Pte.
Ridley, J., 10811, Pte.
Rigby, J. C., 48124, Pte. M.M.
Riley, H., 42090, Pte.
Ringham, R., 9368, Pte.
Roach, T., 11955, Pte.
Roderick, D., 11106, Pte.
Robbins, E. C., 26482, Pte.
Robbins, J. J., 10929, Pte.
Roberts, A., 10709, Pte.
Roberts, C., 8782, Pte.
Roberts, C. W. G., 10257, Sgt.
Roberts, E. P., 9705, Cpl.
Roberts, F., 10815, Pte.
Roberts, J. W., 11592, Cpl.
Roberts, J., 5802, Pte.

Roberts, S., 11771, Cpl.
Robins, J., 6901, Pte.
Robinson, H., 35888, Pte.
Robinson, M., 6453, Pte.
Rogers, E., 7813, Pte.
Rogers, F., 8463, Pte.
Rogers, T. J., 7447, Pte.
Rogers, W. J., 13754, Pte.
Rolfe, G. J., 9242, Pte.
Roscoe, J., 42379, Pte.
Roseman, E., 35577, Pte.
Rowell, L., 25602, Pte.
Royster, A., 13749, Pte.
Ruck, C., 8282, L/Cpl.
Rumsey, W., 22636, Pte.
Russell, A., 42057, Pte.
Ryan, D., 6339, Pte.
Ryan, M., 11577, Pte. D.C.M.
Ryan, R., 15418, Pte.

Samuel, V., 35362, Pte.
Savage, J. H., 9214, Sgt.
Scholes, J., 7892, Pte.
Scothorne, C., 8160, Pte.
Scott, W. W., 9390, Pte.
Scurlock, E. G., 11779, Pte.
Seacombe, A., 11601, Pte.
Sealey, F., 7341, Pte.
Sear, A. W., 7361, Pte.
Selcovitch, H., 49003, Pte.
Sharp, A., 11012, L/Cpl.
Shaw, C, 6945, Pte.
Shea, F., 10331, Pte.
Sheehan, D., 11492, L/Cpl.
Shephard, R. P., 13537, Pte.
Sherwood, A. W., 8826, Drmr.
Short, B. O. P., 29164, Pte.
Shorthouse, H., 11800, Pte.
Shute, W., 31668, Pte.
Sinclair, A., 16473, A/Cpl.
Sinclair, J. H., 46901, Pte.
Singleton, J., 15941, Pte.
Skidmore, G. H., 44340, Pte.
Skidmore, W., 44341, Pte.
Skinner, F., 8690, Pte.
Slade, F., 11917, Pte.
Slater, E. W., 9219, Sgt.
Slattery, M., 13923, Pte.
Smale, R., 11257, Pte.
Smith, E. W., 6228, L/Cpl.
Smith, F., 7916, Pte.
Smith, G. E., 10894, L/Cpl.
Smith, G., 11206, Pte.
Smith, H. T., 9337, Pte.
Smith, J., 11829, L/Cpl.

Smith, J., 15401, Pte.
Smith, J., 11559, Pte.
Smith, R., 14686, L/Cpl.
Smith, T., 13284, A/Sgt.
Smith, T., 14287, Pte.
Smith, W. J., 10954, Drmr.
Smith, W., 7971. L/Cpl.
Smith, W. F., 8759, Pte.
Smith, W. F., 19343, Pte.
Smith, W. J., 13507, Pte.
Smith, W. T., 14822, Pte.
Snow, W., 13916, Pte.
Speke, J. H., 10760, Pte.
Spiller, F., 18483, Pte.
Spink, T. J., 8720, Pte.
Stagg, R., 8329, Pte.
Stanley, J. L., 13664, L/Cpl.
Stanton, J., 7797, Pte.
Stanton, T., 11828, Pte.
Stanton, T., 13220, L/Cpl.
Stenniford, W., 18431, Pte.
Stephens, T. E., 11208, Pte.
Stevens, V. E., 12143, Pte.
Stevens, W., 23405, Pte.
Stock, I., 9169, Sgt.
Stone, W., 7933, Pte.
Stubbins, W. H., 8742, Pte.
Sturdey, G. W., 44698, Pte.
Sullivan, J., 10195, Pte.
Sullivan, P., 10997, Pte.
Sutton, J., 13172, Pte.
Swannell, F. B., 9293, L/Cpl.
Swindlehurst, C. H., 6804, Pte.
Sykes, A. J., 6212, Sgt.
Syll, J., 11945, Pte.

Talbot, W., 36150, Pte.
Tapp, R. T., 25015, L/Cpl.
Tate, F., 45703, Pte.
Taylor, C. E. J., 8462, L/Cpl.
Taylor, J. W., 44533, Pte.
Taylor, R., 8662, Pte.
Teece, A., 10437, Pte.
Terry, T., 6274, Pte.
Thomas, C., 35651, Pte.
Thomas, D., 8261, Pte.
Thomas, E., 24942, Pte.
Thomas, F. H., 11472, Pte.
Thomas, H., 7073, Pte.
Thomas, L. F., 13015, Sgt.
Thomas, S. B., 44609, Pte.
Thomas, T., 12019, Pte.
Thomas, W., 7234, Pte.
Thomas, W., 8037, Pte.
Thomas, W. F., 8515, Pte.

THE ROLL OF HONOUR

Thompson, E., 19356, Pte.
Thornhill, P. T., 8935, Pte.
Thornicroft, H. E., 29423, Pte.
Thorp, G. A. W., 46907, Pte.
Tilley, W., 8664, Pte.
Tipping, G., 44597, Pte.
Tombs, H. A., 7964, Pte.
Tomkins, W. G., 21502, Pte.
Tomlin, G., 8694, Pte.
Toomey, E. J., 9674, Pte.
Tovey, J. T., 11078, L/Cpl.
Tranter, J., 7886, Pte.
Tratman, H., 10912, Pte.
Tremlett, W., 11607, Pte.
Trow, A., 19617, Pte.
Trump, A., 18485, L/Cpl.
Tucker, A. H., 44482, Pte.
Tucker, W., 8432, Pte.
Tucker, W. H., 26169, Pte.
Tugby, T., 7923, Pte.
Turke, G., 46909, Pte.
Turner, A. E., 9515, Pte.
Turner, C. G., 8988, Pte.
Turner, H. A., 35508, Pte.
Tyrrell, E., 35928, Pte.

Upton, T., 13319, Pte.
Upton, W., 10566, Pte.
Urquhart, B., 45729, Pte.
Urry, H. C., 44346, Pte.

Vaughan, A. J., 11367, Pte.
Vearey, G. J., 29610, Pte.
Venn, A. E., 10504, L/Cpl.
Verrinder, W., 13174, Pte.
Vincent, L., 18761, Pte.
Vine, F. W., 11222, Pte.
Virgin, W. C., 11055, Pte.

Waddington, J. W., 9299, L/Cpl.
Wagstaff, G., 35597, Pte.
Wakely, F., 25736, L/Cpl.
Waldie, J., 44347, Pte.
Walker, E. W., 7443, Pte.
Walker, J. W., 10978, Pte.
Walker, J., 19153, Pte.
Walker, T., 10707, Pte.
Wallace, D., 11774, Pte.
Waller, S., 9892, Cpl.
Walsh, R., 45675, Pte.
Walters, E., 13036, Pte.
Walters, F., 11965, Pte.
Walters, M., 8363, Pte.
Walton, H., 28368, L/Cpl.

Walton, J., 6386, L/Cpl.
Wangler, M., 12014, Pte.
Ward, A., 8284, Pte.
Ward, F. T., 8018, Pte.
Ward, J. W., 24872, L/Cpl.
Ward, W., 7783, Pte.
Ware, S., 13572, Pte.
Waring, J., 19354, Pte.
Warner, J., 13063, Pte.
Warren, T., 11195, L/Cpl.
Warrington, T. R., 11413, Pte.
Waterhouse, G. F., 10863, L/Cpl.
Waterhouse, J., 7844, Pte.
Waters, D. J., 13075, Pte.
Waters, E. J., 14595, Pte.
Waters, H. C., 17465, L/Cpl.
Waters, L. E., 8594, Drmr.
Wathen, O., 11031, Pte.
Watkins, A., 8920, Pte.
Watkins, C., 8610, Pte.
Watkins, D., 9383, Pte.
Watkins, E. T., 26225, Pte.
Watkins, G. R., 37584, Pte.
Watkins, J., 11896, Pte.
Watkins, W., 13334, Pte.
Watkins, W. J., 26244, Pte.
Watson, J., 39173, Pte.
Watts, E. F., 9412, Sgt.
Waygood, C. R., 14616, Pte.
Weale, C., 11045, Pte.
Weale, W., 14340, Pte.
Webb, J., 11523, Pte.
Webb, W., 14748, Pte.
Welch, J., 7252, Pte.
Wells, F., 11999, Pte.
Wells, G., 11843, Pte.
Welsh, W., 11726, Pte.
Weston, H., 9019, L/Cpl.
Weyman, W. C., 19307, Pte.
Whatley, A., 4680, C.S.M.
Wheeler, R. J., 26112, Pte.
Whitbread, W., 44351, Pte.
White, G. E., 9523, Pte.
White, H., 8385, Pte.
Whithorn, F. A., 44253, Pte.
Whitney, C., 9373, Pte.
Whittle, A. H., 9402, Pte.
Whitton, F., 10407, Pte.
Wilkins, E., 23852, L/Cpl.
Wilkinson, W. J., 42052, A/Cpl.
Wilks, A. E., 42157, Pte.
Willats, T. J., 8075, Pte.
Willats, W. H., 10436, Pte.
Willey, C., 26098, Pte.
Williams, A., 11443, Pte.

THE HISTORY OF THE SOUTH WALES BORDERERS

Williams, A., 26541, L/Cpl.
Williams, A. C., 21738, Pte.
Williams, A. J., 20460, L/Cpl.
Williams, C., 14814, Pte.
Williams, D., 18930, Pte.
Williams, D., 15388, Pte.
Williams, D., 12021, L/Cpl.
Williams, D., 13131, Pte.
Williams, D. T., 45628, Pte.
Williams, F., 12329, Pte.
Williams, G., 8023, Pte.
Williams, G., 13703, Pte.
Williams, G., 13161, Pte.
Williams, H., 15101, Pte.
Williams, J., 13651, Pte.
Williams, J. H., 7861, Pte.
Williams, J., 11385, Pte.
Williams, M., 13169, Pte.
Williams, P., 8656, Cpl.
Williams, T. J., 11764, Pte.
Williams, W., 8550, Pte.
Williams, W. P., 18852, Pte.
Wilson, J. E., 7837, Pte.
Wiltshire, J., 10949, Cpl.
Windsor, J., 10848, Pte.

Winn, W. J., 10627, Sgt.
Wishart, J. W., 8394, Pte.
Withey, F., 14579, Pte.
Witts, S., 13460, L/Cpl.
Wood, A., 8735, Pte.
Wood, E., 38905, Pte.
Wood, R., 11231, Pte.
Wooddeson, W. H., 8891, Pte.
Woodman, W. J., 9187, Pte.
Woollams, W., 25846, Pte.
Workman, R., 8708, Pte.
Wolstencroft, J. W., 45633, Pte.
Worrall, W., 42080, Pte.
Worthington, C., 46487, Pte.
Worthington, T. C., 26485, Cpl.
Wright, H. J., 11044, A/Sgt. M.M.
Wright, H., 11247, Pte.
Wright, T., 15545, Pte.

Yates, R., 14188, Pte.
Yemm, J., 13735, Pte.
Yend, J., 9485, Pte.
Young, C. H., 8029, Sgt.
Young, F., 8810, Pte.
Young, T. H., 13950, Pte.

2ND BATTALION.

Abbott, C. H., 10657, L/Cpl.
Abel, J. C., 41268, Pte.
Adams, F., 6045, Pte.
Adams, F. B., 21620, Pte.
Adams, L., 24712, Pte.
Adams, W., 13208, Pte.
Angworth, A. V., 45119, Pte.
Allen, B. C., 39527, Pte.
Allen, C., 40580, Pte.
Allen, H., 10166, Cpl.
Allen, W. T., 16067, Pte.
Alline, C., 10897, Pte.
Amies, F., 34222, Pte.
Andrews, A. T., 10667, Pte.
Andrews, F. G., 10880, L/Cpl.
Andrews, S., 15440, Pte.
Anderson, W., 9328, Sgt.
Angwin, V., 29743, Pte.
Ankers, J., 39000, Pte.
Anthony, J., 21585, L/Cpl.
Antill, A. M., 18889, Pte.
Appleton, A., 41360, Pte.
Aries, W., 10128, Pte.
Armitstead, L., 48003, Pte.
Armstrong, G., 24708, L/Cpl.
Armstrong, S., 13573, Pte.
Armstrong, W. L., 15525, L/Cpl.

Arrand, F., 40530, Pte.
Ashcroft, S., 25840, Pte.
Ashton, J., 44111, Pte.
Ashton, T., 28299, Pte.
Ashworth, A. C., 34117, Pte.
Ashworth, S., 24710, Pte.
Aspinall, R., 24527, Pte.
Atack, E., 40550, Pte.
Atherton, G. H., 15615, Sgt.
Atkins, W. D., 10920, Pte.
Atkinson, A., 14130, Pte.
Augustus, D. G. J., 39574, Pte.
Auld, F., 25187, Pte.

Bage, W., 45210, Pte.
Baggs, J., 39462, Pte.
Bailey, H., 9236, L/Cpl.
Bailey, J., 24601, Pte.
Baker, C., 39534, Pte.
Baker, E., 21754, Pte.
Baldwin, A., 40777, Pte.
Ball, C., 9747, Cpl.
Bamber, R. J., 37123, Pte.
Band, R. C., 44659, Pte.
Banks, H., 26487, Pte.
Banyard, O., 15574, Pte.
Barber, G. R., 28986, Pte.

THE ROLL OF HONOUR

Barham, A. C., 44213, Pte.
Baritz, A., 39575, A/Cpl.
Barker, F., 11768, Sgt.
Barlow, T., 39998, L/Cpl.
Barlow, W. R., 40738, Pte.
Barnacle, R., 25060, Pte.
Barnes, A. E., 41843, Pte.
Barnes, E., 9304, Pte.
Barnes, G., 45132, Pte.
Barnes, T., 10750, Pte.
Barratt, W. D., 13997, Pte.
Barron, A., 40587, Pte.
Barry, J., 9010, Pte.
Barry, J., 37752, Pte.
Barry, J., 15715, Pte.
Bartlett, F. C., 8745, L/Cpl.
Bartlett, G., 37583, Pte.
Bartram, G., 24715, Pte.
Bate, P., 34236, L/Cpl.
Bateman, J., 39461, Pte.
Bath, N., 9538, Bndsmn.
Beadle, E. J., 44515, L/Cpl.
Beaty, J. S., 33991, Pte.
Beck, E. J., 11657, Pte.
Beer, J. W., 39530, Pte.
Bendall, T., 9772, Sgt.
Bennett, A. C., 41221, Pte.
Bennett, F. S., 15510, Pte.
Bennett, J., 53910, Pte.
Bennett, S., 8927, Pte.
Benson, F. G., 25050, Cpl.
Bentley, J. M., 53845, Pte.
Bentley, W., 24930, Cpl. M.M.
Beresford, C., 15174, Pte.
Berry, S. E., 19962, Cpl. M.M.
Berryman, W., 45773, Pte.
Bettis, E. J., 10019, Pte.
Betton, A. P., 19991, Pte.
Bevan, C. B., 39659, L/Cpl.
Bevan, J. R., 39645, Pte.
Beynon, A., 44156, Pte.
Bill, R. S., 8265, C.S.M.
Binding, W. J., 39464, Pte.
Bingham, A., 40848, Pte.
Bird, E. O., 10003, Cpl.
Blackwood, W., 40625, Pte.
Blake, V. A. J., 29117, Pte.
Blakeman, A., 35026, A/Cpl.
Blakemore, W., 19425, Pte.
Blane, W., 25046, L/Cpl.
Blease, J., 29255, Pte.
Bloomfield, J. T., 40068, Pte.
Blundell, J. T., 9531, Cpl.
Bonner, G., 10065, Pte.
Boon, F., 12807, L/Cpl.

Booth, F., 39463, Pte.
Boucher, J., 10464, Pte.
Boulter, A. W., 41842, Pte.
Bourne, A., 41166, Pte.
Bourne, J., 37638, Pte.
Bowdery, A. A., 11115, Pte.
Bowles, E., 40662, Pte.
Box, A., 40390, Pte.
Boxall, G., 24635, Pte.
Bracey, A. E., 10740, Pte.
Bradbury, C. T., 34232, Pte.
Bradbury, E., 40651, Pte.
Bradshaw, H. J., 40586, Pte.
Bradshaw, W., 36275, Pte.
Bragg, G. H., 13914, A/Sgt.
Bramley, A. T., 40652, Pte.
Bramwell, W. H., 39621, Pte.
Breslin, R., 41453, Pte.
Brewer, B., 11704, Sgt.
Brierley, R., 42657, Pte.
Brindle, N., 24615, Pte.
Briscoe, W., 13483, Pte.
Britton, F. W., 29651, Pte.
Broadbent, E., 39751, Pte.
Broom, H. E., 9481, Pte.
Brotherston, T. W., 42284, Pte.
Brown, B. E., 37762, Pte.
Brown, E. W., 15589, L/Cpl.
Brown, J., 9609, L/Cpl.
Brown, L. W., 10160, Cpl.
Brown, W., 36027, Pte.
Brown, W. J., 38768, Pte.
Bruford, W., 18446, Pte.
Buck, J., 11200, Pte.
Buckland, W., 10329, Pte.
Buckley, J., 24693, Pte.
Bull, W., 39838, Pte.
Bunton, W., 40802, Bndsmn.
Burgess, S., 34509, Pte.
Burgess, T. G., 14874, Pte.
Burn, A. C., 40983, Pte.
Burns, P., 22685, Pte.
Burrows, A. J., 29661, Pte.
Burrows, W., 19749, L/Cpl.
Bushall, G., 24967, Sgt.
Bussey, H., 45249, Pte.
Butcher, W. R., 10701, Cpl.
Butt, C., 8726, Pte.
Button, H. V., 44215, Pte.
Byard, W. H., 42209, Pte.

Caddick, L., 11767, L/Cpl.
Cain, T., 15402, Pte.
Caines, F. H., 44712, Pte.
Callow, T., 40780, Pte.

549

Campbell, D., 15068, Pte.
Campbell, J., 24897, A/Cpl.
Campbell, W., 25130, Pte.
Campden, T., 39539, Pte.
Campling, A., 22776, Pte.
Carey, C. P., 9164, Pte.
Carroll, J., 14074, Pte.
Carroll, P., 8272, C.S.M. M.M.
Cartwright, Z., 24314, Pte.
Carty, D., 14034, Pte.
Castleman, E. J., 9177, L/Cpl.
Castleton, F. A., 23677, Pte.
Catton, J., 40639, Pte.
Cawley, J., 19625, Pte.
Challinor, E. R., 40564, Pte.
Challis, T., 19120, Pte.
Chamberlain, J., 44269, Pte.
Champion, W., 9660, Pte.
Chandler, J., 24072, Sgt.
Channing, A., 9956, Pte.
Chapman, J., 45798, Pte.
Chaston, F., 5258, C.S.M.
Cheeseman, H. G., 10441, Sgt.
Chignell, A., 10159, Pte.
Chilcott, H., 39980, Sgt.
Chilcott, S., 13740, Pte.
Chivers, W. E., 19939, Pte.
Church, G. T., 19685, Cpl.
Clack, L. G. S., 40189, Pte.
Claffey, J., 6755, Pte.
Clapp, J., 9654, Pte.
Clare, J., 40053, Pte.
Clargo, L., 9719, L/Cpl.
Clark, J. E. Y., 40866, Pte.
Clark, R. W., 45872, Pte.
Clarke, A. J., 15602, L/Cpl.
Clarke, H., 15465, Pte.
Clarke, L., 39541, Pte.
Clarke, W., 39471, Cpl.
Clarke, W. T., 10243, Pte.
Clements, A., 13833, Pte.
Clements, J., 9253, Sgt.
Cleverley, F. J., 10136, L/Cpl.
Clifford, C. P., 44217, Pte.
Cockayne, H., 9893, L/Cpl.
Coils, C., 24733, Pte.
Cole, W. J., 24739, Pte.
Coles, T., 15352, Pte.
Collett, P. J., 10677, Pte.
Collins, F., 40821, Pte.
Collins, J., 22435, Cpl.
Collister, A. N., 26240, Pte.
Connor, A., 45746, Pte.
Connor, J., 10831, L/Cpl.
Connor, P., 45989, Pte.

Conway, A., 9288, Pte.
Cook, E. D., 24970, Pte.
Cook, F., 10356, Pte.
Cook, S., 19888, Pte.
Cooper, J. H., 24571, L/Cpl.
Cooper, T., 41271, Pte.
Cope, J. E., 40764, Pte.
Corcoran, J. W., 19696, Pte.
Corn, H., 39576, Pte.
Cottenham, E., 45250, Pte.
Cottom, H., 41830, Pte.
Cottrell, W. J., 13317, Pte.
Coveny, G., 20999, Pte.
Cowan, P., 41178, Pte.
Coward, G. P., 11224, L/Cpl.
Cowie, L., 38744, Pte.
Cowin, J., 41329, Pte.
Cox, G., 25738, Pte.
Cox, M. T. F., 10230, Pte.
Coxwell, H., 13625, Sgt.
Crabb, W., 19092, Pte.
Crabbe, H. E., 24736, Pte.
Cran, W. E., 9627, Pte.
Crane, E., 42210, Pte.
Crean, J., 13628, Pte.
Crew, F., 36068, Pte.
Critcher, A., 18870, Pte.
Crondace, T., 35383, Pte.
Crook, H. G., 45245, Pte.
Crook, J., 26028, Pte.
Crook, P. J., 45246, Pte.
Cross, J., 6839, Cpl.
Cross, W., 18796, Pte.
Crossdale, G., 24218, L/Cpl.
Crossley, H., 24606, Pte.
Crozier, B., 45262, Pte.
Cullen, A. P., 18627, Pte.
Culley, E., 7421, Pte.
Culverwell, R., 42089, Pte.
Cunningham, F., 24732, Pte.
Cunningham, J., 13161, Pte.
Cunningham, O., 13515, Pte.
Cunningham, T., 45758, Pte.
Curtis, C., 27313, Pte.
Cussick, W., 9557, Pte.

Dale, A. L., 10724, Pte.
Daliday, J. H., 35904, Pte.
Dalton, E., 25132, Pte.
Daniels, H., 14265, Pte.
Dart, A., 14653, Sgt.
Dart, D. B., 26491, Pte.
Davall, J., 39475, Pte.
Davenport, L., 10428, L/Cpl.
Davenport, S., 40163, Pte.

THE ROLL OF HONOUR

Davies, A. B., 39654, L/Cpl.
Davies, A. W., 10574, L/Cpl.
Davies, B., 53861, Pte.
Davies, D., 41455, Pte.
Davies, D. J., 10523, L/Cpl.
Davies, D. J., 39549, Pte.
Davies, D. J., 18637, Pte.
Davies, D. J., 10304, Pte.
Davies, E., 39630, Pte.
Davies, E., 41188, Pte.
Davies, E. D., 41451, Pte.
Davies, F. J., 10674, Pte.
Davies, H., 10689, L/Sgt.
Davies, J., 39902, Pte.
Davies, J., 21726, Sgt.
Davies, J., 18596, Pte.
Davies, J. J., 39551, Pte.
Davies, J., 11966, Pte.
Davies, J. R., 10111, L/Cpl.
Davies, S., 9777, Pte.
Davies, T., 10789, Pte.
Davies, T. A., 33348, Pte.
Davies, W., 39995, Sgt.
Davies, W., 40012, Cpl.
Davies, W. E., 28997, Pte.
Davies, W. H., 39578, Pte.
Davies, W. I., 45776, L/Cpl.
Davies, W. J., 10314, L/Cpl.
Davies, W. J., 14899, Pte.
Davies, W. M., 39579, Pte.
Davis, H. C., 10617, Pte.
Day, F., 10330, Pte.
Day, T., 39022, L/Cpl.
Delderfield, W., 40650, Pte.
Denning, J., 24740, Pte.
Dennis, G. T., 24547, Pte.
Dewsbury, E., 6139, L/Cpl.
Dewsnap, G. O., 42213, Pte.
Dick, W. K., 44219, Pte.
Dingsdale, J., 40070, Pte.
Dixon, G., 7492, Pte.
Doe, C., 19062, Pte.
Douglas, J., 42673, Pte.
Dow, J. H., 36288, Pte.
Dowding, T., 11392, Pte.
Dowsell, R., 19588, Pte.
Dowsett, T. H., 36609, Pte.
Doyle, T., 13632, Pte.
Drake, S., 11806, Pte.
Drane, G. E., 10909, Pte.
Driffield, C., 11334, Pte.
Duckworth, J., 53862, Pte.
Duffield, G. P., 39993, L/Cpl.
Duffield, W. E., 30354, Pte.
Duley, S. G., 45673, Pte.

Duncan, W., 45134, Pte.
Dunn, F. J., 9849, Sgt.
Dutton, W., 40046, Pte.
Dye, S. C., 24583, Pte.
Dyke, R., 16588, Pte.

Eades, B., 25121, Sgt.
Earl, R. H., 22778, Pte.
Eastall, S., 9998, L/Cpl.
Easton, D. H., 44067, Pte.
Eccleston, T., 27655, Pte.
Ede, C. W., 11317, L/Cpl.
Eden, F., 19905, Pte.
Edge, W., 24624, Pte.
Edmondson, J., 38806, Pte.
Edney, F., 40640, Pte.
Edwards, F., 25609, Pte.
Edwards, F., 18519, Pte.
Edwards, S. J., 44222, Pte.
Edwards, W. C., 25557, Pte.
Edwards, W. J., 10077, A/Sgt.
Ellett, F., 25505, Pte.
Elliott, H., 39857, Pte.
Emanuel, V., 36910, Pte.
Emery, H., 25183, Sgt.
Englefield, H., 41212, Pte.
Evans, A. R., 9649, Cpl.
Evans, A. S., 29146, Pte.
Evans, B. C., 24994, Pte.
Evans, D., 18705, Pte.
Evans, D. C., 29290, Pte.
Evans, D. J., 39637, A/Cpl.
Evans, D. T., 11227, Cpl.
Evans, E., 11378, Pte.
Evans, E. R., 39757, Pte.
Evans, G., 21026, Pte.
Evans, H., 10558, Pte.
Evans, H., 10614, Pte.
Evans, J., 23156, Sgt. M.M.
Evans, J. A., 9844, Cpl.
Evans, J. J., 31555, Pte.
Evans, J. W., 28283, Pte.
Evans, L., 22165, Pte.
Evans, P. S., 22534, Pte.
Evans, P., 24938, Pte.
Evans, S., 25554, L/Cpl.
Evans, T. J., 31588, Pte.

Fairbrass, J. S., 9189, C.S.M.
Falconbridge, H., 24746, Pte.
Falls, R., 9391, L/Cpl.
Farmer, W. T., 24939, Pte.
Farr, W., 24944, Pte.
Farrell, E., 18516, Pte.
Farrell, F., 45149, Pte.

Faulkner, F., 29266, Pte.
Feast, G., 18734, Cpl. D.C.M.
Fennell, W., 36572, Pte.
Ferretter, T. J., 45244, Pte.
Fieldsend, E., 40961, Pte.
Finedon, F. A., 40595, Pte.
Finley, M. F., 24744, Pte.
Fisher, C., 8143, Pte.
Fisher, F., 21603, Pte.
Fisher, W., 41210, Pte.
Fitzgerald, E., 10501, Pte.
Fitzhugh, W. C., 40596, Pte.
Flute, W., 40655, Pte.
Flynn, T., 19454, Pte.
Foley, C. J., 10634, L/Cpl. D.C.M.
Ford, F. J., 10629, Pte.
Ford, J., 40069, Pte.
Follett, W., 25162, Pte.
Formby, C., 19172, Pte.
Forster, J., 19430, Pte.
Foster, S. E., 29309, Pte.
Foster, W., 14211, Sgt.
Fox, M., 27468, Pte.
France, R. J., 8756, Pte.
Francis, I. W., 9516, Pte.
Francis, R. M., 10786, Pte.
Friend, B. G., 9022, Pte.
Fry, A., 10307, L/Cpl.
Fury, M., 10358, L/Cpl.

Gall, I., 11720, A/Cpl.
Galloway, J. F., 10678, Sgt.
Gameson, A. A., 20845, Pte.
Gant, W., 9286, Pte.
Gapper, W. V., 32032, Pte.
Gardner, E. W., 41216, Pte.
Garlick, E. L. W., 34249, Pte.
Gaskell, H., 53828, Pte.
Geoghegan, J., 9979, Pte.
George, I., 29082, L/Cpl.
George, L., 13679, Pte.
George, R. A., 42527, A/Cpl.
Gibbs, E. A., 24754, Pte.
Gibbs, W., 9182, Pte.
Giblin, A., 39556, L/Cpl.
Giddings, A. W., 10445, L/Cpl.
Gifford, A. J., 11963, Pte.
Gilby, G. W., 7242, C.S.M.
Gill, J., 24609, Pte.
Gimblett, P., 13678, L/Cpl.
Gittins, E. H., 39760, Pte.
Gittoes, H. J., 42680, Pte.
Goddard, W., 13340, Pte.
Godfrey, J. W., 22782, Pte.
Goldberg, J., 9544, Pte.

Golding, F. J., 24570, Pte.
Goldstone, W. T., 8812, Pte.
Goodenough, A. J., 10462, Pte.
Goodier, J. W., 14790, Pte.
Gooding, T. J., 12502, L/Cpl.
Goodwin, C. W., 19684, Pte.
Gordon, W., 21825, L/Cpl.
Gore, J. A., 31573, Pte.
Gorton, J. J., 31792, Pte.
Gould, J., 13273, Pte.
Goulstone, H., 9723, Pte.
Grace, J., 15708, Pte.
Graham, A., 42683, Pte.
Grange, J. A., 39764, Pte.
Grantham, E., 39558, Pte.
Gray, F., 12054, Pte.
Gray, J. W., 24752, Pte.
Green, A., 9004, Pte. D.C.M.
Green, C., 39763, Pte.
Green, J. T., 10442, Pte.
Green, J., 18448, Pte.
Green, W. J., 42682, Pte.
Greenhill, W. C., 11325, Pte.
Gregory, A., 19895, Pte.
Gregory, T., 39793, Pte.
Griffiths, A. E., 26801, Cpl. M.M.
Griffiths, A. J., 24953, Pte.
Griffiths, D., 32012, Pte.
Griffiths, D. I., 29403, Pte. D.C.M.
Griffiths, E., 18490, A/Sgt.
Griffiths, G. H., 35172, Pte.
Griffiths, H., 10642, Pte.
Griffiths, H., 14993, Pte.
Griffiths, I. J., 11639, Pte.
Griffiths, J., 39580, Pte.
Griffiths, R., 31688, Pte.
Griffiths, R., 11463, Pte.
Griffiths, T., 12071, Pte.
Griffiths, T., 8344, Pte.
Griffiths, W. L., 14515, Pte.
Grindle, T., 40962, Pte. M.M.
Groves, R. A., 24605, Pte.
Gunn, J., 25193, Pte.

Hackett, J., 41449, Pte.
Hadley, T. C., 12232, Sgt.
Haines, J., 13865, Pte.
Hales, A. E., 13153, Pte.
Hall, E., 18679, Pte.
Hall, E., 24767, Pte.
Hall, G. A., 39503, Pte.
Hall, M. A., 8183, Pte.
Halliday, G., 44412, Pte.
Hammond, H., 10043, Pte.
Hanbury, F., 23417, Pte.

THE ROLL OF HONOUR

Hanson, H., 24837, Pte.
Harber, A., 39056, Pte.
Hardaway, A., 37611, Pte.
Hardiman, W. W., 24762, Pte.
Harding, E., 40631, Pte.
Hardy, C., 19593, Pte.
Hargreaves, F., 41375, Pte.
Harries, W., 10789, Pte.
Harris, A., 19599, Pte.
Harris, C. A., 19475, L/Cpl.
Harris, D. T., 39828, Pte.
Harris, D., 48941, Pte.
Harris, J., 19882, Pte.
Harris, J. H., 18911, Pte.
Harris, W., 9125, L/Sgt. M.M.
Harrison, T. G., 14610, Pte.
Hart, N., 10313, Pte.
Hart, W., 19596, Pte.
Hartstone, M., 45185, Pte.
Harvey, S. J., 45663, Pte.
Harwood, R. W., 40791, Pte.
Hassall, J. W., 10621, L/Cpl.
Haworth, W. B., 42687, Pte.
Hayes, H., 11088, Pte.
Hayes, P., 19555, Pte.
Hayward, A., 13427, Pte.
Hearn, G., 29069, Pte.
Hearn, T., 25532, Pte.
Hedgley, T. E., 25164, Pte.
Heel, J., 40785, Pte.
Hemming, T., 44233, Pte.
Henwood, P., 44396, Pte.
Herbert, T. J., 9709, Pte.
Hester, G. J., 10892, Pte.
Hewson, T., 6954, Pte.
Hickman, W., 24562, Pte.
Higham, A., 24759, Pte.
Hill, F. E., 19181, Pte.
Hill, F., 9697, Cpl.
Hill, J., 27383, Pte.
Hill, J., 37610, Pte.
Hindley, F., 18682, Pte.
Hitchings, J. L., 14960, Pte.
Hoar, H., 44420, Pte.
Hobbs, J., 39495, Sgt.
Hobbs, J. T., 19728, Pte.
Hobby, J., 10368, Sgt.
Hodge, S. J., 10143, Pte.
Hodgkinson, W., 24764, Pte.
Hodgkinson, W. T., 39768, Pte.
Hodgson, H., 25165, Pte.
Hodgson, J. D., 24572, Pte.
Hogan, D., 40066, Pte.
Hogg, A., 22560, Pte.
Hogg, H., 9983, Pte.

Holden, W., 24705, Pte.
Holland, H., 11307, Pte.
Hollingworth, H., 45738, Pte.
Hollins, R. H., 40563, Pte.
Holloway, A. F., 9240, Cpl. M.M.
Hood, C. H., 19603, Pte.
Hook, F. H., 8679, L/Cpl.
Hooker, E., 24368, Pte.
Hooker, T., 9527, Bdm.
Hopkins, J., 14873, Pte.
Hopkins, J., 35156, Pte.
Hopkins, W., 15058, Pte.
Hopkins, W. H., 9886, Pte.
Hopkinson, J., 12062, Pte.
Hosking, W., 39620, Pte.
Howard, J., 10027, Pte.
Howard, T., 41348, Pte.
Howcroft, C. E., 13013, Sgt. M.M.
Howe, R. J., 10072, Pte.
Howell, J., 15459, L/Cpl.
Howell, N. T., 38577, Pte.
Howells, V., 25790, Pte.
Hudson, C., 40526, Sgt. M.M.
Hudson, T., 41332, Pte.
Hughes, C., 46808, Pte.
Hughes, D., 14762, Pte.
Hughes, D., 24820, Pte.
Hughes, E., 24300, A/Sgt.
Hughes, G., 13952, Pte.
Hughes, H., 25042, Pte.
Hughes, J. E., 40743, Pte.
Hughes, J. E., 42224, Pte.
Hughes, J. H., 42695, Pte.
Hughes, J. H., 19797, Pte.
Hughes, J. W., 8148, Pte.
Hughes, R., 11343, Pte.
Hughes, T., 19453, Pte.
Hughes, T., 18748, Pte.
Hughes, W., 10554, Pte.
Hughes, W., 15121, Pte.
Hughes, W., 24979, Pte.
Hull, E. D., 40794, Pte.
Hull, H., 24539, Pte.
Humphreys, J. A., 13543, Pte.
Hunt, H., 9211, Pte.
Hunt, R. H., 9725, Cpl.
Hunter, W., 24529, Pte.
Hurle, R., 39497, Pte.
Hurley, J., 19989, Pte.
Hurley, J., 10967, Pte.
Hutchings, W. A., 39570, Pte.
Hutchinson, A., 24582, Pte.
Hyatt, E., 19362, Pte.
Hydes, M. P., 45143, Pte.

THE HISTORY OF THE SOUTH WALES BORDERERS

Iles, A., 42696, Pte.
Ingham, G. E., 18747, Pte.
Irons, J., 8719, C.S.M.
Isaac, T., 6450, Sgt.

Jackson, C. H., 25123, L/Cpl.
Jackson, S., 39518, Pte.
Jackson, T. J., 18440, Pte.
James, D., 24661, L/Cpl.
James, D. G., 39510, Pte.
James, E., 29960, Pte.
James, G. H., 6823, Sgt.
James, I., 29194, Pte.
James, J., 13324, Pte.
James, J., 13748, Pte.
James, N., 13768, L/Cpl.
James, R., 18433, Pte.
James, T., 13951, Pte.
James, W., 25272, Pte.
James, W., 29112, Pte.
James, W. R., 18927, Pte.
Jay, W. T., 39419, Pte.
Jaycock, E. A., 15561, Pte.
Jeffries, S., 25203, Pte.
Jenkins, L., 13380, Pte.
Jenkins, S., 11878, Pte.
Jenkinson, T., 9980, Pte.
Jenner, T. C., 6083, A/Cpl.
Jennings, J., 10303, Cpl.
Jeremiah, W. J., 11099, Pte.
Jinks, W. J., 10668, Pte.
Jobbins, P., 19881, L/Cpl.
John, D., 9737, Pte.
Johnson, A. W., 44080, Pte.
Johnson, A., 9971, Pte.
Johnson, C., 45264, Pte.
Johnson, F. E., 5417, A/C.Q.M.S.
Johnson, G. A., 9881, L/Cpl.
Johnson, H. W., 19590, Pte.
Johnson, H. W., 45257, Pte.
Johnson, T. F., 19177, Pte.
Johnstone, J., 36073, Pte.
Jones, A., 18457, Pte.
Jones, A., 35732, Pte.
Jones, A., 46936, A/Cpl.
Jones, A. W. S., 18504, Pte.
Jones, A. W., 9999, Sgt.
Jones, A., 13257, Pte.
Jones, C., 10560, Cpl.
Jones, D., 39517, Pte.
Jones, D., 11911, Pte.
Jones, D. B., 26572, L/Cpl.
Jones, D. G., 10643, Pte.
Jones, D. J., 13822, Pte.
Jones, D. M., 31657, Pte.

Jones, D. W., 15151, Pte.
Jones, E., 13500, Pte.
Jones, E. D., 41282, Pte.
Jones, E., 41287, Pte.
Jones, E., 29844, Pte.
Jones, E., 18825, Pte.
Jones, F., 35300, Pte.
Jones, F., 41444, Pte.
Jones, F., 25124, Cpl.
Jones, G., 11085, Pte.
Jones, G., 19385, Pte.
Jones, G. T., 10508, Pte.
Jones, G., 10939, L/Cpl.
Jones, G., 30084, Pte.
Jones, H., 13518, Pte.
Jones, H., 40788, Pte.
Jones, H., 10280, Cpl.
Jones, H., 18862, Pte.
Jones, H., 24957, Pte.
Jones, H. J., 10295, Pte.
Jones, H., 10182, Cpl.
Jones, I., 35614, L/Cpl.
Jones, J., 39514, Cpl.
Jones, J., 21755, Pte.
Jones, J. M., 26556, Pte.
Jones, J. T., 14898, Pte.
Jones, J. W., 42225, Pte.
Jones, L., 14081, Pte.
Jones, L., 39592, Pte.
Jones, O., 20767, Pte.
Jones, O., 39772, Pte.
Jones, R. D., 41283, Pte.
Jones, S. F., 41767, Pte.
Jones, T., 39773, Pte.
Jones, T. C., 13454, Pte.
Jones, T. L., 45739, Pte.
Jones, T. R., 15346, Pte.
Jones, W., 9450, L/Cpl.
Jones, W., 42699, Pte.
Jones, W., 9509, Cpl.
Jones, W., 33260, Pte.
Jones, W., 40005, Pte.
Jones, W., 11130, Pte.
Jones, W., 10542, Pte.
Jones, W. H., 13624, Pte.
Jones, W. H., 9811, Pte.
Jones, W. I., 10171, L/Cpl.
Jones, W. J., 26825, Pte.
Jones, W. J., 41284, Pte.
Jones, W. W., 39038, Pte.
Joshua, O., 11769, Pte.
Joyce, W. L., 26741, Pte.

Kay, G., 53890, Pte.
Kay, T., 19572, Pte.

THE ROLL OF HONOUR

Kearns, W., 24098, Pte.
Keast, R., 31979, Pte.
Keefe, E. J., 9866, Drmr.
Keefe, W. G., 9424, Drmr.
Keeling, S., 10338, Pte.
Keirle, A., 10589, Pte.
Kellett, D., 41769, Pte.
Kelly, W. J., 8876, Cpl. M.M.
Kelly, W. M., 48951, Pte.
Kennedy, W. A., 45265, Pte.
Kent, C., 10107, Pte.
Kent, W. A., 7364, Pte.
Kettley, A. W., 39521, Pte.
Kibble, R., 25055, Pte.
Kiley, A., 19171, Pte.
King, A., 41774, Pte.
King, A., 39520, Pte.
King, A., 45205, Pte.
King, J., 45147, Pte.
King, W., 10859, Pte.
King, W. P., 10438, Pte.
Kinsey, J. C., 19178, Pte.
Kinsey, J., 19450, Pte.
Kirby, E. A., 24704, Pte.
Kirkham, I., 19629, Pte.
Kitching, F., 45163, Pte.
Knapp, A. J., 14442, Pte.
Knight, A. G., 44682, Pte.
Knight, C. E. V., 41349, Pte.
Knight, J., 41373, Pte.
Knight, S., 41053, Pte.
Knope, J., 24577, Pte.
Knowles, G. T., 11261, Pte.
Knowles, J., 24511, Pte.
Knowlson, W., 10961, Pte.
Koplik, A., 45148, Pte.

Laing, W., 25120, Pte.
Lambeth, R., 36083, Pte.
Lancaster, P., 44101, L/Cpl.
Lander, A. B., 40601, L/Cpl.
Langridge, P., 12251, L/Cpl.
Lavender, D., 13751, Pte.
Lavender, T., 10992, Sgt.
Lawrence, W. J., 14634, Pte.
Lea, W., 29011, Pte.
Leach, H., 7309, Sgt.
Leavold, S. G., 40632, Pte.
Lee, A., 13816, Pte.
Lee, H., 25184, Sgt.
Lee, S., 41887, Pte.
Lee, S. S., 48095, Pte.
Lee, W., 19184, Pte.
Lennon, R., 25195, Pte.
Leslie, W., 45765, Pte.

Lester, H. F., 24576, Pte.
Lett, C., 41886, Pte.
Levy, H., 39584, Pte.
Lewis, A. H., 9677, Pte.
Lewis, B., 12853, Pte.
Lewis, E., 11802, Pte.
Lewis, F. J., 27410, Pte.
Lewis, G., 8024, Pte.
Lewis, H., 14890, Pte.
Lewis, H., 25032, Pte.
Lewis, J. D., 58428, Pte.
Lewis, R., 38590, Pte.
Lewis, R., 33904, Cpl.
Lewis, T., 10640, Pte.
Lewis, W. G., 19308, Pte.
Lewis, W. J., 13269, Pte.
Leyshon, C., 6888, Pte.
Liddicoat, G., 24687, Pte.
Lilwall, J., 39638, Pte.
Ling, A. E., 11237, A/Sgt.
Lister, S., 13724, Pte. M.M.
Liversage, J. E., 41974, Pte.
Lloyd, D. T., 39662, Pte.
Lloyd, D., 29556, Pte.
Lloyd, F., 10268, Sgt.
Lloyd, H., 13806, Pte.
Lloyd, J., 14961, Pte.
Lloyd, J., 10606, Pte.
Lloyd, L., 12046, Pte.
Lloyd, R., 48953, Pte.
Lloyd, S., 39421, Pte.
Lock, A., 48954, Pte.
Lofthouse, W., 9675, Pte.
Logan, R. C. A., 41773, Pte.
Lowdell, A. G., 26479, Pte.
Lowe, A., 36074, Pte.
Lucas, J., 44509, Pte.
Ludlow, G. C., 41775, Pte.
Luff, W., 35105, Pte.
Lukins, G. H., 46976, Pte.
Lumsden, T., 45201, Pte.
Lunt, J. W., 40533, Pte.

Mabbett, T., 10470, Pte.
Mackinnon, M., 30308, Pte.
Macrow, S., 24786, Pte.
Maddox, G., 34622, Cpl.
Maidment, F., 9395, Pte.
Main, H., 31686, Pte.
Maloney, T. L., 19913, Pte.
Mandall, J., 9035, Cpl.
Manley, W. H., 28346, Pte.
Manns, F., 10450, Pte.
Manton, E., 40622, Pte.
March, R. J., 26373, Pte.

March, T., 29304, Pte.
Marchant, G. T., 44561, C.S.M.
Marsh, F., 10773, Pte.
Marsh, J., 41977, Pte.
Marsh, J. W., 39573, L/Cpl. M.M.
Marshall, A., 7879, Pte.
Marshall, J., 8924, Pte.
Martin, A., 14897, Pte.
Martin, B., 24842, Pte.
Martin, E., 26596, Pte.
Martin, H., 48975, Pte.
Marvesley, Z., 40604, Pte.
Mason, J., 8125, L/Cpl.
Mason, J., 40077, Pte.
Mason, W. H., 10078, Pte.
Maskell, E. A., 24521, Pte.
Matcham, W. F., 10650, Pte.
Mattey, C. J., 30346, Pte.
Matthews, E., 6201, Pte. D.C.M.
Matthews, W., 35125, Pte.
Maycox, W. E., 39009, Sgt.
Mayes, R., 44242, Pte.
McAuliffe, M., 13654, Pte.
McBain, W. A., 10876, Pte.
McCarthy, J., 17760, Pte.
McCarthy, W., 10537, Pte.
McCord, D., 41176, Pte.
McCormick, J., 27617, Pte.
McFarren, F., 9628, Pte.
McGrath, W. H. H., 11949, Sgt.
McMullen, F., 35927, Pte.
McMunn, E., 27388, Pte.
McNulty, J. E., 48963, Pte.
McPhillips, G., 13666, Pte.
McRae, R., 24888, Pte.
McWilliam, A., 30335, Pte.
Mead, R., 13240, Pte.
Meikle, J., 26478, Pte.
Mellors, H., 19125, Pte.
Melton, D., 45821, Pte.
Mesquitta, P. E., 10299, L/Cpl.
Metcalfe, F., 24787, Pte.
Middleton, J., 40800, Pte.
Millard, C., 13677, Pte.
Miller, H. R. G., 8994, Sgt.
Miller, W., 8436, Sgt.
Millichamp, A. H., 6475, C.S.M.
Millington, E. R., 10052, L/Cpl.
Mills, A. J., 9919, Cpl.
Mills, W., 19429, Pte.
Mills, W., 46422, Pte.
Millward, T., 9600, Pte. D.C.M.
Millward, W. C., 10169, Pte. M.M.
Milne, A. G., 10088, C.S.M.
Moaney, F., 41788, Pte.

Molineaux, T., 15613, Pte.
Moloney, R., 46481, Pte.
Moneypenny, C., 18858, Pte.
Moore, J. L., 24792, Pte.
Moore, S. G., 48962, Pte.
Moore, T., 42222, Pte.
Morgan, C., 10675, Pte.
Morgan, D. P., 18724, L/Cpl.
Morgan, E., 26499, L/Cpl.
Morgan, I. T., 31293, Pte.
Morgan, I., 33322, L/Cpl.
Morgan, J. W., 11996, Pte
Morgan, O., 10823, Cpl.
Morgan, R., 10435, Pte.
Morgan, T., 15194, Pte.
Morgan, W., 9547, Pte.
Morris, C., 10170, Pte.
Morris, E. R., 25167, Pte.
Morris, F., 15604, Pte.
Morris, G., 37796, Pte.
Morris, G. W., 39162, Pte.
Morris, S., 46420, L/Cpl.
Morris, W., 39976, Pte.
Morris, W., 13805, Pte.
Morris, W. E., 11055, Pte.
Moss, E., 19630, Pte.
Moss, I., 19474, Pte.
Moulding, W., 24878, Pte.
Mullins, J., 11105, Pte.
Munns, E. A., 13426, Pte.
Murphy, J., 9448, Pte.
Murphy, J., 46427, Pte.
Murray, P., 45708, Pte.
Murray, S., 24600, Pte.

Napper, L., 9809, Pte.
Nash, S. F., 36109, Pte.
Neagle, P., 15213, Pte.
Nelson, S., 23742, Pte. M.M.
New, T. J., 22518, Pte.
Newbury, A., 41214, Pte.
Newman, A. C., 19757, Pte.
Newman, G. C., 19325, Cpl.
Nicholas, W., 12038, Pte.
Nicholas, W., 13700, Cpl.
Nicholson, S., 40753, L/Cpl.
Nightingale, F. J., 19611, Pte.
Noble, A. M., 44244, Pte.
Noble, E., 40061, Pte.
Noble, T. A., 41895, Pte.
Noon, J., 31730, Pte.
Noonan, T., 24947, Pte.
Norris, B. W., 40607, Pte.
Norris, C. R. D., 10087, L/Cpl.
Norvell, A. W. J., 44571, L/Cpl.

THE ROLL OF HONOUR

Nunn, F. W., 10179, Sgt.
Nutter, R., 48978, Pte.

O'Brien, D., 10780, Pte.
O'Brien, P., 9235, Cpl.
O'Connell, T., 10725, Pte.
O'Kelley, R., 13552, Pte.
O'Keefe, C., 25517, Pte.
O'Keefe, T., 11277, Pte.
Ockwell, A. E., 39599, Pte.
Olsen, P., 13775, Pte.
Osbond, S. J., 45791, Pte.
Osborn, H. J. C., 24799, Pte.
Owen, F., 12066, Pte.
Owen, G., 40573, Pte.
Owen, H., 42367, Pte.
Owen, J., 12043, Pte.
Owen, M., 13057, L/Cpl.
Owen, R., 44108, Pte.

Page, C. H., 10717, Pte.
Page, F., 25154, Sgt.
Palliser, W., 40747, Pte.
Palmer, A., 18782, Pte.
Palmer, D., 10910, Pte.
Palmer, J. E., 19156, Pte.
Palmer, R., 25180, Cpl.
Palmer, W. J., 11327, Pte.
Park, J., 18607, Pte.
Parker, A., 24634, Pte.
Parker, W. E., 40571, Pte.
Parkes, D., 14152, Pte.
Parkes, G., 10202, Pte.
Parkin, G., 41801, Pte.
Parrott, C. J., 40657, Pte.
Parry, A. G., 26700, Pte.
Parry, C. M., 27398, Pte.
Parry, E., 14931, Pte.
Parry, E., 27391, Pte.
Parry, J. A., 29429, Pte.
Parslow, L., 41020, Pte.
Parsons, L. S., 10167, Pte.
Parsons, T. A., 41794, Pte.
Partington, A., 53902, Pte.
Partridge, J., 10527, Pte.
Passmore, A. E., 25721, Pte.
Patterson, J., 48110, Pte.
Paull, C., 14336, Pte.
Pavett, C. W. W., 10273, Pte.
Payne, A. G., 7235, Sgt.
Payne, H., 9699, Pte.
Peake, F., 24608, Pte.
Pearce, E., 25077, Pte.
Pearce, E., 13388, L/Cpl.
Pearce, W., 22084, Pte.

Pearce, W. J., 8916, C.S.M.
Pearson, J., 45157, Pte.
Pearson, R., 18741, Pte.
Peattie, A., 24870, Pte.
Pedhale, W., 12292, Pte.
Peel, T. L., 34293, L/Cpl.
Pembridge, P., 21386, Cpl.
Perkins, S., 27276, Pte.
Perks, G., 48987, Pte.
Phillip, J. S., 39605, Pte.
Phillips, A., 10079, Sgt.
Phillips, D., 19903, Pte.
Phillips, H., 29933, Pte.
Phillips, H. G., 25691, Pte.
Phillips, S., 13576, Pte.
Phillips, T., 39207, Pte.
Phillips, W., 13557, Pte.
Pike, H., 25534, A/Sgt.
Pike, H., 13156, Pte.
Pilling, R., 45810, Pte.
Pilling, W., 46439, Pte.
Pine, F., 9570, Sgt. M.M.
Pinney, F. J., 44250, Pte.
Pinnock, W. A., 40620, Pte.
Pitt, B., 19108, Pte.
Platt, J. H., 48114, Pte.
Plummer, W., 15648, Pte.
Poole, R. W., 9598, Sgt. M.M.
Pope, W., 26811, Pte.
Porter, H. A., 9608, Cpl.
Porter, J. W., 41897, Pte.
Portman, G. T., 39945, Pte.
Pounds, C. P., 9478, Pte.
Powell, A., 14771, Pte.
Powell, F., 25145, Pte.
Powell, G., 13548, Pte.
Powell, P., 25574, Pte.
Powell, W., 8963, A/Cpl.
Pownall, T., 40059, L/Cpl.
Poyner, E., 42200, A/Cpl.
Price, D., 11199, L/Cpl.
Price, E. S., 10670, Pte.
Price, G., 44737, Pte.
Price, G., 48118, Pte.
Price, H., 44159, Pte.
Price, I., 6946, Pte.
Price, J., 12080, Pte.
Price, N. L., 29934, Pte.
Price, W. H., 9816, Pte.
Price, W. J., 10575, L/Cpl.
Prince, J., 44110, Pte.
Pritchard, S., 25033, Pte.
Pritchard, W., 39733, Pte.
Pritchard, W., 11097, Pte.
Pritchard, W. G., 41296, Pte.

Procter, F., 41799, Pte.
Prosser, C. H., 25998, Pte.
Prosser-James, L., 15499, Pte.
Protheroe, R., 29294, Pte.
Pryce, T., 41297, Pte.
Pugh, J., 13010, Pte.
Pugh, J., 13695, Pte.
Purcell, T., 24059, Pte.
Purnell, J., 8796, Pte.
Purnell, T., 13810, Pte.

Quinn, P., 11820, Pte. M.M.

Ralph, S., 13993, Pte.
Ramsay, J., 41478, Pte.
Rand, H. G., 8934, Pte.
Raven, A. E., 25146, Pte.
Redford, P., 25147, Pte.
Redgewell, H. C., 19336, Pte.
Reed, W. A., 11431, Pte.
Rees, H., 41304, Pte.
Rees, J., 25535, Pte.
Rees, J. T., 29634, Pte.
Rees, P. A., 13954, Pte.
Rees, S., 30570, Pte.
Rees, T., 44253, Pte.
Rees, W., 13745, Pte.
Rees, W. G., 24413, Pte.
Reeves, T., 15729, Pte.
Reid, R. F., 24861, Pte.
Reilley, W. G., 25198, Pte.
Renshaw, W., 39363, Pte.
Reveley, C., 10317, Pte.
Reynolds, G. E., 18034, Pte.
Rice, J. R., 9964, L/Cpl. M.M.
Rice, T., 46423, Pte.
Richards, B., 39619, Pte.
Richards, R., 31295, Cpl.
Richards, R., 13713, A/Sgt.
Richards, T., 10248, Cpl.
Richardson, A. J., 10060, Pte.
Richardson, E., 29263, Pte.
Richardson, R. E., 48994, Pte.
Richmond, A., 24618, Pte.
Ricketts, T., 40844, Pte.
Ridgway, J., 24703, Pte.
Ridout, H., 14815, Pte.
Riley, P., 24919, Pte.
Ring, W., 38743, L/Cpl.
Risbridger, L. G., 46450, Pte.
Roberts, A., 30166, Pte.
Roberts, D. E., 40750, Pte.
Roberts, H., 41302, Pte.
Roberts, J., 10422, L/Cpl.
Roberts, J. O., 25465, Pte.

Roberts, J., 19972, Pte.
Roberts, J., 40050, Pte.
Roberts, R., 42229, Pte.
Roberts, W. R., 8874, Cpl.
Robinson, B., 26201, Cpl.
Robinson, J. H., 9131, L/Cpl.
Robinson, J., 29451, Pte.
Roby, W., 46442, Pte.
Rogers, E., 14163, Cpl.
Rogers, H., 25053, Pte.
Rogers, W., 8636, Sgt.
Rolph, W. A., 15184, Pte.
Rose, S., 35579, Pte.
Ross, R., 41196, Pte.
Rossiter, F., 24806, Pte.
Rouillier, H. J., 9447, Sgt.
Rowe, F. J., 35718, L/Cpl.
Rowlands, E., 14043, Pte.
Rowlands, W. P., 40749, Pte.
Royle, J. W., 25074, Pte.
Rudd, J., 18548, Pte.
Rudd, S., 46447, Pte.
Rudd, W., 19644, Pte.
Rudkin, J. T., 45192, Pte.
Ruffle, J., 9651, C.Q.M.S.
Rugen, G., 46448, Pte.
Ruscoe, J., 41306, Pte.
Rushforth, S. W., 40643, Pte.
Rutter, T. H., 24675, Pte.
Ryan, D., 14938, L/Sgt.

Sage, E. F., 40759, Pte.
Salmon, P. J., 19194, Pte.
Salter, H., 10112, Pte.
Sanderson, G. S., 9329, Sgt.
Sant, V., 38981, Pte.
Saunders, W., 24561, Pte.
Saunderson, W., 9798, Pte.
Savigair, C., 14666, Pte.
Sawyer, C. B., 9567, Sgt.
Scott, G. W., 27305, Cpl. M.M.
Scott, W., 25299, Pte.
Schofield, W., 33645, L/Cpl.
Scullard, H. J., 24867, Pte.
Seel, W., 25506, Pte.
Selby, H., 19624, Pte.
Sewell, H., 7000, Pte.
Sewell, J. R., 9243, Pte.
Sewell, W., 40756, Pte.
Sexton, J., 39643, Pte.
Shakesheff, G., 6866, Pte.
Shakeshaft, T., 24508, Pte.
Sharp, A. B., 24680, Pte.
Sharp, F., 44300, Pte.
Sharpe, A. W., 10919, Pte.

THE ROLL OF HONOUR

Shakespeare, J., 41807, Pte.
Sharrock, E., 48135, Pte.
Shaw, J., 18475, Pte.
Shearn, G., 15263, Pte.
Shepherd, J., 20301, Pte.
Sheppard, G., 10344, Pte.
Shew, W. E., 39656, Pte.
Shore, J., 10343, L/Cpl.
Short, J., 36566, Pte.
Sibeon, R. H., 45886, Pte.
Sibley, S., 9633, Pte.
Sibley, T. C., 36315, Pte.
Sidgwick, T. A., 24660, Pte.
Sidebottom, J., 19634, Pte.
Silk, G., 9170, Pte.
Silvester, J. E., 25886, Pte.
Simmill, W. H., 29948, Pte.
Simmonds, T. J., 9477, Pte.
Simmons, J., 12256, Pte.
Sivyer, E., 44401, Pte.
Simpson, G., 19095, Pte.
Slinn, H. J., 45814, Pte.
Sloman, A., 24533, Pte.
Smalley, C., 19595, L/Cpl.
Smethurst, J., 41310, Pte.
Smith, A., 8174, Pte.
Smith, A., 40611, Pte.
Smith, A., 40974, Pte.
Smith, A. E., 24019, Pte.
Smith, E. A., 40770, Pte.
Smith, G., 9274, Pte.
Smith, J., 10531, Pte.
Smith, J., 45259, Pte.
Smith, J. R., 9917, Pte.
Smith, L., 11646, Pte.
Smith, M. J., 29061, Pte.
Smith, R., 10755, Pte.
Smith, S. E., 15811, Pte.
Smith, S. W., 24520, L/Cpl.
Smith, T., 9767, Pte.
Smith, T. J., 23529, Pte.
Smith, W., 10023, Sgt.
Smith, W., 31372, Pte.
Smith, W. H., 10417, Pte.
Smith, W. W., 9981, A/Cpl.
Smyth, P., 10298, Pte.
Snape, J., 41330, Pte.
Sparks, G. R., 11824, Sgt.
Spencer, W., 48140, Pte.
Spencer, W., 24816, Pte.
Spinks, A. R., 9121, L/Cpl. D.C.M.
Sprawson, A. W., 24809, Pte.
Starr, H., 40760, Pte. M.M.
Stephens, W. T., 27352, Pte.
Stephenson, A., 25200, Pte.

Stevens, T. A., 30312, Pte.
Stewart, G. A., 41197, Pte.
Stickler, H. J., 7006, Pte.
Stone, J., 34576, Sgt.
Stone, W., 20872, Pte.
Stoner, E. T., 9291, Pte.
Stones, T. A., 44343, Pte.
Straney, G. C., 10229, L/Cpl.
Strange, E. M., 41311, Pte.
Stringer, T., 40557, Pte.
Stuart, D. L., 8898, C.S.M.
Sturgess, I. A., 9912, L/Cpl.
Sullivan, D., 30351, Pte.
Sullivan, J., 18704, L/Cpl.
Summers, S. J., 31891, Pte.
Summons, A. E., 45751, Pte.
Sweet, J., 14011, Pte.
Swindells, F. C., 41355, Pte.
Sydenham, A. G., 9880, L/Cpl.
Symonds, A. H., 30333, Pte.

Tanner, H., 10405, Pte.
Tarrant, P. W., 40779, Pte.
Taylor, F., 26397, Pte.
Taylor, G. H., 40664, Pte.
Taylor, H., 48145, Pte.
Taylor, H. C., 10856, Pte.
Taylor, P. H., 25201, Pte.
Taylor, P., 19285, Pte.
Taylor, R. J., 38896, Pte.
Taylor, T., 13787, Pte.
Taylor, T. S., 45191, Pte.
Taylor, W., 24617, Pte.
Taylor, W., 40653, Pte.
Terrill, A., 10172, L/Cpl.
Thomas, A. E., 29350, Pte.
Thomas, C. J., 10401, Pte.
Thomas, C. W., 10902, L/Cpl.
Thomas, C. W., 23304, Pte.
Thomas, D., 18563, Pte.
Thomas, D. G., 18454, Pte.
Thomas, E., 13207, Pte.
Thomas, E., 15469, Pte.
Thomas, G., 10336, Pte.
Thomas, G., 19901, Pte.
Thomas, G. A., 39626, Pte.
Thomas, H. H., 48141, Pte.
Thomas, H. J., 11373, Pte.
Thomas, H., 31435, Pte.
Thomas, J., 10406, L/Cpl.
Thomas, J., 44255, Pte.
Thomas, J. D., 23235, Pte.
Thomas, J. F., 40037, Pte.
Thomas, J. L., 29524, Pte.
Thomas, J. M., 29500, Pte.

559

Thomas, L., 8226, Pte.
Thomas, L., 25278, Pte.
Thomas, R., 13744, Pte.
Thomas, R. J., 41200, Pte.
Thomas, T. C., 18583, Pte.
Thomas, W. B., 12073, Pte.
Thomson, W., 10326, Cpl.
Thompson, W., 15188, L/Cpl.
Thorburn, J., 24914, Pte.
Thorndick, A. G., 42532, A/Cpl.
Thurlow, A. L., 45969, L/Cpl.
Thurman, R., 24623, Pte.
Tickle, E., 26634, Cpl.
Tickle, H., 24538, Pte.
Tomkins, L., 39444, Pte.
Toole, W., 14750, Pte.
Toothill, J. H., 18525, Pte.
Tordoff, J., 19690, Pte.
Torney, E., 12067, Pte.
Towers, R. B., 40616, Pte.
Townsend, B. E., 39006, Pte.
Tudor, H., 9921, Cpl.
Turland, F. H., 40618, Pte.
Turner, E. H. G., 45794, L/Cpl.
Turner, H. R., 30023, Pte.
Turner, J., 9713, Pte.
Turner, J., 24591, Pte.
Turner, J. H. C., 11147, Cpl.
Turner, W., 18620, Pte.
Turner, W. J., 20896, Pte.
Turner, W. T., 15376, Pte.
Turton, E. R., 45267, Pte.

Upton, W. C., 24817, Cpl.

Vaughan, D. A., 29016, L/Cpl.
Vann, G., 13244, Sgt.
Vinall, A., 9899, Pte.
Vincent, H. T. S., 25040, Pte.
Vizard, R., 10628, Pte.

Wadsell, A. J., 24831, Pte.
Walker, B. L., 39590, Pte.
Walker, C. H., 40730, Pte.
Walker, R. J., 9922, Pte.
Wallace, D. J., 19283, Pte. M.M.
Waller, W., 9682, Pte.
Walsh, P., 25837, Pte.
Walters, G., 11876, Pte.
Walton, G. H. A., 9345, L/Cpl.
Walton, R., 24229, Pte.
Walwin, G. V., 25535, Pte.
Warburton, W., 41906, Pte.
Ward, J., 21803, L/Cpl.

Ward, J. J., 10423, Sgt. D.C.M.
Ward, W., 15342, Pte.
Ware, S. S., 8015, Pte.
Wareing, J. M., 44117, Pte.
Warren, A. E., 24194, Pte.
Warren, G., 24825, Pte.
Washbrook, R., 41169, Pte.
Waters, C., 10080, Pte.
Watkin, H., 24844, Pte.
Watkins, O. G., 25052, Pte.
Watkins, W., 14950, Pte.
Watson, B., 15251, Pte.
Watson, T., 10646, Sgt.
Watts, P., 11827, Pte.
Weaver, J. J., 24834, Pte.
Weaver, W., 15229, Pte.
Webb, C., 45274, Pte.
Webster, J., 41820, Pte.
Webtser, S., 49017, Pte.
Weech, S., 14007, Pte.
Weeks, E., 11686, Pte.
Weller, F. G., 44256, Pte.
Wells, G. A., 8744, Pte.
Welsh, M., 11122, Pte.
West, A. R., 37632, Pte.
West, C. H., 40645, L/Cpl.
West, J., 9952, Pte. D.C.M.
West, J., 41822, Pte.
Westcott, F., 19604, Pte.
Weston, H., 13356, Pte.
Wheeler, J. A., 18566, Pte.
Whitaker, N., 40619, Pte.
White, A., 24866, Sgt. V.C.
White, G., 41202, Pte.
White, W., 41817, Pte.
White, W., 16477, Cpl.
Whittaker, W., 14050, Pte.
Whyatt, A., 45178, Pte.
Whyle, J., 9267, Pte.
Wigfield, T., 18721, Pte.
Wild, G., 41357, Pte.
Wiles, W., 41796, Pte.
Wilkes, A. L., 48148, Pte.
Wilkes, H., 22314, Pte.
Wilkey, E., 13757, Pte.
Wilkins, A. H., 40801, Pte.
Williams, A., 11541, L/Cpl.
Williams, A., 42533, A/Sgt.
Williams, B., 30233, Pte.
Williams, C. H., 19128, Pte.
Williams, D. J., 36119, Pte.
Williams, D. W., 9875, Pte.
Williams, E., 23042, Pte.
Williams, E., 18577, Pte.
Williams, E., 19435, Pte.

THE ROLL OF HONOUR

Williams, E., 13333, Pte.
Williams, E. J., 11548, L/Sgt.
Williams, F., 10059, Pte.
Williams, F., 11608, Pte.
Williams, F., 9766, Pte.
Williams, G., 11943, L/Cpl.
Williams, H. J., 41204, Pte.
Williams, J., 21911, Pte.
Williams, J., 31116, Pte.
Williams, J., 25035, Pte.
Williams, J. D., 25367, Pte.
Williams, J. O., 10873, Pte.
Williams, J. T., 39614, Cpl.
Williams, J., 9763, Pte.
Williams, J., 18469, Pte.
Williams, J., 19911, Pte.
Williams, L. J., 25029, Pte.
Williams, M. C., 41368, Pte.
Williams, O., 44567, Pte.
Williams, R., 24087, Sgt.
Williams, R., 10408, Cpl.
Williams, T., 18464, Pte.
Williams, T., 39646, Pte.
Williams, T., 11748, Pte.
Williams, T., 35598, Pte.
Williams, W., 10566, L/Cpl.
Williams, W., 31474, Pte.
Williams, W., 12079, Pte.
Williams, W. H., 25424, Pte.
Williams, W. M., 16417, Pte.
Willmott, J., 19397, Pte.
Wills, T. E., 9975, Cpl.
Wilmott, F. H., 13759, Pte.
Wilson, A., 14788, Pte.
Wilson, A., 13432, Pte.
Wilson, G. E., 24663, Pte.
Wilson, H., 34608, Cpl.
Wilson, J. H., 14919, Pte.
Wilson, J., 24656, Pte.
Wilson, W., 45195, Pte.
Winrow, H., 45983, Pte.
Winter, F., 24846, Pte.
Wixcey, W. F., 19614, Pte.
Woffenden, A., 9821, Pte.
Wood, A. S., 10824, Cpl.
Wood, J. N., 19505, Pte.
Woodford, F. C., 18875, Pte.
Woodhouse, J., 21549, L/Cpl.
Woods, J., 10354, Pte.
Woods, T., 9813, L/Cpl. D.C.M.
Woods, W., 37118, Pte.
Woolley, E. H., 10103, Pte.
Worrall, J. N., 39959, L/Cpl.
Wright, J., 39823, Pte.
Wright, J., 41363, Pte.
Wrigley, H., 44640, L/Cpl.

Yalden, L., 24848, Pte. M.M.
Yarwood, A., 29591, Pte.
Yerbury, A. E., 40660, Pte.
Young, E., 41962, Pte.
Young, F., 18956, Cpl.
Young, J. W., 15571, Pte.
Young, J., 20547, Pte.

3RD BATTALION.

Alderman, W. J., 35002, Pte.

Baker, C., 19724, L/Cpl.
Belfield, J., 29276, Pte.
Bell, J., 26466, Pte.
Bransfield, P., 19598, Pte.
Broomhead, A. E., 26338, L/Cpl.
Brown, H., 14741, Pte.
Butler, R., 63432, Pte.

Clargo, A. D., 13828, Pte.
Cowles, J. W., 29947, Pte.

Dean, H., 29680, Pte.

Evans, D. R., 27200, Pte.

Fay, E. P., 15144, Pte.
Fincher, J. S., 14148, Pte.
Fisher, S., 13341, Pte.

Griffiths, J., 28837, Pte.
Griffiths, J., 25927, Pte.
Groom, H. S., 31447, Pte.

Holden, S., 37460, Pte.
Hooper, B., 42243, Pte.
Hopkins, W. R., 29807, L/Cpl.
Hough, W., 25470, Pte.
Houghton, S., 29639, Pte.
Howell, F., 9432, L/Cpl.

James, S., 29894, Pte.
Jenkins, J. J., 29542, Pte.
John, J., 19029, Pte.
Jones, A. G., 29015, Pte.
Jones, C. G., 53809, Pte.
Jones, D. J., 29045, Pte.
Jones, M., 63504, Pte.
Jones, W., 27256, Pte.

Jones, W., 29265, Pte.
Jones, W. J., 65190, Pte.

Kelly, P. S., 62952, Pte.

Light, H., 29583, Pte.
Lloyd, W. V., 9293, Pte.
Longman, A. W., 25326, Pte.

McGrath, J., 42059, Pte.
Melluish, C. L., 10672, Boy.
Moore, T. A., 19900, Pte.
Morgan, E., 31682, Pte.
Morris, E. H., 31360, Pte.

Osborne, G., 9362, Pte.

Parry, A, H., 27126, Pte.

Parsons, G., 20727, Sgt.
Powell, E. S., 8048, A/Cpl.
Price, T. H. R., 27277, Pte.

Scourfield, W., 29530, Pte.
Spratt, R., 6484, Sgt.
Stephens, A., 63510, Pte.
Swarbrick, R., 45904, Pte.

Thomas, E., 27303, Pte.
Tricker, E. F., 8322, L/Cpl.
Tucker, F. J. E., 31951, Pte.

Watkins, W. T., 24951, Pte.
Watts, J., 35067, Pte.
Williams, O., 28989, Pte.
Wood, C. H., 25589, Pte.
Wootten, S., 61999, Pte.

4TH BATTALION.

Adey, S., 19804, Pte.
Adnett, J., 19698, Pte.
Alder, P., 12501, Sgt.
Aldridge, G., 12735, Pte.
Allen, E. J., 27741, Pte.
Allen, S. J., 12459, Pte.
Andrews, F. E., 25642, A/Cpl.
Anthony, W., 12838, Pte.
Armstrong, W., 37083, Pte.
Arthur, R., 27639, Pte.
Ashford, C., 27472, Pte.
Ashman, A., 26852, Pte.
Ashwell, W., 12101, Pte.
Atkinson, G. H., 27385, Pte.

Badham, W. J., 12661, Sgt.
Bailey, A. F., 19196, Pte.
Baldwin, J., 18687, Pte.
Ballinger, T., 12616, Pte.
Bartley, J., 33639, Pte.
Barwell, J., 12764, Pte.
Bather, C. E., 27745, Pte.
Beadle, C., 12782, L/Cpl.
Bellamy, G. H., 11300, Pte.
Bellis, H., 19815, Pte.
Bennett, A. G., 12456, Pte.
Bennett, F., 8535, Sgt.
Bentley, F., 13350, Cpl.
Bevan, F. J., 12608, Pte.
Bevan, W., 12609, Pte.
Beynon, W. R., 12972, Pte.
Billingsley, T., 24969, Pte.
Blainey, R., 12345, Pte.
Boulton, F., 15037, Pte.

Bowgen, E. J., 22882, Pte.
Bowkett, J., 27513, Pte.
Bowskill, A., 26951, Pte.
Briddon, F., 26953, Pte.
Bridge, J., 8003, Sgt.
Brindley, W., 12890, Pte.
Britt, S., 24880, Pte.
Broad, E., 12520, Pte.
Brown, C., 19794, Pte.
Brown, H., 7389, Pte.
Brown, H., 27053, Pte.
Brown, T. J., 13117, Pte.
Bulley, W. E., 26948, Pte.
Bush, W. A. W., 13390, C.S.M
Butler, J., 14283, L/Cpl.

Caddy, H., 26846, Pte.
Cadogan, W. A., 26402, Pte.
Caldwell, H., 11358, Pte.
Carpenter, J. G., 30203, Pte.
Carter, W. H., 26888, Pte.
Cartlidge, C., 12772, Pte.
Carvell, I., 12939, Pte.
Cash, G., 44858, Pte.
Caughlin, J., 13931, Cpl.
Cavvell, T. J., 26857, Pte.
Chadwick, C. E., 19813, Pte.
Charlton, W. V., 14272, Sgt.
Chilton, J., 34561, Pte.
Clarke, H., 27752, Pte.
Clarke, W., 27428, Pte.
Clayton, J. W., 26885, Pte.
Clayton, W., 28393, Pte.
Close, W., 12665, Pte.

THE ROLL OF HONOUR

Coles, T., 14259, L/Cpl.
Colman, J., 26641, Pte.
Cook, G., 24865, Pte.
Cook, J., 13091, Sgt.
Cook, S., 13755, L/Cpl.
Cooper, I., 12994, Pte.
Cooper, T., 12629, Pte.
Copping, C., 26514, Pte.
Cording, C., 26858, Pte.
Cornish, A. A., 12752, R.S.M.
Cornwall, W. G., 25879, Pte.
Counsell, F. T., 26859, Pte.
Critchley, W. H., 23390, Pte.
Crocker, W., 44068, Pte.
Crockett, G., 12886, Pte.
Cross, W., 23556, Pte.
Cullum, G., 11742, Pte.
Cunliffe, W. T., 23509, Pte.
Cunnah, J. J., 28390, Pte.

Dale, J., 19777, Pte.
Davies, A. V., 12480, L/Cpl.
Davies, C., 13190, L/Cpl.
Davies, D., 15098, Pte.
Davies, E., 19890, Cpl.
Davies, H., 28395, Pte.
Davies, J., 12295, Cpl.
Davies, J., 13177, Pte.
Davies, J., 12309, Pte.
Davies, R., 14142, Pte.
Davies, S., 30440, Pte.
Davies, W., 12668, Pte.
Davies, W. L., 12792, Pte.
Davis, W., 26860, Pte.
Dearden, S., 27559, Pte.
Dolloway, S., 15544, Pte.
Donovan, P., 12263, Sgt.
Dorrington, W., 28396, Pte.
Dowding, F. A., 27205, Pte.
Downing, T., 19510, Pte.
Drayton, J., 13185, Pte.
Driscoll, D., 14227, Pte.
Driscoll, H., 12449, L/Cpl.
Duckworth, B., 24819, Pte.
Duffield, H., 12530, Pte.
Dunwell, R., 28394, Pte.
Dutton, D., 19829, Pte.
Dutton, J., 19497, Pte.
Dyke, J., 19482, Pte.
Dyson, P., 19868, Pte.

Eastwood, T. E., 26904, L/Cpl.
Edmunds, W., 12374, Pte.
Edwards, B., 13077, Pte.
Edwards, D., 13186, Pte.

Edwards, D. T., 13181, Pte.
Edwards, J. H., 28944, Pte.
Edwards, T., 12776, Pte.
Edwards, W., 13370, Pte.
Edwards, W., 11775, Pte.
Edwards, W. J., 12731, Pte.
Ellis, W. H., 12942, Pte.
Errington, T., 19833, Pte.
Evans, D., 27670, Pte.
Evans, G., 13004, Pte.
Evans, G. T., 12902, Pte.
Evans, G., 12952, Pte.
Evans, J., 28401, Pte.
Evans, J., 12299, Pte.
Evans, J. H., 12671, L/Cpl.
Evans, R., 33672, Pte.
Evans, S., 23267, Pte.
Evans, S., 26831, Pte.
Eyles, H. C., 26845, Pte.

Fidler, T., 14043, L/Cpl.
Finch, H. W., 9095, Pte.
Finch, J., 8903, Pte.
Finnemore, J. T., 19331, Pte.
Fisher, G., 13146, Pte.
Fitzgerald, W., 13271, Pte.
Fives, P., 13459, Pte.
Fletcher, P., 25631, A/Cpl.
Flynn, W., 12267, Sgt.
Fogg, W. J., 44844, Pte.
Ford, C. H., 12839, Pte.
Forrester, D. A., 28403, Pte.
Foster, J., 25515, Pte.
Fox, J. E., 12768, Pte.
Franklin, R., 13076, Pte.
Fry, G., 11959, Pte.
Fynn, J. H., 11220, Pte. V.C.

Garner, F. W., 44062, Pte.
Garratt, J., 19823, Pte.
Gaskell, T., 33949, Pte.
Gateley, A. W., 27659, Pte.
German, J., 24537, Pte.
Gill, S., 24671, Pte.
Gillott, A. L., 33919, Pte.
Gooderidge, J. J., 12898, Pte.
Goodwin, C. H., 26867, Pte.
Gorman, T. H., 12536, Pte.
Gosling, F. M., 35557, Sgt.
Grace, S., 14811, A/Cpl.
Gray, G., 25857, Pte.
Green, F., 13322, Pte.
Green, G., 12504, Pte.
Green, S., 34563, Pte.
Greensmith, G. W., 26962, Pte.

Gresty, J., 19790, Pte.
Greville, A. R., 12945, A/Cpl.
Griffin, J., 12730, L/Cpl.
Griffiths, G. L., 24982, L/Cpl.
Griffiths, M., 13331, Pte.
Griffiths, R., 31444, L/Cpl.
Grimley, J. T., 27641, Pte.
Groves, W. S., 26447, Pte.

Hadfield, J. W., 44759, Pte.
Haines, C., 30237, Pte.
Halford, G., 14048, L/Cpl.
Halford, G., 13852, R.S.M.
Hallesey, W., 30484, Pte.
Hallett, W. A., 26832, Pte.
Hambleton, S., 11885, L/Cpl.
Hamlen, H. G., 24963, Pte.
Hampton, R., 26747, Pte.
Harding, A. J., 44183, Pte.
Harley, W., 27592, Pte.
Harris, D., 11101, Pte.
Harris, G., 22935, Pte.
Harris, J. R., 25772, Pte.
Harvey, R. H., 19883, Pte.
Hayes, H. C., 12823, Pte.
Hayes, I. W. H., 13258, Pte.
Hemmings, G., 12507, L/Cpl.
Hennerley, W., 19832, Pte.
Hennessey, C., 12231, L/Cpl.
Henstock, F., 19839, Pte.
Hewitt, P., 28414, Pte.
Hill, B., 13264, Pte.
Hilton, E., 26892, Pte.
Hines, W., 12837, L/Cpl.
Hockley, G. W., 26909, Pte.
Hodges, A. E., 12728, Pte.
Holroyd, G., 27009, Pte.
Hooper, G. H., 26878, Pte.
Hopkins, E., 26560, Pte.
Houlgrave, W., 37051, L/Cpl.
Howard, F. H., 19904, A/Cpl.
Howell, W. H., 26137, Pte.
Howells, J., 13265, Pte.
Howells, T., 11817, Pte.
Howle, W. D., 27525, Pte.
Howley, C., 27007, A/Sgt.
Hughes, D., 19639, Pte.
Hughes, E., 12505, Pte.
Hughes, J., 24996, Pte.
Hughes, W., 24367, Pte.
Humphreys, A., 12644, Pte.

Iball, G., 26903, A/Cpl.

James, D. G., 30254, Pte.

James, D. J., 30136, Pte.
James, R., 12548, Pte.
James, T., 12383, Pte.
James, T., 12601, A/Cpl.
Jefferies, S., 26327, Pte.
Jeffreys, R., 27488, Pte.
Jenkins, T. W., 34683, L/Cpl.
Jennison, A., 19943, Pte.
John, B., 27111, Pte.
John, T. F., 30012, Pte.
Johns, T., 12498, L/Cpl.
Johns, W., 15396, Pte.
Johnson, A., 25986, Pte.
Johnson, J., 12754, Pte.
Johnson, J., 34537, Pte.
Jones, A., 14213, Pte.
Jones, A. R., 16098, Pte.
Jones, D., 13063, Pte.
Jones, D., 12970, Pte.
Jones, D., 35519, Cpl.
Jones, D. J., 26579, Pte.
Jones, D. J., 28426, Pte.
Jones, D. J., 27778, Pte.
Jones, E. E., 12947, Pte.
Jones, G., 12361, Pte.
Jones, G., 13306, L/Cpl.
Jones, G. E., 28424, Pte.
Jones, H. G. W., 26282, L/Cpl.
Jones, J., 13445, A/C.S.M.
Jones, J., 27774, Pte.
Jones, J., 27773, Pte.
Jones, J., 13067, Pte.
Jones, J. R., 14231, L/Cpl!.
Jones, J. T., 12234, Pte.
Jones, K., 13058, Pte.
Jones, R., 12273, L/Cpl.
Jones, R. W., 12690, Sgt.
Jones, S., 13327, Pte.
Jones, T., 26330, Pte.
Jones, T., 27776, Pte.
Jones, T. M., 27433, Pte.
Jones, T. P., 27511, Pte.
Jones, W., 27583, Pte.
Jones, W., 13166, Pte.
Jones, W. G., 12255, Pte.
Jones, W. H., 12539, Cpl.
Jones, W. J., 13325, Cpl.
Jones, W. L., 12996, Pte.
Jowitt, W., 26911, Pte.
Jukes, E., 14232, Pte.

Kay, A., 25547, Pte.
Kelly, J., 12906, Pte.
Kelly, M., 12789, Pte.
Kelly, T., 11367, Pte.

THE ROLL OF HONOUR

Kelsey, W., 26912, Sgt.
Kempson, T., 13896, Pte.
Kenney, J., 13293, Pte.
Kerton, T., 13279, Pte.
King, C., 37676, Pte.
King, H. I., 27780, Pte.
Kitchener, W., 12125, Pte.
Knight, G., 12727, Pte.
Knowles, F., 44853, Pte.
Kynaston, T., 12969, Sgt.

Lawrence, J., 13052, Pte.
Law, G., 18233, Pte.
Lane, B. A., 27502, Pte.
Lear, P., 12936, Pte.
Lear, W., 12287, Pte.
Lester, J., 19863, Pte.
Lewis, A., 27782, Pte.
Lewis, A., 12543, Pte.
Lewis, E., 30482, Pte.
Lewis, H. S., 19988, Pte.
Lewis, J. H., 28429, Pte.
Lewis, T., 13879, Pte.
Lineham, W. E., 13140, Pte.
Litson, G. W., 13934, Pte.
Lloyd, G., 35216, Pte.
Lloyd, H., 13143, A/Cpl.
Lloyd, R. T., 12290, Pte.
Lock, H. G., 13172, Pte.
Lygo, J. T., 26968, Pte.
Lake, B. W., 30500, Pte.

Maddocks, J., 26463, Pte.
Maggs, F. P., 13116, L/Cpl.
Maidment, R., 27016, Pte.
Mapp, S., 11124, Pte.
Mapstone, E., 13884, Pte.
Marland, W., 19817, Pte.
Martin, A., 13276, Pte.
Martin, E., 36575, Pte.
Masey, W., 24962, L/Cpl.
Mason, A., 27787, Pte.
Matterface, H. T., 22926, Pte.
Matthews, R. J., 30546, Pte.
Matthias, H. G., 12397, Pte.
McCarthy, B., 13958, Pte.
McCarthy, D., 12828, Pte.
McCarthy, W., 12359, L/Cpl.
McCullock, D., 27017, Pte.
McDonald, J., 19827, Pte.
McFarlane, T., 14196, Pte.
McGinley, M., 25584, Pte.
Megson, H., 26896, Pte.
Mercer, J., 44764, Pte.
Meredith, J. C., 13110, L/Cpl.

Metcalfe, J., 27593, Pte.
Milner, J., 33878, Pte.
Mitchell, P., 33669, Pte.
Moffat, R., 19769, Pte.
Moore, H. H., 28436, A/Sgt.
Morgan, A., 24993, Pte.
Morgan, E. T., 12856, Pte.
Morgan, F., 18603, Pte.
Morgan, H. G., 22995, Pte.
Morgan, J., 13839, Pte.
Morgan, J., 12855, Pte.
Morgan, J., 13001, L/Cpl.
Morgan, T., 13684, Pte.
Morgan, T., 14073, Pte.
Morgan, T. G., 12989, Pte.
Morgan, W., 14746, Pte. D.C.M.
Morgan, W., 27794, Pte.
Morgan, W., 30159, Pte.
Morris, H. W., 12229, Pte.
Morris, T., 33940, Pte.
Moseley, M., 13109, Pte.
Moss, A. H., 12496, L/Cpl.
Moynihan, D., 13119, Pte.
Murray, P., 13117, Pte.
Musty, F., 5949, Sgt.
Myerscough, R., 24905, Pte.

Neild, A., 19822, Pte.
Nelson, W., 27075, Pte.
Newman, J., 26941, Pte.
Nicholls, D., 26508, Pte.
Nicklin, H. E., 26974, L/Cpl.
Nightingale, G., 26464, Pte.
Nisbeck, E., 12721, Pte.
Nolan, J., 27020, Pte.
Norris, S., 26873, Pte.

O'Brien, W., 12659, Pte.
O'Grady, P., 12566, Sgt.
O'Neil, J., 22807, Pte.
O'Sullivan, M., 12360, Pte.
Osborne, C., 24997, Pte.
Osmond, H. E., 12833, Pte.
Owen, J. A., 28437, Pte.
Owen, J., 12720, Pte.
Owen, W. E., 34516, Pte.
Owens, D. L., 13928, Pte.

Palmer, A., 12940, Pte.
Parry, E. A., 44846, Pte.
Pateman, F., 12136, Pte.
Peach, A., 28441, Pte.
Peacock, J., 13263, Pte.
Pearce, W. H., 27663, Pte.
Peat, J. G., 14116, L/Cpl.

Peek, E., 15466, Pte.
Peel, R. H., 27029, Pte.
Phillips, F. J., 12662, Pte.
Phipps, H., 12997, Pte.
Pickering, C., 10895, Pte.
Pleace, J., 13129, Pte.
Plumb, C., 34692, Sgt.
Popham, A., 13167, Sgt.
Potter, W., 12799, L/Cpl.
Potts, S. G., 12133, Pte.
Powell, E., 12224, Pte.
Powell, O., 12316, Pte.
Power, W. H., 24981, Pte.
Price, A., 13230, Pte.
Price, J., 25847, Pte.
Price, J., 13957, Pte.
Price, T., 13125, Pte.
Price, W. P., 13036, L/Cpl.
Pritchard, A., 18783, Pte.
Probert, E. J., 10622, Pte.
Proud, H. V., 35343, Pte.

Ralph, V. J., 12138, Pte.
Rees, T., 12681, L/Cpl.
Regan, J., 12222, Pte.
Rendall, A. R., 26855, Pte.
Reynolds, E., 13127, Pte.
Reynolds, H., 12664, Pte.
Reynolds, W. G., 12486, Pte.
Richard, F., 13027, Cpl.
Richards, F., 12742, Pte.
Rintoul, E. W., 27085, Cpl.
Roberts, E., 12770, Pte.
Roberts, F. C., 12716, Pte.
Roberts, G. R., 27645, Pte.
Roberts, H. F., 13132, Pte.
Roberts, W. A., 27809, Pte.
Roberts, W., 28444, Pte.
Robinson, W., 22853, Pte.
Roseveare, F. H., 25025, Pte.
Rudd, T., 11292, L/Cpl.
Rudge, A., 12983, A/Cpl.
Rule, B., 19837, Pte.
Russell, F., 27811, Pte.

Salter, C., 12869, Pte.
Sanders, P. M., 12818, L/Cpl.
Sanderson, E. S., 27035, Pte.
Sandford, J., 26241, Pte.
Sanuders, C., 29782, Pte.
Saunders, J., 14180, Pte.
Saunders, W. M., 14415, Pte.
Savage, W. H., 12563, Sgt.
Saxon, H., 19583, Pte.
Seaman, A., 26838, Pte.

Shanley, J., 13215, Pte.
Sherborne, G., 37057, Pte.
Sill, E., 26922, Pte.
Simon, T., 14745, Pte.
Sirdifield, J., 19197, Pte.
Skegg, W., 26355, Pte.
Slater, H., 27038, Pte.
Slee, F., 24564, Pte.
Smith, G., 19871, Pte.
Smith, G. V., 26597, Pte.
Smith, H. P., 8904, Sgt.
Smith, J. F., 12866, L/Cpl.
Smith, R., 12145, Pte.
Smithers, H., 13138, Pte.
Snell, T., 27646, Pte.
South, F. J., 27629, Pte.
Spencer, C., 13302, Cpl.
Starkey, A. J., 19914, Cpl.
Steele, E., 27033, L/Cpl.
Stephens, A., 18164, Pte.
Stephens, E., 11678, Pte.
Stephens, J., 13221, Pte.   M.M.
Stevens, W., 22851, Pte.
Stinchcombe, A., 12426, Pte.
Stone, J. F., 12962, Pte.
Stone, T., 26853, L/Cpl.
Stonebridge, F., 44065, Pte.
Storey, E., 27034, Pte.
Strauther, G. H., 19755, Pte.
Stubley, P., 26923, Pte.
Sullivan, J., 13446, Pte.
Summerfield, C. W. J., 37693, Pte.

Taker, J., 22799, Pte.
Taylor, A., 13030, L/Cpl.
Taylor, F., 12559, Pte.
Taylor, F. J., 14267, Pte.
Taylor, H., 24684, Pte.
Thaxton, R. S., 45556, Cpl.
Thomas, D. W., 12777, Pte.
Thomas, E., 12751, Pte.
Thomas, F. C., 12588, Pte.
Thomas, H. R., 26412, Pte.
Thomas, J., 14106, Pte.
Thomas, J. H., 24959, Pte.
Thomas, W., 13289, A/Sgt.
Thompson, T., 27040, Pte.
Tillings, A., 12472, Pte.
Tinklin, H. J., 12849, Pte.
Titt, J., 13311, Pte.
Tolcher, J., 13090, Pte.
Tovey, G., 12439, Pte.
Townsend, J. T., 12471, Pte.
Treston, M. H., 12372, Pte.
Trevan, T. H., 34698, Cpl.

THE ROLL OF HONOUR

Trumper, J., 12712, Sgt.
Tudor, T., 26151, Pte.
Turner, G., 26982, Pte.
Tuson, E., 12848, Pte.
Tuson, J., 25504, Pte.
Tyler, A. H., 12817, L/Cpl.
Type, C., 12260, Pte.

Urling, A., 26670, Pte.

Vaughan, E., 33694, Pte.
Venables, A. J., 12673, L/Cpl.
Vickers, H., 26983, Pte.
Vickery, W., 11346, Pte.

Wainwright, C., 28449, Pte.
Wait, G., 19946, L/Cpl.
Walker, F., 26989, L/Cpl.
Walker, J., 27051, Pte.
Walliker, A., 10227, L/Sgt.
Walters, M. J., 27822, Pte.
Walters, T. H., 22920, Pte.
Ward, A., 12711, L/Cpl.
Watkins, E., 13206, Pte.
Watkins, H., 12473, Pte.
Watkins, W. H., 12944, Pte.
Weale, C. J., 26582, Pte.
Wells, E., 26928, Pte.
Welton, J., 26830, A/R.S.M.
Werrett, A. T., 12627, L/Cpl.
West, P., 12147, Pte.
Westby, P., 24847, Pte.
Wheeler, A., 13810, Pte.
Wheeler, G., 25031, Pte.
White, E. J., 44836, Pte.
Whitehead, J., 26991, A/Cpl.

Whitefield, J., 19781, Pte.
Whiteley, A., 27042, Pte.
Whitley, T. H., 26945, Pte.
Whitty, W., 19845, Pte.
Wilcox, M., 13622, Pte.
Wild, J., 25853, Pte.
Williams, A. J., 25022, Pte.
Williams, E., 28451, Pte.
Williams, F., 12560, Pte.
Williams, G., 26117, Pte.
Williams, G., 12995, Pte.
Williams, G. E., 36592, Pte.
Williams, H. J., 28452, Pte.
Williams, J., 14074, Pte.
Williams, J. E., 28453, Pte.
Williams, J., 33675, Pte.
Williams, R. R., 19808, Pte.
Williams, S., 12475, Pte.
Williams, T. J., 13016, Pte.
Williams, W., 12652, Pte.
Williams, W., 14084, Pte.
Willis, A., 22846, Pte.
Willis, T., 12425, A/Sgt.
Wilson, A., 26944, L/Cpl.
Wilson, J. L., 13372, Pte.
Wilson, W., 26993, Pte.
Wood, J., 28454, Pte.
Wood, J., 25796, Pte.
Wright, A. J., 25968, Pte.
Wright, J., 27044, Pte.
Wyatt, G. A., 12984, Pte.
Wyatt, G., 27079, Pte.

Yates, J. E., 12630, Pte.
Young, J., 42294, L/Cpl.
Young, W. F., 12149, Pte.

5TH BATTALION.

Abraham, T., 13882, Cpl.
Adams, D., 21619, Pte.
Adnams, A. H., 14611, Pte.
Alcock, W. G., 16993, Pte.
Amos, W., 14826, Pte.
Anderson, H., 14543, Pte.
Andrews, A., 13903, Cpl.
Andrews, W. H., 40981, Pte.
Ansell, W., 18162, Pte.
Armer, T., 48410, Pte.
Arnold, W., 39323, Pte.
Arnold, W. J., 40950, Pte.

Bailey, W. E., 18080, Pte.
Barber, J., 39886, Pte.
Barlow, S., 33662, Pte.

Barrett, R., 17680, Pte.
Beattie, R., 18385, Pte.
Beckett, H., 18297, Pte.
Benfield, H., 14741, Pte.
Bennett, F. C., 18098, Pte.
Bennett, J. J., 14179, Pte.
Bird, W., 38769, Pte.
Blackburn, T., 46316, Pte.
Blackmore, T. J., 39871, Pte.
Bodman, J. C., 30309, Pte.
Bonner, J., 14540, Pte.
Booth, J., 39287, Pte.
Bowen, J., 18302, L/Sgt.
Bowen, T. J., 14480, Pte.
Boxell, W. E. J., 42512, Pte.
Brittleton, J. W., 33653, Pte.

Broadbent, J., 38644, Pte.
Broadhurst, W. G., 39739, Pte.
Brown, H. J., 42515, Pte.
Brown, P. O., 17491, Pte.
Bryon, S. D., 41657, L/Cpl.
Buckley, J. T., 18963, Pte.
Bull, A., 39835, Pte.
Burgess, J., 46307, Pte.
Bygrave, T., 22880, Pte.
Byrne, M., 39466, Pte.

Capel, J., 14362, Cpl.
Carey, A. L., 22449, Pte.
Carpenter, J., 21130, Pte.
Carruthers, A. E., 41519, Pte.
Casey, P., 17661, Pte.
Chambers, J., 14056, Pte.
Chandler, J. W., 14404, Pte.
Chapman, H., 36048, Pte.
Cheeseman, W., 17950, Pte.
Christopher, T. A., 18392, Pte.
Clark, T. P., 41517, Pte.
Clarke, A., 36155, Pte.
Coburn, J. F., 29790, L/Cpl.
Cocking, T., 14301, Pte.
Cole, E., 14479, Pte.
Cole, T. J., 41514, Pte.
Coleman, T., 20691, Pte.
Colman, F., 14875, Pte.
Conolly, O., 13293, Sgt.
Connor, H., 41518, Pte.
Cook, A. W., 21518, Pte.
Cook, F., 14017, Pte.
Cook, W., 34573, L/Sgt.
Cooke, A. E., 42166, Pte.
Cooper, H., 39782, Pte.
Cooper, W., 25718, Pte.
Cordwell, G. T., 42521, Pte.
Cotterell, P. N., 29296, Pte.
Cotterill, W. C., 34660, Pte.
Cotton, T., 27553, Pte.
Craig, R., 30450, Pte.
Cruttenden, F., 42519, Pte.

Daniels, F., 49550, Pte.
Dart, R., 14058, Pte.
David, W., 32026, Pte.
Davidson, W. D., 14558, L/Cpl.
Davies, C., 14022, Pte.
Davies, G., 17679, Pte.
Davies, G. R., 39875, Pte.
Davies, H., 29613, Pte.
Davies, J., 29566, Pte.
Davies, R. F., 14139, Pte.
Davies, S. E., 18310, Pte.

Davies, T., 18166, Pte.
Davies, T. J., 46192, Pte.
Davies, W., 14024, Pte.
Davies, W. H., 14491, Pte.
Davis, R., 14308, Pte.
Dennis, G. S., 42492, Pte.
Dewhirst, S., 46343, Pte.
Dickinson, A., 40989, Pte.
Diggle, A., 39297, Pte.
Dix, S., 18306, Pte.
Dorcey, J., 13891, Pte.
Drewett, R., 18965, L/Cpl. M.M.

Ebdell, T., 49552, Pte.
Edmonds, J. W., 42150, Pte.
Edwards, E., 14854, Sgt.
Edwards, E., 44137, Pte.
Edwards, E., 14511, Sgt.
Edwards, W. R., 20925, Pte.
Ellery, O. B., 37718, Pte.
Enoch, O., 21753, L/Sgt.
Etheridge, W. G., 40482, Pte.
Evans, E., 14377, Pte.
Evans, E., 14795, Pte.
Evans, J., 28262, Cpl.
Evans, J., 21355, Pte.
Evans, P. J., 27186, Pte.
Everett, R. J., 19370, Pte.
Eynon, J., 14294, Pte.
Exley, A., 24029, Pte.

Feeney, T., 49562, Pte.
Fielding, A. R., 44393, Pte.
Finnigan, L., 39968, Pte.
Fletcher, W. G., 42499, Pte.
Foster, A., 39791, Pte.
Francis, I., 14274, Pte.
Franklin, E., 42497, Pte.
Fry, T., 14834, Pte.
Fuller, H. W., 18266, Pte.

Gallop, J., 18015, Pte.
Gammack, A., 41227, Pte.
Garrard, A. A., 42504, Pte.
Gough, M. S., 26391, Pte.
Gough, W. T., 49565, Pte.
Graves, W. M., 14600, L/Cpl.
Grayson, H. A., 14335, Pte.
Green, F., 14305, Pte.
Gregory, H., 24347, Pte.
Gregory, L., 41683, Pte.
Griffiths, B., 42353, Pte.
Griffiths, C. A., 42503, Pte.
Griffiths, G., 28946, Pte.
Griffiths, R., 41536, Pte.

THE ROLL OF HONOUR

Grimes, A. W., 13890, Sgt.
Gronow, C., 14164, Pte.
Gunn, P., 17959, Pte.

Hall, H. J., 17986, Pte.
Hall, T., 23860, Pte.
Hall, W., 14457, C.Q.M.S.
Hammersley, E., 41545, Pte.
Hancock, W., 26291, A/Cpl.
Hand, T., 39799, Pte.
Harp, F., 14896, Pte.
Harris, T., 14225, Cpl.
Hart, C. W., 19478, L/Cpl.
Hartley, A. E., 29465, Pte.
Haywood, E. T., 42368, Pte.
Hazeldine, A., 45878, Pte.
Heal, W., 42441, Pte.
Hedges, J., 40824, Pte.
Hendrickson, R. J., 14602, Cpl.
Henshall, W. A., 39880, Pte.
Henson, G. T., 23984, Pte.
Hesketh, C., 49571, Pte.
Hibbert, P., 14312, Sgt. D.C.M.
Hickey, J., 34580, Pte.
Hill, F. G., 41039, Pte.
Hill, G., 37122, Pte.
Hillier, A., 14811, Pte.
Hinds, A., 21517, Pte.
Hobbs, F., 14844, Pte.
Hobbs, J. C., 14485, Pte.
Hogarth, R. J., 13930, Pte.
Holden, P., 40964, Pte.
Holland, I. A., 18088, Pte.
Hook, E., 17955, Pte.
Hourahine, A. V., 39740, L/Cpl.
Howe, C., 18284, Sgt.
Howells, R., 14547, Pte.
Hughes, D., 19019, Pte.
Hughes, H. E., 31967, Pte.
Hughes, W., 49585, Pte.
Humphreys, O., 27188, Pte.
Hunt, T., 42440, Pte.
Huss, F. A., 40834, L/Cpl.
Hutcherson, R., 14604, Pte.

Ingham, G. T., 38681, Pte.
Ingham, H., 49588, Pte.

Jenkins, H., 13972, Pte.
Jenkins, D. J., 14069, Pte.
Jenkins, R. B., 16507, Pte.
Jenkins, W. D., 13931, Pte.
Jerrom, D., 36596, Pte.
John, E., 14399, Pte.
Johnson, E., 21576, Pte.

Johnson, J., 49597, Pte.
Johnson, J. B., 24060, Pte.
Johnson, J. W., 17639, Cpl.
Johnston, V., 14315, Sgt.
Jones, D. L., 18255, Pte.
Jones, D. W., 19391, Pte.
Jones, E., 44520, Pte.
Jones, H., 35317, Pte.
Jones, H. W., 27544, Pte.
Jones, I. A., 41009, Pte.
Jones, J., 39418, Pte.
Jones, J. A., 53950, Pte.
Jones, J. W., 23532, L/Cpl.
Jones, R., 14610, Pte.
Jones, S., 14660, L/Cpl.
Jones, S. L. G., 44566, Pte.
Jones, S., 39302, L/Cpl.
Jones, T., 14141, Pte.
Jones, T., 17939, Pte.
Jones, W. E., 49604, Pte.
Jones, W. J., 41662, Pte.

Keen, J. M., 14104, C.S.M.
Kierman, J. L., Pte.
Knowles, F., 25606, Pte.

Lacon, C., 38107, Pte.
Landers, M., 13882, Pte.
Lane, I., 41573, Pte.
Langham, J. H., 49617, Pte.
Langley, A., 18051, Pte.
Lee, G., 19282, Pte.
Lee, W., 41578, Pte.
Lefley, L., 34663, Pte.
Lewis, C. W., 14309, Pte.
Lewis, E., 18313, Pte.
Lewis, E. T., 18422, Pte.
Lewis, G., 14739, Pte.
Lewis, I., 14787, Pte. M.M.
Lewis, J. A., 29792, Pte.
Lewis, W., 14614, Pte.
Lewis, W. B., 18068, Pte.
Lewis, W. S., 18017, Pte.
Lloyd, D., 14492, Pte.
Lloyd, T., 14050, Pte.
Long, F., 18653, A/Cpl.
Lonsdale, R., 16099, Pte.
Lowe, J., 14295, L/Cpl.
Lyddaman, J., 45850, Pte.
Lyddon, G., 14548, L/Cpl.

Marchant, W. A., 21861, Cpl.
Marsden, S. N., 14618, A/Sgt.
Marsh, G., 39328, Pte.
Marsh, T. R., 14118, Pte.

THE HISTORY OF THE SOUTH WALES BORDERERS

Marshall, J. H., 18264, Pte.
Martin, L. H., 41014, Pte.
Masheter, A. E., 49628, Pte.
Matthews, H. T., 29964, Pte.
Mayberry, S., 14705, Pte.
McCoy, J. W., 41585, Pte.
McNamee, L., 18121, Pte.
McNelis, J., 39859, Pte.
Meek, H., 24790, Pte.
Meek, J. B., 14881, Pte.
Mepham, E. J., 45251, Pte.
Millbank, E. G., 19427, Pte.
Mitchell, S. O., 17919, Pte.
Mitchener, W., 13906, C.S.M. D.C.M.
Morgan, C., 39337, Pte.
Morgan, E. T., 39109, Pte.
Morgan, G. E., 26533, Pte.
Morgan, W. V., 29351, Pte.
Morris, C. H. B., 41665, Pte.
Morris, D. R., 41583, Pte.
Motler, F. E., 41586, Pte.
Mulherne, J., 39332, Pte.

Naylor, J., 40501, Sgt.
Newell, J. T., 39304, Pte.
Nicholas, A. F., 13904, A/Cpl.
Norman, R., 11033, Pte.
Notcutt, H. A., 35560, Pte.

O'Connor, J., 13836, Pte.
Onions, W., 23418, Pte.
Outten, D., 39290, Pte.
Owen, A., 39812, Pte.
Owen, J., 39429, Pte.
Owen, J. L., 41677, Pte.
Owen, S., 22443, Drmr.
Owens, A., 39344, Pte.
Owlett, C. S., 40971, Pte.

Parry, E. R., 41601, Pte.
Parry, T., 29620, Pte.
Parry, T. O., 41600, Pte.
Parton, T., 22266, Pte.
Patey, P. J., 24803, Pte.
Pearce, W. E., 21830, Cpl.
Peers, T., 39283, Pte.
Perkins, W. H., 41605, Pte.
Pero, N., 39847, Pte.
Phillips, W., 17943, Pte.
Phillips, W. J., 13916, Pte.
Pinches, J., 26390, A/Cpl.
Plucknett, W., 39349, Pte.
Poole, J., 19444, L/Cpl.
Poole, W., 14794, Pte.
Powell, B. T., 14432, Pte.

Powell, C., 13874, Pte.
Price, G. M., 39816, Pte.
Price, J., 14433, Pte. M.M.
Price, T., 18100, Pte.
Price, T., 39435, Pte.
Price, W. G., 15447, Pte.
Prior, W., 13834, Pte.
Pritchard, T., 39431, Pte.
Pryce, G., 17637, Pte.
Pugh, J. T., 38745, Pte.

Rawlings, F., 16113, A/Sgt.
Read, A., 42467, Pte.
Reason, H., 42468, Pte.
Reece, L. J., 14339, Pte.
Rees, C., 14119, Pte.
Rees, H., 18195, Pte.
Reid, J., 42325, Pte.
Richards, A., 17990, Pte.
Richards, F. H., 22980, Pte.
Richards, J. G. F., 18966, Sgt. M.M.
Ridout, F., 14751, Pte.
Rimmer, S., 39252, Pte.
Roberts, A. D., 14534, Pte.
Roberts, G., 14733, Pte.
Roberts, W., 30277, Pte.
Robey, W. T., 27196, Pte.
Robinson, F., 21612, Pte.
Rock, A. E., 42469, Pte.
Roden, S. J., 39366, L/Cpl.
Rollings, S., 39876, Pte.
Rose, G., 35137, Pte.
Rosser, W., 14429, L/Sgt.
Rothwell, J. W., 41610, Pte.
Ruddick, E., 39367, Cpl.
Ryan, D., 14938, L/Sgt.

Salter, J., 14423, Pte.
Seager, A., 14320, Pte. M.M.
Searle, S., 11230, C.S.M. D.C.M
Shackleton, V., 14187, Pte.
Shattock, J., 39375, L/Cpl.
Skelhorn, J., 29365, Pte.
Skelton, W., 14773, Pte.
Smith, A., 41626, Pte.
Smith, A., 48767, Pte.
Smith, A. J., 26409, Pte.
Smith, C., 39378, Pte.
Smith, E., 22795, Pte.
Smith, H., 19514, Pte.
Smith, J., 18069, Pte.
Smith, P., 39442, Pte.
Smith, W., 14317, Pte.
Smith, W. J., 41620, Pte.
Smithey, G., 14855, Cpl. D.C M.

THE ROLL OF HONOUR

Spanswick, J., 39382, Pte.
Spark, J. J., 14640, Pte.
Spinks, H., 39383, Pte.
Stanfield, H., 41621, Pte.
Steen, G. W., 39371, Pte.
Stowell, J. H., 8440, Cpl.
Stringer, C., 17652, L/Cpl.
Strode, W. J., 39384, Pte.
Sullivan, J., 14892, Pte.

Taylor, E., 20268, Pte.
Taylor, G. H., 39391, Pte.
Taylor, T., 14806, Pte.
Thomas, A., 33006, Pte.
Thomas, E., 29547, Pte.
Thomas, G., 12068, Pte.
Thomas, H. I., 29043, Pte.
Thomas, I. G., 41631, Pte.
Thomas, J., 14635, Pte.
Thomas, K. G., 41670, Pte.
Thomas, T. J. H., 39447, Pte.
Thomas, W. J., 31160, Pte.
Thomas, W. O., 29616, Pte.
Thompson, J., 14006, Cpl.
Thompson, L., 48771, Pte.
Thorpe, A., 18311, L/Cpl.
Thwaites, R. W., 21614, Pte.
Tilton, W. C., 14587, Pte.
Tizzard, A. E., 42479, Pte.
Todd, C., 36560, Pte.
Townson, R., 38618, Pte.
Trehearne, C., 14412, Sgt.
Trickett, F., 31995, Pte.
Tudor, G., 18258, Sgt.
Turner, H., 14647, Pte.
Twiss, F., 36302, L/Cpl.
Tyler, C., 39392, Pte.

Vahey, A. C., 41641, Pte.
Veness, G. F., 41642, Pte.
Verge, T. N., 17655, Pte.
Vigers, S., 14693, Pte.
Vince, J., 39395, Pte.

Wainwright, S., 13881, Pte.
Wall, S. H., 41507, Pte.

Wallace, J., 17527, L/Cpl.
Walker, J. G., 39405, L/Cpl.
Wallwork, J. T., 46483, Pte.
Walsh, J., 41461, Pte.
Walters, G., 39452, Pte.
Ware, D. T., 17576, Sgt.
Warren, H. W., 17966, Pte.
Watkins, F. H., 17989, Pte.
Watkins, I., 39229, L/Cpl.
Watkins, W. J., 17968, Pte.
Weaver, R. J. H., 48778, Pte.
Webster, W. H., 41508, Pte.
Welden, F., 14410, Pte.
Westwood, J., 44403, Pte.
White, J., 15457, Pte.
Whittall, R. W., 41644, Pte.
Willcocks, R., 23858, L/Cpl.
Wilkins, G., 41901, Pte.
Williams, A. I., 25480, Pte.
Williams, D. G., 18260, Pte.
Williams, J., 17981, Pte.
Williams, J. H., 14459, Pte.
Williams, J., 58489, Pte.
Williams, R. W., 15222, Pte.
Williams, T., 13892, L/Cpl.
Williams, W., 39398, Pte.
Williams, W. D., 14520, Pte.
Williams, W. H., 14682, Pte. M.M.
Williams, W. J., 10655, Pte.
Willmott, W. H., 14337, Pte.
Willshire, A. E., 39850, Pte. M.M.
Winch, W., 14864, L/Cpl.
Wincop, A., 41654, Pte.
Wilson, G. W., 39397, Pte.
Wilson, J., 18142, Pte.
Woodbridge, C., 40792, Pte.
Woodcock, R., 41038, Pte.
Woodyatt, T. F., 41502, Pte.
Woolf, M., 42488, Pte.
Woolgar, E., 19051, Pte.
Workman, E., 14408, Pte.
Worrall, B., 39407, L/Cpl.

Young, A. M., 14165, Pte.

Zensz, S., 42489, Pte.

6TH BATTALION.

Addison, E., 19702, Cpl.
Ainsworth, E., 16903, A/Sgt.
Alders, M., 42269, Pte.
Allman, E. J., 40160, Pte.
Anderson, W. J., 40855, Pte.
Andrews, A. J., 16419, Pte.

Arding, C. L. S., 48865, Pte.
Armstrong, R., 40854, Pte.

Bailey, S., 41699, Pte.
Baines, R., 29376, Pte.
Baines, W., 31170, Pte.

Baker, C., 42397, Pte.
Balme, S., 48876, Pte.
Banwell, F., 29702, Pte.
Barker, J., 48885, Pte.
Bate, E., 29749, Pte.
Bath, J., 25821, Pte.
Baxendale, G., 41696, Pte.
Beashel, N., 19968, Pte.
Beddington, T. W., 17098, Pte.
Bell, J., 53957, Cpl.
Bennett, A. J., 45276, Pte.
Bilsborough, W. T., 41704, Pte.
Binns, N., 19232, Pte.
Birchenough, H., 40079, Pte.
Blake, R., 48872, Pte.
Blunt, F., 14494, Cpl.
Bonnell, H. G., 19713, Pte.
Boswell, W. S., 26639, Pte.
Bowtell, H. C., 45796, Pte.
Braithwaite, R. P., 40538, Pte.
Brems, B., 40860, Pte.
Brothwood, E., 17201, Pte.
Brown, A. E., 48882, Pte.
Brown, H. G., 41710, Pte.
Brown, J., 16546, Pte.
Brown, R., 40859, Pte.
Brown, W. H., 17560, Pte.
Buckingham, G. J., 45282, Pte.
Buckley, J., 29679, Pte.
Burnie, R., 48878, Pte.
Burtonshaw, N., 16981, Pte.
Bustin, F., 16990, Pte.
Bywater, J. C., 40082, Pte.

Caddy, R. E., 30151, Pte.
Campbell, T., 21546, Pte.
Carbin, T. W., 17269, L/Cpl.
Carter, T. J., 19380, Pte.
Carthy, F. J., 41718, Pte.
Cater, J. P., 40089, Pte.
Charles, I. T., 39247, Pte.
Charlton, J., 17557, Pte.
Chattington, T. H., 16470, Sgt. M.M.
Chesworth, W. E. K., 29486, Pte.
Chipman, F. A., 40864, Pte.
Clark, F. J. H., 42399, Pte.
Clarke, W. H., 14452, Pte.
Clement, G., 48889, Pte.
Clements, C., 17068, Pte.
Cole, A. B., 45284, Pte.
Coleman, H. J., 36570, Pte.
Coles, C., 17066, Sgt.
Coles, W. J., 17187, Pte.
Collier, C., 17221, Pte.
Collins, J., 17347, Cpl.

Coombs, G., 17548, Pte.
Coombs, T., 17288, Pte.
Cooper, W., 41717, Pte.
Compton, S., 17459, Pte.
Corcoran, J., 16385, Pte.
Cottam, R. H., 19673, Pte.
Cox, A. J., 39474, Pte.
Cox, J., 17606, Pte.
Coyle, P., 16848, L/Cpl.
Crane, A., 10822, Cpl.
Crane, G., 19652, Pte.
Critchley, W. A., 48892, Pte.
Crompton, J., 48899, Pte.
Croxton, H., 42391, Pte.

Dancey, G., 40137, Pte.
Dark, G. A., 19683, Pte.
Dart, G. K., 16852, Pte.
Davenport, A., 41734, Pte.
David, G. F., 29176, Pte.
Davies, C., 41720, Pte.
Davies, G. H., 17621, Cpl.
Davies, G., 16338, Pte.
Davies, I., 48903, Pte.
Davies, J., 17075, Pte.
Davies, J., 19880, Pte.
Davies, R., 16421, Pte.
Davies, R. T., 41728, Pte.
Davies, W., 16412, Pte.
Davies, W., 40144, Pte.
Davies, W. H., 39298, Pte.
Davies, W. J., 17280, Pte.
Davies, W. M., 39565, Pte.
Dean, A., 29253, Pte.
Delves, W. H., 41045, Pte.
Donovan, E. T., 16461, Pte.
Dorkings, E., 16762, Pte.
Downs, P., 41736, Pte.
Drew, E., 17030, Cpl.
Driscoll, J., 9620, L/Cpl.
Drummond, A. J., 46006, Pte.
Dunn, H., 29284, Pte.

Easthope, W. E., 24165, Cpl.
Eddleston, B., 17237, Pte.
Edgerton, J., 42333, Pte.
Edwards, G., 40093, Pte.
Egerton, W. T., 41740, Pte.
Ellis, R., 39270, Pte.
Ellis, V. C., 40875, Pte.
Elsdon, E. W., 42404, Pte.
Elston, W. F., 41741, Pte.
Emanuel, F. J., 39288, L/Cpl.
Entwistle, W., 39212, Pte.
Evans, A. H., 42252, Pte.

THE ROLL OF HONOUR

Evans, G., 29189, Pte.
Evans, J., 17623, Pte.
Evans, M., 27403, Pte.
Evans, T., 39248, Pte.

Fallon, L., 17202, Pte.
Farrington, G., 41747, Pte.
Farthing, A. G., 40876, Pte.
Fawcett, J. T., 48921, Pte.
Fellows, J. T., 17106, L/Sgt. M.M.
Field, H., 40096, Pte.
Finch, H. W., 41746, Pte.
Fletcher, F., 16346, Pte.
Fletcher, J. H., 41745, Pte.
Ford, A. L., 30251, Pte.
Foster, A., 41044, L/Cpl.
Foster, J., 39197, Pte.
Foulkes, D., 16955, A/Sgt.
Francis, I. G., 27357, Pte.
Franklin, A., 23859, Pte.

Gallagher, J., 42322, Pte.
Gallimore, G., 53810, Pte.
Gardiner, W., 31977, Pte.
Gardner, L., 40483, Pte.
Garrard, E. S., 36590, Pte.
Gibbon, T. J., 23319, Pte.
Glenister, A., 9388, R.S.M.
Goff, E. F., 39679, Pte.
Goodman, W. H., 16401, Sgt. M.M.
Goodwin, A., 36153, Pte.
Goulding, J. W., 15121, Pte.
Grandorge, M. W., 41001, Pte.
Grant, G., 18126, Pte.
Green, C., 42293, Pte.
Greenway, F. J., 29421, Pte.
Griffiths, H., 38665, L/Cpl.
Griffiths, P. D., 48925, Pte.
Griffiths, R. W., 40170, Pte.
Guy, B., 19049, Pte.
Gunning, S., 39283, Pte.

Hadley, E., 17143, Pte.
Hall, J., 16498, Pte.
Hallworth, A., 29699, Pte.
Hammond, A. G., 17571, Pte.
Hampton, J., 44415, Pte.
Hancock, A. W., 19896, Pte.
Hargreaves, C., 17350, Pte.
Hargreaves, R., 45979, Pte.
Harris, G. W., 40130, Pte.
Hawkins, G. T., 17015, L/Cpl.
Head, G., 40882, Pte.
Head, J., 16850, Pte.

Heap, A. E., 38574, L/Cpl.
Heath, A. G., 42408, Pte.
Heath, E., 29223, Pte.
Hemmings, A., 16997, Sgt.
Henson, R., 16818, Pte.
Herbert, F., 34545, Pte.
Hern, D. J., 17139, Pte.
Hickey, J., 16258, L/Sgt.
Hicks, C., 42279, Pte.
Higgins, T., 42295, Pte.
Hitchings, W. L., 15597, Sgt.
Hogg, J. M., 40895, Pte.
Holliday, W., 16760, Pte. D.C.M.
Hollis, H., 53808, Pte.
Hopkins, D., 16931, Pte.
Hopkins, E., 17624, Pte.
Houlding, C. V., 42264, Pte.
Howden, J., 42321, L/Cpl.
Howell, G., 40156, Pte.
Howell, W. J., 17550, Pte.
Hudson, H. S., 39210, Pte.
Hughes, H. V., 60025, Pte.
Hughes, O. J., 46969, Pte.
Hughes, P. J., 40889, Pte.
Hughes, T., 19712, Pte.
Hughes, W., 40686, Pte.
Humber, M., 42249, Pte.

Jackson, E., 45182, Pte.
James, A., 29195, Pte.
James, D., 17846, Pte.
James, G. F., 16532, Pte.
James, J. E., 31589, Pte.
James, W., 16986, Pte.
Jefferies, J., 19649, Pte.
Jenkins, C. L., 39309, Cpl.
Jenkins, R., 17070, Pte.
Jenner, W. J., 17608, Pte.
Jennings, W., 39271, Pte.
Jones, C. T., 34722, Pte.
Jones, C. W., 17036, L/Cpl.
Jones, D., 14379, Pte.
Jones, D. R., 16947, Pte.
Jones, G., 17480, Pte.
Jones, H., 40109, Pte.
Jones, H., 40692, Pte.
Jones, P. B., 40164, Pte.
Jones, R. E., 17455, Sgt
Jones, T., 17344, Pte.
Jones, T. J., 17315, Pte.

Kavanagh, T., 19382, Pte.
Kelly, H. E., 36497, Pte.
Kelly, W., 16820, Pte.
Kidd, W., 40898, Pte.

573

Lacey, W., 17249, Pte.
Lamb, F., 16975, Cpl.
Lander, W. E., 17176, Sgt. M.M.
Lane, R. W., 48806, Pte.
Latham, J., 40696, Pte.
Laycock, W. E., 39234, Pte.
Leah, F., 40016, Pte.
Lee, E., 42412, Pte.
Lee, L., 40694, Pte.
Lees, E., 39203, Pte.
Lester, I. P., 16880, Pte.
Lewis, B. J., 16794, Pte. M.M.
Lewis, D. W., 39525, Pte.
Lewis, E. H., 29232, Pte.
Lewis, R. A., 29652, Pte.
Lewis, L., 17246, Pte. M.M.
Lewis, S. R., 21966, L/Cpl.
Lindsay, T., 17281, Pte.
Livermore, T., 42393, Pte.
Llewellyn, C., 16121, Sgt.
Lloyd, C. F., 42413, Pte.
Lloyd, R., 41075, Pte.
Lloyd, T. J., 16951, Pte.
Lubick, I., 42411, Pte.
Lumley, G., 40902, Pte.
Luttrell, J. H., 35164, Pte.

Mainwaring, A., 22178, Pte.
Mahoney, J., 17279, Pte.
Malan, J., 37841, Pte.
Marsh, W. S., 42308, Pte.
Martin, S., 42318, Pte.
Mazzie, A., 17042, Pte.
McCollom, R., 42715, Pte.
McCrory, J., 17585, Pte.
Melling, G. H., 24580, Pte.
Mercer, S., 42713, Pte.
Miller, A., 17135, Pte.
Mills, F., 40905, Pte.
Moorcroft, H., 39243, Pte.
Morgan, H. A., 16796, L/Cpl.
Morgan, L., 40556, Pte.
Morgan, M. H., 45588, Pte.
Morris, C., 22889, Pte.
Morris, D., 39329, L/Cpl.
Morris, J. T., 16950, Pte.
Morris, R. H., 31907, Pte.
Morton, S. O., 40906, Pte.
Mulloy, E., 39340, Pte.
Muris, W., 40910, Pte.
Murphy, W., 40903, Pte.
Myers, H., 42418, Pte.

Neale, O., 48852, Pte.
Neate, C., 41082, Pte.

Nelson, H., 45806, Pte.
Nethercott, W., 17506, Pte. M.M.
Norgrove, G., 29382, Pte.
Norris, J., 16943, Cpl.

O'Connell, S., 17552, Pte.
Osmond, W. H., 15601, L/Cpl.
Owen, D. T., 25385, Pte.
Oxley, H. H., 32100, Pte.
Oxton, G. H., 41496, Pte.

Paddock, A., 15209, Pte.
Panting, W. R., 17165, Pte.
Parker, D. G., 17619, C.S.M.
Paulin, S., 40914, Pte.
Pearson, S., 17183, Pte.
Perkins, C., 42281, Pte.
Perkins, W. C., 31578, Pte.
Perkins, W., 40121, Pte.
Perry, J., 17204, Pte.
Phillips, E., 31572, Pte.
Phillips, L., 14553, Pte.
Pink, A., 17341, Pte.
Porter, S., 40132, Pte.
Powell, D. R., 29212, Pte.
Price, A. C., 13769, Pte.
Price, W., 29930, Pte.
Priest, W. J., 41325, Pte.
Prince, B. H. R., 29802, Pte.
Prince, I., 29040, L/Cpl. M.M.
Pudner, W. B. L., 26375, Pte.

Quick, J., 17320, Pte.

Ranson, J., 19223, C.S.M. M.M.
Reacher, F., 42289, Pte. M.M.
Rees, I., 31882, Pte.
Rees, J., 15966, Pte.
Rees, J., 16428, L/Cpl. M.M.
Rees, L. T., 29573, Pte.
Rees, W. E., 29882, Pte.
Reynolds, W. T., 17529, Pte. M.M.
Richards, D., 17367, L/Cpl.
Richards, J. H., 44447, Pte.
Richardson, J., 17346, Pte.
Rider, W. V., 39199, Pte.
Rigby, R., 45997, Pte.
Ring, W. J., 39219, Pte.
Robbins, R. T. J., 30313, Pte.
Roberts, A., 39182, Pte.
Ryan, M., 17488, Pte.

Salter, S., 40849, Pte.
Seaton, V. F., 38747, Pte.

THE ROLL OF HONOUR

Skym, M., 16871, Pte.
Snelling, T., 45170, Cpl.
Snowball, T. W., 40927, Pte.
Spoors, L. T., 40923, Pte.
Stacey, E., 19648, Pte.
Stagg, C. A., 18390, Pte.
Stapleton, A. L., 31804, Pte.
Stephenson, W. T., 25273, Pte.
Sully, A., 17592, Cpl.
Sullivan, J., 17420, Pte.
Sumpter, J., 40710, Pte.
Swales, W., 40926, Pte.

Tagell, F., 29219, Pte.
Taylor, C., 40725, Pte.
Taylor, R., 16845, Cpl.
Terry, W., 16725, Sgt.
Theobald, E., 17082, L/Sgt.
Thomas, F., 39232, Pte.
Thomas, G., 16752, Pte.
Thomas, J. W., 297828, Pte.
Thomas, N., 17077, Sgt.
Thomas, S. V., 48409, Pte.
Thomas, W., 17627, Pte.
Thomas, W., 14491, Sgt. M.M.
Tobin, J., 40933, Pte.
Tolman, A., 39179, Pte.
Tomkinson, J. E., 40724, Pte.
Tonks, I., 17124, Pte.
Troy, J., 39227, Pte.
Turberville, J., 13054, Cpl.
Turnbull, R., 40932, Pte.
Turner, C. W., 16360, Sgt.

Venn, S., 22367, Pte.

Vimpany, E., 42251, Pte.
Viney, L., 39217, Pte.

Wakefield, H., 40940, Pte.
Wall, W., 25679, Pte.
Walters, D., 16783, Pte.
Walters, T. H., 17189, Pte.
Walters, W. H., 25520, L/Cpl.
Walton, J. R., 40853, L/Cpl.
Ward, G., 19782, Pte.
Ware, D., 17490, Pte.
Watkins, T. J., 17582, C.S.M.
Watt, R., 17110, Pte.
West, E., 42266, Pte.
Weston, T., 14086, Pte.
White, J., 16790, L/Cpl.
Whittaker, T., 29239, Pte.
Wigmore, H., 17117, Pte.
Wilde, R., 33173, Pte.
Williams, A., 16329, Sgt. M.M.
Williams, A. T., 17418, Pte.
Williams, G., 17492, L/Cpl.
Williams, J., 39240, Pte.
Williams, J. A., 40352, Pte.
Williams, P., 16972, Pte.
Williams, S., 54140, Pte.
Williams, W. T., 16911, Pte.
Williams, W. T., 40731, Pte.
Wilson, T. A., 40938, Pte.
Winterscale, P., 46634, Pte.
Woodhall, J. J., 17099, L/Cpl.
Woodward, H., 39257, Pte.

Youcks, J., 41056, Pte.
Young, L., 18353, Pte. M.M.

7TH BATTALION.

Abel, F. J., 64091, Pte.
Abraham, B., 28376, Pte.
Armitage, P., 45414, Pte.
Askey, C., 37646, Pte.

Baker, A., 36244, Pte.
Ball, J., 16906, Pte.
Beddow, O., 15515, L/Cpl.
Bell, J., 45948, Pte.
Benjamin, H. B., 22893, Pte.
Bennett, E., 15596, Pte.
Bennett, G. E., 14954, Pte.
Bishop, J., 27543, Pte.
Braddock, F., 48223, Pte.
Brannan, D., 64060, Pte.
Bratt, M. A., 19272, Pte.
Braund, T., 28333, Pte.

Broad, W. R., 64225, Pte.
Brown, M., 14921, Pte.
Brown, W., 45417, Pte.
Buck, T., 18357, Pte.
Budgett, E., 13455, Pte.
Burrell, H. W., 19312, Pte.
Burrows, A., 15848, Pte.

Challenger, J., 28375, Pte.
Chappel, A. S., 15606, Pte.
Collinge, L., 46230, Pte.
Cooke, W., 14079, A/R.S.M.
Connors, T., 15457, Sgt.

Davies, E., 19010, Pte.
Davies, J., 46183, Pte.
Davies, J. H., 15498, Sgt.

THE HISTORY OF THE SOUTH WALES BORDERERS

Davies, T. L., 26752, Pte.
Dicken, L., 15649, Pte.
Didcott, F., 17880, L/Cpl.
Donovan, P., 10399, Pte.
Drew, S. F., 14054, L/Cpl.

Edwards, D. J., 15678, Pte.
Ellison, G., 64036, Pte.
Evans, F., 44943, Pte.
Evans, H. E., 21069, Pte. M.M.
Evans, W. J., 19094, Pte.

Farley, S. G., 44997, Pte.
Fear, J. H., 15297, L/Cpl.
Fogarty, J., 48365, Pte.
Fowler, G., 15346, Cpl.

Garrity, E., 18001, L/Cpl.
George, A. C., 15191, Pte.
Gibb, J., 15320, Pte.
Griffiths, W., 38986, Pte.
Greenhill, E. A., 11337, Pte.

Hall, W., 64068, Pte.
Hansom, J., 48272, Pte.
Hardman, J., 42218, A/Cpl.
Harrington, J., 15722, Pte.
Heath, P. T., 17896, A/Cpl. M.M.
Henderson, E. T., 14114, Pte.
Hibberd, J. A., 18225, Pte.
Hill, J. H., 64032, Pte.
Hillier, W., 21715, Pte.
Hiscox, C., 15400, Pte.
Holliday, W., 48328, Pte.
Hookham, S. R., 48319, Pte.
Huxtable, W., 15078, A/Cpl.

Illing, W. B., 44994, Pte.
Ingram, J., 19462, Pte.

Jackson, L., 64058, Pte.
Jackson, S., 16765, Pte.
Jacob, W. J., 18231, Pte.
Jacobson, W., 19265, Pte.
James, F. C., 34776, Pte.
James, J., 15960, Pte.
Johnson, H., 64034, Pte.
Jones, B., 15129, Pte.
Jones, D., 48235, Pte.
Jones, J., 15688, A/Sgt.
Jones, P., 39039, Pte.
Jones, W., 44971, Pte.
Jones, W. B., 14135, Pte.
Jordan, E., 19467, Pte.
Joseph, I., 18254, Pte.

Lee, G., 15343, Pte.
Leech, H. B., 45432, Pte.
Leigh, A. E., 48382, Pte
Letts, T. F., 64061, Pte.
Lewis, A. W., 27459, Pte.
Lewis, H., 45805, Pte.
Lewis, J., 15436, Pte.
Lloyd, D. W., 16090, L/Cpl.
Lloyd, E., 48304, Pte.
Lloyd, W., 26799, Pte.
Lotz, H., 44615, Pte.
Lowe, J. T., 24628, L/Cpl.

Mannion, T., 27618, Pte.
Martin, F., 64071, Pte.
Martin, T., 12724, Pte.
McDermott, J., 15733, Sgt.
Merrick, A. F., 18355, Sgt.
Miller, W. R., 45059, Pte.
Mills, J. F., 14921, Sgt.
Mills, W. K., 31592, Pte.
Moremon, T. H., 45049, Pte.
Morgan, T., 45060, Pte.
Morris, J., 19046, Pte.
Morris, T., 15041, L/Cpl.

Naylor, H., 48341, Pte.
Newbound, J., 18318, Pte.
Newell, W., 15395, L/Cpl.
Newman, B., 44959, Pte.
Norman, W. H., 9081, L/Cpl.

Ogden, W., 64038, Pte.
Orwin, T., 64094, Pte.
Owen, I., 15202, L/Cpl.
Owen, W., 30214, Pte.
Owens, J., 45055, Pte.

Patterson, W. J., 45851, C.S.M.
Pegler, W., 14995, Pte.
Percy, J., 26616, Pte.
Phillis, E., 15305, Pte.
Phillips, W. J., 27447, Pte.
Price, G. W. T., 46237, Pte.
Probert, R., 27101, Pte.
Procter, B., 19202, Pte.

Rackham, J. J., 19079, L/Sgt.
Rawle, R., 19021, Pte.
Reddall, S., 18247, Pte.
Redding, J., 14944, Pte.
Reid, G., 15667, Pte.
Reynolds, H., 14964, Pte.
Richards, I., 15244, L/Cpl.
Richards, T., 13852, Pte.

THE ROLL OF HONOUR

Roberts, G. A., 22539, Pte.
Rosser, E., 18158, Pte.

Shakespeare, S., 64067, Pte.
Shand, D., 46240, Pte.
Shellard, W. H., 15285, Pte.
Simister, G., 48383, Pte.
Simpson, J. D., 15060, Pte.
Slade, F. H., 15264, Pte.
Smith, D., 25812, Pte.
Smith, F., 18746, Pte.
Stanley, G. W., 44993, Pte.
Steventon, A., 39201, Pte.
Stott, W. H., 15559, Cpl.

Taylor, A. P., 45838, Pte.
Taylor, G., 15423, Cpl.
Taylor, R., 18986, L/Cpl.
Thomas, W. E., 28476, Pte.
Tippins, S. J., 42174, Pte.
Tyrrell, J., 18328, A/Cpl.

Vine, H. C., 15549, Pte. M.M.

Walker, R., 7845, Sgt.
Ward, O. G., 19262, Pte.
Warner, J., 46185, Pte.
Watkins, J., 15246, Pte.
West, W., 64069, Pte.
Wheeler, W. H., 15470, Pte.
Whines, B., 15683, Sgt.
Whitehouse, W. A., 48209, Pte.
Williams, A. M., 44975, Pte.
Williams, A., 15128, Sgt.
Williams, C., 19257, A/Cpl.
Williams, E. J., 27440, Pte.
Williams, H. E., 15462, Sgt.
Williams, H. O., 44982, Pte.
Williams, R., 20502, L/Cpl.
Williams, S., 18834, Pte.
Williams, T., 18323, Cpl.
Williams, T., 44951, Pte.
Williams, W. G., 16295, L/Cpl.
Windsor, A., 18252, Pte.

8TH BATTALION.

Arthur, T., 14599, Sgt.

Beynon, D. J., 16058, Cpl.

Chambers, E. G., 18211, Pte.
Charles, R. E., 17406, C.Q.M.S.
Coffey, T. H., 31843, Pte.
Cooper, W. R., 16713, Sgt.
Cowdry, H., 18205, Pte.
Cox, C. F., 18122, Sgt.

Davies, D. V., 24524, Pte.
Davies, E. D., 15936, Pte.
Davies, J., 38193, Pte.
Davies, R. W., 17808, Pte.
Davies, R., 16526, Cpl.
Davies, S., 16631, Pte.
Davies, W. H., 16018, Pte.
Durant, F. C., 16694, Pte.

Evans, W., 18476, A/Cpl.

Fletcher, T. H., 46289, Pte.

Gilmore, W., 16411, Pte.
Green, T. F., 19319, Pte.

Hart, G. F., 12819, Pte.
Hill, F. H., 17702, Pte.

Hollister, J., 16229, Pte.
Hopkins, T., 16251, Pte.
Hughes, T., 20151, Pte.

Jackson, T. C., 16565, Pte.
James, D. E., 16308, Pte.
James, J., 16161, Pte.
Jenkins, J., 16445, L/Cpl.
Johnson, C., 48280, Pte.
Jones, I., 15989, Pte.
Jones, T., 17748, Pte.

Kiley, J., 16266, Pte.
Kite, G. J., 16190, Pte.

Lees, R., 45375, Pte.
Lewis, T., 15874, Pte.
Lihou, W., 16083, Pte.
Lingard, R., 17723, Pte.
Longshaw, A., 19534, Pte.

Makin, A. E., 28934, Pte.
Malsom, C., 17832, Pte.
McCarthy, D., 16064, Pte.
McKeown, J., 19530, Pte.
Morgan, D., 17751, Pte.
Morgan, D., 13365, Pte.
Morgan, G. W., 16665, Pte.
Morris, D., 15914, Pte.
Morris, T., 16281, Sgt.

Oldham, J., 13603, Pte.

Paget, G., 33338, Pte.
Pask, R. T., 15893, Pte.
Perrin, W., 16012, L/Cpl.
Phillips, I., 16874, Pte.
Pitt, S., 16659, Pte.
Pope, E., 16533, Pte.
Price, S., 12413, Pte.
Purdue, T., 37672, Pte.

Reynolds, B., 15849, Cpl.
Rodgers, W., 46796, Pte.
Rosser, E. J., 46245, L/Cpl.
Rothin, W. J., 11016, L/Cpl.

Sanderson, E., 23691, Pte.
Seary, G. F., 17378, Pte.
Senior, A., 26614, Pte.
Shell, H. A., 26716, Pte.
Smith, H., 19020, Pte.
Solway, H. J., 27563, Pte.
Stanley, J., 16081, Pte.

Stevens, A. E., 45389, Pte.
Sullivan, J., 16443, Pte.
Sullivan, J., 16422, Pte.
Sullivan, M., 24416, Pte.

Taylor, W., 15768, Pte.
Thomas, H., 33637, Pte.
Thomas, S., 16157, Pte.
Travis, J. H., 34508, Pte.

Watkins, J., 16050, Sgt.
Watkins, W., 15616, Pte.
Watts, T. J., 15973, Pte.
Webber, J., 15780, Pte.
Wheeler, F., 16628, Cpl.
Whittington, H. J., 25860, Pte.
Wiggins, P., 16269, Pte.
Wigglesworth, W. L., 21999, Sgt.
Wilcox, F., 14972, Pte.
Wilkinson, W., 16687, Pte.
Williams, B., 13827, Pte.
Williams, I., 44086, Pte.
Williams, W., 13281, Pte.
Woodford, W. H., 45408, Pte.

9TH BATTALION.

Thomas, D. J., 13213, Pte.

Virgo, P., 14947, A/Sgt.

10TH BATTALION.

Adams, C., 21338, Pte.
Aldred, T. H., 45978, Pte.
Allcock, C., 22045, Pte.
Ames, A. C., 22916, Pte.
Andrews, S., 48436, Pte.
Armitage, J., 46300, Pte.
Armstrong, J., 46301, Pte.
Ashcroft, N. E., 44599, Pte.
Ashman, D. L., 32226, Pte.
Aston, J. T., 49360, Pte.
Aston, T. E., 32185, Pte.
Atherton, J., 24682, Pte.
Attwater, B., 10426, Sgt.
Austin, J. J., 44355, Pte.
Ayres, H. C., 20482, Cpl.

Badham, A., 20914, Cpl.
Baggs, W. F., 31940, Pte.
Baker, R., 39687, L/Cpl. M.M.
Ball, H., 29380, L/Cpl.
Baney, G. E., 39698, L/Sgt.
Banks, G. E., 40310, Pte.
Barlow, A. V., 42180, Cpl.
Barnett, J., 23209, Pte.

Batten, E., 23045, Pte.
Baxendale, R., 46310, Pte.
Baxter, R., 48028, Pte.
Beale, A. E., 48642, Pte.
Beard, A., 40400, Pte.
Beard, E. B., 33098, Pte.
Beechey, P., 29568, Pte.
Bennett, E., 20282, Pte.
Bennett, T., 21174, Pte.
Benson, T., 45855, Pte.
Berridge, W., 40382, Pte.
Berry, M., 48650, Pte.
Bethell, S., 21009, Pte.
Bishop, E., 33099, Pte.
Bishop, G. H., 21064, Pte.
Bishop, H., 21472, Pte.
Blair, H., 44155, Pte.
Blick, A. E., 23256, Pte.
Bodenham, C., 38780, Pte.
Bodley, G., 23255, Pte.
Booker, C. P., 40226, L/Cpl.
Boothman, E., 48446, Pte.
Bracey, J., 20164, Pte.
Bradley, J., 48191, Pte.

THE ROLL OF HONOUR

Brewin, H. J., 44649, Pte.
Brickell, J., 20971, Pte.
Briggs, W. O., 38486, Pte.
Brinkworth, W. J., 23259, Cpl.
Brinn, W. G. P., 48457, Pte.
Brown, C. J., 23085, L/Cpl.
Brown, J. J., 44731, Pte.
Buckley, J., 48451, Pte.
Burke, F., 26318, Cpl.
Burrows, A., 40318, Pte.
Butterworth, J., 20318, Pte.

Callow, W., 30534, Pte.
Carson, F., 38328, Sgt.
Carter, W. S., 21404, Pte.
Cartwright, H., 38655, Pte.
Chalcroft, H. G., 39695, Pte.
Challenger, C. R., 20601, L/Cpl.
Challenger, L., 20898, L/Cpl.
Challis, R., 20332, Pte.
Cherrill, R. A., 24170, Pte.
Chorley, F., 23091, Pte.
Clark, J. S., 21377, Pte.
Clarkson, J. S., 19237, Pte.
Cleasby, J. W., 20312, Pte.
Clissold, C. F., 20104, C.S.M.
Cobb, F., 10047, L/Cpl.
Codrington, F., 21337, Pte.
Colburn, J. H., 48653, Pte.
Cole, F., 42272, Pte.
Cole, R., 49378, Pte.
Coles, F., 20976, Pte.
Collins, C. J., 40414, Pte.
Coombs, F., 33104, Pte.
Corbridge, H. H., 38656, Pte.
Corden, E., 38653, Pte.
Cornish, W., 22391, Pte.
Cornock, E. C., 20448, Pte.
Cosgrove, E. J., 23092, Pte.
Cowan, D., 48469, Pte.
Cox, S., 58686, Pte.
Cox, W. S., 24242, Cpl.
Cudmore, G., 40241, Pte.
Curry, T., 31577, Pte.
Causon, A. E., 15305, Pte.

Daniels, E. A., 33266, Pte.
Davies, A., 20538, Pte.
Davies, D. J., 49411, Pte.
Davies, E. B., 48657, Pte.
Davies, F. C., 30088, Pte.
Davies, H., 23023, Pte.
Davies, J., 41113, Pte.
Davies, L. W., 20068, Pte.
Davies, O., 21791, Pte.

Davies, S., 20241, L/Cpl.
Davies, W., 33029, Pte.
Davies, W. E. M., 44146, L/Cpl.
Davies, W. L., 23074, Pte.
Davis, E. W., 48664, Pte.
Day, J. E., 20383, Sgt.
Deanheart, F., 33202, L/Cpl.
Dobbins, W., 33058, Pte.
Dobbs, G., 21419, Pte.
Donoghue, T., 20243, Sgt.
Donovan, W., 35668, Sgt.
Down, B. G., 37814, Pte.
Downs, G., 20280, Pte.
Dransfield, J. C., 38554, Pte.
Dray, W. E., 21421, Sgt.
Drury, H., 40385, Pte.
Dunn, A., 20380, Pte.
Dunn, W., 49274, Pte.
Dyer, E., 23194, Pte

Eastwood, F., 48161, Pte.
Edwards, J., 21068, Pte.
Edwards, J., 20517, Pte.
Edwards, L., 33272, Pte.
Edwards, R. H., 42563, L/Cpl.
Edwards, T. B., 20536, Sgt.
Edwards, T., 38557, Pte.
Edwards, W., 49310, Pte.
Edwards, W. T., 20315, Pte.
Elliott, H. B., 20986, L/Cpl.
Elliott, S., 20676, Pte.
Evans, E. W., 20451, Pte.
Evans, J., 20333, Pte.
Evans, O., 44132, Pte. M.M.

Farley, S. H., 39489, A/Cpl.
Farquharson, W., 23189, Pte.
Featherstone, G., 34148, Pte.
Fidler, J. S., 29310, Pte.
Fletcher, G., 44467, Pte.
Flowers, H. D., 40386, Pte.
Foster, T., 40387, Pte.
Freeland, W. P., 40245, L/Cpl.

Gardiner, A., 21644, Pte.
Gardiner, G. W., 30411, Pte.
Gash, F., 40285, Pte.
Gash, W. A., 40284, Pte.
Gingell, E., 21859, Pte.
Godden, A. E., 22852, Pte.
Godfrey, W., 20981, Pte.
Goode, J., 30393, Pte.
Gough, W. H., 34560, Pte.
Grant, P., 20955, Cpl.
Green, D. J., 44543, Pte.

Griffiths, J., 51873, Pte.
Griffiths, L., 21290, Pte.
Griffiths, N., 26239, Pte.
Griffiths, P., 20718, Cpl.
Griffiths, R., 21473, Pte.
Griffiths, W., 48682, Pte.
Gwatkin, W. R., 58309, Pte.
Gwilt, P. J., 49397, Pte.

Haines, R., 20436, Pte.
Hall, A. W., 23084, Pte.
Hall, C. H., 20561, Pte.
Hall, E., 28992, Pte.
Hamer, D., 23656, Pte.
Hamer, J. C., 38571, Pte.
Hampson, A., 41047, Pte.
Harrison, G., 35601, Pte.
Harrison, J., 34289, Sgt.
Harrold, S. F., 40598, L/Cpl.
Hartley, A. W., 33975, Pte.
Harwood, O., 48690, Pte.
Hawkins, S., 38567, Pte.
Hayes, J. J., 33778, Pte.
Henderson, J., 24900, L/Cpl.
Heywood, J., 29384, Pte.
Heywood, W., 40357, Pte.
Hickling, W., 38568, Pte.
Hill, A., 23517, Pte.
Hill, J., 20344, Pte.
Hitchins, G., 20493, Pte.
Hodgson, L., 21191, L/Cpl.
Holbrook, E., 20421, Pte.
Holmes, G., 20128, Pte.
Holmes, W., 40296, Pte.
Hooper, H. J., 21075, Pte.
Hopkins, A., 58303, Pte.
Hornby, J. A., 41555, Pte.
Hoskins, W., 40429, Pte.
Howells, D. J., 32041, Pte.
Howells, J., 21363, Pte.
Hudson, L., 23651, Pte.
Hughes, A., 20149, Pte.
Hughes, F., 20526, Pte.
Hughes, J., 23037, Pte.
Hughes, W., 20588, Pte.
Hulse, H., 40196, Pte.
Humphreys, L., 20833, Pte.
Hunt, C. J., 39717, Pte.
Hutton, W., 45926, Pte.
Hyde, W., 20513, Pte.

Ince, A., 23197, Pte.
Inman, E., 20345, Pte.
Ivory, H., 40376, Pte.

Jacob, A., 38684, Pte.
James, G. G., 21362, Sgt.
James, J. H., 23150, Pte.
James, S., 21550, C.S.M.
Jayne, E., 21111, Pte.
Jefford, A. J., 40641, Pte.
Jenkins, A., 21942, Pte.
Jenkins, B., 20438, Sgt.
Jenkins, H. C., 20378, A/Sgt. M.M.
Jenkins, T. H., 30058, Pte.
Jenkins, W., 21319, Pte.
Johnson, D., 20216, Sgt.
Jones, A., 30352, L/Cpl.
Jones, A. R., 58721, Pte.
Jones, D., 31234, Pte.
Jones, D., 20560, Pte.
Jones, D., 58236, Pte.
Jones, E., 20801, L/Cpl.
Jones, E. E., 20362, Pte.
Jones, F. J., 35425, Cpl.
Jones, G., 18173, Pte.
Jones, G., 23135, Pte.
Jones, H., 31111, Pte.
Jones, H. J., 23973, Pte.
Jones, J., 51817, Pte.
Jones, J. T., 39685, L/Cpl.
Jones, M. L., 39686, L/Cpl.
Jones, P., 20184, Pte.
Jones, P. E., 49589, Pte.
Jones, R., 41135, Pte.
Jones, S., 58651, Pte.
Jones, T., 20171, Pte.
Jones, T. A., 17705, Pte.
Jones, W. L., 20966, L/Cpl.
Joseph, T., 20500, Sgt.

Kellett, N., 24006, Pte.
Kelly, T., 51819, Pte.
Kerchey, A. G., 21175, Pte.
King, J., 45778, Pte.
Kinnock, W. H., 10526, Pte.
Kirby, A. E., 40372, Pte.
Knight, E. J., 49234, Pte.
Knowles, G. T., 48706, Pte.

Lancaster, W., 38687, Pte.
Lang, A. C., 30389, Pte.
Lawrence, H., 21387, Pte.
Leadbeater, R., 23755, Pte.
Ledger, J., 33034, Pte.
Lee, C., 23111, Sgt.
Leeslie, W., 40201, Pte.
Lewis, J. H., 20310, Pte.
Lewis, J. H., 23043, Pte.
Lewis, P. T., 31083, L/Cpl.

THE ROLL OF HONOUR

Lewis, P., 20188, Pte.
Lewis, R., 20220, Pte.
Lewis, W., 20992, L/Cpl.
Light, A. T., 20107, Pte.
Littlemore, W. G., 36466, Pte.
Lloyd, F., 42560, Pte.
Lloyd, T., 20598, Pte.
Lock, O. G., 27270, Pte.
Lomax, L., 33044, Pte.
Longden, W., 22408, Sgt.
Lovell, A., 21066, Pte.
Loveridge, W., 23010, Pte.
Lowe, G. H., 51824, Pte.
Lowe, W., 44239, Pte.
Ludlow, F., 20414, L/Cpl.

Manns, B., 40391, Pte.
Marley, G., 20530, Pte.
Marsden, J., 48721, Pte.
Masters, W. C., 21374, Pte.
Matthews, J., 20882, L/Sgt.
Maydwell, A., 39723, Pte.
Mayersbeth, G. H., 10480, Pte.
McCarthy, T., 21292, Pte.
Miles, G. T., 40277, Pte.
Mitchell, G. H., 20920, Pte.
Moon, F. E., 35515, Pte.
Morgan, B., 21314, L/Cpl.
Morgan, L. J., 32167, Pte.
Morgan, T. J., 58630, Pte.
Morgan, W., 20859, Pte.
Morris, E., 21285, Pte.
Morris, T., 9759, L/Cpl.
Moss, J. W., 30801, Pte.
Munckton, E. J., 21439, L/Cpl.
Munday, B. C., 40459, L/Cpl.
Musker, P., 40335, Pte.

Nelson, E. F., 42270, Pte.
Nevitt, T., 40384, Pte.
Newcombe, I., 20625, Cpl.
Noble, H. G., 58510, Pte.
Nott, A. F., 23094, Pte.

O'Boyle, M., 38693, Pte.
Oppenshaw, J., 35652, Pte.
Osborne, S. J., 20011, Sgt.
Osland, M., 32156, Pte.
Owen, A. P., 20854, L/Cpl.
Owen, D., 48735, Pte.
Owen, D. G., 31325, Pte.
Owen, T. R., 27554, Pte.

Pace, T., 40360, Pte.
Paddock, A. G., 51831, Pte.

Pardon, R., 38871, Pte.
Parker, W., 20118, Pte.
Parry, H., 42171, Pte.
Parry, W., 21373, Pte.
Parson, A. J., 40256, Pte.
Paulk, W. J., 21400, Pte.
Payne, A. E., 21371, Pte.
Payne, J. G., 21465, Sgt.
Payne, W. G., 9996, Pte.
Pedlar, P., 20084, Pte.
Pembrey, W. I., 20256, C.Q.M.S.
Pepper, H. A., 31794, Pte.
Perry, W., 22025, Pte.
Pinches, A. F., 20122, L/Cpl.
Platt, J., 38601, Pte.
Pleece, E. W., 20305, Pte. M.M.
Poole, G. C., 39946, Pte.
Potter, A., 40258, Pte.
Powell, A., 33293, Pte.
Powell, A. E., 40360, Pte.
Powell, E., 21045, Sgt.
Powell, W. J., 49363, Pte.
Powell, W. J., 20359, Pte.
Price, F. A., 20286, Pte.
Price, G., 58570, Pte.
Price, W., 20787, Pte.
Prosser, E. T., 30555, Pte.
Purnell, T., 21281, Pte.
Pym, S., 30319, Pte.

Ratcliffe, S. E., 48126, Pte.
Read, J., 40259, Pte.
Read, T., 20101, Pte.
Reed, T., 33190, Pte.
Reed, W. H., 21034, L/Cpl.
Rees, S., 20441, Sgt.
Renshaw, J. H., 48758, Pte.
Richards, G. V., 40417, Pte.
Richards, J. H., 21405, Pte.
Richards, M. M., 31467, Pte.
Richards, O. J., 31357, Pte.
Rider, F. C., 45941, Pte.
Roach, J., 20116, Pte.
Roberts, A., 42561, Pte.
Roberts, H., 42201, Pte.
Roberts, J. P., 44152, Pte.
Roberts, R. A., 44136, Pte. M.M.
Roberts, T., 20956, Pte.
Roe, L. L. J., 40379, Pte.
Rogers, T. H., 20387, Sgt.
Rose, C. C., 40427, Pte.
Rose, H., 20587, Pte.
Rowlands, W., 58614, Pte.
Ruddick, R., 20232, Pte.

Russell, T., 45934, Pte.
Ryan, P., 21469, Cpl.

Saint, J., 30395, Pte.
Salmon, A. T., 20836, Pte.
Salt, G., 40235, Pte.
Scrivens, W., 20868, Pte.
Selby, J. H., 21464, Pte.
Sessarago, J. J., 42136, L/Cpl.
Sheldrick, J., 40406, Pte.
Shrubb, O. J., 40281, Pte.
Silk, E. H., 30208, Pte.
Skegg, W. J., 39707, Pte.
Skillman, T., 40614, Pte.
Slocombe, J. T., 21110, Pte.
Smart, A. J., 20736, Sgt.
Smith, A. E., 20939, Pte.
Smith, E. H., 40287, A/Cpl.
Smith, G. A., 44696, Pte.
Smith, W. L., 20095, Pte.
Smith, W. T., 23260, Pte.
Snellgrove, F., 23208, Pte.
Spanswick, D., 23064, Pte.
Springfield, G., 40279, Pte.
Steele, J., 51883, Pte.
Stevens, G. C., 21651, L/Cpl.
Stokes, W. J., 58758, Pte.
Stone, E. V., 40435, Pte.
Strange, J., 39110, Pte.
Strettell, J., 45949, Pte.
Surrell, W. H., 42173, Pte.
Sutton, E. W., 21022, Pte.
Swatman, T., 15258, Pte.
Sweet, A., 21408, Pte.

Tamplin, J., 20156, Pte.
Taylor, C. F., 40265, Pte.
Taylor, J., 40341, Cpl. M.M.
Thissen, W. J., 29937, Pte.
Thomas, A. C., 40306, Pte.
Thomas, H. J. W., 30410, Pte.
Thomas, J., 58427, Pte.
Thomason, W., 48570, Pte.
Thompsett, A., 40266, Pte.
Thompson, F. W., 40280, Pte.
Thomson, R., 45638, Pte.
Thorne, A. H., 14762, Pte.
Thornton, F. H., 44642, A/Sgt.
Tovey, E., 20468, Pte.
Townley, C., 20020, L/Sgt.
Townson, E., 38619, Pte.
Trump, C., 58719, Pte.

Turner, E., 36495, Pte.
Turner, E., 49379, Pte.
Tyler, G., 36188, Pte.

Venn, A., 21112, L/Cpl.
Vickers, W. E., 37534, A/Cpl.
Vowles, E., 42193, Pte.

Walker, F., 20248, Pte.
Walker, H., 37639, Pte.
Walton, J. T., 40346, Pte.
Wardley, W., 41476, Pte.
Warren, H. S., 40381, Pte.
Waters, A. E., 30381, Pte.
Watkins, J., 23149, Pte.
Watson, H. T., 40289, Pte.
Watts, H. J. J., 40452, Pte.
Watts, J., 20150, L/Cpl.
Webster, A., 35010, Sgt.
Webster, W., 40437, Pte.
Welsh, J., 23210, Pte.
Werrett, W., 21381, Pte.
Whatley, E., 20252, Pte.
Wheeler, B., 23134, Pte.
Wheeler, C. E., 42177, Pte.
Wheeler, J., 21496, Pte.
Whisken, W. R., 20346, Pte.
White, F. H., 40269, Pte.
White, H. W., 44707, Pte.
White, J. E., 21015, Pte.
Whiteman, E. E., 58720, Pte.
Whitson, B., 20820, Pte.
Whittingham, E. W., 25360, Pte.
Wilce, S., 35859, Pte.
Williams, C., 58317, Pte.
Williams, E. H., 32189, Pte.
Williams, E. J., 20866, Pte.
Williams, G., 20105, Pte.
Williams, G. R., 21148, Pte.
Williams, H. H., 25442, Pte.
Williams, I., 21032, Pte.
Williams, J. H., 58837, Pte.
Williams, O., 25379, Pte.
Williams, R., 20766, Pte.
Williams, S., 20375, Pte.
Williams, T., 23106, L/Cpl.
Williams, W. J., 20903, Pte.
Woolcock, I. C., 48139, Pte.
Woolfenden, A., 48152, Pte.

Yapp, R., 20413, Pte.

THE ROLL OF HONOUR

11TH BATTALION.

Adams, T. G., 27565, Pte.
Almond, P. T., 34044, Pte.
Attwood, J., 40409, Pte.
Ayling, E. J., 29417, Pte.

Baker, W. G., 40481, Pte.
Baldwin, T. G., 24595, Pte.
Barker, C., 33794, Pte.
Bassett, J., 22067, Pte.
Bellis, W., 22603, L/Cpl.
Bennett, E., 21771, Pte.
Berrill, A., 37704, Pte.
Berry, G. W., 22134, Pte.
Bettle, A. G., 20568, Pte.
Bevan, H., 44444, Pte.
Beynon, T., 30078, Pte.
Bignall, W. J., 22932, Pte.
Blackwell, A., 18628, Sgt.
Blackwell, J. E., 22540, Pte.
Bowen, W. H., 21701, Pte.
Boyes, S., 40507, Pte.
Bradnock, T. G., 38541, Pte.
Bronton, W. J., 21743, Cpl.
Brown, A., 29791, Pte.
Bull, J., 20374, Cpl.
Bundy, A., 22422, Cpl.
Burns, J., 21524, Sgt.
Butler, R., 23273, Pte.

Chapman, E., 22348, Pte.
Chard, J., 33016, Pte.
Charrott, E., 36070, Pte.
Cheese, F., 44380, L/Cpl.
Clarke, R. J., 22484, Sgt.
Coates, R., 22357, Cpl.
Colligan, C., 22564, Pte.
Collins, T., 20640, Pte.
Coombs, E. C., 20579, Pte.
Coombs, F. B., 28475, Pte.
Corfield, H., 22200, Sgt.
Corless, R., 46337, Pte.
Court, S., 30152, Pte.
Cousins, T., 22253, Pte.
Crawford, A., 37843, Pte.
Creese, J. D., 40490, L/Cpl.
Crompton, F., 46329, Pte.
Crook, E. C., 44386, Pte.
Cross, C., 30024, Pte.
Cross, W. S. J., 20018, Sgt.

Dadey, T., 33487, Pte.
Daly, J., 22119, Pte.

Dallow, J. D., 23247, Pte.
Darby, J. H., 21716, L/Cpl.
Dart, S., 20032, Pte.
Daniels, A., 33483, Pte.
Davenport, G., 34151, Pte.
Davies, A. E., 22317, Cpl.
Davies, C. J., 22965, Pte.
Davies, D., 22236, Pte.
Davies, J., 20067, L/Cpl.
Davies, J., 44388, Pte.
Davies, S., 21764, Pte.
Davies, S., 42131, Pte.
Davies, T., 22302, Pte.
Davies, W., 22128, Pte.
Davies, W., 22606, Pte.
Davies, W. A., 21804, Pte.
Davis, H., 22548, Pte.
Dawson, J. W. H., 22640, Pte.
Dicker, H., 42143, Pte.
Dillon, T., 27619, Pte.
Dobson, W., 22122, Pte.
Dodgeon, A. E., 38724, Pte.
Downey, J., 22073, Pte.
Dring, W., 45998, Pte.
Dudley, T., 21775, Pte.
Dunster, J., 40228, Pte.
Dunthorne, E. R., 39190, Pte.
Dutton, G. H., 28305, Pte.

Earp, J. A., 44404, Pte.
Emmanuel, J., 44554, Pte.
Evans, B., 22130, Pte.
Evans, D. J., 44548, Pte.
Evans, E., 22315, Pte.
Evans, J., 21665, Pte.
Evans, J. E., 31141, Pte.
Ewins, A., 33087, Pte.

Fernley, P. E., 36010, Pte.
Flood, W., 40510, Pte.
Flowers, A., 33248, Pte.
Foley, W., 31800, L/Sgt.
Frost, J., 44408, Pte.
Furness, C. A., 21529, Sgt.

Geeves, W. C., 21623, Pte.
Giles, A., 44411, Pte.
Gilmore, A., 22688, Pte.
Gleave, H., 28315, Pte.
Gore, A., 22506, Pte.
Gossage, J., 41121, Pte.

583

Graham, C. R. F., 40499, Cpl.
Gunner, T., 22150, Pte.
Gwynne, A. W., 35915, Pte.

Hale, G., 22924, Pte.
Hancock, H. B., 21892, Pte.
Hannell, W., 37713, Pte.
Hanson, W., 44416, Cpl.
Harries, H. H., 22085, Sgt.
Harries, W., 21539, Pte.
Harris, E., 21640, L/Sgt.
Hatherall, H. J., 22343, Pte.
Hawkins, C. J., 22596, Pte.
Hawkins, G., 27610, Pte.
Hemmings, F., 21883, Sgt.
Henwood, B., 22763, Pte.
Hills, E. A., 36020, Pte. M.M.
Hingley, A., 21783, Cpl.
Hodges, J., 21940, Pte.
Hogan, J., 21617, Pte.
Hogarth, H., 38630, Pte.
Holder, W., 20005, Pte.
Hopkins, W., 21778, Pte.
Horne, W. D., 44395, Pte.
Howell, J. A., 38675, Pte.
Howells, A. V., 33475, Pte.
Hughes, D., 45947, Pte.
Hulbert, T., 20012, Cpl.
Humphries, H. T., 21806, Pte.
Hunt, E., 21600, Cpl.
Hunt, F., 36585, Pte.
Hunt, J. A., 22065, Pte.

Jackson, A. E., 44422, Pte.
James, J. H., 22300, A/Cpl.
James, J. O., 41132, Pte.
James, T., 28257, Pte.
Jay, A., 22188, Cpl. M.M.
Jenkins, J. C., 33234, Pte.
Jones, A., 25403, Pte.
Jones, C. S., 20001, Cpl.
Jones, D., 25454, Pte.
Jones, E., 21552, Pte.
Jones, E., 44135, Pte.
Jones, H., 25485, Pte.
Jones, H., 25473, Pte.
Jones, H., 21653, Pte.
Jones, I. W., 21951, Pte.
Jones, J., 22536, Pte.
Jones, J., 22482, Pte.
Jones, R., 22401, Pte.
Jones, S., 22616, Pte.
Jones, T., 22349, L/Sgt.
Joynson, J., 37007, Pte.

Kear, A. W., 21931, Pte.
Kear, H. S., 22112, Pte.
Key, H., 21582, Pte.
Killingback, H., 22103, Pte.
Kirk, H., 44397, Pte.
Knight, B., 21924, Pte.

Lancaster, C., 44429, Pte.
Lane, W. E., 22226, Sgt.
Lawless, P., 21609, Sgt.
Leonard, W. J., 21926, Cpl.
Lewis, D., 28270, Pte.
Lewis, E. E., 29865, Pte.
Lewis, F. A., 21777, Pte.
Liggitt, A. E., 22978, Pte.
Llewellyn, D., 16635, Pte.
Llewellyn, G., 21671, Pte.
Llewellyn, I. J., 33320, Pte.
Llewellyn, T., 21590, A/Sgt.
Lloyd, D., 33119, Pte.
Luke, H. G., 22259, Pte.

Mansfield, E., 33310, Pte.
Marsden, E., 24209, Pte.
Marshall, J., 21613, Pte.
Mash, F., 22969, Pte.
Meats, F. J., 18666, Cpl.
Millington, E., 25432, Pte.
Mills, J. W., 22556, A/Sgt.
Mitchell, F., 22998, Pte.
Morgan, A., 22403, Pte.
Morgan, J. C., 22679, Pte.
Morgan, W. L., 29469, Pte.
Morris, F., 22531, Pte.
Morris, R., 22276, Sgt.
Morton, C., 35903, Pte.
Moseley, R., 21717, Pte.
Mosley, A., 44434, Pte.
Moss, W., 21779, Pte.
Murray, W., 23240, Pte.

Nanney, J. H., 36513, Pte.
Nash, C., 21776, L/Sgt.
Newland, J. A., 22445, Pte.
Newman, A., 22416, Pte.

O'Connell, J., 22428, Pte.
O'Leary, J., 21513, Pte.
Oliver, E. F., 21723, Pte.

Packer, T., 22043, L/Cpl.
Palmer, A. A., 22570, Pte.
Parry, R., 29563, Pte.
Parsons, H., 46324, Sgt.
Pattemore, S., 22206, Pte.

THE ROLL OF HONOUR

Paul, W. H., 40494, Pte.
Peterson, C., 20037, Pte.
Phillips, D., 22446, Pte.
Phillips, M., 22429, L/Cpl.
Pike, T. J., 22700, Pte.
Pilgrim, A. A., 35511, Pte.
Plummer, G., 22014, Pte.
Pointon, F., 29843, Pte.
Poland, D., 22568, L/Cpl.
Pole, E. J., 21527, Pte.
Postle, T., 22376, L/Cpl.
Power, J., 21945, Pte.
Price, E. W., 21813, L/Cpl.
Price, E., 22003, Pte.
Price, S., 21657, Pte.
Prout, C. G., 12489, Sgt.

Quinn, J., 42165, Pte.

Raby, W., 22342, Pte.
Rea, W. J., 18822, Sgt.
Reece, R., 19560, Pte.
Rees, R., 21947, Pte.
Rickard, A., 22202, Pte.
Richardson, A., 21559, Pte.
Riley, W., 21642, Pte.
Robbins, E. J., 29856, Pte.
Roberts, A., 39104, Pte.
Robins, D. J., 22592, Pte.
Rogers, S., 44400, Pte.
Rustell, C., 40512, Pte.

Saint, T., 38888, Pte.
Salathiel, S. L., 21557, Cpl.
Sargent, F. W., 22378, Pte.
Saunders, A., 29893, Pte.
Saunders, N., 22473, L/Cpl.
Savage, J. H., 33273, Pte.
Sawyers, F. J., 21741, Pte.
Scammel, C., 33469, Pte.
Scott, J. W., 40236, Pte.
Shaw, G. M., 27690, Cpl.
Shelmerdine, G., 33481, Pte.
Shepherd, D. C., 29862, Pte.
Shields, W., 22535, Pte.
Simcox, W., 21696, L/Cpl.
Smith, S. A., 29886, Pte.
Smith, W., 33263, Pte.
Spencer, W. A., 44342, Pte.
Steel, H., 42138, Pte.
Stephens, E., 22529, Pte.

Storton, A. W., 34180, Pte.
Straus, I., 37746, Pte.
Sullivan, M., 22684, Pte.

Taylforth, C., 22600, Sgt.
Thomas, R., 21772, Pte.
Thomas, W., 37656, Pte.
Thomas, W. G., 21988, Pte.
Thomas, W. J., 22701, Pte.
Thompson, J., 21639, Pte.
Tierney, J., 21632, Pte.
Tilley, J. S., 21594, Pte.
Tomlinson, W., 25575, Pte.
Tout, E. J., 44474, Pte.
Treherne, R., 15920, L/Cpl.
Turner, A., 22094, Pte.

Usher, E., 39107, Pte.

Vaughan, A., 22207, Pte.
Vaughan, W. J., 13568, Pte. M.M.
Venn, G. T., 33164, Pte.
Vigdosky, H., 35722, Pte.

Wade, J. T., 29536, Pte.
Walker, C. E., 37728, Pte.
Walker, E., 22359, Pte.
Wall, R., 22117, Pte.
Walters, D. R., 42141, Pte.
Walters, J., 30568, Pte.
Walwin, A. H., 20017, C.S.M.
Warr, A., 27455, Pte.
Warwicker, W. J., 37772, Pte.
Weal, J., 36061, Pte.
Weeks, W. F., 25487, Pte.
Wells, A. J., 37714, Pte.
Wheeler, W. A., 44060, Pte.
Wheeldon, J., 29695, Pte.
White, A., 22427, Pte.
Whitehead, W. A., 36189, Pte.
Whittaker, H. S., 22686, Pte.
Williams, A. H., 21739, Pte.
Williams, J., 20950, Pte.
Williams, J., 21985, Pte.
Williams, T., 29912, Pte.
Williams, W., 22554, L/Cpl.
Williams, W. G., 22493, Pte.
Withers, J. C., 33035, Pte.
Workman, A. P., 22344, Pte.

Yapp, A., 20410, Pte.

12TH BATTALION.

Abbott, E. A., 35636, Pte.
Allen, W., 39883, Pte.
Allison, J., 35183, Pte.
Andrews, A. G., 42370, Pte.
Ash, J., 23907, Pte.

Baird, W. G., 44638, Pte.
Baker, J., 29366, Pte.
Banks, C., 35139, Pte.
Bardwell, H. H., 35401, Pte.
Barnes, F., 24030, Pte.
Barnett, A. E., 23868, Pte.
Baxter, E. J., 23775, L/Cpl.
Beaman, W. H., 23565, Pte.
Beard, F., 30628, Pte.
Bevan, R. G., 24421, Pte.
Bishop, J. R., 35516, Pte.
Bosworth, R., 24249, Pte.
Bowden, T., 22771, Pte.
Bradburn, B., 22772, Pte.
Brennan, J. J., 35174, Pte.
Brooks, W. C. A., 23350, Cpl.
Brown, T., 23992, Pte.
Brunning, P., 45856, Pte.

Capewell, T. S., 24039, Cpl.
Carpenter, T., 45873, Pte.
Carter, A. J., 23847, Pte.
Casey, D., 23809, Pte.
Cashman, J. A., 29519, Pte.
Cater, F., 45857, Pte.
Catling, S., 23904, Pte.
Chance, S., 22777, Pte.
Chard, S. F., 23353, A/C.S.M.
Cheeseman, R., 23790, Pte.
Chivers, T., 23422, Pte.
Clark, H., 44663, Pte.
Cleverly, N. H., 35158, Pte.
Collins, J., 24482, Pte.
Corbett, I. C., 39967, Pte.
Coultson, T. J., 24061, A/Sgt.
Crockett, E. H., 41263, Pte.
Cully, A., 24093, Pte.

Davies, B., 41265, Pte.
Davies, E., 39899, Pte.
Davies, F., 23889, Pte.
Davies, F. A., 45611, Pte.
Davies, H., 24380, Pte.
Davies, I., 45632, Pte.
Davies, P., 30418, Pte.
Davies, W. R., 24373, Pte.

Day, C. P., 45859, Pte.
Day, J., 24182, Pte.
Dean, J., 39080, Pte.
De-Fen, R. J., 24423, Pte.
Dobre, A. R., 35571, Pte.
Douch, H., 23330, Pte.
Draycott, F., 24161, L/Cpl.
Dunn, G. J., 23646, Pte.

Edmonds, W. R., 35387, Pte.
Ellis, J., 23901, Pte.
Elson, W. A., 39904, Pte.
Evans, H., 22780, Pte.
Evans, J. T., 24375, Pte.

Farrar, W., 23772, Pte.
Fearne, E., 35160, Pte.
Foster, S. J., 24320, Pte.
Foulke, H., 23928, Pte.
French, J., 24281, Pte.

Gibbons, F., 24028, Pte.
Glanville, R. T., 24363, Pte.
Goddard, F., 24438, Pte.
Grace, C. H., 23835, Pte.
Grahad, T., 35239, Pte.
Grant, W., 23733, Pte.
Graves, H., 24153, Pte.
Greaves, W., 24378, Pte.
Griffiths, D. W., 13163, Pte.
Griffiths, T., 23864, Pte.
Grummett, T., 22707, Sgt.
Gurney, L., 23432, Pte.

Haines, F., 23490, Pte.
Hancock, J., 35339, Pte.
Harding, S., 25220, Pte.
Hardy, T., 23954, Pte.
Harris, C., 24171, Pte.
Harris, F., 25221, Pte.
Harris, F. C., 45616, L/Cpl.
Harris, G. H., 24301, Pte.
Harris, L. E., 23727, Pte.
Harrison, F., 29431, Pte.
Harrop, J. H., 23782, Pte.
Hathaway, R., 25223, Pte.
Hawcroft, J. H., 24033, Cpl.
Hawker, F., 23632, Pte.
Hawyes, S., 35389, L/Cpl.
Hayward, F. J., 15539, Pte.
Hemingway, R., 24259, L/Cpl.
Hemmings, E., 23384, Pte.

THE ROLL OF HONOUR

Hernon, P., 24238, Pte.
Hill, W., 24017, Sgt.
Hobbs, T. W., 24357, Pte.
Hope, J. J., 22785, Pte.
Hopkins, C. E., 22759, Pte.
Horton, W., 23832, Pte.
Howard, W., 24444, Pte.
Howells, W., 39572, Pte.
Hughes, T., 31381, Pte.
Hunt, J., 45834, Pte.
Hurle, H., 15136, Pte.
Hurst, J. W., 22716, Pte.

Ingham, J., 34323, Pte.

Jacques, R. W., 23574, Pte.
James, C., 24044, Pte.
James, T. G., 41242, Cpl. D.C.M.
Jamieson, C., 24128, Pte.
Jeffries, G. J., 24126, Pte.
Johnson, C., 23978, Pte.
Jones, C. V., 35242, Pte.
Jones, E., 35565, L/Cpl.
Jones, L., 35163, L/Cpl.
Jones, R. D., 24479, Pte.
Jones, T. J., 25228, Pte.
Jones, W. H., 31181, Pte.

Kemp, E., 23721, Pte.
Kenyon, J. A., 23616, L/Cpl.
Kilby, E., 39932, Cpl.
King, W., 35127, L/Cpl.
Kirky, F., 23581, Sgt.
Knight, A., 23526, Pte.

Leadbeater, C., 24251, Pte.
Lee, J. W., 35187, Pte.
Lerigo, W., 24042, Pte.
Lewis, C. I. A., 39524, Pte.
Lloyd, R. T., 23726, Pte.
Lown, C. A., 35202, L/Cpl.

Maidment, A. R., 35540, Pte.
Maloney, M., 23751, Cpl.
Manville, J., 45936, Pte.
Marsden, C., 23822, Pte.
Matthews, F., 25337, Pte.
McTernan, F., 23881, A/C.S.M.
Miles, W., 24399, Pte.
Miller, A. R., 25235, Pte.
Millinship, W. H., 23336, L/Cpl.
Minchin, H., 24116, Pte.
Mitchell, A. R., 35512, Pte.
Moore, R., 23949, A/Sgt.
Morgan, G. F., 23453, Pte.

Morris, J., 35395, Pte.
Myatt, L., 24267, Pte.

Nelson, J., 23570, Sgt.
Newman, F. S., 23510, Pte.

Ogden, W., 23944, Pte.
Oliver, J. C., 23497, Pte.
Olley, B. J., 45808, Pte.

Peed, J. T. E., 24187, Pte.
Perrett, S. W., 35207, Pte.
Pipe, A., 24271, Pte.
Platt, C. R., 25254, L/Cpl.
Pollard, H., 39942, Pte.
Pollard, S. C., 30452, Pte.
Powell, J. C., 12047, Pte.
Price, W. J., 16170, Sgt.
Pritchard, W. G., 23485, Pte.
Purdy, G., 29057, Pte.

Randels, A., 22808, Pte.
Rawlinson, W. E., 23472, L/Cpl.
Reynolds, A., 24127, Pte.
Richards, G., 23359, Pte.
Roberts, W. J., 35126, Pte.
Robinson, F., 23527, Pte.
Rustage, W., 24201, Pte.

Sandilands, A., 45160, Pte.
Sebright, F., 24148, Pte.
Semmens, T. H., 35542, Pte.
Sergent, T., 24345, Pte.
Shatford, T., 23388, Pte.
Shaw, F., 17668, Pte.
Sheargold, J. R., 23523, Pte.
Simpkins, W., 23496, Pte.
Singlehurst, J. G., 25239, Pte.
Smeaton, J. T., 24106, Pte.
Smith, F. C., 41236, Pte.
Smith, J., 28306, Pte.
Sorrell, F. C., 30297, Pte.
Spencer, C. W., 23811, Pte.
Spray, P., 23305, L/Sgt.
Stalker, J., 23572, Pte.
Stevenson, J., 23612, Pte.

Tanner, G. W., 30296, Pte.
Taylor, W. E., 23553, Pte.
Terrett, H. G., 31260, Pte.
Thomas, O. H., 24415, Pte.
Thorpe, E., 23714, L/Sgt. M.M.
Turner, E., 23557, Pte.
Turner, F. H., 22736, L/Sgt.
Turner, G., 34581, Pte.

THE HISTORY OF THE SOUTH WALES BORDERERS

Vickery, J. S., 30267, Pte.
Voake, G. F., 34617, A/C.Q.M.S.

Wall, T., 24080, Pte.
Walters, D. J., 23381, Sgt.
Walters, E., 24474, Pte.
Watkins, W., 24400, Pte.
Way, F. J., 45617, Pte.
Weare, E., 23534, L/Cpl.
Weaver, A. G., 25542, Pte.
Webb, R. F., 41248, Pte.
Weekes, J., 39954, Pte.
Wesson, E., 23446, Pte.
White, F., 16173, Pte.

Whittle, J. B., 23704, Cpl.
Williams, A., 24484, Pte.
Williams, I. H. C., 39955, Pte.
Williams, J., 35572, Pte.
Williams, J., 38530, Pte.
Williams, T., 35340, Pte.
Willoughby, A., 22804, Pte.
Wilson, W., 45603, Pte.
Wood, J., 23706, Pte. M.M.
Wood, J., 39962, Pte.
Wood, J. W., 23695, Pte.
Wood, R. F. C., 39958, Pte.
Wright, J., 25253, L/Cpl.
Wright, R., 24215, Pte.

13TH BATTALION.

Austin, J. J., 33580, Pte.
Blain, B., 33365, Pte.
Davies, J., 33056, A/Cpl.
Emmett, C., 20046, Pte.

Jones, W. J., 33548, Pte.
Monks, H. T., 42237, L/Cpl.
Stoker, E., 23845, A/Cpl.
Walsh, T., 33442, Pte.

14TH BATTALION.

Bastin, C. H., 23826, Pte.

Edwards, H., 35811, Pte.

51ST BATTALION.

Austin, B. V., T.R.4/2465, Pte.
Atkinson, J., T.R.4/6918, Pte.

Bridge, G., T.R.4/4023, Sgt.

Jones, J., T.R.4/44388, Pte.
McCartney, W. T., T.R.4/67044, Pte.
West, A., T.R.4/4063, A/Sgt.

52ND BATTALION.

Forward, G. S., T.R.4/64728, Pte.

Jenkins, F., T.R.4/66821 Pte.
Jones, H., T.R.4/66399, Pte.

53RD BATTALION.

Dodd, J. W., T.R.4/67908, Pte.
Hewitt, G. J., T.R.4/14116, Pte.
Jones, O., T.R.4/67840, Pte.
Maddocks, G., T.R.4/64250, Pte.
Raimo, W., T.R.4/67987, Pte.
Roberts, R. J., T.R.4/67849, Pte.
Rogers, G. E., T.R.4/67895, Pte.

Sheppard, W. J., T.R.4/67866, Pte.
Smouth, F. P., T.R.4/67415, Pte.
Suller, A., T.R.4/68037, Pte.
Symonds, L., T.R.4/68068, Pte.

Walsh, V. O., T.R.4/67999, Pte.
Walsh, M., T.R.4/68480, Pte.
Williams, J., T.R.4/68090, Pte.
Williams, W. H., T.R.4/67794, Pte.

THE ROLL OF HONOUR

Brecknock Battalion.

Appleyard, A., 200511, Pte.

Bareham, C. M., 202477, A/Cpl.
Baylis, J., 202488, Pte.
Beardsley, I., 202502, Pte.
Blaney, C., 3166, Pte.
Brown, R., 1707, Pte.

Campbell, R., 202479, Pte.
Coombe, P. A., 1781, Pte.
Crompton, C., 1688, A/Sgt.
Cunningham, A. E., 200062, Sgt.

Davies, C., 201586, Pte.
Davies, W. E., 2345, Pte.
Dean, R., 202443, Pte.
Denny, F. A., 202475, Pte.
Drew, P., 1933, Pte.
Dunn, E., 200536, Pte.

Edwards, F, C., 201517, Pte.
Evans, W., 202621, Pte.

Flye, J. J., 200864, Pte.
Frankham, E., 201842, Pte.

Gough, J., 200510, Pte.
Green, E., 2308, Pte.

Hardy, A., 202507, Pte.
Harris, H., 200515, Pte.
Hayden, J., 201389, Pte.
Hicken, J., 200591, Pte.
Hubert, A. L., 202490, Pte.
Hughes, P., 30, Sgt.

Isaac, C., 2316, Pte.

Jacomb, P, H., 202454, Pte.
James, T. M., 201101, Pte.
Jenkins, G., 1370, L/Cpl.
Jenkins, J. J., 201648, Pte.
Jones, A., 201362, Pte.
Jones, D. G., 202083, Pte.
Jones, G. H., 1518, Pte.
Jones, R. T., 2212, Pte.
Jones, W. J., 201713, Pte.

Kennedy, P. G., 200612, Pte.
Kint, R. L., 34818, Pte.

Langston, S., 202498, Pte.
Lewis, C., 1775, Pte.

Lewis, C., 2967, Pte.
Lewis, F. J., 201636, Pte.
Lewis, T., 201100, Pte.
Lewis, W., 200660, Pte.
Lloyd, H., 1478, Pte.
Lloyd, W., 1319, Pte.

McKellar, D., 61798, Pte.
Monk, S., 202472, Pte.
Morgan, W., 2383, Pte.
Morgan, W., 200409, Pte.
Morris, J. H., 200521, A/Sgt.

Owen, P., 201869, Pte.
Oxenham, W. F., 2135, Pte.

Parsons, H., 201306, Pte.
Patient, J. G., 202446, Pte.
Pinch, G. H., 202259, Pte.
Price, B., 201458, Pte.
Price, J., 6, Sgt.
Price, J. T., 200590, Pte.
Prosser, I. G., 201304, Pte.
Prout, T. J., 1840, Pte.

Reynolds, G. C., 200415, Cpl.
Rumtey, J. T., 201225, Pte.

Saunders, C. J., 200476, A/Sgt.
Shaw, F., 202550, L/Cpl.
Skan, F. R., 200697, Pte.
Smith, J. H., 813, Cpl.
Smith, W. J., 201218, Pte.
Stringer, W., 202597, Pte.
Symonds, C. E., 2305, Pte.
Sullivan, T. J., 201855, Pte.

Thomas, J., 202060, Pte.
Tyrrell, G. W., 202476, Pte.

Vaughan, R., 2646, A/Sgt.

Waddell, R., 202453, L/Cpl.
Walker, F. W., 202444, Sgt.
Watkins, E. W., 201278, Pte.
Whittaker, A., 200882, Pte.
Williams, C., 201740, L/Cpl.
Williams, C., 2272, Pte.
Williams, J. R., 2285, Pte.
Williams, R., 2047, L/Cpl.
Williams, W., 200917, Pte.
Woodyatt, C., 487, A/Sgt.
Woolforde, L., 3238, Pte.

DEPOT.

Allcock, H., 14785, Pte.

Berry, A., 16769, Pte. M.M.
Brute, W., 15613, Pte.

Castree, H., 9802, Pte.
Conley, J., 46950, R.Q.M.S.

Fisher, B., 21881, Pte.

Gough, T. H., 25256, Pte.

Higgins, D., 14855, Pte.

Lang, W., 38448, Pte.

Mann, H., 15518, Pte.
Mine, M., 15446, Pte.
Morris, R., 17722, C.Q.M.S.

Parry, J., 15270, Pte.
Parsons, A. L., 18565, Pte.

Samuels, D, J., 14973, Pte.
Sisam, A., 16791, Pte.
Smith, O. C., 10833, Pte.

Waters, R., 21959, Pte.

INDEX OF PERSONS

The Casualty List and List of Honours and Awards are not indexed.

Ackerley, Lt. R. O., 141, 145, 244, 417, 457
Ackerman, L/Cpl. T., 370
Adams, Pte. W., 91
Addams-Williams, 2/Lt. D. A., 127, 161, 162
Addison, Major A. M., 65, 170, 258, 262
Agate, Capt. E. (R.A.M.C.), 253
Ainsworth, Lt. B. L., 419, 420, 421, (Capt.) 506
Allbutt, Lt. and Q^{r}Mr J., 71, 230
Allen, L/Cpl. J., 309
Allenby, Gen. Sir E., 503
Allsopp, Lt. R. D., 269
Amos, 2/Lt. A. L., 171
Amos, 2/Lt. E. C., 173, 175, 227, (Lt.) 386, 409, 416, 427
Anderson, 2/Lt. J., 445
Andrews, R.S.M. E. C., 279, 483, 493
Angell, 2/Lt. S. W., 298
Angus, Major J. R. (Welch), 339, (Lt.-Col.) 389
Anstey, 2/Lt. C. W., 4, 32
Apps, L/Cpl. S. G., 477
Apsden, Sergt. J., 307
Archdale, Brig.-Gen. E. M., 63
Arnold, 2/Lt. H. G., 382, 415
Arnold, Sergt. J., 277, 278
Arthur, Cpl. R., 483
Ashe, 2/Lt., C. V., 445, 447
Austin, Lt. T. C. M., 127, 159, 160, 161, 189, 190, (Capt.) 194, 200, 201, 205
Avery, C.Q.M.S., 230

Baggallay, 2/Lt. G. T., 300, (Lt.) 352, 355
Baillie-Hamilton, Major N. A. B. (Black Watch), 346
Baker, 2/Lt. C. A., 4, 32, (Lt.) 98, 215, (Capt.) 434, 506
Baker, Cpl. R., 333
Baker, Lt. W. G. (Som. L.I.), 199
Ballantine, 2/Lt. A., 182, 183, 198
Bancroft, 2/Lt. L. G., 256
Banks, Sergt., 216
Baratoff, Gen., 319
Bardoe, R.Q.M.S. H. A., 177
Barker, C.S.M. A., 507
Barker, 2/Lt. J. M. W., 359, (Capt.) 392
Barker, 2/Lt. W. R., 318

Barnardiston, Brig.-Gen. N. W., 74–6, 82, 83
Barnes, Pte. W., 171
Barraclough, Capt., 500
Barratt, Cpl. J., 198
Barry, 2/Lt. E. W., 204
Barry, Capt. G. T. J., 34, 38, 40
Barry, R.S.M. J., 70, (Lt. and Q^{r}M^r) 177, 178, 230, 290
Bassett, Pte. F., 439
Batty, 2/Lt. D. A., 267
Bayliss, 2/Lt. A. N., 251
Beach, Pte. G., 229
Bean, Sergt. S. D., 116, 118
Beardshaw, 2/Lt. R. D., 186, 267
Beary, L/Cpl. M., 166, 198
Becker, Brig.-Gen. C. T., 59
Bees, 2/Lt. F. H., 415
Beeston, Lt. C. N., 215
Behrens, 2/Lt. R. P., 73, (Lt.) 105
Belcher, 2/Lt. W. H., 228
Bell, Lt. A. F., 127, 161, 162
Bell, Sergt. F., 126
Benfield, Lt. W. T., 482, 489
Bennett, Lt. H. S., 467
Bennett, Capt. J. B. S., 384, 408, 415
Benson, Major T. C., 66, 170
Bentley, L/Cpl. W., 345
Benzie, Major R., 302, (Lt.-Col.) 361–363, 391, 392
Beresford, Major M. de la P., 58, 127, 160, 166, (Lt.-Col.) 190, 192, 194, 198
Beresford-Ash, Lt.-Col. W. H., 233
Berger, 2/Lt. S. H., 118
Berry, Pte. A., 265
Berry, Pte. F., 488
Best, 2/Lt. F. H., 317
Best, 2/Lt. S. W., 317, 320, 326
Best, C.S.M., 131
Bethell, C.Q.M.S., 71
Bevan, Lt. F. H. V., 171
Bevan, Pte. J., 331
Beynon, 2/Lt. W. C., 298
Bickford-Smith, Lt. W. N. V., 127, 158, (Capt.) 209, 318, 496
Bill, Capt. J. H., 4, 93, 94, 99
Birch, Major F. W., 59, 117, 129, 167, 206–7
Birkett, Capt. G. H., 73, 83, 102, 105
Black, Pte. R., 53
Blackader, Maj.-Gen. C. G., 310, 329
Blackall-Simonds, Lt. G., 28, 30

591

INDEX OF PERSONS

Blair, Sergt T., 382
Blake, Lt. A. J. (R.A.M.C.), 102, (Capt.) 220, 296, 369–370
Blake, Lt. F. S., 165, (Capt.) 220, 238
Blaxland, Capt. J. B., 127, 211, 316
Blomfield, Lt. C. G., 173, (Capt.) 175
Blowen, 2/Lt. F. E. V., 68, (Capt.) 179, 232
Bloxham, Lt. W. V., 64, (Capt.) 173, 496
Bodenham, Lt. H., 171, 377
Bodley, Lt. O. C., 186, 220, 258
Boggett, Pte., 240
Bond, Capt. W. F., 180
Boobyer, L/Cpl. J. 363
Bourne, Lt. S. M. (R.F.), 204
Bowden, C.Q.M.S., 175
Bowen, Major A. L., 291, 389, (Lt.-Col.) 440, 447
Bowen, Pte. T. J., 240
Bowen, 2/Lt. W. L., 428, 439
Bowyer, 2/Lt. G. H., 238
Boys, Captain H. H., 64–6
Bradbury, Major P. H. (Welch), 278, 376, 483
Bradley, Lt. J. F., 118, 124
Bradstock, Capt. J., 73, 81–3
Braithwaite, Lt.-Gen. Sir W. P., 450
Breene, 2/Lt. T. F. (R. Warwickshire), 218
Brewer, 2/Lt. E., 391
Brice, Sergt. F., 388
Bricknell, 2/Lt. E. T. S., 287
Bridges, Maj.-Gen. G. C. M., 225, 265, 269
Bridgewater, Sergt., 223
Broacker, Lt. E. W., 69
Bronham, 2/Lt. T. C. R., 460, 461, 462
Brooke, Sergt. H., 265
Brooking, Maj.-Gen. H. T., 497, 500
Brown, 2/Lt. H. J., 230, 291, (Capt.) 391
Brown, Lt. M. W., 171, (Capt.) 483
Brown, Capt. W. E., 230, 359, (Major) 361–3, 391, 392
Brown, Pte. W., 342
Browning, 2/Lt. C. E., 176, (Lt.) 178, (Capt.) 244, 247, 291, (Major) 481, 482
Bruce, Major D. W. (R.W.F.), 278, (Lt.-Col.) 377
Brunker, Pte. J., 488
Bruntnell, R.S.M. W., 52, 179
Bryant, Lt. and Q^{r}Mr J. W., 143, 286, (Capt.) 386, 454, 510
Bryant, 2/Lt. T. H., 333

Buchanan, 2/Lt. A., 127, 158, (Lt.) 191, (Capt.) 194, 198, 203, 204, 211, 317
Buckley, 2/Lt. F. A., 151, 215
Buckley, 2/Lt. (Cheshire), 125
Budd, 2/Lt. W. J. C., 122, 124
Budgen, 2/Lt. H. K., 177
Bull, Sergt. L. G., 333
Bullen, Pte. P., 293
Bullock, 2/Lt. G. F., 333
Bülow, Gen. von, 6, 8, 10, 11, 20
Bunce, 2/Lt. G., 102, (Lt.) 118
Bundy, 2/Lt. C. A., 448
Burges, Lt.-Col. D. (Gloucestershire), 376, 488, 490
Burgess, Pte. G., 349
Burn, Lt. W. A., 170, (Capt.) 276, 277, 376
Burrell, 2/Lt. P. E., 118, 167
Bury, 2/Lt. E. P., 127, 162
Bush, C.S.M. T., 127, 161, 189
Butcher, Pte. D. J., 307
Butler, Brig.-Gen. R. H. K., 88, 90
Byng, Maj.-Gen. Sir J., 36
Byrne, Lt. E. J. W., 87, 91, 184, (Capt.) 220, 221

Cable, Pte. G., 198
Cadoux, 2/Lt. B. J., 170
Cahill, Pte. M., 251
Cahusac, Lt. A. N., 73, 81, 141, 142, (Capt.) 191, 192, 194, 197, 200, 205
Cain, 2/Lt. H. C., 369
Caldwell, Lt. R. N., 190, 198, 205, (Capt.) 309, 334, 372, 385, 386, 483, (Major) 490, 493
Callaghan, C.Q.M.S., J., 127
Campbell, Capt., R.A.M.C., 349
Cardwell, 2/Lt. G. E., 171, 278, 373, 377, (Lt.) 493
Carless, Capt. A. L., 131
Carlyle, 2/Lt. G., 430
Carpendale, Lt. H. M. St. J., 228, 450
Carrington, 2/Lt. R. C., 247
Carroll, Sergt. P., 363
Carruthers, Major P. J. O., 66
Carter, Lt. and Q^{r}Mr A., 377, 483, 493
Carter, Lt. F., 64, (Capt.) 173, 175, 233
Carter, Pte. F. L., 335
Case, Lt. and Q^{r}Mr A., 173, (Capt.) 429, 430
Casey, Capt. C. L., 171, 279
Casey, R.S.M. E., 64, 173, 288, 305
Casey, Pte. P., 240
Cashman, R.S.M. W., 64, 171, 273, 279
Cass, 2/Lt. H. L., 118, 122, 123

592

INDEX OF PERSONS

Cassell, Lt. (U.S.A.), 477
Casson, Col. H. G., 2, 73, 83, 106-9, 115, 118, 119, 130
Cavan, Brig.-Gen. Lord, 51, (Lt.-Gen.) 326
Cayley, Maj.-Gen. B. E., 322
Chamberlain, 2/Lt. W. J., 102, 105
Chaplin, C.S.M. J., 284
Chapman, 2/Lt. A. N., 385, 391
Chapman, Cpl. J., 419, 421
Charlton, 2/Lt. G. F. H., 70, (Capt.) 177, 289, 290, 309
Charton, Lt. W. C., 173
Chatfield, Q.M.S. F., 173
Cheyne, Sergt. J. D., 482
Choinier, Capt. E. C., 173, 255, 288
Claffy, Pte. T., 178
Clark, Sergt. G., 482
Clarke, 2/Lt. H. Y. C., 298
Clarke, Pte. W., 240
Clausewitz, Gen., 16
Clayton, 2/Lt. A., 177
Clent, Pte. T., 118
Clevey, Sergt. J., 279
Clissold, C.S.M. C. F., 178, 340
Cobb, 2/Lt. W. T., 332 (Capt.) 388, 389, 506
Cobbe, Maj.-Gen. Sir A. S., 211, (Lt.-Gen.) 503
Cochrane, 2/Lt. I. E. M., 185, 186, (Capt). 493
Cochrane, Pte. H., 363
Cockcroft, Capt. E. F., 131, (Major) 514
Codling, C.S.M., 230
Coe, Capt. F. A., 170
Coghill, 2/Lt. J. K. B., 251
Coker, Lt. C. J., 4, 30, 31
Cole, 2/Lt. R. H., 169, 251
Cole, 2/Lt. W., 169, 251
Colley, Pte. W., 325
Collier, Capt. B. W., 2, (Major) 151, 179, (Lt.-Col.) 213, 214, 216, 251, 282
Connolly, Cpl., 424
Constantine (King of Greece), 479
Cook, Sgt. W. R., 198
Cooke, Brig.-Gen. H. F., 376
Cooke, Major S. FitzW., 58, 59, 143, 169, 220
Cooke, 2/Lt. E. S. W., 186, (Lt.) 356-7, 370
Cool, C.S.M., 178
Cooper, C.S.M. A. E., 178
Cooper, 2/Lt. F. N. N., 357
Cooper, Sergt. J., 377
Cooper, 2/Lt. L. G., 127, 159, 161

Copner, 2/Lt. C. J. P., 4, 58, 59, (Capt.) 143, 343, 346, 381
Corfield, Lt. L. V., 171
Cornish, C.S.M. A. H., 127, (R.S.M.) 129, 210
Cottam, 2/Lt. H., 70, 177, (Lt.) 331-333, (Capt.) 390
Cottrell, Lt. and Q^{r}Mr G. J., 440
Coulter, 2/Lt. F. C., 240
Cousmaker, Lt. A. B., 254, 267
Cowburn, Major A. B. (Border), 423
Cox, Brig.-Gen. H. V., 120, 161
Cox, Lt. and Q^{r}Mr A., 310, (Capt.) 418
Cox, Sergt. C. F., 482
Cox, R.S.M. J., 386
Cox, 2/Lt. R. M., 173, 264, (Lt.) 288, (Capt.) 305, 307
Coxhead, L/Cpl. R. H., 40
Cracroft-Wilson, Lt. C. W., 211
Crake, Major R. H. (K.O.S.B.), 318, 496
Crawford, Capt. G. S., 143, (Major) 287, 309, 335
Crawford, Major W. L., 438, (Lt.-Col.) 478, 510
Creary, 2/Lt. H. J., 130
Creighton, Pte. J. T., 358
Crewe-Read, Capt. R. O., 43, 45-7, 50, 51, (Major) 496, 504, 513
Crisp, Pte. T., 198, 239
Crocker, Major (Cheshire), 316, 318
Croft, Lt. D. W., 143, (Capt.) 169, 223, 224, 253, 304, (Major) 385, 395, 396, 399, 407, 454
Crossdale, Pte. G., 359
Crossland, Pte. A., 262
Crowder, Capt. A. E., 415, 423, 435
Crum, Sergt. T. J., 401
Cullimore, 2/Lt. S., 70, (Capt.) 178, 230
Cuff, 2/Lt. J. W., 465
Curgenven, Capt. W. C., 4, 32, 36, 38, 40
Curling, 2/Lt. T. E., 278
Currall, Major W. B. (L.F.), 278
Curtis, Capt. C. M. D., 143, 169, 224, 287

Dadey, Pt. R., 247
Dakeyne, Lt.-Col. H. W. (R. Warwickshire), 510
Daniel, 2/Lt. H. J., 142
D'Arcy, Capt. de B., 170
Darcy, C.S.M. W. H., 331
Dare, Sergt. J., 380, 419, 421
Dart, Pte. R., 144
Darwent, Pte. C., 251

INDEX OF PERSONS

Davenport, 2/Lt. H. H., 177, 247, 331, (Capt.) 388, 389
Davenport, C.S.M. T., 230
David, 2/Lt. A. W., 449
Davidson, Captain (R.N.), 103
Davidson, 2/Lt. A. W., 282
Davidson, Lt.-Col. C., 65, 66
Davidson, 2/Lt. C., 217
Davies, Cpl. A. E., 172
Davies, 2/Lt. B. E. S., 178, (Capt.) 331–333
Davies, Lt. B. J., 142, 185, (Capt.) 186, 218, 253, 267, 298, 299
Davies, 2/Lt. C. A., 487
Davies, 2/Lt. D. C., 247
Davies, Pte. D. J., 247
Davies, 2/Lt. D. S., 170, 172, 274
Davies, 2/Lt. D. T., 445
Davies, Pte. E., 171
Davies, 2/Lt. E. O., 363
Davies, 2/Lt. G. L., 318
Davies, 2/Lt. G. A., 382, 462
Davies, Lt. H., 427, 428, 429
Davies, Capt. H. A., 130
Davies, Lt. H. C. A., 173, 175, 226, (Capt.) 363
Davies, 2/Lt. H. C. S., 151, (Capt.) 457–9
Davies, 2/Lt. H. E., 230
Davies, 2/Lt. H. H., 349
Davies, Brig.-Gen. H. R., 140, 148
Davies, 2/Lt. J., 437
Davies, 2/Lt. J. H., 310
Davies, Lt. J. H., 309
Davies, Pte. P. S., 247
Davies, 2/Lt. T. H., 247
Davies, Capt. W., 409, 415
Davies, C.S.M. W., 178, 247, (R.S.M.) 341, 389
Davies, 2/Lt. W. F., 267
Davies, Pte. W. H., 284
Davies, Lt. W. T., 416
Davis, 2/Lt. H., 398
Davis, 2/Lt. J. H., 296
Dawes, Lt. A. J., 70, (Capt.) 178, 229, 244
Dawes, 2/Lt. H. D., 4, 32
Dawson, Sergt. W., 227
Day, 2/Lt. W. H., 143, 241, 268
Deacon, Lt. E. T., 349
Deacon, Capt. T., 143, 169, (Major) 224, 287
Deane, 2/Lt. L. C. W., 173, (Lt.) 175, (Capt.) 288, (Major) 386, 397, 398, 406, 415, (Lt.-Col.) 426, 429, 438

De Freyne, Capt. Lord, 86, 94, 139
De Lisle, Maj.-Gen. Sir H. B., 121, 344
Dendy, Capt. R. (A.S.C.), 385, 415, 424, 460, 470, 471
Dick, Lt. W. T., 170, 274, 375, 376, (Capt.) 377, 487
Dickie, Lt. M. A. M., 171, (Capt.) 373, 377, 483, 493
Dickinson, 2/Lt. D. C., 437
Dickinson, Capt. F. G., 296, 299
Dickinson, 2/Lt. F. J. T., 220, (Capt.) 486
Dickinson, Capt. W. V. D., 423
Dilloway, 2/Lt. W., 381, 391, 419, 420,
Dix, C.Q.M.S. A., 480
Dixon, 2/Lt. L. F., 424
Dobbs, Lt.-Col. H. R. (R.I.F.), 377, 482, 483, 489, 490, 491, 492, 512
Dold, Capt. (R.A.M.C.), 459
Don, 2/Lt. D. F. (Foresters), 238
Donald, Maj.-Gen. C. G., 232
Donald, Capt. (R.A.M.C.), 487, 488
Doran, Sergt. J. E., 377
Dorchester, Sergt., 70, (C.S.M.) 178, 333
Dorrington, 2/Lt. J. W. H. (K.R.R.C.), 215
Dover, Pte. G. G., 388, (Cpl.) 471
Down, Capt. H., 171, 279
Doyle, Pte. D., 140
Drewett, L/Cpl. R., 240
Driscoll, L/Cpl. J., 483
Drury, 2/Lt. P. H., 86, 150
Duckin, Sergt. A., 382
Duffy, Sergt. G. S., 31
Duncan, Maj.-Gen. J., 277, 378, 488, 490
Dunham, 2/Lt. E. V., 308
Dunn, Sergt. J. H., 471
Dunne, R.Q.M.S. A., 170, (Lt. and Qr Mr) 272, 483
Durand, 2/Lt. A. E., 197, 198, 204
Dutton, 2/Lt. C. F., 186, 237, (Lt.) 460, (Capt.) 470
Dwain, Sergt. W. J., 46

Eames, 2/Lt. W. S., 360, 363, 392
Easterbrook, Capt. L. F., 173, 227
Ede, 2/Lt. C. M., 173, (Lt.) 241
Ede, 2/Lt. H. S., 173, 255
Ede, Pte. W. T., 174
Edmonds, 2/Lt. E. T., 447
Edmonds, 2/Lt. H. S., 230
Edmunds, Sergt. F., 488
Edmunds, Pte. T., 231

INDEX OF PERSONS

Edwardes, Sergt., 247
Edwards, 2/Lt. E., 358, 363
Edwards, 2/Lt. H. J., 369
Edwards, 2/Lt. H. T., 355
Edwards, Corpl. J., 91
Edwards, 2/Lt. J. R. T., 349
Edwards, Sergt. R., 245, 247, 291
Edwards, Corpl. T., 388
Edwards, 2/Lt. T. J., 186
Edwards, 2/Lt. W. G., 227
Edwards, Sergt. W. T., 290, 291
Edwards, Sergt. W. S., 178
Edwards, 2/Lt. (R.W.F.), 141, 142
Edwards, C.Q.M.S., 131, 178
Egerton, Lt.-Gen. Sir R., 500
Elgee, Capt. H. F., 125, 126
Ellaway, Pte. J., 227
Ellis, Capt. A. H. J., 73, (Major) 185, 288, 305, 309
Ellis, Major A. J., 478, 510
Ellis, 2/Lt. J., 333, 445, 447
Elliot, Capt. (R.A.M.C.), 4, 26
Elliott, Sergt. T. W., 377
Elridge, Lt. and Q^{r}Mr R. W., 57, 131
Elsdon, Corpl. J., 416
England, Capt. J. R., 171, 464, 465
Enright, 2/Lt. H. P., 230, 292
Eskell, Lt. R., 173, 175, 241
Esmond, 2/Lt. G., 424, 425
Evans, C.S.M. A., 131
Evans, Capt. A. J., 440
Evans, 2/Lt. C., 209
Evans, 2/Lt. D. L., 253
Evans, Capt. E. (R.A.M.C.), 247, 291
Evans, 2/Lt. E. S., 268
Evans, 2/Lt. E. S. J., 343, 427
Evans, 2/Lt. F. F., 317
Evans, Corpl. F. J., 488
Evans, Lt. G. S., 278
Evans, Pte. H., 388
Evans, 2/Lt. H. E., 355
Evans, Brig.-Gen. H. J., 244
Evans, 2/Lt. H. P., 129, 165, 185, 238
Evans, Pte. H. S., 229
Evans, 2/Lt. I. T., 143, 225, 240, (Lt.) 286, (Capt.) 343, 386, 399, 407, 410, 416, (Major) 437, 454, 510
Evans, 2/Lt. J. L., 241
Evans, 2/Lt. N., 251
Evans, 2/Lt. N. V., 300, 338
Evans, Pte. O., 331
Evans, Sergt. P. F., 290
Evans, 2/Lt. R., 316
Evans, Pte. R., 464
Evans, 2/Lt. R. G., 381, 452

Evans, Capt. R. H., 4, 58, 290
Evans, Lt. R. T., 70, (Capt.) 230
Evans, Lt. T. B. (R.A.M.C.), 177
Evans, 2/Lt. T. G., 173, 241
Evans, 2/Lt. S., 173, 175, 226, 227
Evans, Capt. W. G., 173-180
Evans, 2/Lt. W. H., 330, 333
Evans, 2/Lt. W. M., 254, 267, (Lt.) 361, 363, 392
Evans, Pte., 227
Everett, 2/Lt. R. T., 204, 206, 209, 211, 500, 501
Everton, 2/Lt. M. J., 247
Excell, 2/Lt. C. B., 442, 447

Fairs, 2/Lt. C., 483
Fairweather, Capt. J., 127, 189, 211, (Major) 316
Farnall, 2/Lt. E. L., 251
Farrier, 2/Lt. A., 86, 92
Farrow, Lt. J., 127, 159-61, 189, (Capt.) 190, 194, 198, 200, 201, 205
Fasken, Maj.-Gen. C. C. M., 59
Fearby, Capt. S. A., 341
Feast, Sergt. G., 70
Ffrench, Lt. K., 118, 124, 185, (Capt.) 198
Field, Lt. A. C. H. (R.F.), 204
Field, Lt.-Col. J. A. F., 232
Fisher, Lt.-Col. H. T., 233
FitzClarence, Brig.-Gen., 42, 47, 48, 51
Fitzpatrick, Lt.-Col. T. N. (R.E.), 386, 397, 406, 409, 415
Fitzpatrick, Pte. J., 257
Fleming, Lt. (R.A.M.C.), 161
Fletcher, 2/Lt. A. S., 244
Foley, L/Cpl. C. J., 82
Foote, Pte. E., 333
Ford, 2/Lt. C. B., 204
Ford, 2/Lt. R. M., 98, 169, 304
Foreman, Capt. J. W., 180
Forsythe, Pte. R., 363
Foster, Capt. W. G. L., 359, 392, 440
Foster, Drummer A. W., 39, 40
Fountaine, Capt. P. G., 498
Fowkes, 2/Lt. C. C., 42, 45, 47, 50, 54, (Lt.) 238, (Capt.) 419, 421, 451
Fowler, Capt. H. G. C., 86, 87, 90, 118, 122, 179, (Major) 233, 346, 349, (Lt-.Col.) 380
Franchet d'Esperey, Gen., 489
Francis, 2/Lt. E. H., 230, (Lt.) 302, (Capt.) 381
Francis, R.S.M. J., 386
Francis, Cpl. W., 92, 96, 97

595

INDEX OF PERSONS

Francis Ferdinand, Archduke, 1
Franklin, C.S.M. H., 214
Franklin, 2/Lt. W. V., 171, (Lt.) 272, (Capt.) 377, (Major) 481, 483, 490
Franks, 2/Lt. P. H., 382
Franey, 2/Lt. G. J., 445
Fraser, 2/Lt., 396
Fraser, 2/Lt. I. K., 409
Frayne, Pte. L., 335
Freeman, Sergt. J. J., 217
Freeman, Capt. J. W., 230
French, 2/Lt. Hon. E. A., 299, (Lt.) 333
French, 2/Lt. Hon. G. P., 96, 138, 140
French, Field Marshal Sir J., 8, 16, 35, 49, 87, 140, 145, 178, (Lord) 233
Galsworthy, Capt. A., 177, 244, 247, 331, 332
Garner, 2/Lt. G., 462
Garnett, Lt. H. G., 87, 92, (Capt.) 221, 254, (Major) 284, 310, 336, 344, 368, 369
Garnett-Botfield, 2/Lt. A. C. F. (R.B.), 86, (Lt.) 140
Garnons-Williams, 2/Lt. A. A. C., 250, 251
Garro-Jones, 2/Lt. G. M., 177
Gaussen, Lt.-Col. J. R. (3rd Horse, I.A.), 177, 179, 229, 246, 247, 290, 291
Gawler, Sergt. W. J., 281
Geary, Sergt. R. J., 257
Geldard, 2/Lt. S. H., 118, 129
George, 2/Lt. D. F., 331, 333
George, Pte. W., 278
Gibbon, 2/Lt. E. M., 337, 344, (Capt.) 352, 366, 367, 369
Gibbs, Sergt. G., 506
Gibbs, 2/Lt. J. E. A., 382
Gibbs, 2/Lt. R. R., 130, (Lt.) 163, 185
Gibson, 2/Lt. G. F., 300, 344
Gibson-Watt, Major J. M., 55, 290, 389
Gilbee, 2/Lt. E. O., (R.F.), 204
Gilbert, Lt. H. A., 28, 35
Giles, Lt. H. R., 66, 170
Giles, 2/Lt. W. G., 349, 449
Gill, 2/Lt. E., 177, 228, 247, 444
Gillespie, Major F. M., 2, (Lt.-Col.) 57, 58, 127, 155, 156, 157, 161, 413
Gilmore-Ellis, 2/Lt. P. D., 170 (Lt.) 376
Givons, Capt. A. D., 177, 229, 460, 461
Glanusk, Col. Lord, 2, 132, 327
Glazebrook, 2/Lt. F. E., 184
Glenister, R.S.M. A., 386, 429
Glover, Lt. A. N., 436, 470

Glynn, R.Q.M.S., 272
Godsal, Lt. J., 177
Godwin-Austen, Lt. A. R., 58, 59
Godwin-Austen, Capt. R. A., 230, 294
Going, Major J., 73, 108, 115, 118, 122, 123, 131, 164, (Lt.-Col.) 185, 221, 283
Goldsmith, Lt. E., 178, 229
Golightly, C.S.M. W. H., 178
Goodchild, C.Q.M.S. R. J., 127
Goodman, Lt. D., 359, 363
Goodman, Sergt. W. H., 265
Goodship, Capt. W., 359
Gordon, Maj.-Gen. Hon. F., 173
Gorringe, Maj.-Gen. G. F., 201, 208
Gotelee, 2/Lt. G. H., 142, (Capt.) 487
Gottwaltz, Capt. P., 170, 276 (Major) 277, 374, 376, 377, 483
Gould, 2/Lt. R. B., 315
Graham, Lt. E. M., 34, 45, 46
Gransmore, Major F. W. (Welch), 316
Grant Dalton, Major E. F. (W. Yorks), 177, 178, 229
Graystone, Capt. H., 181
Greaves, Lt. L. B., 392, 490
Green, Pte. A., 82
Green, R.S.M. C., 57
Green, 2/Lt. H. S., 300, 509
Green, Sergt. T., 415, 416
Greenway, Capt. T. C., 73, 109, 115, 119, 121, 198
Greenwood, Lt.-Col. Sir H., 69, 177–178
Greenwood, C.Q.M.S., 178, (C.S.M.) 229
Grey, Capt. R. F., 200, 209
Griffith, Lt. H. B., 325
Griffiths, L/Cpl. A. E., 284
Griffiths, 2/Lt. C., 209, (Lt.) 312, 314
Griffiths, Cpl. H., 488
Griffiths, 2/Lt. H. C., 118
Griffiths, 2/Lt. H. E., 411, 412
Griffiths, 2/Lt. H. J., 320
Griffiths, 2/Lt. I, 462
Griffiths, 2/Lt. J. H. C., 70, (Lt.) 178, 230, 318
Griffiths, 2/Lt. N., 170, 228, 241
Griffiths, Lt. R. J., 343
Griffiths, R.S.M., 72
Griffiths, Pte., 227
Griffith Jones, 2/Lt. J. S., 177
Grimwood, Captain J., 65, 66, (Major) 170, (Lt.-Col.) 278, 376
Gronow, L/Cpl. W. J., 166
Grylls, 2/Lt. H., 76

INDEX OF PERSONS

Guillaumat, Gen., 479, 484
Gunter, Pte. H. C., 33
Gwynn, Capt. R. S., 4, 30, 31, 43, 45, 47, 50, 97, (Major) 142, (Lt.-Col.) 148, 149, 151
Gwynne, 2/Lt. B., 304

Habershon, Lt. C. B., 73, (Capt.) 102, 110, 112, 129
Hadley, Lt. R. B., 4, 38, 42
Haig, General Sir D., 5, 8, 20, 32, 97, 145, 212, 225, 226, 248, 281, 283, 296, 303, 328, 352, 357, 370, 426, 441, 444, 451, 468, 474
Haig-Brown, Capt. A. R. (Midd'x), 180
Hales, R.S.M., 513
Hales, Drummer, J., 333
Halford, R.S.M. G., 127
Halil Pasha, 205
Hall, 2/Lt. A. R. C., 424
Hall, Lt. C. E. L., 143, 225, 240
Hall, 2/Lt. J. E. K., 184, 185
Hall, 2/Lt. J. H., 434
Hall, C.S.M. P., 277, 377
Hamer, Lt. T. P., 178, 244, 290
Hamilton, Major E. G. (Connaught Rangers), 327
Hamilton, General Sir I., 103, 119, 157, 163, 182
Hamilton-Jones, Major A. H. M., 65, 170, 233, 272, 279
Hammond, Lt. T. E. (R.A.M.C.), 197
Hampton, Sergt. H. A., 361, 363
Hancock, Col. H. E., 60, 170
Hancock, Pte. D., 309, 416
Hanford, Pte. T., 251
Hankey, Major E. B. (Worcestershire), 48
Hanna, 2/Lt. W. H., 308, 335, 398
Hannay, Lt. H. H., 170
Hardwick, Lt. A. W., 383, 509
Hardy, 2/Lt. C. J., 470
Hardy, 2/Lt. F. W., 470
Harford, 2/Lt. J. H., 267
Harries, 2/Lt. J. E., 298
Harris, Capt. J. B., 170, 276, 493
Harris, Sergt. P., 247
Harris, L/Cpl. W., 185
Harris, Lt. W. T., 178, 290, (Capt.) 333, 381, 450
Harrison, Lt. J. P., 293
Hart, 2/Lt. O., 385, 391, 416
Hartley, Lt. F. L., 363
Hartley, 2/Lt. F. W., 462
Harvey, 2/Lt. C. A. L., 171, (Capt.) 371, 493

Harvey, Major C. D. (Foresters), 177, 178, 229, 245, 246, 247, (Lt.-Col.) 289, 290, 340, 425, 511
Harwood-Banner, 2/Lt. W., 96, (Capt.) 142
Hathaway, L/Cpl., 292
Hausen, Gen. von, 8
Havard, Capt. W. T. (C.F.), 177, 309
Haydon, Lt. G. M., 171, 279, 300, (Capt.) 336, 338
Hayes, Lt. H. H., 34
Hayes, 2/Lt. J. R., 141
Haywood, Cpl. H., 361, 363
Hazard, Capt. S. C. J., 171
Heal, 2/Lt. C. H., 102, 116, 118
Hearder, 2/Lt. S. F., 369, 405
Heath, Pte. P. T., 277, (L/Cpl.) 483
Hemingway, Lt. S., 127, (Capt.) 203, 204
Hendy, L/Cpl., 110, 118
Heppel, 2/Lt. R. M., 247, 304
Herbert, 2/Lt. H. M., 318
Hewett, Lt.-Col. E. V. O., 66, 173, 228, 265, 288, 381, 386
Hewitt, 2/Lt. C. J., 141, 142
Hewitt, Pte. J., 361, 363
Heyworth, Brig.-Gen. F. J., 142
Hibbert, L/Cpl. P., 223
Hibbins, 2/Lt. A., 177
Hicks, C.S.M. H., 47, (R.S.M.) 52
Hicks, 2/Lt. S., 468
Hill, 2/Lt. E. O., 308
Hill, Lt. F. A., 165
Hill, 2/Lt. H. R., 358
Hill, Capt. P. A., 296, 297
Hillbourne, 2/Lt. E. E., 247
Hillier, C.S.M. F., 382
Hillier, 2/Lt. S. N., 398
Hind, 2/Lt. W. E., 318, (Lt.) 513
Hipkiss, R.S.M. T., 68
Hipkiss, C.S.M., 509
Hiscock, Pte. C., 333
Hitch, R.S.M., 180
Hitchcox, Capt. C. W., 386
Hitchings, 2/Lt. A., 177
Hitchings, Pte. J., 342
Hoffmeister, Lt. C. E., 71, (Capt.) 180, 232, 443
Hogg, Pte., 103
Holden, 2/Lt. F. (R.W.F.), 141
Holland, Maj.-Gen. A., 169
Holliday, Cpl. W., 161
Holliday, Pte. W., 397, 398
Holyoake, Lt. G. N., 382
Homfray, Lt. J. R., 4, 45, 50, 52

597

INDEX OF PERSONS

Hooper, 2/Lt. A. W., 54, (Capt.) 127, 161, 189, 496, 504
Hooper, 2/Lt. E. J. J., 363
Hooper, C.S.M. G. J., 305, 307, 432
Hopkins, 2/Lt. D. J., 298
Hore, Major C. B. (R. Warwickshire), 180, 230, 293
Horne, Lt.-Gen. Sir H. S., 292
Hornsby, 2/Lt. J. P. S., 177, (Capt.) 341, 443, 445
Horrobin, Pte. J., 335, 398
House, C.S.M. H. G., 458
Howarth, 2/Lt. B. J., 425, 443
Howater, R.Q.M.S., 68
Howcroft, Sergt. C. E., 222
Howe, Sergt C., 223
Howell, 2/Lt. W. E. G., 230, (Lt.) 359
Huggett, 2/Lt. W. W., 229
Hughes, Capt. A. A., 222, 237, 238
Hughes, Sergt. H. L., 390
Hughes, 2/Lt. P. C., 487
Hughes, 2/Lt. W. P., 443
Hulbert, 2/Lt. C., 451
Hulbert, Sergt. O., 333
Hullah, Pte. A., 39, 40
Humphries, 2/Lt. W. J., 333
Humphreys, Major E. J. (D.C.L.I.), 483, 489, 493
Hunter, Col. F. C. K., 3
Hunter-Weston, Maj.-Gen. Sir A., 103, 105, 118, 121, (Lt.-Gen.) 219, 220, 238, 254, 263, 382

Ingledew, Lt. and Q^rM^r J. R., 69, 170, 290
Inglis, 2/Lt. J. J., 118, 121, 151, (Capt.) 213, 214, 256, 257
Inglis, Lt. R. C., 118, 121
Ingram, C.Q.M.S., 131
Irons, C.S.M. J., 353
Isaac, Major T., 57

Jackson, 2/Lt. E. P. (R. Warwickshire), 93, 140
Jackson, Sergt. W., 184, 198
Jacob, Lt.-Gen. Sir C., 334
Jacobs, 2/Lt. G., 308
Jacques, Pte. J., 302
Jakeway, 2/Lt. G. B., 409
James, Lt. A. E. L., 4, 31
James, Lt. A. S. B., 86
James, Sergt. D. J., 217
James, Capt. T. G., 362
James, C.Q.M.S., 127
James, Lt. F., 475
James, 2/Lt. G. C. B., 300, 355
James, Pte. H., 293
James, Capt. J. N. A., 173
James, Cpl. J. V., 333
James, Lt. T. N. B., 171, 279
James, Cpl., 377
Jamieson, Lt. G. D. (R. Scots), 501
Jarman, Capt. (R.A.M.C.), 277
Jeffcoat, 2/Lt. E. R., 339
Jeffreys, Maj.-Gen. G. D., 343, 510
Jenkins, 2/Lt. A., 416
Jenkins, Capt. C. F. B., 178, 330, 333
Jenkins, 2/Lt. D., 173, 335, (Capt.) 406, 416
Jenkins, Capt. E., 359, 363
Jenkins, 2/Lt. R. D. P., 86, 93
Jenkins, Lt. T. M., 127, 159, (Capt.) 326
Jenkins, C.Q.M.S. H.C., 178
Jeremiah, Sergt. H., 419, 420, 421
Jewell, 2/Lt. W. J., 447
Job, C.Q.M.S. W. H., 230
Joffre, Marshal, 5, 11, 16, 87, 101, 281
John, 2/Lt. I. G., 151
John, Pte. T., 223
Johns, 2/Lt. S. B., 86, 92, (Lt.) 176, 212
Johnson, Capt. D. G., 73, 82, 83, 105, 197, (Major) 380, 381, (Lt.-Col.) 474, 475
Johnson, Lt. M. T., 4, 24, 27
Jones, 2/Lt. A. D., 359
Jones, Lt. B. H., 332, 333
Jones, 2/Lt. B. I., 197
Jones, 2/Lt. B. I. L., 118, 123
Jones, Lt. B. O., 143, 144, (Capt.) 385, 386, 396
Jones, 2/Lt. B. R. B., 173, (Lt.) 178
Jones, 2/Lt. B. R. S., 184, 186
Jones, 2/Lt. D., 465
Jones, Pte. D., 262
Jones, 2/Lt. D. L., 317, 320
Jones, C.S.M. D. T., 325, (2/Lt.), 491
Jones, 2/Lt. E., 363
Jones, Lt. E. C. H., 143
Jones, 2/Lt. E. G., 254, 487
Jones, Major E. W., 73, 102, 118, 119, (Lt.-Col.) 496, 498, 499, 503, 504
Jones, 2/Lt. G. W., 173, 227
Jones, 2/Lt. H., 383, 415, 471
Jones, 2/Lt. H. O., 333
Jones, 2/Lt. H. R., 230
Jones, 2/Lt. H. T., 477
Jones, 2/Lt. I. D., 407, 416
Jones, C.S.M. J., 159
Jones, Sergt. J., 251
Jones, Capt. J. A., 309, 465

INDEX OF PERSONS

Jones, 2/Lt. J. R. L., 386, 399 (Lt.), 410, 416
Jones, Lt. J. R. O., 180, 232
Jones, Sergt. J. T., 227
Jones, 2/Lt. L. R., 383
Jones, 2/Lt. R., 255
Jones, Pte. R., 293
Jones, 2/Lt. R. C. M., 268
Jones, Lt. R. H., 463
Jones, C.S.M. T., 361, 363
Jones, 2/Lt. T. G., 197, 204
Jones, 2/Lt. T. L. R., 205
Jones, Lt. T. O., 230, 293, (Capt.) 300, 301
Jones, 2/Lt. T. O., 308
Jones, 2/Lt. V., 298
Jones, Capt. W. O., 177, (Major) 341
Jones, Sergt. W. J., 240
Jordan, Capt. A., 232
Jordan, Lt. J., 122, 123
Jordan, 2/Lt. T. C., 357, 369
Joyce, 2/Lt. F. G., 344
Joyce, Pte., 377

Kamio, Gen. (Japan), 75, 76
Karran, 2/Lt. J. B., 186, 222, 238
Kay, Brig.-Gen. Sir W. A., 451
Kaye, Major A. M. R., 65, 66
Kaye, Lt. W. G. C., 171, 279, (Capt.) 482
Kearns, R.Q.M.S. W., 309
Keen, C.Q.M.S., 178, (C.S.M.) 229
Keighley, 2/Lt. F. W., 183, 206, 208
Kekewich, Maj.-Gen. R. G., 59
Kelly, Capt. B. J. R., 267
Kelly, 2/Lt. W., 222, 238
Kendrick, Lt. W. J., 430
Kenny, 2/Lt. H. St. J., 171, 278, (Lt.) 483
Kenslade, Lt. and Q^{r}Mr R. J., 290, 389
Kent, 2/Lt. H., 334
Kent, 2/Lt. L. V., 334
Kent, 2/Lt. T. H. 430
Kenward, Lt. R., 177, (Capt.) 309, 332, 333
Kerley, 2/Lt. B. F., 335
Kerr, Lt. D. (Cheshire), 124, 126
Key, Sergt. A. R., 370
King, 2/Lt. L. R. (Monmouthshire), 449
King, Capt. M. H., 332
King, 2/Lt. R., 458
Kitchen, 2/Lt. F. T., 430
Kitchener, Lord, 101, 170, 182

Kitchin, Capt. C. E., 58, 127, 155, 159, 160, 162, 166, 167, (Major) 190, 192, 194, 198, 199, 201, 202, 206, 208, 209, (Lt.-Col.) 316, 336, 327, 496, 503, 513
Kite, 2/Lt. E. W. S., 308
Kluck, Gen. von, 6, 10, 11, 12, 14, 16, 17, 18, 19, 20, 21, 22
Knight, L/Cpl. A., 370
Knowles, Lt. J. A. (Cheshire), 129, 165
Knott, Pte. L., 217

La Capelle, Gen., 344
Lacey, C.S.M. D. J., 177
Lake, Capt. J. S. R., 42, 43, 215, 217
Lakin, Lt. C. H. A., 271, 279
Laman, Lt. and Q^{r}Mr E. K., 73, 118, (Capt.) 220, 382, 435
Lancaster, 2/Lt. M. W. H., 332
Lancaster, Pte, 293
Landon, Brig.-Gen. H. J. S., 1, 18, 31, 37, 43, 45, 88
Lane, L/Cpl. J., 390
Langlands, 2/Lt. A., 98, 120
Lanrezac, Gen., 6, 8, 9, 11, 13
Laurie, Lt. F. E. W., 377, (Capt.) 493
Lawrence, Capt. F. G., 4, 36, 41, 98, (Major) 142
Lawrence, Major W. L., 4, 30, 31, 36, 45, 46
Leach, Lt.-Col. H. E. B., 1, 4, 26, 38, 43, 45, 46, 47, 48, 49
Letts, C.Q.M.S., 178
Lewin, Brig.-Gen. A. C., 191, 503, 504, 513
Lewis, 2/Lt. A. T., 296
Lewis, Pte. A. W., 277
Lewis, 2/Lt. C., 300
Lewis, Col. D. F., 60, 66
Lewis, Lt. J. S., 230, 293, 301, 415
Lewis, Capt. L. R., 178, 247
Lewis, Sergt. L., 483
Lewis, Pte. R., 91
Lewis, 2/Lt. T. C., 316
Lewis, Capt. T. E., 143, 144
Lichfield, R.Q.M.S. E., 171, 272
Light, 2/Lt. F., 314, 315, 499
Lightfoot, 2/Lt. W. R., 481
Lillington, 2/Lt. W. H., 177
Linnell, C.Q.M.S., 131
Lipyeart, Pte. F., 335
Little, 2/Lt. K. J., 391, 392
Littleton-Geach, 2/Lt. H. W. A., 143, (Capt.) 410, 454
Livesay, Lt. G. A. B., 143

599

INDEX OF PERSONS

Llewellin, 2/Lt. W. M., 434
Llewellyn, 2/Lt. H. A., 171, 220
Llewellyn, Sergt. C., 227
Lloyd, Capt. A. M. O. J., 57, 85, 90
Lloyd, Capt. E., 445
Lloyd, 2/Lt. E. A., 415
Lloyd, 2/Lt. E. C., 459
Lloyd, Capt. E. L., 173, 227, 277, 374, 483
Lloyd, 2/Lt. G. D. O., 54, 85, (Lt.) 212, 300, 310, 338
Lloyd, Lt. H. C., 230, (Capt.) 293, 300, 359, 391, 392
Lloyd, Capt. J. C., 139, 140
Lloyd, Col. J. D. A. T., 60
Lloyd, 2/Lt. J. E., 357
Lloyd, 2/Lt. Ll., 178
Lloyd, 2/Lt. L. R., 331
Loch, 2/Lt. A. A. F., 84, 95, 96, (Capt.) 149, 214
Lochner, Lt. C. B., 143, 152, 225, (Lt.) 224, 225, 286, 287
Lochner, 2/Lt. R. G., 4, 58, 59, (Capt.) 143, 224, 287, 348, 349, 417, (Major) 435
Lockie, R.S.M. G., 176, 177, 310, 341, 425
Lockwood, Pte. J., 361
Lomas, Pte. L., 215, 349
Lomax, Maj.-Gen. S. H., 1, 23, 27, 31, 37, 49
Long, Capt. H. M., 177, (Major) 280
Lougher, Pte. O., 251
Loxton, 2/Lt. C. E. H., 392, 444
Loxton, Pte. W., 315
Lovett, Lt.-Col. A. C. (Gloucestershire), 49
Lowe, 2/Lt. A. D. W., 169, 244, 285, 344
Lucas, Brig.-Gen. C. H. T., 365, 366
Lucas, 2/Lt. C. M., 127
Lucas, Sergt. E., 126, (2/Lt.) 480, 487
Lush, 2/Lt. W. C., 307
Lynn, Thomas, 2/Lt. C. I., 151

Macaulay, Lt. C. A., 205
Macaulay, Pte. D. M., 151, 216, 450, 467
MacGregor, 2/Lt. C. R., 74, (Lt.) 118
Macpherson, Lt.-Col. A. D. (Camerons), 376
Magness, C.S.M., 131
Maher, C.S.M. J., 127
Mahoney, Pte. P., 333
Malins, 2/Lt. E. D., 415
Manley, Capt. W. J., 348, 349, 381
Mann, Capt. (R.A.M.C.), 398, 428

Manners, 2/Lt. G., 227
Manning, Sergt. T. C., 450
Mansbridge, Pte. P., 447
March, 2/Lt. G. W., 205
Margesson, Major E. C., 73, 83, 105
Marle, Capt. H., 290
Marr, 2/Lt. H., 54, (Capt.) 208, 314, 325
Marshall, 2/Lt. B. S., 227
Marshall, Brig.-Gen. W. R., 100, 108, 110, (Lt.-Gen.) 211, 322, 323, (Gen.) 498, 500, 501, 503
Martin, Cpl. D., 483
Martin, Lt. and Q^{r}Mr G., 64, 170, 272
Martin, 2/Lt. H. F., 458
Martin, R.Q.M.S. J., 54, 179
Martin, Pte. W., 373
Martin, C.S.M. W. J., 273, 483
Mason, L/Cpl. A., 302
Mason, 2/Lt. D. C., 349
Mason, Sergt. H. E., 344
Mason, 2/Lt. W. M., 186, 238
Massy, 2/Lt. G. W., 348, 349
Masters, 2/Lt. R. A., 97, 140, 142
Mathias, 2/Lt. D. E., 482
Matthews, Pte. E., 122
Matthews, 2/Lt. L. N., 333
Matthews, Capt. W. F., 285
Maude, Maj.-Gen. F. S., 167, 200, (Lt.-Gen.) 211, (Gen.) 312, 313, 314, 316, 318, 319, 321, 322, 325, 497
Maughfling, 2/Lt. T., 143
Maund, R.Q.M.S., 72
Maunoury, Gen., 16, 17, 19, 20, 22
Mayger, 2/Lt. F. J. L., 186, 239, (Lt.) 337, 338, (Capt.) 342, 354, 356, 357
Maynard, Capt. J. C. D., 343
Mayne, 2/Lt. V. C. M., 98, (Lt.) 214
Mayou, 2/Lt. J. W., 470
Maxwell, Capt. I. B., 42, 45, 47, 50
Maxwell-Heron, Major G., 233
McCarthy, Pte. L., 198
McCormick, Pte. J., 365
McDonald, Corpl. D., 377
McLaren, Capt. R. J. (Cheshire), 238
McMullen, 2/Lt. J. F., 197
McNaught Davis, 2/Lt. J., 85
McPherson, Sergt. N., 377, (2/Lt.), 509
McShane, Lt. V. (N.F.), 130, 165
Meller-Hallett, 2/Lt. S. A., 178, 230, 244
Miller, C.S.M. A., 216
Miller, Lt. H., 503
Miller, Lt. J. H., 127, 159, 161
Millichamp, C.S.M. A. H., 116
Mills, Lt. E. E., 170, (Capt.) 487

INDEX OF PERSONS

Mills, Capt. J. E., 178, 229, 376
Millward, L/Cpl. T., 117, 118, 198
Milne, Gen. Sir. G. F., 378, 488, 512
Mitchell, 2/Lt. A. C. O., 326
Mitchener, C.S.M. W., 286, 430
Moffatt, Pte. C. W., 363
Monro, Gen. Sir C. 182
Montague, 2/Lt. R. M., 374
Monteith, 2/Lt. T. H. I., 7, (Capt.) 178, 244, 290, (Major) 425, 440, 464, 465
Montgomery, Maj.-Gen. R. A., 67
Moore, Sergt. A., 434
Moore, Pte. F., 377
Moore, 2/Lt. G. H., 289, 290, (Lt.) 294
Moore, Cpl. P. S. 284
Morgan, 2/Lt. A., 390, 425
Morgan, 2/Lt. A. E., 142, 180
Morgan, Lt. and Q^{r}Mr C. B., 171, 273
Morgan, Lt. C. H., 170
Morgan, Capt. D. J., 247, 333
Morgan, 2/Lt. F. E., 302, 363
Morgan, Capt. I. A., 176, 290, 385, 415, 421
Morgan, 2/Lt. J. L., 284
Morgan, 2/Lt. M. C., 74, 82, (Capt.) 185
Morgan, Capt. S. C., 173, (Major) 225, 241
Morgan, Lt.-Col. S. W., 2, 55, 179, 233
Morgan, Capt. T. H. (Major) 177, 230, 389, 426, 437, 438
Morgan, Sergt. T., 482
Morgan, 2/Lt. T. H., 421
Morgan, Pte. W., 198
Morgan, Lt. W. B. C., 226
Morgan, 2/Lt., W. H., 383, 415
Morgan, Pte. W. J., 198
Morgan, 2/Lt. W. R., 169, 214, 215
Morgan Owen, Lt. J. G., 205
Morgan Owen, Capt. L. I. G., 59
Morland, Lt.-Col. C. B. (Welch), 25, 42, 47
Morris, C.S.M. G. J., 416
Morris, 2/Lt. H. H., 341
Morris, 2/Lt. H. S. F., 142, 150
Morris, 2/Lt. I. T., 430
Morris, 2/Lt. L. R., 178
Morris, 2/Lt. N. D., 173
Morris, Lt. O. D., 230, 293, (Capt.) 300, 301, 302
Morris, Capt. W. A. C., 510
Morris, 2/Lt. W. H. (1), 382, 383
Morris, 2/Lt. W. H. (2), 424
Mosey, L/Cpl. J. R., 315
Moss, C.S.M. M. G., 325

Mottram, Pte. J. A., 363
Mumford, 2/Lt. C., 97, (Lt.) 129, 165, 186, 228, (Capt.) 255, 264, 309, 328, 343, 354, 355, 370
Mundy, Lt. P. R. M., 58, (Capt.) 127, 155, 156, 160, 198, 215, 285, 483, 487, 488
Murphy, Capt. B. F., 230, 292, 293, (Major) 294, 359
Murphy, Pte. P., 287
Murray, 2/Lt. H. R., 430
Murray, 2/Lt. J. C., 238
Murray, Capt. T., 3
Murray, C.S.M. W., 198, (R.S.M.) 210, 500
Musgrove, Capt. E. H., 133
Myles, Sergt. W., 161, 196, 198

Napier, 2/Lt. J. W. L., 127, (Lt.) 209, 211, 326
Napier, 2/Lt. V. J. L., 458, 467
Napier, Major Sir W. L., 60, 127, 161
Neale,, Lt. T. J., 173, 288
Nelson, Brig.-Gen. H., 366
Nelson, Sergt. S., 259
Netherclift, 2/Lt. H. K., 298, 352, 369
Nevile, 2/Lt. H. G., 102, 110, 165
Newman, Lt. A., 230, 231
Newman, 2/Lt. A. L., 298, (Lt.) 460, 461
Newmarsh, Capt. O. H. M., 143, 169, 253
Nicholas, 2/Lt. C. H., 118, 124, 170
Nicholas, 2/Lt. E. O., 445, 462
Nightingale, 2/Lt. W. B., 298
Nisbet, 2/Lt. D. G., 93, 96, (Lt.) 224
Nivelle, Gen., 281, 296, 426
Norman, Cpl. J., 377
Norris, Pte. W., 445, 447
Norton, Lt. and Q^{r}Mr G. (R.W.F.), 290, 309
Nott, 2/Lt. C. W., 348, 349
Noyes-Lewis, Lt. D., 170
Nowell, Cpl., 299

O'Grady, Cpl. D., 198
O'Kelly, Major E de P. (R.W.F.), 291, 339, 389
O'Neil, 2/Lt. T. J., 467
O'Neil, C.S.M. P. J., 241, 265, 288
O'Neill, Sergt. H., 377
Orford, R.S.M. E. E., 176, (2/Lt.) 177, (Lt.) 247, (Capt.) 309, 389
Orr-Ewing, Capt. (R.A.M.C.), 91
Osborn, 2/Lt. A. G., 230, (Lt.) 302
O'Sullivan, Capt. (R. Inniskillings), 122

INDEX OF PERSONS

O'Toole, Sergt. D. P., 91
Owen, Capt. C. P., 296
Owen, Pte. D. J., 247
Owen, Lt. E. H. (Lincolnshire), 86, 92
Owen, 2/Lt. G. C., 333
Owen, 2/Lt. G. M., 127, 161
Owen, 2/Lt. J. C., 171, (Capt.) 288, 305, 406, 416
Oxley, Major H. C., 266, 386, 416, 454

Pace, Pte. E., 363
Paddock, Pte. A., 265
Page, Capt. G. D., 339
Page, 2/Lt. W. F., 185, (Capt.) 293, 294, 300, 382, 415
Palmer, Lt. and Q'M' J. E. W., 70, 177
Palmer, Capt. R. J., 73, 104, 110
Parfitt, 2/Lt. N. H., 420, 421, 458
Parish, C.S.M. C., 127
Park, Pte. M., 340
Parker, C.S.M. J., 230
Parker, 2/Lt. L. R., 458
Parker, Cpl. R. H. 409
Parker, Capt. W., 143
Partridge, Major J. E. C. (Welch), 389
Parry, 2/Lt. E., 428
Parry, Lt. R. B., 247
Parry, 2/Lt. W., 274, (Capt.) 493
Parry, 2/Lt. W., 415
Parry, 2/Lt. W. S., 382, 383, 415
Parry-Davies, 2/Lt. T. M., 186, 221
Parry-Jones, Capt. P. E. H., 253
Pashley, Pte. T., 247
Paterson, Lt. C. J., 4, 23, 28, 33, 34, 44
Paterson, 2/Lt. R., 504
Patrick, Sergt. S. W., 340
Patterson, Capt. C. C., 123
Patterson, 2/Lt. R. A., 129
Pearce, 2/Lt. A. G., 308, 397, 398
Pearson, Capt. N. G., 386, (Major) 409, 415, 416, 455
Pearson, C.S.M. J., 406, 416
Pearson, R.S.M. P. F., 177, 178, 290
Peel, Lt. H. L., 326
Pellé, Gen., 432
Pemberton, 2/Lt. W. J., 383, 415
Pembrey, C.Q.M.S. W. I., 443
Pembridge, 2/Lt. F. R., 340, 451
Perceval, Capt. A. P., 171
Petre, Lt. R. L., 73, 82, 83, (Capt.) 100, 102
Petts, Lt. L., 307, 398, 409
Philips, Lt. C. G., 349
Phillimore, Lt. G. W. (H.L.I.), 214
Phillips, Lt. C. D., 71, (Major) 339, 381

Phillips, 2/Lt. D. C., 338
Phillips, Lt. D. S., 127, 166
Phillips, 2/Lt. R., 298
Phillips, 2/Lt. T. C., 467
Phillips, Lt. T. O., 381
Phillips, Pte. W., 214
Philpott, Lt. F. O., 122, 165, (Capt.) 313, 324
Pickett, Pte. R., 292
Picton, Lt. A. G. C., 504
Pierce, 2/Lt. F., 258
Pierson, Capt. W. H. M., 299, 336, 337, 342, 356, 357
Piggott, Lt. G. F. L., 96
Pink, Lt. S. T., 307
Pitten, Major W. H., 67, 176, (Lt.-Col.) 179, 232
Pitten, 2/Lt. W. H., 392
Platt, R.S.M., 180
Playford, 2/Lt. A. B., 98, 99, (Capt.) 148
Pleece, Cpl. E. W., 333
Plumer, Gen. Sir H., 175, 508
Plummer, Pte. F., 360, 363
Pollock, 2/Lt. M. V., 98, 138, 140
Pollock, 2/Lt. W., 302
Ponsonby, Maj.-Gen. J., 392
Pope, Lt.-Col. E. A., 71, 230, 302
Poole, Pte. R., 185
Porter, Lt.-Col. J. R., 70, 177, 233
Porter, Pte. S., 198
Potter, Pte. E. J., 359
Potter, 2/Lt. L. B., 142, 151
Powell, Lt. D. B., 178, 359
Powell, 2/Lt. H. J., 220
Powell, Lt.-Col. T. G., 72
Powell, 2/Lt. W. T., 363
Power, C.S.M. J., 251
Power, Sergt. P., 445, 447
Pozzi, Lt. F. W., 381, 401, 421
Pratt, Lt. J. H., 382, 424
Pratten, Sergt. B., 216, 257
Prescott, L/Cpl. A., 361, 363
Preston, Pte. P. J., 247
Price, Sergt. A., 475
Price, Cpl. A., 46
Price, 2/Lt. G. W. B., 178, 358, 363
Price, Pte. J., 335
Prichard, Capt. W. O., 4, 5, 13, 30, 31
Primavesi, C.S.M., 178
Prince, Pte. J., 302
Pritchard, Lt. A. J., 470
Pritchard, Lt. C. M., 180, (Capt.) 230, 292
Probert, C.S.M. W. J., 375, 377

INDEX OF PERSONS

Proctor, 2/Lt. W. J., 230
Prosser, C.Q.M.S., 131
Ptolemy, 2/Lt. J. B., 482
Pugh, Cpl., 53
Pugh, 2/Lt. H. L., 258
Purvis, Lt. A. G., 209, (Capt.) 500

Quinn, L/Cpl. J. D., 302
Quinn, Pte. P., 216
Quinton, Sergt. A. J., 335

Radice, Lt.-Col. A. H. (Gloucestershire), 291, 331, 339
Raikes, Capt. G. T., 199, (Major) 238, 283, (Lt.-Col.) 197, 336, 356, 366, 368, 369, 370, 382, 384, 413, 414, 509
Raikes, Lt. W. T., 148
Ralph, 2/Lt. A. J., 177, 230
Ralston, Capt. W. R. C., 66
Ramsden, Lt. V. B., 4, 45, 47, 48, 50, 51, (Capt.) 142, 169, 282, (Major) 346
Randolph, 2/Lt. I. G., 173, 227
Rattenbury, Lt. G., 173
Raymond, 2/Lt. W. C., 304
Rayner, Lt.-Col. R. R., 468
Rayner, 2/Lt. G. W., 425, 465
Ravenhill, Pte. A., 216
Ravenhill, Sergt. A. E., 506
Rawle, Lt. T. F., 142, 169
Rawle, Lt. W., 73, 81, 120, 121
Rawlings, Sergt. E., 458
Rawlins, Lt. R. S. P., 453
Rawlinson, Lt.-Gen. Sir H., 35, 147
Rebsch, 2/Lt. R. F. W., 143, (Lt.) 240, (Capt.) 253, 286
Reddie, Major A. J., 4, 45, 47, 49, 50, 52, 89, 90, 91, 96, (Lt.-Col.) 142, (Brig.-Gen.) 147, 148, 506
Reecher, Pte. F., 335
Reed, 2/Lt. C. N., 177, 363
Rees, 2/Lt. A., 377
Rees, Sergt. A. L., 306, 307
Rees, Capt. E. T., 177, 229, 247, (Major) 290, 291, 329, 389
Rees, Lt. H. C., 71, (Capt.) 230, 292
Rees, Sergt. I., 330, 333
Rees, 2/Lt. R. R., 300
Rees, Sergt. W., 247
Rees, 2/Lt. W. S., 475
Rees, C.Q.M.S., 178, (R.Q.M.S.) 291
Rees, Pte., 223
Reeve, 2/Lt. H., 392
Reeves, 2/Lt. J. E., 230

Regan, Cpl. J., 488
Reid, 2/Lt., J. S., 338
Reid-Kellett, Capt. A., 255, 305, 308, (Major) 335, 386, 426, 429, 438
Renwick, Major G. A., 255, 288, 308
Renwick, Lt. H. A., 169, 224
Renwick, 2/Lt. J. M., 230, 241
Rhys Jones, 2/Lt. W., 267
Rice, 2/Lt. F., 185, 238
Rice, Pte. J. R., 198
Richards, 2/Lt. A. L., 396
Richards, 2/Lt. J., 178
Richards, 2/Lt. J. H., 335, 409, 416
Richards, 2/Lt. M. G., 4, 27
Richards, Sergt. J. G. F., 424
Richards, Cpl. T., 370
Rickards, C.Q.M.S., 282
Ricketts, C.S.M. W. H., 428
Roberts, 2/Lt. A. D., 308
Roberts, 2/Lt. D. C., 308
Roberts, 2/Lt. H., 333
Roberts, 2/Lt. J. C., 185, 186
Roberts, 2/Lt. L., 70, (Lt.) 178
Roberts, Capt. N., 435, 437
Roberts, Lt. W., 487
Roberts, Pte. W., 325
Roberts, 2/Lt. W. J., 465
Robertson, Capt. G. A. N., 185, 186, 310, 338
Robertson, 2/Lt. T. P. N., 151
Robinson, 2/Lt. C. G., 170, 173
Robinson, 2/Lt. J., 238
Robinson, C.Q.M.S., 131
Rogers, Cpl. A. H., 388
Rogers, 2/Lt. F. O., 343
Rogers, 2/Lt. H. M., 197
Rolls, L/Cpl., 401
Rose, Lt. L., 143, 152, (Capt.) 253, 287, 343, 416
Ross, 2/Lt. W., 102, 116, (Lt.) 218, 253, 299, (Capt.) 336, 338
Round, Lt. C. J., 487, 488
Rowlands, 2/Lt. F. T. R., 356, 357
Rowlands, Sergt. J., 481
Rowles, L/Cpl., L. J., 416
Ruffle, C.Q.M.S. J., 356
Rumbelow, 2/Lt. A., 416
Runham, Lt. W. K., 342, 343, (Capt.) 410, 416, 454
Russell, 2/Lt. E. F., 382, 421
Russell, 2/Lt. H. R. (Gloucestershire), 96
Russell, R.Q.M.S. E., 509
Ruther, 2/Lt. T. H., 468
Ryan, Pte. M., 450

INDEX OF PERSONS

Salathiel, 2/Lt. E. G., 244
Salmon, Lt. H. M. B., 19, 41, 45, 46, 51, (Capt.) 94, 97, 142
Salt, Pte., 284
Samuda, Major C. M. (Somerset L.I.), 173, 227
Sanders, Sergt. G., 257
Sandys Thomas, 2/Lt. W. J., 285
Sargent, Pte. G. H., 335
Sarrail, Gen., 270, 371, 479
Saunders, C.S.M., 506
Saunders, 2/Lt., L. D., 141, 149
Sayce, Lt. R. V., 178, 330, 333
Schofield, 2/Lt. H. F., 447
Scott, Lt.-Col. (R. Sussex), 411, 412
Scott, Pte. J., 298
Scott-Napier, Capt., 66
Seager, 2/Lt. J. E., 382, 384
Seager, 2/Lt. W. H., 177, 229
Searle, C.S.M. C., 386
Seden, 2/Lt. R. N., 258
Segers, R.Q.M.S. C., 173, 309
Sellicks, Lt. and Q^{r}Mr H. S., 377
Settle, 2/Lt. T. F., 342, 343
Sharp, Capt. C. H. C., 171, (Major) 279, 377
Sharpe, Capt. S. A., 363
Shaw, Maj.-Gen. Sir F., 167
Shaw, 2/Lt. B. L., 298
Shawcross, 2/Lt. P., 363
Shawson, 2/Lt. H., 476
Shearman, 2/Lt. H. J., 373, 374
Sheehan, Sergt. T., 257
Shepherd, Sergt. W. J., 335
Sherer, 2/Lt. S. F., 462
Sherman, Sergt. D., 377
Shermer, C.S.M. J., 265, 305
Sherwood, R.S.M., 64
Shipley, 2/Lt. C. W. C., 52, (Capt.) 506
Shirley, R.S.M. J., 9, 98, 506
Shulstra, Capt. (R.A.M.C.), 210
Siddle, 2/Lt. T., 173, 175
Silby, 2/Lt. T. S., 340, 387, 388, 448
Silcox, Sergt. J., 225
Silk, 2Lt. M. G., 4, 48, 50, (Lt.) 102, 110
Sills, 2/Lt. C. C., 4, 30
Simmonds, 2/Lt. R., 142, 150, (Lt.) 177
Simmons, L/Cpl. H. W., 198
Simons, Lt. E., 143, (Capt.) 208, 307
Simpson, 2/Lt. G., 363, 445, 447, 448
Skeath, Pte., 377
Skelton, Pte. R. B., 223
Skinner, 2/Lt. H. F. C., 251
Smeathers, 2/Lt. A. R., 431

Smith, Brig.-Gen. W. E. B., 172
Smith, 2/Lt. G., 471
Smith, 2/Lt. G. E., 458
Smith, Pte. G. E., 363
Smith, Pte. (1), 40
Smith, 2/Lt. G. F., 382, 415
Smith, 2/Lt. J., 169
Smith, Sergt. J. S., 325
Smith, 2/Lt. R., 316
Smith, C.Q.M.S., 230
Smith-Dorrien, Gen. Sir H., 10
Smithey, Cpl. G., 416
Smyly, Major P. R., 59, 60, 67
Snelson, 2/Lt. L. V., 358
Snow, Pte. G., 82
Solomon, R.S.M., 318
Somerville, Lt. D. H. S., 72, 82, 109, 110, (Capt.) 125, 185, 198, 220, 238, 345, 356, 368, 369, 370, (Major) 382, 405, 408, 415, 423
Southey, Major E., 141, 142
Spanwick, Pte. D., 290
Spartali, 2/Lt. M., 118, 121
Spence, R.Q.M.S. H., 513
Spinks, Pte. A. R., 110, 118
Squibb, C.Q.M.S., 230
Staite, R.S.M., 513
Stanborough, 2/Lt. W., 102, 116, 118
Staples, 2/Lt. E. G., 127, 161, 189, (Lt.) 211, (Capt.) 324, 326
Starr, Pte. H., 376
Stephenson, 2/Lt. F. A., 363, 487
Stevens, L/Cpl. M., 284
Steward, Lt. C. K., 4, 29, 45, 47, 50, 52, (Capt.) 212
Stickler, Capt. D. H., 409, 416, 427, 439, 455
Stockton, Pte. J. H., 363
Stockwood, 2/Lt. J. H., 127, 208
Stone, C.S.M. H., 361, 363
Strickland, Maj.-Gen. E. P., 458
Swanson, 2/Lt. J., 465
Swift, Pte. T. E., 344
Sword, Lt.-Col. W. D. (N. Staffords), 170, 172, 278, 279
Sykes, Major A. R. (King's), 440, 467
Symes, 2/Lt. J. R., 71, (Lt.) 230, (Capt.) 360, 361, 363

Talmage, R.S.M. C., 64, 170
Tamplin, Pte. H., 151
Tanner, Sergt., 293
Tarrent, Sergt. C. F., 377
Taylor, Lt.-Col. C. L., 282, 346, 348, 381, 419, 420, 421, 506

INDEX OF PERSONS

Taylor, Pte. E. C., 370
Taylor, Lt. E. R., 392, (Capt.) 450, 474
Taylor, Lt. G. D., 66, (Capt.) 170, 276, 277
Taylor, Lt. G. H., 409
Taylor, Cpl. J., 390
Taylor, 2/Lt. J. N., 376
Taylor, 2/Lt. J. R. W., 230
Taylor, 2/Lt. O. P., 230
Taylor, 2/Lt. R. P., 247
Taylor, 2/Lt. T. T., 289, 290, 341
Taylor, 2/Lt. W. (King's Own), 86
Taylor, 2/Lt. W. J., 230
Temple, Capt. R. D. (Worcestershire), 94
Tessier, Lt. N. Y., 127, 211
Thain, Sergt. O., 377
Theobald, C.Q.M.S., 509
Thesiger, Brig.-Gen. G. H., 140
Thomas, Sergt. B., 377
Thomas, 2/Lt. C. L., 425
Thomas, 2/Lt. C. R., 437
Thomas, Major D. W. E., 56, 327
Thomas, 2/Lt. E. D., 415
Thomas, L/Cpl. E. J., 458
Thomas, Lt. F. B., 173, (Capt.) 241
Thomas, Pte. G. A., 229
Thomas, Capt. G. C., 2, 56, 98, (Major) 304
Thomas, Capt. H. F., 143, 225
Thomas, 2/Lt. H. L., 398
Thomas, C.S.M. H. M., 54
Thomas, Pte. J., 450
Thomas, Capt. J. I. P., 131, 133
Thomas, 2/Lt. J. R., 360, 363
Thomas, 2/Lt. L., 363
Thomas, 2/Lt. M., 298
Thomas, Lt. M. F., 57, (Capt.) 327
Thomas, 2/Lt. P. E., 178
Thomas, Lt. R. P., 442
Thomas, 2/Lt. R. I. V. C., 360
Thomas, Lt. R. W., 226
Thomas, Sergt. W., 227
Thomas, 2/Lt. W. A., 348
Thomas, 2/Lt. W. W., 171, (Capt.) 493
Thomas, R.Q.M.S., 180
Thoms, L/Cpl. R., 240
Thorne, Capt. A. F. A. N. (Grenadiers), 47
Thorp, Capt. L. T., 64, 171, 272, 279
Thorpe, Pte. G., 302
Thunder, Major A. F. G., 173
Tilby, R. S. M., 177
Tilley, Pte. J., 247
Tippetts, Capt. C. M., 73, 111

Tomlinson, C.S.M., 230
Torney, Sergt. J. M., 488
Townley, Dr. (R.A.M.C.), 132
Townsend, Pte. F., 363
Townshend, Maj.-Gen. C. V. F., 200, 204, 205, 208
Tragett, Lt. J. C. B., 129, 165, (Capt.) 366, 367, 369
Travers, Lt. H. H., 4, 36, 95, 99
Travers, Brig.-Gen. J. H. du B., 59, 154, 155, 159, 191
Travis, 2/Lt. E. A., 247
Treglown, Lt. C. J. H., 66, (Capt.) 170, 276, 277, 457, 488
Treloar, 2/Lt. P., 332, 434
Tring, C.S.M. H. F., 285, (R.S.M.) 509
Trower, Col. C. V., 59, 99, 143, 169, 178, 225, 241, 252, 269, 281, 286, 401, 402, 431, 453, 454
Trower, 2/Lt. E. B., 143, 287, (Capt.) 386, 416, (Major) 430, 431, 437, 454
Tunnicliffe, 2/Lt. H. E., 420, 421
Turner, Lt.-Col. G., 57
Turner, 2/Lt. H. J., 140
Turner, 2/Lt. P. H., 118, (Lt.) 126, 185
Turrell, Pte. J., 185
Turton, L/Cpl. J., 384

Usher, Lt. C. G., 189, 205, 318, (Capt.) 324, 325, 496, 500, 513

Vanderpump, 2/Lt. F. L., 142, 257, 258
Vatcher, R.S.M. H., 71, 230, 435
Vaughan, Sergt. A. C., 432
Vaughan, Pte. W. J., 262
Venizelos, M., 479
Ventris, Maj.-Gen. F., 63
Vernon, 2/Lt. J. M. L., 4, 25, 27
Vick, 2/Lt. R. I. (Hampshires), 141, 150
Viliesid, Lt. D. (R.A.M.C.), 230
Villar, Capt. P. L., 170, 276, 374
Vine, Pte. H. T., 274
Vizer, 2/Lt. J. H., 330, 332, 333

Wakefield, Major G. W. H., 170
Wakefield, C.Q.M.S., 127
Waldron, Lt. and Q^{r}Mr T. H., 435
Wales, H.R.H. the Prince of, 283, 511
Wales, 2/Lt. O. M., 142, (Lt.) 349, 381, (Capt.) 434
Walker, Major C. E. Fitz G., 3
Walker, Lt. R. K. B., 73, (Capt.) 102, 116, 122, 165, 185, 188
Walling, Major A. J., 68

605

INDEX OF PERSONS

Walshe, 2/Lt. F. W., 169, (Capt.) 251, 256, 259
Wannell, Pte. G., 251
Ward, Major E. B., 170, 273
Ward, Capt. G. B. C., 4, 25, 29, 36, 39, 40, 41, 45, 50, 52
Ward, Lt.-Col. T. (Denbigh Yeo.), 130
Ward Jones, 2/Lt. F. V., 151, (Lt.) 216, 249
Wardle, 2/Lt. G. R., 254
Wardle, L/Cpl. J. T., 198
Watkins, 2/Lt. D. F., 421
Watkins, 2/Lt. H. H., 34, 39, 40, 54
Watkins, Pte. T., 333
Watts, Maj.-Gen. H., 244, 286
Watts, 2/Lt. W. J., 230
Watts-Morgan, 2/Lt., 177
Webb, 2/Lt. L. M., 169, 251, 267
Webber, 2/Lt. F. E., 284
Weeks, 2/Lt. H. W. M., 284, (Lt.) 354, 355
Welby, Major, G. E. E., 4, 9, 30, 32
Welford, Lt. G., 358
Wells, 2/Lt. T. M. R., 238
Welsford, Lt. P. S. J., 170
Welsh, 2/Lt. A. C. R., 251
West, Pte. J., 92
Westhorpe, R.Q.M.S., 71, 230, 392
Westlake, R.S.M. H., 122, 165, 220
White, Sergt. A., 299, 310
White, 2/Lt. C. W. H., 386, 396, 401, 407
White, Sergt. F., 198
Whitehorne, 2/Lt. W. J., 487
Whitehouse, C.S.M. T., 96, 97
Whittaker, 2/Lt. F. C., 244
Whitworth, Capt. E. A. A., 180, 230, 300, 301, 415, 424, 435
Whitworth, Lt. and Q^{r}Mr W., 389, 427
Whyte, 2/Lt. W. J., 459
Widdington, Lt.-Col. B. F. (K.R.R.C.), 172
Wigley, Major A. B. (R. Sussex), 327
Wilcox, Sergt. W., 94, 96
Wileman, 2/Lt. G. W. B., 169, 257
Wilkins, 2/Lt. W. H. A., 178
Wilkinson, Lt.-Col. S. J., 229, 244, 247
Willan, L/Cpl., 293
Williams, Lt. A. E., 73, 83, (Capt.) 100, 102, 124, 164, 185, (Major) 198, 199
Williams, Lt. C. E., 170, 278, 375
Williams, 2/Lt. D. A., 173, 251
Williams, Lt. D. R., 230, 301
Williams, C.S.M., E., 279
Williams, Cpl. E., 94, 96
Williams, Pte. E., 257
Williams, 2/Lt. E. H., 289
Williams, R.S.M. F. C., 425
Williams, 2/Lt. F. F., 425
Williams, Capt. F. T., 373, 483
Williams, 2/Lt. F. T., 415
Williams, 2/Lt. G. E. P., 374
Williams, 2/Lt. H. C., 247, (Lt.) 407
Williams, Capt. H. C. W., 178, 230
Williams, Sergt. H. J., 333
Williams, 2/Lt. J. P., 197, 198
Williams, Cpl. J., 377
Williams, Pte. J. C., 340
Williams, 2/Lt. J. G., 465
Williams, Sergt. J. H., 246, 247, (C.S.M.) 464
Williams, 2/Lt. J. J., 177
Williams, 2/Lt. L., 98, 142
Williams, 2/Lt. L. G., 332, 333
Williams, Lt. L. V., 170, (Capt.) 374, 375
Williams, Brig.-Gen. R. B., 63
Williams, Pte. T., 279
Williams, 2/Lt. T. G., 333
Williams, Lt. T. R., 352, 382, 425
Williams, 2/Lt. W., 298
Williams, 2/Lt. W. F., 448
Williams, 2/Lt. W. G., 70, (Lt.) 176, (Capt.) 178, 477
Williams, Capt. W. H., 430
Williams, 2/Lt. W. J., 358
Williams, Cpl., 278
Williamson, L/Cpl., 240
Wilson, Lt. J., 64, 170
Wilson, Lt. and Q^r Mr W. R., 4, 45, 50, 98
Wilton, 2/Lt. C. I., 267
Windsor, 2/Lt. J. S., 367, 369
Wingard, Lt. H. S., 170, 172, 273, 293
Winn, Sergt. W., 251
Winston, Sergt. T. C., 386
Witherall, Pte. A., 302
Witts, Cpl., 247
Wood, 2/Lt. J. B. V., 270, 292
Wood, Major J. P., 173, 179
Wood, Lt. T. G., 171, 377, (Capt.) 493
Wood, Pte. J., 302
Woodcock, 2/Lt. G., 178, 224
Woodhall, L/Cpl. S. J., 247, (Sergt.) 291
Woodhouse, Cpl. W. G., 247
Woodliffe, Capt. H. D., 131
Woods, Pte. T., 122
Woodward, 2/Lt. R., 140
Woodward, 2/Lt., 381
Woolley, 2/Lt. C. C., 171, (Lt.) 377, 483
Woolley, 2/Lt. W. L., 487

INDEX OF PERSONS

Woolveridge, 2/Lt. C. L., 297, 357
Woosey, 2/Lt. T. H., 180
Woosnam, Capt. R. W., 318
Wright, Major C. V. R., 59, 143, 169, 224
Wright, Sergt. H. J., 251
Wynne, 2/Lt. F. R., 209

Yates, Pte. F., 227

Yates, Capt. R. P., 57, 127, (Major) 187, 190, 198
Yatman, Major A. H. (Somerset L.I), 170, 272
Yeatman, Capt. M. E., 4, 26, 27
Yonge, 2/Lt. F. H., 247
Yorath, 2/Lt. G. L., 363

Zacharias, 2/Lt. F. H., 261, 262

INDEX OF UNITS

Artillery

L Battery, R.H.A., 100
39th Brigade, R.F.A., 24
66th Brigade, R.F.A, 321
147th Brigade, R.F.A., 100

Brigades

1st, 19, 23, 38, 39, 40, 41, 42, 43, 48, 52, 88, 90, 91, 95, 146, 147, 149, 248, 249, 256, 258, 456–7, 475
2nd, 19, 23, 91, 137, 146, 147, 213, 250, 256, 311, 381, 451, 475
3rd, see 1st Battalion
4th (Guards), 8, 41
5th, 25, 26, 27, 86
7th, 242, 405, 406, 427, 429
19th, 14
20th, 43
21st, 41
34th, 128
38th, 44–6, 313–16, 318, 323, 324, 325, 497, 498, 500, 501
39th, 194, 196, 204–6, 208, 313, 316, 319, 320, 321, 503
40th, see 4th Battalion
56th, 252, 305, 344, 395, 432
57th, 178, 240, 252, 305, 307, 394, 396, 399, 431
58th, 59, 194, 240, 305, 394, 395, 399, 407
65th, 271, 279, 372, 481, 485, 488, 490, 491
66th, 485, 487
67th, see 7th and 8th Battalions
75th, 242, 394, 396, 415
77th, 485, 488, 489
83rd, 490
86th, 109, 110, 123, 124, 129, 163, 235, 236, 285, 336, 353–7, 365–7, 408, 437, 452, 460, 469–71, 472
87th, see 2nd Battalion
88th, 110–12, 115, 119, 124, 126, 130, 163, 295, 297, 339, 353, 365–6, 452, 460–2, 469, 471, 478
113th, 244, 329, 340, 442, 443, 444, 445, 447, 448, 449, 465, 468, 477
114th, 244, 245, 290, 329, 442, 443, 444, 447, 448, 465
115th, see 10th and 11th Battalions
119th, see 12th Battalion
120th, 300
121st, 360–363
125th, 115
130th, 69
156th, 123, 186
157th, 130, 187
203rd, 181
14th Reserve, 180
South Wale˜ Infantry (T.F.), 2
6th Indian Cavalry, 500
7th Indian Cavalry, 314
7th Indian Infantry, 207
8th Indian Infantry (Jullundar), 87, 88, 207, 208
9th Indian Infantry (Sirhind), 98, 207
29th Indian Infantry, 118, 119, 120, 131, 154, 161, 162, 165
35th Indian Infantry, 317, 318, 322, 324, 496, 499
36th Indian Infantry, 314
37th Indian Infantry, 500
N.Z. Infantry, 116, 183
2nd Australian Infantry, 116
4th Australian Infantry, 157
South African Infantry, 407–410

Cavalry

Scots Greys, 466
9th Lancers, 86
15th Hussars, 362
18th Hussars, 86
Denbigh Yeomanry, 130
Lovat's Scouts, 188
Montgomeryshire Yeomanry, 261
Welsh Horse, 261
Aden Troop, 131, 132

Colonial, etc.

Ceylon Planters, 129
Guernsey L.I., 366
King's African Rifles, 423
Newfoundland Regt., 237, 238, 295, 367, 368
N.Z. Mounted Rifles, 165
West African Regiment, 285

Corps

First, 5, 8, 9, 10, 11, 13, 14, 17, 18, 19, 28, 33, 35, 36, 40, 50, 51, 53, 85, 86, 87, 93, 146
Second, 5, 6, 8, 9, 10, 11, 14, 17, 18, 19, 33, 35, 50, 51, 85, 86, 87, 308, 334, 335, 459

INDEX OF UNITS

THIRD, 14, 18, 35, 85, 87, 351, 353, 357, 364
FOURTH, 35, 85, 87, 97, 146, 359, 394
FIFTH, 351, 393
EIGHTH, 219, 254, 289
NINTH, 154, 187, 426, 430, 432, 449, 450, 451, 456, 466
TENTH, 228, 472
ELEVENTH, 149, 150, 178
TWELFTH, 273, 371, 372, 484, 485, 489
THIRTEENTH, 437, 466
FOURTEENTH, 310, 329
FIFTEENTH, 242, 300, 304, 410
SIXTEENTH, 485, 492
SEVENTEENTH, 230, 242, 468
EIGHTEENTH, 295, 329
NINETEENTH, 459, 460, 472
INDIAN CORPS (*afterwards* FIRST INDIAN), 85, 87, 97, 143, 200, 318, 503
THIRD INDIAN CORPS, 211, 312, 314, 316, 500
TIGRIS CORPS, 209, 211
ANZAC CORPS, 154, 187
IInd AMERICAN, 466

DIVISIONS

GUARDS, 142, 150, 178, 310, 329, 336, 362, 365
FIRST, see 1st Battalion
SECOND, 5, 7, 12, 19, 22, 23, 33, 36, 40, 41, 48, 51, 93, 97, 137, 140
THIRD, 5, 6, 7, 226
FOURTH, 10, 14, 21, 344
FIFTH, 5, 408, 414, 435
SIXTH, 24, 263, 353, 368, 449, 450, 456, 466
SEVENTH, 35, 36, 40, 41, 42, 43, 45, 48, 51, 140, 146, 148, 242, 246, 256, 280, 286
EIGHTH, 137, 140, 224, 225, 239, 240, 300, 302, 334, 335, 427
NINTH, 405, 407, 413, 435, 436, 459, 469, 470
TENTH, 154, 189, 270, 271, 375
ELEVENTH, 164, 269, 305, 307, 340
TWELFTH, 150, 151, 240, 241, 353, 402
THIRTEENTH, see 4th Battalion
FIFTEENTH, 146, 149, 257
SIXTEENTH, 305, 391
SEVENTEENTH, 226, 284, 298, 444, 445, 448, 449
EIGHTEENTH, 268, 441, 444
NINETEENTH, see 5th Battalion

TWENTIETH, 333, 339, 341, 353, 365
TWENTY-FIRST, 246, 248, 427, 428
TWENTY-SECOND, see 7th and 8th Battalions
TWENTY-THIRD, 240, 248, 255
TWENTY-FOURTH, 149
TWENTY-FIFTH, see 6th Battalion
TWENTY-SIXTH, 271, 273, 275, 372, 485
TWENTY-SEVENTH, 485, 493
TWENTH-EIGHTH, 271, 485, 491
TWENTY-NINTH, see 2nd Battalion
THIRTIETH, 430, 438, 455, 472
THIRTY-FIRST, 391, 408, 409, 414
THIRTY-SECOND, 228, 239, 241, 310, 449, 458
THIRTY-THIRD, 294, 409, 413, 465, 467, 468, 477
THIRTY-FOURTH, 239, 240, 405, 406, 409
THIRTY-FIFTH, 460
THIRTY-SIXTH, 305, 360, 381, 469
THIRTY-SEVENTH, 334
THIRTY-EIGHTH, see 10th and 11th Battalions
THIRTY-NINTH, 166
FORTIETH, see 12th Battalion; also 403, 405, 408
FORTY-FIRST, 385, 394, 395, 396, 462, 472
FORTY-SECOND, 115, 119, 283, 302, 396
FORTY-SIXTH, 151, 449, 456, 458, 459, 466, 475
FORTH-SEVENTH, 146, 212, 227
FORTH-EIGHTH, 242, 247
FORTY-NINTH, 241
FIFTIETH, 282, 405, 411, 412, 427, 438, 462, 463, 464
FIFTY-FIRST, 252, 253, 329, 353, 355, 359, 360, 362, 411
FIFTY-SECOND, 123, 186
FIFTY-THIRD, 161, 163, 184, 188
FIFTY-FOURTH, 163
FIFTY-FIFTH, 403, 404, 417
FIFTY-SEVENTH, 390
SIXTIETH, 275, 372, 375
SIXTY-FIRST, 469
SIXTY-SECOND, 359, 363
SIXTY-THIRD (R.N.D.), 115, 392, 439
SIXTY-EIGHTH, 181, 234
YEOMANRY, (Dismounted), 163
THIRD INDIAN (Lahore), 87, 91, 98, 137, 206–8, 316, 319, 495, 500
SEVENTH INDIAN (Meerut), 58, 91, 137, 138, 140, 202, 204, 206, 208, 318, 495, 500
FOURTEENTH INDIAN, 313, 496, 497, 498

INDEX OF UNITS

Fifteenth Indian, 497
Third Indian Cavalry, 312, 313, 318, 321, 322
New Zealand, 262, 401, 448

Infantry

Grenadier Guards, 4th Batt., 176
Scots Guards,
  1st Batt., 41, 44, 46, 47
  2nd Batt., 339, 362, 363
Irish Guards, 1st Batt., 52, 150
The Queen's,
  1st Batt., 8, 17, 18, 19, 23, 36, 37, 38, 43, 45, 46, 52
  2nd Batt., 42
Buffs, 5th Batt., 135, 319
King's Own,
  2/5 Batt., 390
  6th Batt., 160, 188
  7th Batt., 253
  9th Batt., 482, 488, 489, 490, 491
  11th Batt., 391
  12th Batt., 362
Northumberland Fusiliers,
  17th Batt., 253, 266
R. Warwickshire,
  9th Batt., 396
  10th Batt., 253, 401
R. Fusiliers,
  2nd Batt., 366, 469
  12th Batt., 305
King's,
  9th Batt., 147
  10th (Liverpool Scottish) Batt., 418
Norfolk,
  5th Batt., 242
  7th Batt., 389
Devons, 51st Batt., 509
Suffolk, 1st Batt., 512
Bedfordshire, 4th Batt., 392
R. Irish, 2nd Batt., 6
Lancashire Fusiliers,
  1st Batt., 114, 124
  15th Batt., 449
R. Scots Fusiliers, 2nd Batt., 41
Cheshire,
  8th Batt., 59, 192, 203, 209, 210, 316, 317, 321, 476, 498
  11th Batt., 309, 396, 406
  14th Batt., 123
R.W.F.,
  2nd. Batt., 443, 444, 445, 464, 465, 476
  4th Batt., 94
  2/7th Batt., 181
  8th Batt., 59, 127, 204, 315, 321, 324, 325, 501
  9th Batt., 152, 395
  10th Batt., 63
  11th Batt., 63, 272, 278, 374, 483, 486, 487
  17th Batt., 246, 329, 330, 331, 442, 444, 445, 464, 465, 476
  19th Batt., 233, 360
  21st Batt., 233

South Wales Borderers (Twenty-Fourth Foot)

1st Battalion; 1; mobilized, 4; crosses to France, 4; in advance to, retreat from Mons, 5–15; in battle of Marne, 16–20; in battle of Aisne, 21–33; transferred to Flanders, 34; in First Ypres, 35–53; 85–87; in battle of Festubert, 88–92, 93; in defence of Givenchy, 94–96, 97–99; in attack at Rue du Bois, 137–140; 141–142; at Loos, 146–152; 168–169; trench-warfare before the Somme, 212–217, 235; moved to Somme, 248; in action at Contalmaison, 249–253; near High Wood, 255–258; near Flers, 261–262; during winter of 1916–1917, 281–283, 302; moved to Flanders, 303; moved to coastal sector, 304, 310; in Le Clipon camp, 311, 342, 345–346; in action on Goudberg Spur, 346–349; in Ypres Salient, Dec. 1917–April 1918, 379–382; defence of Givenchy (April 1918), 419–421, 423; during summer of 1918, 433–535; transferred to Fourth Army, 449; attack on Maissemy (Sept. 1918), 450–451; attack on Hindenburg Line (Sept.–Oct. 1918), 456–459; attack on Wassigny (Oct. 1918), 466–467; in action on the Sambre (Nov.), 474–476; in advance to Rhine, 505–506; return home, 506; its record, 507

2nd Battalion; 1; mobilized, 79; at Tsingtao, 74–83; returns to England, 84; in Twenty-Ninth Division, 85, 100, 101; move to Gallipoli, 102; landing at " S " Beach, 103–107; in first attack on Krithia, 108–110; at

INDEX OF UNITS

"Y" Beach, 110–112; at Cape Helles, 113–126, 129–130; at Suvla, 163–165; back to Helles, 185–187; at evacuation of Helles, 193–194; move to Egypt, 199; in Egypt, 217–218; move to France, 218; trench-warfare before the Somme, 219–222; attack on Beaumont Hamel (July 1st, 1916), 235–239; 250, 253; moved to Flanders, 254; in Ypres Salient, 262–263; return to Somme, 263; in action at Le Transloy, 268–269, 283–285; in action at Monchy le Preux, 295–299; moved to Flanders, 300, 310, 311; attack at Langemarck (Aug. 1917), 336–339, 344–345, 350; in battle of Cambrai (Nov. 1917), 352–357; counter-attacked at Cambrai (Dec. 1917), 364–370, 380; in Ypres Salient, Jan.–April 1918, 382–385; repulse of German attack (March 11th, 1918), 383; in battle of the Lys (April, 1918), 405, 408–409, 413–415, 421; at Vieux Berquin, 423–425, 435–437; in advance on Lys (Sept. 1918), 451–452; attack East of Ypres (Sept. 1918), 459–462; attack on Ledeghem, 469–472; advance over Scheldt, 428; on the Rhine, 507–508; return home, 509; its record, 509

3rd (S.R.) Battalion; 2; move to Pembroke Dock, 3, 54–56, 178–179, 233–234, 507

Brecknockshire Battalion [later 1/1st Brecknocks]; 2, 56; forms Home Service unit, 57; proceeds to Aden, 57, 72; at Aden, 130 ff.; advance to Lahej, 132–136; transferred to India, 136, 327; in 1918–1919, 513–514; returns home, 514

Brecknockshire Home Service Battalion [later 2/1st Brecknocks]; formed, 56, 74, 181; disbanded 236, 261

3/1st Brecknocks; formed, 181; 234

4th (Service) Battalion; formation ordered, 4; early days, 57–59, 61–62, 67, 126; proceeds to Gallipoli, 137; at Cape Helles, 127–129, 154; in action at Demakjelik Bair, 155–163; at Hill 60, 165–167, 183; at Suvla, 187–192; evacuation of Suvla, 191–193; at evacuation of Helles, 194–198; move to Egypt, 199; sent to Mesopotamia, 200; operations for relief of Kut, 201–209, 209–211; return to front, 312; operations for recapture of Kut, 313–318; advance on Baghdad, 318–319; operations North of Baghdad, 319–326; action of the Boot, 323–326; in summer of 1917, 495–496; Jebel Hamrin operations, Oct.–Dec. 1917, 497–499; winter 1917–1918, 499–500; operations in Kurdistan (1918), 500–503; final operations of 1918, 503–504; return home and demobilization, 512–513

5th (Service) Battalion; formed, 59; early days, 59–60, 62, 67–68, 142; proceeds to France, 143, 144; in action at Loos, 152, 169; trench-warfare before the Somme, 223–225, 235, 239; in action at La Boisselle, 240–241, 248, 250, 251; in action near High Wood (July), 252–253, 258; at Wytschaete, 265–266; in action on Ancre, 267–269, 280; during winter of 1916–1917, 285–287; at Ypres, 304–305; battle of Messines, 305–308, 334, 342–343; winter 1917–1918, 385–386, 391; in the "March Retreat" (1918), 393–402; transferred to Flanders, 403; in battle of the Lys (April 1918), 404–416, 421; sent to the Aisne, 426; in German offensive on Aisne (May 1918), 430–432, 437–438, 451; Col. Trower vacates command, 453–454; in action on the Selle, 468–469, 477–478; after the Armistice, 509–510; disbanded, 510

6th (Service) Battalion; formed, 60; early days, 63–66, 173; proceeds to France, 174, 175; trench-warfare before the Somme, 225–228, 235, 239; in action on the Somme (July 1916), 241–242, 248, 250; in action in Leipzig Salient, 255, 258; in action near Thiepval (Sept.), 262–264; at Ploegsteert, 288; battle of Messines, 305, 307–309; in action at Westhoek, 334–335; winter 1917–1918, 386–387; in the March Retreat (1918), 343–402; transferred to Flanders, 403; in battle of Lys (April 1918), 404–416, 421; sent to the Aisne, 426, in German offensive on Aisne (May 1918), 417–430; posted to Thirteenth Division, 430, 438–439, 451, 455, 472–473, 478;

INDEX OF UNITS

after the Armistice, 509–511; disbanded, 511

7th (*Service*) *Battalion*; formed, 60; early days, 63–66, 170; proceeds to France, 171, 172; transferred to Salonica, 173; reach Salonica, 270; in Salonica defences, 271–272; advance to Doiran, 272; on Vardar-Doiran front (winter 1916–1917), 273–278; operations of 1917, 371–378; raid on Krastali, 374; in 1918, 478–484; in attack on Grand Couronne, 485–488; after the Armistice, 492–493; amalgamated with 8th Battalion, 493; its record, 493–494; in Army of the Black Sea, 512, disbanded, 512

8th (*Service*) *Battalion*; formed, 60; early days, 63–66, 170; proceeds to France, 171–172; transferred to Salonica, 173; reach Salonica, 270; in Salonica defences, 271–272; advance to Doiran, 272; on Vardar-Doiran front (winter 1916–1917), 273–275, 278–279; operations of 1917, 371–378; in 1918, 479–484; transferred to 65th Brigade, 481; raid on Flat Iron Hill, 481–482; attack on " P " Ridge, 488–489; in pursuit of Bulgarians, 489–492; after the Armistice, 492–493; absorbed into 7th Battalion, 493; its record, 493–494

9th (*Service*) *Battalion*; formed, 56; early days, 68; becomes a " Second Reserve " battalion, 68, 127, 179, 231–233; becomes 57th Training Reserve Battalion, 232; re-numbered 52nd (*Graduated*) Battalion, S.W.B., 233 n., 506

10th (*Service*) *Battalion* (1st *Gwent*); formation authorised, 69; early days, 69–70, 175–177; proceeds to France, 178; trench-warfare before the Somme, 228–230, 235; at Mametz Wood, 242–247, 253, 254; transferred to Flanders, 255; in Ypres Salient (1916–1917), 288–292, 309–310; attack on Pilckem, 329–374; at Langemarck, 339–341; moved to Armentières, 341, 342; Sept. 1917–March 1918, 387–389, 390; on the Ancre (summer 1918), 417, 430, 431; in advance from Ancre to Tortille (August–Sept. 1918), 432–447; at Gouzeaucourt, 448–449; attack on Villers-Outreaux, 462–464; in action on the Selle, 467–468; in action in Forest of Mormal (Nov. 1918), 476–477; after the Armistice, 511; disbanded, 511; its record, 511–512

11th (*Service*) *Battalion* (2nd *Gwent*); formation authorised, 69; early days, 70–77, 175–177; proceeds to France, 178; trench-warfare before the Somme, 228–230, 235; at Mametz Wood, 242–247, 253, 254; transferred to Flanders, 255; in Ypres Salient, 288–292, 309–310; attack on Pilckem, 329–334; at Langemarck, 339–341; moved to Armentières, 341, 342, 381; Sept. 1917–Feb. 1918, 387–389; disbanded (Feb. 1918), 389; detachment engaged at Merville (April 1918), 410–412

12th (*Service*) *Battalion* (3rd *Gwent*); formation authorised, 69; early days, 71–72, 178, 180–181; proceeds to France, 230; introduced to trench-warfare, 231; in Loos Salient, 292–293; on the Somme (Sept.) 294; in action near Gouzeaucourt, 300–302, 342, 350, 358–359; in battle of Cambrai, 360–363, 370, 381, 383; in Bullecourt sector, 391; disbanded, 392

13th (*Local Reserve*) *Battalion*; formed, 177, 180; becomes 59th Training Reserve Battalion, 232

14th (*Local Reserve*) *Battalion*; formed, 177, 180; becomes 65th Training Reserve Battalion, 232

51st, 52nd, 53rd (*Graduated*) *Battalions*; 233 n., 506, 508

K.O.S.Borderers,
  1st Batt., 100, 104, 110–112, 123, 163, 164, 296–298, 338–339, 353–357, 365–366, 436, 460, 471
R. Inniskilling Fusiliers,
  1st Batt., 100, 108, 109, 122, 123, 163, 164, 187, 220, 235, 284, 298, 299, 353–354, 365
Gloucestershire,
  1st Batt., 4, 24, 33, 37–39, 51, 89–91, 94, 137, 151, 214, 258, 417, 450, 451, 457–458, 475
  2nd Batt., 73, 493
  10th Batt., 142, 147, 231
Worcestershire,
  2nd Batt., 48, 49, 50, 413

INDEX OF UNITS

3rd Batt., 241, 255
4th Batt., 184, 295
9th Batt., 162
14th Batt., 392
East Lancashire,
  7th Batt., 265
  9th Batt., 481, 483
D.C.L.I., 2nd Batt., 73
Duke of Wellington's,
  1st Batt., 211
  2/6th Batt., 363
Border,
  1st Batt., 100, 108, 109, 114, 115, 120, 121, 124, 164, 220, 235, 237, 284, 298, 336, 353, 365, 383, 405, 417, 452, 460, 461
  8th Batt., 396
  9th Batt., 377, 492
R. Sussex, 2nd Batt., 381, 474, 475
Hampshire, 2nd Batt., 107, 369, 369
Dorsetshire,
  6th Batt., 448
  7th Batt., 67
South Lancashire,
  1st Batt., 514
  2nd Batt., 396, 406
Welch,
  2nd Batt., 7, 24, 25, 28, 30, 37-39, 43-46, 51, 90-92, 94, 95, 137, 147-149, 231, 249, 252, 258, 420, 474
  8th Batt., 59, 62
  9th Batt., 152, 343, 396
  10th Batt., 63, 389
  11th Batt., 276, 278, 486, 487
  14th Batt., 184
  16th Batt., 242, 246, 329, 340
  17th Batt., 302
  18th Batt., 180, 294, 361, 392
  19th Batt., 180, 229, 294, 391
Black Watch,
  1st Batt., 49, 95, 139, 147, 149, 261, 456-458, 466
Oxfordshire L.I.,
  2nd Batt., 36, 52
  7th Batt., 373, 374
Essex, 1st Batt., 295
Loyal North Lancashire,
  2nd Batt., 349
  9th Batt., 175
Northamptonshire, 1st Batt., 138, 250
R. Berkshire,
  1st Batt., 93
  8th Batt., 142, 147
R.M.L.I. (Plymouth Batt.), 104, 110-112

K.S.L.I.,
  4th Batt., 432
  7th Batt., 63
  10th Batt., 435
K.R.R.C., 2nd Batt., 213, 281
Manchester, 1st Batt., 88, 89
Wiltshire,
  1st Batt., 241, 255
  5th Batt., 62, 67, 154, 157-159, 187, 192, 202-206, 208, 209, 313, 316, 322, 324, 325, 499, 501, 503
  6th Batt., 152
N. Staffordshire,
  7th Batt., 155
  8th Batt., 223
H.L.I., 1st Batt., 90, 207
Cameron Highlanders,
  1st Batt., 24, 31, 147
Connaught Rangers,
  5th Batt., 161, 165, 166
Argyll and Sutherland Highlanders,
  14th Batt., 362, 392
R. Munster Fusiliers,
  2nd Batt., 10, 52, 91, 92, 137, 138, 149, 236, 261, 281, 311, 347, 349, 463
R. Dublin Fusiliers,
  1st Batt., 107, 119, 124, 125, 128, 163
Herefordshire, 1st Batt., 161
London Regt.,
  1/14th (London Scottish), 147, 151
  2/14th (London Scottish, 439
  2/19th, 455
  25th Batt., 514
  28th Batt. (Artists), 392
Monmouthshire, 2nd Batt., 253
50th Provisional Battalion, 181
14th Sikhs, 118, 119
23rd Sikh Pioneers, 132
36th Sikhs, 73, 77, 80, 83
47th Sikhs, 208
109th Infantry, 132-134
126th Baluchis, 132, 134
6th Gurkhas, 118, 119

* * *

GERMAN UNITS

1st Army, 6, 12, 13, 14, 20, 21, 22
2nd Army, 6, 8, 14, 21, 22
3rd Army, 6, 8

CORPS

II   16, 17
III   16

INDEX OF UNITS

IV   16, 17
IV Res.   16, 17
VII Res.   22
XV   52
XXIII Res. 40
XXVII Res. 45

Divisions

2nd Guard Reserve, 385
3rd Reserve, 385
25th Reserve, 31
46th Reserve, 37
51st Reserve, 39
54th Reserve, 45
6th Bavarian Reserve, 43–46

Brigades

25th Reserve, 24
50th Reserve, 31

Regiments

Guard Fusilier (Cockchafers), 334
9th Grenadiers, 331

Turkish

XIIIth Corps, 319, 321, 322
XVIIIth Corps, 319, 320, 321, 322

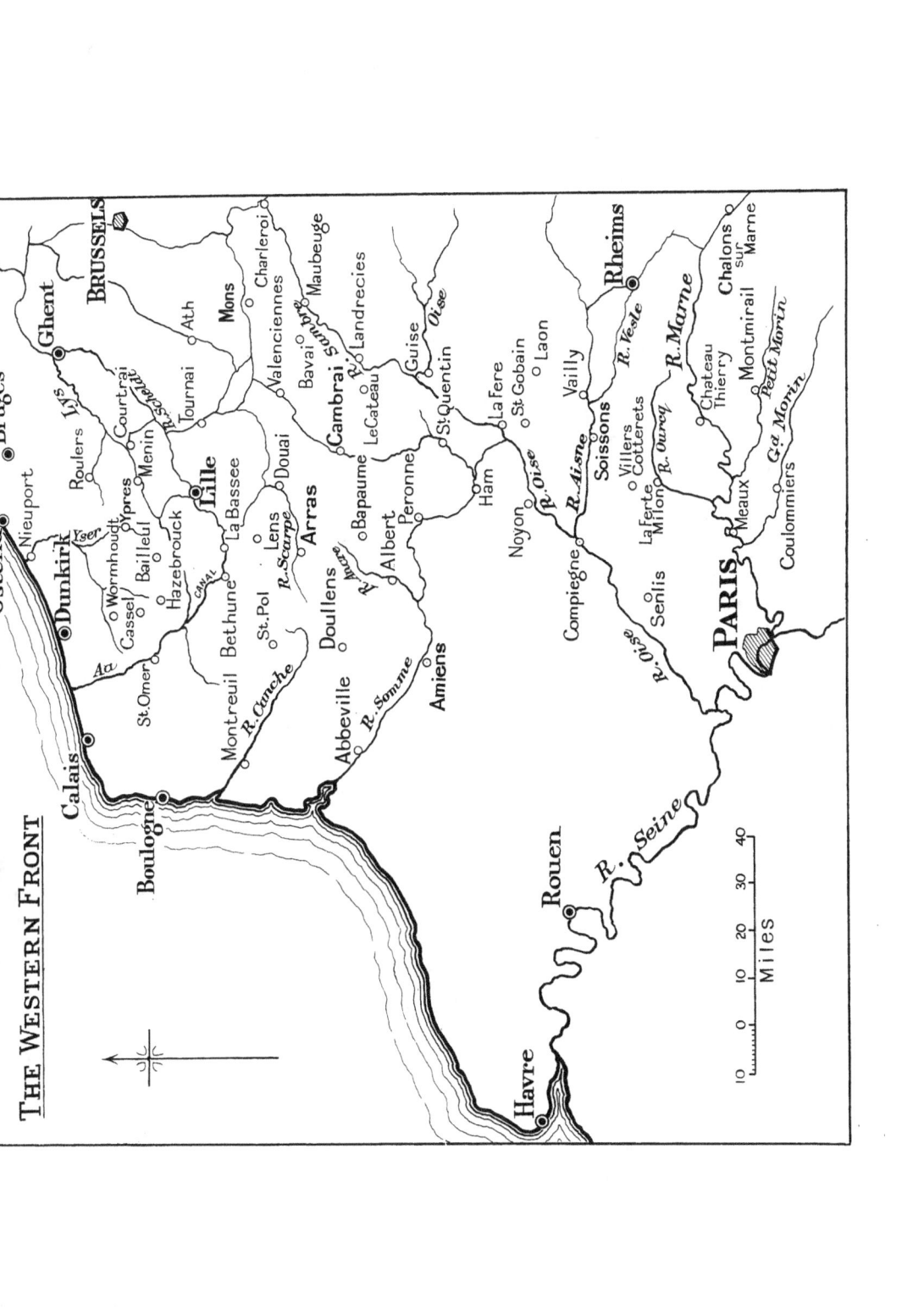

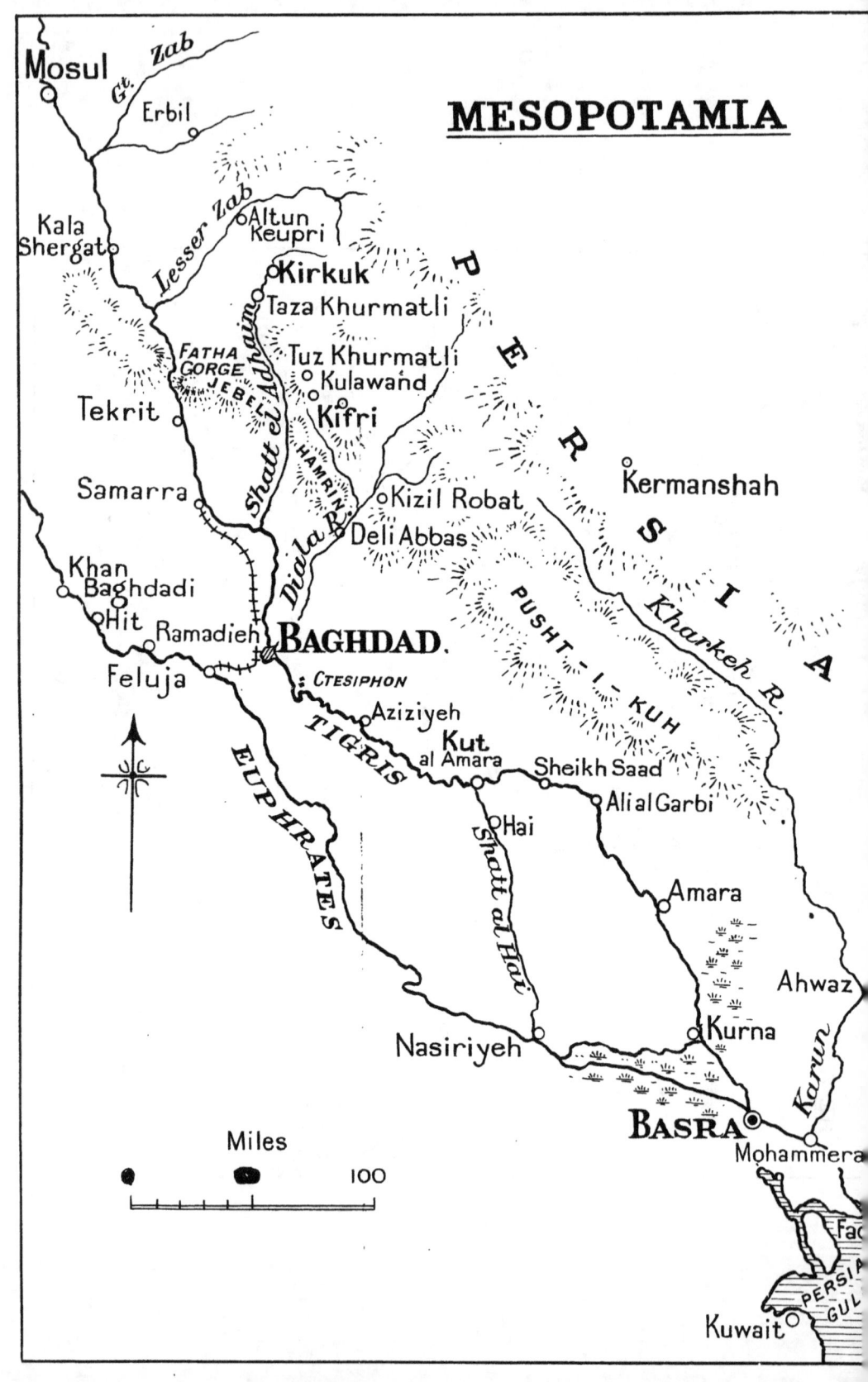